THE THEATER IN SOVIET RUSSIA

The Theater
in Soviet Russia

By NIKOLAI A. GORCHAKOV

TRANSLATED BY EDGAR LEHRMAN

BOOKS FOR LIBRARIES PRESS
FREEPORT, NEW YORK

Library of Congress Cataloging in Publication Data

Gorchakov, Nikolai Aleksandrovich, 1901-
    The theater in Soviet Russia.

    ([BCL/select bibliographies reprint series])
    Translation of Istoriia sovetskogo teatra.
    1. Theater--Russia--History. I. Title.
[PN2724.G5912 1972]   792'.0947   72-2996
ISBN 0-8369-6869-7

PRINTED IN THE UNITED STATES OF AMERICA

ACKNOWLEDGMENTS

THE PREPARATION OF THIS BOOK, as well as other works in the Slavic field, was made possible by a grant from the Rockefeller Foundation to the Department of Slavic Languages, Columbia University, and the translation of the manuscript by a grant from the Russian Institute, Columbia University. Funds to meet part of the cost of publication have been provided by the Committee for the Promotion of Advanced Slavic Cultural Studies, Inc. The Institute for the Study of the USSR, Munich, Germany, has also contributed to the publication of the volume. For this varied and generous aid, we are deeply grateful.

ERNEST J. SIMMONS
General Editor

INTRODUCTION

IF THE SOVIET THEATER of today is examined only from the quantitative standpoint, its state of well-being might seem unparalleled in the history of mankind. Certainly, the Soviet government has not spared its resources wherever the theater was concerned. This is true on both the professional and amateur levels, in cities and towns, on collective farms and construction projects, for the Russian and non-Russian parts of the Soviet population alike. The healthy state of the Soviet theater is also evidenced—among other ways—in the performances, the productions, and the huge number of books on the theater that appear in the Soviet Union.

It is true, moreover, that there is no unemployment among Soviet actors, and the numerous institutes and technical schools cannot train theater personnel quickly enough to keep up with the demand. Whereas on this side of the Iron Curtain theaters and theater companies go bankrupt and have to close, the generosity of Soviet governmental subsidies prevents such closings.

There is more to the theater, however, than such statistics show. One must also consider quality and examine what goes on behind the luxurious façades of Soviet theaters. One must study the spiritual decline of a theater that has been distorted into a living oil painting that illustrates the catchwords of the Communist Party. The real reason for the generosity of the Soviet government then becomes apparent. Its millions of rubles are spent not only to patronize Melpomene but also to support the gigantic governmental propaganda machine.

The price that the Soviet theater pays for governmental assistance, therefore, is a terrible one. Creative freedom has been largely lost. Free art, which strives for truth, is incompatible with Bolshevik ideology. The Communist Party dominates the Soviet repertory; hence, the Soviet theater sees Bolsheviks—and even their secret police—through rose-colored glasses exclusively. Historical characters, such as Ivan the Terrible, are used as means to justify Soviet policy. Alexei Tolstoy's portrayal of Peter the Great—created because of a "social command" —emerges as a prototype of Stalin. The classics too are often tailored to suit Bolshevik propaganda. Monarchs, people from high society, and clergymen are among the characters who are re-evaluated in the process. Of course, the same process of adaptation is present in productions deal- ing with the "capitalist West," especially since 1947. The entire Soviet theater is weighted down by a standardized "socialist realism"; there is little freedom for innovation or experimentation.

The tragedy is that the Soviet theater arts once flourished brilliantly. They were indivisibly bound up with the brilliant innovators active dur- ing the first quarter of the twentieth century. The contributions of these people antedated the revolutions of 1917. All Russia seemed to be interested in the theater. Factories, villages, and even army units had their own "dramatic circles," which produced the plays of Molière and Gogol and other national and foreign dramatic works. Performances were used in the curricula of schools on the pre-university level. This creative upsurge was of mysterious origin. Russia's religion and culture made her one of the lands least likely to be the leader in theater in- novations. And the time was not a period of national cultural renais- sance—quite the contrary. Hunger, civil war, and devastation were present instead. But prosper the theater did. The native Russian de- velopments, however—the new contributions and the widespread formal- ism of the 1920s—have long since been wiped out. Statistically, the Soviet theater of today holds many records; artistically, it is in a state of decline.

A study of the developments in the Soviet theater can serve many good purposes.

First, the causes both of the Golden Age of the Soviet theater and of its decline have not been the subject of careful analysis.

Second, many of the trends, aims, ideas, and innovations of those years are still but slightly known outside the Soviet Union. They have not penetrated the great wall with which Bolshevism has separated the peoples of Russia from the rest of the world. Many ideas that the Revolution brought to the Russian theater remain vital for the non- Russian theaters of our time, but Bolshevism has stifled principles and practices that would contribute to the development of the theater every- where.

Third, people who intend to defend human freedom from dictatorial oppression must be interested in the history of how one of the greatest theaters of our age was mercilessly and systematically sapped of its vitality and enslaved. A study of this destructive process will serve to confirm the age-old truth of the indivisibility of art and freedom.

Fourth, objective historical research is necessary to counteract the unscrupulous writings of Soviet theater "experts." The Marxist-Leninist-Stalinist approach to history is the only one permitted in the Soviet Union; history is viewed as party policy "spilled into the past."

All totalitarian regimes, including Bolshevism, falsify history in the most shameless way to suit themselves. Of course, this falsification has been widespread in Soviet studies of the theater and its history. The form is always the same: before 1917, there were gloom, terror, the tsarist censorship, the suffering proletariat of actors, the drunken impresarios, the ruin of talent, the stifling of free art, and a theater that was only a "place of digestion for the bourgeoisie"; after 1917 came the bright world of Soviet history, the beginning of all crusading quests, of the "revolution in the theater," of the glorious ascent toward today's "socialist realism."

This book intends to disprove—with historical facts—the Bolshevik myth that the revolution in the Russian theater began only after the cruiser *Aurora* had fired on the Winter Palace in Petrograd.

Finally, therefore, an objective study of the Soviet theater is needed for still another reason. Many people this side of the Iron Curtain view anything connected with the post-Revolutionary Russian theater as the work of Satan. This position allows them to negate all the good, individual features of the Soviet theater and every positive aspect of the Soviet government's attitude toward it. These people believe that Bolshevism not only creates evil, but that it also paralyzes all the good that Russian masters of art have been continually producing.

The time is ripe to destroy the myth that the Russian theater offered no resistance of any kind to Bolshevism, that it entered the service of its new masters silently and willingly, and that it lacked any ideals or principles of its own. Few people know that the resistance was prolonged. The time has come to offer the first investigation of what many playwrights and theaters did in this connection.

An objective history of the Soviet theater cannot be written in the Soviet Union. The Bolsheviks have erased from history one of the greatest innovators in the Soviet theater—Vsevolod Meyerhold—as an "enemy of the people"; it would have been truer to call him an enemy of Stalin's regime. Alexander Tairov, a second great pioneer in the theater, was branded as a "class alien," and his artistic endeavors were constantly obstructed by the government. Other "enemies of the people" included such major innovators as Nikolai Evreinov, Feodor Komisarzhevsky, and Mikhail Chekhov. The orthodox Bolshevik theater experts would either have to omit or to distort the significance of such a great playwright of post-Revolutionary Russia as Mikhail Bulgakov, of such talented dramatists as Yuri Olesha and N. Erdman. Bolshevik historians would have to disown even such an orthodox, hundred-percent Communist as Kirshon—generally believed to have been executed by the NKVD. Can Soviet critics write more than a few standard imprecations about Nataliya Sats, that most talented creator of the Soviet children's theaters?

Can Soviet theater experts give an impartial history of such major Soviet theater phenomena as the Proletcult (a shortened form of the Russian words meaning "Proletarian Culture"), with its numerous theaters and studios, its manifold aims, and its theories of a "proletarian theater"? Can they give a just treatment of RAPP (the Russian Association of Proletarian Writers), with its "theatrical front," its numerous dramatic critics and theoreticians, with its important periodical, *Teatr*, and its TRAM (the Theater for Young People) tendency of employing a collective, rather than an individual, as the protagonist? All of these brought about a new era in the political theater of the Komsomol.

One cannot understand the history of the Soviet theater, however, without a basic knowledge of nineteenth-century developments and of the pre-Revolutionary Russian theater of the twentieth century. One must study Konstantin Stanislavsky's Theater to be able to evaluate correctly such innovators as Meyerhold, Tairov, and Evreinov; they arose in opposition to the revolution of Stanislavsky and Vladimir Nemirovich-Danchenko. One cannot correctly decipher what the innovations in the Soviet theater mean without analyzing the aims and the new ideas of the pre-Revolutionary opposition to the Moscow Art Theater; by far the greater part of this opposition began long before 1917. This history of the Soviet theater begins, therefore, with that necessary background material.

CONTENTS

xii CONTENTS

LIST OF ILLUSTRATIONS

PART ONE

THE RUSSIAN THEATER
BEFORE THE REVOLUTION

CHAPTER I

THEATER CONDITIONS
IN THE NINETEENTH CENTURY

IN 1897, SEVERAL MONTHS before the historic meeting at which Konstantin Stanislavsky and Vladimir Nemirovich-Danchenko decided to organize the Moscow Art Public Theater (as it was then called), the First All-Russian Conference of Theater People took place in Moscow. There were two Imperial theaters in Russia at that time: the Alexandrinsky in St. Petersburg and the Maly in Moscow. The actors from these citadels of glamour were meeting with other actors from all over Russia for the first time.

The speeches made at the conference gave a rather gloomy picture of the Russian theater as it was then. A. A. Potekhin, for example, declared: "Bit by bit, the theater is being sacrificed to business and mercantile enterprises. It has lost its instructive and artistic significance. The present contingent of theater people contains many persons who have no relationship to art and who see it only as a means for their own existence." [1]

THE ACTORS

The invasion of the Russian stage by unsuitable and untalented amateurs was undoubtedly why the artistry in acting deteriorated. A. I. Yuzhin-Sumbatov, the actor and playwright, complained:

We are now getting masses of ignoramuses, every kind of jack-of-all-trades. . . . Why is the theater—an educational organization—being made into a storehouse for ignorance and a special asylum for all human failures? [2]

Twelve years of study are needed before a person can be eligible for a judicial post; nine are required for a second lieutenancy. For actors, who are called upon to embody the joys and sorrows of judges and second lieutenants both, is it enough to have been expelled during the second year of high school? [3]

One of the outstanding actors and directors of the time was A. P. Lensky. Voicing his opinion of the great majority of actors from the rostrum, he declared that they "have nothing in common with art and paralyze every worthwhile undertaking of the gifted and intelligent minority." Lensky was one of the most reserved and cultivated of the actors and teachers at the Maly Theater. Yet he appealed to the theater experts to unite against the hordes of dilettantes and ignoramuses who were invading the theater: "The salvation of the theater . . . must begin with the painful but inevitable amputation of its sick and infected members. Any slackening of these efforts will indubitably have a harmful influence on restoring the sick organism of art to good health." [4]

A man such as Lensky expressed himself in that manner because idlers, uneducated persons, and people who sought quick success and easy money could get on the stage easily at that time. What did a potential "actor" need? Height, a sonorous voice, plus a mixture of insolence and easy manners. An "actress" needed a pretty face and a good figure. In the three or four "rehearsals" that took place, one had to get used to repeating half-correctly whatever sounds emanated from the prompter's box and to remember when and where the entrances and exits were made and where to stand onstage. One only needed to avoid any shyness in public and to behave pertly. The result would be applause, flowers, success, and salary increases from the general manager. Why finish school, race to class, or spend years at a university? Why begin a difficult and slow life after school at a provincial hospital, a notary's office, or in some government department? In the theater, glory, money and votaresses were won for very little—assuredness and a minor strain on the vocal cords. What else was needed? To find an effective costume, to ask the hairdresser to get hold of a somewhat better wig, and put on good-looking make-up. There was only one feeling in the entire performance —to seem to play something through, not to fall flat, not to be hissed at. The plot called for loving someone, hating somebody else, and there was nothing left but to copy one's memories of work done by other craftsmen. There were scenes of "wrath," "jealousy," "tenderness," or copying the poses of whoever conducted the rehearsals.

But these were not the expressions of feelings that were needed on the stage. They were only the stereotypes of external expressions of feelings. The artisans in the theater had to accomplish a creative act on the stage, and this act, despite all their wishes, was beyond their powers. They could neither copy nor borrow the experience and the creative process. All they could do was adopt the external appearance of feeling and the outer result of someone else's creative work. The stereotype was a way in which the artisans of the stage, who were neither gifted nor sensitive, could commit a legal form of plagiarism.

Generally speaking, stereotyping is a very old phenomenon. No one knows how many centuries some clichés have been going on—such as pressing the palm against the heart to signify the vowing of love, grasping the hair to express despair, or beating one's breast to indicate inner torment. Life itself gives the theater a multitude of firmly established clichés in feeling, intonation, and gesticulation because people outside the theater are apt to react in a standardized way when shocked into sudden emotion. Then, too, artisans of the stage can collect numerous trite expressions for all human feelings in good and in bad literature. Some clichés in acting last for centuries because they are stale copies of what had once been brilliant discoveries by the great actors of the past. Formerly they had evidenced the genius in intonation and gesticulation of Tommasso Salvini, Ernesto Rossi, Mikhail Shchepkin, Eleonora Duse, or David Garrick. Since then, these devices have been coarsely copied in all theaters, and now they are old, worn-out, lifeless masks freezing intensely emotional experiences.

Stanislavsky characterized such clichés brilliantly:

With the aid of mimicry, the voice, and movement, the artisan-actor presents only external stereotypes on the stage, as if they expressed the inner "life of the human spirit" to be found in the role, or a dead mask of feelings that do not exist. For such external performances, a large assortment of devices has been worked out to depict all possible occasions. . . . The artisans have a special manner with which to approach their roles—that is, through voice, diction, and phrasing. (They exaggerate and raise their parts, with a specific tremolo in their acting or with a special, florid, and intricate use of the voice.) . . . There are devices for mimicking entire characters and types of characters from the various strata of society. Peasants spit on the floor and wipe their noses; soldiers clink their spurs, and aristocrats use lorgnettes. There are devices for eras: operatic gesticulations are used to depict the Middle Ages, and a mincing gait is used for the eighteenth century. Devices to depict plays and roles are also rather common.[5]

The prevalence of mechanical attitudes testified to the decline in the theater arts. Responsible for this decline were not only the miserable artisans of the stage but also the outstanding actors of the period, for even they contributed to the disintegration of the realistic school of acting founded by Mikhail Semyonovich Shchepkin (1788–1863).

When Shchepkin began acting, stilted declamation and grandiloquent gesture dominated the Russian stage, in imitation of the Western European theater. Years later, he wrote:

Let me recall, to the best of my ability, what was then considered excellent acting. No one spoke in his natural voice. Acting consisted of tortured declamation. Words were uttered as loudly as possible; almost every one of them was accompanied by gestures. Lovers especially declaimed so passionately that it is ridiculous even to recall it. The words "love," "passion," and "betrayal" were screamed with as much strength as the actor possessed, but facial expressions were not used. The face remained in the same tense and unnatural position it had been in when the actor had come on stage. Or again, when an actor approached the end of any powerful monologue after which he had to leave the stage, the rule was that he had to raise his right hand and withdraw in that fashion.[6]

Shchepkin found great joy on the stage. He was the first to speak simply and naturally instead of declaiming with false pathos. "I felt that I had spoken some words simply—so simply that, had they been uttered in life rather than in a play, I would have said them in just that way. And every time I succeeded in talking that way, I enjoyed it. . . . I felt good." [7]

Shchepkin brought life into the twilight world of grandiloquent hypocrisy. He swept away the dust that had settled on the threadbare decorations and brought in sunlight and fresh air. He understood that artistic truth lies beyond the theater walls, in ordinary life. And he thirsted to know ordinary life, with its real people, rather than shadows that uttered long and bombastic monologues. He sought to study living characters anywhere and everywhere, with their weaknesses, their greatness, their wretchedness, and their laughter:

Shchepkin's entire life, even outside the theater, furnished a constant flow of material for his art. Everywhere he found something to observe and something to study: naturalness, faithfulness of expression (to whatever was being done), the endless variety and special features of that expression, the exclusive attributes of each individual character, and the action of those traits on the others. Everything was observed; everything was transmuted into art; everything enriched the spiritual resources of the artist.[8]

Although he learned artistic truth from life and studied human beings carefully, Shchepkin did not become a mimic or a copyist of life. From antiquity on, there have always been many comedians who have brilliantly imitated the foibles of living people. They are the naturalists of human trivia. The power of Shchepkin's realism enabled him to penetrate the outer shell and generic details and get to the depths of human character. He brilliantly accomplished what Stanislavsky was later to call "the chief task of a character": he played the "kernel of the role"—that is, the basic, internal mainstream of human character. Any partisan of the stage who has nothing in common with realism can play the truth in part. Shchepkin's power consisted in his ability to play the truth in its entirety, and only that truth can create a living person on the stage.

Shchepkin was the ancestor of that great school of incarnation and experience that was later to be expanded by Stanislavsky and Nemirovich-Danchenko. Eyewitness reports of his acting impress the reader as having been written about the players of the Moscow Art Theater. "What struck me first was the unusual truth and simplicity in his enactment of a role," A. A. Stakhovich wrote. "Involuntarily I compared him with other actors; Shchepkin alone lives on the stage, while all the others play-act—as Alexander Ostrovsky has stated. . . . I never saw such acting before Shchepkin." [9]

Shchepkin's greatness did not lie merely in the external and realistic devices of his acting, but they proceeded rather from his revealing of the truth of the internal, spiritual nature of the character on the stage. He acted about eight hundred roles, of which the overwhelming majority were intellectually and spiritually poverty-stricken. Yet Shchepkin possessed the gift of ennobling and humanizing the roles that were assigned him. He never indicted the characters whom he created on the stage but instead defended them. His work was a search for the good and noble in everyone. This is what Stanislavsky later suggested in his brilliant formula, "When you play a scoundrel, first of all, look for his good traits."

But Shchepkin's legacy was forgotten in the latter part of the nineteenth century. His devices were transformed into the very stereotypes that his imitators used. Not only the painstaking study of life and society, but even thorough work on the role began to be considered incompatible with "creative acting." Only Inspiration, come down from Apollo on high, it was felt, could aid an actor on the stage.

An actor of that period believed only in the "internal." The "internal" actors considered that thorough work on a role, on inner technique, on gesticulation, on facial expression and voice—that any intense use of the brain, of reason, or of calculation—would be ruinous in staging works of art. Everything was delegated to Inspiration, which had to condescend to the actor and raise him aloft on its wings while carrying the playgoer along. Training, technique, and loathsome reason could only frighten Inspiration. Everything had to be conceived in "internal" darkness and mystery.

Magical Inspiration, however, who visited even a genius but rarely, did not always wish to visit ordinary mortals at precisely eight o'clock in the evening. And as the actor had to perform every evening, the poor, lazy artisan was reduced to resorting to force in order to dig resisting "inspiration" out of his vitals. The actor tried to dredge out his "inspired feeling" from within by means of a cry, a convulsive gesture, by racing about the stage, or—most frequently—by consuming alcohol. But if he did succeed in tearing something out from his insides, it was not creative inspiration, of course, but rather a very primitive kind of hysteria, neurosis, and muscular overexertion. About this violent method Stanislavsky wrote:

Only by strenuously moving my arms and legs was I able even for a second to incite muscular stimulation and then I moved without any reason and confusedly and got mechanically stirred up, and immediately it [the motion] died out. It was like a watch that isn't running properly.[10]

In a moment of great enthusiasm, which I took for inspiration, I did not direct my body; on the contrary, it directed me. But what can the body do when creative feeling is needed! At such times, the will becomes powerless, the body strains, and there is an abnormal tenseness everywhere, in all the different centers of the body, which ties you in knots and gives you cramps, thanks to which your feet fall asleep and you can hardly walk, your hands grow numb, you lose your breath, you get a tight feeling in your throat, and your entire body grows stiff. Or, on the contrary, anarchy attacks your whole body because you do not control your feelings: your muscles move involuntarily, causing an infinite number of motions, of unthinking poses and gestures, of nervous tics, etc. Feeling itself flees from this chaos and hides in some secret place. Can one create and think under such conditions?[11]

In these passages, Stanislavsky has given a clinical description of "internal" acting. Performers who were so inclined needed artificial stimulants to awaken their "stage temperament." Some, before making their entrances, persuaded the stagehands to hold them fast so that, in tearing themselves away from them, the actors could work themselves into a rage and dash onto the stage.

A certain irresponsibility on the stage was called by the artisan-actor "nerve," "something internal," "temperament," and "inspiration," but these catchwords can be replaced by a phrase that is easier to understand—stage hysteria. Indeed, it was essentially only the form—artificially provoked—of stage hysteria and stage epilepsy, the ability to get oneself worked up to the limits of one's nerves. The "internal" actors substituted hysteria and stage epilepsy for experience and the creative act.

"Tragedians" of this type could get themselves so worked up that passion gurgled in their throats. They yelled on the stage hoarsely and deafeningly; they raced about like persons possessed; they tore "a passion to tatters." But the feelings that they depicted during the course of the action—hate, wrath, love, and joy—were in no way distinguished from each other. And the "talents" in this "internal" school were distinguished from one another only by the power with which this or that "tragedian" could bring on his stage hysteria.

Of course, the modest, level-headed, and relatively healthy theatergoer was accustomed to the normal gestures and voices of life around him. Frequently, however, upon seeing the fits of hysteria taking place on the stage, he would think: "Most likely, this is high art, because there are no such heart-rending wails in life." But a perceptive contemporary of that theater, C. Vertinsky, testified that the hysterical school of acting, freed from any kind of training and rationalism, was only a conspiracy of lazy artisans: "The habit of playing from inspiration . . . was aided by its complete correspondence to the lazy Russian nature. The flood was felt especially on the provincial stage where it ruined not a few talents completely." [12]

Indeed, many in that theater were convinced that one must not touch enigmatic feeling on the stage with a cool technique or consciousness, nor frighten the sensitive and magical bird from the nocturnal mist of the subconscious with any training. This led the actor, in practice, to reject any work whatsoever on either his role or himself. Moreover, such a system harmonized very well with the leanings of the entrepreneurs because with only two rehearsals one could give so many more premières. This belligerent dilettantism led to the most complete decline of technique: the actor combined both skill and raw materials in himself; he renounced the search for self-perfection as an artist. At the same time, he allowed his raw materials—his body, voice, nerves, and expressions—

to run wild and grow coarse. This is the estimate of Yuzhin, the leading actor of the Maly Theater:

Recently, our development of acting techniques has deteriorated. This is the result of prolonged admiration for the notorious "internal" [school]. Current tastes have long encouraged a herdlike aspiration toward that unconscious state of mind which has now received its most subtle development. At every step, technique is regarded almost as a felony, and this prejudice has gradually done away with the discipline that the great artists of our day have worked out. It is strongly reflected in the present generation of actors. Genius and talent can be polished only by work, but this has been completely forgotten.[13]

Their Training. The deterioration in the art of acting and the inroads of dilettantes on the stage also show that theatrical schooling was quite haphazard toward the end of the nineteenth century. The best Russian actors of the time had long since known that the art of acting had to be linked with a deep comprehension of the drama and with a subtle analysis of the psychology and character of the people depicted on the stage. This called for a high degree of intellectuality in the actor, and it demanded educational qualifications. The best actors of the time knew that performances had to be bad as long as half-trained, high-school products and others with little formal schooling dominated the stage.

As early as 1881 Ostrovsky indicated to the Imperial theaters and to others who were interested that a school was needed on a higher level:

[The purpose of such an institution would be] to furnish the stage with actors whose strict preparation would allow them to develop their own capabilities, and to perfect themselves . . . to create characters full of artistic truth. . . .

Actors who go on the stage without technical preparation do not have at their disposal the material for making the characters whom they depict come alive; they deceive the playgoers and themselves in suggesting that they are depicting any kind of living person. Hence, their playing of a given character is a performance that neither penetrates the outer surface of the actor nor transforms the part into a clearly defined character. The acting by untrained performers is not impersonation; it is only, more or less, a presentable reading of the role, accompanied by futile, incoherent efforts to make one's body harmonize with the words of the role.[14]

Instruction in the schools of the Imperial theaters took place in the old-fashioned way.[15] Classes were assigned to first-rate actors. These performers were important and celebrated on the stage, but most of them could in no way be regarded as born teachers. They coached future actors according to the devices and the glittering mechanics that they knew perfectly but that their students were powerless to copy. Training began with classes in diction where poetry had to be memorized. The students were coached in singing out declamations—for example, they spent much time warming up on the hexameters of Homer's *Iliad*. The students' diction was corrected by rule of thumb, and the instruction was quite primitive. Dancing, fencing, and drama classes were also taught. What were these drama classes—the most important part of theater training—like?

V. N. Davydov was a great actor of the Imperial theaters. In the training school at St. Petersburg, he tried to transmit to the students the successful devices he used in his acting. Sometimes he would discuss and demonstrate how the great actors of the past—such as Samarin, Shumsky, and Sadovsky—played some role. But this practice exhibited only individual devices, the end results of someone else's work. The main thing—the creative path leading to these results—was not shown the students. Instruction was carried on by illustration. Of course, Davydov demonstrated with wonderful skill, but he was unable to reveal the creative laws upon which his technique had been based by teaching students how to copy. Frequently, L. Freidkina reported:

His voice would ring out during the lessons: "Live, live, my dear girl!" "It has to be felt!" "You must cry over the role!" and so on. But Davydov was never able to instruct his students in how to make a role live, how to blend with the character, how to acquire an obedient technique in order to live the life of the character depicted on the stage. One of his former students recalls that he would demand that the actors do a role immediately as well as he did it himself. "You know" [he would say], "it is so simple. Only open your eyes, take the wax out of your ears, and be sincere." [16]

The most important dramatic coaches in Moscow at the time were G. N. Fedotova, Lensky, Yuzhin, and—of course—Nemirovich-Danchenko. In 1883 Stanislavsky studied for a short time at the training school where Fedotova was teaching. This is his comment on the experience:

They told us ably and very graphically what a role and a play had to be— that is, about the end results of the work—but they were silent about how to attain these results, about what creative method to use in approaching the aims desired. They taught us to act in general or to do a given role in particular, but they did not teach us our art. There were no basic rules and no systematization. Practical devices were not verified by scientific research. I felt like some kind of dough from which they were baking rolls of a definite look and taste.

They taught the students to read almost with the voice [alone], and to act with the aid of demonstrations. Hence, each one of them tended more than anything else to copy his teachers . . . students had to repeat whatever their teachers did. And they repeated the very same thing, only—of course—considerably worse.[17]

Litovtseva, a student of Fedotova's, reminisced thus:

[Fedotova] was concerned with the voice exclusively. This system brought much to a given role but little to the further perfection of the actor, because no matter how well a student might play a given role after he or she had grasped the precise intonations of a great teacher, all the training was limited to that role alone.[18]

About Yuzhin's teaching at the Moscow Philharmonia, a periodical of the time wrote, after a performance by his students: "The attempt to copy Yuzhin has sometimes even reached photographic reproduction." [19] And N. L. Tiraspolskaya, one of Yuzhin's students, declared:

He was able to give very wise and useful advice about principles. He analyzed a play profoundly and cleverly ridiculed the false pathos and the overworked posing of the student. His illustrations glowed with a magnificent skill. But, in the strict sense of the word, Yuzhin was never a teacher. Obviously, he understood this himself and left the Philharmonia training school never to return after he had spent three or four years there.[20]

Instruction in the theater at the end of the last century was, therefore, in the main, dilettantism. The basic method used, the pose, was manifestly false. It only increased the number of artisans and copyists on the stage, who were coached in clichés and stereotypes, and the Russian stage already had enough of such people and such devices.

Their Status. In addition to the decline of standards in his craft, the actor's status in society was lowered. Ostrovsky's dramas depict several unfortunate Russian provincial actors of the 1870s. To this group belong Arkashka Neschastivtsev in *Les* ("The Forest"), Shmaga and Neznamov in *Bez viny vinovatye* ("Guilty without Guilt"), and Robinzon in *Bespridannitsa* ("The Girl with No Dowry"—sometimes called in English "The Poor Bride"). How hungry, despised, nomadic, and persecuted Russian provincial actors were! The attitude of society toward actors, declared Yuzhin, was a mixture "of condescension and a certain insultingly cautious treatment that places some special, subtle obstacle between the public and actors." [21] Players were put on almost the same level as criminals under police surveillance. They were deprived of the right to change their living quarters—lest the scoundrels abscond after having swindled the entrepreneur. Yuzhin wrote this about the effect of society's attitude on the women in the theater: "Even if an actress is chaste in her personal life, she will not become respected by society until the word 'acting' becomes as respected by public opinion as the words 'doctor,' 'professor,' and 'writer.' " [22] Yuzhin's words are especially valuable because he had come from the *haut monde* himself and was really Prince A. I. Sumbatov.

What was the milieu of the ordinary actor at the provincial run-of-the-mill theaters at rehearsals and performances? Stanislavsky left us this picture:

Remember the conditions under which actors lived, particularly in the provinces. They frequently did not even have their own spots in the wings. Three-fourths of the entire building was given over to the audience, with buffets, tea rooms, snack bars, fine checkrooms, the lobby, smoking rooms, men's and women's rooms with wash basins and warm water, and corridors for the promenade. Only one fourth of the building was at the disposal of the theater arts. Here were the decorations, the stage properties, the electrician's equipment, the offices, the workshops, the costumers' place, and the tailor's shop. Was there much left for the actor? A few narrow stalls under the stage, with no windows or ventilation, but always dusty and filthy.[23]

At the time under discussion, actors did not have their own spots or foyers, which were extremely rare in the theaters, and they had to seek refuge somewhere else, and for that reason the servants of beauty and aesthetics had to loaf in the filthy wings, along the cold corridors, in the bathrooms, while waiting to go on. The uninterrupted smoking, the cold snacks, the sausages, herring, and ham on the newspapers spread out on their laps, the gossiping and the vulgar flirting, the slanders and the anecdotes were a natural result of the inhuman conditions to which the actor was being subjected. The actor spent three-fourths of his life in such surroundings.[24]

These Augean stables of backstage life—this terrible, seamy side of the stage—were ruinous for acting. How could one talk about concentration, about becoming lost in thought and experiencing a role under such conditions? Actors did not even have the solitude that they needed before going out on the stage to perform. And they got almost no help and little sympathy from their supervisors in the theater—not even in the cities.

MANAGERS

The Imperial theaters were managed by people chosen by the Ministry of the Court. Their choice frequently was haphazard, and they had no talent or anything else in common with art:

The trouble was that [these] persons were unsuitable. All power, including the artistic, was concentrated not in the theater but in the office. The office did not serve the theater, but vice versa, and the result was that, for the troupe, the office became a swearword and, for the office, the theater became a revolutionary element. . . . Out of poor art, one obtained a "theater department." [25]

An example of such a manager was a certain Pchelnikov, who directed the Moscow office of the Imperial theaters between 1882 and 1898. He was not only indifferent to questions of art but simply did not understand art, and he was notorious for his abysmal ignorance. He reported to St. Petersburg about Leo Tolstoy's *Power of Darkness* that the play did not bring in money and that this is explained by its complete lack of artistic and literary qualities! Half the plays in the repertory of the Maly Theater during the years of Pchelnikov's administration were put on because he knew their untalented authors.

A. A. Maikov—a cousin of the famous Russian poet with the same surname—was another manager of the Imperial theaters in Moscow. His tenure was short, but nevertheless his stupidity has immortalized him:

Altani hands him a paper to the effect that the musicians of the orchestra need music stands for the second violins. Maikov makes the decision: "The Imperial Theater is rich enough to have only first violins."

The celebrated Samarin died, and the role of Famusov was open. "Why is *Gore ot uma* ["Wit Works Woe"] not being played?" Maikov asked the director. "Lensky isn't ready for it yet." "Lensky? Lensky? You have an actor named ———— who is the same height and weight as Samarin. Let him play it, and the old costume will fit him." [26]

And such "administrators" were complete autocrats. They were surrounded with kowtowing esteem, and their every word was law for the theater.

DIRECTORS

The stage director of the period, on the other hand, was an unassuming corporal of the guard. According to Nelidov, the work of the director in the Imperial Maly Theater ran along these lines:

Having received a play, he assigned the roles. It would seem that this deserved some thought, but the troupe was so rich in talent that any play-goer could have done this without making a serious error. Furthermore, the director wrote the headings and the bare outlines of the stage directions: *"dramatis personae,"* "décor," "furniture," "costumes," "wigs," "properties," "effects" (there were about nine or ten headings). . . . Under "furniture," [he wrote] "poor" or "rich." Costumes were "urban" or "historical." Wigs were "bald," "gray," "red," etc.

The office carried out all this. The director and the actors frequently did not see the set before the dress rehearsal, and sometimes not before the performance itself, for it was felt that if they simply knew the plan of the stage—that is, that a door would be in one particular place and a writing table in another—it would be enough.

Rehearsals were carried on simply. They came onstage with their note-books in hand; they read the roles and assigned places, that is, they settled that X would stand here and Y would sit there. . . . After the third re-hearsal, the notebooks were taken away. The role had to be learned by heart, for which one, two, or three days were allotted, depending on its scope. . . . And that was the entire work of the director.[27]

On the crown stage, this kind of corporal-of-the-guard director was a protector of clichés and routine. A. Kugel, a critic, said that such a direc-tor reminded him of Sancho Panza after he was appointed governor: "He is a creature of caprice, and his supposed power continues as long as the joke is enjoyed, but his ideals, even if they are placed on the table fried, are immediately taken away at a sign from the doctor in the inter-ests of His Excellency's health." [28]

THE DÉCOR

The theater suffered, as a result of such uninspired leadership, from unimaginative décor. Set designs for all the plays of the world were confined to three trite frameworks. "Gothic" was for Shakespeare, Racine, Schiller, and all the "classical" and "costume" dramas—every-thing that smacked of pathos, romanticism, and poetry. Then there was the "Gogolian" assortment, used for all Russian plays whose action took place between the end of the eighteenth century and the middle of the nineteenth. Finally, there was the "urban" set. All these "Gothic," "Gogolian," and "urban" sets were banged together on the stage without the slightest regard for fidelity to life. Stanislavsky said this about stage design in those days:

At the time, the question of décor in the theater was usually solved quite simply: the backdrop, four or five archways in perspective upon which had been painted a palace hall with various passageways, an open or closed terrace, a view of the sea, and so forth. In the center of the stage was a smooth, filthy, theater floor and as many chairs as there were performers. In the gaps between the wings, a crowd of stagehands, extras, hairdressers, and tailors was visible, wandering around or staring at the stage. If a door was needed, they set it between the wings; no one cared that above the door there was an empty space. When it was necessary, they painted a street in perspective on the backdrop or side scenes; it contained an enormous square, empty of things and of people, with a fountain, mountains, etc. . . . The stage contained the luxurious pavilion of the Empire or rococo periods, in stereotyped form, with canvas doors that would shake when one opened or closed them.[29]

But the décor described by Stanislavsky was a magic luxury of the theater arts compared to the status of decorative art at such a model theater as the Imperial Maly in Moscow. This is how the administrator of the Maly Theater troupe described staging conditions there:

New décor was an event. . . . The décor current for all plays included: a living room, rich or poor; a study of the same kind; a prison; a hut; woods in the winter or summer; and "open air," that is, sky-blue linen for depicting open spaces. If a bedroom or an office—or something else of that nature—was needed, they tried to combine whatever they already had on hand.

The classical plays of Shakespeare, Schiller, and Hugo made use both of the "Gothic" decorations and of their variants. King Lear divided his kingdom, Hamlet spoke "to be or not to be," Elizabeth signed the death warrant of Mary [Stuart] in the identical "Gothic" décor.

The furniture situation was no better. In the first place, it belonged directly to the plot, that is, it could in no way be done without because the artist used it during the course of the play; secondly, there was always one of two kinds of furniture sets—rich and poor. In the rich sets, springs came through and the lower linings stuck out. And the playgoer, seated in the orchestra of the theater, saw the sets on the stage with the stuffing coming out of the furniture. This is why the backstage expressions for poor and rich furnishings were "poor" and "pregnant." [30]

There were three kinds of lighting effects: white light and light seen through a dark blue or a red glass set before the footlights. Morning and night came on as if at the equator—they would lower the dark blue glass at once and put on the red one, or vice-versa, and it was ready.[31]

THE PUBLIC

Undoubtedly there must have been some basic cultural and social causes for this decline in the theater arts in the nineteenth century. One of the most threatening factors was the evaporation of the more subtle group of playgoers. The Russian theater had been born and had matured as a court theater, a theater for a tiny group of playgoers from the highest strata of society. In the time of Shchepkin and Ostrovsky, the theater attracted the civil servants, the *raznochintsy* (intellectuals and other city dwellers from nonaristocratic backgrounds), the merchant class, and the students. Toward the end of the nineteenth century, the lowest economic strata of the cultivated public grew even poorer, and the theater lost more of its public every year. Back in 1882 Ostrovsky wrote that the Maly was the only theater in Moscow; with its high prices and its few seats, it could serve only the "wealthy public." There was no theater for the students, the sales clerks, the artisans, or those who lived in the "outlying quarters of Moscow." Yuzhin was right in declaring:

This is not the *public*. It is a *small group* of thinking and educated people, but this is precisely why the theater is too dependent on a number of moods and trends that are extraneous to the theater as an institution, which is mainly popular and demands for its evaluation freedom from any preconceptions and a large, ardent, and sensitive crowd. Our large public is both poor and ignorant. Meantime, it does not support the theater.[32]

The fact that less than one percent of the Moscow population went to the theater had a depressing effect on the quality of both the productions of the plays and of the plays themselves.

New plays had to be given with increasing frequency for the small contingent of playgoers. The quantitative increase in the repertory lessened the period of preparation for the opening nights until there were only a few rehearsals. Even the Imperial Alexandrinsky Theater devoted only eight rehearsals to preparing such an extremely complicated work as Goethe's *Faust*. What more could be expected from the private and provincial theaters where the classics went on after two or three rehearsals? And even in the Imperial theaters there were generally only six to eight. Not much could be expected, of course, of the staging nor could the actors even be expected to know their parts, let alone play them well.

THE REPERTORY

The abundance of premières and short runs demanded a great quantity of new plays. The classics were infrequently put on because they had been played so repeatedly that they were no longer good box-office attractions. There has never been an unlimited assortment of good new plays, and so many second- and third-rate works were produced to meet the great demand for material in nineteenth-century Russia. To lure the gentlemen who purchased theater tickets, their taste had to be catered to. This drastically cheapened the dramatic fare because taste and a fat purse very rarely go together. That Russian public viewed the theater as a pleasant little place, not without its comforts and its satisfactions. Some went to the theater to see others and to be seen; others went, as Yuzhin put it, "to laugh a bit, to get tight, and God knows what else." These children of the *fin de siècle* period demanded a gay, carefree, diverting repertory that would be piquant and titillating—and, please, with no world problems or other boring material. To beguile this public, cheap melodrama, farce, and trivia dominated the stage.

The soiling of the repertory with bad plays was felt in the provinces, in the private theaters of St. Petersburg and Moscow, and even in the Imperial theaters of those two cities. In his article on the First All-Russian Conference of Theater People, Yuzhin described the situation thus: "In recent years, the despair of critics and playgoers has reached the limits of grief because of the rivers of Babylon; the word 'dramatist' in the elegant language used by some organs of our press is for the most part accompanied by such epithets that, in private conversation, would provoke a challenge [to a duel]." [33]

The repertory of plays on contemporary themes may be compared to steps on a ladder of falsehood and banality. At the top was the phenomenon that, in the early twentieth century, was called "Krylovism"—after the immoderately productive stager of minor plays with petty morals, V. Krylov. Lunacharsky said about this kind of drama:

Along with the diverting role, it often sought another, more pitiful aim— to teach, to moralize. The moral verities of these plays were so insignificant that one blushes to admit that, for showing the offense of stealing handkerchiefs from the pocket of one's neighbor or of raping poor girls [the dramatist] had to and was able to write four acts of adroitly sewn, dramatic shilly-shallying. [34]

These are the plays that Treplev discusses in Chekhov's *Sea Gull* (Act I):

When the curtain goes up and, in a room with three walls, at twilight, those great talents, the priests of sacred art, depict how people eat, drink, make love, walk, and wear their jackets; when, out of these banal pictures and phrases, they try to fish out a moral—a little moral—which is understandable and useful in the family circle; when they hold up to me a thousand variants of one and the same thing—one and the same thing—then, I run and run, as Maupassant ran from the Eiffel Tower, which weighed on his brain with its banality.

Even lower than Krylovism were the plays made up of adroitly tailored little intrigues and minor plots, both of which were empty and aimed only at diverting people from boredom, at gently titillating their nerves and petty feelings. And, behind these, came the floods of translated farces and both native and foreign melodrama.

It was to fight this all-pervasive and progressive decline in all aspects of the Russian theater that Stanislavsky and Nemirovich-Danchenko came together to establish the Moscow Art Theater. The history of that new theater is most significant in the history of the entire Russian theater of our century. The birth of the Moscow Art Theater, its creative path, all its prolonged searches for truth on the stage, are directly and indissolubly bound up with all the quests of the Soviet theater. This is so true that it is impossible to understand the Soviet theater without studying the history of the theater established by Stanislavsky and Nemirovich-Danchenko.

CHAPTER II

THE MOSCOW ART THEATER
FROM 1898 TO OCTOBER, 1917

IN THE SIXTY YEARS since its founding, the Moscow Art Theater has presented more than 130 productions, 62 of which antedate the Revolution. The pre-Revolutionary years must be considered more fruitful than the Soviet period, both in the scope of the innovations and in the number of productions. The spirit of search and of experimentation began to wither and die after Stanislavsky's retirement, which happened shortly before his death in 1939.

The Theater has acquired an unwieldy official title in our time—"The Moscow Order of Lenin and of the Toilers' Red Banner Art Academic Theater of the U.S.S.R. Named for M. Gorky." It is now in exactly the same gloomy and decadent state that the Imperial theaters were in toward the end of the nineteenth century, the state against which Stanislavsky and Nemirovich-Danchenko had rebelled in the first place. The heritage of Shchepkin had been forgotten then, and the Moscow Art Theater has either lost or distorted the traditions of Stanislavsky now. The repertory of the Moscow Art Theater has been littered with the works of the Soviet propagandistic playwrights, and its search for new forms ended long ago. Again like the Imperial theaters of the past—and possibly to an even greater extent—the Theater is stifling and suffering from the abundance of governmental bureaucrats whose control over it is quite unbending.

ORIGINS

Stanislavsky and Nemirovich-Danchenko decided on a night in June, 1897, to found a new theater. They were in a private room of the Slavic Bazaar Restaurant on Nikolskaya Street in Moscow. "It was decided that we would create a national theater with approximately the same aims and plans that Ostrovsky had dreamed of," Stanislavsky said.[1] He then summarized their complaints against the theater of their time:

We protested against the old manner of acting, against theatricalism, false pathos, declamation, artificiality in acting, bad staging and décor conventions, the emphasis on new productions that spoiled the ensemble work, the whole system of presentations, and the insignificant repertoires of the time.[2]

The rich merchant Alexeyev who adopted the name Stanislavsky had begun to speak and work for reforms in the theater as early as 1877, first in his own group—Alexeyev's Circle—and then in the Moscow Society for Art and Literature. The "protestantism" of both Stanislavsky and Nemirovich-Danchenko was based on the aspirations and work of other men of the Russian theater and also of other European theaters. Let us trace, therefore, first what Stanislavsky did during the twenty years of his so-called "dilettantism" before the founding of the Moscow Art Theater and then the work of Nemirovich-Danchenko. We shall see that both men had discovered most of the Moscow Art Theater's formulas long before 1897 and that the theater people and the public in Moscow knew about them.

When Stanislavsky staged Potekhin's *Prakticheskii gospodin* ("A Practical Gentleman"), here is how he arranged for himself and the other actors

to live not according to their own personalities but according to those of the characters they were playing and in the conditions of the life shown by the play. In order not to encounter the real life around us, we would either go for a walk, gather mushrooms, or go boating. We had to be guided by the circumstances indicated in the play and to depend on the state of each character's own frame of mind.[3]

Thus, in producing *A Practical Gentleman* Stanislavsky and the Alexeyev Circle found a method for becoming immersed in their roles. In their *Mikado,* which they staged in 1885, the troupe first attempted a prolonged, profound, and thorough familiarity with the era, the flavor, and the atmosphere associated with the work. And twenty years before Vsevolod Meyerhold's first experiments with stylization Stanislavsky inserted this special scene in his production of the *Mikado:*

Red, green, and yellow fans of small, medium, and enormous size . . . flew through the air. . . . Many little platforms were heaped up so that it was possible, from the foreground (where the actors were lying on the floor with their fans) to the background (where they were standing at the highest points) to use the fans as a complete arch on the low stage; the arch covered the stage just like a curtain.[4]

Thirty years before the famous innovations of Alexander Tairov in rhythm and in associating the gestures of the actors with music, Stanislavsky did something similar in his production of the *Mikado:*

A number of gestures had been composed and inserted in the score of the production just like notes of music. . . . Every passage, measure, and stressed note determined gestures, movements, and actions with the fans. On the stage everything was connected with the music in a kaleidoscope of groups that were constantly changing and flowing into one another.[5]

During these years as an amateur Stanislavsky also began to realize the great significance of ensemble work. He tried to have all the participants and creators of a presentation subordinated to one, general creative aim.

A. F. Fedotov staged Pushkin's *Skupoi rytsar'* ("The Covetous Knight") in 1889. He used the resources of the Moscow Society for Art and Literature, which Stanislavsky had founded, and Stanislavsky played the lead in the presentation. He observed the work of Fedotov, who was a veteran director, and formed his first conclusions about directing that went into the making of the methods he was to use in the Moscow Art Theater. "Directors are talented in explaining what they feel that the play needs," Stanislavsky said. "But they are interested only in the end result. They criticize and also point out what is not needed. But they remain silent about *how* to attain what they want." [6] Stanislavsky concluded that even an excellent demonstration by a director to an actor of how to act a particular spot is pernicious; it causes pitiful imitation rather than creative independence. The "copy and profit!" of a Fedotov was the formula for the entire school of posing and coaching.

Stanislavsky also acted in Pisemsky's *Samoupravtsy* ("Autocrats") in 1889. He discovered then what may be considered most significant in his philosophy of acting, his outlook on life, and subsequently the point of view of the Moscow Art Theater. "When you play a villain," the great director declared, "seek the places in which he is good." He continued:

Having spoken this aphorism by accident, I sensed that the role of General Imshin had suddenly become clear to me. I had made the same mistake as my companion. I had played a beast—but that [element] is not eliminated from the role, so there is nothing to worry about; the author himself worried about it immoderately, and I had only to seek the places in which he [General Imshin] was good, loving, tender, suffering, remorseful, and self-denying.[7]

This discovery of Stanislavsky was more profound than he himself realized at the time. It is a philosophy that justifies human beings, that seeks the good and the divine in them. For decades in the Moscow Art Theater it has attracted millions of Russian playgoers, who have been deeply influenced by the idea of universal forgiveness. This philosophy was the source of the ethical greatness of the Moscow Art Theater.

Aside from purely moral greatness, however, the formula contained the embryo for a completely new method of working with the actor on his roles. It revealed a new dimension in the art of acting. Stanislavsky's formula opened a door in the imprisoning wall of theater routine and showed the actor the way to psychological independence and to the innermost secrets of the role he was doing. This formula was to produce a theater of psychological profundity, which is what the Moscow Art Theater became. From this profundity came the "subtext," the "kernel of the role," and the special searches for the internal characteristics that have made the Stanislavsky System famous.

A major influence on Stanislavsky during this time when he was acting and teaching was the arrival of the Duke of Meiningen's Company in Moscow, under the direction of Kronek. Stanislavsky wrote:

I considered what the Meiningen people brought us to be good, that is, their directorial devices for showing the essence of a production. For that, I shall be most grateful to them. It will always live in my art. In the life of our Society [for Art and Literature] and particularly in myself, the Meiningen people brought about a new and important phase.[8]

Stanislavsky grasped Kronek's brilliant teachings both about staging a play thoroughly and about profoundly revealing the era and the spirit of the work through directorial devices, and some Russian dramatic critics stated that Stanislavsky was merely the unimaginative disciple of the Duke of Meiningen's Company. This estimate has been repeated by such masters as Vsevelod Meyerhold and Alexander Tairov, but it is unfair and unobjective.

There was a decided difference in the methods of Kronek and Stanislavsky. Kronek used sumptuous, authentic, historical costumes, furnishings, and background material to surround—and often to cover completely—actors of the old stamp who used the posing and the stereotyping of German bathos. There was a dissonance between the truth of the environment and the false theatricality of the acting. Furthermore, the actor was on a subordinate level in the German company; the director and the historian were more important. Stanislavsky's theater, however, introduced the actor into a realistic stage setting. There was a single style of truth to life. Most important of all, the Moscow Art Theater was—and remained—a theater of the actor, not a theater of the director.

When he produced Tolstoy's *Fruits of Enlightenment* in 1891 Stanislavsky first introduced strict rules for artistic discipline among the actors of the semiprofessional Society for Art and Literature. He struggled against the banality of backstage life and introduced the ethics of acting and everything else that became the special part of the Moscow Art Theater atmosphere.

In that same year the Society staged *Selo Stepanchikovo* ("The Village of Stepanchikovo and Its Inhabitants"), which was based on the short novel of Dostoevsky that has appeared in English under the title *A Friend of the Family*. Stanislavsky played the role of the Uncle, and for the first time in his acting career he experienced boundless joy at blending himself with his role, at bringing it to life, and in making its life his own. He later wrote: "I *became* the Uncle, while in other roles I had—to a greater or lesser extent—'teased' (that is, copied, mimicked) my own or someone else's mannerisms." [9]

The playing of this role marked an important development in Stanislavsky. He began to wonder if the joy, the creative glow, that he had experienced in bringing the role to life was no chance miracle but had occurred with the aid of certain devices of internal technique. He wondered if this genuine experiencing of a role could become permanent and usual for an actor. We must here seek the sources of those tortuous searches that Stanislavsky undertook over the course of many years. They resulted in his book *Rabota aktëra nad rol'iu* ("An Actor Prepares"), which presented a syntax for the inner technique of the actor and allowed him a permanency in his blending with the character and a stabilization of the role. [10]

Stanislavsky's enormous talent as a director had already been developed as early as his production of Gutzkow's *Uriel Acosta* (1893). The regisseur had mastered the color and the complete truth to life of the mass scenes; every supernumerary played his own role, which had been worked out thoroughly. Stanislavsky recalled: "They began saying that our show glorified—and even seemed to have a patent on—crowd (*narodnyi*) scenes." [11]

This was some years before the opening of the Moscow Art Theater. It was also before the time when symbolical, mystical, and fanciful works appeared in Stanislavsky's theater side by side with productions of the most profound psychological realism. These semiprofessional works of the director revealed his great talent for the unreal.

In *Le Juif polonais* by Erckmann-Chatrian (Emile Erckmann and Alexandre Chatrian)—a play that Leopold Lewis translated into English under the title *The Bells*—Stanislavsky added an intrusive motif. This was the sound of the sleigh bell belonging to the plundered and murdered Jew. Like an aural hallucination, it hounds the burgomaster and develops into a delirious sound-phantom, which drowns out everything else, and it finally drives the murderer insane. Stanislavsky transformed his directorial discovery—the sound-phantom—into the protagonist. The intrusive sound, like Fate, metes out punishment and lacerates the burgomaster. The entire production was subordinated to the music, which was dominated by the sound-phantom.

The ghost of the criminal appears in the blue-gray light. The black shadows of the courtroom rise against a foggy green background; during the inquest they rise up at the vision of the dead and cremated Jew like nightmares. Stanislavsky filled the stage with ghastly chimeras from a profound delirium. "The transformation of the room into a court," he later wrote, "proceeded almost unnoticeably and produced the impression of a nightmare to such an extent that, at almost all the performances, nervous ladies left the auditorium and some fainted—of which I, who invented the device, am very proud!" [12]

Gerhart Hauptmann's *Hannele's Himmelfahrt* gave Stanislavsky even more scope for his experiments with the mystic and the fantastic or—to use the language of these days—the surrealistic. In this production Stanislavsky found wonderful devices for transforming the actors into shadows. The stage was lost in darkness. A dark blue beam, narrow and bright, came from behind the stage and caused the actors whom it illuminated to produce very lengthy shadows. The shadows

lay on the floor and climbed the walls and ceiling. And when they moved, the actors seemed to be silhouettes and their shadows ran, came together, separated, blended, dispersed, and intermingled, while the actors themselves became lost among them and also seemed to be shadows. . . . I taught them to speak and move as happens in our dreams or when we have a high temperature and are delirious, when someone whispers certain words in our ear. . . . A word is broken off in the middle. . . . There is a long pause. . . . It is suffocating. . . . Again, a slow, jerky, way of talking with the words frequently stressed—rising and falling the entire gamut of the chromatic scale. . . . And again a pause, a fading out, an unexpected whispering . . . the slow monotonous swaying by a crowd of shadowlike beggars who stand in one place as if glued to the floor. . . . Shadows moving along the wall and ceiling.[13]

At first the shadows began to run; then everything became intermingled —as if one were giddy; after that, everything congealed in an agonizing pause. When Hannele's coffin was carried out, a whispering began that grew into a hurricane and blended with the nightmare of whirling shadows. Stanislavsky created these purely surrealistic devices back in 1895!

Stanislavsky's production of Hauptmann's *Die versunkene Glocke* on the stage of the Society for Art and Literature was also fanciful. He played havoc with the floor of the stage and heaped up a variety of platforms for the actors. This was many years before the innovations of others such as Meyerhold and Tairov, but twenty-five years later a host of Russian innovators and constructivists were to make a great to-do about who could claim priority for them.

One must also note Stanislavsky's production of Shakespeare's *Othello* in 1896. He used Meiningen-style thoroughness in conforming to the historical truth of the entire presentation. This was later to be one of the special features of the Moscow Art Theater, which distinguished it from the primitive lack of taste shown by the other Russian theaters in doing historical plays. Stanislavsky took a special trip to Italy in connection with this *Othello*. He sought and purchased old objects, brocade, needlework, ornaments, and furnishings.

This is but a cursory survey of Stanislavsky's work before the founding of the Moscow Art Theater. It should suffice to show that his revolutionary program for the Russian theater in 1897 was not the chance discovery of a genius and was not hit upon suddenly. It was the logical climax to his twenty years of work before the so-called rebellion.

An abyss divided the work of this supposed dilettante from the arts of the so-called professional Imperial Maly Theater, which was working in the same city at the same time. Whereas Stanislavsky was indefatigable in his tortuous search for ways to raise the theater to the heights of genuine art, the productions at the Maly were characterized by haste, poor taste, stereotypes, slovenliness, bureaucracy, and routine. At the Maly even the idea of seeking new ways was close to sacrilege. The people there imagined themselves to be a caste of faithful priests in the temple of the Russian theater, but in reality they were only conservative bureaucrats in the Department of the Theater.

It was not strange, therefore, that the rumors about the founding of the Moscow Art Theater greatly disconcerted and frightened the priestly caste of the Imperial stage. One of the most cultured actors and directors of the Maly Theater—A. P. Lensky—cried out that now the Maly would be overtaken and conquered by Stanislavsky. And the genuine defeat that a free man in the free land of the theater inflicted upon the Imperial theaters clearly proved that the age of the "crown stage" was finished. An age was beginning in which the leaders of the stage would be the private theaters.

The creative identity of Vladimir Nemirovich-Danchenko, the second founder of the Moscow Art Theater, had also been established long before June, 1897. He had become one of the most profound directors and teachers in the Russian theater.

Nemirovich-Danchenko began as a dramatist at the Maly Theater in 1882, and this began his long association with that Theater. Subsequently he served both as a director for his own plays and as a member of its repertory committee. From the beginning he struggled against the stultifying routine and the standardization of the Maly Theater—an organization he greatly loved and respected. In 1891 he turned in a memorandum to the management in which he pointed out that hasty and careless productions were ruining the artistic prestige of the Theater. "A play does not always need the identical amount of time to be staged," he said, "and the number of rehearsals should not be determined from the use of costumes alone. That number must depend on but one fact: a play can be acted when it is ready, and not before." [14]

Nemirovich-Danchenko went on to suggest many urgent measures to stop the decline in theater arts and the narrow-mindedness that was then corroding the Imperial theaters. These recommendations included: introducing dress rehearsals; creating new décor, costumes, and furnishings for every production (rather than mounting them haphazardly from whatever happened to be in storage); and staging plays with some idea of their periods and coloring (rather than using the so-called rich, poor, and Gothic set-ups). He indicated that new trends in writing plays should become public property and that the theater should become associated with the outstanding literature of the time.

In 1891, too, Nemirovich-Danchenko published instructions for directing his own play *Novoe delo* ("Something New"), in which he first stated the principles that would characterize his future work as a director. He asserted that the chief task of the director must be not to explain the settings but rather to analyze the characters, especially in their relationship to the general idea of the play. "Any setting, gesture, or movement by an actor," he declared, "must depend directly on his internal, subjective, life on the stage. The actor's crossing the stage from right to left and vice versa must flow from the conduct of the character correctly conceived." [15] In the same year Nemirovich-Danchenko began his teaching activities by holding a class on the drama at the training school of the Moscow Philharmonia.

In a number of articles Nemirovich-Danchenko asserted the urgency of educating actors. In one such article he defended his school from the gibes of actors and newspapermen. In those times most actors and many critics were firmly convinced that schooling was useless, and even ruinous because it could suppress original talent, nervous power, and inspiration. Nemirovich-Danchenko argued that a school does not strive to manufacture talent but to eliminate natural shortcomings, to perfect values, and to improve artistic taste. L. Freidkina declared about him:

He was sure that schooling could release the actor from ignorance, develop his artistic taste, and acquaint him with the classics—which the provincial stage could not do because ignorance and bad taste were enthroned there, presentations went on after two rehearsals, and good acting consisted of captivating the public with outbursts that were frequently extraneous both to the play and to the role.[16]

Nemirovich-Danchenko was the first to transfer the center of gravity from surface memorization to inner technique. As early as 1891 he expressed ideas in which one can see the outlines of the methods to be used by the Moscow Art Theater:

When I look at students, I am little interested in their successes in the techniques of theater arts. Those can be acquired. I look first of all for sincerity and a serious groundwork in art. The task for a professor of courses in the drama is to notice the specific talent of the student and to give it genuine guidance, that is, to teach how to ponder over the characters depicted, to show how a student must adapt himself to the role.[17]

With the old methods work began with notebooks containing the role at the very first "individual" rehearsals. Nemirovich-Danchenko introduced the prerehearsal phase of working on a play, the so-called "table" work. This phase profoundly analyzed the inner world of the play and its characters. During it he asked the students to set forth their own ideas about the play, its themes, roles, and essence. He made the students reflect, meditate, and dream about the roles and then tell in their own words the lives of the characters not only during the time of the play but beforehand and afterwards. Nemirovich-Danchenko made the students talk about the personages in the play as if they were dealing with living persons whom they knew well. In this way each student grasped the entire sense of both play and his role. He sensed the life of the character whom he was to depict on the stage before memorizing the text, before the production, and even before he took his first step on the stage.

Thus the great significance of Nemirovich-Danchenko's teachings during those years consists in his having created lofty and more exact methods for training actors and preparing them for the revolution in the scenic arts that was to begin in 1897. Suffice it to say that Nemirovich-Danchenko's classes at the Moscow Philharmonia gave the Moscow Art Theater such cherished performers as Ivan Moskvin, Olga Knipper-Chekhova, Meyerhold, and many other fine artists who were among the founders of the new theater.

TRUTH-TO-LIFE ON THE STAGE

The Moscow Art Theater opened on October 14, 1898, with a production of Alexei Konstantovich Tolstoy's play *Tsar Feodor Ivanovich*—something of a revolutionary event in the history of the Russian theater. Instead of simplified stereotypes for the boyars, the Russia of 1600 came to life on the stage, reproduced with loving thoroughness and truthfulness. The Tsar's palace, the Arkhangelsk Cathedral, the customs, costumes, ornaments, and furnishings—all were genuine, unprecedented, and unmistakably truthful. This lifelike quality extended to the slowness of motion, gesture, and pronunciation. The audiences enjoyed this new and unusual sincerity in the acting and found themselves present at a miracle. It was as if some kind of time machine had returned them to the life and environment of old Russia. Nelidov said the production was

not a presentation like those generally seen before, but life itself in its artistic interpretation, not the reality of life, not a photograph of life, but the truth of life . . . strengthened by a timeless dogma: first of all, they acted not the role but the play, and secondly, they acted truthfully, artistically, according to the enviroment, the time, and the mood.[18]

A number of people in the theater, however, reproached the creative new workers for using too much historical accuracy and for cluttering up the stage with too many real objects.

During the preparatory period for the production of *Tsar Feodor Ivanovich* Stanislavsky used methods unprecedented in the Russian theater. As for *Othello,* he began his directorial work with an expedition to those cities where he might uncover old objects. Numerous sketches were made in all the museums, and he even spent the night in the ancient rooms of the Kremlin at Rostov Yaroslavsky in order to "catch the mood." He studied the belfry and the chiming of the bells especially. This was not a whim or eccentricity in Stanislavsky. He was seeking authentic objects of the period of the production. This was a new method for using historical accuracy and authentic objects to reach inner truth, spirituality, and the flavor of life in the past. Thus, the feeling of the period was sought persistently and with unparalleled thoroughness. The extremes of Stanislavsky's naturalism and historical emphasis can be evaluated correctly only if it is understood that material objects were not, as his enemies charged, introduced as ends in themselves. They were only a means for the actor to reveal on the stage the truth of life and of human existence. In order for an actor to depict not diagrams or masks of feelings but really to experience emotion and use it to reveal the truth about the spiritual world of a person, he had to be surrounded with real objects on the stage. This and this alone can explain the unending searches by Stanislavsky for naturalistic details in his stagings.

The Moscow Art Theater introduced its own make-up technique and even its own palette of make-up paints in order to have the terrible masks that had been daubed on in the past disappear from the stage. Make-up to suit an actor's natural coloring was applied, and not only was the public scarcely aware of the make-up of an actor—neither were the other performers. The gaps in the side-scenes were eliminated. Conditions resembling reality were constructed on the stage: rooms had ceilings; large halls had stucco molding; entire suites of rooms led out of an apartment. Stanislavsky created the convention of the fourth wall; a mirror on the stage was turned toward the public and considered as a wall. Corners, projections from rooms, and furnishings did not face the audience in the worn-out manner of the old theater but were arranged in realistic patterns. Frequently the furniture faced away from the front, and this curbed the actor's compulsion to face the audience.

The old stage had neglected the fact that a human being is constantly surrounded not only by material objects but by a world of sounds, noises, and rustlings. Their vibrations have a great effect on his moods, emotions, and experiences. The rhythm in wind gusts, the patter of rain, the sound of birds in the night, distant singing, or chaotic rustlings often not only shape a person's mood but even direct the currents of his thoughts. And this is what the enemies of Stanislavsky failed to understand when they ridiculed the sound effects that he introduced. For the first time, the Moscow Art Theater created a laboratory to seek new sound effects for the theater and to expand the variety of sounds that surrounded the actor.

In his passionate quest for truth to life on the stage Stanislavsky fell into extremes of naturalism. He acknowledged this himself:

External material truth is evident right away; you see it and you grasp it at once—and you take it for an achievement of real art, for a fortunate discovery, for a new victory over the old. Having hit upon external realism, we followed the line of least resistance. Justice makes us state that a very important creative essential, the basis of any art, was concealed—we may not even be conscious of this—but still present among all our mistakes of the time. This was the striving for genuine artistic truth. This artistic truth was rather external for us at that time; it was the truth of sounds, costumes, properties, stage lighting, furnishings, material objects, the exterior of the actor's face, and his external physical life; at least we succeeded in doing one thing, in bringing authentic—even if only external—artistic life to a stage where false theatricality was then reigning, and this unveiled certain prospects for the future.[19]

All the unfriendly critics and fanatical opponents of the Moscow Art Theater among the "leftist" directors could also see, however, that Stanislavsky stood on a new and higher psychological plane then did any of the other Russian directors then active. Unlike the others, he was the first to understand profoundly that sets, sounds, lighting, and material objects were closely connected with the psychic and physical state of the human being in their midst. He realized that they not only acted on the human soul but were able to reveal it. He realized that the authenticity of material objects, the truth of the material surroundings aided the actor to believe in the reality of life on the stage and in the "ego of the role." Truthful settings engendered truthful emotions. Later on, Stanislavsky transferred the center of gravity to a psychological realism of the inner world. The naturalism of material objects were no longer significant just in themselves: the staging of a play was transformed into a means for revealing the psychology and the way of life of the people moving on the stage.

The struggle of Stanislavsky and Nemirovich-Danchenko for truth to life on the stage enriched the Russian theater with a great and new method of stage expression, a new means for revealing the human heart. This was *mood*. For the first time, a troupe deserved to be called a "theater of moods." The Moscow Art Theater showed that one and the same experience could be painted in an infinite number of different tints and shades, depending on the spiritual condition of the person at the given moment and the influence of the given inner and outer circumstances. The new theater showed that mood exists as a certain tonality of experience, as an internal leitmotif that subordinates and colors all human sensations. Dutch-tile stoves, snow beyond the windows, the sound of crickets, and lighted candles were used to achieve an atmosphere of warmth and coziness on the stage. The patter of rain, the splashing of horses' hooves in puddles, and dim light filtering in from the window created the atmosphere of autumn boredom. The Moscow Art Theater utilized all these means to produce a definite inner mood in the performers so that the setting and the heart would be in unique harmony.

This new, inner dimension was born of the search for outer truth. Mood and atmosphere did more for the Russian theater than to open up new ways of expression. They impelled it to seek something completely new and psychologically much more profound. This was the inner technique of acting.

THE BIRTH OF THE STANISLAVSKY SYSTEM

Another major development in the Russian theater during the pre-Revolutionary period of the Moscow Art Theater was the birth and refinement of the Stanislavsky System. Inasmuch as this System has recently been acknowledged as the basic creative method for the Soviet theater, we shall have to study the basic phases of its development.

In the summer of 1906 Stanislavsky tore himself away from the endless chain of rehearsals, productions, and worries about the theater and took a vacation in Finland. There he began to ponder the reasons for his recent woodenness and lifelessness on the stage. He faced the problem squarely and came to the conclusion that clichés had been accumulating within himself that were akin to those against which he had rebelled some eight years earlier. "I copied naïveté, but I was not naïve. I took short steps in walking, but I sensed no internal haste producing them, etc. I was playing more or less artificially, imitating the outer phenomena of action and experience itself." [20] With staggering realization he understood that he, too, was playing only the outer results—the hackneyed motions that did not come from the actor's heart.

[I] had made a great discovery and realized the old truism that the inner emotions of an actor on the stage before the thousands in the audience and with the footlights turned on were unnatural and the main obstacle to working in public . . . that in such a physical and spiritual state, one can only pose, perform, and seem to experience, but cannot possibly live or give himself up to feeling.[21]

It became clear to Stanislavsky that an actor needs some kind of "spiritual attire," something leading into the "spiritual atmosphere that alone makes the creative sacrament possible." [22] He understood that all his experiments in planting the outer truth of life on the stage had not solved the knottiest problems in the theater—helping the actor to bring real emotion to his part. He wondered whether an actor could be taught to evoke creative inspiration on the stage whenever he wanted to.

Stanislavsky began the period of experiencing through suffering. He observed himself and his fellow actors on the stage. He examined the state of the actor at rehearsals. He tortured the actors with all kinds of experiments. He wrote: "They grew angry; they said I was transforming the rehearsals into the efforts of an experimentalist, that actors were not to be studied like rabbits." [23]

The first and most important conclusions that Stanislavsky came to from this set of tests was that bodily freedom plays an essential role in the inner emotion of creation. By bodily freedom, he meant the absence of tenseness in the muscles, the complete subordination of the actor's physical apparatus to the commands of his will. As an actor, Stanislávsky sought to free his muscles from tension. When he succeeded, he felt happy and free.

Quite by accident, Stanislavsky made another discovery that was to play a decisive role in his new system of inner technique. He found that when his attention on the stage was absorbed in experimenting with his "freedom of the muscles" he lost the feeling that there was an audience on the other side of the footlights, and he stopped fearing it. For minutes at a time, he forgot that he was on the boards, and it was at just those periods that his inner, creative emotion was especially good. Hence, along with the first rule about "freedom of the muscles," a second rule was discovered: the actor's powers of concentration were especially important for the inner, creative feeling. The actor's work, Stanislavsky stated,

includes, first of all, *complete concentration of his entire spiritual and physical nature*. It embraces not only sight and hearing, but all the five human senses. Furthermore, it includes the body, thinking, the mind, the will, feeling, memory, and imagination. The entire spiritual and physical nature must be directed at creating whatever is taking place in the heart of the character being depicted.[24]

It would be difficult to overestimate the importance of this discovery. Let us remember that it gave rise to such parts of the Stanislavsky System as the "circle of attention" and the even more important phenomenon of "public solitude." The absorption in inner action was the lever used to isolate the actor from the audience, to create in him a feeling of solitude before the crowd, and only in this way could the actor completely immerse himself in the thoughts and experiences of the role.

Timidly but persistently, Stanislavsky kept seeking new links for his System. He discovered the magic formula of "if." Stanislavsky considered the "if" to be the principle of creative acting:

From the time when the *if* appears, the actor is carried away from the plane of real life to that of the life that he is imagining. Once he believes it, the actor can begin to work. The stage is the truth in which the actor sincerely believes, and even an obvious falsehood must become the truth in the theater in order to be art.[25]

(In the future, the Bolsheviks would make brilliant use of Stanislavsky's final conclusion to transform the obvious lies of propaganda into the truth on the stage.)

From the very beginning, the Stanislavsky System linked the problems of acting with a knowledge of human psychology. And this was one striking difference between Stanislavsky and other theater people during the *fin-de-siècle* period. Most of the others considered the intrusion of science into the sacred realm of Apollo to be coarse blasphemy. Stanislavsky repeatedly asserted that if such a great, pure, and inspired art as music has long had profound, scientific, and theoretic bases, then the art of acting has no reason to avoid science. The misfortune of the theater was that it had no scientific foundations of its own before.

The point of departure for the Stanislavsky System was the psychology of Théodule Ribot (1839–1916); a Russian translation of this Frenchman's *Psychologie des sentiments* (1896) had appeared in the year when the Moscow Art Theater was founded.[26] Ribot explained that the final ideal of any memory consists in preserving the imprint of anything that one has already experienced, so that it might be comparable in strength to the original impression. Ribot's ideas were not generally applicable to acting, because they state that a person completely understands all the aspects of the emotions reproduced. Stanislavsky, however, frequently observed the distinction between experience on the stage and in life. Were it not for this difference, Stanislavsky declared, the actor playing tragic roles could hardly depict the genuine torments of his heart every day and die a tragic death because of them. He noted that, unlike individuals in real life, actors direct their highly excited emotionalism according to the design intended for the role. Their consciousness always controls their experiences, and it does not at all let them lose themselves in those experiences. Despite this, very many of Stanislavsky's opponents persistently advanced a charge that was not true: that his System made no distinction between life and the stage and was therefore defective.

Stanislavsky went further and deeper than Ribot on the subject of recalling highly excited emotionalism. Such memories were a powerful weapon in his System for taking an actor away from clichés and stereotypes.[27] Since not only an actor's heart recalls the experiences it has lived through, but his body also remembers whatever it was doing at such times, he is naturally led to the complexity of genuine experience. He therefore grew used to considering whatever he had personally gone through as being more valuable than what was borrowed or copied. A feeling that he had experienced belonged authentically to life itself and his recalling of it erected a firm bridge between himself and truth to life.

The complicated spiritual process of returning to what he had lived through gave the actor a fine edge and made him a more subtle psychologist. Stanislavsky did not limit the significance of intense emotion to the actor's personality alone. His knowledge of his own heart and emotions also made the actor a connoisseur of the psychology of others, led inevitably to a deeper and keener understanding of the feelings and psychology of the people around him in life. And this awareness of self and others in the Stanislavsky System was the basis upon which the Moscow Art Theater later grew into a theater of psychological realism.

The mechanism of highly excited emotionalism was also the real strength that enabled the actor easily to reproduce all the experiences that had been discovered at rehearsals. Stanislavsky explained that an actor does not create a role through a single inspiration—as some theoreticians mistakenly think—but through a number of inspirations that are evoked and set at rehearsals and repeated in accordance with the intense emotions that the actor feels at the time he is working.

But Stanislavsky did not limit the inner technique of acting to the naturalistic process of merely recalling highly excited emotionalism. Everything acquired through memory, association, and deeply felt personal experiences is only the seed. The seed can be made fruitful only through creative fantasy and imagination. The memory of intense emotion is but the raw material for a genuine creative act.

In the first outline of his System, Stanislavsky divided the actor's work into six basic processes: (1) The preliminary *wanting*—the wish to work is aroused; (2) *seeking*—the capabilities that have been aroused by the actor's wish to work find the raw material for his task both inside and outside himself; (3) *experiencing*—the actor creates and lives through the inner and outer character of what he has created, even if at first only in his dreams; (4) *impersonating*—the actor creates an outer covering for the character thus envisioned; (5) *blending*—experience and impersonations are interwoven; (6) *influencing*—the work of the actor before the public compels the audience to share the actor's experiences.

Work on a presentation at the Moscow Art Theater began with a long period of table work, which preceded the rehearsals. The director and actors analyzed the play profoundly and sought its *trunkline of action*—that is, the mainstream of its action with which the tributaries of the separate characters are blended. The trunkline of action is established through each of the roles. The trunkline of action in *Hamlet,* for example, consists in revealing and punishing the murderer of the Prince's father. The next step is to ferret out the interplay between the trunklines of action for all the characters, with their struggles, defeats, and victories as their wills clash.

Before Stanislavsky, both the stage directions of the playwright (such as "jealously," "madly," "happily," and "lovingly") and the instructions of the directors from the old school demanded that the actor depict emotion from the very first rehearsal. The actor was told that his jealousy in a given scene should be mad, that wrath rather than malice was needed, or that a person had to be depicted who was deeply in love, and so forth. It was primitive, barbarous, and illiterate, however, to demand the end results of a complex, psychological process in the human spirit straight off. An actor could respond only with an artisanlike portrayal, a rigidly stamped product of the given experience. He had to show "love" right away, so he held his hand to his heart and made his voice grieve sweetly, but he did not experience love itself. At the first rehearsal an actor was asked to exhibit "terror," so he rolled his eyes and backed up clumsily, but his heart lacked even a semblance of fright.

Stanislavsky replaced the idea of emotion—which had always defined the result in the theater—with *experience,* a more accurate word that deals with the action, the process. At first glance, this change seems unimportant, but it concealed a major improvement of inner technique. A static stereotype was replaced by a process; it made the actor realize that this process had to have a beginning—the hypothesis that engendered it. Stanislavsky showed the actor that feelings and passions are the result, the final link in the chain of complex inner actions. And he found the vital link in the mysterious chain of the origin of emotions. He made it basic, simple, and comprehensible to any actor. This link is ordinary human desire. He revealed to the actor that any emotion is divided into cells of desire and that the complex nature of the end result—of emotion —comes from conflicts, from the success or failure in realizing the various wishes. The magic word "desire" was one of the firmest bridges to the truth of real life; for human existence is an infinite chain of wishes and anxieties, and at any moment of his conscious life a person is either striving toward something or trying to get away from it.

The subtext, with its desires and tasks, was also a potent means for transferring the art of the stage from the external art already in general existence to the complex depths of the human psyche. Stanislavsky thus created a theater of psychological realism that most subtly revealed the recesses of the human soul. This theater was two-thirds inner action, which was linked to the subtext during the long and thorough analysis of both the play and the roles at the preliminary period of table work.

The general theater practice had been for actors to memorize their roles almost as soon as they saw the text. The Stanislavsky System, however, kept postponing the memory work, and thus it prevented acting clichés. The actors of the Moscow Art Theater began by analyzing the psychological design of the role and mastering the heart and soul of the character. The Stanislavsky System made the actor invent a biography for the character, which included his "prehistory"—his life before the play—and his life after the play. The actor had to improvise all kinds of situations from the life of his character that the dramatist had not mentioned in the play. These methods made an actor feel at home in the play. He memorized not the text but the spirit of the character he was playing. After this phase the actor began to study, to outline, and to improvise upon the trunkline of the action, the bits, and the desires that go with the role. The important preliminary—or "pre-text"—work gave the actor a much greater comprehension of the character and his psychology. He was in a position to play any situation suggested by the life of the character, including the circumstances proposed by the playwright.

At first, the Stanislavsky System, like the initial phases of any other great discovery, met with ridicule, rejection, and resistance. Even the company of the Moscow Art Theater considered it as so much eccentric and ridiculous experimentation on the part of the restless Stanislavsky. The System was too revolutionary and incomprehensible even for the troupe of the outstanding theater in Russia, and Stanislavsky needed years to win his own theater over to his System.

In December, 1909, Stanislavsky scored the first victory for his System when he applied it in staging Ivan Turgeniev's play *Mesiats v derevne* ("A Month in the Country"). One of his letters tells about this triumph: "Understand what it is worth to turn the entire troupe straight off to the direction in which we have been going gradually and systematically. This made everyone pay attention to my system, which I had adequately prepared even before those years." [28]

Turgeniev's play was a good choice for the debut of the System. It was rather motionless, like a watercolor of the outer world, but it was rich in the portrayal of the inner life of the characters and in the complexity of their emotion. "The play was so subtle in its psychology," Stanislavsky wrote, "that it permitted no setting. Come, sit on a bench, and undergo experiences with almost no gesturing. The inner design of the play had to be worked out to an unprecedented degree." [29] This presentation also marked a major advance by the Moscow Art Theater towards psychological theater.

The Stanislavsky System finally became part of the Moscow Art Theater after the production of Leo Tolstoy's *Redemption* in 1911. At that time, Nemirovich-Danchenko—who had completely failed to share Stanislavsky's enthusiasm—addressed the company of the Theater and insisted that Stanislavsky's methods be studied by the actors and accepted by the Theater in its future productions.

THE DIRECTOR AT WORK

Stanislavsky and Nemirovich-Danchenko were the first to raise the director's toil to the heights of creative independence. They made the director the guide of the theater's ideas and the composer of the presentation. They discovered that producing a play called for much work about which the Russian theater workers of the time were ignorant. Stanislavsky and Nemirovich-Danchenko started using a period of preparation, the prerehearsal period. The director studied in museums during this time and examined the literary, historical, and iconographical materials that characterized the period, the people, the places, and the ways of life portrayed in the play. He made expeditions to places that would show him the environment in which the characters moved and lived. For example, trips were made to the countryside for the production of Leo Tolstoy's *Power of Darkness* and flophouses were visited when the Moscow Art Theater worked on Gorky's *The Lower Depths;* Rome was visited before the presentation of *Julius Caesar*. At the same time, the director demanded that the performers read historical and literary materials in preparation for their roles.

The play was analyzed more broadly and profoundly than in the past and in other theater companies. The director did more than reveal the idea of a dramatic work: he established the trunkline of the action and "supreme task" of the play as a whole and of each separate part in it. The Moscow Art Theater developed the orchestration of a complex, symphonic presentation. Stanislavsky's directorial notebooks—such as the one for *The Lower Depths*—are striking because they list all the stage effects exactly and exhaustively. They not only contain sketches of all the sets, but they even predetermine the acting of all the roles. In this respect, Stanislavsky's copies of the dramatic texts may be compared to the "ironclad shooting scripts" of motion pictures in the recent past.

The notebooks for *The Lower Depths* also reveal the rich possibilities that Stanislavsky discovered for scoring the presentation. Before the start of every act, the director's copy had a heading called "mood." Stanislavsky's artistic power made this an example of his collaborating with the playwright. Thus, the mood at the start of Act IV is described as follows:

Night. Warm, springtime, moonlit. Stuffy—even the outer door has been thrown open. Quiet, both in the flophouse and outside. In the yard only a dog is howling . . . far off in the distance one can hear the noise of a belated carriage passing by. At times there is the distant whistling of a train. The whole city is sleeping. The flophouse too. Wheezing and snoring permeate the entire cellar. Just a group of rummies—night owls—who have been whooping it up. A child has awakened and begun crying. The sleepy mother feeds him from her withered breast. Toward morning the Suspicious Lady returns. Behind her, Aleshka the Tramp. . . . The flophouse is lit by a single lamp hanging above the plank beds downstage. In the back the light is out, and the patches of moonlight coming through the windows and the open doorway give the cellar an ominous look.

Stanislavsky and Nemirovich-Danchenko were the first Russian men of the theater to have laboratories for seeking new stage effects. In the new directorial art the décor, costumes, make-up, furnishings, properties, and stage equipment were no longer requisitioned from whatever happened to be in storage. Instead they became paints on the great palette of the director. He used them creatively to reveal his own concept of the presentation. The director worked closely with the designer. For the first time, trial maquettes and numerous sketches were used in seeking décor. Stanislavsky himself did not hesitate to show his ideas of staging to the designer. The Moscow Art Theater asserted that every object on the stage was itself a role, a part of the theater arts. The Theater felt that bad décor, tasteless furnishings, or unimaginative stage effects could destroy the artistic value of a presentation just as bad acting could.

The new type of directorial work also improved the staging of crowd scenes. Prior to the work of the Moscow Art Theater crowd scenes were understood only quantitatively, and the host of supernumeraries was disorganized and responded chorally and primitively to the action. Stanislavsky made the crowd a gathering of individuals, each with his own characteristics and idiosyncracies. Every extra must be an artist, he felt, and play a mature, polished, definite, and characterized role. His new method of staging crowd scenes helped create the unified ensemble at the Moscow Art Theater. The group was harmoniously subordinated to a single concept and a single creative will.

The new Moscow Art Theater asserted the symphonic quality of a play. The presentation—rather than the role or the acting—was the work of art. The director in the Moscow Art Theater was like a composer in that he brought artistic unity to scenic heterogeneity. He subordinated the separate bits, scenes, colors, and effects to a particular idea. He brought his own rhythm to the action in its shadings of intensity, its rising and falling, and its pauses. He treated the presentation like a symphonic work of the most complex rhythm and melody. The noise of the wind, the shadows of the clouds, every piece of décor, all the objects, and the actor's complete performance—his silences as well as his words—were all of great importance in scoring the production for the stage.

Stanislavsky's affirmation of the art of directing in the Russian theater engendered a mighty school of new directors—the monarchs of the theater. The autocratic extremes of the directors—which have also existed in Soviet times—had both their positive and negative aspects. The history of the Soviet theater is indebted to the "theater of the director" for many productive innovations and for a great revolution in form.

REALISM VS. FANTASY

Hostile criticism of the Moscow Art Theater and its constellation of pioneering directors increased. The theater of Stanislavsky and Nemirovich-Danchenko was charged with being an absolutely naturalistic organization that copied reality. Stanislavsky himself, however, admitted certain extremes of naturalism and soon eliminated them. The Moscow Art Theater then became, basically, an organization of lofty psychological realism. This was shown in one of its first productions—Chekhov's *The Sea Gull*. The Theater did not superficially reproduce the outer naturalism depicted in the play. The production revealed the complex human spirits, with deeply subtle psychological changes, and the truth of living experience inherent in Chekhov's work.

This psychological realism, however, was not the only way in which the Moscow Art Theater influenced the Russian stage both before and after the Revolution. The Moscow Art Theater was the first Russian theater to begin looking for the dimension of the unreal in fantasy, mysticism, and symbolism. This line of development should be studied if only because it nurtured such major reformers of the stage as Vsevolod Meyerhold, Feodor Komisarzhevsky, and Alexander Tairov—to say nothing of the many trends in the "leftist" theater after the Revolution.

The plays of Hauptmann, Ibsen, and Maeterlinck, which were new to Russia, were produced by the Moscow Art Theater in its search for new forms of scenic expression far removed from the devices of naturalism. This Theater sought and found the devices of the symbolic and the impressionistic stage. Stanislavsky, however—unlike some later reformers in the Russian theater—considered that the symbols could be revealed only through the lofty realism of the actor's experiences:

Symbolism, impressionism, and all the other refined "isms" in the art belong to the superconscious and begin where the ultranatural leaves off. But the superconscious emerges from its secret hiding place only when the actor's spiritual and physical life is developed on the stage naturally and normally, in accordance with the laws of nature itself. With the slightest coercion of nature, the superconscious hides in the depths of the heart, fleeing from the coarseness of muscular anarchy.[30]

This was a statement of the most profound importance. Later reformers, such as Meyerhold and Tairov, favored symbolism, mysticism, fantasy, and other forms of the unreal on the stage. They, however, were always faced with an unpleasant fact: their notions were hindered by the real, live, three-dimensional body of the actor and the reality of his experiences. They sought issue from this contradiction in their attempts to "stylize" the actor, to subordinate his living body, voice, and feelings to a predetermined and unreal scheme and concept. They wanted to transform the actor into an affected marionette, whose motions, intonations, and deeds belonged to a world of unreal dimensions. They had an unsolvable problem. They never succeeded in dematerializing the actor and thus transforming the living person into an abstraction, a chimera, or a diagram. The actor always interfered with their conventionally symbolic décor and their abstract constructions on the stage. He was an alien bit of genuine reality.

Stanislavsky's attitude toward the fantastic, the symbolic, and the unreal was deeper, truer, and directed more toward the future. Like Edgar Allan Poe, Stanislavsky asserted a certain reality within the fantastic. The power of Poe's fantasy arises through a person remaining human and real in a mystical and fantastic situation. The same was true about Stanislavsky, for whom everything unreal had its profound, inner justification. The power of the unreal at the Moscow Art Theater lay in the fact that the unreal was made real, while living, natural persons were left alone. It has been asserted that to engender the unreal in living persons is both possible and legitimate. Just as a person journeys to a magical and improbable world in his dreams and remains alone there, so symbolism, mysticism, and folk tales are journeys by the living to a world of other dimensions.

This does not mean, however, that all of Stanislavsky's decisions were good ones. In dealing with fantasy, he found the real nature of phantasmagoria in *Die versunkene Glocke* and *The Snow Maiden*. In dealing with mysticism, his productions of Hauptmann's *Hannele's Himmelfahrt* and a number of plays by Leonid Andreyev were deeply justified. In dealing with symbolism, however, some of his experiments made the identical errors and brought him to the same blind alleys to which Meyerhold was later brought by his experiments.

The huge success of the Moscow Art Theater's realism in the period from 1898 to 1904 did not compel Stanislavsky to rest on his laurels or to be satisfied with what he had already discovered. He was obsessed by the fear that the Theater might enter the blind alley of naturalism, and he sought ways to depart from depicting the daily life of the philistines and their everyday feelings on the stage. What forms could the theater use to transmit the superconscious, the lofty, and the noble from the life of the human spirit? "Why is it," Stanislavsky asked, "that we, the actors of the drama, cannot renounce materialism and attain incorporeality? It must be sought!" [31] He was obsessed by a wish to create a laboratory for seeking new forms having nothing in common with the victorious psychological realism of his theater. These new forms would be able to express "lofty feelings, the sorrow of the world, the feeling of the secret of existence, [and] the eternal." [32]

He brought back Meyerhold, who had left the Theater in 1902.

Meyerhold had gathered a troupe together in the provinces with which he was searching for new paths in the theater arts. In 1905 the "Theater Studio" of the Moscow Art Theater came into existence on Pozharskaya Street in Moscow. Stanislavsky defined its aims as renewing dramatic art through new forms and devices of scenic performance:

The *credo* of the new Studio, in short, comes to this: realism, and [depicting] the way of life have outlived their age. The time has come to stage the unreal. Not life itself, as it occurs in reality, must be depicted, but rather life as is vaguely perceived in fantasies and visions at moments of lofty emotion. This is the spiritual situation that must be transmitted scenically, in the way that painters of the new school use cloth, musicians of the new trend write music, and the new poets, poetry. The works of these painters, musicians, and poets have no clear outlines, definite and finished melodies, or precisely expressed ideas. The power of the new art lies in its combinations of colors, lines, musical notes, and the rhyming of words. They create general moods that carry over to the public unconsciously. They create hints that make the most unobservant person create with his own imagination.[33]

It is not difficult to realize that Stanislavsky and Meyerhold were seeking impressionistic devices for the theater. The experiments included Maeterlinck's *La Mort de Tintagiles* and Hauptmann's *Schluck und Jau*. Let us mention here only that the Studio lasted but a short time. Stanislavsky became disillusioned with its experiments and closed it. For him, they only asserted the hegemony of the director and the designer over the stage and transformed the actors into marionettes. The search for impressionism, Stanislavsky declared,

came not from within, from inner experiences, but merely from the eyes and ears, from external imitation of the new forms. . . . It is easy to say that we should bring to the stage whatever we see in music, painting, and the other arts that have gone far beyond us. Good for them! The artist's canvas accepts all the lines and forms that quaint fantasy makes appear. But what do we do with our physical body?[34]

Stanislavsky did not consider that Meyerhold's experiments solved the antinomy between the "left" décor and devices in the directing and the "right" natural body of the actor. Stanislavsky objected to Meyerhold's treatment of actors as clay with which to give form to his ideas.[35] Thus Stanislavsky, despite his own tendencies in that direction, expressed opposition to the theater of the director.

The failure of the Pozharskaya Street Studio did not stop Stanislavsky. He continued his dangerous journey to the land of the unreal. In 1907 he staged Andreyev's *Zhizn' cheloveka* ("Life of a Man") at the Moscow Art Theater. The play itself was something of an experiment, a departure from the realistic portrayal of existence to a world of shadows and patterns. The entire stage was hung with black velvet to emphasize the gloomy and mournful action of the whole drama. This made the black parts of the characters' costumes seem to disappear against the walls and the floor, and the protagonist—Someone in Gray (personifying Fate)—appeared even more somber. Stanislavsky created designs for the décor to suit the sketchiness of the dramatic material. White lines on the black velvet merely sketched the rooms, windows, chairs, doors, and tables. Beyond these outlines, one could sense boundless mist. Lines of the design were also painted on the costumes, parts of which were made of black velvet to blend with the background. This isolated separate portions of the actors' bodies and gave the characters somber and grotesque shapes. Instead of using living voices and living intonations, the actors spoke drily, as if making official reports. Both life and people appeared on the stage suddenly and disappeared unnoticeably, dissolving into the fog. This is Stanislavsky's description of Act III:

A great ballroom, testifying to the luxurious life of the rich Person, is outlined in golden string. A shadowy orchestra conducted by a phantom; despondent music; the ghastly dances of two people whirling around and, downstage and along the footlights, a number of monstrous old hags, millionaires, rich young maids and swains, and well-dressed ladies. . . . Rich, somber, black and gold fabrics with flashy, colored spots on the women's dresses; black, gloomy, frock coats; dull, smug, motionless faces. . . . "How beautiful! How splendid! How rich!". . . . The guests waxed lifelessly rapturous.[36]

The production of the last scene, the death of the drunken Man at the inn, was especially powerful. Stanislavsky says:

The black Parcae with long cloaks are reminiscent of long-tailed rats, creeping across the floor; their senile whispering, lisping, coughing, and grumbling inspires terror and is foreboding. Then, way downstage, drunken figures are born of the fog both singly and in groups, and disappear in it. They speak hoarsely, gesture despairingly or stand motionless in a drunken stupor, like a vision during a feverish delirium. At one moment, they fill the room with a shout, and then fall silent again, retaining only some muffled sighs and drunken breathing as the residue. At the moment when the Man dies, a multitude of huge, human figures grows to the ceiling and flies in the air; below, from under the floor, creeping reptiles appear. . . . A complete bacchanale is created which, probably, seems a severe agony to the dying man. And then comes the final, terrible, resounding blow which penetrates mind and body—and the life of the Man is over. Everything disappears: the Man himself, the phantoms, and the drunken nightmare. Only, against the bottomless, boundless mist, again the huge figure of Someone in Gray appears and grows larger until, in a fateful, iron, irrefutable voice he utters the judgment of all mankind once and for all.[37]

Stanislavsky's production of *The Life of a Man* can be considered to be the beginning of the gloomy and grotesque impressionism of the Russian theater. It will frequently be met with in the work of Meyerhold (both before and after the Revolution) and in many productions by Soviet directors, including so brilliant a reformer as Eugene Vakhtangov. The formula for the ball scene in *The Life of a Man* was to be used by many Soviet directors to determine the characters for the corpses of the capitalistic world.

Nemirovich-Danchenko's production of an adaptation from Dostoevsky's *The Brothers Karamazov* in 1910 also enriched the Russian theater through its new devices. It was the zenith of the Moscow Art Theater's achievements in its subtle methods of revealing the most complicated windings of human psychology. The absolute economy used in the outer staging of this production showed that a striking presentation could be given on an almost barren stage. Thus, a tree and a mild suggestion of a path were the décor for a field. A table, a dozen chairs, and a cloth suggested a dining room. There were other examples as well. The presentation was staged against a background of neutral cloths, hints, and details that created a symbol for wherever the action was taking place. In future years the theater would utilize this technique with increasing frequency. It permitted the concentration of all power on the inner revealing of the drama through the acting—leaving a naked actor upon the naked earth.

The experiments of the Moscow Art Theater in nonrealistic presentations included the production of Shakespeare's *Hamlet* by Gordon Craig, the famous English director and innovator, in 1911. Stanislavsky's boldest experiment was to invite Craig to the Moscow Art Theater. Craig had already rejected experience as a criterion for the stage. He dreamed of replacing the actor with a supermarionette.

Craig rejected flat décor, asserting that the actor's three-dimensional body demanded sculpture and architecture on the stage. Basically, Stanislavsky and Nemirovich-Danchenko had already learned this long before: in their struggle against falsehood in the theater they had risen up against painted, two-dimensional décor. Craig's contribution to the Moscow Art Theater—and through it to the Russian theater—was the abstract primitivism of three-dimensional shapes on the stage. The basic element of Craig's Moscow *Hamlet* consisted of screens of coarse, undecorated canvas, sometimes covered with gold. The various combinations of the huge but narrow screens hinted at corners, towers, palace halls, narrow streets, and other places. These square, neutral shapes served to augment Craig's various lighting effects. Craig asserted the need for blending the music, the lighting, and the movement of the architectural forms into a single musical quality. The synthesis of music, lighting, and architecture was also new for the Russian theater.

Craig also brought a special hyperbole to the Moscow Art Theater. His great intensification of the stage effects, his introducing of gigantic chimeras, influenced the techniques of Meyerhold and Tairov, not to mention many other innovators in the Russian theater both before and after 1917. There would always be a relationship between Craig's devices and Meyerhold's, and many of Tairov's productions would also bear the stamp of his apprenticeship with Craig.

SOCIAL AND POLITICAL THEMES

Another way in which the Moscow Art Theater differed from the Russian theaters that preceded it was that the theater of Stanislavsky and Nemirovich-Danchenko consciously and consistently chose plays by contemporary dramatists that dealt with important political and social problems. The Imperial theaters were apolitical in principle. The Moscow Art Theater spoke for civic virtues and, in a number of productions, preached socialistic ideas.

The democratic ideas of the Moscow Art Theater remained with it from the time it was founded. Stanislavsky and Nemirovich-Danchenko declared then that they were establishing a *national* theater. The fact that national theaters were restricted in their choice of plays by the censorship made the two men officially limit their tasks in art to those of a *public* theater. This in no way altered their steady course of service to the nation. In one of his speeches Stanislavsky declared that the Moscow Art Theater "cannot and does not have the right to serve pure art alone; it must respond to social currents, explain them to the public, and be the teacher of society." [38] The Theater has always remained true to this principle.

The Moscow Art Theater showed the Russian public nine dramas by Ibsen and four plays by Hauptmann.[39] Most of them dealt with the struggle against injustice and the dream of improving human society. Thus, the Moscow Art Theater opened a window from monarchist Russia to the world of Western democracy and its socialistic teachings.

Stanislavsky remarked about Ibsen's *An Enemy of the People:* "For us, [Dr.] Stockmann was neither a politician nor a soap-box orator, but only a just and honest man with an idea, a friend of his country and people—which is what every sincere and honest citizen of a nation must be." [40] The Moscow Art Theater was precisely such a just theater with an idea and the friend of the people. But there was a clear-cut distinction between the "social and political line" of the Moscow Art Theater— the phrase is Stanislavsky's—and the reality of the political parties in those times. Before the Revolution the Theater was never a megaphone for any party at all. It never lowered itself to crude forms of biased propaganda and agitation. Stanislavsky observed: "Art and tendentiousness are incompatible; each precludes the other. Once art even approaches tendentiousness, utilitarian or other nonartistic designs, it withers—like the flower in Siebel's hands." [41] This is almost prophetic of the terrible fate to which his Theater would be subjected in the years of Stalinism.

The Moscow Art Theater brought to Ibsen, Hauptmann, and Gorky not a party line but whatever the Theater found in those playwrights for accomplishing its lofty mission as a "teacher of society." The Theater defended the poverty-stricken and the oppressed and indicated that a time was coming when a system would be created—even in Russia— that would be subordinated to the principles of social justice.

The public of the Moscow Art Theater consisted of students and the national intelligentsia. There was reason for its dangerous repertory to be under constant surveillance by the tsarist secret police and censorship. The Theater served as a nucleus for everyone who was a decided free-thinker or socialist in Russian society. And some of its presentations took place in a charged political atmosphere. Thus, in the days when the students' general strike was suppressed on Kazanskaya Square in St. Petersburg, the Theater was touring the city with *An Enemy of the*

People. This served as the reason for a demonstration in the playhouse. Stanislavsky recalled:

The audience at that presentation consisted of select intellectuals; there were many scholars and professors. I remember that there were only gray-haired people in the orchestra seats. In view of the sad events of the day, the hall was aroused to the limit, and grasped at the slightest hints of freedom, and responded to every word of protest by Stockmann. That is why explosions of tendentious applause burst out at the most unexpected places in the action. It was a political presentation. The atmosphere in the hall was such that the closing of the theater and arrests were expected at any minute. The censors were present at all the performances of the play, and were watching to see that I—who was playing the lead—spoke according to the censored copy, and they usually found fault with every word that had not been permitted by the censorship; this time, they watched me with doubled attention. Special care was called for. When sections of a role have been repeatedly struck out and restored, it is easy to become confused or to say something extra. In the final act of the play, when Stockmann is setting his apartment in order after the crowd has sacked it, he finds the black frock-coat which he had worn to the public meeting the evening before amid the general mess. Seeing a hole in it, Stockmann tells his wife: "You ought never to wear a new suit when you go out to fight for freedom and truth."

The people in the playhouse involuntarily associated this sentence with the slaughter that had taken place on Kazanskaya Square where also, most likely, not a few new suits had been torn in the name of freedom and truth. After these words such an outburst of applause occurred in the hall that the performers had to wait. A few people jumped out of their seats and raced down to the footlights to offer me their hands. On that day I learned from my own experience the powerful influence which a genuine and authentic theater could have on a crowd.[42]

The regime greatly hindered the Moscow Art Theater's production of *Philistines*—Gorky's first play—in 1902. The Theater was under suspicion; the author, under police surveillance. The play was forbidden by Sipiagin, the Minister of Internal Affairs. Stanislavsky writes:

The times were politically confused and turbulent. The police and censorship watched our every step. . . . At first, they did not want to permit the play. A lot of hustle and bustle began. Witte struggled more than anyone else to have it allowed. *Philistines* was permitted, but with corrections.[43]

In the clash between the "fathers and sons" in *Philistines* Gorky showed the conflict between the old, outdated, and bankrupt social system and the new and more just one which ought to replace it. Gorky was born among the dregs of society, and his plays featured the life of poor, humble, and oppressed persons. Yet, even this man and his dreams were close to the Moscow Art Theater. His *Philistines, Lower Depths,* and *Children of the Sun* all had one aim—to protest against the injustices of Russian society. The Moscow Art Theater greatly modified Gorky's protest against the greedy and banal "landlords of life" of that time; the Theater strove for objectivity and did right by the villains, even seeking the good in them. As for the *Philistines,* however, even after the censors had crossed out a good deal of what the Theater had left in, the authorities still considered the play dangerous. Only subscription audiences were allowed to see it, and the governor of the city used detachments of police to check the tickets. Only after Nemirovich-Danchenko had insisted upon it to the officials in charge did the policemen start wearing frock coats and white cotton gloves in order not to frighten the public. One glance at policemen in frock coats was the comedy sensation of the time.

Another protector of the disinherited was the leading dramatist associated with the Moscow Art Theater—Anton Chekhov. His plays also forecast social tempests. Stanislavsky described that quality thus:

In the literature of the past age Chekhov was one of the first to sense the inevitability of revolution when the latter was only in embryo. . . . He was one of the first to sound the alarm. Who, if not he, began to chop down the flowering and beautiful cherry orchard, knowing that its time had passed, that the old life had been consigned to the junkpile irrevocably? Always trying to go forward, Chekhov could not have stayed in one spot. On the contrary, he evolved together with life and the age. As the atmosphere grew heavy and the revolution approached, he kept becoming more and more positive.[44]

The name of Chekhov brings us to what is greatest and most valuable in the pre-Revolutionary Moscow Art Theater.

"THE HOUSE OF CHEKHOV"

It is no exaggeration to state that everything that is most significant in the pre-Revolutionary Moscow Art Theater is indissolubly connected with the name of Anton Pavlovich Chekhov. A white sea gull has become the trade-mark of the Moscow Art Theater. Even today, the emblem decorates the Theater's curtain and posters; all the personnel of the Theater wear the device in their buttonholes. This has been a natural and legitimate development. Along with Stanislavsky and Nemirovich-

Danchenko, Chekhov must be considered the third founder of the Moscow Art Theater. The fact that "The House of Chekhov" these days has been named for Maxim Gorky results from the sad circumstances of Soviet life. Side by side with the sea gull emblem, they have placed the great name of a playwright who was closer to Bolshevism.

The Moscow Art Theater discovered its own identity and style during its very first year when it produced Chekhov's *Sea Gull*. Later, *Three Sisters, Uncle Vanya, Ivanov,* and *The Cherry Orchard* solidified and sharpened the creative method of the Theater. "We took Chekhov to our hearts," Nemirovich-Danchenko stated, "we lived and breathed the very same thoughts, worries, and emotions as he did." [45]

Chekhov's plays are the most valuable and original part of the entire work done by the Moscow Art Theater. They encouraged Stanislavsky profoundly to work out the problems of life on the stage and to seek a new inner technique of acting experience. Later, the Moscow Art Theater was to transfer the methods of Chekhov to its productions of all other playwrights, both classical and contemporary.

What did Chekhov bring to the Moscow Art Theater? First was his poetry of the commonplace—the revelation of the hidden beauty of man's inner world in the prosaic context of everyday life. The playwright also brought to the Theater a hatred for inner and outer falsehood, and he engendered in it a thirst for the truth that came from the secret recesses of the human heart, from sounds, silences, and implications. Chekhov created the art of "inner dialogue" in his plays, enriching the stage with a pregnant pattern of silences and pauses. He discovered the enormous world of new potentialities for revealing the human spirit through the theater of mood. More important, his plays, which are filled with the most profound sympathy for all the characters, confirmed the Moscow Art Theater in its tendency to justify the human being. Under Chekhov's influence the Theater tended to set high standards in choosing and producing its repertory.[46] And finally, his plays laid the basis for what Stanislavsky termed "the social and political line" of the Moscow Art Theater—the presentation of the negative aspects of the existing order and of hopeful dreams of a more just social order in the future.

Perhaps it was Chekhov's dream of a bright future, for which one had to keep suffering, rather than the Bolshevik program, that was most important after the Revolution in furthering the other revolution to which Stanislavsky, Nemirovich-Danchenko, many actors of their Theater, and numerous individuals in other theaters had been leading. The Moscow Art Theater accepted Chekhov's protest against the existing system, which was grinding down the lives of good people. This impulse to a better and more just future caused Chekhov's ideology to become that of the Theater.

The legacies of the great dramatist and of the reformer in the Russian theater were brought by "The House of Chekhov" through the Revolution and into the Soviet period. As will be seen below, the Moscow Art Theater always used the light and warmth of Chekhov's methods to ennoble and humanize the crude, false, ponderous, and frequently misanthropic works of Soviet drama. This was the great Christian meaning of the Theater's work. It was based on the reflected glow of the Sermon on the Mount. We shall see, however, that the Theater also used the faith of Chekhov as its inner justification for Soviet reality and that the troupe became sincerely partisan to Bolshevism. At first, the company did not understand that there was an impassable abyss between Chekhov's "two or three hundred years from now, life will be . . . wonderful" and the Bolshevik myth about building a Communist paradise on earth.

CHAPTER III

THE GREAT INNOVATORS OF THE PRE-REVOLUTIONARY THEATER

IN ADDITION TO STANISLAVSKY and Nemirovich-Danchenko, there were four other important creators in the pre-Revolutionary Russian theater —Vsevolod Meyerhold, Nikolai Evreinov, Feodor Komisarzhevsky, and Alexander Tairov.

VSEVOLOD MEYERHOLD

Vsevolod Emilievich Meyerhold began his spectacular career as an actor at the Moscow Art Theater. From 1898 to 1902 he performed a number of excellent roles there, including Vasily Shuisky in A. K. Tolstoy's *Tsar Feodor Ivanovich,* Konstantin Treplev in Anton Chekhov's *Sea Gull,* Malvolio in Shakespeare's *Twelfth Night,* Ivan the Terrible in A. K. Tolstoy's *Smert' Ivana Groznogo* ("The Death of Ivan the Terrible"), and Tusenbakh in Chekhov's *Three Sisters.*

Meyerhold left the Moscow Art Theater in 1902 and founded an association of actors with which he set off touring the southern provinces of Russia. It was there that he undertook directing for the first time. Between 1902 and 1905 his productions in the provinces were not especially original, being based for the most part on the realistic principles of the Moscow Art Theater. Not even his productions of "modern" plays so much as hinted at his later genius as a director.

Stanislavsky invited him to join the Moscow Art Theater Studio in 1905. This may be considered the first important phase of Meyerhold's directorial work. For the Theater Studio he set about producing Maurice Maeterlinck's *La Mort de Tintagiles* and Gerhart Hauptmann's *Schluck und Jau.* In these plays his rebellion against the creative methods of the Moscow Art Theater began to take shape. This was the time that the Russian theater began to split into two hostile camps, a division that would be the cause of so many trends both before and after 1917. The foundations were being laid for the theater in which the director rules, a trend that Meyerhold himself personified clearly and brilliantly.

Meyerhold rejected the three-dimensional, realistic décor of the Moscow Art Theater, and he returned to two-dimensional flatness and painted panels. Together with the designers—Sapunov, Sudeikin, and Ulyanov—he reveled in the iconography from the periods of *La Mort de Tintagiles* and *Schluck und Jau*. His aim in doing this was not to reconstruct the truth of the life and the mores of the past *a la* Stanislavsky, but rather to awaken his own creative fantasy. He wanted to create a feeling for the period through symbols and stylization. He decided, for example, to do *Schluck und Jau* in a stylized "age of powder." Court ladies were seated in bowers along the footlights; they were using outsized needles to embroider a ribbon en masse. The queen's chamber had a bed that was ornate and grandiose—including an extraordinary canopy—to the point of being ridiculous.

All trifles were abolished in a Meyerhold production. The basic point alone was transmitted. Meyerhold's method was to render period, style, and emotion through some brilliant characteristics. He neither copied exactly nor overloaded the stage with historical properties and trivia. He intended to do *La Mort de Tintagiles* in the style of living frescoes. He wanted to flatten the actors out and to construct the dialogue against a musical background.

Stanislavsky and Nemirovich-Danchenko approached their work with the actors psychologically and realistically, using the logic of experience. Meyerhold's point of departure was to saddle the actors with a definite, directorial concept. The actors were subordinated to a clear-cut pattern of movements and intonations arising from the director's fancy. The pattern was symbolical, stylized, and abstract.

In his very first effort Meyerhold asserted the hegemony of the director in the theater. The discord between the "theater of the actor" and the "theater of the director" led to a conflict between Stanislavsky and Meyerhold. As a result, neither *La Mort de Tintagiles* nor *Schluck und Jau* was presented to the public. The Studio was closed, and Meyerhold left the Moscow Art Theater for good. From then on, he opposed it fiercely.

The "theater of the director" was completely alien to Stanislavsky. Though he tolerated opposition to the realism of his theater, he rose up against the results of that opposition, against transforming the actor into a fragment painted into the décor. Stanislavsky considered the actor the sole bearer of the theater arts. The actor was alive and as wonderful as life itself. He was a player rather than a puppet. Stanislavsky described Meyerhold as a "talented director" who "tries to surround himself with actors who, in his hands, are ordinary clay for molding beautiful groups and settings that he uses to realize his interesting ideas." [1] Stanislavsky went on to explain his position in the conflict thus:

It would be possible to create a studio for the director and his work on productions. But at that time, the director interested me only insofar as he aided the work of the actor and not insofar as he concealed the bankruptcy of the latter. Hence, the studio of the director—fine as it might be—did not respond to my dreams of the time, especially when you realize that I was then disillusioned with the stage work of the designers—on cloth, in paints, in cut-outs [kartony], and in the external methods of staging—and with the tricks of the directors. All my hopes were directed towards the actors, towards working out solid bases for their work and technique.[2]

Meyerhold's work and split with the Moscow Art Theater Studio took place twelve years before the October Revolution. This period was permeated both with his rebellious struggle against naturalism and with his great discoveries in the theater of the unreal. A thorough analysis of all the facets in his work during this time lies outside the scope of the present study. We shall limit ourselves here to those reforms of his that would later have a major influence on the development of the Soviet theater.

Meyerhold left Moscow for a long time. In 1905 his St. Petersburg period began, which was one of the most productive in his life. He entered the Komisarzhevskaya Theater. Vera Fëdorovna Komisarzhevskaya was a leading actress of the day. She abandoned the stultifying routine of the Imperial theaters and created her own company. Like Meyerhold, she too dreamed of a "theater of the spirit," which would be free from the materialism of life. "Reproducing the way of life realistically has now become . . . uninteresting and unnecessary," she wrote, and "must disappear from the stage." [3] One of the most important presentations opposed to a realistic reproduction of life was Meyerhold's production of Henrik Ibsen's *Hedda Gabler*. This took place at the Komisarzhevskaya Theater on Ofitserskaya Street in St. Petersburg. The date of the première was November 10, 1906.

For Meyerhold, Ibsen's text was merely a pretext for an impressionistic and symbolic composition. Meyerhold rejected the way-of-life approach, the specific time, and the realism of objects and psychology, and he subordinated everything to his impressionistic stylization. All the stage furnishings served the mood that the director desired to transmit. A participant described it as follows:

The stage seemed enshrouded in a haze that was a mixture of blue, green, and silver. The backdrop was blue. At the right, an enormous French window extended the entire height of the stage. Through the window, one could see the greenish-indigo sky with its twinkling stars (in the final act). To the left of the curtain, an indigo tapestry showed a gold-and-silver lace. On the floor was a greenish-blue carpet. The furniture was white. The piano was white. The vases were a greenish white and contained white chrysanthemums. There were white furs on the strangely shaped divan. And, like sea water, like the scale of a sea serpent, the dress of Hedda Gabler appeared.[4]

The costumes were simplified and purified of realistic details, so that they were but colored spots in the general composition. Every character had his own color. The motions of the actors were also subordinated to the same stylization. They too opposed the way-of-life approach. The economy of movements and the sculptured quality were extraordinary. Every character also had his leitmotif in posing. The intonations had to be rhythmically blended with the lines and colors.

Meyerhold revealed a new method for staging in this presentation. He interpreted it not according to Ibsen's stage directions but according to his own ideas. In the future this assertion of the director's vision would be applied widely to the classics as well as to contemporary plays. After Meyerhold, Tairov of the Kamerny Theater, Eugene Vakhtangov, and many other Soviet innovators would use this method.

Meyerhold's first productions revealed a special feature that was to be found in all his work—the chief means that his directorial imagination used to arouse the public was the fine arts. In asserting his idea of a production, he always submerged himself in old engravings, bas-reliefs, frescoes, and medieval pictures or miniatures. He did this in his first experiment with La Mort de Tintagiles.[5] Meyerhold's stylization and his Uslovny teatr (Symbolical Theater) developed out of iconography. Furthermore, he was the first person in the Russian theater to hand the stage over to the designer. The painter was the most important orchestral section for the scenic symphonies that Meyerhold composed. He began to subordinate the Russian stage to the artist—something that would typify it during the first decade after the Revolution.

Having handed over the theater to the painter, Meyerhold for many years tried as hard as he could to flatten out the three-dimensional body of the actor, to transform it into a bas-relief, into part of a fresco, or even into a colored spot. He wished "to insert" the actor against a background of remarkable panels created by the brilliance of Russian impressionism.

In staging Maeterlinck's *Soeur Béatrice* at the Komisarzhevskaya Theater—the première was on November 22, 1906—Meyerhold created a chorus of nuns that seemed to have stepped out of the bas-reliefs in a medieval cathedral. The groupings in the scene showing Béatrice's death used as their point of departure old paintings. In order not to destroy the similarity to the ancient iconography, Meyerhold clothed the chorus in a single kind of gray garment, and he made it move constantly in half turns, endowing it with gestures that were few and monotonous.

Despite this harsh effort to make the actor two-dimensional, Meyerhold succeeded in transmitting a most religious feeling. He was aided by the settings, which were reminiscent of primitive miniatures. The production soared high above the trivia of everyday life. His version of *Soeur Béatrice* clearly showed both that the theater arts had potentialities beyond realism and that the Russian theater had not known about them.

Meyerhold discovered the best formulas for rejecting naturalism, formulas that were directed against the Moscow Art Theater. For many years his ideas became the common property of many innovators in the pre-Revolutionary and Soviet theaters. In Meyerhold's opinion the theater was supposed to offer hints to set the imagination of the audience in motion. Stanislavsky was trying to create the illusion of real life on the stage, but the theater is not life but art, Meyerhold replied, and the laws of art are profoundly different from those of life. He found support for his esthetic theory in the symbolist works of Maeterlinck, Bryusov, Alexander Blok, and Vyacheslav Ivanov.

Meyerhold's theory of the Symbolical Theater was of great importance in establishing a solid link between his early quests and the later "leftist" experiments in the Russian theater. Although Meyerhold himself acknowledged that "the [Moscow Art] Theater Studio undertook the first experiments in creating the Symbolical Theater," [6] it was his refinement of the tendency that was used by other creative directors of both the pre-Revolutionary and the Soviet theater.

The basic method of the Symbolical Theater consists in making the audience a creator of the presentation alongside the dramatist, the actor, and the director. Its staging gives the theatergoer an opportunity to use his imagination in inferring whatever is implied on the stage. Furthermore, in Meyerhold's words, the audience at the Symbolical Theater "never forgets for a minute that it is seeing actors who are playing, and the actors [never forget] that an auditorium is before them, a stage is beneath them, and décor is along the sides." [7]

The décor itself gives only hints: a window replaces a room; two trees, a forest; a cut-out with coarsely painted patterns of stones, a tower. Only those furnishings and properties are used that are absolutely necessary for the course of the action. The stage is not overladen with ornamental objects. And this is how Meyerhold defined the technique of the actor in the Symbolical Theater:

1. What is needed is the cold minting of words, completely liberated from the tremolo and the weeping of the actors' voices. Never tenseness or gloominess of tone.

2. The sound must always have support, and the words must fall like drops into a deep well. In stage speeches there must be no howling of the endings as if one were reading decadent verses. . . .

3. A mystical trepidation is stronger than the temperament of the old theater. This last was always unbridled, externally coarse (with its swinging of the arms, and its striking of the breast and thigh). The inner quivering of mystical trepidation is reflected in the eyes, in the lips, in the sounds, and in the way that the words are uttered. It depicts an outer peace in the presence of a volcano inside there. And everything is easy, without tension.

4. The experience of deep emotions and all its tragedy is inalienably connected with form, which is an integral part of content.

5. Epic calmness does not preclude tragic experience. Tragic experiences are always majestic.

6. Tragedy with a smile on one's face. . . . [8]

In connection with the plastic movements of the actor of the Symbolical Theater, Meyerhold asserted the primacy of motion over talk, an idea to which he would be faithful throughout his life. "Gestures, poses, glances, and silence," he wrote "determine the sincerity of the interplay between people." [9] Several years later, he asserted that motion, pantomime, is the basis of the theater.[10] In Meyerhold's formulation of the bases for the sculptured motions within the Symbolical Theater, we see once again the repetition of an idea to which his entire directorial career would be faithful: the dependence of staging conceptions and settings on the paintings of the old masters, from whom he mined the secrets of plastic harmony. Meyerhold felt that the director in the Symbolical Theater must know how to link the lines and the angles of the actor's motions with the lines and angles of the entire decorative idea. He must know how to renounce in part the changes in groupings and how to attain the secret of motionlessness. If a decorative panel is the background for the acting, the director must know how to apply the methods of simplifying the groupings; if the play has no décor, he must know how to apply the sculptured method.

In Meyerhold's theoretical bases for the Symbolical Theater, we first find his statement about the hegemony of the director. He called this the "triangular theater" because the audience perceives the actors' work through that of the director. (The playwright was, of course, the first creator in the process, but in Meyerhold's view he was not involved in the production.) The audience and the actor are the base angles of the triangle, while its apex is the director. In this theater the director reveals his concepts to the actors and rehearses them until the time that he hears and sees the play as he heard it and saw it when he was working alone on it. Meyerhold always remained faithful to his "triangular theater."

He, of course, saw more in his Symbolical Theater than a form of protest against the naturalism that he hated. It was more to him than a mere embodiment of the new, symbolist drama. He considered it the way to revive the theater of antiquity, which he considered the highest and most ideal theater form that has ever existed on earth. In that theater the audience participated actively in a sacred action. The audience saw its own fate in the masks of the tragic heroes and in their fortunes. That theater infected and transformed the audiences over the course of centuries. Later it went into a most complete decline and became a pitiful spectacle in which the audience passively "gaped" at whatever was happening on the other side of the footlights that separated it like an impassable abyss from what was happening on the stage.

Meyerhold considered that the Symbolical Theater, in its primordial forms, was similar to the theater of antiquity:

If the Symbolical Theater wants to eliminate décor, . . . does not want footlights, subordinates the playing of the actors to the rhythm of diction and to the rhythm of plastic movements, . . . if it anticipates a renascence of the dance and attracts the audience to active participation in its work, will such a Symbolical Theater not lead to a renascence of Antiquity? . . . Yes. . . .[11]

Thus began Meyerhold's lifelong struggle. The return to the forms used by the folk theater in the past, the stubborn struggle with the illusions of the scenic box, the forcible removal of its finery, the unveiling of the "kitchen" (that is, the technical work that goes into a presentation), the baring of the stage, the advancing of the proscenium, the removal of the curtain and the footlights, the filling up of the orchestra pit, the construction of steps and gangways to the auditorium and the transferral of action to it, the compulsory participation of the audience in the action, and the hundreds of Meyerhold's other clever devices would galvanize the audience of the intimate theater and aim at making them the fourth creator of the theater.

We have seen that Meyerhold set forth on his quest by using the ideas of others, which he never rejected, as his point of departure. That his starting point was not original with him is also shown by the fact that, two years before he wrote down his theory of the Symbolical Theater, he became acquainted with George Fuchs's book *Die Schaubühne der Zukunft*. Fuchs was a leading figure in the Munich Art Theater. His work influenced Meyerhold greatly, and Meyerhold acknowledged this.

In his book *O teatre* ("On the Theater") Meyerhold told how the first push toward determining the path of his art was given by a lucky invention of the planes of action in Alexander Blok's wonderful *Balaganchik* ("Farce"). *Farce* had its première at the Komisarzhevskaya Theater on December 30, 1906. This was a most important date both for Meyerhold's work and for the history of the Russian theater during that period. This production contained the roots of the phantasmagoria and the "tragic farce" that would be the leitmotif of all Meyerhold's future work. We shall also encounter it in the Soviet theater.

The plot of Blok's lyrical and symbolist drama can be told in a few words. The mystics are awaiting the arrival of Death. In Death, Pierrot recognizes his beloved. But his age-old rival, Harlequin, who is full of wild, earthly happiness, arrives and takes her—Columbine—away with him to the carnival. She later comes back in the guise of Death. The play is constructed not on action but on confused and brittle experiences. It served Meyerhold as a basis for creating a presentation that evoked storms of enthusiasm and indignation.

Meyerhold found in *Farce* illusion, unfaithfulness, duality in the characters (which is typical of Blok), and the trivia of the terrible "real world." At the end of the play, Pierrot lies on the floor of the empty stage without knowing whether his experiences have been real or only a drama of ghosts, a tragedy of phantoms created by his imagination. And were the torments that he bewailed phantom torments or were they real emotions? Neither he nor the audience at *Farce* could answer that question.

Here for the first time was the Meyerhold of evil irony, pitiless jeering, and grotesque buffoonery. The mystics sat solemnly in cardboard frock coats. Harlequin hurled himself through a window against a limitless blue world that turned out to be painted paper, a "counterfeit" that he tore up and cast upon the floor. Suddenly, the décor flew up to the fly-galleries. Living people died suddenly in distorted poses, as if they were only cut-out clowns crumpled by some unseen hand. As they died, they emitted cranberry juice. This malicious stressing of the cardboards, the painted and coarsely farcical world would be revealed in many of Meyerhold's future works. And Pierrot's last words in *Farce*—"I am sad. And are you amused?"—was like Gogolian laughter through bitter pain. It became a special feature in many Meyerhold productions, both of comedy and of his favorite genre, the "tragic farce."

The invisible dividing line between the real and the phantom (on which the play is developed) and the theme of the double (of the were-wolf Columbine-Death) attracted Meyerhold. The frightening theme of the werewolf and the double would in the future stir up and breathe a cold mysticism into his productions of Lermontov's *Maskarad* ("Masquerade"), of Sukhovo-Kobylin's *Death of Tarelkin,* and of other plays.

In *Farce* Meyerhold used a number of devices that were to be of great future importance. He did away with the traditional coulisse and hung all the walls of the stage with a dark blue canvas. In the center of this blue space there was a very small theater building. Since the top part of the building was not covered by "harlequin" the public could see how the décor of the farce was raised to the fly-galleries. All the lively action took place on the proscenium. The décor was changed in full view of the audience. There were also other examples of rejecting scenic illusion, of baring the "kitchen of the stage." The prompter, for example, crawled into his box and lit his candle.[12]

In *Farce* one must also seek the sources of Meyerhold's teachings about the "eternal farce," his renunciation of the theater of mystery plays, and his transition to the theater of "mask and farce," of *"cabotinage,"* and of the "grotesque." With *Farce,* too, Meyerhold began to leave his principle of flattening the actors into details of the panel and bas-reliefs in his productions.

His new attitude became stronger when he staged Leonid Andreyev's *Life of a Man* at the Komisarzhevskaya Theater in 1907. The following distinguished this production: the revelation of the magic of gray, smoky space into which the characters dissolve; new devices for lighting the stage with but one source of illumination (a lamp behind the divan in the first scene, a chandelier at the ball, a lamp hanging over the drunkards' table in the final scene); a reduction of the set-up to an absolute minimum; the use of furnishings and accessories of exaggerated proportions, and make-up, costumes, and poses to make the characters of the play stand out sharply. Meyerhold's "giganticism of things" began with his work on *Schluck und Jau* and was used later in many of his other productions.

One of his last productions at the Komisarzhevskaya Theater was his work on Frank Wedekind's *Frühlings Erwachen, eine Kindertragödie,* in 1907. Meyerhold here unveiled the device of dividing the stage into several short and isolated episodes by illuminating limited bits of the scenic platform. The décor for all eighteen scenes was established from the very beginning of the presentation. In complete darkness the spotlight picked out a bed and a chair. A short dialogue ensued. The light went out, and a minute later it was turned on in a glade upstage. This device allowed the rapid change of scenes and helped concentrate the attention of the audience. Thus, a device was prepared that would be of great use in the Soviet theater, a technical device that developed into a completely new type of drama and that enabled the playwright to write a huge number of short episodes. The places of action could be varied without limit and permitted the stage to adapt motion-picture devices, such as the concentration of the audience's attention on details, the influence of montage for the various episodes, and the opportunity for simultaneous action in different parts of the stage.

The production of *Frühlings Erwachen* was not a public success. Meyerhold's production of Maeterlinck's *Pelléas et Mélisande*—his final work for the Komisarzhevskaya Theater—was also a failure. Meyerhold in this production returned to motionlessness, paucity of gesture, and monotony of tone. He was stubbornly aiming to bring everything to "flatness" and "motionlessness," to a theater of dolls and marionettes in the hands of a mercilessly experimenting directress who distorted her theater into a laboratory for directorial effects. Komisarzhevskaya considered further work with Meyerhold impossible, and parted with him for good.

As Meyerhold had not gotten along with Stanislavsky in the past, so did he now not get along with Komisarzhevskaya. He was too demanding, unbending, merciless, and obsessed in his attitude toward the arts. Alexander Golovin, the designer, told V. A. Teliakovsky, the general manager of the Imperial theaters, that Meyerhold was dismissed from the Komisarzhevskaya Theater because he almost shot down everyone who was not attracted by innovation. There was always a storm raging around Meyerhold. From his first efforts in the theater the director acquired a good many enemies, whose malicious howling was heard throughout all of his great life. But this criticism was food for his soul.

One need only recall the reviews by the critic Kugel, dating from 1907, to realize the zeal with which certain adherents of the theater arts attacked Meyerhold. Kugel considered it his duty to protect the actors, and the "age-old potentialities of the human spirit, into which this directorial pike has sunk its hooks." [13] A violent opponent of the "theater of the director," Kugel felt that in Meyerhold's theater the author loses his originality and is presented to the actor in the colorless guise of the director-interviewer. He believed that the actor of the Symbolical Theater was chained in iron fetters by the director. Kugel declared: "Meyerhold, with his incorporeality, his negation of realism, and his contempt for life, is a very great and innate enemy of the theater." [14]

Meyerhold was denounced, not only by such "rightists" as Kugel, but by the "socialists" as well. Thus, Anatoli Lunacharsky—who was to become the People's Commissar for Enlightenment during the Soviet period —published an article against Meyerhold in 1907 called "On Art and Revolution." He termed Meyerhold's theater a theater of intellectuals gone sour, a center for decadent art.

On the one hand, all the attacks on the theater of directorial absolutism and the defense of the actor against the encroachments that transformed him into an experimental puppet seem, at first glance, to be justified. But, on the other hand, the "unenslaved" actor could never, through his own powers, have moved the Russian theater away from its dead stop or guided the search for new forms to advance the art of the theater as a whole. The enslavement of the actor to the director was and always would be the Achilles' heel of Meyerhold. But it would be unfair to state that he never did anything to discover new ways for revealing acting skill. An examination of his later experiments will clarify the contribution that he made to the art of acting.

In 1908 the mutineer and furious experimentalist was suddenly invited to be a director in the realm of tradition and routine—the Imperial theaters of St. Petersburg. He was personally invited by Teliakovsky, the general manager of the Imperial theaters.

Meyerhold produced Richard Wagner's *Tristan und Isolde* at the Imperial Marinsky Theater at St. Petersburg in 1909. The production contained new devices for building the movements of the actors on a musical basis and for blending the sculptured side of the production with rhythm. These were the principles upon which Tairov was to base many a production at the Kamerny Theater during Soviet times.

In Meyerhold's statements about his plans for staging *Tristan und Isolde* we encounter the idea that the stage had to be constructed as if it were a pedestal for sculpture, that is, in three dimensions, like the body of the actor.[15] Meyerhold declared that the director should also be a sculptor and architect and that in method the actor should correspond completely to a sculptor. Every gesture of the actor's, every motion, contains the form and lines of sculpture. Meyerhold departed from using the even floor of the stage, declaring that the floor of the stage should be uneven and transformed from a wide field to a compact series of planes having different heights.

One of Meyerhold's most significant productions for the Imperial Alexandrinsky Theater was Molière's *Don Juan* in 1910. The designer was Golovin. It was as if a storm had burst over all the traditions of that venerable theater. Meyerhold decided to recreate the atmosphere in which the presentation had taken place during the times of the Sun King and Molière. He unveiled the flavor of the sixteenth and seventeenth-century theaters, "jingling the bells of pure theatricality." But this, of course, was no reconstruction, but Meyerhold's own first love for the purely theatrical element, with which he was to be long obsessed. This production of *Don Juan* was a turning point in his work; he turned to the "theatrical theater," to a world of magic that had nothing in common with reality.

In this *Don Juan* we find devices everywhere that Meyerhold loved and that would survive the last days of his theater in Soviet Moscow. He removed the curtain and the footlights. He created a semicircular proscenium that cut deeply into the auditorium. He left the lights on in the hall throughout the presentation, lowering them only for certain pathetic passages. The stage was illuminated by huge, standing candelabra and by chandeliers with real candles. Meyerhold wanted to use all methods to remind the audience that it was merely seeing a presentation that was symbolic and deliberate. As one of his most remarkable means for stressing the conventions of the theater, he chose a "kurambo"—a proscenium attendant from the Japanese theater of the sixteenth and seventeenth centuries—whom he dressed fancifully for Molière's *Don Juan*. Negro boys in livery performed the roles of these "people in black." They arranged the stage in full view of the audience; they snuffed the candles. They were always present on the stage, silently performing a good number of tasks. They called the public by ringing a silver bell and notified the audiences of the intermissions. Two prompters, in wigs and stylized costumes and in full view of the public, came out of the wings and sat down behind ornate screens on both sides of the stage. The audience saw the prompters moving the curtains on the windows of the screens in order to do their work. This theatricality stressed that characters, going on a journey, simply walked around the large, semicircular proscenium, chatting with the public. It also emphasized that the "hell fire" was definitely an effect. When the stone guest appeared, the Negro attendants hid beneath the table that had been set for supper.

This production was enormously successful with both the press and the public. In *Don Juan* Meyerhold revealed new possibilities in the proscenium, which would henceforth enter his arsenal of devices. This flood of light, this free expanse of the proscenium to which the actor is very close, demands a special technique of motion from the actors, a filigreed clarity and a vividness in their gestures and pantomimes, that Meyerhold sought in his Studio shortly afterwards.

Meyerhold staged Gluck's *Orfeo ed Eurydice* at the Imperial Marinsky Theater on December 21, 1911. This had a great revolutionizing influence on the development of opera in Russia. It also contained a number of significant innovations that were later transferred to the stage. Here Meyerhold intensified the device of constructing his interpretation, not on revealing the period to which the dramatic material belongs (ancient Greece in this case), but on creating the flavor of that period in which the author lived and wrote. He thus continued what he had begun with *Don Juan*. Meyerhold discarded the search for the illusion of antique reality and decided to revive the "antique" style of the artists who were Gluck's contemporaries in the eighteenth century. This device would become quite widespread in the treatment of the classics by the Russian theater.

Meyerhold separated the other devices found in *Orfeo ed Eurydice* into two parts. The first was the painted background, and the second was that the proscenium was adorned with an embroidered fabric. The separation of the stage into a "passive" background and an "active" proscenium was a further development of the idea of emphasizing the proscenium. Along with Michel Fokine, the balletmaster, Meyerhold for the first time constructed the group movements, not according to their points of contact with the music, but according to an independent pattern, a parallel musical fabric, which appeared like a certain kind of sculptured and melodramatic declamation.

Meyerhold offered Richard Strauss's opera *Elektra* on February 18, 1913, at the Imperial Marinsky Theater in St. Petersburg. This production contained a typical contradiction arising from Meyerhold's characteristic revising of authors. He wanted to correct the shortcomings in the modernistic stylization of antiquity to be found in Hugo von Hofmannsthal's libretto. Meyerhold tried to link the opera to Sophoclean antiquity. He thus lost sight of the fact that Strauss's impressionistic music corresponded to antiquity even less than did Hofmannsthal's libretto. (Meyerhold did not build on traditional antiquity either but transferred the action to the Mycenaean culture that had been excavated between 1903 and 1909 by Sir Arthur Evans, the English archaeologist.) He was still atavistically attracted by the archaeological quality that he had borrowed from Stanislavsky, and he became obsessed with a passion for reconstructing the recently discovered Creto-Mycenaean culture. He consulted an archaeologist and, in clay boards and frescoes, set up façades that borrowed architectural motifs from the throne room at Cnossos and the palace at Aestos. The critics were right in pointing out the dissonance between the directorial devices and the music of the opera.

Elektra furthered the expansion of Meyerhold's directorial work. He had begun by rejecting Ibsen's stage directions for *Hedda Gabler*. In *Orfeo ed Eurydice* and *Elektra* he asserted that the director had the right to transfer the place of action to a period which, in his opinion, would better suit his conception of revealing its idea. In Soviet times the continuation of this line has led not only to "revisions," reworkings, and the "transmontage" of classical texts but has even introduced scenes from the author's rough drafts (as in Gogol's *Inspector-General*) and the idea that the director was the "author of the presentation."

None of Meyerhold's pre-Revolutionary innovations had such a great influence on the Soviet theater as those devices that he had discovered by reviving the acting techniques of the *commedia dell'arte* and other national theaters of the past. It would be almost impossible to list all the Soviet productions that used the principles of the Italian improvisational comedy, which Meyerhold had revived. In the first years of the Soviet regime Sergei Radlov's Theater of National Comedy arose in Petrograd. This organization used, for the most part, what Meyerhold had discovered in his experiments of 1917 and 1918. Nikolai Evreinov, Alexander Tairov, Eugene Vakhtangov, and many other outstanding masters of the Russian theater turned again and again to the immortal forms of the improvisational comedy and the technique of the old national theaters.

The static symbolism of Meyerhold's first productions seemed alien to Russian society on the brink of World War I. Profound, powerful, and dynamic changes were already rocking Russia below the surface. The thirst for motion seized Meyerhold. He tried to reject the sculptured quality. He wanted not to show art to a bored theater, but to force the art of the theater to bloom within the very midst of the audience.

His turning to dynamism in the theater, to the *commedia dell'arte,* was legitimate. The old market place theater, the theater of the fairs was itself motion. Its genealogy comes from the games of the old Russian *skomorokhi* (wandering buffoons and performers), the mimes and histrions of Rome, and the theater organically bound up with the essence of the Italian people. This ancient national theater was loud, noisy, and happy, like children released from the schoolroom. In the seventeenth century it conquered the "learned comedy" (*commedia erudita*) of the schoolmen, which sacredly observed the three Aristotelian unities. The art of the beggarly, wandering comedians of Italy began its triumphal procession from the market places through the palazzi of the grandees to the courts of Europe. Count Carlo Gozzi gave it its exact literary form in the eighteenth century, when he resurrected the art that had started to decline. Meyerhold accomplished a second renaissance of the *com-*

media dell'arte. He used it as a weapon against both the naturalism of the Moscow Art Theater and the literary junk that had conquered the stage in his own times.

The *commedia dell'arte* that Meyerhold discovered had a great number of strata. The first stratum was the crude theater of masks and of market place comedians, whose art originated with the Roman mimes. A second stratum was the *commedia dell'arte* of Jacques Callot's engravings, which were grotesque and malicious. Then came the comedies of masks by Goldoni, ennobled by realism, psychology, and details pertaining to the way of life. Over that came the stratum of "tales for the theater" by Gozzi, ennobled by poetics, magic, and a fairy quality. The top stratum of interpreting the *commedia dell'arte* came from E. T. A. Hoffmann, and was found in such stories as "Princess Brambilla." Hoffmann's tales contained a masked and transformed mysticism, interplay between doubles, and phantasmagoria. In them, the real is closely connected with what lies beyond reality. Meyerhold revived all the strata of the *commedia dell'arte,* with the sole exception of Goldoni's realistic type of work. His spirit was most akin, however, to Hoffmann's treatment, and, in general, the Hoffmannesque principle is strongest in Meyerhold's work.

In the autumn of 1910 Meyerhold established Interlude House at 33 Galernaya Street in St. Petersburg, a special studio in which he preached the techniques of the market place theater. His participation in the Imperial theaters did not permit him to use his own name when working with other theaters, and so he chose "Dr. Dapertutto" as his pseudonym. He published a wonderful magazine of the theater arts called *The Love for Three Oranges* (taken from one of Gozzi's tales for the theater), and he translated a number of scenarios for improvisational comedy.

In Interlude House, which lasted until the spring of 1911, there were no footlights. The stage was gradually united with the auditorium. The actors played on the proscenium, in the auditorium, and among tables behind which visitors were seated, and they provoked the audience into participating in the action. The actors entered and exited through the auditorium, and they took seats among the audience or on the stairways leading to the proscenium. A notable production at Interlude House was *Columbine's Scarf,* a pantomime by Schnitzler and Dohnanyi, as set by Sapunov. Its première was on October 9, 1910.

The leitmotif that began with *Columbine's Scarf* went through many of Meyerhold's later productions. This was the theme that people are only pitiful puppets in the hands of Fate and of powers that are not of this world. This leitmotif was doubtlessly taken by Meyerhold from Maeterlinck. But whereas Maeterlinck tried not to inspire terror before Fate and preached reconciliation to it, Meyerhold stressed the malicious irony in life, and he frequently treated the puppet-people as a terrible, soulless, and mechanical crowd.

Gozzi had defined the grotesque as a manner of exaggerated parody. Meyerhold, however, expanded this definition.[16] The grotesque, he said, "is ignorant of details and acts merely from its own originality, appropriating everything that corresponds to its *joie de vivre* and to its capricious and scoffing attitude toward life." [17] If the method of stylization is analytical, then the method of the grotesque is synthetic. "The grotesque uncompromisingly disregards all trifles," Meyerhold wrote, "and creates the entire fullness of life (under, of course, unprecedented conditions)." [18]

He also emphasized another special feature of the grotesque: "What is basic in the grotesque is that the audience is continually led from the plane that it has guessed to another one that it does not expect." [19] In later years Meyerhold asserted the grotesque as a basic trait of the theater:

[The grotesque is] a deliberate exaggeration and reconstruction (distortion) of nature and the unification of objects that are not united by either nature or the customs of our daily life. The theater, being a combination of natural, temporal, spatial, and numerical phenomena, is itself outside of nature. It finds that these phenomena invariably contradict our everyday experience and that the theater itself is essentially an example of the grotesque. Arising from the grotesque of a ritual masquerade, the theater inevitably is destroyed by any given attempt to remove the grotesque—the basis of its existence—from it.[20]

From these quotations, we see how Meyerhold transformed the grotesque from a capricious and scoffing attitude toward life to the basis of the theater's existence in the fundamental style of his directorial work.

The *commedia dell'arte* was Meyerhold's means of revolting against himself. He would always reject mercilessly whatever he had done earlier. How could he do otherwise than to assert the complete dependence of the theater on literature? How could he not strive to place the actors under the director's heel, to transform them into trivial, obedient, and almost motionless puppets? It was a revolt against Meyer-hold's scholasticism, against his own *commedia erudita,* against the Symbolical Theater, which called for a complete liberation from the director's oppression and from words alien to the author.

The *commedia dell'arte* was a realm in which the actor was enthroned. He 'created the plot of the comedy. He improvised on the text every evening, according to his mood. He launched the *lazzi*—the jokes pe-culiar to the theater—that he had devised according to his inspiration. No one other than Meyerhold himself, the "despot of the theater," was the first to wish passionately that the actor be emancipated.

Between 1912 and 1914 Meyerhold's Studio on Borodinskaya Street in St. Petersburg became increasingly freer of plans for reconstruction. Work on the devices of the old national theaters was considered as an accumulation of new acting techniques needed to revive the Russian theater. The Studio studied other traditions besides the *commedia dell'arte.* The actors mastered the devices of tomfoolery, farce, com-pletely about-face impersonations, and so forth.

Meyerhold's program to educate the actor for the new theater was built on the primacy of the sculptured aspects in acting. He taught the actors how to make the most use of the acting platform. He believed that the form and pattern of the actors' motions and gestures should embrace the basic value of the stage. He taught the actors how to live in the form of a design, how to move in a circle, a square, or a rectangle in a room or in an open spot. As a support for motion, Meyerhold in-troduced rhythm. His students would improvise all kinds of pantomimes to music and numerous variations on the themes of wordless scenes.

He was fascinated by the use of hands and arms on the stage from the time he first became acquainted with the Japanese theater. He considered them the finest and most expressive instruments at the actor's disposal, and he thought up numerous ideas merely to develop the sculptured tech-nique of hands and arms. His Studio also stressed exercises using real objects. He made a point of inviting some touring Japanese jugglers and other performers to his Studio who told his students the secrets of their art. Hundreds of things became themes for the magical scenes of the actors. The gestures and motions of the actors with real objects un-covered a new world of possibilities for the stage. The Studio developed suppleness, musicality, rhythm, melodiousness, and adroitness on the part of the actor.

Meyerhold worked out the acting scenes step by step in conjunction with his students. He discovered the collectivism of the theater arts for the first time. He introduced a single kind of clothing to the Studio during 1914, and the actors got dressed openly. The second time we encounter this in Meyerhold's theater, it was called blue "productional clothing." This was during the staging of *Le Cocu magnifique* by Fernand Crommelynck at the GITIS Theater in Moscow during 1921.

Meyerhold turned away at this time from the decadent theater, which was for selected and consecrated audiences. He turned firmly toward the most democratic theater, the theater of and for the people, with its coarse, frivolous, but healthy humor, with its serious and unashamed actors who, according to the rules, give each other enemas, grasp at wooden phalli, and depict scenes of castration and seduction with unbridled "Attican" devices. One must admit there was a kind of prophetic intuition in Meyerhold's turning, sudden and unexpected as it was, to the devices used by the folk theaters of Italy, Spain, France, Japan, and China. He anticipated the arrival of a new period, in which the theater that had belonged to privileged decadents and esthetes would become the property of the entire nation.

In the year when World War I broke out, Meyerhold presented the Russian theater with a most subtle masterpiece of directorial art. He produced Blok's *Neznakomka* ("The Unknown Woman") with actors from his own studio. He also revived his production of *Farce* at the same time. *The Unknown Woman,* like *Farce,* was a most subtle "lyrical drama," in which, as Blok has stated, the experience of an individual spirit, the doubts of passion, and failure are represented only in dramatic form.

There were three scenes in *The Unknown Woman.* The first took place on a drunken evening at a cheap eating place. The third took place in a bourgeois living room. Both depicted human pettiness, which Meyerhold treated with his typical grotesque style. Between the two scenes there was a bit that was phantomlike, blue, and snowy—a fairy tale world of the unreal and unearthly. It contained a brittle, arched bridge, beyond which two masks held poles for a sky of blue tulle, with twinkling stars scattered upon it. At the highest point of the bridge, there was an astrologer who calculated the time when the Star of Mary fell. When this began, one of the proscenium attendants hoisted a long, flaming, bamboo pole to the ceiling and used it to show the parabola of the shooting star against the sky, while another proscenium attendant extinguished the flame in a dipper full of water. The star became incarnated in the Unknown Woman whom the poet encountered at the high point of the delicate bridge.

All Meyerhold's productional devices were filled with a childlike belief in the magic of acting, which transforms a rag into a flying carpet and a bit of crumpled paper into a monster. The breadth of the bamboo canes in the hands of the proscenium attendant sometimes created a background for the action, sometimes caused unnecessary objects and details to disappear, and sometimes took on the forms of naïve allegories. A character, strewn with snow, was wrapped up in a white shawl and, like a child in his deep belief in the acting, experienced the cold of the layers of snow. During the intermissions small Chinese children regaled theatergoers with their unpretentious tricks and scattered oranges among them.

Meyerhold may have taken some of his staging devices for *The Unknown Woman* from the Chinese theater, but he succeeded in using these modest seeds to grow something completely new, subtle, and spicy. The new poetic quality was inspired by theatricality. *The Unknown Woman* also marked the first production in which Meyerhold introduced a bridge as a piece of "construction." It was an apparatus for acting, with no realistic resemblance to a bridge, and was like an illusory decoration.

In 1915, when dark clouds were beginning to gather over Russia and there was failure at the fronts and shortages of fuel and food, Meyerhold staged Ostrovsky's *Storm* at the Imperial Alexandrinsky Theater. He tried to transmit what he considered the "authentic Ostrovsky," cleansed from the qualities of genre painting and mores that had been attributed to the playwright. He believed that overemphasizing the slang words and the way of life in the *Zamoskvoretskaya* (the quarter of Moscow in which Ostrovsky's merchant families tend to live) had hidden the playwright from the audiences. Ostrovsky was an expert on types, characters, and the tragic. Meyerhold tried to reveal deep and mysterious passion, along with tragic fate, by stressing the fate of Katerina, the heroine. He interpreted the play as a Russian, romantic drama.[21]

Meyerhold and Golovin—the designer—interpreted the most important fourth act (when Fate administers its own justice) in a completely new manner. The author's stage directions make a landscape with a view of the Volga mandatory for all productions of *Storm*. Instead of this, Meyerhold and Golovin transferred the action to the center of a half-destroyed church on the walls of which the remnants of ancient frescoes are to be seen. The figure of a Horseman from Judgment Day is still well preserved. Under it, the scene of Katerina's lacerating struggle with her own conscience was presented. So was the scene of the mad young lady with the two lackeys who personify the voice of Fate in the drama.

Meyerhold's "revision" of a Russian classic was greeted with a multitude of abusive reviews. In the future their tone would be adapted by Soviet dramatic critics in discussing every effort of this genius to approach the classics of the Russian drama in a new way.

Note must also be taken of a production by Meyerhold during the early years of World War I that was not completed. This was his presentation of *Ogon'* ("Fire"), a work for which he had written the scenario himself. He used a background of events from the start of the war in his desire to create a spectacle that could awaken heroic feelings in the audience.

This abortive production used directorial devices that were linked to the theme of world war and introduced industrial motifs in constructing the staging. Constructivism in industrial motifs had been thought up by Meyerhold as early as 1914. It was realized in *The Land Is on Edge*, although—it is true—with completely different political aims. Instead of treating the officers and soldiers of the Entente as heroes, this work satirically scoffed at the "imperialists," the generals, and the monarchs. The soldiers were called upon to throw away their weapons, to end the war by "fraternization" and by other charms of the front that the Bolsheviks had thoroughly propagandized.

Meyerhold's production of Lermontov's *Masquerade* was his outstanding production before the Revolution. At that very time, the February Revolution was already beginning, and there was shooting on the streets of Petrograd.[22] The première of *Masquerade* took place on February 25, 1917.

The production of Lermontov's play was the pinnacle of Meyerhold's mysticism. He made the ominous figure of the Unknown Man the most important character in Lermontov's drama. This individual held all the threads of the intrigue against Arbenin. The Unknown Man was the demonic principle. Minor devils, like Shprikh and Kazarin, who wove the plot, were subordinated to him. The Unknown Man was clad in a black, Venetian costume, with his face covered by a white "bautta" from carnival time. He had a sharp beak, as if he had stepped out of a canvas by Pietro Longhi. He was present throughout the play, and his terrible shadow passed behind the transparent fabric of the mournful curtain in the finale.

Meyerhold broke up the four acts of *Masquerade* into ten scenes. Together with Golovin, he considered the stage to be an architectural continuation of the auditorium at the Imperial Alexandrinsky Theater. A semicircular proscenium was pushed into the auditorium and was fenced off by bannisters; two staircases led down to the orchestra. On the sides of the proscenium were sculptured portals above which were loges shut off by closed, red, silken curtains. The architectural motifs of the portals were a continuation of the auditorium; the mirrors on both sides of them reflected the auditorium and thus strengthened its connection with the stage. There were divans at the limits of the proscenium throughout the action. Numerous curtains of a different color served as symbolical backgrounds for emphasizing the moods of the various scenes. They also served to pick out the action in separate scenes and bits. They permitted the stage to be rearranged without the use of intermissions. The number of actors used was unprecedented. There were about two hundred of them.

For the first time, Meyerhold discovered the device of the "crowded setting." A large number of actors were amassed in a small space. This was reminiscent of the composition in the group portraits of the baroque masters. In the two scenes around the gambling table, he wove the heads and the arms of the gamblers, the cards, and the colored banknotes into a single composition, illuminated from above and against a background of red wood. These devices of the "crowded setting" achieved perfection in his productions of *Gore ot Uma* ("Woe from Wit") and *The Inspector-General* in Soviet times.

The most powerful and effective part of the production was the masquerade scene. This was realized with the full brilliance of Meyerhold's genius. The drama of Arbenin grew heated in the currents of the ominous, masked crowd. Znosko-Borovsky stated:

Myerhold developed the small scene of the masquerade into a picture of complete and nightmarish terror. It was as if fate itself hounded the jealous husband as he thrashed about in the circle of his suspicions and in the circle of the dancers. The masks became bent. The horns were frightening. The fateful circle that surrounded him kept growing smaller. There was general rejoicing, joking intrigues, and spontaneous dancing which acquired a strange and foreboding aspect, as the danger kept growing greater; a whirlwind and a windspout spun about the stage. It was as if we were among some unlikely monsters created by the sick, troubled imagination of a husband who has a blameless wife and does not believe in her innocence. He handed the poison to her himself in order to kill not her, but rather his own dark thoughts which had acquired such frightening reality.[23]

There was something dark and prophetic about this *Masquerade* in the Western capital of Russia on whose cold and empty streets the first shots of the Revolution were booming out. The production was unsurpassed in the luxury of its costumes and décor and in the number of its actors. It was also prophetic in that Meyerhold seemed to be taking his leave forever from the audiences of that stratum of life that made luxury and refinement possible. This glitter of a worldly masquerade would never again be repeated in a Russia that was to sink into the chaos of war, hunger, beggary, and devastation. Also prophetic was the crowd of creatures who had lost their reality and were transformed in full view of the audience that evening into mere phantoms and masked chimeras. This is the way, on the morrow or within the week, resplendent reality would be transformed into pitiful and terrible shadows of the past. The mysticism of the presentation on the eve of the Revolution was even more subtle and more profound. The innocent Nina is to be killed at the instigation of the demonic forces conspiring with the Unknown Man. The ugly faces at the masquerade bait Arbenin and kindle the madness of murder within him. In Nina's character and in those ugly faces, there was a prophetic link with an idea of foreboding. Certain dark powers, at the instigation of some Unknown Man, were murdering innocent Russia and plunging her into long years of chaos and Satanism.

This was Meyerhold's farewell presentation within tsarist Russia. He showed himself to be a finished master whose long quests had brought him his own unique style in directing. But let us recapitulate briefly his discoveries between 1905 and 1917. They were to have an enormous influence on the development of the Soviet theater.

Meyerhold created formulas for rejecting the naturalistic theater. Asserting the incompatibility between the theater and life, he believed that the theater had its own language and that time and space are affected by different laws from those of reality. He worked out the bases and forms of the Symbolical Theater. He accomplished a renascence of absolute theatricality on a grandiose scale at a time when realism and naturalism dominated the Russian theater.

He declared that the director was the leader in the matter of theatrical innovation, the author and composer of the presentation, and he infinitely expanded the right of the director to revise the classics and to interpret dramatic material freely. Meyerhold revived the magic in the theater of the masks, and he discovered inexhaustible springs for the theater of the future in the forms and devices used by the old theaters of Europe and Asia. He stubbornly sought to revive the theater with these forms from the past, and his students and disciples would continue this search in the Soviet period. More than any of the other Russian directors of his time, Meyerhold sought to make the theater democratic, to link its forms to those of the national theater through reviving the devices of the past. He also taught the Russian theater, however, to relate its own developments with the formal revelation of the outstanding new works in literature and painting.[24]

Meyerhold stated the primacy of the sculptured aspect in the art of acting over speech and plot, and from this many schools and trends would develop in Soviet times. In his Studio he laid the foundations for new methods of theatrical pedagogy that completely contradicted the old school and the Stanislavsky System. He expanded the program of educating the actors and introduced new discipline to motion and to the study of devices used by the comedians of the past. The basis of his pedagogy would lead to the Soviet theatrical training during the years of experimentation.

Meyerhold turned over the stage to the designer and thus revealed new potentialities for enriching the art of the theater. In a number of brilliant productions he discovered the need for three-dimensionality on the stage, along with architectural and sculptured qualities in acting skill. He was the first to work out the vivifying idea of the proscenium that would typify all the innovating productions of the Soviet theater. He destroyed the footlights, bared the stage, constructed bridges into the auditorium, and struggled against the antiquated forms of the intimate theater. He was the first to introduce experiments in construction, by transforming the décor into an apparatus for acting. He made unrealistic and unconventional lighting one of the most potent tools of the stage. His use of lighting enabled him to find new devices for dividing the acts and scenes, for individualizing episodes and details (in the Soviet period he would create a new form for constructing a play on the basis of a great number of minor episodes and little scenes). Believing the audience to be the fourth creator of the theater, for long years Meyerhold conducted numerous searches for making the audience active and drawing it into the acting process.

Finally, Meyerhold was an eternal rebel and a bold reformer, who paid no attention to the criticism of traditionalists. He kept performing new and most risky experiments on the Russian stage and exerted an enormous influence on the work of the new, revolutionary generation in the Russian theater. This new generation strove to follow his example in its great use of innovation and experimentation.

NIKOLAI EVREINOV

In the winter of 1906 another innovator appeared in the Russian theater whose quests had a major influence on his colleagues, including even Meyerhold. Like Meyerhold, Evreinov began by rejecting realism, which, he thought, led to a most complete decline in the theater arts. He began to fight for a revival of the theater by asserting the need to bring to the Russian stage the productional devices and acting styles in use during the most theatrical periods of the past, when the art of the stage did not aspire so shamefully to copy life.

This is how the idea of the "Old Theater" was born.[25] Several notable individuals in the Russian theater associated themselves with this idea, among whom were N. V. Drizen and K. M. Miklashevsky. The first cycle of work at the Old Theater included these presentations: *Tri volkhva* ("The Three Magi"), an eleventh-century liturgical drama; *Deistvo o Teofile* ("A Play about Theophile"), a twelfth-century miracle play; *Igra o Robene i Marione* ("A Play about Robin and Marion"), a thirteenth-century work by Adam de la Halle; *Dva brata* ("Two Brothers"), a fifteenth-century morality play; and two sixteenth-century farces —*O chane* ("About a Tub") and *O shliape-rogache* ("About the Cuckold's Hat") by Jean Dabondance.

These productions reconstructed the scenic technique of presentations of the past. An atmosphere was created for them like that in which the ancient acting had taken place. The liturgical drama, for example, had been played in olden times before the portals of a cathedral. In staging it the theater presented a prologue that Evreinov had written. The prologue showed the awakening of a sleeping crowd, with conversations about miracles. Then flagellants appeared whose self-torture brought the crowd to a pitch of ecstasy. The prologue also prepared the audience for the liturgical drama, which transpired in reaction to the living comments of the crowd on the stage. A three-tiered stage was reconstructed for the production of the twelfth-century miracle play; it included "hell" and "paradise." In staging *A Play about Robin and Marion* Evreinov recreated the entire flavor of a presentation at a knight's castle.

The second cycle of work at the Old Theater took place in 1911 and 1912. It concentrated on the Spanish theater of the seventeenth century. The works staged were: *Chistilishche sv. Patrika* ("The Purgatory of St. Patrick") by Calderón; *El gran duque de Moscovia y emperador perseguido* ("The Grand Duke of Muscovy and the Persecuted Emperor") by Lope de Vega; *Fuente Ovejuna,* also by Lope de Vega; *Marta la piadosa* ("Pious Martha"), a comedy by Tirso de Molina; and *Dva boltuna* ("Two Chatterboxes"), an interlude by Miguel de Cervantes.

These productions showed much love and resourcefulness in reviving the flavor of the milieu that was contemporary with the plays. Znosko-Borovsky wrote:

At times, the audience saw [parts of] the presentation by torchlight, in the royal park *Buen Retiro,* in the garden scene (set off by an ornate curtain), or in the stiff and ceremonious acting. The actors wore make-up and costumes from the quaint and fantastic Orient or were clad luxuriously according to the paintings of Velasquez. At other times, the poor, wandering company coarsely acted out a rapid comedy on the pitiful boards in an inn yard, or on balconies accommodating some members of the audience who interrupted the presentation with their own uncomplicated observations. At still other times, there was a luxurious stage for a presentation at the court of Philip IV; it had three portals and a raised platform, with rich stage effects, such as clouds racing by. Then, the new, wandering company dispersed around the square, and smashed the boards of the stage into barrels or logs.[26]

The two seasons of the Old Theater in St. Petersburg—1907–1908 and 1911–1912—were joyful and unparalleled events, and not for the Russian theater alone. Nothing like them had ever been seen in the theaters of other nations either. They revived the magic of the fine forms connected with the old theater, dust-covered forms that had been forgotten for centuries. The productions of the Old Theater were a great success.

The Russian stage, both before and after 1917, is greatly indebted to the Old Theater. Its main contribution was the resurrection of acting devices from periods of pure theatricality. The directors of the Theater, including Evreinov, began their experiments in reviving devices from the theaters of the distant past even before Meyerhold's experimentation with the idea. Unlike Meyerhold, they did not seek to submerge the actor in the concepts of the director. Instead of trying to turn the actor into bas-reliefs, circles, and cubes, they approached the player with great piety because they considered him the prime foundation of the theater. In the Old Theater, therefore, the player was again the sovereign of the theatrical world. Although the Old Theater was indubitably second to Meyerhold in the power and scope of its directorial art, it came closer than he to solving the problem of "who is most important in the theater."

For Evreinov, the Old Theater made it possible, not only to revive the theatrical devices of the distant past, but also to revive the separate forms of interplay between the stage and the audience. His slogan was "the reconstruction of the audience" and of its craving for the theatrical. Evreinov's searches to discover the secrets of theater audiences would be carried on long and persistently. He found the audiences, as we shall see, more important than the actor and dramatist of the Old Theater. The audience craved a transformation and had an instinct for the theater. Evreinov was to seek the playgoer's secret in all forms that had not lost their freshness or their spontaneous connection between the audience and the stage. Among such forms were the puppet theater, the shadow theater, the Turkish "karagez," the farce, folk rituals, operettas, harlequinades, the grotesque performances in cabarets, and the *guignol*.

The Old Theater was decisive in Evreinov's work. But his *Apologiia teatral'nosti* ("Apologia for Theatricality"), which was printed in 1908, was destined to be even more important in the Russian theater, both before and after 1917, than the Old Theater. In this work Evreinov rejected both naturalism on the stage and Meyerhold's Symbolical Theater. He sharply separated the limits of the theater from reality. The theater, he wrote,

is thoroughly symbolical and has never been—nor can it ever be—otherwise, no matter how ultranaturalism is cultivated on its boards. . . . In art everything is symbolical, and this is the source of its charm and joy for us. Art creates fine new values. Art fascinates because it does not wish to hire anything, however cheap the thing might be, but daringly creates its own heaven, which is at times even more heavenly than the real sky.[27]

Some years later, Evreinov rose up against the truth of experiences and sincerity, which is what Stanislavsky considered most important in the theater:

The contemporary leveling of experiences, and sincerity of social intercourse has produced complete boredom. There is some question as to how long these apologetics will be highly esteemed. Are we not on the eve of a wonderful age of masks, poses, and fine phrases? The most sensitive persons have already understood that sincerity is a peculiar form of ignorance, pettiness, the lack of creative potentialities, and poverty. It is an impudent intrusion on someone else's house, not so much to help as to poison.[28]

Evreinov swept aside realism on the stage and rejected the fixed quality of Meyerhold's Symbolical Theater also. Meyerhold's theater was venomously characterized by Mme Teffi, the author, as being something halfway between metaphysics and the ballet. But Evreinov rejected the fact that Meyerhold's theater saddled the stage with symbolism and enslaved the theater to literature and to nontheatrical tasks.

To assert that the main task of the new scenic art is to reveal secrets to the audience, to explain inner dialogue and so on, is to saddle art with a definite subject of expression that is useless and harmful to an art that is essentially free. Is it not all the same regardless of whether the philosophical significance is serious or not? Once theatricality of expression is ignored, no matter how beautifully this is done, the audience cannot be rescued from boredom.[29]

Our art critics to this day imagine that the main thing in the theater is the literary play, the style, the faithfulness to the period, the feeling of measure, the beautiful décor, the bow-ties, etc. But I assert that for the theater all this is beautiful trash and nothing more. None of it can exist on the stage because none of it makes the theater a theater.[30]

A theater must be neither a temple, a school, a "tribune of fighters for freedom," a "pulpit of humble loyalty," nor a "mirror." A theater must be only a theater. Evreinov laid the foundations for his philosophy of the theatrical and developed them in his work *Teatralizatsiia zhizni* ("Making Life a Theater").

Evreinov's starting point in his philosophy of the theatrical is that human beings have a pre-esthetic instinct of transformation among their basic instincts, along with the sexual and the maternal instincts. Using anthropological data, Evreinov asserted that even in their initial stages of development people possessed this craving for transformation. The caves of the period following the Ice Age show that primitive man had the accessories for transformation. These included the jaws of bears, fixed with thongs so that they could be hung from one's face, colored pastes for making up the face and body, and so forth. The most primitive savage covered himself with strange necklaces and rings, painted himself fantastically, and adorned himself with feathers and animal skins. He acted from esthetic motives, from his instinctive desire for transformation, his craving to be something else. This instinct for transformation, this thirst for theatricality, is contrasted by Evreinov with art, which tries to express not a mask but the very personality of its creator. This thirst to be not oneself but someone else, this instinct for acting, does not disappear among people who are cultured and civilized. It can be traced down to our own days. All the court ceremonies, from antiquity to our own times, all the devices, attire, worldly customs, rites, and rituals are for us merely examples of the many forms in which the instinct for transformation has asserted itself.

The very naturalness of contemporary man can be questioned to a major extent. Everyone plays a good number of roles in his life that have nothing in common with his real self. Some play brilliantly, some satisfactorily, and some are beneath criticism, but our entire lives are saturated with acting and playing under a mask. Evreinov saw this acting in children's games, in our dreams, crimes, drunken orgies, hysteria, and madness. According to Evreinov, even the church and religion is a form of the same theater, and without theatrical conviction, neither saints, prophets, nor preachers would have succeeded in flourishing down to our own times.

The theatrical, the acting instinct in mankind, according to Evreinov, is broader than man's craving to transform himself. It is an instinct for transforming life in general, the wish to create something unprecedented. Only a transformed and theatricalized life gives man meaning and makes of his life something that can be loved. Nature and human existence, Evreinov thought, are shadows of that real existence that is renewed by the creative fancy of mankind. Evreinov pushed the limits of the theatrical instinct to almost cosmic proportions. He expanded the ancient idea that "all the world plays comedy" to link it with everything human, with the acting of masks and the craving for play. Thus, his relationship to the theater as art becomes unclear. He debased the theater by calling it a survival of a primitive, gregarious feeling:

What had previously been considered as the "theater" is nothing more than one of the numerous, vulgar forms for satisfying theatrical feelings. In the end result, it is but an insignificant episode in the universal history of theatrical culture.[31]

In other works, however, Evreinov placed the theater on a pedestal. The theater must help to turn "the monstrous surface of life into something of unprecedented and unparalleled beauty." He wrote:

> The theater will be the new teacher. To make a theater of life is the duty of every artist. A new kind of director will appear, the director of life.[32]
>
> I assert and insist that the stage must not borrow so much from life as life borrows from the stage. [An actor must impress the public] by the beauty of his diction, his facial expressions, and his sculptured quality to such an extent that people in life will want to use what the stage has given them.[33]
>
> We must not lower the theatrical heroes in their stage roles to ourselves, but rather we must raise our own conduct to the loftiness of theatrical heroes.[34]

The "super-director" aspired to remove the confining band of footlights and instead, with a handful of actors, tried to soar upwards to the limits of the sky. He wanted no more of "players" and "contemplators," but rather a blending of the sociological tasks of the theater, "making a theater of life." Life must be clad in the holiday attire of the theater. It must be filled with acting, masks, and transformations. And as a result, life would become more beautiful and easier. Evreinov promised us all a heaven on earth that could be achieved with the simple aid of the theater.

Evreinov discovered still another magic trait in the theater—the doctoring of the human race. He asserted the "therapeutic theater" and proclaimed that theater people hold one of the means for making mankind healthy. He traced theatrical devices for curing the ill from antiquity to our day. Wizards, sorcerers, and the shamans of primitive peoples, he argued, utilize the theater widely in their very clothing and in their "medical paraphernalia." The medieval medical man cured the ill not so much through his knowledge and drugs as through the hypnosis of his theatricality. The contemporary therapeutic measure of "a change of environment" is also a theatrical means of curing. It changes the décor and cast on the stage of life. According to Evreinov, the American method of "faith healing" is built on exactly the same theatricality.

Evreinov's play Samoe glavnoe ("The Main Thing") was practical propaganda for "theatro-therapy." He reveals the idea of the work in an article which he wrote for its production:

The main credo of my play *The Main Thing* is that it makes socialism something intimate by using actors experienced in the art of transformation. The main character of my play is Paracletes (which, translated from the Greek, means "adviser, helper, consoler"), who appears during the course of the drama under different guises and invites the actors of a local, provincial theater to demonstrate their talents not on the stage of a theater but on "the stage of life," where so many of our neighbors have been deprived of the most natural joys because of wretchedness in the body or mind. "If we cannot give happiness to the disinherited," says Paracletes, "we can at least give them the illusion of it." In the end, it turns out that illusions on "the stage of life" are much stronger than on the stage of a theater, from which it follows that the actors and "actresses of mercy" must play an important social role in the very near future.[35]

Evreinov saw something more important than sociology in this mission of the theater, in the staging of happiness for the debased and unfortunates. In his unrestrained elaboration on the subject, he came to give theatro-therapy a religious role. He conceived the mission of the theater to be the cleansing of the audience's accumulated forces for evil and transgression. Society frees itself of secret desires to sin by seeing its desires portrayed on the stage:

It is, as it were, a purgatory to which the soul is taken . . . and in which man sees naked, secret fears and passions that are as ancient as the world. It is a dream, an exhibition, in which acting gives a way out to the elemental forces of nature that have been hidden in the human soul under the organized structure of culture, the systems of rules in society, and the gloss of decency.[36]

Evreinov passionately sought the means by which the audience could be transformed from passive contemplators to active participants of the theater. He was drawn to a new form, the *monodrama*. He delivered a speech called "An Introduction to the Monodrama" (Moscow, 1908) in which he set forth the idea that there was a new kind of dramatic presentation in which the audience would be transported within the drama itself and become an "inner factor of the drama." Evreinov started from the principle that the world exists only in our notion of it. This principle led him to drama in which events and people are given only as the hero perceives and evaluates them.

In the monodrama the audience is made to feel everything that happens through the experiences of the protagonist. If the hero closes his eyes on the stage, darkness must descend on the playgoer also. When the hero is in love, the entire stage is filled with sunlight and rosy tints, but when terrible thoughts enter his heart everything on the stage is seen in a dark light.

Evreinov tried to realize his monodramatic principles in his directorial work at every opportunity. When he staged *Francesca da Rimini* at the Komisarzhevskaya Theater, he introduced novel lighting effects that followed his principles. He divided the stage diagonally into light and dark sides, and he concentrated the positive characters in the light part and the negative ones in the dark portion. He selected a color of light for each act to characterize the action. In his production he did not strive for historical accuracy but for a legendary quality that was related to the action as pictured in the popular imagination. For Evreinov, the playgoer was the most important participant in the theater.

Except for some of his productions at the Krivoe Zerkalo ("Crooked Mirror") Theater, Evreinov's principles of monodrama did not take hold in Russia. Similar devices are occasionally used in "psychoanalytical" dramas and surrealistic motion pictures, however, and perhaps the future will make more use of Evreinov's monodrama.

Evreinov's monodrama was also a bridge for him to reach his favorite genres—the grotesque, parody, and caricature. He practiced them at the Crooked Mirror Theater and at the Vesëlyi teatr dlia vzroslykh detei ("The Happy Theater for Grown-up Children"). He used these theaters of "minor forms" as laboratories in which he continued his efforts to seek a living link with the audience. He was also by this means able to continue his efforts to depose the professional theater by using the powers of the theater itself rather than a pen. Like Stanislavsky, who had protected the birth of the "Bat" cabaret within the walls of the Moscow Art Theater, Evreinov raised forms of theater from third-rate entertainment to the heights of art. In the theater of "low style" Evreinov discovered the sources of sublime and vital theatricality. His parodies at the Crooked Mirror Theater became a campaign against the dramatists, directors, and actors of the old theater. His parody of the various directorial treatments of *The Inspector-General* and his caricature of operatic stereotypes, *Vampuka,* have taken their place in the history of the Russian theater as brilliant stage productions of the cabaret theater.

Evreinov's pre-Revolutionary innovations exerted a considerable influence on the Soviet theater. Russian knowledge of the theater was enriched by his enormous contribution to the study of the acting principle

in human life and the study of theatricality in all its manifestations.[37]
He shed much light on the matter of attracting playgoers to acting in the
theater and making them participants in the action. The Soviet theater
would expend much time and energy on these problems. His theories
about man's instinct for transformation influenced the growth of mass
plays, fanciful plays, and dramatizations that took place in primary and
secondary schools. His principle of "making a theater of life" helped
to produce the mass spectacles and celebrations and the Soviet carnivals
and other forms of group art.

Evreinov's work was continued in large measure by the Left-Fronters
(LEF), headed by the poet Vladimir Mayakovsky. Echoes of his theories
also entered the platforms of the Proletcult movement and RAPP. His
research on the theatricality of Russian rituals furnished the basis for
the "Obriadovyi teatr" (Ritual Theater), and his Crooked Mirror
Theater was the ancestor of many "theaters of minor forms," theaters
of parody and satire, during the Soviet period.

FEODOR KOMISARZHEVSKY

Feodor Fëdorovich Komisarzhevsky began his connection with the stage
at his brilliant sister's theater, where he was in charge of the montage.
It was upon his initiative that Meyerhold was invited to that theater,
and Meyerhold's productions were a school for the future director.
Komisarzhevsky sympathized with Meyerhold's revolt against naturalism,
but he did not approve of the extremes to which Meyerhold was brought
by his enthusiasm for stylization and the Symbolical Theater. Komisarzhevsky soon began to oppose Meyerhold's innovations. After Meyerhold finally broke with Vera Komisarzhevskaya, her brother began his
own independent work as a director.

Komisarzhevsky was the most profound thinker of all the pre-Revolutionary innovators. He established his own theory of the theater and of
directing, which had a considerable influence on the Russian theater.
Like Evreinov, he rejected both naturalism and Meyerhold's Symbolical
Theater. He disliked the way in which the director of the Symbolical
Theater deprived the actor of a soul and transformed him into a puppet
or a detail of the decorative background. He rejected Meyerhold's directorial method, which made every dramatic work merely an òccasion
for the director to realize his own fantasies and ideas. He rose up in

defense of the actor, and he brought the greatness of the author back to the stage. He made the director the philosopher and interpreter of the dramatist's outlook on life. The director, Komisarzhevsky said:

reveals an author on the stage and must use all the resources of the stage, both internal and external, to express his own conception of the dramatist's outlook on life and his own conception of the philosophical contents of the play staged.[38]

A scrupulous analysis of a play's text by the director is not enough to stage it, Komisarzhevsky felt. The director should be aware of the philosophy of the dramatist's complete works, for the staging of a separate play must be a philosophical portrait of the author's entire work. And a director should stage only those writers whom he finds sympathetic to his own outlook on life. Only then can a director, who has perceived an author's outlook on life through his own *ego* discover the *ego* of the author.

Komisarzhevsky's treatment of Ostrovsky deserves to be mentioned in this connection. For this director, Ostrovsky was not a limited "depicter of mores" (Oitovik), or the poet of the merchants' "Kingdom of Darkness." The playwright was rather an artist who revealed the struggle between the individual and society, between mind and matter. His sympathies were with those who represented light and virtue. Rather than the accusatory quality that has been attributed to Ostrovsky's style, Komisarzhevsky found that the author was in love with the flavor of Russian life, and of Russian customs, and gloried even in the petty tyrants.

In Molière, Komisarzhevsky found a link between the playwright's schematic and puppetlike characters and the market place theater from which they had sprung. He considered it a mistake to treat Molière's comedies realistically, because the dramatist considered his characters merely as generalizations, symbols, and marionettes with which to reveal and illustrate his thoughts.

Between the prism of the author's outlook on life and the audience, Komisarzhevsky interposed a second prism—the way the director and interpreter perceived the style and philosophy of the author. The audience, therefore, had two subjective outlooks to contend with: that of the author and that of the director's conception of the author. Komisarzhevsky's philosophical interpretation of plays, for example, frequently furnished examples not so much of his revealing an author's outlook on life but of his subordinating it to his own outlook. Yet, he rendered an undoubted service to the Russian theater by affirming the theater of thought and the romantic theater.

Komisarzhevsky solved the problems of acting and of directing in the theater with equal profundity. The actor was a free actor in his theater because the director did not force ready-made forms of expression upon him. The actor was subordinated to the general idea of the presentation, but he was free in his work. The director's work was to unify the experience.

One of Komisarzhevsky's most remarkable productional devices was his method of "psychologized décor." This resembled Evreinov's devices for the monodrama. At one point in the production of the play based upon Dostoevsky's "Skvernyi anekdot" ("A Sordid Story") the hero has nightmares. These are reflected in the broken lines of the décor, the falling outlines of the houses, the convulsive movements of the characters, the sudden interruptions in speech, and the subordination of the entire rhythm to that of a feverish delirium.

For the play adapted from Charles Dickens's *A Christmas Carol* Komisarzhevsky found a form for intimate acting. He created "the impression of a pastel in glass, in which voices do not seem to be heard, and in which colors are sometimes bright and sometimes hazy." [39] He staged Tschaikovsky's opera *Eugene Onegin* by having the décor resemble the vignettes and illustrations of Pushkin's time. He treated the motions of the actors on the stage also like graphic illustrations for Pushkin's poem.

Komisarzhevsky asserted the complete independence of the theater from reality. He felt that art should be neither tendentious nor utilitarian. The aim of art is art itself, the manifestation of the creative power that lives within the artist. Komisarzhevsky created a theater in which he broke out of the magic circle of who was most important in the theater. He knew how to blend the author, the director, and the actor to depict the same idea in the presentation.

Komisarzhevsky left Russia and therefore did not participate in the Soviet theater. His theory of the theater has been reflected in Soviet practice in a distorted manner only. Not so much attention is paid to the outlook on life of the author as to the treatment of his dramatic works from the philosophical viewpoint of Marxism alone. Komisarzhevsky's form of theater came into being during the Soviet period, however, under the title of the Romantic Theater, and it existed for a number of years. His experiments with the synthetic theater are undoubtedly connected with the experiments of Soviet directors—such as Tairov—in the same vein.

B. G. Sakhnovsky, a disciple, brilliantly carried on the conception of the director as a philosopher in the Soviet theater. Together with Komisarzhevsky, Sakhnovsky founded the Komisarzhevskaya Theater of Moscow in 1914. He, too, was a director who was a thinker.

ALEXANDER TAIROV

Alexander Yakovlevich Tairov was the last of the pre-Revolutionary innovators in the Russian theater. He was trained on the experiments of Stanislavsky, Meyerhold, Evreinov, and Komisarzhevsky. The Kamerny Theater of Moscow, with which Tairov was connected, occupies a special place in the Soviet theater arts, but Tairov's productions there were by no means his first. The way to the Kamerny Theater passed through studying, apprenticeship, and many mistakes. The character of the Kamerny Theater was shaped gradually. Tairov came out with his own theory of the theater only in 1921, when his book *Zapiski rezhissëra* ("Notes of a Director") was published.

The Moscow Art Theater stood for psychological realism and truth to life on the stage. The grotesquerie of Meyerhold carefully blended reality with phantoms. Evreinov called for making life into a theater, and Komisarzhevsky sought a philosophical theater. Tairov, however, accomplished the complete emancipation of the theater. He separated it from life and transformed it into a festival of the arts on the stage.

The first presentation at the Kamerny Theater in Moscow took place in 1914. This was a production of *Sakuntala,* an ancient Hindu drama by Kalidasa, probably dating from the fifth century before Christ. It contains the key to all of Tairov's work. For Tairov, the theater was a myth, a fairy tale, a different existence, something happy and festive that was elevated above the earth and was connected with the sacred dances of priestesses in a temple.

In *Sakuntala* Tairov introduced one of his first innovations. He stripped the actor's body, painted it, covered it with scanty bits of colored cloth, liberated it from heavy costumes, and thus revealed new potentialities in scenic expressiveness.[40] Using the body on the stage with a "free chastity" and extracting expressiveness from it was a more difficult art than learning how to wear a costume. From that time on, the Kamerny Theater and its imitators were characterized by a love for the bare body of the actor and the rhythm of his motions. It is true that this often led Tairov to extremes. He sometimes chose artists' models of both sexes rather than people of talent for his theater.

Everything that would later typify all of Tairov's work was present in *Sakuntala*. The setting was most subtle and of exquisite taste. The composition was brilliant. The rhythm in the construction of the mass scenes was profound. At times, the production looked like a finished painting; at other times, like masterfully modeled sculptured groups. The first review of *Sakuntala* remarked upon the pictorial quality of Tairov's setting. N. Krashenninikov wrote:

The chariot and horse, and the fine face of the tsar, and the slow nobility of his words and movements. . . . The hermits and the maids, the sacred conversations, rites, and singing. . . . If one may exaggerate, the number of Hindu scenes increased before one's eyes from 149 to 285. I am not joking, for each scene was not only a scene for the *stage*—of which there were 13 or 14 (I no longer remember)—but every motion of the characters, every one of their poses was a scene of its own kind. When the girls sit under the marvelous trees, it is a scene; when they get up and take the pitchers, it is another scene; when the tsar comes in and they take fright, it is again a scene.[41]

Beaumarchais's *Le Mariage de Figaro* was produced by Tairov in 1915. One felt the influence of Meyerhold's stylization and of his finding the flavor of the dramatist's period. (Meyerhold's production of Molière's *Don Juan* at the Imperial Alexandrinsky Theater is a case in point.) The reviews of the time remarked upon it: "One of the heads of the Kamerny Theater has declared that, in its production of *Le Mariage de Figaro*, the Theater intended to express Beaumarchais's era." [42] Meyerhold's influence was also present in Tairov's directorial devices.

Particolored curtains are parted one after the other, like the curtains of centuries; shepherdesses in powdered wigs start coming down a gilded staircase towards the audience, along with Negroes in gilded camisoles, *paysans, paysannes,* harlequins, judges, and a ballet. It was a living and colorful collection of symbols from a bygone age. It was not merely a beautiful spectacle but the concept behind the entire production. . . . The comedy was not played so much as it was shown, and was not shown so much as it was presented. The theater openly gloried in its whimsical reincarnation of Beaumarchais's era.[43]

Even before the Revolution, Tairov sought an organic link between the presentation and music. He did not think of a single production without music written for it by a composer born for the theater.[44] The Russian theater, and perhaps the contemporary European theater as well, is indebted to Tairov because it was he who brought music into the playhouse, subordinating the entire structure of the presentation to its rhythm.

In any of Tairov's productions the rhythm was the most important element in the architectonics of the entire presentation. Even when the orchestra was silent, or when no band accompanied the production, the developing action in Tairov's production was perceived as a musical composition. The actor's motions, gestures, and intonations were always subordinated to a definite rhythm. So were the costumes and décor. In revealing character on the stage, in the gestures, in the composition of the crowd scenes, Tairov always sought a definite rhythm.[45] The style of speech on his stage was somewhere between prose read as verse, melodramatic declamation, and singing. It was to become one of the main attributes of the Kamerny Theater in Moscow. In Alice Georgievna Koonen (Tairov's wife), the theater had a leading lady who was a brilliant representative of that style. Her speech was always intoxicating music. Nevertheless, the "melodiousness" of the Kamerny Theater was always an inexhaustible source for attacks by the critics.

Tairov made still another specific contribution in the four pre-Revolutionary years of the Kamerny Theater. If speech in his theater was half-singing, then the movements of the actors were half-ballet. The actor's hands, gait, gestures, and bodily motions also sing and are subordinated not only to rhythm but to a definite melody as well. And if the half-singing of the actors at the Kamerny Theater had few followers in the other theaters of the Soviet Union, the gentleness of motion found quite a few imitators.

Tairov was seeking a miracle in his productions. He was trying to make music a real object on the rhythmically constructed stage. He called it "the keyboard for the actor's playing." [46] Later, Tairov found a fine musician for the settings in Georgy Yakulov. Yakulov's settings for *Signor Formica, Princess Brambilla,* and *Giroflé-Girofla* were music arranged in color, line, and sweep.

One of Tairov's finest productions at the Kamerny Theater before the Revolution was of Annenkov's *Famira Kifared.* This was a real "program" presentation in which the style and devices of the new theater were shown powerfully and brilliantly. Most important of all was the dissolving of everything connected with the stage in the solvent of the rhythmical element.

Tairov constructed his tragedy on the clash between the cults of Dionysus and Apollo, on two rhythms: the Bacchic and the tragic (the latter was clear and smooth-flowing). Tairov, together with Alexandra Ekster—the designer—subordinated the entire stage platform and all the acting to the two rhythms. The smooth-flowing and peaceful Apollonian rhythms were placed in the center upstage. The other areas were given over to the various cubes and platforms that were piled up for the rhythm of Dionysus.

One must note something special among the other important discoveries in the production of *Famira Kifared*. Tugenkhold described it thus:

Here, for the first time, the European stage used the principle of "sculptured décor" for the countryside, which was reduced to several simple forms: blue steps of different widths; black, conical cypress trees; and black and gold, cube-shaped stones and cliffs. Instead of a painted background, a simple cloth served as a translucent backdrop. Thanks to Zaltsman's special system, there was a great variety in the shadings, from a moon-like blue to a reddish purple. None of the sculptured forms remained un-utilized in the presentation. The bodies of the Bacchantes wriggled on the broad steps; the satyrs climbed into the cypress trees. The majestic and sorrowful figure of Kifared, the protagonist of the play, bent harmoniously to the stones of the cliffs.[47]

Tairov and Mme Ekster continued the use of the nudeness of the actor's body, which had been begun with *Sakuntala*. In *Famira Kifared,* however, they applied make-up to the bodies of the Bacchantes and satyrs. The brushstrokes set the main muscles and lines of their figures in relief.

The four-year pre-Revolutionary period of the Kamerny Theater was quite productive for Tairov. He staged about fourteen premières. Another basic tendency of Tairov's came out during this work—he created a theater of great range. He directed everything from tragedy to buffonades and operettas. In addition to all his innovations, moreover, Tairov's pre-Revolutionary theater protested against philistine trivia and naturalistic degeneration in the repertory of the Russian theaters. It offered a choice of dramatic works representing high taste.

Of the five great innovators in the pre-Revolutionary Russian theater, four belong to the school of "the performing theater."

The mask and the grotesque were in the center of Meyerhold's theater. Evreinov had Harlequin with a rattle, intended to make all life a spectacle. Komisarzhevsky found the philosophy and the abstract ideas of the author more important than the living human being on the stage. For Tairov, the theater was only the festival of a different existence, in which the actor was above mankind. Only for Stanislavsky was the human being the center of the theater. The human being was alive and unique. The shadings of his experience very frequently seemed completely ordinary, but his pitifulness and his grandeur, his joys and his sufferings, always bore the divine spark within them.

Meyerhold, Evreinov, Komisarzhevsky, and Tairov were linked by their common fencing off of the theater from life and by their proud assertion that the theater was better and nobler than life. Only Stanislavsky did not look at life with detachment from a high pulpit in the temple of art. He perceived life with love and enthusiasm and as a friend—a friend of the common man, whose spiritual treasures it is the duty of art to reveal.

It seems to us that the high value that the West placed upon the Soviet theater—especially on the Kamerny Theater—in the first decade after 1917 is the result of an error. Aside from the Moscow Art Theater, the Russian theaters never went abroad before the Revolution. The great majority of the innovations in them remained completely unknown outside of Russia. In the 1930s the Kamerny Theater, the Meyerhold Theater, and the Vakhtangov Theater did tour abroad. Their productions created a sensation, were an incomprehensible miracle, which Westerners hastened, however, to ascribe to the beneficial influence of the Soviet regime on the nature of the theater itself. The West lost sight of the link between the Soviet and the pre-Revolutionary theater. The attainments of the three theaters just mentioned were only continuations —and by no means the most brilliant ones—of pre-Revolutionary innovations.

The West became acquainted with Meyerhold through the production of Sergei Tretyakov's *Rychi Kitai* ("Roar, China") by the director's student, Vasily Fëdorov, and through three of Meyerhold's own productions: the purely experimental *Le Cocu magnifique* by Fernand Crom-melynck; the quite debatable *Les* ("The Forest") by Ostrovsky; and the—truly—brilliant production of Gogol's *The Inspector-General*. But the West remains ignorant to this day of such masterpieces of Meyer-hold's staging as *Farce, The Unknown Woman, Don Juan,* and *Masquerade*.

The West saw Gozzi's captivating *Turandot* as produced by the Vakhtangov Theater. Yet it never managed to see a single work of Komisarzhevsky's or of Evreinov's Old Theater in the years before the Revolution. Westerners saw Tairov's production of *Salome* but not his *Sakuntala* or his *Famira Kifared*. And finally, the people in the West have remained unaware of the huge number of ideas and theories of the theater that were brought forth before the Revolution and from which the innovations of the Soviet theater have developed.

PART TWO

THE FIRST DECADE, 1917 TO 1927

CHAPTER IV

FEBRUARY TO OCTOBER, 1917

ON THE NIGHT OF FEBRUARY 26, 1917, the audience returned from Meyerhold's production of Lermontov's *Masquerade* through side streets and alleyways because trucks and bullets were racing through the main thoroughfares. By the next day the February Revolution had taken place. Yet the theaters remained full. Apparently people wanted either to be distracted from what they did not yet believe or to get away from their homes lest their nerves be jangled by the sounds of shooting, rioting, and impending horror.

THE REVOLUTION TOUCHES THE THEATER

How did the theater people of Russia react to the overthrow of the tsarist regime? In different ways. Many of them did not yet believe that all the old foundations of society were breaking up. They thought that the "disorders" would be only temporary and that the old life, along with the old regime, would be resumed. The majority of the actors at the Imperial theaters, of course, feared what was happening. They did not want the chaos of revolution to destroy their peaceful and noble work at the "best of the best" theaters. The actors and directors at the private theaters greeted the revolution with hope. It promised to free them from annoying difficulties with the censorship, from the ban on acting during Lent, from the shameful position of being second-rate theaters, and from the imperial control over the crown theaters. The Revolution promised the poorest actors that their material situation would be improved and that accounts would be squared with the theater managers. Meyerhold, Tairov, and Komisarzhevsky—the most important innovators in the theater—greeted the February Revolution with joy and hope. They themselves were revolutionaries in art, and they had been persecuted by the press of the former regime. They hated the conservative and titled dignitaries who had constituted their public and who had frequently squirmed and sneered at the work of the creative directors. There is pathos in Tairov's statement:

Motor vehicles, troops, and guns swept past us. Powerful waves of workers rolled by, flooding the snowy streets, while we were standing on the sidewalks, behind lines of chains, the audience at an incomprehensible Mystery play which was taking place before our eyes! Stirred up, with exultation in our hearts, we quiveringly greeted the future freedom, but our feelings—the feelings of the public at the world theater—were reflected in the arena where the architects of the New Russia were creating a new life. What could be more tragic for an innate actor, proud of his calling, than to be a member of the audience at a time of national action, to come down from the boards upon which all his life had been spent and to turn up in the amphitheater? An actor who has become a member of the audience is like a sailor with no deck beneath him or a horseman at the corpse of his mount.[1]

E. K. Malinovskaya promised the eternal freedom of art to an assemblage of actors from the Petrograd theaters. This was the same woman who was later to become the Soviet manager of the Bolshoi Theater in Moscow. She would zealously carry out the subjugation of art to the Communist Party.

Komisarzhevsky was finally able to speak out and say everything that had been building up within him against the Imperial theaters:

The crown theaters are reactionary. They are conservative. Their trend in the theater arts is autocratic. They have always been dominated by the strong, by those who have "privilege." . . . The repertory was established and the roles were allotted for these leading men, even though they were rather less gifted than all the "subordinate actors." For their benefit, such bases of the theater arts as the spirit of the presentation and the inner ensemble were destroyed. A system of servility, toadyism, and oppression of the junior members was introduced. . . . Conventionalism and routine were supported in all ways within the crown theaters. Their directors, managers, and others used art to create sinecures for themselves.[2]

Boris Glagolin, the famous actor and director, came out with a plan for "socializing the theater." He suggested the establishment of "a toiling group of actors, a Theater Lodge that would aim to unite those devoted to the theater on the basis of religious service." A monastic order of begging actors would be contented with alms donated by the public. "Any surplus, should there be one, would be used for charity." The main theme in the repertory of this Lodge would be, in Glagolin's words, "the culture of the human personality in God." [3]

The Moscow Art Theater greeted the Revolution with more profundity and sincerity. The Theater saw the Revolution as an opportunity for realizing all its ideas and dreams of a better lot for Russia. Together with Anton Chekhov, this Theater had been instilling these dreams in its actors for many years.

It would be a mistake to think that only the Revolution of 1917 made Russian theater people articulate about democracy and service to society. Anatoli Lunacharsky had published his work on the socialist theater as early as 1908. Certain other definite statements were made in the Russian theater press just before the Revolution. A. R. Kugel, for example, wrote:

The present impoverishment [results from the fact] that we are on the eve of self-determination for the new democracy, for the new social and national strata. . . . I am not undertaking to judge whether this new renaissance is close by or far off, but it is inevitable. It is organically connected with a new social stratification.[4]

And I. Rabinovich, the designer, declared:

Only the new public can revive the theater and give it back its earlier power and its past brilliance. This public is still timid in overcoming a number of external and internal obstacles and in taking row after row of barbed-wire entanglements. It is drawing close to the theater. Making the theater democratic is the slogan that can do for the theater what contact with the earth did for Antaeus of antiquity—give it new strength.[5]

The Revolution immediately brought something new both to the stage and to the auditorium. Political participants in the February Revolution were present at the performances. During the intermissions they would frequently deliver speeches from their places about a free art in a free nation and on themes of political moment. They extolled the Revolution and provoked ovations. The public demanded the *Marseillaise*. Sometimes the presentations would be interrupted by meetings at which the theater personnel participated. A new form appeared for the first time in the Russian theater of those days. This was the "concert-meeting." Performances by actors and opera singers would alternate with speeches by political workers and with the playing of music.

The theater took its first halting steps to join the revolutionary street crowds. It was aided by the rostrums erected near the theaters for May Day. Passers-by would get up on these platforms and make speeches, to which the actors would respond with other speeches. The opera chorus would perform the *Marseillaise*. Actors in make-up and costume used trucks or hastily erected platforms to participate in the "Freedom Loan" drive.

Eight months separated the February Revolution from the Bolshevik seizure of power. During this period the Russian theater was unable to begin either a basic change or the staging of new socialist presentations. Nevertheless, during the short period when the regime was both democratic and republican, there were a number of significant developments with respect to the theater.

In the first place, the theater was freed from the strict control of censors, police, and clergy. A number of plays were staged for the first time. They dealt with Russian monarchs, the court, the officers, and the orthodox clergy. Included among them were such works as Dmitri Merezhkovsky's *Pavel pervyi* ("Paul I"), A. K. Tolstoy's *Smert' Ivana Groznogo* ("The Death of Ivan the Terrible," which previously had been heavily cut), Pisemesky's *Poruchik Gladkov* ("Second Lieutenant Gladkov") and Protopopov's *Chërnye vorony* ("Black Crows").

The Revolution also removed the ban from plays that the Orthodox Church had forbidden. Among the works affected were *Tsar' Iudeiskii* ("King of Judaea") by "K. R." (the pen name of Grand Duke Konstantin Konstantinovich), and *Salome* by Oscar Wilde. Plays that had been banned for moral reasons were also permitted. Such works included *Leda* by Anatoli Kamensky, *Der Reigen* ("La Ronde") by Arthur Schnitzler, and both *Tsar' Golod* ("King Hunger") and *Anatema* ("Anathema") by Leonid Andreyev.

The theater was permitted performances both on fast days and on various church holidays. It was allowed to touch upon religious questions and to show the seamy aspects of the clergy upon the stage.

For the first time, there was great discussion within the theater about democratic civil liberties. The theater itself obtained freedom of speech and of assembly, the right to use the stage to propagandize different political, religious, and philosophical positions. It became responsible for its productions to the judiciary alone, and not to administrative organs of the regime.

The "overthrow of autocracy" resulted in something else as well. The Imperial theaters lost their privileged position. Five theaters had been receiving substantial subsidies from the Palace Department. These included the Alexandrinsky, the Marinsky, and the Mikhailovsky in Petrograd, and the Bolshoi and the Maly in Moscow. The tsarist government had not helped the private theaters, which included the Moscow Art Theater, the Komisarzhevskaya Theater, and the Kamerny Theater.

Many questions relating to the theater were discussed in the press, at meetings, and at assemblages. These included: the right of the former Imperial theaters to government aid; the closing of such a purely court theater as the French troupe of the Mikhailovsky Theater; the need to make the Moscow Art Theater a state theater, and the establishment of state-subsidized theaters. The programs for these new state theaters would be laid down by the government, but they would be in charge of private individuals.

The critics' fire wrecked the entire structure and all the customs of the former Imperial theaters. It destroyed the "servile, civil-servant actor," the "star system," the absence of ensemble work, "the extravagant fees of the stars," and the whole atmosphere of subservience to rank, titles, influence, and position. Instead, the actor became a free artist and citizen. Some stated that the Imperial theaters, like Carthage, had to be destroyed, that their entire personnel had to be examined severely and purged of "ballast." This word denoted the untalented actors present only because they were protected by those in power. Such persons had to be replaced by gifted actors from the private and the provincial theaters.

The subscription system had let "only the nobility and the privileged group" go to the theater. It was replaced by a general sale of all tickets at cheaper prices. *Russkaia volia* ("Russian Freedom"), a completely middle-class newspaper, wrote at the time:

The subscription system in our finest opera house represents, in its own way, the chains of absolutism which have heretofore dominated all the rest of our life. . . . The time to free the Marinsky Theater from all its medieval feudal lords arrived long ago.[6]

This period is significant more for its new systematization within the theater than for the struggle to show new content on the stage.[7] A number of questions were dealt with by the post-February reforms. These included new ways to administer the state theaters, the principle of elections, the general administration of the theater by itself, the complete autonomy of artistic corporations, and the concession to the state of only the general right to control and regulate the theaters. Thus, the projected regulations for the "Union of Personnel of the Alexandrinsky and Mikhailovsky Theaters Based on Principles of Social Self-Administration" were considered the highest authority for directing those two theaters. This was a general assembly of actors, including representatives of the directors, technical personnel, workers, and attendants. This assembly elected a Union Council in which artistic questions could be decided only by the votes of the actors and directors. Every guild had to have its own professional committee. The general manager of the theater was elected by the troupe. He had executive authority and was responsible for contact with the government. Each theater elected its own "repertorial and artistic committee." These committees invited new people to join the troupe, assigned roles, and selected directors. The actors were stormily approaching complete autonomy.

"The Provisional Position of the State Theaters" was introduced in May, 1917. This constitution for the theaters was based on the regulations of the Comédie Française. An autonomous association of actors under the control of a government-appointed director was established. The French regulations were changed and made more democratic. All the guilds were allowed to participate, including the stage hands. The rights of the electoral organs were also expanded. "The general sense of all these reforms," Bezpalov said, "was this: 'You, that is, the government, give us money—big money—and we, the actors, will be autonomous and will take care of the administrative aspects ourselves.' " [8]

V. A. Teliakovsky, the former general manager of the Imperial theaters, continued in his post for a short while after the February Revolution. Bezpalov said about him and the situation:

V. A. Teliakovsky became acquainted with the wishes of the troupes. He characterized them well when he stated that from then on the actors would recognize the theater administration's duties in only two particulars: turning the box-office receipts over to the autonomous troupe, and sweeping the halls of the theater.[9]

The actors of that time were greatly attracted by "the principle of universal suffrage" in all fields. They fell into extremes. They struggled against one-man management in the theater and confused it with the struggle against autocracy. They transformed their electoral organs into parliaments. They brought up very many petty issues. Meetings were turned into endless and fruitless talkathons. Within the theaters themselves, there were hostile little groups and "parties." The issues became lost in the competition and disagreements, and so they remained undecided.[10]

The acting world reflected all the tragic mistakes made after the February Revolution in miniature. It was submerged in talk, speeches, meetings, contests, words, and rationalism—until the Bolsheviks throttled it. The Bolsheviks acted with no scruples as to means, while their enemies grew intoxicated and passionate in their new parliament.

The February Revolution had struggled for the right of the toilers to trade unions. The wish to apply this to the theater was both good and natural, and valuable attempts were made to set up unions among the theater personnel. These were hindered by the extremists—people whom freedom had made tipsy. Some of the extremes in the first trades union of Russian actors have become legendary. The opera company of the Marinsky Theater, for instance, did not wish to admit the ballet dancers of the same theater into their organization. After all, opera can manage quite nicely without the ballet was their argument. The ostracized dancers advanced arguments to the contrary. Most operas were successful because of the ballet alone (such as Borodin's *Prince Igor*, with its Polovtsian Dances). Some of the extremes were more somber. Alexander Tairov wrote the regulations of the "Union for Moscow Actors," and he asserted the "class antagonism" between the actors and the theater managers—as if the actors were to be equated with the "proletariat" and the managers with the "capitalists." If necessary, the Union would "undertake an organized struggle according to the general principles of the struggle of the toiling masses" against the managers.[11]

THE THEATER APPRAISES BOLSHEVISM

In August, 1917, there was an All-Russian Conference of trade unions connected with the theater. It was held in Petrograd, and Tairov presided. A periodical of the times declared:

The leitmotif of the orators was that the actors were proletarians, that their movement was entirely a class-movement of the proletariat, and that the theater managers were class enemies of the actors.[12]

The managers, however, created the theater in the Russian provinces. The entire theater press came to their defense, stating that the managers discovered actors, sponsored a highly artistic repertory, and sometimes incurred losses. In an article entitled "Teatral'nyi bol'shevizm" ("Bolshevism in the Theater"), E. Stark wrote that the persecution of the managers by the actors "cannot be termed anything but an organized campaign of serried mediocrity against a few individuals with brains and talent."[13]

The Bolsheviks organized a human slaughterhouse on the Nevsky

Prospekt and at the Public Library in Petrograd during July, 1917. This had a sobering effect on the actors and the other intellectuals who had been attracted by "Marxist" formulas and "class" movements. The first blinders were removed from people's eyes, and they began to understand the real essence of Bolshevik "class warfare." This may explain why, toward the end of the summer, the actors left the workers' Soviets and began to defend the Provisional Government. They banished from their unions not only the Bolshevik formulas but also the people "on the other side of the footlights." This last group included the cloakroom attendants, the ticket collectors, the workers, and the attendants. The actors thus resisted the Bolshevik "proletarianization" of their unions. The "Resistance Movement" against Bolshevism within the Russian theater had therefore begun even before the Bolsheviks seized power in Petrograd.

In the summer of 1917 some skits critical of the "Communist Comrades" were put on. In June Shabelsky's one-act satire *Dezertir* ("The Deserter") was staged in the Tauric Gardens. This play "boldly revealed the thorough propagandizing of the slightly conscious soldiers by extremist agitators." [14] This was followed in July and August by *Troitskii Fars* ("A Trinity Farce"), *Partiinyi Fars* ("A Party Farce"), and *Bol'shevik i burzhui* ("The Bolshevik and the Dirty Bourgeois"). Such pieces were hits. V. Lin's Theater staged on July 10 *Ivanov, Pavel—anarkhist* ("Ivanov, Pavel—Anarchist"), by Rapaport. This was a malicious parody on a meeting of "green youths" infected with "leftist" and "revolutionary" ideas. The *Tragediia glupykh liudei* ("Tragedy of Stupid People") by someone named Epikur was staged at "Luna Park" on August 17. It was an important review that depicted Lenin, Roshal, and Gorky negatively. On September 22 the Zbrozhek-Pashkovskaya Theater staged Teffi's *Napoleon*. This work presented people with no convictions in a ridiculous light. Such persons adhered to the Bolsheviks and anarchists for the sake of careers and preached the continual butchery of the officers.

A month before the Bolsheviks seized power, the Troitsky Theater scored a hit with Mirovich's *Revoliutsiia v Golovotiapove* ("Revolution in Bunglerville"). This was a satirical skit about some stupid philistines who created their own "regional republic" somewhere in the provinces. A contemporary Khlestakov—a Bolshevik—played a major role in the production. (Khlestakov is the main character in Gogol's

Inspector-General; he is something of a rogue and a parasite.) A critic wrote about Mirovich's play:

Ridicule of these stupid people, these revolutionaries with neither sense nor understanding, is petty at a time when the heart grieves because the Revolution has been distorted not by idiots but by blind fanatics who are undermining the foundations of freedom. The whips and arrows of satire are needed here.[15]

The struggle against the Bolsheviks and the "leaders of the proletariat" was carried on through farce, satire, ridicule, and parody. It was expanded by the "ad libs" of the actors in operettas and by the versifiers and storytellers at clubs and cabarets. Koshevsky, a comedian, was performing in an operetta entitled *Osennie manevry* ("Autumn Maneuvers"), the theme of which had nothing to do with those times. He supplemented his role with very astute political ad libs: "the very latest about current happenings—including Lenin." [16] At the arty cabaret called the "Comedians' Rest," Nikolai Evreinov led a "chorus of Bolshevik versifiers." On the same program with *Revolution in Bunglerville,* the Troitsky Theater presented Goriansky's skit *Poet i proletarii* ("Poet and Proletarian"). It showed a "skillfully cut-out figure of a symbolic 'proletarian' threatening to overpower poetry." [17]

In the third supplement to the catalogue of works produced by the Union of Dramatic Writers during 1917, we find many sketches, farces, and grotesque pieces on anti-Bolshevik themes. Some titles include *Anarkhist—telegrafist* ("The Anarchist Telegrapher"), *Anneksiia i kontributsiia* ("Annexation and Contribution"), *Bol'shevik i men'shevik* ("The Bolshevik and the Menshevik"), and *Dvorets baleriny* ("The Ballerina's Palace").[18]

These minor theaters and these skit writers must be awarded the honor of having seen through Lenin and the Bolsheviks even before the upheaval of October, 1917. These theaters and playwrights were among the first to oppose Lenin and the other mortal enemies of Russia within the theater. They deserve to be included in a history of the twentieth-century Russian theater.

Some weak plays were also put on, however, such as Evtikhi Karpov's *Zarevo* ("Glow") and E. Milyukova's *Altar' Svobody* ("Altar of Freedom"). These last two authors sincerely wished to respond thematically to the February Revolution. Mikhaelis' *Revoliutsionnaia svad'ba* ("A Revolutionary Wedding") was put on at Saburov's Theater in April,

1917. This was a second-rate play whose plot had been taken from the French Revolution. The rest of the repertory between February and October of 1917 was quite miserable. Some theaters specializing in farces or short sketches put on poor skits on such "vital" themes as *Rasputin, Krakh doma Romanov i Ko* ("The Fall of the House of Romanov and Co."), and *Tsarskosel'skie blagodati* ("Bliss at Tsarskoe Selo"). These pieces provoked irate indignation in the press, which declared that the direction of such works was "not to the lofty heights of freedom and reason, but to the stinking atmosphere of the old serf-holding society in which the serfs, once out of their masters' sight, would gossip about the latter." [19]

Some dramatic critics tried to explain the lack of good revolutionary dramas in terms of the terrible conditions produced by the collapse of the old regime. B. Nikonov, for example, wrote:

Not a single real talent has yet spoken out in the language of freedom during this "free period." . . . The talents remain silent, agitated, and frightened by the terrible lees, the confusion, and the disorder that our revolution has cloaked. . . . Can songs of beauty and light conceivably be sung when the spectacle of a shameful struggle against our country is going on? This struggle has almost become a slogan of the day. The spectacle can make one cry out from pain, or swear, or tear his hair, but it cannot make him write songs or create inspired works of art! . . . Something incomprehensible has occurred. . . . The hopes have been crushed underfoot by criminals. People have grown stupid, wasted their humanity, cremated their souls, and run away from the enemy at the front, and here they sing savage songs during the nights. . . . One does not feel like believing that this is life itself.[20]

The terrible time in which the Bolsheviks had thoroughly propagandized the soldiers deserting from the front, the increase in disorders, and civil war all left their imprint on the theater press. This press appealed for resistance to the anarchy unleashed by the evil gravediggers of Russia. The critic Kugel wrote:

Right now, the most genuine and important work for the actor and, I would say, his great historical task, is to set out for the front to counterbalance the corrosive and ruinous sermons about peace with Germany, or—what is the same thing—ignorance about the war against her, or—what is still worse (because it is more senseless)—the transformation of a national army in wartime into a weapon of the International. The actors should establish concert-meetings of a patriotic character. . . . Every actor who feels that he is a son of Russia . . . can and must turn all the fire of his heart and talent toward inspiring people to perform exploits and toward awakening feelings for our country. . . . Go then, actors, if love of your country is alive within you, go to the front, to the soldiers, arouse that emotion and raise their spirits! And you, oh tender and fragile actresses, go there and use your soft and womanly voices to appeal for a struggle on behalf of the honor and dignity of Russia.[21]

The most perspicacious Russian theater people spoke out with increasing persistence and loudness in favor of resisting the anarchy that Lenin's staff was instigating. A periodical of the day wrote that the theater had to carry on propagandistic work within the army. The theater, it said,

must strongly oppose the preaching of anarchy and disintegration and all the rotten defeatist propaganda that dark powers are using to lead our country to its death. . . . The stage personnel of our country must realize that their main civic duty is to go to the masses with catchwords of healthy, patriotic art, with all the zeal and nobility of their talent, and with a readiness to endure even the greatest sacrifices for the sake of their great task.[22]

These were the final appeals of the most honest people in the Russian theater. Respectfully, we preserve them on the pages of its history.

CHAPTER V

BOLSHEVISM ASSIGNS
A ROLE TO THE THEATER

DID THE COMMUNIST PARTY have any ideas of its own about the role of the theater before the Revolution of October, 1917? It had a few statements by Karl Marx and Friedrich Engels on the ideology of the theater and a very few scraped together—for the most part—from the pre-Revolutionary issues of *Pravda*. To supplement their shortcomings in this field, the Bolsheviks appropriated remarks by Rousseau, Robespierre, Feuerbach, Belinsky, Dobroliubov, Rolland, and Wagner. A great deal of the "legacy of the Marxist classics" on the ideology of the theater comes from a letter of Engels, which he wrote to Ferdinand Lassalle about Lassalle's drama *Franz von Sickingen:*

The great profundity of ideas, perceived in the historical sense, which you— and not without foundation—ascribe to the German drama, will probably be blended with Shakespearean vitality and effectiveness only in the future and then, perhaps, not by the Germans. In any case, I see the future of the drama in just such a blending. . . . [Its heroes] will be motivated not by trivial individual whims but by the historical current bearing them along.[1]

Then there were the pre-Revolutionary statements of Anatoli Lunacharsky. In the Soviet period Lunacharsky became the first People's Commissar of Enlightenment of the R.S.F.S.R. He was in charge of Soviet theater policy for a number of years, and he was also—to some extent—a Bolshevik theoretician of the theater arts. As early as 1908 the liberal conditions of the tsarist censorship permitted Lunacharsky to write an article anathematizing the "bourgeois" theater of those days. He repudiated the "bourgeois" theater—that is, the entire Russian theater from start to finish—as a theater of mere entertainment. "This entertainment is sometimes beautiful and elegant," he wrote, "and contains some shadings of ideas, but it is more often coarse, base, and vulgar." [2] Lunacharsky was astonished that such a "socialistic thinker" as Georges

Sorel dared to express the heresy that the poor worker grows tired toward evening and does not want presentations with "ideas" but desires fairy scenes and light, glittering entertainment.

Lunacharsky felt that the theater of the future would be a "powerful, energetic, courageous theater of a generation under the red banners." It would be

a theater of rapid action, major passions, rare contrasts, whole characters, powerful sufferings, and lofty ecstasy. Yes, it will be a theater of ideas. [This ideal] new theater will get rid of nuances, details, and all the flavors needed by the refined and hysterical palates of our "cultured" public. It will thunder, glitter, be noisy, rapid-flying, and crude both for the nervous young ladies and the soured "cream" of society. Its satire will strike one's cheeks loudly: its woe will make one sob. Its joy will make one forget himself and dance; its villainy will be terrifying.[3]

As we shall see, few of Lunacharsky's dreams have come to life in the Soviet period. The "socialist theater," which is ideal in every sense, has not been achieved. But one of Lunacharsky's statements in 1908 has become basic to Soviet theater policy:

The task is clear: to appeal to all the young, fresh, and healthy in "cultured" society to create a lofty socialist art, to resurrect Shakespeare, Schiller, and many of the other past titans in order to link great art with the great lords of the future—the people.[4]

EARLY SOVIET POLICY

The Bolsheviks set up the Theater Section as part of the People's Commissariat of Enlightenment in January, 1918—two months after they had seized power. The tasks of the Theater Section included

the general guidance of theater work in the country on a broad nationwide scale; . . . to give localities directives of a general character on administering theater work, in the interests of unifying this last and aiming at a systematic and (insofar as is possible) a uniform application to life (within the limits of local conditions) of the Theater Section's tasks . . . to create a new theater connected with the rebuilding of the state and society upon the principles of socialism.[5]

This organ of the Soviet regime intended not merely to administer the theaters but to direct their content and direction as well. This is borne out by the very first point in the program of the Theater Section— namely, "The Theater Section will cooperate in unifying all creative and research forces concerned with theater ideology."[6]

Lenin signed a decree of the Council of People's Commissars that was published on August 26, 1919. It was entitled: "Ob ob'edinenii teatral'nogo dela" ("On the Unification of Theater Work").[7] It nationalized the property of all the theaters of Russia.[8] It centralized—in a bureaucratically Bolshevik manner—the entire theater economy and subordinated it to the "Tsentroteatr" (the Central Theater Committee).[9] This Committee was given responsibility for subordinating the theaters to the Bolshevik ideology and for giving them "indications of a repertorial character to link them with the popular masses and their socialistic ideal." [10]

There were many theater people during the first years of the Soviet regime whose acceptance of Bolshevism was largely conditioned on a comparison with the romanticism of the French Revolution. This parallel was accepted even by the Communists. The French Revolution, however, considered the idea that "The freedom of the theater cannot be constrained without encroaching on freedom of thought" to be inviolable.[11] The Council of the Commune was granted the administration of the theaters and control of the plays staged therein only at the Convention of August 14 to 20, 1793—four years after the fall of the Bastille. The Soviet regime, however, seized the theater in its very first months. Bolshevism seized the theater hastily and avidly and imposed "thought control" upon it. The Soviet attitude was similar to the French attitude formalized in the decree of the Paris Commune dated May 17, 1871, which defined dramatic productions as a method of instructing in all the civic virtues and forthwith placed all the theaters under the control of "delegations of enlightenment."

The Soviet theater policy during the first years of the new regime was completely two-faced. As soon as they had seized power, the Bolsheviks realized quite well that the theater was a mighty weapon for influencing the masses. Nationalizing the theaters completely was not enough, therefore. The theater companies had to be assigned the mission of carrying out the Communist Party's tasks. But Bolshevism could not take possession of the Russian theater immediately because the resistance movement against the usurping regime was still quite strong among theater people. Before the Revolution there had been no "proletarian theater" in Russia and not even one Bolshevik among the actors. The only Communist supporters had been among the stagehands and the wardrobe people. Because of this all the participants in the Russian theater were included among the "bourgeois intelligentsia." [12] To have permitted the Cheka to chase away and liquidate all the hostile elements in the Russian theater would have meant the end of that theater. The "processing" and training of the old intelligentsia by the new regime required years, patience, compromise, and a feigned liberality.[13] An examination of the lists of those who directed the Theater Section in those first years shows how liberal the Bolsheviks were then. The Petrograd Theater Section included Vsevolod Meyerhold as deputy chief and the symbolist poet Alexander Blok as chairman of the repertorial subsection. The Moscow Theater Section was largely a collection of mystics and symbolists, such as Vyacheslav Ivanov, Andrei Bely, Valery Bryusov, Georgy Chulkov, and Eugene Vakhtangov.

During these early years the Bolsheviks tried to win over the masses of people who followed the Mensheviks, anarchists, and Leftist Socialist Revolutionaries. Hence, they had to tolerate those parties and their representatives in the Soviets, and they had to conduct a liberal ideological program. This explains why one could still read direct and open attacks on the Bolsheviks in the press—including the theater press—during the period 1917 to 1922.

Bolshevism was unable to swallow all the theaters of Russia because of organizational and economic difficulties. A huge number of commissars faithful to Lenin would have been needed to subordinate the enormous number of theaters to the propaganda of the Communist Party, and the cadres faithful to Bolshevism were barely enough for the army and the Cheka. Bolshevism was economically unable to maintain the numerous theaters that it had seized because the Soviet state treasury had more important financial burdens, especially the fighting of the Civil War.[14]

There were many different views during the first years of the Soviet regime about the path the theater should follow. All the new ideologists of the theater, however, proceeded from the same basic problem—the relationship between the people and the theater.

Some started from the premise that understanding of the classics and high art was beyond the capacity of the common people. Those of the theater felt that art had to be simplified and lowered to the people's own educational level, and so they became seekers after new forms of "national comedy" and reconstructors of the old national theaters. They included those who went back to the rural roundelays and farces and those who wanted to base the Soviet theater on the pre-Revolutionary "theater for the people." A few Bolsheviks rebelled against this view of the Soviet theater, however, considering it to be an underestimation of the toiling masses and apolitical, petty-bourgeois culture.

Others asserted that the old theater was completely unsuitable, and that a theater had to be organized that would be new from start to finish. This viewpoint was shared by Meyerhold, the Proletcult (Proletarian Culture movement), and the Futurists under Vladimir Mayakovsky, although they all had different nuances and special features.

A third group asserted that the great theater classics alone were able to instruct and educate the people. This was the view of such fine theater experts as Stanislavsky, Nemirovich-Danchenko, Yuzhin-Sumbatov, Alexander Blok, and a majority of the outstanding actors on the crown stage.

What was the official Soviet viewpoint during that period? It was not so "revolutionary" as that maintained by the ideologists of the new "proletarian culture" movement. Moreover, it was quite conservative in those times. The Soviet regime's theater policy was mainly "protective." It decided to maintain the oldest and most valuable theaters. It categorized them as so-called "academic theaters" and isolated their administration from that of the others. Lunacharsky explained this as follows:

I personally introduced a resolution in the Council of People's Commissars that a certain sum must be allocated, not just for maintaining the traditional theaters, but for giving substantial aid to the new theaters as well. I was answered that the state was so poor in its central budget that we can take into our boat only the most valuable old theaters from the general current of culture in which the old values are submerged.[15]

The support given by the Soviet regime to the "traditional theaters" alone has, of course, been explained by a more important factor than the central budget. Lenin's artistic tastes were conservative. Dictatorships, including that of the Communist Party, are always conservative in their tastes, and the reason is not so much that dictators fail to grasp esthetic feelings but that they are mortally afraid of freedom of thought. Bold, "leftist," and experimental innovations in the theater arts are basically flights of free thought, which any tyranny or dictatorship hates and considers "subversive."

Neither Lenin, his Party, nor the Soviet regime in general was interested in new paths for art. Their maximum aim was to preserve some of the old artistic values.[16] The search for new forms and potentialities was carried on by people who had nothing in common with Bolshevism. Under a regime that protected only the "academic theaters," they sought some air vents and loopholes through which to force their way to the new theater.

The only one who loudly rose up against the protective policy of the Soviet regime was Meyerhold. He created the "Teatral'nyi Oktiabr'" (October in the Theater) movement whose slogan was "make the theater political." He struggled angrily against the Bolshevik policy of giving privileges to such conservative theaters as the Alexandrinsky and the Maly, while refusing to aid the theaters engendered by the Revolution. Meyerhold, with his inherent maximalism, demanded that the old things of the "intimate" bourgeois theater be cast overboard and that all strength be devoted to creating a theater whose themes and forms would harmonize with the Revolution. He found a stubborn opponent in Lunacharsky, who strongly defended the academic theaters. Lunacharsky wrote:

Now that the tiny theatrical October is arriving, it would, of course, be ridiculous to give it the valuables which were preserved not without great labor at the time of the gigantic tempests in the real October [of 1917]. . . . I can entrust Comrade Meyerhold with the destruction of what is old and bad and with the creation of what is new and good, but I cannot entrust him with preserving whatever is old and good.[17]

It would be a mistake to think that the encroachments of the Bolsheviks on the theater (which they sought to turn into a weapon for Communist propaganda) were impeded during Lenin's lifetime by his conservative tastes. It would be a mistake to assume that these Bolshevik efforts were defeated by his good intention of enlightening the ignorant masses of Russia through the great and immortal classics and the best actors of the old Russian theater. No, even the cultural and artistic policy of Lenin himself was also two-faced.

During the first years of the Soviet regime no one advanced slogans about the complete subordination of art, culture, and education to the tasks of building Communism as much as Lenin did. Thus, we see perfectly clear indications of what was in store for art in the land of the Soviets in one of the resolutions adopted by the Eighth Congress of the

Communist Party in 1919. This took place under the complete guidance of Lenin. The resolution read:

There are no forms of art or science which should not be linked to the great ideas of Communism and the infinitely variegated work of creating a Communist economy. [All nonscholarly education of the masses, including the theater] must touch Communist propaganda.[18]

In the second year of the Soviet regime, the Russian theater learned that art might be subjected to the "national economy" and to "Five-Year Plans." Lenin himself wrote the draft for the resolution "O proletarskoi kul'ture" ("On Proletarian Culture"). This stated:

In the Soviet Workers' and Peasants' Republic, every educational endeavor, both in politics and in education generally—and in art particularly—must be permeated with the spirit of the proletariat's class struggle for successfully accomplishing the aims of its dictatorship.[19]

The Party's effort to enslave the theater was expanded at the Twelfth Congress of the Communist Party in 1923:

The question of utilizing the theater in systematic mass propaganda in favor of the ideas of struggling for Communism must be stated in a practical form. Suitable forces must be attracted, both in the capital and in the provinces, to strengthen the creation and selection of a suitable revolutionary repertory. . . . The theater must also be utilized as a means for antireligious propaganda.[20]

Later, following Lenin, Lunacharsky was to start the slogan of "new content in old forms." For many years this was the attitude of the Soviet government toward the theater.[21]

The Theater Section of the People's Commissariat of Enlightenment was set up in Petrograd during the fall of 1918. It was later transferred to Moscow, when the Soviet government moved to the Kremlin. The head of the Theater Section was O. L. Kameneva, and her deputy was Meyerhold.[22]

There was great scope and there was pathos in the Theater Section during its first years. Not all its astronomical plans turned out to be feasible, and very few were carried out successfully. Let us list the basic projects that the Theater Section undertook. This should indicate the scale upon which Russian theater people were attempting to build theaters. Let it be understood that most of these ideas and fine plans came not from the Bolsheviks but rather from the non-Communists associated with the Russian stage, Russian art, and Russian letters. The group in question included Vsevolod Meyerhold, Eugene Vakhtangov, Vyacheslav Ivanov, and Alexander Blok.

Blok was in charge of the repertorial subsection of the Theater Section. The country had been devastated completely; there was a paper shortage, and the printing presses were all overloaded with Communist Party literature. Despite all this, Blok managed to publish more than one series of the world's dramatic classics. Lists of the best plays were published to help the provinces and the amateur theaters both in the countryside and in the towns. Such plays were recommended for production. The pedagogical subsection, for the first time in Russia, raised questions about the children's theater as a weapon for education. In all their scope, it raised and investigated problems dealing with the children's theater and the young people's theater. It organized the first theaters and companies for young audiences. The Theater Section created many state studios, courses, and schools. These included such excellent educational units as the courses for mastering stage presentations and the school for acting mastery.

The historical-theater subsection tried to organize a "single, scientific theater." It summoned all the theoreticians, historians, and theater specialists to participate in working on a *Theater Encyclopedia*. It set up a Theater University. It did much work in collecting materials on the history of the Russian theater, and it published many scholarly works. It created a special "workers'-and-peasants'-theater subsection," which carried on its stormy work with the amateur and mass theaters.

Vakhtangov, the highly gifted head of the directorial subsection, set up courses for directors. He organized both experimental workshops and laboratories as well. "Time, and perhaps a good deal of time," he said, "is needed before people can turn up from the very heart of the nation. That is why firesides from which they can appear must be created first." [23]

Despite the nationwide paper shortage an unprecedented number of theater journals and newspapers were published in Russia between 1918 and 1923. In Petrograd and Moscow alone there were over forty titles. Before the Revolution there were fewer than a dozen such magazines. This is their approximate total at present also. The early years of the Soviet period have, in this regard, never been equaled.

Even if you discount the Utopian dreams, the harebrained schemes, and the temporary nature of many enterprises and magazines, one new fact emerged from all this hubbub. The theater had become the center of cultural and educational work in Russia. All the Russian theater people, heatedly and inspiredly, undertook to educate the masses through the theater. It was as if they were repeating one of the appeals from the French Revolution: "Convince yourselves, like us, to admit the moral importance of the theater arts. The question is how to erect a social school which will serve virtue and elegance of taste in equal degree." [24]

The people who did the working and planning within the Theater Section had, for the most part, nothing in common with the Soviet regime. What did the best Russian symbolist poets—such as Blok, Ivanov, Bely, and Chulkov—who worked in the Theater Section have in common with it? They were strangers, and the Communists of those years considered them "class-alien elements." What was there in common between the great scope and ideas of such poets, who wanted to elevate the theater arts to a school for society, and the governmental statute setting up the Soviet Theater Section as an organ of "general guidance and observation"? The best part of the Theater Section's work was accomplished in spite of the Soviet regime and by getting around it. And we shall almost always encounter this evasion in the history of the Soviet theater's best accomplishments.

Before Russian intellectuals could participate warmly in the Theater Section, however, certain changes had to take place within it. There had to be a new platform for them to be able to work together with the Bolsheviks. This platform was first proclaimed by Lenin and Lunacharsky. It consisted of making the world's classics national property.[25] The intellectuals may not have accepted the Soviet regime, but many of them did work with it and cooperate with it in a limited way. What could be finer than to enlighten the people by producing the best of the world's classics? Is not this what every real theater person dreams about? Russian theater people considered this mission a hundred times nobler and purer than all of Bolshevism, with its antihuman "class struggle," its coercion, coarseness, plunder, and terror.

The theater as a potent means for national education was the platform for "fellow traveling" and cooperating with the Soviet regime. As soon as this educational program was eclipsed by the propagandistic tasks of the Communist Party, the literary intellectuals began to leave the theater. Some of them emigrated, and many of them resisted and participated in the "inner emigration"—remained in their homeland but refused to cooperate with the regime.

Such a great artist as Eugene Vakhtangov based his recognition of the Soviet regime on a profound love for his people. "Mankind does not have a single genuinely great work of art," he said, "which fails to incarnate the summit of the creative powers in the nation itself. The really great is always what the artist has overheard in the spirit of the people." [26]

Another movement to justify what was happening in Russia was "Scythianism," a philosophy connected with the name of Alexander Blok. His verses—"Yes, we are Scythians, we are Asiatics"—appeared in 1918, and they started a movement to justify the historical need for Bolshevism. Scythianism came from a hatred of bourgeois civilization, from a conviction that western culture, with its humanism and its philosophy, was already breaking up. Scythianism preceded Oswald Spengler's *Decline of the West* by several years, but it was filled with the same foreboding of doom and belief that barbarism would inevitably replace a civilization that had outlived its day and a culture that had grown decrepit. But the arrival of the Scythian barbarians yielded a synthetic primitivism.[27] The peasant masses, tortured by Bolshevism, turned out to be the barbarians, the gravediggers of decrepit bourgeois civilization, the twentieth-century Scythians.

It must be admitted that the Scythianism that seized Russia contained some good. A simplification and a return to primitive origins occurred in both the culture and the economy. The Scythian influence can be traced in Russian philosophy [28] and in the prose and poetry of those days.[29] It is also apparent in the numerous experiments of the theater, in the return to the early and spectacular folk forms such as the roundelay and the national comedy, and even in the manifestos of the innovators.[30]

Lunacharsky had hailed the arrival of the barbarians even before Blok had. As early as 1908 he asserted that the theater of the future would be a barbarian theater, for "the salvation of civilization is in its barbarians. They are the bearers of real culture; they discover the light, long paths, while the so-called rotten society withers away." [31] And Scythianism has not died out yet. In Europe today there are enough "estheticians" and "intellectuals" praying for the Bolshevik "steppe horses" to arrive and to destroy a society that does not give these failures any recognition or high fees. And who among us can guarantee that the monstrous mistakes that the West has made in dealing with Bolshevism during the past thirty-five years—mistakes that enabled Bolshevism to expand and to engulf the countries of Asia and Eastern Europe—are only slip-ups on the part of stupid politicians and not the senile impotence of a tired civilization incapable of further resistance?

THE "MASSES" DISCOVER THE THEATER

The ordinary actors did not share the Scythian philosophy or believe the refined analogies or lofty motivations of the intellectuals. The national audience furnished their reasons for accepting what was going on. Before the Revolution the actors were familiar with success, flowers, devotees, and applause. These were given them by the ordinary playgoer at the old theater. But the audiences to whom they were now playing were extraordinary. These audiences were made up of workers and peasants in uniform or wearing their own torn jackets and homespun coats. These people were sailors and Red Guardsmen, all the "dregs" of society, the most ordinary people who were at one time considered ignorant. But the poor, torn, and hungry people were strikingly different from those pre-Revolutionary audiences that had watched the actors coldly and quietly. The people was obsessed with the theater. The new audience did not merely look on. It chose many actors to be "instructors" at private "dramatic circles." The people wanted not so much to watch the presentations as to argue, to shout, and to swear about the plays and the performances. The people not only craved productions for themselves but fervently wanted to construct a theater and to bring it to the most ignorant and godforsaken places in the Russian provinces. And the people's fervent enthusiasm for the theater, which had become accessible for the first time, was the most warming and the most moving reason why the actors accepted what was going on. They worked enthusiastically for the people. The actors craved both to enlighten the people and to work while rejoicing in the people's love for the theater. This alone can explain the successes that have been ascribed to the Soviet theater policy during the first years of the Communist regime.

The times were incredibly bad. Almost to a man, the city dwellers became "bagmen"—speculators who made excursions to the countryside in search of food. On the overcrowded trains, the roofs of the railroad cars, the buffers and the footboards, in frost and rain, herded in the stations by Bolshevik police and Red Guards—people still undertook very dangerous expeditions to the countryside. There they exchanged frock coats and morning coats for sacks of groats and formal gowns for bottles of sunflower-seed oil. Petrograd and Moscow were hungry. The Red Army men would sit at the concerts in unheated theaters while wearing their uniforms and fur caps, holding their rifles, and cracking their sunflower seeds. Every night someone was arrested "at the expense" of the Cheka. It was a terrible world, woven of frost, spoiled herring, patched rags, typhus, arrests, queues, and armed soldiers. Yet, in this world there was première after première. Every evening the public packed the theaters. The lobbies disappeared in the thick gray fog from cheap tobacco and human respiration. The chilly, enormous auditoriums of the theaters warmed up toward the middle of the performances from the heat of the crowd. Quite frequently the lights would go out because the current had been shut off. There was a coal shortage. At that time, Isadora Duncan danced to the light of torches brought out on the stage, as the tune "Smelo, tovarishchi, v nogu" (Boldly, Comrades, in Step) was sung by thousands of voices, hoarse from the cold, coming out of the dark auditorium. At operas the musicians sat in their fur coats with their fur caps pulled down over their ears. The tubes of the woodwinds and brasses, like locomotives, belched forth steam. The stages were icy and drafty; the frosty props were in the corners. Yet, ballets were danced in transparent tulle, in light tights, and in tutus, as they had never been danced before. The salaries of the performers were almost nil, but never did a single curtain go up late.

Moscow and Petrograd were hungry and frozen through. Yet, the number of studios, theaters, societies, lectures, publishing houses, periodicals, and exhibitions multiplied incredibly. It was like an epidemic. After a succession of roaches and rag fairs, at which shirts were bartered for either a handful of cheap tobacco or for several lumps of sugar, people would go participate in lengthy and learned discussions on such themes as "The Cult of the Archangel Michael in the Middle Ages." Instead of throwing bombs or confiscating property, the Socialist Revolutionaries would meekly visit Maeterlinck's play *Marie Magdaleine* and would write about it in their periodical, *Znamia bor'by* ("Banner of the Struggle"). The Belgian's work reminded them of "the glistening beauty in the socialism of the first Christian communities." Everyone acted, danced, sculptured, and covered canvas with paint. How did these "maîtres," "maestri," and "masters" live? Victor Shklovsky wrote:

I burned my furniture, my sculptor's bench, my bookcases, and my books— books that were priceless and innumerable. If my hands and feet felt like wood, I would warm them and wait interminably for the arrival of spring. One friend of mine burned only books. His wife would sit at the small, smoky stove and fed it magazine after magazine. In other places they burned the doors and furniture that was not theirs. . . . People slept in their overcoats and almost in their galoshes as well. Everyone gathered in the kitchen. Stalactites were multiplying in the other rooms. . . . We ate strange things: frozen potatoes; rotten turnips; and herrings, the heads and tails of which had to be cut off lest they stink. We cooked in the oil used to dry paints (*olifa*), in the boiled oil for paints, and in boiled lead salts. We ate unshelled oats with horse meat that was soft because it was already decomposing. . . . Had there been a slave market where one could have sold himself for bread, it would have been busier than all the shops that carried saccharine. . . . At our dark apartments—oh, the darkness, the soot from the tiny night lamp, and the anticipation of light!—we would gather to go to the theaters. We looked at the stage. Hungry actors performed. Hungry writers wrote. Scholars were working. . . . We assembled and sat in our overcoats by stoves that were burning books. Our legs were injured; our crockery broke because of the grease shortage. And we talked about rhythm and literary form.[32]

Perhaps there is no example that is more devastating to the Bolshevik idea that "being determines consciousness" than the creative obsession of the Russians in general for art in the days when "being" could engender only cannibalism and crawling around on all fours—in which case no treasures of the spirit would be created. But let us leave the heroism of the urbanites and examine what the people itself was doing with the theater in those terrible days. The national obsession with the theater was a general epidemic.[33]

The peasants yielded schools, sheds, and large huts for theaters. In the remote villages where there were no standard plays, the peasants who had no "instructors" at all staged Russian songs. They themselves wrote plays, and—what is even more interesting—they frequently wrote plays collectively. Examples of this last are *Prervannyi pir* ("The Interrupted Feast") and *Muzhitskii Oktiabr'* ("The Muzhik's October"), which Dragobuzh's Peasant Studio staged in 1918.[34]

There was no plant or factory in the country that did not have its own dramatic circle. At the time of the Civil War there were about 3,000-odd professional troupes in the R.S.F.S.R. alone. Studios and dramatic schools mushroomed up in the cities and were filled to overflowing by those who craved to learn the secrets of theater mastery. And "there was literally not a single studio or circle that would not have sworn that it had itself discovered the philosopher's stone of revolutionary art." [35] The town of Kargopol in the Olonets Province of northern Russia may be considered as typifying those times extremely well. There were under 4,000 inhabitants in the town, and yet in 1918 it not only organized a resident company but even published a theater bulletin.

Even in 1920, when the "theater epidemic" was beginning to subside, the Red Army and Fleet had over 1,800 clubs to which 1,210 theaters and 911 dramatic circles were attached. Shklovsky wrote:

> Every unit has its little theater. There is a theater attached to almost every organization. We even have a school of instructors in theater work with a section for preparing prompters attached to the Baltic Fleet. . . . I would not be astonished if the Murmansk Railroad or the Central Nail Factory were to begin training actors, and not just for themselves but for others as well.[36]

Plays written by semiliterate Red Army men made the rounds of thousands of regimental dramatic circles. Everything that was printed or mimeographed in Moscow and Petrograd was sold out down to the last copy and distributed throughout the vast expanses of Russia.

In the primary and secondary schools "dramatizations" and "stagings" became an ordinary part of the curriculum. Teachers fervently discussed "the theatrifying of instruction." [37]

The obsession with the theater spread and gripped the entire nation. How can this "theater psychosis" be explained? It possessed the country during the years of hunger and devastation. The Freudian solution was a convincing explanation for some. This maintained that it was a psychosis that caused people to flee into the mania of an illusory life. Shklovsky, for example, wrote:

> Life is hard and its hardness cannot be concealed. And in this hard life, are we not like Selenites . . . seated in barrels, from which only tentacles— useful for the collective—are allowed to grow? . . . Willy-nilly, man would be happy wherever it was easier, wherever there were nothing but soft pillows and there was always fuel for heating water. But, of course, the road to yesterday is blocked off.

And so, man flees to the theater, to the actors, as (according to Freud) we take refuge when we have a psychosis in any mania as if it were a monastery, that is, we create our own illusion of life, an illusion of reality, instead of the difficult reality of reality.

In all probability, you recall Dostoevsky's description of a theater in his *Notes from the House of Death*. To cover one's shaven head with a wig, to dress up in gray clothes, to enter into someone else's life—all these were what captivated the prison laborers at the theater. Dostoevsky says that they turned out to be good actors. . . . These millions of [dramatic] circles must not be closed; man must not be forbidden to rave.[38]

Let it be understood that in those years there were many people for whom an "artificial life"—such as the theater—was a place of refuge from the terrible reality that they neither could nor would acknowledge. For the most part, however, this applied to the intellectuals. The somber comparison with the forced laborers in the *Notes from the House of Death* does not explain why ordinary people were obsessed with the theater.

The reasons for this were brighter and happier. For the first time, the magical and captivating art of the theater had become the genuine property of ignorant and unfortunate people. It was the time of their flaming first love for the theater. The nation greedily took enormous and unbridled pleasure in a world that was different from its own humdrum life and better as well.

This obsession, this love, this almost childish exultation in the joys of the theater can also explain the enthusiasm and the immeasurable sacrifices with which, under conditions of the most cruel hunger and devastation, Russian actors brought the people the art for which it was praying and which it craved. Under a regime that was alien and hostile in spirit, in theaters that were unheated, risking the loss of their voices and going hungry, the actors sang and played for the people and fervently built and expanded the Soviet theater. This was not done for Bolshevism but rather for the welfare of the people of Russia who had for the first time burst into the theater auditoriums.

The subsequent blossoming of the Russian theater during the first Soviet decade cannot be explained without admitting that many theater people sincerely accepted the Revolution and were protagonists of the new regime. They accepted the Soviet government. Like Vakhtangov, they associated it with what the people were creating. Vakhtangov declared: "What the people contribute is immortal. And right now the people are creating new forms of life. They are creating them through the Revolution." [39]

Many theater people accepted the new regime that hourly asserted its manumission of the slaves, its defense of "the injured and the insulted," its liberation of the people from hunger, beggary, ignorance, and the lack of rights. These people believed the assertions literally. And the words of the new regime indeed were fine. Its decrees, the speeches of its leaders, its slogans and proclamations were filled with appeals for enlightening the ignorant Russian countryside, for bringing culture to both the rural districts and to the urban proletariat, for educating the people and improving them. Who could deny the Russian actor's patriotism and charity to both beggars and the ignorant? The time had not yet arrived when the abyss between the elegant words of the Bolshevik slogans and the morbid crimes that the Communists committed would grow clear. This was to come years later. Many people would then understand to whom they had sold their souls in exchange for a platitude.

Actors were called upon to teach the nation, to use their art for instructing the countryside, the factory barracks, and the soldiers' barracks. They responded to this mission with joy and pathos—actors have always been idealists.

Part of the theater personnel also sincerely believed the Communist myth that a "new life," a "new society" was under way, in which each would give according to his abilities and receive according to his needs. They were asked to create a bright future, with gigantic, open-air theaters for tens of thousands of people. They were summoned to a future resembling the kingdom of light, virtue, and charity. There, there would be neither injured nor insulted, neither beggars nor slaves. Only the hardened heart of a confirmed misanthrope could have failed to respond to such an appeal.

The Soviet government wanted, at one nod of its head, to transform Arkashka and Shmaga (who wandered along the railroad ties from town to town), the beggarly, touring comedians, and the functionaries from the "Department of Melpomene" into the builders of a Communist paradise on earth, into lofty and respected participants in culture. Actors were in very great demand. Suddenly, they became some kind of Salvation Army soldiers in a land of hunger, despair, epidemics, and devastation. They were greatly needed and sought in smoky barracks, at the dinner-time halts in factories stinking of iron and burning coke, in thousands of dramatic circles where they would teach the arts of the stage, and in hundreds of unheated theaters. And everywhere they went, there was a crowd of common people awaiting them, craving their art. They realized that the people were seeing Shakespeare and Gogol for the first time. They saw the joy with which the world of the theater was accepted by the people, who now had access to it. For the first time, the actors realized that such things as pay, food, clothes, and comforts lost all their value and significance when compared to the happiness of bringing a noble art to people who were hungry, tormented, and huddled together in dirty and unheated halls.

Yes, the Russian theater people saw the coarseness, the cruelty, and the ignorance of the newly made commissars and leaders around them. They realized that the country was hungry, terrorized, and devastated. But there were many intellectuals who believed that the Revolution could be humanized. They thought that the commissars and the Red Guards could be tamed, if one did not grumble or bear malice against the "uncouth" ravishers. These dreamers settled down to re-educate such people.

There were many factors that went into the blossoming of the Soviet theater. Not the least of them was an illusion which many theater people believed in that Bolshevism could be influenced for the good and that the Soviet regime could be humanized if the theater would undertake its main mission with love and enthusiasm. That mission consisted of teaching the masses of the people, of educating them, improving them, and perfecting them.

THE PROFESSIONAL THEATER

Certain Western European dramatic critics and theater theoreticians have long considered the brilliant innovations of the Soviet theater to be an indisputable result of the Bolshevik regime. Bolshevizing estheticians possess such naïve illusions because they know nothing about Soviet reality. Right after its seizure of power, however, Bolshevism became unalterably opposed to experimentation, innovation, and all the other "leftist" efforts in the theater. Bolshevism takes the same attitude today. Every remarkable achievement of the Soviet theater connected with the new forms of the theater arts has been accomplished in spite of the Soviet regime. They have all been done behind the government's back, while the Bolshevik critics swore and anathematized. They have all contradicted Soviet theories about the theater.

Lunacharsky and the Bolshevik theater theoreticians and dramatic critics observed that most of the innovations in the Soviet theater were continuations of what had been going on before 1917. According to Bolshevik terminology, the entire pre-Revolutionary theater was "bourgeois" and "alien to the proletariat." Hence, any innovations were considered the backwash of bourgeois theories and ideas.

Bolshevism considered the "new" art of the Soviet theater to consist not in experimenting with new forms but rather with the old forms of "classical realism." These would be filled with a "new content reflecting the experiences of the proletariat and of the working masses in general. . . . Revolutionary content . . . would reject all the so-called American subterfuges and would make the theater as convincing as it has always been." [40] Hence, most of the experimentation within the theater during the period of War Communism was done against the wishes of the Soviet regime.

One of the first experimental theaters of the time was established with the participation of Vsevolod Meyerhold in Petrograd. This was the so-called "Hermitage Theater." It began to perform in the Hall of Arms at the Winter Palace. Its public consisted of Red Army men and of workers. The theater opened by presenting Molière's *Le Médecin malgré lui* on July 12, 1919.[41] Its most interesting production, however, was of Leo Tolstoy's *The First Distiller,* which was directed by Yuri Annenkov. Tolstoy's play was realistic and true to life, and it was aimed at the "kulaks" who encouraged drunkenness in the countryside. Annenkov tried to create a new form of spectacle for the people. He included elements of both the circus and the farce.[42]

Annenkov expanded the fantastic element in the play, introducing "imps," "the old devil's fool," and a "vertical devil." He entrusted these roles to such circus performers as clowns, pairs of acrobats, etc. This first attempt to blend the theater and the circus was, perhaps, inspired by F. T. Marinetti's Futurist manifesto.[43] It was the first step toward turning the theater into a music hall. Later, other innovators in the Soviet theater would try to do this, including such a major experimentalist as Sergei Eisenstein.

The production of *The First Distiller* raised a question that would later divide Russian theater people into two camps. Is it right to "patch up," to rework, and to "restage" the classics? A problem arose as to the nature of a classical play. Is it something sacred, or merely a scenario? The majority would wax indignant at the "blasphemous shredding of the classics." The minority, including Meyerhold, would maintain its right to deal freely with classical texts. Meyerhold had first begun "to revise" the classics before the Revolution. The minority almost considered its freedom to edit as one of the gains won by the Revolution.[44]

The leftist artists at work in the Hermitage Theater made the first efforts to construct stage platforms based on "urbanism" and "dynamism." The theater was soon closed. The Soviet regime had no intention of supporting purely "bourgeois" efforts at making the classics contemporary.

The Theater-Studio was set up in Petrograd during 1918. Among the directors connected with it were Sergei Radlov, Konstantin Tverskoi, and K. Landau. It concentrated on seeking new forms from the national and the children's and the puppet theaters. The Theater-Studio, according to the declarations of those who organized it, was descended from the "entertainments of the old Russian wandering minstrels and the merry men" and it had to be nomadic.[45]

Radlov, Tverskoi, and Yuri Bondi had once worked under Meyerhold at "Dr. Dapertutto's" Studio. They used the Theater-Studio to practice Meyerhold's pre-Revolutionary discoveries in experimentation and to develop them further. The Theater-Studio, however, was closed in 1919. Some of its actors, along with Radlov, went over to the newly organized Folk Comedy Theater. This was the most serious experimental theater in Petrograd during those years.

The State Exemplary Theater was set up in Moscow during 1919. It reflected two trends in which the best people of the Russian theater took part. One group desired to use all its powers and skills for educating the nation through the great classics. The other group tried to find refuge upon the "mountain tops" of the classics from whatever it disliked about both Soviet reality and the "revolutionary repertory." The founders of the Exemplary Theater were F. A. Stepun, M. F. Lenin (the actor at the Maly Theater), V. Massalitinova, I. Khudoleyev, Pevtsov (the popular actor), and V. G. Sakhnovsky (the director). Stepun was the idea man of the theater.

The founders did not fence themselves off from the Revolution. They considered that they had to be closely associated with the historical developments that were taking place in the country. The repertory of such a theater must include both Shakespeare and the tragedies of antiquity:

To the possible question from Party echelons as to why we have decided to take such a path, I offer the answer that, considering the proletarian of the future to be a kind of "superman," we could hail its accession to power in no worthier way than with the super-art of the past.[46]

Let it be understood that the Exemplary Theater was allowed to exist, not because its participants isolated themselves so boldly and honestly from the mythical conception of "proletarian culture," but merely because the classics that they promised to stage in this "costumed and heroic" theater suited the Lenin-Lunacharsky theater policy.

This Theater opened by staging Shakespeare's *Measure for Measure*. The production was by Khudoleyev, and the décor was by Georgy Yakulov. The presentation was well received by the Soviet public. Stepun recalled: "The workers and soldiers reacted in an especially lively fashion to the dialogue between the hangman and the fool. Perhaps they sensed that these figures were contemporary." [47]

The Theater's most programmatic presentation was Stepun's version of Sophocles' *Oedipus the King*. The idea behind the presentation was that ancient Thebes showed the tragedy of contemporary Russia. Stepun wrote:

Nothing is to be made archaic. Our task is to "show" not ancient Greece but contemporary Russia. We are revealing our own tragedy in Sophocles' only because the contemporary Russian drama is insufficiently profound and monumental to reflect all the profundity of our own days. An impenetrable fate hangs over Russia, like over ancient Thebes. And the wisest of us, those who—like Oedipus—having once guessed the riddle of the Sphinx, do not know what to do. Typhus, like the plague, cuts people down, and there are moans throughout the land. Like the King of Thebes, we do not know what our guilt is made up of, but we feel its burden upon our shoulders. Blinded, our faces wet with blood, we go out into the darkness of the night. . . . Oh Lord, what will become of us? That is what must be gotten across to the audience.[48]

The presentation experimented with new forms that did not reconstruct antiquity naturalistically. In accordance with Stepun's plans, Yakulov designed a somewhat abstract "construction" based upon ancient Hellenic architecture.[49] Stepun found an interesting form of speech in his attempts to overcome the stereotypes of pseudo-pathos and falsely

classical declamation in tragedy. Such declamation was alien to the
religious and liturgical essence of tragedy. Stepun declared:

[We] applied the metrical system of the Orthodox divine service to the performance of ancient tragedy. Of course, we are not talking about simply
transferring the scheme from church to stage, but about adapting it freely and
differently for the main figures and for the chorus. Most of all, I felt like
getting away from the arbitrariness of psychological individualism, which is
alien to the religious essence of tragedy, and to try getting a reading free of
any affectation. The reading would be sincere, profound, and simple, and
would be interrupted only rarely by irate, sorrowful, exultant, and passionate
exclamations from within. On the surface, however, it was as strictly
shackled in the canonical framework of the music as the cries of the arch-
deacon are in a church.[50]

But all efforts to create a national theater for the great classics, whose
forms would be new rather than stagnant or traditional, were crushed.
Meyerhold, now the deputy chief of the Theater Section, was sent to the
Exemplary Theater. He addressed the company and accused it of having
"a reactionary ideology and an eclectic and decadent repertory." This
pressure from the Theater Section forced Stepun to leave the Exemplary
Theater. Later, Lunacharsky became the "idea man" of the Theater,
and Sakhnovsky became its chief director. After Stepun's departure, the
Exemplary Theater failed to contribute a single major innovation to the
Soviet scenic arts.

In those days there were many studios. The theater manifestos promised much and were frequently funny.[51] Many organizations sprang up,
but they broke up and disappeared very quickly. There were also some
experiments with the forms and aspects of a new people's theater that
were quite valuable.

Even before the Revolution, Vyacheslav Ivanov had been preaching
a theater "of audience participation" that would be a "national theater"
beyond esthetics.[52] Ivanov's idea was to remove the boundaries between
the actors and the audience. Everyone would participate in a mystical
and religious communion (*sobornost'*). In Ivanov's "national theater"
the playwright becomes the teacher of the nation who creates myths that
would transform life to a higher reality. Ivanov was supported by
Meyerhold, who felt that the independent creativeness of the masses
could cause "the blooming of myth-making and of authentic improvisation" within the theater.

V. N. Vsevolodsky-Gerngross, the historian of the theater, spoke to a conference of workers and peasants at the start of 1919. He believed that the theater had to return to its primordial sources in Russian folk rites and roundelays. This return to the primitive would permit a revival of the purely folk and purely Russian theater whose development had been interrupted by civilization.

A theater must be created in which the folk would not remain merely a passive observer, but would take part in the work. . . . The Russian folk has tried to create such a theater in the past—such as, for example, the folk festivals on St. John's Eve, the holiday in honor of the god of spring, the roundelays, etc. The further development of this theater was hampered by various foreign influences. Beginning with the times of the Empress Elizabeth Petrovna (1741–1762) the Russian theater became enslaved to the French theater. Such is its present status [as well], and this is why it is alien to the spirit of the Russian people. What must the people be given in order to have them accept the theater as their own? No *Inspectors-General* and no Ostrovskys will help. The people must create a theater from their own, restored folk rituals. The basis of the future rural theater must be the performance of the roundelay.[53]

Some of Vsevolodsky-Gerngross's ideas influenced Soviet theoreticians of the rural theater. They herded the poor Russian peasants into "ideologically tolerable" roundelays and masques. This theoretician had some influence in the return to the times of the pagan Slavic gods Perun and Yarilo, which was undertaken by the Folk Comedy Theater in Petrograd and by certain other innovators in Moscow.

The Folk Comedy Theater opened in 1920 at the Iron Hall of National House in Petrograd. It was headed by Radlov and Soloviëv. These two had been among Meyerhold's most prominent colleagues at his Studio. Their Theater was an interesting attempt to use the devices that had been discovered in Meyerhold's Studio. Their creative method was to revive the acting techniques used in the old national theaters and to improvise upon them.

The Folk Comedy Theater is a striking example of how the actors, directors, and theoreticians of the Soviet theater sought ties with the folk tradition. This was not done, however, in the manner that the Communist Party and the Bolshevik critics preferred but in accordance with the values held by the theater people themselves and in a way that enabled them to be honest with the folk. There was no need to lie or coerce one's spirit. Meeting the folk could be based on the fine and true democratic forms of the old national theaters.

Theater men and women felt that the scenic arts had, for the first time, become completely accessible to the Russian folk. The theater needed to be "national." It could be built by restoring the national theaters of olden times and giving them new power and polish. Those theaters had died out and vanished without using all their potentialities. The aim was not to reconstruct the devices of the improvised, market-place theater, but to revive them. They would then be developed and strengthened within the one country in the world that possessed a folk regime.[54] This movement can be traced in almost all the "folkifying" efforts of the Russian theater during the first years of Bolshevism. Soviet critics christened it "esthetic democratization." It was an effort to find the way to democracy without renouncing esthetics.

The numerous and, for the most part, completely sincere attempts by major specialists in theater history and by estheticians to establish a new folk theater all ended in failure. Such individuals created their "folk theater" in their beakers and laboratories, but the people did not under-stand it and remained indifferent. The people eyed this artificially nur-tured theater with some interest, but they were unable to consider it theirs. No living folk theater has ever been created in a laboratory. There is a reason for this. The experimentalists sought to include the farce, the circus, the pantomime, the eccentric, the traditional playing with masks, and—in short—*visual* forms in general. The secret of the Russian folk theater, however, is that it has always been a theater of the "bon mot," of the witticism, and—basically—of speech. Let us take the bril-liant Russian folk tales, the comic folk epos, the bon mots, the flourishes in the fairy tales, the urban folk rhymes, and the stories. Everywhere, we find the love and the great talent of the Russian people for a sharp, quick, and striking "expression." The real Russian folk theater had to be a theater of the word and not of motion or visual attractiveness. Labora-tories could not create this, despite all the good intentions of the experi-mentalists.

The Folk Comedy Theater existed for two years, from 1920 to 1922. During that time it undertook a large number of varied experiments. In Radlov—as in the post-Revolutionary Meyerhold—we have a director with a Soviet turn of mind. He quickly passed through "fellow-traveling" to a complete acceptance of the Communist platform and the class strug-gle. Most of his productions at the Folk Comedy Theater are permeated with the same leitmotif. He stressed hatred of the dirty bourgeois and of the capitalists. His very first "circus comedies" were based upon the Italian improvised comedy. He wrote the scenarios for *Nevesta mertvetsa* ("The Corpse's Bride") and *Obez'iana-donoschitsa* ("The Monkey That Was an Informer"). Everywhere we encounter Communistic "social satire of the enemies of the working class." Radlov transformed Panta-loon, in the traditional mask, into J. P. Morgan, the banker. The latter warbled primitive verses resembling those on the Bolshevik propaganda posters from the times of War Communism.[55]

Shakespeare's *Merry Wives of Windsor* was the first major production of Radlov. The director sought to shake off realism. He considered it superficial and "a barbarous memorial from the barbarous end of the nineteenth century." He did not try to indicate real and concrete places for the action but instead aimed at "charming and uninterrupted action, with a constant flow." [56] This attempt to "make Shakespeare dynamic" or—more accurately—to use the uninterrupted action of the motion pictures typified very many of Radlov's productions. He was the first to transfer various devices from the screen and from "urban eccentricity" to the stage. He considered "urban eccentricity" to be "a new aspect of the comic outlook on life, created by Anglo-American genius." [57] He mixed it with the characteristically Russian desire to make it completely acceptable for the folk theater.

This "eccentric urbanism" and "motion-picturizing" of the theater was especially sensed in Radlov's production of *Priemysh* ("Adopted Child") during August of 1920. This was a detective story with adventures woven in. It takes place in a capitalistic city. An extensive manhunt is under way for an individual who has stolen a document that is extremely important to Soviet Russia. There is a complete assortment of devices from detective films. These include rioting in a restaurant, the climb of Serge—the gymnast who stole the document—up to the fifth floor, his jumping out of a fifth-floor window, and his rescue from the police through a rope let down from an airplane. The entire action was de-veloped at "cinematographic tempi" and the concern with tricks eclipsed the Soviet theme matter completely.

Another Radlov play was entitled *Liubov' i zoloto* ("Love and Gold"). He staged it in the same way during January of 1921:

[It included] rogues, Apaches, prefects of police, underground hatchways, short scenes transferring the action from the sinister quarters of Paris at night to the compartment of the courier's train. Everything was blurred in a special and mysterious haze.[58]

This melodrama was also based on adventure films. There were five acting platforms on the stage, all of different heights. Frequently the action would take place on three of them simultaneously.

The Folk Comedy Theater also continued to revive the devices of the old theaters. In these productions, as in their predecessors, it was not seeking any forms of the national theater that were in accord with the Bolshevik notions on the subject. The Theater was soon liquidated, therefore, because it had failed to justify the hopes of the Soviet regime. Nevertheless, the devices that it had popularized in the Soviet theater remained very much alive. We shall encounter them frequently.

Soloviëv, Meyerhold's old colleague, was in charge of establishing the Ligovsky Dramatic Theater in Petrograd. Many people who had participated in "Dr. Dapertutto's" Studio now worked in this, among whom were such persons as Dmitriev, Tverskoi, Derzhavin, Gripich, and Alpers. The "industrial program" of the Theater declared:

The contemporary theater is really alien to the working class in general, but not at all because of any special traits in its repertory. Repertory never has any independent significance. . . . The contemporary stage—with its photo-scenic box, its footlights, its illumination, and so forth—is really, at this moment of transition, the chief obstacle to the actor's rapid appreciation of the psychology of a given auditorium. . . . The actor is removed from the play-goer inasmuch as he has no real opportunity to base his work on the support of the auditorium.[59]

During the 1922–1923 season the Ligovsky Dramatic Theater was renamed The Theater of New Drama. It then departed from many of the points made in its manifesto and leaned toward expressionism. Insofar as innovation was concerned, the Theater remained second-rate. Its chief distinction was that two of its members—Gripich and Alpers—later took part in organizing the Theater of the Revolution in Moscow. In its last program this last Theater accomplished many things that the manifesto of the Ligovsky Dramatic Theater had called for.

A theater that sympathized with the Proletarian Culture Movement was established in Petrograd during February, 1919. This was the Red Army Workshop for the Theater and Playwrights, which was attached to the Political Administration of the Petrograd Military District. Its first chief was N. G. Vinogradov. He was succeeded by Pëtrovsky, who was later to become an outstanding theoretician and historian of the Soviet theater. The task of this Workshop was to establish a new, heroic, and monumental theater permeated with the spirit of the proletariat's class struggle and to prepare cadres of instructors who would be able to transfer the principles of mass, heroic, theatrical action to the units of the Red Army. As for the new drama intended for the era of the proletarian dictatorship, the Workshop modestly decided to have its dramatists create works that would surpass Aeschylus by as much as the ideas animating the proletarian Red Army surpassed the ideas of the slaveholding society in ancient Athens.

Vinogradov himself wrote a "folk tale" that he called *Tragediia o tsare Petre* ("A Tragedy about Tsar Peter"). This was a weak attempt to create something like the dithyrambs of antiquity. It made an interesting contribution to the "mass spectacle." On March 12, 1919, the Workshop staged a mass play entitled *Sverzhenie samoderzhaviia* ("The Overthrow of the Autocracy") before the Soviet Workers', Peasants', and Red Army Men's Deputies in Rozhdestvensky Hall. Later, this "mass show" was renamed *Krasnyi god* ("The Red Year"). It included scenes entitled "Kerenskyism" and "October" and was staged not only in buildings but also at the front, and it was even put on in the lobby of the Winter Palace in Petrograd.

The performers at this "mass show" were ordinary Red Army men. They played both themselves and their enemies—the Tsar, the generals, the police, the capitalists, the judges, and so forth. All the "enemies" were coarsely caricatured and made into buffoons, and the "revolutionary" scenes included manifestos by the workers and battle episodes. The street warfare, for example, showed bayonet attacks and the storming of the Winter Palace. These scenes attracted the Red Army men in the audience despite themselves. Weapons in hand, they joined the "performers" involuntarily. The crowd improvised the text itself, borrowing words from speeches delivered at meetings during those days.

Among the experiments performed by the Workshop were also: a "street show" entitled *Tretii Internatsional* ("The Third International"), which was performed on May 1, 1919, and was a spectacle constructed of singing, pantomime, and the "shifting of allegorical figures" around an enormous "globe"; and *Krovavoe voskresen'e* ("Bloody Sunday"), which was staged at the Iron Hall in National House, Petrograd, on January 9, 1920.

The Red Army Workshop for the Theater and Playwrights did not last long. Nor did any of the other experimental undertakings during the years of War Communism. It did give impetus, however, to "mass shows" and "mass spectacles." These were new forms, born of Soviet reality. We shall discuss them later in this chapter.

Four presentations may be considered as undoubtedly the most important ones given during the first three years of the Soviet regime. The first of these was Meyerhold's production of Vladimir Mayakovsky's *Mystery-Bouffe* in Petrograd. This was a noisy demonstration of the brilliant director's transition to Bolshevism. The second was his production of Verhaeren's *Les Aubes* at the First Theater of the R.S.F.S.R. in Moscow. This laid the basis for the new Soviet theater, which was to be a political theater. The third was Alexander Tairov's production of Oscar Wilde's *Salome* at the Kamerny Theater in Moscow. This was a declaration of that Theater's esthetic program—which was completely alien to all the Bolsheviks' ideas about the theater. The final presentation was the Moscow Art Theater's production of Byron's *Cain*. This work sounded a profound human protest against the fratricide of civil war and the brutalities of the "class struggle" that the Bolsheviks had unleashed throughout Russia.

The first anniversary of the October Revolution was celebrated from November 7 through November 9, 1918. At the Petrograd conservatory building, Meyerhold, in conjunction with Mayakovsky, staged *Mystery-Bouffe*. Meyerhold termed this work a "heroic, epic, and satiric depiction of our period done by V. Mayakovsky." [60] The poster advertising *Mystery-Bouffe* sheds some light upon its contents:

Scene 1: Whites and blacks flee from the red flood. Scene 2: An ark. The clean foist a tsar and a republic on the unclean. . . . Scene 3: Hell, in which the workers send Beelzebub himself to the devil. Scene 4: Paradise, an exchange of words between a farm hand and Methuselah. Scene 5: A commune, a sunny holiday of things and workers.

"Seven pairs of clean people" were the "representatives of the parasitic and exploiting classes." The protagonists were "unclean people"—a smith, a farm hand, a miner, a raftsman, a seamstress, and so forth. The "unclean people" throw out of the ark the Negus of Abyssinia, a Turkish pasha, an American, a German officer, a priest, and other "exploiters." A new Messiah, "the common man," appears on the stage. (This role was played by Mayakovsky himself.) He shows the "unclean people" the way to the Promised Land of Communism. He utters a derisive and blasphemous new "Sermon on the Mount" that is directed against religion, and he proclaims the "single and highest truth—the truth of the real struggle on earth against the exploiters." "The common man" appeals to "the unclean people": "Blow up everything that you have respected and respect now!"

In both content and devices this production was the first Soviet "political review." It was posterish, coarsely propagandistic, and "fighting on the side of the revolutionary proletariat." There was also something else to it, however. Mayakovsky's innate attitude—that of a rebelling anarchist and Bohemian—was also present.

Meyerhold made broad use of his pre-Revolutionary experiments in this production, but in a new and purely Bolshevik way. He utilized farce, grotesque, and buffonade to aid him in achieving an unsparing satire and ridicule of the "clean people" in the ark scene. Mayakovsky and Meyerhold laid it on thick in their malicious caricatures of persons who supported the February Revolution. Mayakovsky brought up the overthrown democratic republic in order to use a catchword: "One gets the bagle, the other gets the hole—that is a democratic republic!" The designer for the production was K. S. Malevich, a suprematist—a member of that art group concerned with the arrangement and inter-relation of nonobjective forms. The suprematists would use his skill to start turning out propaganda posters and staging revolutionary festivals. Many new productions would inevitably use these costumes and decorations.

Both the "left" and the "right" reacted negatively to *Mystery-Bouffe*. From the right, *Mystery-Bouffe* was attacked because of its antireligious rowdyism and its violent attempt to use all its powers for the new regime.[61]

Two years later, Mayakovsky himself termed the first variant of his *Mystery-Bouffe* "nastiness." He reworked it, brought in new characters, and introduced even more malicious things.[62] The playwright supplemented the work with a new act: "The Land of the Clouds." This concerned the struggle of the Soviet regime against devastation. It also dealt with speculators, sabotaging "specialists," bureaucrats, and the electrification of the country. Meyerhold staged the new edition of *Mystery-Bouffe* at the First Theater of the R.S.F.S.R. in Moscow on May 1, 1921. It had a major influence on all the later efforts dealing with Soviet political reviews of the day and on Soviet satire on the stage.

Meyerhold's production of Verhaeren's *Les Aubes* also took place at the First Theater of the R.S.F.S.R. He organized an exemplary heroic spéctacle. Its theme was revolutionary, and it was in accord with the Bolsheviks' slogans about the class struggle.

It was up to Meyerhold to "Sovietize" Verhaeren. Erenian, the protagonist, weakly incarnates Bolshevik ideas about the mass and the individual. He is too indecisive, too ready to yield, too ready to be a "conciliator." Meyerhold reworked Erenian into a model Bolshevik leader. In Verhaeren's text the proletarian mass was very passive and decorative. It did not "make history," but Bolshevik writings maintained that it should. Meyerhold inflated the role of the masses beyond all limits and introduced many crowd scenes of his own. Verhaeren showed no "class enemies" at all against whom a rebellion could take place. Meyerhold brought in scenes showing the "sovereign of the Great City." There was in particular a scene depicting the Senate in session "by the light of swaying candles." Cannon salvos and the din of rebellion were also heard. He depicted the terror of the businessmen on the Stock Exchange and in Parliament as they sense their doom. Verhaeren's play was directed against militarism, imperialism, and parliamentarianism, but the proletarian poet had not foreseen that Bolshevism and a Soviet regime would appear in the world. This mistake was corrected: words were "inserted" about the "dictatorship of the proletariat" and about expanding the rebellion into a "world-wide proletarian revolution." The finale contained a radio broadcast about the victory of the Revolution in the republic of the "Stellar Flag." This last was a romantic pseudonym for the Soviet regime in Russia. Meyerhold went even further in making Verhaeren "contemporary" and "Sovietizing" him. At every performance a messenger would turn up to read the latest dispatches from the fronts, both of the Civil War and of the war against Poland. This had to be followed by a meeting in which the public took part. Actors were placed in the orchestra seats, dressed in the ordinary urban dress clothes of the times. They were to "initiate" the contact between the public in the auditorium and the actors on the stage.

Meyerhold's coauthor in revising Verhaeren's text was Georgy Chulkov. His codirector in staging the result was V. Bebutov. V. Dmitriev, the designer of the production, rejected all illusions in the décor. He erected a number of flats and silvery-gray cubes upon the bare and enormous stage. Cables, reaching from the floor to the flies, divided the darkness of the upstage area like rays of light. The air of the stage was filled with many hanging "contre-reliefs," triangles, bits of bent tin, and a pair of red and gold disks. It was abstract both in form and in composition. The actors were dressed in silvery gray uniforms. They seemed to mingle medieval armor with the wide cavalry breeches that were so popular in those days.

The First Theater of the R.S.F.S.R. was given the building on Sadovo-Triumfalnaya Square that had belonged to the old Zon Operetta Company. Meyerhold removed the curtain, the cornices, and the coulisses, so that the stage became cold, empty, and enormous. The auditorium was stripped in the same way. B. Alpers wrote:

It was an ordinary meeting hall, with damp spots on the walls, and a damp and bluish atmosphere. There were no ticket collectors at the doors of the theater. . . . They were wide open and, in the winter, snowstorms would sometimes invade the lobby and the corridors of the theater and make the audiences turn up their overcoat collars. . . . The railings were stripped off the loges. The seats and benches for the audience had been greatly knocked about, and they were no longer arranged in rows. One could crack nuts or smoke cheap tobacco in the lobby. Red Army units and groups of young workers constituted the new audiences. They received their tickets by allotments, and they filled the theater with noise and excitement.[63]

The new playgoers found the presentation strange and incomprehensible. *Les Aubes* began Meyerhold's personal tragedy. He had given himself and his art completely to the "victorious proletariat." He strained and labored to create new forms and presentations for the proletarian mass audiences. Each of his new conceptions could have in itself sufficed to begin a new school of the theater arts. Fights among the critics bubbled over his shows; every première evoked moans of protest, swearing, and enthusiasm in the theater press; but the people —"the people is silent." The extremely brilliant director had joined the Party and given all his creative strength to the Party theater. He now turned out to be alien, too wise and incomprehensible for the proletarian "supermen," and so he worked alone.

The critics also disliked *Les Aubes*. The "leftist" critics considered that Meyerhold's basic device—the activizing of the audience through heroic and revolutionary presentation—had failed.[64] These critics caught him in errors and contradictions within the production itself.[65]

The Bolsheviks did not like *Les Aubes* either. Natalia Krupskaya—Lenin's wife—attacked Meyerhold's production in *Pravda*. She began the article by accusing Meyerhold of trying to change a symbolist play into a revolutionary presentation by purely mechanical means:

Instead of "the beggars," and "the oppressed," substitute "the proletariat"; instead of "the government," "the bourgeoisie"; instead of "hostile troops," "imperialistic troops." The "Regime of the Soviets," the "Social Revolution" and other such things appeared on the stage. And a wonderful tale is turned into a trivial farce, while all the charm of *Les Aubes* disappears. The action takes place outside of time and space; it deals with the adherents of Erenian, who concludes a compact with the government and simply acts with insufficient prudence. In a Russian environment, in the environment of the class struggle, Erenian is a traitor, a traitor who has taken the bait of flattery. A hero outside of time and space can be overlooked, but to have the Russian proletariat act like Shakespeare's crowds—whom any conceited fool can lead wherever he feels like it—is an insult.[66]

Such was the sharp tone which Mme Lenin took to Meyerhold, who wished to give the proletariat its own theater.

Les Aubes was a most valuable experience in terms of form. It was the first presentation on a revolutionary theme that had been abstractly worked out and staged. It formed a link to Meyerhold's later experiments with constructivism on the stage. The stage had already been stripped of costumes and décor for it, so that only abstract frameworks and "contre-reliefs" remained. Despite all the affected and propagandistic pathos in *Les Aubes,* it was still a brilliant scheme for constructing revolutionary and heroic presentations. It had only to be covered—like a skeleton—with living and organically connected dramatic material. The framework of *Les Aubes* undoubtedly influenced Soviet playwrighting strongly. We shall meet many revolutionary tragedies written by people who understood quite well the lessons that Meyerhold had taught at the First Theater of the R.S.F.S.R.

The Kamerny Theater in Moscow reopened its doors after the October Revolution. Its first presentation was Tairov's version of Wilde's *Salome*. The designer was Alexandra Ekster. Tairov considered this production to be the first step towards solving "the problems of the dynamic changes in the atmosphere of the stage." The décor was only supposed "to accompany" the acting and not to illustrate the locales.[67] It was changed, but not for reasons of descriptiveness or background. The purpose in this was merely to stress the changes of emotion and the dynamics of action. The changes were intended as an element of the stage action.

In order to stress the "dynamic changes in the atmosphere of the stage," Tairov staged *Salome* with curtains of different colors and of different textures. The tragedy begins with the dull prophecy of Iokanaan, at which time a silvery-black curtain is torn. This reveals a tank, in which the prophet is languishing and which becomes the center of action for the whole thing. When Salome finally agrees to dance for Herod, the movement of the rear curtain, the appearance of the backdrop, and the blood-colored moonlight all underscore both Herod's joy and the meaning of the dance. At the end of the tragedy the soldiers approach Salome and crush her beneath their shields. Then the atmosphere vibrates with "the black wings of devastated carcasses, as if the moon has cast a funereal canopy on the tomb of Salome, which has been shut by the shields." [68]

Mme Ekster brought to the theater her laboratory experiments with painting. She sought the dynamic through the rhythm of colors.[69] Here, she succeeded on a mass scale in confirming all the conclusions that she had reached about ease, flatness, and repose in color and about its dynamics.

Mme Ekster's most valuable innovation left a very great impression on the Soviet theater. It was to become a major influence on many designers. She created "dynamic costume." In constructing costumes her point of departure was the dominating rhythm of the characters' motions and gestures and the connection between this rhythm and the rhythm and tempo of the entire play. She conceived of costume as "make-up for the body" and a "mask for the face." Hence, she used her lines and paints to bring out a person's basic rhythm. In some measure, her costumes "move." She achieved these dynamics by putting them together from pieces of different materials. Thus, velvet creates the impression of delay; silk, of agility and glitter of speed.[70] A second means of making costumes "dynamic" was, of course, color. All her experiments in making paints move were broadly applied to costumery. She used "quiet" and "disquieting," "heavy" and "light" paints to clarify a character's rhythm and to intensify the force of his gestures. She considered stage costumery to be "living, colorful sculpture." For the first time, costumes were "sketched out." They were decorated with paint. Their lines were emphasized either through color or through rigid frameworks to keep the costumes within the forms and rhythms of the designer's lines. The weave and fabric of the costumes became a method of composition. They gave the costumes definite and clearly expressed rhythm.

Mme Ekster's maquette for *Salome* was based on the principles of architecture. There were two diagonal scaffoldings, with steps on the stage. Between them, there was a spiral staircase going up into the wings. The quite meager—and almost abstract—steps and staircases, however, were not the main feature of this production. What was newest and most important in *Salome* were the bits of material of different colors and forms, the "moving décor." These wedge-shaped and rectangular forms fell, were piled up, were put way downstage, were hoisted, and were moved aside. They were not intended to illustrate the place of action. Their pure dynamics were to intensify the stage action and its culmination. Mme Ekster was the first person in the Russian theater to assert something that was even more important. This was the pure "element of color." "Color harmonies" can independently influence the emotions of the audience. As if accomplishing what Goethe had dreamed about in his "Study of Painting," she revealed new theater possibilities in the music of paints. Paints can influence the audience's psychological, physiological, "physical, and moral" nature. Theories and experiments were to appear many years later that aimed to accompany a performance with the "music of paints," with lighting and color effects painted specifically for the "scoring of the colors." Mme Ekster's innovations furnished the starting point for all of them.

Wilde's text for *Salome* was spiced with colors, rhythms, and costumes. It was recherché and refined. Of course, it had nothing in common with the "regime of the Soviets" or with the "dictatorship of the proletariat." It was exotic. Moscow was dirty and devastated when the Bolsheviks seized power. This strange and unprecedented coloring seemed to have come from another world to the land of terror, hunger, and purges. It would characterize the Kamerny Theater under the Soviet regime for a number of years.

It was no accident that the Moscow Art Theater chose to stage Byron's *Cain* during Soviet times. The Theater used *Cain* to protest against the fratricidal war that the Bolsheviks had unleashed throughout Russia. The Bolsheviks realized that it was a protest quite well and quite quickly.[71] All the official critics joined with all their power to declare it a mistake and a failure for the Theater. The production remained in the repertory of the Moscow Art Theater for only a very short period. In addition to its value as an act of civic courage, however, it included the new and major aims that Stanislavsky had set for himself and for the Russian theater.

With *Cain,* the Moscow Art Theater took another step forward in experimenting with unreal forms. Perhaps in none of his previous works had Stanislavsky so broadly raised questions about the sculptural method, the three-dimensionality of the architectural elements in the stage action, and the dissolving of the entire action within the rhythm. He filled the stage with figures done by N. A. Andreyev, the sculptor. Thus, in the scene of hell, spirits of Great Beings who had once lived were represented by gigantic statues scattered about the stage against a hazy background. A special light of its own illuminated every figure, and the entire stage was quite awe-inspiring. The characters were grouped and arranged according to the principles of sculpture. In the second scene, Stanislavsky used brilliant stage effects to achieve an impression of reality when Cain and Lucifer fly among the enormous, extinguished planets. Stanislavsky did not succeed in carrying out all his remarkable devices because many of them were precluded by the devastation in the country. Black velvet, for instance, was unobtainable—and many unrealistic stage effects demanded it. The gigantic columns at the gateway to Paradise were unforgettable. The columns had been built by beings that had once inhabited the land. Stanislavsky wrote:

This time, I understood particularly well that sculpture and architecture are most important for the actor. Indeed, what use is it to me, an actor, that behind me, behind the actor's back, there is a backdrop hanging that was painted by a great master? I do not see it. It does not help me. On the contrary, it hinders me because it binds [me] to blend in with the background, that is to be not less brilliant, but even more brilliant than the master designer himself in order to stand out and be noticed against the colored cloth. The sculptor and, in part, the architect put objects and reliefs downstage that we can use for our own expressive aims to incarnate the life of the human spirit. . . . The sculptor's tasks are closer to us, the actors. . . . The sculptor is used to sensing the real body of the human being, with its physical ability to bring out the internal life.[72]

The sculptural method gave Stanislavsky the impetus to examine the speech, motion, and rhythmic life of the actor on the stage. Stanislavsky would spend many years experimenting with the laws of stage rhythm that he had begun with *Cain.*

THE PROPAGANDISTIC THEATER

New ways were found for using the theater during the first years of the Soviet regime. These may be termed the "applied theater arts." The most important projects were undertaken by non-Communist Russian theater people rather than by Bolsheviks. Alexander Blok, for example, conceived a magnificent plan for using the theater to educate the people. He wanted to stage "theatrical panorama" to illustrate the development of human history.[73] Marietta Shaginian, the writer, proposed during those years that the *Iliad* and other epics be staged. Eugene Vakhtangov dreamed about putting on scenes from the Bible.

All these fine plans were inspired by the desire to help educate the masses of people, and yet they received no material aid from the Soviet regime. During the first years after the Revolution the Bolsheviks did not consider their most important task to be the raising of the national cultural level. Instead they tried to win the workers and peasants over to their side. The stage was used to propagandize the nation rather than to educate it. The applied theater arts were used to stage all the holidays of the Soviet Revolutionary Calendar and all the possible "campaigns" of the Communist Party. All the forms that came into existence at the time were essentially but different aspects of the "propagandistic" theater. Let us examine its principles.

The propagandistic theater as a genre appeared in Red Army units during the Civil War. Disseminated by the political administration of the Red Army to raise the morale of the combat troops, it included both professional actors and amateurs from the army. Sometimes the Red Army units were visited by "propagandistic brigades" (*agitbrigady*) composed of professional actors sent by the Political Administration, which prepared their repertory. At other times concerts and such presentations as propagandistic skits (*agitki*) were shown to the troops. These shows had been prepared by amateur dramatic circles of Red Army men, guided by an instructor who was a professional actor.[74]

The most common form of propagandistic theater work was the staging of vital political issues of the day, as stressed by the Communist Party. *The Campaign of the Entente* was replaced by *The Fight against Typhus. The Plots of the Counterrevolution* followed *The Toilers'· Army.* This genre was further typified by such titles as *The Work of the Committees of the Poor, The Fight against Bagmen,* and *The Intrigues of Finance Capital.*

The second most common form was the "propagandistic trial" (*agitsudy*). Party members thought up the most varied topics, such as *The Trial of Admiral Kolchak.* General Yudenich, General Wrangel, and other leaders of the White Army were also "tried." So were the "murderers" of Karl Liebknecht, illiterates, the typhus louse, drunkenness, landed proprietors, Mensheviks, and so forth. As a genre, the "propagandistic trial" was borrowed from the pre-Revolutionary theater courts in which actors and public figures had both participated. The characters made speeches that were partly rehearsed and partly improvised against a background of the usual legal proceedings. The "defendants" and "witnesses" wore make-up and costumes. Props were used in the productions also. The "propagandistic trial" afforded much opportunity for involving the audience. The latter was allowed to make occasional comments on the "legal proceedings" and to take the floor as "witnesses" and "sufferers."

Another very common form of the propagandistic theater was the staging of reports and debates. The speeches were illustrated by pantomimes, conversations, "living diagrams," "living placards," choruses, or individuals acting on the platform. The debates staged a clash between the two points of view. They brought in various characters who defended their ideas during the discussion, including priests, kulaks, "Nepmèn," and White Guardsmen. They appeared in costumes and make-up to enact the roles that they had rehearsed.

The "animated poster" was another minor form used by the propagandistic theater. An enormous political poster was placed on the stage in which holes had been cut for the arms and heads of living performers. These people would recite their speeches, dialogues, or verses in this position and accompany them with gestures. Mischievous Russian folkrhymes were also used by the propagandistic theater. A "political folkrhyme" came into being. This was sung by its author, by a chorus, or by an accordian player. The people loved the scoffing quatrains of the folkrhymes, and the propagandistic theater used them to contrast two purely political ideas.

There were as yet no Soviet plays and no Soviet literary figures. Foreign plays on social themes were insignificant in number, unwieldy for the amateur theaters, and far removed from the objectives of Bolshevik propaganda. The Revolutionary verses of proletarian poets and translations from such socialist poets of the West as Emile Verhaeren and Walt Whitman began to appear in the very first days of the Soviet regime. Verse furnished the first literary means by which dramatic circles reflected Revolutionary events. Hence, verse became part of the propagandistic theater.

The "staging of verses" was a genre that began in the Proletarian

Culture Theater and spread throughout the amateur dramatic circles. Revolutionary verses were acceptable for many reasons. They needed no décor or acting technique, and the infrequent conversations of the "soloists" could be staged against a choral background. Its poetics (if the word may be used) responded to the bathos and stiltedness with which many people tried to adorn the terrible Revolution. The great and faceless mass was symbolized abstractly, and the abstract and allegorical Super-Proletarian was extolled. The quality of the "Revolutionary verses" was frequently wretched. They were overstuffed with flattery of the proletarians, and the "proletariat"—womanlike—was completely susceptible to this approach. The staging of verses produced a new genre called "collective declamation," with the protagonists in a chorus.

"Literary montage" also received its start in the propagandistic theater and spread to many amateur theaters. Like the staging of verses, "literary montage" came into being because purely Bolshevik material for the amateur stage was so rare. It mixed a variety of texts and visual genres, and applied them to the stage. Examples of "literary montage" include "1905," "Lenin," "October," "War," and "Karl Marx." These were made up of selections from such sources as letters, documents, police dossiers, memoirs, political speeches, resolutions of the Communist Party congresses, slogans, and verses. Later, the author would treat his material the way a motion-picture director treats film montage. He assembled textual bits of different length and character. Extracts from police dossiers interrupted public speakers. Stanzas of verse or some prose broke into selections from articles or diaries. The authors and directors of literary montage used such devices as repetition, association, and leitmotifs (which increased the similarity to the motion pictures).

The staging of "literary montage" mixed various visual devices also. The main reader and the orchestralike chorus would declaim in responsive reading. Individual readings would be followed by pantomimes in which either separate characters or a crowd would take part. Calling back and forth gave way to masked acting and dancing, which could be either comic or serious.

Vladimir Yakhontov, an actor, director, and author with refined tastes, worked with "literary montage" between 1926 and 1936. His choice of literary and documentary selections was always excellent. His montage was original, dynamic, and full of effective contrasts. His acting was a model of grotesque virtuosity.

The "living newspaper" was a leading form in amateur dramatics for a number of years. It began in Soviet clubs and spread. Originally, the "living newspaper" was presented in the clubs of Red Army men, factory workers, or villagers. Several individuals would go up on the dais and read ordinary newspaper texts. Even this primitive and completely untheatrical form proved a powerful weapon with which the Bolsheviks could propagandize the masses. It replaced the Soviet newspaper in the countryside, where illiteracy was quite common. In many towns with no newspapers of their own, this form enabled local material on topics of vital interest to be introduced.

The progressive "animation" of this form through the amateurs at the clubs took place gradually. The text was divided between an individual and a chorus, who conversed with each other. Slogans were shouted into a megaphone. Sometimes the performers in the "living newspaper" would put on masks or head-dresses or would change their clothes. Characters, in make-up and costume, were introduced to illustrate the texts. A small number of performers could thus impersonate many characters.

The "living newspaper" was compounded from the operetta, choral singing, folk-rhymes, songs, dancing, gymnastics, acrobatics, declamations, and pantomimes. It used lantern slides and bits of film or scenes from the "living film." It thus approached a revue, a political cabaret theater, or a theater of miniatures. The "living newspaper" could be performed on any premises; its décor and properties were uncomplicated (consisting of some shields, projectors, megaphones, and screens). It was therefore very practical. Its dynamic quality, rapid tempos, and variety of changing genres made it most suitable for club audiences, and it became a powerful weapon for Bolshevik propaganda. The young people from the Komsomol constituted the "living newspapers." Their military zeal, sonorous voices, and supple bodies—which let them proceed from acrobatics to pantomimes or happy choruses—attracted the club audiences more than the boring Communist texts and slogans that they shouted between "attractions."

Later on the "living newspaper" became very professional. Professionals began writing words and music for it. Directors began staging it in the theaters. Finally, a "living newspaper" appeared with professional actors in it that was entitled *The Blue Blouse*. This was even closer to a revue and the music-hall. Countless professional and amateur imitators of *The Blue Blouse* appeared in the country. A journal began to appear that was also called *The Blue Blouse*. It printed words, music, and sketches, both for staging programs and for the costuming of all the "blue blouses" in the Soviet Union.

The expansion of the "living newspaper" was gradually followed by its decline. It died out because the audiences in the club began to grow tired of its rantings and its elementary and importunate propaganda. By 1927 the "blue blouse" had almost completely disappeared from the amateur theaters.

MASS SPECTACLES

The demonstration was one of the first forms of the Soviet mass spectacles to contain elements from the theater. Of course, a procession bearing slogans to an assembly point was no invention of the Bolsheviks. They borrowed it from Western democracy, where demonstrations, however, were generally directed against the existing regime. Soviet demonstrations, on the other hand, were inspired and organized by the regime itself to create the impression among the people that the "broad masses" identified themselves with some action or campaign of the Communist Party.

The demonstrations used the theater arts in many ways. They staged political slogans with décor, props, costumes, and make-up—often on top of a truck that had brought the performers to the spot. The allegorical scenes included in the Soviet demonstrations were either still-lifes or had movement. If they were motionless, they resembled an animated political placard. If they moved, the performers shouted their lines, played on their prearranged sets, and used their platforms and props to good effect—that is, they turned a slogan into a primitive play.

Two styles were used for staging the demonstrations. The first style was naturalistic. Workers, peasants, and Red Army men would appear in their usual dress with real props, such as hammers, picks, plows, sickles, rifles, and machine guns. They acted out scenes and created new pictures. The second style was theatrical. The participants acted roles that were not theirs in real life and that stressed the purely theatrical, satirical, and semifantastic.

Crude farce was a favorite device for such theatrified demonstrations.

The masks and characters of the allegories and the caricatures became standardized in the very first years. Almost all the demonstrations of those years used the same masks for the "enemies of the Soviet regime." These included "Curzon," an "imperialist," a "banker," a "kulak," a "priest," a "White-Guard general," and a Menshevik "conciliator."

In addition to shows atop trucks, there were also farces and allegories acted out in the midst of the demonstrating throng itself. A certain theatrical element appeared in the very first Soviet demonstrations that later became standard. The demonstrators were grouped according to their factories, enterprises, institutes, or unions. Every detachment included a unit of marchers in costume and make-up. The people in these units organized roundelays, costume dances, choruses, and the singing of folk-rhymes.

Sometimes, the devices from the theater drew the mass itself into the symbolic play. An example of this took place at the May Day parade in Petrograd during 1919. "An anvil was set up on the 'Field of the Victims of the Revolution' as a focus for the festival, and the leaders of the marching columns struck it with a hammer as they passed by to show their faith in the revolution." [75] The May Day parade in Samara during 1920 featured an enormous globe inscribed "Long Live Toil." It was surrounded by young people wearing ribbons and emblems. An "Altar of the Proletariat"—a hammer and sickle—had been set up near the globe. The demonstrators passing by lowered their "toilers' symbols" and shouted greetings, and the children threw flowers and ribbons upon the "altar."

The Bolsheviks wished to identify their illegal seizure of power with such a great national revolution as the one in eighteenth-century France. They bent all their efforts to find flattering parallels between the events of 1789 and their own overthrow of the Provisional Government. This craving was shown with special clarity in the way the Soviet regime organized festivals for the "revolutionary calendar." But the drabness and primitiveness of these festivals prompted Lunacharsky to remark bitterly: "In this respect, we have turned out to be less alive and less talented both in terms of organization and in terms of responding to the masses than the Frenchmen who lived toward the end of the eighteenth century." [76]

Both right after the Bolshevik Revolution and later on, the regime was not successful in freeing the demonstrations that it staged from boredom or from the obvious hand of the government. This was the result despite the fact that the leaders of the regime used all their power and all their enormous resources to avoid this. The reason for such an outcome was simply that it is impossible artificially to create boisterous and spontaneous happiness within a nation when the mood does not already exist.

The experiment of giving spectacle to the national masses was, however, more interesting. "Mass performance" indicates open-air staging with an enormous number of participants and onlookers. It was the most important form of spectacle that Bolshevism had engendered. "Mass performance" was new both in scope and content, but not in acting techniques. It borrowed its devices from the magical pantomimes and the dumb shows of historical battles. These are encountered in the history of almost all the European theaters and took place frequently in Russia between the eighteenth century and the year 1917. Magical pantomimes on patriotic motifs and mass battle scenes were frequently given in St. Petersburg, Moscow, and the provinces. They contained allegorical "living pictures" and apotheoses.[77] The Soviet contributions included: a theme that always involved the revolutionary struggle of the proletariat; timing the shows for the holidays of the "Red Calendar"; the great scale of the stagings; open-air performances; and the active participation of the audience.[78]

The unities of time and place were not observed in the historical and revolutionary or "symbolical and allegorical" themes of these "mass stagings." These "living panoramas" might begin with the Paris Commune of 1871, include World War I, and February Revolution, the Bolshevik upheaval, and—to close the production—an ideal "world commune" of the distant future.

The characters would be divided into two unequal camps—a huge mass of identical proletarians and a small group of their enemies. The latter would include cruel and bloodthirsty generals, capitalists, "social democratic traitors," policemen, and clergymen. The acting techniques used in the "mass performances" were quite primitive. It was impossible to have many rehearsals with such a huge mass of performers. This precluded any refinement in acting technique. The open-air presentations took place on huge platforms and afforded no opportunity for relying on the roles, speeches, and conversations of individuals. The content of what was going on was transmitted to the audience mainly through choruses, shouting into megaphones, and the movement of the masses.

The most immense "mass performance" during the first years of the Soviet regime was the *Mystery-Play of Liberated Toil*. This was first performed on May Day of 1919 outside the Stock Exchange in Petrograd. It was repeated on the following July 19, in honor of the Second Congress of the Third Internationale, which was then taking place in the city. On November 7 of the same year, the anniversary of the Communist Revolution, *In Favor of a World Commune* and *The Taking of the Winter Palace* were staged in front of the Winter Palace.

The Mystery-Play of Liberated Toil was dedicated to May Day. It was staged by Yuri Annenkov and A. R. Kugel. The designers were Mstislav Dobuzhinsky and V. A. Shchuko. Over 2,000 persons took part in this "mystery." They were Red Army men, students at training schools for the theater, actors, opera singers, and circus performers. There were about 35,000 persons in the audience.

The mass performance *In Favor of a World Çommune* was written and directed by N. V. Petrov, Sergei Radlov, V. N. Soloviëv, and A. I. Pëtrovsky. The Stock Exchange was specially decorated for this "mass performance," but the décor did not use perspective. Instead there was bunting of orange and red, and there were huge banners inscribed with greetings in several languages for the delegates to the Communist Congress. The place of action was illuminated by spotlights from destroyers in the Neva and from the Fortress of SS. Peter and Paul. More than 45,000 people were in the audience.

The "mass performance" most impressive in scope was the staging of *The Taking of the Winter Palace*. The director-in-chief was Nikolai Evreinov. The production used more than 8,000 Red Army men, sailors, workers, and actors. The chief place for the action was the oval of buildings at the Arch of the General Staff, and the square in front of the palace nearby. The audience took their places in the square. Evreinov wrote about the production:

An artillery shot sounds. Light breaks through to the white platform and illuminates the worn-out stones of the olden hall. On a dais, the Provisional Government, with Kerensky at its head, accepts pledges of loyalty from the former dignitaries, generals, and financiers, as the band plays a false *Marsellaise*. On a red platform, against a background of brick factories, the *Internationale* starts up, and, to this music, individuals in the throng and then hundreds of voices yell out: "Lenin! Lenin!" . . . While those on the white platform spend their time at all kinds of meetings, the proletariat on the red platform begins to unite around its leaders.[79] . . . Then comes a depiction of General Kornilov's revolt in July. After this, the Provisional Government is protected only by military cadets and the Women's Battalion, and it flees to the Winter Palace. Then, the windows of this last citadel of Kerensky light up. The Reds have now organized their own military detachments and point the Winter Palace out to each other. . . . Machine guns crackle, rifles fire, and the artillery thunders. . . . There is a continuous din for two or three minutes. . . . But suddenly, a rocket goes up and everything instantly becomes quiet, so that the air can become filled with new sounds. A chorus of 40,000 voices is singing the *Internationale*. Five-pointed red stars start to light up above the darkened windows of the Winter Palace. An enormous red banner is raised above the building itself. . . . The show is over, and the Red forces begin to parade.[80]

"Mass performances" brought about a completely special technique of directorial command over the staging. Every thousand participants was divided into units of ten, and each unit had its own "foreman." The rehearsals took place, for the most part, with only the directors and the "foremen" present. The latter would then train their groups and take charge of them for the show. Furthermore, there were leaders for every group of characters, for every episode in the action, and for every part of the square during the show. The "mass performance" was divided into short, effective bits, such as entrances, turns, and individual gestures. There were 170 such "measures" used to stage *In Favor of a World Commune*. They were all included in the "score" of the mass action that the director's staff used to indicate the development of the plot and the movements of groups and characters. The staff took their places on the captain's bridge and were connected with all the platforms of action through a system of signal lights and field telephones. The guides would receive the signal from the captain's bridge and would pass it along to their "foremen," who—in turn—would pass it along to their own subordinates. The director was on the podium, and he controlled tempos, rhythms, pauses, retards, and accelerations.

Arguments and theories arose in those years about "mass performances." Some considered that the intimate theater had to be tossed overboard by the Communist Revolution. They felt that the future belonged to the outdoor theater alone, with its large-scale spectacles for the nation. Victor Shklovsky dreamed of large-scale "mass performances," in which "actors must be hoisted above the Neva by cranes, foreshadowing those brothers of mine—H. G. Wells's Martians. And a spotlight will direct all the orchestras of the world and all the drumming guns." [81] He asserted that all these first "mass performances" were merely a substitute for the theater, for they have both performers and audiences. A real mass performance would transform all the onlookers into participants:

The mass holiday of the nation, the review of the forces, the joy of the crowd, are assertions and apotheoses of today. They are legitimate when no one looks at them through the windows of a special stand, otherwise they will degenerate into a parade, into a ballet of serfs with a band. And that is why they are now neither masquerades nor theater.[82]

The theoreticians' prophecies that "mass performances" would eclipse the forms of the old theater were not fulfilled. Aside from the period of War Communism and from some attempts in the years following, the mass, outdoor staging—the "theater of the squares"—did not catch hold. It disappeared from Soviet usage. The most important prerequisite for such a theater was lacking—a mood of genuine and boisterous happiness among the people.

THE AMATEUR THEATER

The "amateur theater" is a nonprofessional theater. This theater was not an invention of the Soviet regime—it antedates the professional theater in even very ancient countries, and it existed and exists in all countries. There was scarcely a single city in pre-Revolutionary Russia without its "amateur dramatic circle." [83] People from all strata of Russian society took part in these dramatic circles of "zealots and connoisseurs," and even the amateur theater of workers, peasants, and soldiers was not new.[84]

These amateur dramatic circles multiplied in an unparalleled fashion after the October Revolution and assumed the proportions of a "theater epidemic." At the start these theaters had nothing in common with the Soviet regime. They were an elemental phenomenon, and the popular desire for the theater was uninhibited. The enormous enthusiasm of the amateur theaters between 1917 and 1919 continued the apolitical and educational trend that had characterized the pre-Revolutionary theater in Russia. The plays enacted in the villages and factories at the time were generally classics. The people staged and watched such dramatists as Ostrovsky, Gogol, Chekhov, and Leo Tolstoy with love and zeal.

A purely Soviet amateur theater, closely identified with Bolshevism, began only later. This was when the Communist Party attempted to use this spontaneous movement for its own propaganda. Then the amateur theater, fettered by Communist policies, became the starting point for the "amateur art of the masses." The amateur theater no longer staged the classics. It ceased to rejoice in theater work and repressed its desire to liberate all the acting instincts. The Communist Party used it to make propaganda in the countryside, the army, and the factories. "Apolitical" plays were routed from all the dramatic circles. The Komsomol activists forced the dramatic circles to become a weapon of propagandistic art. The basic job of the amateur dramatic circles was now to stage such things as political campaigns, revolutionary holidays, demonstrations, and *subbotniks* (voluntary work Saturdays).

Earlier, workers and peasants had been drawn into dramatic circles because they wanted to become acquainted with a different life, about which they knew nothing, and plays dealt with that different life. The persons involved used a "different world" as a shelter from the hunger and grimness of reality. They sought release for their humor, their acting instincts, and their wishes to be "masked" and different. Earlier, the amateur theater stirred the workers and peasants personally. Now, the non-Party participants in the amateur theater felt cold, bored, and unfriendly under the constant pressure to become regular Communist Party agitators. They had to yell themselves hoarse proclaiming the virtues of the *subbotniks* while, in the meantime, the exhausted workers were driven every week to toil without pay for the Soviet regime under the Soviet *corvee*. They had to show that the forcible requisitioning of grain, the various kinds of exorbitant "deliveries," and the "excess produce taxes" levied against their fellow-villagers were just and sacred. They had to point out that giving one's last copper to the Soviet "loan" was a highly conscientious action. They had to show that God and the religion in which they and their fathers had been reared could only be abused, ridiculed, and spat upon.

The amateur theater, once a pleasure, under the Communist regime became "social work." As might have been expected, most of the amateurs lost interest in their dramatic circles immediately and began to leave en masse. Therefore, members were frequently recruited for these organizations. Participation in a "dramatic circle" was considered one kind of "active social work." Without such work on one's service record, one could join neither the Komsomol nor the Communist Party. The circles thus became assembly points for potential Soviet "activists" and careerists rather than for real theater fans.

Perhaps what was most moving about the history of the Russian amateur theater was the flourishing of the rural theater after the October Revolution. Winter in the Russian countryside is lonely; it gets dark at three in the afternoon. Crowds of peasants, young people, and children "performed" in illuminated huts during the winter evenings. Shouting, arguments, and sometimes even fights over the lack of space preceded almost every rural show. Not everyone who craved the theater could fi' into the "reading rooms." Many people would not manage to get in, and so they would stand outside in the frost all evening, glued to the glass windows, trying to catch a glimpse or a word.

The "stage" did not generally exceed five yards in width. Sewn sacks or bast matting served as a "curtain," and smoking kerosene lamps provided the "lighting." Frequently, there were no wigs at all, and the make-up was amateurish. The paint was made of crushed cranberries, burnt cork, coal (for the "moustaches"), and burnt matches (for eyeshadowing). If luck was with the performers, they found a rural painter of some kind to draw a "forest" or a "garden" on burlap. And generally the Police Commissioner's house in Gogol's *The Inspector-General* and the garden in Ostrovsky's plays and the merchants' mansions would be one and the same corner of the hut, hung with burlap. The groups would send "messengers" off to the cities on foot to obtain plays. Sometimes they staged whatever happened to be in the shabby "libraries" of the schoolmistresses and the rural doctors, or whatever remained on the ruined estates of the landed proprietors.[85] When even these sources were not available, the groups "created" for themselves or "dramatized" classical tales for which they supplied the necessary texts.

The theater movement in the countryside arose spontaneously and was not at first subordinated to the Soviet regime. Soviet statistics indicate the enormous extent to which the peasants developed the rural theater. By 1926 there was scarcely any reading hut without its own dramatic circle. One survey of 130 reading huts disclosed that only 13 percent had "political circles"—which were, of course, most important to the Soviet regime—but 74 percent had dramatic circles and staged shows. The R.S.F.S.R. had about 20,000 rural dramatic circles with about 250,000 amateur actors. The peasant dramatic circles played to over 25,000,000 people a year.

According to Lunacharsky, "at the start of the Revolution, the peasants' amateur theaters developed with an almost feverish rapidity. The phenomenon then calmed down and almost seemed to freeze to death." [86] Obviously, there were important reasons for this catastrophic decline. One of them was the Bolshevik offensive against the peasants' amateur theaters. The Department of Agitation and Propaganda reached out for the rural theater in 1927. From that time on, as the Communist captors of the peasant theater have asserted, "the influence of the dramatic circles on the villages was not spontaneous. We have seized them, and they are now proceeding under our instructions." [87] This "seizure" began with the repertories. The "instructors of the rural theater" began to hound "apolitical" plays out of the dramatic circles. The groups were forced to take special propagandistic plays that were published in Moscow or written by "active" adherents of the Soviet regime in the countryside as "social work."

The Department of Agitation and Propaganda created 400 plays for the countryside—85 percent of which were propagandistic skits, 10 percent plays true to life, and the other 5 percent mixtures of the two types. The Communist leaders of the "construction of the rural theater" admitted that 70 percent of the total had little artistic value, 20 percent were mediocre, and only 10 percent were "satisfactory"—that is, "we are compelled to term them satisfactory." [88] Even worse were the "plays" concocted by local "activists," and in many regions "plays of local origin were staged almost exclusively. They were terribly illiterate." [89]

The peasantry protested this violation of the rural theater by propagandistic skits. The Soviet press did not publish many of the protests, but the bits that did see print clearly show what the amateurs of the rural theater were fighting for and against. "The constant outcry of the most devoted representatives of the peasantry [was] 'Give us the real theater . . . because you are preparing something very uninteresting for us.' " [90]

The mass exodus from the dramatic circles and the resistance in the countryside forced the Bolsheviks to retreat for a while. Some people stated that the peasants' craving for the classics was after all a healthy phenomenon and that the plays shown in rural districts had to be first-rate. Without surrendering its control over the rural theaters, the Party and the Soviet regime expanded the "rural houses of amateur art." Polenov House in Moscow trained special instructors for the rural theater. It published plays that contained comments by directors and detailed descriptions for staging and for preparing the props, décor, and costumes. Sketches of the mise-en-scène, the costumes, and the make-up were appended. No easing of the pressure in the propagandistic play, however, could replace the peasant theater that had arisen so spontaneously throughout the countryside. The rural theater thereafter remained merely a crippled creature of the Soviet government.

The enslavement of the workers' club theater in the Soviet Union followed approximately the same pattern. The amateur factory theaters grew rapidly during the first years of the Soviet regime. Basically, however, they remained what they had been long before the Revolution—that is, organizations of enlightened and apolitical amateurs. More than five hundred Russian professional actors helped the workers enthusiastically after the Revolution. They aided in organizing dramatic circles and in staging shows more than the Soviet officials did. The workers' amateur theaters staged the European and Russian classics, and sometimes even presented religious works.[91] Hence, the amateur theaters of the factories were by no means purely proletarian. The factory intellectuals—white-collar workers, engineers, technicians, and their families —took part in them along with the laborers.

The amateur theater of the factory clubs continued to be apolitical during the first years after the Communist Revolution. It was controlled by the intellectuals. This evoked Lenin's indignation. At the extra-scholastic congress in 1919, he declared:

The first shortcoming [of the educational work in the factories] is the abundance of bourgeois intellectuals who inevitably view the newly created educational establishments of the workers and peasants as a most suitable field for their own personal philosophical and cultural notions. They present the most absurd affectations as something new while they offer the supernatural and the awkward under the guise of a purely proletarian art and culture.[92]

Lenin's outburst before the "political educators" forced them to accelerate the speed with which the Party seized control of the amateur theaters. His attack on "affectations" signaled the beginning of a battle against those who sought new forms for both the amateur and professional theaters.

There were several thousand troupes in the clubs that played to about 50,000,000 people a year. These were potentially a mighty weapon for Bolshevik propaganda. The amateur theaters in the factory clubs did not exceed the professional theaters in number alone. In contrast to the professional theater, its auditoriums were more uniform, its worker-actors, being more akin to the audiences, could catch the mood of the working masses more rapidly and could adapt to them and exert a much greater influence upon them. But again the Bolsheviks changed what had been entertainment, relaxation, and education into a means for cramming Communist slogans into the minds of the many millions who attended the amateur theaters.

The apolitical and classical repertory went into a total eclipse. Party members began saying, in the press and at assemblies, that the old plays were "alien to the working class." They began announcing that the worker who was an amateur actor could not, of course, depict the characters of a Molière or a Goldoni or any other characters from the distant past. They had to limit themselves exclusively to their own, Soviet way of life.[93] Finally, "administrative" measures were taken to "purify" the repertory:

The reportorial committee must scrutinize this aspect [that is, the repertories of the club theaters]. . . . There, measures of administrative influence—banning, ought, perhaps, to be adapted. . . . We have reached an understanding with the administrative organs [that is, the OGPU] that one comrade is to be made responsible for the repertory in each club.[94]

A "purge" began of the individuals who headed the dramatic circles, and all those who were adjudged "apolitical" were chased out. Hence, "directors must not be invited without a preliminary check on their ideology and other things." [95]

The sole activity of the amateur theaters in the factories now became the "staging" of Soviet holidays, meetings, demonstrations, and various Communist propaganda campaigns, and so the circles were overworked. Some of them staged a dozen "productions" and as many as sixty performances a month. Instead of dramas, the audiences were treated night after night to "living newspapers," propagandistic skits, boring and clumsy stagings of Party slogans, "political" folk-rhymes and choral singing, and verse declaimed about the issues of the day. The amateur actors found their earlier joy in the theater missing. Instead, they were now harnessed to heavy, hasty, and most tiresome toil. What happened is what might have been expected. The audiences of working people fled the clubs, while the amateur performers left the dramatic circles. The Communist Party had to face the fact that amateur art had been crushed by its politics and propaganda.

The Bolsheviks had cut the theater off from its own supply line. To give it a little new life, they were forced to make a concession, and to stage the classics and other plays once again. The very same Party comrades who had removed plays from the clubs the day before now began confusedly to preach that the amateur theaters had to stage both the classics and costume plays. These would "show not only our present life, but—to speak roughly and pointedly—other periods, other peoples, and other customs as well." The day before, the comrades had purged the amateur circles of the actors and directors who had been staging apolitical plays. These same comrades now expatiated pharisaically:

Why indeed do our clubs . . . not stage plays without problems, plays which produce a happy and cheerful impression, which are interesting for simply technical reasons, which intrigue the audience, which have brilliant denoucements, and which—it must be said—were numerous in Goldoni's time.[96]

One must not, however, conclude from this that the Bolsheviks, having acted stupidly, were now coming to their senses and returning a certain degree of freedom to the amateur theaters of the Soviet Union. Less than three years later, the peasants began to be herded onto the collective farms and the terrors of "constant collectivization" and "constant industrialization" began. Instantly all the former slogans and theories were tossed overboard, and once again the amateur theater was completely subordinated to the Party and government, which wanted propaganda and "the building of the five-year plans."

And this makes it abundantly clear that Bolshevism has never intended to create or utilize any definite theory and ideology within the theater. It has not created and does not create any theater.

THE PROLETARIAN CULTURE MOVEMENT

The full title of the Proletarian Culture Movement was the "Central Committee of Proletarian Cultural and Educational Organizations." The rise, flourishing, and fall of this movement is a most remarkable phenomenon in the history both of the Soviet theater and of Communist Party policy toward the arts.

Actually the Proletarian Culture Movement antedated the February Revolution. After the October Revolution it declared its independence of the Soviet regime and opposed the cultural policy of the Communist Party as carried out by the People's Commissariat of Enlightenment. It considered itself a "purely class organization of the proletariat," and set itself above the Soviet regime and even superior to the Communist Party. It considered the Soviets merely a political bloc composed of classes that are completely different, and hence not a pure dictatorship of the proletariat. . . . To place the organization and the independent cultural work of the proletariat under the guidance and control of ideologists for the peasantry, the army, the Cossacks, and the *Lumpenproletariat* means at least a major debasement of the cultural value of the working class.[97]

Such an organization was predestined to a sad end. It was the creation of a "party over the Party," with its own "Central Committee," and a disdain for peasants, soldiers, and the middle classes. Bolshevism would never make peace with any priestly caste of proletarians set above it.

The very first manifestos and declarations of the Proletarian Culture Movement showed that its semi-intellectuals had delusions of grandeur with an inferiority complex. Sharply and arrogantly, the Proletarian Culture Movement cut itself off from the "impure" and "lower" classes in art. It proclaimed that the entire intelligentsia had to be tossed overboard because it was a product of the "damned bourgeoisie." It declared that proletarian culture had to be built by proletarians themselves in a wilderness cleansed of the bourgeois culture of the past, which was to be razed. Its Central Committee announced that "in questions of culture, we are immediate socialists," and called for a complete "break with the bourgeois past." [98] One of its members declared: "We must not compromise. We will create our own culture steadily, with no waverings, and from the standpoint of our own class." [99] Another one stated: "The tasks of building a proletarian culture can be accomplished only with the forces of the proletariat itself." [100] One of its periodicals asserted: "The workers will know how to forge the bases of a true proletarian art in our proletarian culture organizations." [101] There were many other examples of these attitudes as well.

The Movement advanced the slogan that the new socialist theater could be built only by "machine-tool workers": "Any effort to establish a socialist theater with even the most brilliant bourgeois actors would be as fruitless as analogous efforts [would be] to organize, for example, a socialist magazine with the aid of bourgeois writers." [102]

The actors of the Russian theater were all "bourgeois." The Proletarian Culture Movement tossed these professional actors overboard, and replaced them with workers, who would tend their machines during the day and act during the evenings. "Only by standing at his machine, by remaining a worker, can the worker become the genuine creator of the proletarian theater." [103] Only in the distant future, "when the period of peaceful construction of socialism arrives, can there be talk about specialized workers in the arts and about professionalism in the theaters." [104]

Some participants in the "proletarian theater," such as V. Kerzhentsev, went further than rejecting the professional theater. They even denied that the theater was art. Kerzhentsev wrote: "The task of the proletarian theater is not to train good professional actors who would be able to enact socialist plays successfully, but rather to give issue to the creative artistic instincts of the broad masses." [105]

The manifestos of the Proletarian Culture Movement were extraordinarily loud and arrogant. It proudly asserted that it alone was creating a perfectly new culture, art, and socialist theater on a universal and proletarian scale.

The first Proletarian Culture theater was the one in Petrograd. It began by staging the verses of the proletarian poets. The protagonist in these melodramatic declamations of proletarian culture was the abstract figure of the new Superman—the Proletarian, the sovereign to whom the entire world belongs.

This theater's style consisted of symbolically exaggerating the Sovereign of the Universe—the Proletarian—and was unbearably false.[106] A. A. Mgebrov, an actor, who was the founder and the first director of the Petrograd Proletarian Culture Arena, described it thus, however:

From the original chaos . . . there arose a symbolic figure of a worker who represented the entire significance and power of the collective which had been created by overcoming the desire for freedom. The bared muscles of the arms, the aspiring pose, the sickle, the hammer, the anvil, the blow frozen in space, the well-set head—everything is the simultaneous animation of a genuinely great inspiration.[107]

The Super-Proletarian smith symbolized the Sovereign of the World in proletarian art for a number of years. Sometimes he was stripped to the waist and wore a brand-new leather apron. At other times, he was almost entirely naked, and covered with only fig-leaves bearing the emblem of the hammer and sickle. Why it was the smith who was to become the Superman and even the Messiah [108] has remained the secret of the Proletarian Culture Movement to this day.

The Movement did not merely stage the proletarian poets' individual pieces. Sometimes, it managed to put on an entire book of verse in one evening.[109] The repertory of the Proletarian Culture Arena Theater included poems and verses by Walt Whitman and Emile Verhaeren, which were also crammed full of "Revolutionary symbolism." Contemporary sources say that these stagings of verse by the Movement were popular with the workers, soldiers, and Red Guardsmen en route to the front. The reasons for this, of course, lay not in the lack of taste in the audience nor in the charming style of the proletarian poets. The audiences understood not even 10 percent of the hundreds of pompous "symbols." [110] What the audience liked was the boundless extolling of the Proletarian. This, of course, was pleasant and cheered the hearts of the workers.

Mgebrov proceeded from staging verses to producing plays. In December of 1918 he staged a symbolical play by a proletarian poet named Bassalko. It was entitled *Kamenshchik* (The Stonemason). Bassalko wanted his play to be compared with Ibsen's *The Master Builder*. *The Stonemason* asks: Who is greater, the architect or the stonemason? The answer, of course, is the stonemason.

The architect in the play is pedantic, old, full of "senile lisping," and "thinks that he is most important in building." He is contrasted with a "young, handsome, zealous stonemason." These two symbolize the "old" and the "new" world. Mgebrov himself wrote: "The judge of the two worlds, and of the two men, is a woman [the architect's wife], who is the elemental principle of life, which is based on spontaneous attraction and is free of false and dogmatic prejudices." [111] This free creature falls passionately in love with the stonemason, who is younger than her husband. She incites her sickly husband to climb to the very top of the scaffolding. "I cannot," she says, "love builders who do not go to the top of their own buildings, and you are one of them." He is vulnerable, and decides to do the dangerous deed. "I will show that the creator is greater than the creation," he says. As one might expect, weakness and vertigo lead him to fall and die. The tricky wife then marries the stonemason who, in the apotheosis of the final act, "has mastered culture and science." After the Revolution, the mason builds a "tower of the commune."

This play was naïve and extremely weak. Yet, the critics wrote that it "finely and sharply expressed the idea of proletarian class culture." Mgebrov used all the devices of the mass, allegorical spectacle and filled the stage with stonemasons all dressed alike to symbolize the "collective."

The peak of "revolutionary symbolism" in the Proletarian Culture Movement was the production of Kozlov's *Legenda o kommunare* ("Legend of a Communard"). Suffice it to quote Mgebrov's description of one scene to sense the entire flavor of the Proletarian Culture Movement. Mgebrov, incidentally, was enthusiastic about the work:

The first scene shows the completely fantastic birth of the Communard. This takes place somewhere on a mountain overgrown with some sort of invisible forest which is not unlike the columns of a cathedral, a water plant, or an octopus [so the author himself describes the forest]. On the mountain and in the woods . . . there is (of course) a cave, and in the cave is a sage. An ancient volume lies before him. Next to the sage, leaning on a sword, is Thought. Below is an anvil upon which the Son of the Sun and the Son of the Earth are working on a piece of steel from which they are forging the Communard's heart. Dark forces move and hiss maliciously behind fantastic bushes. They keep appearing and disappearing, so that one can imagine the fantastic world from which the author extracts his idea of Communism. The Sage, Thought, the Son of the Earth, the Son of the Sun, and, finally, Happiness, give birth to this idea. They bear it through hammer blows on the same anvil about which the ancient volume bears witness. The dark forces tremble, but the Son of the Sun and the Son of the Earth keep forging. Happiness throws flowers on the anvil, and Thought awaits the sunrise.[112]

Mgebrov staged this collection of cheap operatic and theatrical tinsel in 1919. Not even the "leaders" of the Proletarian Culture Movement could abide it. They clashed with Mgebrov, and he had to leave the Arena. Only after the *Legend of the Communard* did the critics declare for the first time that the entire symbolism of the Proletarian Culture Movement (or, more accurately, of Mgebrov) was purely "petty bourgeois." They declared it to be a new version of the "god-seeking" that the pre-Revolutionary Social Democrats indulged in. Mgebrov had made a fetish of the "collective," and this was now considered alien and harmful to the working class. Even Kirillov, whose books of verses had been staged by Mgebrov, took arms against him. Kirillov stated: "The collective reading is permeated from start to finish with a strained and unnatural drum-major's attitude to action. Hysterical and noisy bathos is not proletarian at all, but purely of the intelligentsia." [113]

Mgebrov's productions were really guilty only of a lack of taste. His ideology had been borrowed in its entirety from Bogdanov, the leader of the Movement. Bogdanov had turned the collective into a fetish with his theory of empirio-symbolism and his "ideas as characters." Lenin successfully attacked Bogdanov, "Bogdanovism," and the Proletarian Culture Movement. (We shall return to this assault shortly.)

The Movement had loudly sworn not to take a thing from the old bourgeois theater for its own proletarian theater. It wanted "to create an unprecedented variety of our own, new genres that would show all the special features of proletarian style." All this stayed on paper. The Movement invented nothing new. It staged melodramatic declamations, living pictures, and allegories that had been known long before. It brought its audiences not the best of the old theater but the worst and most stereotyped garbage.

The Proletarian Culture Movement in Moscow chose a different path from the one in Petrograd. It was headed by V. Smyshliayev, a director at the First Studio of the Moscow Art Theater. In its initial stages the Moscow Proletarian Culture Theater was clearly influenced by the Moscow Art Theater, with its principles of "starting from life." These were diametrically opposed to the methods of Mgebrov, who started from the idea, the allegory, and the symbol.

Sergei Eisenstein, a talented pupil of Meyerhold's, replaced Smyshliayev in 1922. He demanded that the actors in the Proletarian Culture Theater possess the techniques of circus acrobats and contortionists. He produced Ostrovsky's *Na vsiakogo mudretsa-dovol'no prostoty* ("Enough Stupidity in Every Wise Man," also called "The Diary of a Scoundrel"). He turned this realistic Russian classic into a circuslike, music-hall spectacle. He even used some motion-picture excerpts, which caused many arguments and scandals. Eisenstein's production of Sergei Tretyakov's *Protivogazy* ("Gas Masks") was less successful. He tried to play the show not on a stage but in a factory, among the real machines, tools, and equipment which the characters utilized. The effort was a failure. The acting and the text itself turned out to be too false when seen against the real machinery. The acting was too conventional, deliberate, and "visual" in its own way. The "workers" did not begin to move about their machines in the course of the action, for the stage technique of the actors in the Proletarian Culture Movement had nothing in common with the genuine naturalism of the shops themselves. No doubt Stanislavsky and his students would have been more successful with such an experiment.

Lenin's destruction of the Proletarian Culture Movement was the first great Bolshevik offensive against the freedom of theater work, and the freedom of trends and thought in the Soviet theater arts as a whole. Orthodox Bolsheviks termed Bogdanov's ideas, upon which the Movement was based, "idealistic" and "vulgarized" Marxism. Bogdanov invented "organizational science." According to his tectonics, original proletarian culture was "the process of organizing the collective experience" of industrial workers. Such workers alone are capable of creating the new culture. This divided the factory workers from the peasants and from other strata of society. Hence, Lenin assaulted the Proletarian Culture Movement and "Bogdanovism."

The Proletarian Culture Movement was punished and "dispersed." Lenin wanted to intimidate the "100 percent proletarians," the "people who had originated in bourgeois milieus," and who had dared to set themselves over the leaders of the Communist Party. There was also an attempt to rein in the conceited failures who wanted to patent the construction of the new culture. The Proletarian Culture Movement's successors, such as the Theater of Young Working People (TRAM) and the Russian Association of Proletarian Writers (RAPP), were later punished by Stalin. The reasons for this were purely political. Extolling a "proletarian dictatorship" and its hegemony in art and literature became superfluous and dangerous in Stalin's time. The regime had been changed from a dictatorship of the proletariat to a cruel dictatorship over the proletariat.

THE "THEATER OF THE FUTURE"

All the extremist trends and theories in the theater, which were so abundant during the earliest years of the Soviet regime, had begun before the Revolution. Although they all differed, they did have one idea in common—they believed that the "old" theater was obsolete and had to be removed to clear the way for whatever was "new" "socialist," and "contemporary."

Even before 1917 a great deal had been written that aimed at "subverting" the theater of the time. Books, articles, and speeches at numerous panel discussions showed general indignation over the "old" theater and great hopes for the "theater of the future." The rebellion had begun in 1908 with the appearance of an anthology entitled *Kniga o novom teatre* ("A Book about the New Theater"). A second collection of articles, entitled *Krizis teatra* ("The Theater Crisis") followed, and then came Aikhenvalid's book *Otritsanie teatra* ("A Denial of the Theater"). In these books and in the many separate articles and panel discussions on the subject the reasons for condemning the theater varied greatly.

Some stated that the "intimate theater"—the theater for the few—had no future. Others declared that a theater could exist only in a period when an ethical struggle was seething within society; therefore, inasmuch as (in their opinion) there was nothing to fight for in contemporary Russia, and since no one wanted to see the stage depict the death-struggle between good and evil, the theater was dead. Lunacharsky, the socialist, and the Marxists, forecast that the theater would die because it was a toy of the doomed bourgeoisie. Aikhenvalid rejected the theater purely because it was not self-sufficient but was parasitic on the dramatists. He felt that it was nobler and purer to read a play than to watch it being debased upon the boards. The visions about the "theater of the future" were even gaudier. The symbolist poets imagined a theater based upon the entire nation. New myths would be created, and the theater itself would blend vocal and instrumental music with poetry and the drama, providing a new Renaissance of the theater of the Greeks. Lunacharsky also foresaw a "social theater." This, he thought, would become "a place for the collective staging of tragedies to raise the spirit to religious ecstasy—either violent or philosophically peaceful." But "side by side with the theater for the tens of thousands, with the theater of dazzlingly brilliant productions and of great 'operas,' the 'intimate' theater would also be most important." The "terrible sensitivity of the spirit would unwind in the theater world of the future." [114]

Leonid Andreyev believed that the theater of the future would deal both with the problem of the Individual and the Collective, and with the Universality of the Collective. It would replace the theaters of the present. The theaters today, he stated,

have doorways with policemen stationed at them; they will be [replaced] by other theaters, perhaps theaters based on the entire nation . . . the walls of the theaters will fall, but the theater will remain. And this theater will play only what is lofty and tragic.[115]

Painters had begun to fight realism, rationalism, and "plot construction" before the Revolution. They continued to seek the irrational and the "transsense" under the Soviet rule. Under the old regime very many Futurists and "leftists" of various shades had been rejected and derided.

These people now hoped to gain Soviet support as "victims of the old regime," but they were to be disappointed.

At the very left flank of the extremists was the "transsense theater." In 1923 it staged *Predsedatel' Zemnogo Shara* ("The President of the World") by Velemir Khlebnikov, a poet. This highly gifted individual was the most extreme opponent of the rationalism that was quite widespread in poetry. He opposed the sense, the logic, and the semantics of words. Words were to become "abstract" and to retain only a purely esthetic beauty. He thus applied the ideas of abstract painting to poetry. The motto was: "The world is an abstraction."

The "Leftist Front"—the outstanding movement among the Futurists after the Revolution was headed by Vladimir Mayakovsky and Osip Brik. Brik wrote an article in 1918 entitled "Drainage for Art" and used it to set forth his basic ideas. These would later develop into the leftist theory of "productionalism." The task of the artist under a proletarian dictatorship would be, according to Brik:

Not to distort, but to create. And not brain waves, but material things. The bourgeois artists depicted woods, the sun, the mountains, and the sea; they made people and animals from clay and marble. Why? All this exists already; it moves, is alive, and is a thousand times better than the painted canvas and the cloying blocks of marble. "We have given the idea of things." [So says the bourgeois artist, but we answer:] "We do not need your ideas. We love our living and material life, our life of the flesh. . . . If you, the artists, can create, create our human nature and our human things for us." [116]

The artist had to construct not ideas, phantoms, or illusions, but rather things that were both new and real. Brik continued:

Plants, factories, and workshops are waiting for artists to come to them and give them models of things that have never been seen before. . . . Everyone who can create something material must participate in the creation of these genuinely proletarian centers of art and culture. [117]

Punin and others worked out and expanded the "productional" theory of Brik. They declared: "The chief task of proletarian art is to eliminate the concepts of 'free, creative work' and 'mechanical labor.' They must be replaced by one idea: 'creative toil.' . . . What matters is not the decorations but the creation of new artistic things. For the proletariat, art is no holy temple suited only for lazy contemplation,[118] but toil—a factory, turning out objects of art for everyone." [119]

The declarations of the Leftist Front are loaded with crude and uncompromising rejection of all past artistic values. Those in the Leftist Front wished impetuously to be super-Communists and to assert the complete utilitarianism of the new "art of the commune." Take the section of their first manifesto entitled "Whom Does the Leftist Front Bite Into." There, the Communist Futurists formulated their rejection of the old art in these terms: "We will struggle with all our strength against transferring the methods of work used by the corpses [that is, the classics] to the art of today."

The positive part of the Leftist Front program was neither so long nor so inspired as its "destructive" element. It stated:

We are waiting only for the acknowledgment that our esthetic work is true before we joyfully dissolve the little "we" of art within the enormous "we" of Communism. . . . In the work of strengthening the gains made by the October Revolution and of reinforcing leftist art, the Leftist Front will propagandize for an art with the ideas of a commune, blazing the trail for art to tomorrow. . . . The Leftist Front will struggle for an art that is the builder of life.[120]

The rulers of Bolshevism, however, took a dislike to the Communist Futurists. Lenin rejected them, and Lunacharsky declared: "The Futurist artists have served our festivals greatly during the first years after the Revolution. But it is still very debatable as to whether they decorated our streets and squares or disfigured them." [121]

Most Soviet critics also took a negative attitude toward the Leftists. Some of them accused the Leftist Front of mechanically transferring to art the Marxist thesis that, in a socialistic society, the professions will become obsolete. Futurism was accused of attributing artistry to every worker and of distorting art into the production of utilitarian things. It did not deal with such essential questions as the relationships among people and the psychology of the new human being at all. Others—and they were not all wrong—considered the Leftist Front a new and militant formalism. Its program advanced such a point as this:

The aim of art is to influence matter in order to gain power over it, for the aim of art is included in art itself and does not depend on any conventional ideas about the condition of mankind. The aim of art is always the attainment of the most perfect forms.[122]

Still others saw in the Leftist Front something more dangerous to Bolshevism than formalism. According to them, the Leftists sought to take art away from the proletariat, to discard art as an effective weapon of ideas in the class struggle, to transform it into an inoffensive construction of new forms, and to turn a form of "class consciousness" into abstract "thingism."

Did the theories of the Communist Futurists and the Leftist Front influence the Soviet theater of those years at all? They dreamed that work would be transformed into art and filled with the rhythms and creations of art. They dreamed that the power of the theater would build a new and fine existence. All of this remained a paper tempest on the pages of periodicals. The application of the Leftist theories to the theater produced nothing special, save for a primitive use of venerable acting forms in areas that were boring, saturated with politics, and completely removed from the joy of the theater arts.

CHAPTER VI

ACCEPTABLE SUBJECTS
FOR ACCEPTABLE PLAYS

THE BOLSHEVIKS SEIZED POWER, nationalized the outstanding Russian theaters, and waited for the stage to applaud the "October Revolution." They had a comparatively long wait. Most of the major Russian playwrights of the time were neither enthusiastic nor prepared to hail the new regime. Even Maxim Gorky—whom the Bolsheviks have since placed upon a pedestal as the sole classical writer in Soviet literature—never wrote even a single play with a Soviet subject.

THE CLASSICS

Alexander Blok, in charge of the repertorial subsection during the first years of the Soviet regime, stoutly asserted that the classics alone could furnish the foundation upon which a new regime could arise over the ruins of the old.[1] Blok justified the need for the classics by stating that the theater was national property in the first place; the nation had to be given those treasures from the world drama that it did not yet know. He also felt that, in times of social cataclysms, one must look for the answers in the great works of the past. In such periods old values were reexamined and art too had to be "reviewed." People should therefore check over the greatest works created by the titans of the past.

In this regard, Blok remained constant to his idea. Beyond the uproar, the failures, and the chattering of the February Revolution, beyond the treason and the refuse of the October coup, beyond the shell of events and politicking, he saw something immeasurably greater. He saw the collapse of the entire old world and the end of its senile civilization. The scope of its collapse was apocalyptic. Blok envisioned a kind of Judgment Day for the ruined old world and its values. The scale of the cataclysm dictated gigantic themes for the theater and a reexamination for art. The Bolsheviks were accidental puppets of fate and mattered little.[2]

In those days Gorky also felt that the classics alone could respond to the "stormy" and heroic age.[3] Many classics were staged at the time, especially plays that showed individuals in a heroic struggle against the current and in revolt against society. They included: Schiller's "republican tragedy" *Fiesko* and his *Wilhelm Tell, Don Carlos,* and *Die Räuber;* Lope de Vega's *Fuente Ovejuna;* and Shakespeare and Sophocles.

This kind of classic, however, was against tyranny and "sympathetic to revolution"; it therefore turned out to be a double-edged sword. Its heroes were glowing, humanistic, and most honest—utterly unlike the engineers of the October Revolution. The classics attacked usurpers with soliloquies and other speeches, and Russian audiences were reminded of those who had seized power in the fall of 1917.

The drama of the world was examined thoroughly in the search for a more harmonious repertory. For the first time, Russian translations were staged of Mérimée's *Jaquerie,* Sardou's *Thermidor,* Büchner's *Danton's Tod,* Lassalle's *Franz von Sickingen,* Schnitzler's *Der grüne Kakadu,* and the plays of Romain Rolland. Foreign plays were used which contained any kind of social theme at all. Among such dramas were Hauptmann's *Die Weber* and *Fuhrmann Henschel,* Galsworthy's *Strife,* Kaiser's *Gas,* and Herman Heijermans's *Op Hoop van Zegen* ("The Good Hope").

During this period many miserable Russian plays that somehow dragged in the workers or revolution were also staged. These included Karpov's *The Workers' Quarter* and *Glow,* Skitalets's *Volunteers,* E. P. Milyukova's *Altar of Freedom,* and Tatyana Mayskaya's *Above the Land.* In these, sentimental tripe and cheap eroticism were mixed with intellectual conversations about the "socialism of the future." Some theaters staged many of Gorky's plays. Finally, room was found for plays which depicted Russian monarchs unfavorably, such as Merezhkovsky's *Paul I, Alexander I,* and *Nikolai I.*

This stage—the presenting of plays from world drama that were "socially sympathetic"—preceded the beginnings of the Soviet drama itself.

THE SO-CALLED HISTORICAL PLAYS

The scenarios for the mass spectacles and the mass performances were the first works of Soviet drama. They included *The Mystery-Play of Liberated Toil, In Favor of a World Commune,* and *The Taking of the Winter Palace.* These presentations contain the main element distinguishing the Soviet plays from their pre-Revolutionary predecessors—their purely Bolshevik attitude. Events were examined from the viewpoint of the class struggle. The scenarios sharply delineated the "righteous" nation and the capitalist, imperialist, and autocratic "sinners." They all contained the "original sin" of Soviet drama, that is, the narrow Communist scheme for falsifying human relations, history, and the struggles of individuals.

In the open-air spectacles a world took shape that was constructed according to the scholastic scheme of Bolshevism and bifurcated into white (the proletariat) and black (the "others"). The "people" and its "sons" are always fine and endowed with all the virtues. The "others"—the "enemies of the people"—are afflicted with all the existing (and nonexistent) vices of this world. The "class struggle" and "class interests" are invariably behind everything human.

Everything from the past was depicted in a somber light. It was saturated with the clinking of chains, with enslavement, and with all the other abominations that mocked mankind. October, 1917, marked the beginning of light. The mass performances started the Soviet myth about building paradise on earth by referring to the "Bright Commune of the Future."

Bolshevism, which evidences a kind of inverted snobbishness, spared no effort in "socially commanding" every mercenary genealogist of history or literature to compile hastily a magnificent "family tree." Communists began their search for ancestors among the Greek and Roman slaves, the medieval serfs, the sans-culottes, the Parisian Communards, and the soldiers of World War I. With every year, the quasimegalomaniacal bluntness of Bolshevism has its genealogical tree branch out further. The tree now includes all the great thinkers and fighters of the past, both distant and recent; it shows a direct blood-tie to all the great Russian military leaders, such as Peter I and even Ivan the Terrible. They all turn out to have been precursors of Bolshevism.[4]

This falsification of history for the greater use of Bolshevism began with the very first Soviet historical plays. Soviet drama idealizes the rebellions of the past. An example of presenting history as "policy spilled over into the past" is furnished by two plays about the seventeenth-century rebel Stenka Razin. The first one, entitled *Stenka Razin*, was written by Vasili Kamensky, the Futurist poet. In its posterlike language and its mixture of verse with political slogans, this play is a development of the mass spectacle. Its characters are divided coarsely and sharply into two camps. The first, the rebellious paupers, has all the author's love and enthusiasm. The second contains boyars (who are scoundrels), merchants, and princes. Kamensky considered the Bolshevik Revolution to be a peasant revolt, the advent of those Scythians who would remove all the complexity of bourgeois civilization (so hateful to his Futurist heart) and assert a primitivism akin to his own verses. And he spills this peasant and Scythian idea over into the past. The violent and rebellious mass of muzhiks almost totally eclipses Stenka Razin, the hero. Throughout the play, there is an obvious "politicalization" of history according to the Bolshevik catch-phrases.

Stenka Razin was an original propaganda play on a historical subject. The end of the play stresses the slogan of "historical succession." After Razin is executed at the block, a crowd with red banners surrounds Red Square in Moscow, where the event had taken place, and someone shouts: "Each of us is Stenka Razin. We have been suckled on his struggle. And later on, we shall go with him to the sunlit expanses of a universal brotherhood for all mankind." [5]

Yuri Yurin's version,[6] a more complex treatment of the same subject, appeared a year later. Instead of the muzhiks being stereotypes, as in Kamensky's play, Razin and his entourage were individualized. Tints and shades replaced the crude "blacks" and "whites." But Marxist "sociology" loomed over Yurin's entire tragedy. Everywhere, the playwright tries diligently to revise history and facts and to append "social premises." Razin's adventures in robbery turn out to have been a legitimate historical process caused and anticipated by social conditions; the thief himself is shown as the wise and popular leader of a peasant revolution in old Russia; he leads the masses against Moscow in a "systematic and organized fashion" to seize power over the entire nation. In Yurin's tragedy, the relationship between the hero and the masses is associated with the Marxist attitude towards the relationship between the individual and the mass.

V. Volkenshtein's *Spartak* ("Spartacus") also revised the history of a rebellion.[7] *Spartacus* was written in good poetry and had the worthy intention of reviving the form of Roman tragedy and of pouring revolutionary content into it. It was badly received by the Soviet dramatic critics. The most valuable thing in *Spartacus* was its attempt to depict the theme of a Roman slave rebellion in an ancient dramatic form. This was declared vicious, and the work was viewed as unnecessarily restorative and as devoid of genuine revolutionary pathos.[8] As a tried and true member of the Communist Party remarked, Spartacus posed and declaimed rather than led a rebellion. Even the Marxist critics derided Volkenshtein's effort to give the "social essence" of the patricians (according to Marxian formulas) by having them count up their profits from the fights of the gladiators.

Zagmuk, a play by Anatoli Glebov, must be considered the most distant excursion into the debris of history.[9] Glebov, a Communist playwright, set the action of his play in Babylon during the eighth century B.C. The Zagmuk was an annual festival during which the slaves of Babylon were freed for eleven days and chose their own king, while the masters were transformed into slaves. After this, the king had to pay for his short reign with his life. Such was the theme of the tragedy. The slaves in the city of Larak decided to make serious use of the Zagmuk festival by seizing power and holding it permanently. Zer Siban is chosen "king" and becomes the leader of the rebellion which is later drowned in blood by the joint efforts of the Assyro-Babylonian slaveowners.

Zagmuk continued the theme of "early popular revolutions" and premature revolts, a theme that had been started in *Stenka Razin* and *Spartacus.* Plays of this kind occupy an impressive niche in the Soviet drama. In all of them, the heroes are condemned to death. Inevitably they break out in moving soliloquies: though we are condemned to death, our cause will not fail; in the future the Bolsheviks will come to complete our work.

The critics detected a failing in *Zagmuk* from which the Soviet drama would never be able to shake loose. The villains of the piece were more lifelike than the heroes. All the "popular leaders," revolutionaries, superproletarians, and titans—to use the vocabulary of the Soviet dramatic critics—show traces of abstract and undisguisedly posterish social characteristics. The failure of Soviet playwrights in this regard was inevitable. All the "heroes" were—and are—created in the retorts at the government laboratories. The vices of such heroes are removed, and only the cloying virtues are left. Hence, only "the enemies of the people"—the monarchs and White Guardsmen (who are endowed with vices and shortcomings exclusively)—are singularly alive when compared to the "heroes." This is not surprising as vice is more picturesque than the drabness of concocted virtue. Later, the Soviet playwrights would make desperate efforts to enliven their "heroes." They would seriously consider mechanical methods:

It has reached the point where one of the proletarian writers, speaking at a public meeting in the company of his fellow-dramatists, discussed the way in which we must write plays nowadays to preclude people's finding fault with them. One has to give three villains and five positive figures, and then a certain kind of balance will be observed and the play will be accepted. And when I portray a Communist, I must give him one negative trait and five positive ones.[10]

Soviet dramatists will go through agonies in thinking up other methods "to create a heroic figure who is also realistic, and acts according to the will of the people and for its good, but without depriving the hero or the people of their individuality, and without simplifying the relationships between them." [11] This is what Marxian criticism has demanded, but the Soviet stage has never achieved it.

The plays of Anatoli Lunacharsky were among those which revised the past from the Soviet viewpoint by looking for precursors of Communism. It is comforting to note, however, that the great erudition and superior taste of this author distinguished his works from most of the historical plays by other Soviet dramatists. His plays are also striking because they are not schematic. Their heroes and villains are depicted as people, with virtues and vices. Lunacharsky's humanism evoked a most coarse attack on him by the "hundred percent" Marxian critics. His play *Oliver Cromwell* (1920) was their special target. The orthodox critics accused it of extolling the role of the individual in history, which contradicted the Marxian attitude towards the question. They attacked Lunacharsky for his "apotheosis of the leader," and because his protagonist—rather than the people or the levelers—founded the English bourgeois state. Not a few Communists demanded at the time that administrative measures and severe penalties be imposed against the playwright, who was the People's Commissar of Enlightenment. They wanted *Oliver Cromwell* to be taken off the boards immediately, and desired the State Publishing House (which had printed the play) to be punished.

Why had *Oliver Cromwell* called forth the wrath of the orthodox Bolsheviks? Lunacharsky's Cromwell was a strong man who profoundly understood the historical situation. He knew how to rise above the current of history and how to guess its course before anyone else did. He was strong enough to force the people living under his regime into the current of history. In winning the revolution that he had led, Cromwell did not hesitate to step over the corpses of those with whose aid it had been started. His punishment of the leveler leaders was demanded by historical necessity. Cromwell was depicted as towering above a nation that had not yet matured sufficiently to understand revolution. Unlike most characters in Soviet plays, Lunacharsky's Cromwell was variegated. He was cruel, but pure of spirit; he was wise, but narrow-minded; his leadership was strong, but he had doubts about the end result of the revolution.

The odes to *Oliver Cromwell* in various Soviet books about the theater of the recent past are directly contradictory to the fury of the Communists against the liberal commissar in Lenin's time. This is easy to understand. In 1920 extolling a revolutionary leader who stepped over the corpses of his "liquidated" contemporaries was a challenge to Soviet democracy. Later, however, Stalin's dictatorship and purges eclipsed those of both Cromwell and Robespierre. Hence, Lunacharsky's play became positive and almost prophetic for Stalinist dramatic criticism.

Quantitatively speaking, the "revision of history" from the theoretical Bolshevik viewpoint was of major importance to Soviet drama. Many playwrights were willing to denigrate the tsarist history of Russia. A list of merely the better works of this type is quite impressive. It includes: A. N. Tolstoy's *The Empress's Conspiracy* (1924) and *Azef* (1926); Konstantin Trenëv's *Pugachev's Rebellion* (1924); N. Lerner's *Catherine II and Gregory Orlov* (1922), *Peter III and Catherine II* (1923), and *The Mistress of Peter I* (1924)—Lerner specialized in the secrets of the imperial bedchambers; A. Kugel's and K. Tverskoi's *Nicholas I and the Decembrists* (1925); V. Venkstern's *In 1825* (1925); M. Yakhontava's *Decembrists* (1925); N. Shapovalenko's *Georgy Gapon* (1926) and *1881* (1925); V. Shkvarkin's *Degayev's Treason* (1925); D. Smolin's *The Seven Wives of Ivan the Terrible* (1925) and *The Tsarina Elizabeth* (1925); I. Platon's *The Days of Arakcheyev's Power* (1926); and S. Mstislavsky's *On Blood* (1927).

The centennial of the Decembrist Uprising in 1925 brought many plays on the subject to the dramatic market. As a rule, their quality was low—they were anniversary potboilers. The Bolshevik "social command" for the centennial was roughly as follows: make the Decembrists into precursors of Bolshevism so that their halo of glory might somewhat illuminate the somber edifice of the Soviet state. Earlier, the Decembrists had been considered as lone rebels, as dreaming knights who perished because they had failed to perceive their total lack of support. Bolshevism now demanded that they be viewed as a "revolutionary movement" rooted in the people and linked with later revolutionary trends in Russia from Herzen to Lenin.

Kugel and Tverskoi wrote a play based on Merezhkovsky's novel *December 14.* Their main figure was Nicholas I, whose despotism and ownership of serfs was stressed. They did not succeed, however, either in making the Decembrists come alive or in connecting them with the people. Theirs was an attempt to falsify history by staging and adroitly juggling quotations from transcripts and other documents, but it failed. Even the Bolshevik critics admitted the wretchedness of the work, and they felt that almost all the plays on this topic lacked "inventiveness"— that is, a bolder distortion of history.

The history of the workers' movement in Russia was also subjected to this kind of "revision" by the dramatists, examples of which were Shapovalenko's *Gapon* and *1881.* The many plays on this subject, however, were completely primitive and false. The working masses were depicted as being all of the same stamp; the characters in the plays were not worked out, and all of them spoke in one and the same governmental language. Their bias was quite open, and framework of these plays was very evident. Most of the dramas consisted of mechanically staged episodes.

Such plays as *Degayev's Treason* by Shkvarkin, *Azef* by A. N. Tolstoy, and *On Blood* by Mstislavsky offered a later and more advanced stage of the dramatists' use of the revolutionary movement in tsarist Russia. Works by these playwrights avoided a montage of "reports" by the characters, quotations from proclamations, brochures, documents (to be declaimed), and a feebly mechanical joining of episodes. These authors were the first to use the elements of adventure in the lives of their revolutionaries. Secret agreements, underground activities, shadowings by the police, and the preparation for acts of terrorism were all depicted. This made their plots interesting and even gripping.

These three writers were more talented than their predecessors (which certainly helped their plays to score hits with the Soviet public). Both Count Alexei Tolstoy and Prince Mstislavsky handled their plots skillfully. They knew how to transmit the Russia of the past with all of its flavor and material truth and how to make every character talk in his own fashion.[12]

Azef and *On Blood* were chronicle plays, a genre that Soviet audiences have always loved and that is quite important in the general Soviet repertory. They were written by literary masters who were profound connoisseurs of that past in which they themselves had once lived. But public success does not connote success with the "regime of the repressed." The orthodox Bolsheviks disliked these plays. Although the spirit of the period had been given with only relative justice and accuracy, this did not suit the Bolshevik critics. They wrote about *Azef:*

The class character of the Socialist Revolutionary Party, its antisocialist nature, and its reactionary adventurings were not revealed socially and artistically. The interest of the play is concentrated on the bright details of the adventures of Azef himself, a provocateur and a lowly, acquisitive individual.[13]

Tolstoy did not succeed in blackening the Socialist Revolutionaries in the way that the Bolsheviks wanted. He failed to show that "the practice of terror brilliantly showed the falseness of the Socialist Revolutionary theory about the struggle against tsarism" or that "the structure of a protective police force nourishes such poisonous fruits as entrapment by the authorities."[14]

On Blood dealt with the year 1905, when St. Petersburg had a strike in October, Moscow had an uprising (which was repressed) in December, and the Bolsheviks went underground. The Bolshevik critics discovered that the playwright had shown the "crisis of the peaks" (to which he himself had belonged) rather than the uprising of the workers.[15] They accused Prince Mstislavsky of making the high circles and the officers—whom he had known and been close to—alive and pithy, while the revolutionaries (whom, of course, he had not known) were "schematic and stereotyped."

Pugachëv's Rebellion, by Trenëv, was one of the outstanding Soviet historical plays about popular revolutions. This tragedy, written in 1925 and produced years later, is one of the best examples of Soviet falsifications of history.

Of all the peasant revolts that took place in the distant past of Russia, Pugachëv's rebellion was the most important. The Bolsheviks considered Emilian Pugachëv a kind of ideological forebear, worthy of being

1. Stanislavsky and Nemirovich-Danchenko opened the Moscow Art Theater in October, 1898, with A. K. Tolstoy's *Tsar Feodor Ivanovich*.
2. Chekhov's *The Sea Gull* brought recognition to the Móscow Art Theater in 1898. Often called "The House of Chekhov," the Theater chose as its trade-mark a white sea gull, an emblem which even today decorates its curtain and posters and which all its personnel wear in their lapels.

3. From its earliest days, the Moscow Art Theater was concerned with social and political themes. This scene is from Gorky's *The Lower Depths*, 1902.
4. Another production of a Chekhov play by the Moscow Art Theater was *The Three Sisters* in 1901. Meyerhold played the part of Tusenbakh.
5. Griboyedov's classic *Woe from Wit* was produced by the Moscow Art Theater in 1906. The scene is from Act III; the décor by Dobuzhinsky.

6. In his production of *Farce*, by Alexander Blok, in 1906, Meyerhold already was experimenting with parody and the grotesque. *Farce* appeared at the Komisarzhevskaya Theater, décor by Sapunov.
7. Alexander Golovin's sketch for Act III of Ostrovsky's *The Storm*, staged by Meyerhold in 1915 at the Imperial Alexandrinsky Theater.
8. Alexander Golovin, stage designer, and Vsevolod Meyerhold.

9. Alexander Tairov presented Annenkov's *Famira Kifared* at the Kamerny Theater in 1916. The designer was Mme Alexandra Ekster.
10. Oscar Wilde's *Salome* was produced by Tairov at the Kamerny Theater in 1917.

11. Mme Ekster used unusual combinations of fabrics and the accent of different paints to make her costumes for *Salome* dynamic and to intensify the force of a character's gestures.

12. Mme Ekster's set for *Salome* was almost abstract—with wedge-shaped and rectangular forms that could be piled up, moved downstage, hoisted, or lowered.

13. Alexander Tairov, who founded the Kamerny Theater in 1914.

14. Mass spectacles staged in city squares were calculated to rouse the public to enthusiastic support of the new regime. "The Taking of the Winter Palace," directed by Evreinov in 1918, used more than 8,000 Red Army men, sailors, workers, and actors.

15. Anatoli Lunacharsky, first People's Commissar of Enlightenment, guided Soviet theater policy for twelve years.

16. The "living newspaper" and the "animated poster" were favorite Bolshevik uses of dramatic forms for propaganda purposes. One of the most popular was *The Blue Blouse*.

17. In order to dramatize Bolshevik slogans about the "class struggle," Meyerhold completely "Sovietized" Verhaeren's *Les Aubes,* which he produced at the First Theater of the R.S.F.S.R.

18. Sergei Eisenstein, a Meyerhold pupil later to become famous as a director of motion pictures, demanded that his actors possess the techniques of circus acrobats in Ostrovsky's *Enough Stupidity in Every Wise Man.*

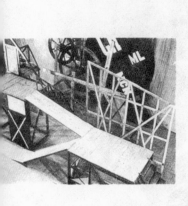

19. In 1922, Meyerhold abandoned traditional staging and turned to constructivism. The stage was stripped down to the unplastered brick walls. In Sukhovo-Kobylin's *Death of Tarelkin,* many of the devices resembled those found in a circus.

20. For Crommelynck's *Le Cocu Magnifique,* another constructivist production of 1922, an abstract scaffolding was built to represent the miller's house. The function of the disk, which spelled out the playwright's name (vowels omitted), was to whirl furiously as the rages of the jealous miller increased.

21. Seated: Composer Dmitri Shostakovich and Meyerhold; Standing: playwright Mayakovsky and Rodchenko, an exponent of construc-

22. For his constructivist productions, Meyerhold invented a new acting system which he called "biomechanics." He believed that the proletarian theater should be regarded as a factory, the motions of the actors as clean-cut and defined as those of a machine.

23. The calculated gestures of "biomechanics" bordered on dance techniques.

24. Meyerhold somewhat modified constructivism but still omitted backdrops in 1924 when he turned Ostrovsky's gentle comedy *The Forest* into a malicious satire on the landowners of the old regime.

25. Another imaginative Meyerhold presentation: Faiko's *Bubus the Teacher,* 1925. During the entire performance, one of the finest pianists in Moscow sat on a high platform overlooking the stage, playing Chopin and Liszt.

26. Meyerhold's production of Gogol's *The Inspector-General* in 1926 is often considered his masterpiece. This presentation alone is enough to give him a permanent place in the history of the theater. His wife, Zenaida Raikh, a famous actress in her own right, played the role of Anna Andreyevna.

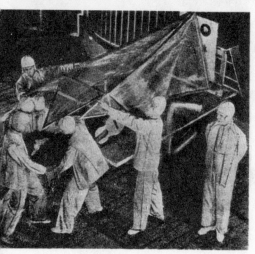

27. The staging of the "bribery scene" in *The Inspector-General* was Meyerhold at his creative best.
28. Meyerhold was an ardent believer in Communism but felt that the ideas of the Revolution had grown thin while the new Party functionaries had grown fat. He dealt bureaucratic "yes-men" a frontal blow with his presentation of Mayakovsky's *The Bug* in 1929
29. Meyerhold at work on his notes for Griboyedov's *Woe from Wit*.

30. The sophisticated productions of Tairov were always refined, well-coordinated, brilliantly staged, masterfully costumed, and excellently furnished. An example is his treatment of E. T. A. Hoffmann's *Princess Brambilla*, given at the Kamerny Theater, décor by Yakulov.

31. Tairov believed in the "theatricality" of the theater and found inspiration in plays of fantasy and imagination. His production of Lecoq's operetta *Giroflé-Girofla* in 1922 was an ebullient buffonade. Again the décor is by Yakulov.

32. Tairov was one of the few directors to schedule contemporary Western plays. In 1924 he produced Chesterton's *The Man Who Was Thursday*. A model of the complicated set of *The Man Who Was Thursday*, designed by Krzhizhanovsky.

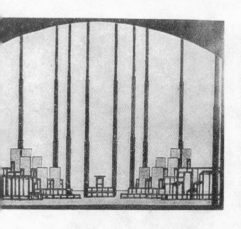

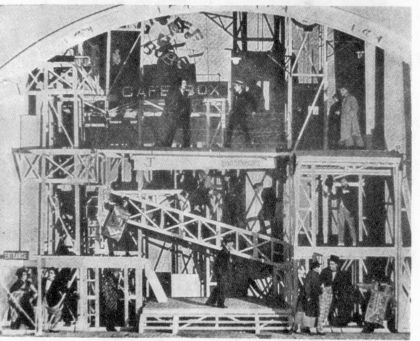

33. A sketch by the Stenberg brothers for the set of Shaw's *Saint Joan*. Tairov's wife, Alice Koonen, one of the outstanding actresses in Russia, played Joan.

34. In 1924 Tairov produced Ostrovsky's *The Storm*, a play whose realism he hated. He tried to escape its true-to-lifeness with a fanciful set by the Stenberg brothers.

35. In *The Man Who Was Thursday*, Tairov tried to bring out "the symphony of the big city."

36. In 1926 Tairov produced Eugene O'Neill's *Desire Under the Elms*. The décor is by the Stenberg brothers.
37. The Kamerny Theater always stressed the imaginative and the sophisticated. This extremely modern looking sketch for a set is by Alexandra Ekster.

38. A world-famous figure in the theater, Konstantin Stanislavsky, shows approval at a rehearsal.

39. Co-founder and co-director of the Moscow Art Theater, Vladimir Nemirovich-Danchenko. He was responsible for the literary quality of the Theater's repertory as Stanislavsky was for its high standard of acting.

40. Bulgakov's *Days of the Turbins* was indeed rare in that it portrayed soldiers of the White Army as anything other than monsters. The Moscow Art Theater produced it amid great criticism in 1926.

41. Maeterlinck's *Le Miracle de Saint Antoine,* 1921, was a satire on bourgeois society wherein greedy relatives impatiently await the death of a wealthy aunt. It was presented by Eugene Vakhtangov, director of the Third Studio of the Moscow Art Theater, which was eventually named for him.

42. Vakhtangov did not live to see the first actual performance of his brilliant production of Gozzi's *Turandot.* First given in 1922, it remains in the repertory of the Vakhtangov Theater to this day exactly as Vakhtangov conceived it. Décor by Nivinsky.

43. Vakhtangov chose neither the absolute naturalism of Stanislavsky nor the symbolism of Meyerhold, but made the widest possible use of all theatrical forms.

immortalized by a Soviet playwright.[16] Pugachëv's rebellion was first treated by Alexander Pushkin in his *Istoriia pugachëvskogo bunta* ("The History of Pugachëv's Rebellion," 1834) and *Kapitanskaia dochka* ("The Captain's Daughter," 1836). Pushkin, with the consent of Nicholas I, was the first to gain access to the secret material in the archives, and he even journeyed to the scenes of the action. The poet supplemented his historical study with traditions and the testimony of the living, and his objectivity on the question of Pugachëv is indisputable. The Pugachëv in his *History of Pugachëv's Rebellion* is alive and most complex, but scarcely fit to be canonized as a hallowed revolutionary. Pugachëv begins as an "unknown tramp' who stands out because of the boldness of his language He is an adventurer, who has confused people with his false tales about riches hidden on the frontier and with his story that some "pasha" has promised him five million rubles to support the Cossacks. Later on, Pugachëv turns himself into an autocrat and proclaims himself to be Peter III. Plans for rebellion take shape within him only later.[17] Pushkin does not spare facts or documents in testifying to Pugachëv's monstrous cruelty. As a historian, Pushkin is not reverent toward the rebels. He generally refers to them as "rabble" and does not identify them with freedom at all, although the love of liberty is found throughout Pushkin's work. He mentioned as the most important aspect of Pugachëv's rebellion the spontaneity with which the peasants revolted. Such was Pushkin's objective idea of this event. Let us now compare it with Trenëv's conception and—most important of all—with the falsification that Bolshevik criticism demanded.

At the start of his tragedy Trenëv wanted to retain at least a fraction of the historical truth. He wished to show a Pugachëv who, although idealized and cleansed of his inherent cruelty, was still a bandit who liked to lie, had his weaknesses, and possessed the dark and light sides common to all men. Later, Trenëv wanted to show Pugachëv's development into a leader of the rebellious peasants. Such a transformation of Pugachëv into a heroic leader had little in common with the truth of history, but at least it was good theater. The growth of a character and his complex development during the course of the action made the role authentically dramatic and attracted actors. (For an actor the most terrible role is a static one.) But Trenëv's good intention of painting Pugachëv in both tints and shades evoked the wrath of Soviet critics. Sobolev wrote that Trenëv's Pugachëv has "features that cancel out and contradict each other. A braggart, a fibber, a ladies' man, and a cynic in the first scenes, Pugachëv develops in the last ones into a romantic hero who is the acknowledged leader of the rebellion." [18] The badgering was so strong that the play was banned as ideologically uneven. Only the efforts of Nemirovich-Danchenko, who staged *Pugachëv's Rebellion* at the Moscow Art Theater, led the State Academic Board to reconsider the decision and to revoke the ban.[19]

Trenëv's Pugachëv becomes, in spots, a sort of Communist leader. He not only destroys, he builds and even dreams of a socialist paradise. "And my duma," he says, "will be the first to bring the kingdom of light to the ignorant nation"—that is, to the proletariat. Trenëv Bolshevized the peasantry in his play. The peasants began to divide the landowners' estates according to the Bolshevik catch-phrases, just as if they had been alive in 1917 rather than in the Age of Catherine. Trenëv could not manage without setting up a "bridge to Bolshevism" at the end of his play. In the final scene, Emilian Pugachëv hints at the inevitable arrival of the Bolshevik Revolution: "Farewell, oh tortured nation, oh great orphan! . . . My last hour has struck. And when your first hour comes, rise up and listen!" But the author's intentions did not suit the Soviet critics who considered him merely "an illustrator for a bygone national tragedy. . . . Thanks to his concentration on naturalistic details, the illustrations have been turned into a special kind of snapshot showing historical events and occurrences that were true to life." [20]

In *Pugachëv's Rebellion*, one clearly senses not so much the tragedy of Emilian Pugachëv as that of the Russian playwright who tried to adjust his work to the paper doll types demanded by the Soviet censorship. He wanted to remain faithful to the truth of history and to realism, so he created a Pugachëv who was a vindicative bandit with all the shady aspects inherent to such a person. He created rebellious Cossacks and living muzhiks who were scarcely "conscious revolutionaries" or prototypes of the Bolsheviks. Trenëv knew, however, that such a conception would not pass the censorship, and so he began to compromise and to falsify. He changed Pugachëv into a wise Bolshevik rebel leader and depicted the landed proprietors and the officers in a manner that came strictly from Bolshevik propaganda. But all his attempts to please the Bolsheviks failed because he did not know all the principles of falsifying history according to the Bolshevik formulas. He made a mistake in concentrating on the "leader" and pushing the people aside. The

Bolshevik canons of falsifying the past insist on making the people—consciously inclined toward Bolshevism—the protagonist of tragedy.[21]

Let us omit those plays whose aim was to give the proletarian audiences the satisfaction of rummaging about in the dirty linen of the tsars. We then have only the most important and serious efforts to look at history through Soviet eyes. We can discern that the great bulk of these plays followed the historical school of Mikhail Pokrovsky (1864–1932).

Some years later, Pokrovsky's school would be considered "anti-Marxist." It would be stated as a maxim that writers ought to depict the phenomena of social life in their broad and many-faceted unity of opposites. The falsification of history and reality would remain in the drama, however. It would even become the sole method of the Soviet drama. Despite the hallowed commandments of the founders of Marxism and Leninism, the Bolshevik Department of Agitation and Propaganda would issue the social command to falsify history with increasing frequency. The stage needed such counterfeits in order to deceive the masses of Soviet people during the years of complete collectivization, industrialization, Stalin's dictatorship, and the war.

Quotations from Dmitri Ivanovich Pisarev (1840–1868), the Russian critic and publicist, were brought in to affirm that the center of gravity in the Soviet historical drama must be in the "mass" rather than in the characters. A writer must, Pisarev wrote,

be interested not in an external sketching of the events, but in the inner aspect of history . . . how and why this or that important historical event took place . . . what impression it produced on the mass, how the mass understood it and reacted to it. . . . It is obvious that every historical event takes place either because the people want it or because the people cannot or do not know how to stop it. It is also obvious that any historical event that deserves to be termed major takes place either to the advantage or to the disadvantage of the people; this means, as a general result, that it either lulls or, on the contrary, produces and develops in the people the opportunity for understanding truly, wishing strongly, and insisting firmly.[22]

But against the heaps of quotations shorn from the classics that seem to support the falsifying of history for the benefit of the Communist Party, one can pile up whole Everests of quotations from the classics in support of the exact opposite. The tendency may be answered with the indisputable observation of Alexander Pushkin's, which in a few words depicted the real aim of the dramatic chronicler:

What does a writer of dramas need? Philosophy, impartiality, the statesman-like mind of a historian, ingenuity, and liveliness of imagination. No prejudice or favorite ideas of any kind. *Freedom*.[23]

WAR COMMUNISM

The second enormous division of Soviet drama during the first decade concerns plays dealing with the Russian Civil War of 1917 to 1922. This field borders upon the historical drama inasmuch as it treats of the historical origins of the Soviet state, but it also betrays a Bolshevik falsification of history.

A most important play dealing with the times of War Communism is Vladimir Bill-Belotserkovsky's *Storm,* which appeared in 1925 and in which the playwright reveals a power that had not been evident in preceding Soviet dramas. *Storm* shows a provincial town during the Civil War threatened by destruction—by typhus, counterrevolutionary conspiracies, and the break through of General Denikin's White Guard troops.

A dozen awe-inspiring scenes are given in the play, and the shadow of an iron Bolshevik stalks through all of them. The protagonist of the play is the anonymous Chairman of a District Committee of the Communist Party, through whom the author shows the ideal and iron Bolshevik of the period. He is self-denying and vigilant, knows how to spot enemies, and is merciless in sending opponents, one after the other, "to the reckoning"—to be executed. Unbending, he never leaves his captain's bridge for a minute until a bullet gets him.

Bill-Belotserkovsky melodramatically depicted the terrors of civil war. The typhus epidemic soon has the dead lying beside the living. Thieves, drunks, traitors, and counterrevolutionaries sell shirts that have been taken from the ill to those not yet felled by typhus. Fear of the epidemic causes a rebellion in the Red Army barracks. There is hunger and a raid on the town by White Guardsmen.

Storm was powerful. Many of its sixty characters are alive rather than schematic. In a number of places the play did not fear to give the truth even when critical of Bolshevism. But *Storm* was the first authentically Bolshevik Party play. Its hatred for the intelligentsia was unbridled, and the great majority of the intellectuals were depicted as rascals, self-seekers, and complete counterrevolutionaries.

Storm was first staged in 1925 at the Theater of the Moscow Council of Trades Union. The public liked it,[24] and the press hailed it. The play began a triumphal procession through all the amateur and professional theaters of Soviet Russia. *Storm* is still considered a classic of the Soviet drama.

The second outstanding play on the Civil War was Trenëv's *Liubov' Iarovaia* ("Lyubov Yarovaya"), which appeared shortly after *Storm* did. Technically speaking, its plot is not particularly strong. It is a "survey" or a chronicle rather than a drama.

The action takes place in a southern Russian town under encirclement by the White Army. A group of Bolsheviks is sent to blow up a bridge and gets captured. The remaining Bolsheviks—Commissar Koshkin, the sailor Shvandia, and the others—have gone underground. Like the Bolsheviks who have left, this group struggles to prevent the Whites from hanging the prisoners. Lyubov Yarovaya, a schoolmistress, plays the main role in the struggle. She is a "non-Party Communist." Yarovoi, her husband, is a lieutenant in the White Guards and is assigned to punish the Bolsheviks.

The contest for the prisoners lying in jail is the main theme of the plot. Its basic tragedy lies in the transformation of the heroine's love for her husband to fierce hatred. But the situation at the front changes, and it becomes the turn of the Whites to retreat. At the last moment before the evacuation, Lieutenant Yarovoi wants to carry out the sentence, but a detachment of workers headed by his wife frees the Bolsheviks from jail. In contrast to Yarovoi, who has saved his wife from arrest and prison, Lyubov Yarovaya is instrumental in the capture of her husband at the end of the play, and he is led off to be executed.

The quality of *Lyubov Yarovaya* is none too high. It is essentially a propaganda play, and its plot and structure are naïve and artificial. Trenëv distinguished himself over other early Soviet dramatists, however, in that he endows most of his characters—including the transients—with a pithy way of speaking that manages to typify them. A second value of Trenëv's play is that his Lieutenant Mikhail Yaravoi, a serious and fanatical enemy of the Soviet regime, is presented in depth. A third —and perhaps the most important—value of the play lies in its comic characters.

When *Lyubov Yarovaya* appeared, the Bolshevik critics found many weaknesses in it. They discerned chaos in the action, the piling up of "crowd scenes," and a "steel and concrete scheme" for Commissar

Koshkin, the chief of the Communists. Trenëv himself found his play quite weak. He wrote that when he "measured" what he had written for the stage, he despaired; it responded so little to the conventions of the theater and the demands of the stage. "This is a poem, a story, or anything else you like—but it is not a play." [25] The dramatist states that he tried "to give first of all the political and social background, and against this and organically dependent upon it, the history of the drama, of heroine and hero." He therefore created a survey and not a drama.[26]

Armored Train 14–69 by Vsevolod Ivanov was one of the most outstanding Soviet dramas to deal with the Civil War. The action of the play begins in a Russian town on the Pacific Ocean. The White Guardsmen are trickling back into it under pressure from the Red Army in Siberia. Captain Nezelasov's armored train is the last detachment covering against the Bolsheviks and partisans advancing from the West. It is also the only means for breaking through to the Japanese and American units that the partisans have cut off and surrounded in the *taiga*.

In fleeing from the prison of the coastal town, Peklevanov, a devoted Bolshevik, has succeeded in winning Nikita Egorych Vershinin, a hunter, over to his side. Vershinin is most influential among the rural population, and he is a strong and loyal man. His going over to the Bolsheviks is anticipated when he receives the news in town that the Japanese have burned his village and cremated his two children in it.

Vershinin becomes a partisan leader in the *taiga*. He gathers countless peasants and they undertake to capture Armored Train 14–69 and to use it in moving against the final stronghold of the Whites. This is the coastal town in which Peklevanov is preparing for a revolt by the workers in order to push both the Whites and the foreign interventionists into the ocean.

One of the best scenes in the play takes place on a railroad embankment along which Captain Nezelasov's armored train must pass. Vershinin and his partisans must take the armored train "alive" and without destroying the rails (there is no time and no way to repair them). They must not damage the train either, because they need it to attack the town. In order to stop the train, the partisans decided that one of them must lie on the rails and pretend to be dead. The "old regime" engineer must stop his train in accordance with the railroad manual and remove the corpse from the rails. But if the engineer does not notice the man lying there, it would cost the volunteer his life. After lengthy arguments among the many who wish to sacrifice their lives, the palm is awarded to Sin Bin-u, a Chinese, for, in Vershinin's words: "The Chinese wants to show his importance to Russia. . . . He wants to show his great spirit." The "old regime" engineer actually does stop the train, for which his reward is a bullet in his head. The engineer was the only White who knew how to drive a locomotive. After a seventy-two hour battle, the White soldiers break down from exhaustion. The partisans succeed in capturing the armored train and they find a polytechnical student capable of replacing the dead engineer.

Peklevanov has heard nothing from Vershinin, but he believes in him and starts a revolt. At the very beginning of the uprising, Peklevanov is shot by a Japanese spy. The armored train, however, forces its way into the town together with the partisans and they continue Peklevanov's work victoriously. They push forward to storm the fortress with the corpse of their Bolshevik leader replacing the red flag on the cow-catcher.

The three main characters in the play are Vershinin, Peklevanov, and Nezelasov. Ivanov depicts them skillfully and in detail, which contrasts with the other Civil War plays of the period. Vershinin is thickset and illiterate, but he is a wise muzhik of the *taiga* who develops into a leader of the partisan movement. Peklevanov is a round-shouldered and bespectacled intellectual, a wise Party member, and a brilliant organizer of rebellion. Captain Nezelasov is a cocaine addict, broken and lacerated inside—the "last of the White Guardsmen."

Armored Train 14–69 was the Moscow Art Theater's first production of a strictly Soviet topic. It was presented in 1927 to celebrate the tenth anniversary of the Soviet regime, and it marked a turning point in the history of the Moscow Art Theater. Its première began the "Sovietization" of that Theater and Stanislavsky's acceptance of the existing government.

The Moscow Art Theater worked over Ivanov's play and humanized it. The author was made to change much that was false and conventional. Ivanov was completely indebted to the Moscow Art Theater and to its gifted actor, N. Khmelëv, for dissociating Peklevanov from the stereotyped "iron Party-members." Khmelev said:

Every tendency to declamation was removed from the character. Peklevanov appeared on the stage unpretentiously, spoke in a low voice, was nearsighted, and seemed odd, but beyond his outer unsociability, there were concentration, a good mind, and a gentle spirit. All this seemed much more convincing than theatrical heroism, pathos, and declamation.[27]

All the Soviet dramatic critics were enthusiastic about the scene in which Vaska Okorok, a partisan, "propagandizes" a captured American soldier. The scene was naïve, and the raptures of the critics can be explained only by the fact that this was the first mention of Lenin's name on the Soviet stage. Okorok does not know a single word of English, and the American does not know a word of Russian. Yet, the partisan succeeds in thoroughly converting the American in a scene that contains neither truth nor imagination:

Okorok (Suddenly waves his arms happily, beckons the American towards him, and yells right in his face): Hey, you, fellow! Listen . . . Le-nin . . . Lenin . . .
American: Lenin. . . . Hurrah!
Okorok (Strikes his own chest): We, you bum, we're the Soviet republic.
American: Republic. . . . Hurrah!

This scene takes place on the roof of a church, and Okorok fetches out of the church building an icon of "Abraham bringing Isaac to be Sacrificed," which he uses to illustrate this conversation:

Okorok: Listen. This one here, with the knife—that's a bourgeois. And this one here, this young fellow lying tied to the logs—that's the proletariat. Savvy? Proletariat. . . .
American: Proletariat? I am worker from Detroit automobile works. Worker. . . . I . . . worker . . . automobile!

And a moment later, the American is already a Bolshevik and cries out in pristine Russian: "Down with imperialism."

The Soviet dramatic critics praised *Armored Train 14–69* because it showed a partisan leader who was "simultaneously a leader and an ordinary muzhik. . . . He does not exactly lead, but merely personifies the will of the entire mass as it pushes forward." [28] Another reason for approving the drama was that Peklevanov was a "truthful and convincing figure of a Bolshevik." He was wise, modest, and unwavering. As Khmelev remarked about his own enactment of the role, he tried to endow Peklevanov with a number of traits that had been borrowed from Lenin.

However not all critics praised Ivanov's play. Some Communist critics found no trace of revolution in it. But not a single Soviet critic dared to point out its main weakness—the false picture of the Whites. They were shown as stupid, whining, and nonsensical—constantly bewailing their fate and exhibiting their spiritual impurities.

We now come, however, to a unique work of the Soviet drama, a play that made a heroic attempt to show White Guardsmen objectively, with verisimilitude, and as living human beings. This is Mikhail Bulgakov's *Dni Turbinykh* ("The Days of the Turbins"),[29] a play that was most severely criticized by the Bolshevik press and about which the most prolonged debates were held.

Bulgakov was slandered as a White Guardsman and an "anti-Soviet dramatist." He was put under strict "surveillance" and was baited by the Soviet press to his dying day. What was he guilty of? He was by no means a "White Guardsman" or a "monarchist" in his work. His play was based on a strictly Soviet attitude toward the White movement—he considered it condemned to death and forced to yield to the Soviets. Purely Soviet also was Bulgakov's farcical and satirical treatment of the Hetman Skoropadsky, his milieu, the Germans von Stratt and von Dust, the adherents of Petliura, and the leadership of the White movement. Bulgakov even gave a purely Soviet ending to the play: Captain Myshlayevsky is ready to serve the Bolsheviks and announces: "In front are the Red Guardsmen, like a wall; to our rear are the speculators and every kind of riffraff with the Hetman; and in between am I. Your humble servant. I am fed up with being used like dung to fill in ice holes. Let them [the Bolsheviks] mobilize me! At least I know that I shall be serving in the Russian Army."

Bulgakov was the first and last Soviet dramatist who was honest and courageous enough not to depict the White Guardsmen as animals in uniform, the way they were shown in the other plays dealing with the Civil War. He showed them as living Russians, with their contradictions, their awareness that they were in a blind alley, their decay, their death —and their brightly human side as well.

In the fate of the Turbin family and their friends, Bulgakov depicted the terrible collapse that took place during the first years of the Revolution. Kiev was occupied by the Germans, whose bayonets created a "Ukrainian state" with Hetman Skoropadsky on the throne. The play is the tragedy of the Russian officers who joined the Hetman to stave off approaching anarchy and civil war. The revolution in Germany during 1918 forced the Germans to abandon the Ukraine. The Hetman runs off with them because he is not strong enough to maintain his regime without their support, for the peasantry is following the Ukrainian nationalist Petliura. The Russian officers, cadets, and secondary-school volunteers are betrayed and left to the mercies of Petliura's forces. Bulgakov uses their resistance and struggle, which is predestined to fail, in order to show the bright and dark aspects of the people in the White movement.

Colonel Alexei Turbin of the Guards is the oldest son, a man with an enormous desire to fight and one who stays at his post although he sees the inevitability of his death. Only at the gates of death itself does he realize that he has followed the wrong course. Then, there are Captain Myshlayevsky, a talkative scapegrace, and Lieutenant Shirvinsky of the Guards. Shirvinsky is a poseur and a "nice little guardsman," but battle proves him to be a brilliant Russian officer. There is Nikolka Turbin, a cadet yesterday and soldier in the White Army today; he is romantically and passionately seeking battle, although he does not understand what he is fighting for. Let us not forget Captain Talberg, the husband of Elena Turbina; he is a timeserver, a coward alien to the Russian land, and he easily throws over both wife and country to flee with the German army of occupation.

The Soviet dramatic critics accused *The Days of the Turbins* of all the mortal sins, including even Russian chauvinism. After all Petliura's adherents were painted in blacker colors than were the White Guardsmen.[30] Bulgakov was greatly libeled by the Marxist critics. They called him an "artist expressing the right-wing bourgeoisie" and the "bard of counterrevolution."

The production of *The Days of the Turbins* at the Moscow Art Theater was a great event in the theater life of the capital. There was a long line of Muscovites at the ticket window in the evenings. That part of Russian society whom the Bolsheviks had termed "former people" made their pilgrimage to the Moscow Art Theater. These were people who had lost their relatives in the Civil War and in the Terror. Some of them had themselves served in the White Army, and they included people whose relatives had gone into exile with the Whites. Such individuals hoped that this production heralded a peace between the Soviet regime and its enemies and an end to the terror of new repressive measures. They filled the auditorium of the Theater, eager to recognize with love and sadness the sufferings of individuals whom they held dear. Very often, after the scene with the White soldiers in the secondary school, some people in the audience would grow hysterical; the women would bewail their sons and husbands and some fainted, and the ushers would carry them out to the snow in the theater courtyard.

These were not playgoers but palmers, and their pilgrimage was to see a stirring miracle in a land of terror and "class hatred." For many years the stained misanthropy of Bolshevik propaganda had covered the "White bandits"; now, they suddenly turned up—alive and wonderful, erring and terrible, but yet fine Russian people. One could make a pilgrimage to this presentation, for it was filled with the miracle of Christian forgiveness; it called for extending one's hand to the defeated enemy of yesterday.[31]

With Bulgakov's *The Days of the Turbins,* something unusual took place that was quite typical of Stalin's dictatorship. According to the official version of Lunacharsky, the play was permitted through an error of' the repertorial committee, after which the Moscow Art Theater prepared the presentation. Then, the entire repertorial committee saw a closed preview of the production and became terror-stricken; they categorically forbade it. But the Theater had spent much money on it, and the oversight had been on the part of the repertorial committee. Hence, the People's Commissar of Enlightenment insisted that the ban be removed.[32] But this version is really false. Stanislavsky reacted to the ban on the play by the repertorial committee by complaining to Stalin, who personally ordered the ban to be lifted. Later, difficulties again arose over whether to restore the play to the repertory of the Moscow Art Theater, and Stalin expressed himself approximately thus: "And why must it be forbidden? I do not see anything bad in your playing *The Days of the Turbins.* The play shows an intelligent and powerful enemy. That is good. We must show the enemy as he is." [33]

This later craving of Stalin's to see an "intelligent and powerful enemy" on the stage seems highly dubious. What this really was was a *beau geste* by Stalin to win over the most important of the Russian theaters, with their world-wide reputation. Stalin was not wrong in his calculations. Stanislavsky was suborned, and during the following year the Moscow Art Theater staged *Armored Train 14–69.* Instead of the justification for the White Army that was found in *The Days of the Turbins,* Stanislavsky demanded that Ivanov's play show the White officer, Captain Nezelasov, as a "cruel and intelligent enemy. He cost Russia hundreds of thousands of lives." [34]

Stanislavsky's treatment of a number of roles in *Armored Train 14–69* was based on Soviet preconceptions and directly contradicted his own System. For the first time, he convinced the actress who played Varia, a White sympathizer, that she had to hate the character whom she was depicting: "You are our young actress and a Soviet artist. . . . Do not become infatuated [with Varia], but rather learn to hate her. You should want the audience to grow indignant at such an empty-headed person." [35] The strictly Soviet treatment of *Armored Train 14–69* by the Moscow Art Theater led the playgoers of the time to say that the Theater was expressing its loyalty and asking forgiveness for *The Days of the Turbins*. The real state of affairs was not so simple, however. By compromising in part, the Moscow Art Theater wished to earn the right of bringing the truth to a different part of its repertory.

DOMESTIC THEMES

Many plays during the first decade of the Soviet regime dealt with the construction of the Bolshevik state in rural districts. The chief enemies of the regime were not the former dignitaries, the landed proprietors, or the capitalists, because for the most part such people had been "liquidated" by the Cheka. They were not the outstanding Russian intellectuals because the old intelligentsia had been suppressed, were under constant police surveillance, or had been "reworked" and "re-educated" by the Bolsheviks. They were not the "Nepmen" because they were always tightly enmeshed by taxes. The most dangerous domestic foe of Bolshevism was the peasantry, and so it remained for a number of years. The peasants were not passive; they struggled stubbornly and mightily against Bolshevism. Their uprisings were numerous, and they terrorized the rural henchmen of the Soviet government. Later, millions of them participated in a heroic and unequal struggle against collectivization.

Bolshevism could not permit the truth about the countryside to be told in the Soviet theater because it would be devastating. It would have shown that the great majority of the people in the huge land—the peasants—was opposed to the Soviet regime. Hence, the very first plays devoted to the subject set the pattern of deliberately falsifying reality. The Communist Party issued a "social command." Change the peasants' stubborn resistance to the Soviet regime into a struggle with the "kulaks" alone. Make them seem like battening spiders. Show them as the confirmed enemies of the poor and middle farmers. Use these biased plays to make believe that most peasants are in favor of the Soviet government, with its wise and incredibly humane commissars and "activists."

The first important play to deal with the countryside was L. Seifulina's *Virineya,* which the Vakhtangov Theater staged in Moscow during 1925. The action of the play begins during the February Revolution, and it attempts to show that most of the peasants were Bolsheviks even before the upheaval of the following October. Virineya, the heroine of the play, becomes the leader of the rural poor and is sympathetic to the Soviet regime in the countryside. Seifulina has her soldiers, together with the solidly pro-Revolutionary young people of the countryside, carry out a "rural revolution."

The authoress read her play to a number of directors and producers in Moscow, most of whom considered it crude propaganda. After its production, however, it was awarded something greater than a prize or medal. Stalin saw the play and deigned to write the following historical words in a book containing reviews of the Vakhtangov Theater's work: "In my opinion, the play is a piece of life that is true to living life. . . . On the whole, it is good—even first-rate." [36]

The Vakhtangov Theater also presented the second outstanding play on a peasant subject. This was Leonid Leonov's *Barsuki* ("The Badgers"), which was put on in 1927. *The Badgers* portrays the clash between two forces: the conscious will of the revolutionary proletariat, and the petty-bourgeois and anarchistic element of the peasant masses. B. Zakhava, who directed it, wrote:

On one side, we have the city, the proletariat, reason, organization, a constructive struggle to build a socialist society, Communism, and a better future for all mankind. On the other side, we have petty private interests with instinct instead of reason, chaos instead of organization, and personal interests instead of the universal good of the toilers.[37]

One of the central figures in the play is Semën, a leader of the peasant movement. He is contrasted with Paul, his brother, who incarnates the organizing will of the Communist Party. Paul is a "monolithic character." His brother, Semën, is a split personality with a dual psychology that seemed to typify the entire peasantry, for the peasants both toil and own private property.[38] After the shedding of blood, Semën realizes his fatal error in rebelling for the interests of people who are different. He goes to his brother and surrenders to the Soviet punitive organs. The play asserted a legend that the Bolsheviks needed. This was the inevitability and the historically predestined complete capitulation of the "petty bourgeois" element within the peasantry to the dictatorship of the proletariat.

There were many plays produced between 1917 and 1927 that dealt with domestic topics and Soviet-created relationships between the individual and the state. Among them were: Nikolai Erdman's *Mandat* ("The Warrant," 1925); Boris S. Romashev's *Konets Krivoryliska* ("The End of Krivorylisk," 1926); Alexei Faiko's *Evgraf—iskatel' prikliuchenii* ("Evgraf the Adventure-Seeker," 1926); Mikhail Bulgakov's *Zoikina kvartira* ("Zoika's Apartment," 1926); and Vladimir Bill-Belotserkovsky's *Shtil'* ("Calm," 1927).

Romashev pretentiously termed *The End of Krivorylisk* a "satirical melodrama." He presented a portrait gallery of "villains," "philistines," and outdated opponents of the Soviet regime, and his villains were more alive and convincing than his heroes both in the text and in the presentation. The "former people" eclipsed the hothouse "heroes" of Soviet life.

Evgraf the Adventure-Seeker was the first link in a long chain of Soviet plays that dealt with the petty-bourgeois intellectuals during the Bolshevik Revolution and under the Soviet state. This group of plays was always reviewed most scathingly by Bolshevik critics. They dealt with different aspects of the same question: the right of the individual to approach the Bolshevik Revolution and the "building of Communism" in his own way. This theme is present in all Soviet drama even if carefully masked under a loyalty to the Soviet regime. "The right to dream" contained a muted appeal by the authors to Bolshevism not to stifle the personality completely but to leave it some safety valve, even if only a few last extraterritorial blobs of spiritual freedom.

Evgraf is in love, but not so much with Betty—the acrobatic dancer —as with the enigmatic world of a "beautiful life" that she represents (or that exists in his own imagination). This world has nothing in common with the drab boredom inspired by the government in Soviet daily life. The play was put on by the Second Moscow Art Theater. It called for Soviet life to find room for the Evgrafs, not to punish them or to consider them enemies merely because Soviet reality did not satisfy them. The Evgrafs dreamed, raved, and sought things that—ridiculous and pitiful though they might be—were "different" and outside the strict limits of the proletarian dictatorship and the iron formulas of Marxism. The Soviet critics damned the play.

Bill-Belotserkovsky's *Calm* treats of those who had been heroes in the harsh times of War Communism. These people accepted the "NEP" with difficulty and endured inner struggles. The restoration of "free trade," merchants, and speculators impressed them as surrender and as treason to the October Revolution for which they had shed their blood. The hero of *Calm* had also appeared in *Storm;* this was the "pal" —the bellicose, one-legged sailor in the Red Guards. The NEP makes him "in practical terms, heartsick." Gradually, however, under coercion from the Communist author (who is "loyal to the general Party Line"), the "pal" becomes reconciled and even admits that the "calm" of reconstructing agriculture makes him ill. "At sea, a calm means that one storm is over; prepare for another."

Zoika's Apartment was staged by the Vakhtangov Theater and provoked a certain tempest among the Soviet critics. They declared that the bourgeoisie will make fun of all our shortcomings by attending Bulgakov's play. The critics blasted the play so completely that it was soon withdrawn. The author's intentions were noble; he wanted to satirize the Soviet philistines who were becoming evident, along with the many speculators, adventurers, and other wretches. After *The Days of the Turbins,* every new play by Bulgakov was considered to be a counterrevolutionary conspiracy masked by the forms of the theater.

Nikolai Erdman's *The Warrant* was given at Meyerhold's Theater in 1925. This play is a genuine masterpiece, similar in theme to *Zoika's Apartment,* but towering above all the other plays of the period.

The language of *The Warrant* is harshly comic, and this quality—like part of its plot—makes it reminiscent of Gogol's *Inspector-General.* Its hero is a rogue and philistine named Guliachkin, a Soviet version of Gogol's Khlestakov. He spreads a rumor among certain Moscow burghers and "former people" that he has a "warrant" enabling him to do anything and to obtain everything. A terrible array of "former people" clings to Guliachkin. They give him their daughters to wed and rally around him to rebel against the Soviet regime. They want to restore the good life, with its dancing to band music. All kinds of misfits hide in the houses of the district. Like Khlestakov, Guliachkin gets carried away by his own lies and almost goes so far as to say, while he is in his cups, that the Politburo itself trembles before him. At the climax of the wedding dance held to celebrate Guliachkin's marriage, the band is tooting away. After the toasts, just as if they and their waiterlike tailcoats had come from an exhibit, the "former people" among the guests lose their senses because of the phantoms that they envision in the future. In honor of the "reigning people," they fawningly kiss the bride's dress. For them, she is the hallowed spouse of the one who will bring them the Resurrection. The whole bubble bursts when Guliachkin's warrant turns out to be a slip of paper from a Soviet office that is completely worthless.

In form and in theme, *The Warrant* took place on two levels. On the one hand, it maliciously satirized the revolt of the philistines against the Revolution. Its sharpness thus seemed to be directed against the "former people" and covert philistines waiting behind their muslin curtains, left-overs from the past. On the other hand, however, it was directed against the Soviet regime. It showed that every day brought more scoundrels with "warrants" for the "successful construction of socialism." Hence, the cringing terror before papers bearing the government seal and the Soviet bureaucracy's growing stronger from day to day. The blow against these people ricocheted against the Soviet regime. The Soviet philistines, the petty officials of the Party and of the trade unions, supported this set-up fanatically and with the most obtuse, stupid, and terrible power. They were the victors. They later became the legislators of the nightmarish Soviet lack of taste in everything and solidly supported Stalin's dictatorship. They were the most important cog in the Soviet bureaucratic machine.

Erdman's talent was enormous. Even Gorky termed this keen and unsparing satirist "our new Gogol" and "our new Shchedrin." He was the first-born of the Soviet theater, but he was not fated to find room for himself under Stalin's dictatorship. His uncompromising satire was too dangerous for the "enthronement of universal silence." His second play, *Samoubiitsa* ("The Suicide"), continued his treatment of "former people" in Soviet society. This work, however, was not produced and, shortly afterwards, the author himself was exiled and disappeared from Soviet literature for a long time.

FOREIGN THEMES

The first decade also saw one last kind of play—counterfeit dramas about "the decadent and perishing capitalist West." This category grew from year to year. There were two circumstances which enabled false-hoods about life abroad to be depicted successfully and in accordance with the stereotypes and slogans of the Communist Party. First of all, Soviet dramatists found it easier to strike bargains with their consciences in dealing with the nonexistent terrors in foreign countries than in falsifying what both they and their audiences saw daily. The older generation of dramatists had once been linked to the "Scythian" theory of Alexander Blok, which had condemned bourgeois civilization to inevitable decay, and so they could follow this trend easily. The younger generation of Soviet playwrights had never known anything about the real West aside from the official falsehoods printed in the Soviet press, and so they could swim with the current even more easily. There were also many non-Communist literary men who were democratically inclined but who did not sympathize with capitalism at all. Secondly, the Soviet masses had been fenced off from the rest of the world by a strong "Chinese wall" that had come into existence after 1917. They had never seen the West with their own eyes. The country did not have a single organ to transmit objective information about events abroad. For years, Russians had been constantly given only biased items sifted from the gloomy facts about life in the rest of the world. People who could read only the Soviet governmental press found it still easier to believe the falsehoods of the dramatists.

The truth about how toilers lived outside the realm of Bolshevism would have made any Soviet person realize the hungry, beggarly, and miserable level upon which the "construction of socialism" was taking place. It would have instantly and permanently destroyed the myth about "world revolution" and the idea that the toilers of the West dreamed day and night of accomplishing at home what the Bolsheviks had done in Russia during October of 1917. Soviet people would have immediately lost the pathetic belief which the Bolsheviks were continually warming over for all the workers. This was the idea that the proletariat of the entire world loved them and was wholeheartedly on their side. The truth about the West would have been a mortal danger to the rank-and-file Communists as well. They would have seen that "damned, rotten, and perishing capitalism" had no wish to rot away and was not preparing either to putrefy or to perish despite the forecasts of Marx, Engels, and Lenin. They would have seen that the "classic authors of Marxism" were not far-sighted politicians and were even less prophets. The great majority of the opposition within the Communist Party itself was composed of people who had known and seen the real West. This also shows how extremely dangerous an objective knowledge of it was to Party members.

There were several responses to the command for counterfeiting the world beyond the Communist frontiers. These included: *Trest D. E.* ("The Give-Us-Europe Trust") by M. Podgayetsky, which was based on Ehrenburg's novel *Daësh Evropu!* ("Give Us Europe!"); Faiko's *Uchitel' Bubus* ("Bubus the Teacher"), and *Rychi Kitai* ("Roar, China") by Sergei Tretyakov, the poet.

The Give-Us-Europe Trust shows Europe perishing and transformed into a desert because of a conspiracy by predatory American capitalists. *Bubus the Teacher* showed the fate of an honest man in an eastern European hotbed of capitalism. *Roar, China* showed the coolies, hungry and tortured by exploitation, as innocent and holy victims of capitalism. Alongside them, it gave terrifying caricatures of British "imperialist vampires."

Such plays and Faiko's *Ozera Liul'* ("The Lakes of Liul") began the "All-Soviet competition" of dramatists and directors to see who could show the "decomposition of the bourgeoisie" in its most loathsome form. *The Lakes of Liul* appeared some years later, and was staged by Meyerhold at the Theater of the Revolution in Moscow. The bourgeoisie was rotting and decomposing in *The Give-Us-Europe Trust;* it was depicted as a lifeless puppet, writhing in a "dance of death" to the howling of Negro jazz. *The Lakes of Liul* was especially crude and false. It depicted two worlds: the enslaved proletariat and impotent capitalism which was drowning in a sea of liquor and lechery. Both *The Give-Us-Europe Trust* and *Bubus the Teacher* had the same propaganda ending—the Red Army appears in the finale to free the world from decay and the fox trot. Tretyakov's *Roar, China* presented the standard lies about "the struggle of the oppressed peoples against colonial imperialism" that have not changed from that day to this. A comparison between the cruel behavior of the English and the Americans to the Chinese in *Roar, China* with the falsehoods in the dramas about bestial Americans in Korea during 1952 shows that the stereotype worked out in the 1930s is clearly made of cast-iron.

PUBLIC AND CRITICAL RESPONSE

The Soviet theaters and the Soviet audience of the first decade must be given their due—they stubbornly resisted the dissemination of counterfeit dramas on the stage. At the 1927 session on theater questions called by the Central Committee of the CPSU, the People's Commissar of Enlightenment complained about it to Party members:

Some people are saying that the plays that our repertorial committee passes are sometimes not accepted by the theaters themselves. . . . Of course, no theater will say: "We do not want to take your play because we find it revolutionary." A loyal theater will say: "We are not accepting it because it is not artistic." The theaters can be hypocritical about it.[39]

Litovsky, the Communist critic, spoke even more clearly at the same meeting. The theaters, he said "are obviously not accepting our revolutionary playwrights. Anything which smacks of the class struggle is not accepted." [40] R. Pelshe, the head of the Political Enlightenment Division of the People's Commissariat of Enlightenment, shed even more light on this resistance;

I have a complete portfolio of complaints made by our revolutionary playwrights . . . about the theater directors. They are complaining that many of the theaters in Moscow are not staging their plays despite the fact that they have not only been found ideologically useful, but are even sufficiently artistic. Some plays have been reviewed by the official organs or by individual Communist authorities on the theater arts, but nevertheless many of them have not been produced in the city of Moscow. What is the reason? . . . To a large extent, it is a certain desire by the large theaters not to stage works whose class nature is expressed clearly.[41]

The directors of the resisting theaters were, of course, repeatedly summoned to the People's Commissariat of Enlightenment and were finally presented with an ultimatum: The theater which you, Comrade Director, are in charge of is a state theater. It is maintained completely by the Soviet regime, and you will therefore take pains to stage plays in it that propagandize for the regime which gives you your subsistence.

The theaters capitulated and staged "ideologically useful" plays, plays which falsified according to the formulas of the Party. Even after this, however, Soviet plays were subjected to a plebiscite. The voters were not delegates, but ordinary playgoers who bought tickets at the box-offices. There was reason for the then current expression that "the playgoer votes with his ruble." As a result of this "plebiscite," presentations of "ideologically useful" dramas played to empty houses and the theaters suffered deficits.[42] The state pressured the theaters to put on Communist propaganda, but that propaganda affected the national treasury because enormous sums were needed to cover the deficits of the theaters.[43]

The provinces were far removed from the surveillance of the Repertorial Committee and the People's Commissariat of Enlightenment. There, the position of Soviet plays was even worse. Most of the provincial theaters "paid their own way," and they either received no financial support from the state or were allotted some niggardly stipend by the local Soviets. An empty auditorium in such places would mean bankruptcy and closure. The Bolsheviks kept harping on the theme that the provinces played only "box-office" plays.

The birth of an authentically Soviet drama was thus accompanied by a resistance to it. This resistance was shown in the somber and terrible emptiness of the auditoriums. And this plebiscite was more secret than any ballot. Playgoers simply did not buy tickets, and no one could make them open their purses to throw money away on counterfeit and propagandistic drivel.

The Bolshevik state then resorted to something completely unprecedented. It created an institute of "organized playgoers." Tickets to Soviet plays were purchased by the cultural and educational sections of the trade unions at the plants and were given away to the workers gratis. And, of course, there are people willing to see anything "for nothing." Essentially, the "organization of working playgoers" indicated that the sowing of falsehood on the stage had broken down completely. The state was transferring its money from one pocket to the other.

Even the system of organizing the working playgoers, however, soon ran into a dead end. The free tickets to propaganda plays did not enjoy any special success, and the workers began to demand with increasing persistence that tickets to the classics, the operas, the operettas, and so on also be distributed. The Soviet regime could not do this.[44]

These were the strained and complex circumstances that accompanied the birth of Soviet drama. On the one hand, it was under constant pressure to fulfill the "social command" given by the Department of Agitation and Propaganda, the entire press, and the critics. On the other hand, the theaters and the audiences put pressure on it with all their might. The people wanted to be spared the sorry sight of spectacles inspired by the Communist Party.

CHAPTER VII

HEYDAY

THE GREAT PERIOD OF INNOVATION and creativity in the Soviet theater began approximately in 1921 and lasted until about 1929 or 1930. It was unparalleled in the history of the international stage. Its lavishness and luxury were almost fabulous, and its schools and techniques not only enriched the Soviet theater alone but benefited the theaters of many other peoples as well. It was almost a miracle that such activity could take place amidst hunger, typhus, poverty, and total destruction, and right after a fratricidal civil war.

If we try to explain this miracle by historical and social causes, we must bear a number of things in mind. Most of those active within the theater were convinced that the Revolution had begun to construct a completely new society, which would need a completely new theater. Then, too, the bold methods of revolution, which had destroyed the old social structure and were constructing the new, were transferred to art. Masses of people came into the auditorium for the first time, and their passionate love for drama nourished the inner enthusiasm of the theater experts. There was joy over the fact that the sinful bloodletting was over in the land. There was hope that Lenin's NEP would lead the country from hunger and poverty to normal economic conditions, abundance, and prosperity. Finally, there were material conditions that the other theaters in the world did not possess. Almost all the Russian theaters were subsidized by the state and hence had no sword of Damocles hanging over their box-offices. They could experiment without fear of bankruptcy or even deficits.

The great masterpieces of the Soviet theater innovators had nothing in common with Soviet subjects, however. This also applies to the best works of the Soviet drama, as we have seen. As a rule, the great masters of the Soviet theater chose either the classics or Western European dramas for their epoch-making reforms. These included: *Le Cocu magnifique* by Fernand Crommelynck, *Turandot* by Carlo Gozzi, *Phèdre* by Racine, *Adrienne Lecouvreur* by Eugene Scribe and Ernest Legouvé,

Hamlet and *Romeo and Juliet* by Shakespeare, *Le Mariage de Figaro* by Beaumarchais, *Princess Brambilla* by E. T. A. Hoffmann, *Giroflé-Girofla* by A. C. Lecocq, *Erik XIV* by August Strindberg, various plays by George Bernard Shaw and Eugene O'Neill, and such Russian classics as *The Forest, The Storm,* and *A Burning Heart* by Ostrovsky, *The Inspector-General* by Gogol, and *Woe from Wit* by Griboyedov. Only three plays on Soviet themes can be added to this distinguished list, but even they did not treat things "in Soviet style"—Nikolai Erdman's *The Warrant,* Mikhail Bulgakov's *The Days of the Turbins,* and Vladimir Mayakovsky's *The Bug.*

This suggests that any outstanding Soviet director could show his talent and imagination in all their fullness only when he treated plays that were remote from the aims of Communist propaganda. Although directors staged non-Soviet plays with Soviet money, they regarded the subsidies as money from the people and not from the Communist Department of Agitation and Propaganda. Such an outlook could have taken place only in the days when the experts still chose their plays and their experiments in freedom and the theaters still had some freedom of choice.

The Soviet theater flourished in the years when a little freedom of thought still existed (which is no mere coincidence). This period began under Lenin and continued through the period of NEP. During those years even Mensheviks, anarchists, leftist Socialist Revolutionaries, and the opposition within the Communist Party could still defend their views in the press. Stalin's dictatorship, however, came along to pump the spirit of freedom out of the country, and the Soviet theater faded correspondingly.

We shall sketch in brief the outstanding theatrical reforms during the flourishing of the Soviet theater. We have grouped the productions according to the leading theaters and have arranged these last according to their contributions to innovation within the theater. In the vanguard of all the reforms during this wonderful period was, of course, Meyerhold's Theater.

MEYERHOLD'S THEATER

Vsevolod Meyerhold's Theater was the Soviet theater that launched the period of *Sturm und Drang.*[1] Its first experimental work was its production of Crommelynck's *Le Cocu magnifique,* the première of which was

pril 15, 1922. Meyerhold's forms and devices in this production exer-
:ed a profound and prolonged influence on both the Soviet and non-
·viet European theaters. He asserted two completely new ideas in the
:eater: constructivism and biomechanics.

How could Crommelynck's "tragic farce" have attracted Meyerhold?
ie plot shows that Bruno, the miller, was jealous of his wife, Stella.
iis scarcely harmonizes with the end of the Civil War and the "October
the Theater" programs that Meyerhold headed. There was not even a
ice of the "social conflicts" so dear to the hearts of Marxists. Ivan
ksenov's translation was painful and inaccurate, and it often slid over
to "transsense" language. The only feature of the play drawing the pre-
evolutionary—but not the post-Revolutionary—Meyerhold was that
alousy was reduced to an absurdity.[2]

Basically, Crommelynck's tragic farce was an abstract orchestral score
at merely furnished a pretext for the extremely abstract treatment given
by Meyerhold. In *Le Cocu magnifique* he dealt a most merciless and
·structive blow to the old "intimate" theater with its threadbare devices
ıd its handling of the stage like a box-camera. The enormous portal of
ιe Zon theater stage was laid bare. The curtain, the coulisses, the
·rnices in front of the soffits, the soffits themselves, and even the fly
ιlleries were stripped completely. There was a gloomy haze on the
ιormous stage, beyond which rose unplastered brick walls. Radiators
·r central heating hung in the heights of the fly galleries.

Meyerhold then removed all the machinery for creating scenic illusions.
·e had the actor stand alone on the stage, with no make-up, no wig, and
ɔ colored finery on his costumes. He was starting all over again. It was
ke the first day of creation. No one tried to hide the spotlights from the
ıblic or to pass them off as "sunlight" or "moonlight." Babanova,
ynsky, and Zaichikov enacted Crommelynck's tragic farce without a
rop of the "tragic." They used the gay mockery of mischievous come-
ians and circuslike devices.

This was Meyerhold's most telling blow against "theatricality" and the
ıost "leftist" point in his work. It marked the birth of constructivism
·ithin the Russian theater. It was the only time in his career that he came
lose to denying the magic of the theater completely. The experiment
:eked of the laboratory. It resembled an anatomic theater containing
nly the skeleton of the living person. He destroyed all the ingredients
f the theater, save only the actor—its final and indestructible nucleus.

He wanted to say that almost everything else in the theater could
removed or replaced, but if the actor remains on the bare stage
greatness of the theater stays with him.

The constructivism that Meyerhold discovered in this presentati
merely continued the stripping of the illusory flesh and sinews from
skeleton of the theater. The skin of illusion was removed from the déc
and only the ribs—the skeleton of the technical construction—remain
There were two stands on the stage, each as tall as a one-storied hou
They were connected by a board which also ran down to the stage flo
There were two staircases and a ramp to glide down along. Beyond
stands were the skeletons of stage properties, from which the can
coverings had been removed. One of the stands had turnstiles above a
below, while a number of crossbeams on the other stand created windo
The driving wheels of the mill were placed beyond the construction, a
the enormous disk was also utilitarian rather than decorative. The s
function of the disk was to start turning furiously when the madness
the jealous Bruno began to fume. CR-MM-L-NCK was written in lar
white, Latin letters on the disk so that the public would notice
rotation. The disk itself and the shafts supporting it lacked the lett
"O," "E," and "Y" to complete the playwright's name.

Such was the external appearance of the first "machine for acting"
the Russian theater. This was the abstract construction that the magic
acting virtuosity transformed into the miller's house. One and the sa
place beneath the stand represented a courtyard where the furiou
jealous peasant women want to square accounts with Stella, a dining ro
in which guests are gathering, and an office in which Bruno dictates
verses to Estrugo. One spotlighted flower in Stella's hands furnished
sole stage property for the entire production; it sufficed, however, to tu
the bare platform into a terrace that was filled with flowers and bathed
the morning sun. The production was one of Meyerhold's most power
and it revived the pure art of acting on the stage.

Meyerhold had made motion, gesture, and pantomime omnipotent
the theater. His *Le Cocu magnifique* was the first practical realization
a grand scale of the theories and plans that had matured within h
back in the days of "Dr. Dapertutto's" Studio. These ideas dealt w
the supremacy of motion over language and illusion. There is a dir
connection between *Le Cocu magnifique* and all of Meyerhold's p

evolutionary experiments at Interlude House and "Dr. Dapertutto's
studio.

The "Leftist Front" Futurists considered Meyerhold's work on *Le
Cocu magnifique* a mere continuation of their own ideas about "productionalism in art" and "constructivism in painting." [3] They asserted:

In the theater, constructivism united constructive furnishings—such as the
decor, the props, and the costumes—designed to show things themselves, or at
least their models, with "constructive" gestures, motions, and pantomimes.
This last was the biomechanics of Vsevolod Meyerhold; the actors were organized according to rhythms. [4]

The reference to "biomechanics" in the quotation calls attention to
another aspect of the production of *Le Cocu magnifique,* an aspect that
was to distinguish Meyerhold's later productions. It was a new system
of acting that started with the supremacy of motion, which was calculated in a way resembling circus acrobatics. It was diametrically opposed to the Stanislavsky System. Meyerhold's concept was called
"biomechanics" and stood for the power of pantomime.

Meyerhold rejected the Stanislavsky System as having overemphasized
the "spirit" and "psychologizing" at the expense of the actor's "body."
He felt that the actors at the Moscow Art Theater, for all their refined
souls and experiences, were completely incapable of motion. He was
striving to restore the lost equilibrium. He wanted to use his biomechanics for creating actors whose bodies would be supple and obedient
and who would be highly proficient in gesture and pantomime. He
wanted to break with the acting art that used priestly draperies, the fog
of the subconscious, the intuitive, and everything else that smacked of
mysticism and spiritual charlatanism. He wanted to confirm the harmony
of acting through the algebra of reason. In all the rare statements by
Meyerhold and his collaborators on the theory of biomechanics, the
emphasis is on rationalism and on a mechanistic understanding of the
creative process. They tried to base everything on the simple and
elementary laws of the reflexes. Two theoretical works of Meyerhold's
appeared in the year he staged *Le Cocu magnifique.* They are especially
important because they served as a declaration of his new acting system.
These works were called *Amplua aktëra* ("The Actor's Role") and
Aktër budushchego ("The Actor of the Future"). Their approach to the
art of acting is decidedly mechanistic. He wrote:

A necessary and special trait in actors is their ability to respond to stimu applied to their reflexes. . . . The stimulus is the ability to fulfill an assign ment received from the outside through feelings, motion, and language. T coordinate the reactions to stimuli is what constitutes *acting*. The separa parts of this are the *elements of acting*, each of which has three stages: 1 Intention; 2) Accomplishment; 3) Reaction.

Intention is the intellectual perception of the assignment received from the outside (from the author, the dramatist, the director, or on the initiativ of the performer himself).

Accomplishment is the series of volitional, mimetic, and vocal reflexes

Reaction is the lowering of the volitional reflex in accordance with th realization of the mimetic and vocal reflexes. The volitional reflex is prepare to receive a new intention and proceeds to a new element of *acting*.

The actor must be able to respond to stimuli. The reflex stimulus is th process of reducing the perception of a task to the minimum ("the ordinar reaction time").

A person who possesses the necessary ability for reflex stimuli can be or ca become an actor; he can fulfill one of the roles in the theater in accordanc with his natural and physical talents. He can be given a position that i determined as appropriate by the stage functions.[6]

One must know Meyerhold, with his burning contempt for the ol theater and the Stanislavsky System, to understand all the charm of hi sarcasm. He considered the new theory of acting a stylistic mixture o the "Regulations for the Military Disciple" and a textbook for algebra He reduced all the subtle complexities of the actor's creative activity t the fullfillment of an "assignment received from the outside" and reduce all the mysterious greatness of acting talent to the presence of thos "reflex stimuli" possessed by every person and every animal.

These theoretical works set forth the bases of biomechanics that sough to tailor the actor's motions, to subordinate them to the same method used to organize labor processes scientifically. Biomechanics aimed a removing superfluous and unproductive motions and rhythms and a correctly locating the center of gravity in the body and finding balance Meyerhold wrote:

The motions constructed on these bases are distinguished by a *dansan* quality. The labor process used by experienced workers always resembles the dance. Here, work verges on art. The sight of a person who is working cor rectly produces a certain satisfaction.

This applies completely to the work of the actor in the theater of the future. We are always dealing in art with the organization of material. Constructivism demands that the artist become an engineer as well. Art must be based on scientific principles; all the work done by the artist must be conscious.[7]

All this "stage algebra" and predominance of mechanics becomes
omprehensible only if we realize that Meyerhold also decided to try
omething else in his production of *Le Cocu magnifique*. This effort was
uite important but has been little discussed. He wanted to link the
heater arts with the age of the proletarian dictatorship, and so he struck
ut sharply and mercilessly against the acting "priesthood." A stage is
ot a temple, he asserted. Its brick walls and "machines for acting" do
ot distinguish it in any way from a factory. An actor on the stage is
 member of the actors' guild and wears the same proletarian "street
othes" as any worker. His work contains no bourgeois obscurantism
 any sort. It is based on materialist science and is subordinated to
ethodology principles known to every Soviet worker.

This was what Meyerhold, the Communist and the leader of the
October in the Theater" movement, contributed to the presentation.
t the time, he considered that the theater of "experiences," of "psy-
ologizing," and of the philistine drama was obsolete. He thought that,
 a nation with a proletarian dictatorship, the task of the theater would
 to present the ideal person of the new period on the stage. The new
erson would be a fine model of a human being, whose motions and
bor processes were clean-cut and skilled. This would be the human
eing at work. The theater would have to infect the audiences with a
 aving to imitate this dextrous and well-organized hero of the age.[8]

The practice, teaching, and staging of biomechanics in the form it
ok for *Le Cocu magnifique* was much more interesting, however, than
e dry and pseudoscientific statements on the subject by Meyerhold and
s associates.

First of all, biomechanics was a rebellion that Meyerhold launched
gainst the conversational theater of the day. In that theater people
ore frock coats or jackets and sat around on armchairs or couches
hile talking incessantly.[9] It was an angry revolt against a theater in
hich philosophizing had destroyed the motions of acting. The actor had
tained only the right to step forth on the stage, to bow, to sit at a
lace which the director had indicated, and to begin his speeches.

Biomechanics marked the first great break-through on the stage of
e tremendous experimental work that Meyerhold had accumulated in
s laboratories and studios before the Revolution. He had been seeking
 revive pantomime and all the richness of motion possessed by co-
edians. Biomechanics attempted to contrast the subtle and psycho-

logical actor (anemic in his motion) with the tempestuous comedi
who loved life. The latter was nourished on all the wealth of the pant
mimes in the great theaters of the past. He knew about the Roma
mimes, the jugglers, the acrobatic virtuosi of the Italian *commed
dell'arte*. Biomechanics thus used the gold reserves to be found in tl
traditions of the old comedians' art.

There was another element to biomechanics that has not been di
cussed in other writings on the subject. Devices were borrowed fro
the Chinese and Japanese theaters—theaters that were unsurpassed
accuracy or in their graphic quality. Gestures were calculated so pr
cisely that they verged upon dancing techniques and circus acrobatic
It was no accident that Inkinzhinomov, a Mongol connoisseur of tl
Asian theater, was one of the founders of biomechanics in Meyerholc
Theater and one of its best teachers. Biomechanics induced the actor
study the secrets of plasticity from the cat family,[10] which Meyerhold fe
possessed the highest degree of inborn feelings for economy, accurac
calculation, suppleness, and lightness in motion.

This new concept was important, not for its influence on the theori
of others, but in its results upon the stage. And the results were tl
lively, mischievous, and unbridled gaiety of the comedians who enacte
Le Cocu magnifique with a controlled virtuosity over their bodies.
was as if the band of comedians had just raced out of a sunny squa
into the gloomy theater, had joined in tossing all the trashy rags o
into the street, had taken the stage in battle, and, in unrestrained ha
piness at having the space of an open stage under their control, ha
given themselves up to the most "crazy jokes of the theater." It furnishe
clear and convincing proof that the actor himself contained the mag
power of transforming the wasteland of the stage and the abstract co
structions into something living.

In 1922 Meyerhold also staged *Smert' Tarelkina* ("The Death
Tarelkin"), a comedy by Alexander Sukhovo-Kobylin (1817–1903
in which the director sharpened and deepened his methods of constru
tivism. The designer, V. F. Stepanova, aided Meyerhold in creating
number of apparatuses that resembled the devices and contrivances use
by circus performers. Again like circus devices, these contraptions we
strictly utilitarian—they were all covered with a neutral white and we
not ornamental in the slightest. The furniture was altered and used fe
different tricks during the course of the action, according to the pri

ples used by clowns in the circus. When an actor sat on the constructivist furniture, he would either be tossed into the air by a spring
in the seat or a torpedo would go off under him, the chair would somehow turn into a board, a policeman would jump out like a jack-in-the-
box.

This was Meyerhold's second production of *The Death of Tarelkin*.
In 1917 this tragic farce about a man mistakenly put on an obituary
list had served as the basis for a presentation by him at the Alexandrinsky Theater in Petrograd. Sinister and fantastic colors were used, in the
style of E. T. A. Hoffmann. In 1922, however, Meyerhold seemed to
be mocking his own earlier mysticism. He now presented the work with
the bold and happy devices of circus buffoons, which had nothing in
common with Sukhovo-Kobylin's gloomy comedy. In the play Tarelkin
is a minor and forgotten functionary—like Akaky Akakievich Bash-
machkin in Gogol's "The Overcoat." In his second production, however,
Meyerhold transformed Tarelkin into a merry prankster who makes fools
out of the police. He flies across the entire width of the stage on a cable,
like an acrobat, in order to get away from the police.

As he had done with *Le Cocu magnifique,* therefore, Meyerhold
viewed the text of Sukhovo-Kobylin's play as a technical excuse for
his unique staging ideas. He believed that the object of presenting the
play was to show that a construction could bear the same relationship
to actors that it did to stars of the circus—that is, it contained devices
useful for the presentation. The actors of Meyerhold's Theater found
The Death of Tarelkin to be a kind of "textbook." They learned how
to use the "machines for acting" to good effect as virtuosi; they learned
to work with things and to calculate their motions and tricks with the
preciseness of circus performers.

In 1923 the centennial of Alexander Ostrovsky's birth was celebrated,
and in connection with this event Anatoli Lunacharsky, the People's
Commissar of Enlightenment, advanced a new slogan: "Back to Ostrovsky!" This, he declared, was the policy of the Soviet government
toward the theater.[11] Meyerhold considered such a slogan reactionary
and defeatist. It called for the restoration of truth to life, of naturalism,
and of psychologizing. The director rebelled against these things throughout his life.

He answered Lunacharsky's slogan in January, 1924, with a production that provoked quite a few tempests in the press and in theater

circles. The play was Ostrovsky's *The Forest,* a very popular work. Th
production was clearly polemical, as Meyerhold used it to assert h
own views. He thought that the Soviet theater must not go "back" t
Ostrovsky but must bring Ostrovsky forward, make him contemporar
and revise him in accordance with the attainments of the theate
Ostrovsky must not be transformed into a relic, but the material in h
plays must be used for the tasks of the present. Meyerhold proclaimed
most daring revision of the great pre-Soviet dramatist and then carrie
it out.

The presentation began something new, first in Soviet Russia and the
in other countries as well. A powerful wave of innovation began tha
was based, for the most part, on the most daring revisions, "tailorings,
and reworkings of the old classics. Hence, it will be worth our whi
to examine this version of *The Forest.*

Meyerhold was no novice at re-evaluating the classics. He had dor
that quite often before the Revolution, including his important produc
tion of Ostrovsky's *The Storm* on the imperial stage. With *The Fores*
however, he did something new. He not only destroyed both the trea
ment given by the author and the flavor of the period, but he rose u
against the inviolability of the classical text. He made himself th
coauthor of the classic.[12] Meyerhold cut the comedy and changed th
order of its scenes, dividing it into thirty-three independent episodes. H
revision changed *The Forest* from a comedy, in which the "good" an
the "bad" people are depicted rather gently and quite humanly, into
malicious satire on the Russia of the landowners. This was *The Fore*
as seen by a Bolshevik, with his enormous hatred for the departe
world of the Russian gentry.

The "leftist" theoreticians in the Soviet theater and the "leftist" criti
hailed Meyerhold's aggression against the classics enthusiastically. The
considered this presentation to be a deserved blow against the "reac
tionary elements who have protected the age-old traditions in th
theater." They felt it was directed against those who, "in connectio
with the anniversary of the man who created the true-to-life dramas o
the Russian burghers," allowed themselves to hope "for reaction withi
the theater." [13] There were even those who subscribed to the idea tha
"there can be no doubt that if Ostrovsky were alive today he coul
object to nothing in Meyerhold's edition of *The Forest.*" [14] They fe
that Meyerhold had acted correctly in destroying "the principle that

literary text is inviolable, in changing that text in accordance with the feelings influenced by the events of the Revolutionary years, and in casting aside respect for the supposedly 'eternal' values of the poet-priests." [15] They felt that a majority of even Shakespeare's greatest works contain strata, insertions, and corrections that the actors and directors do not know about.

Meyerhold's real genius was as a director, however, not as a collaborator of Ostrovsky's. In *The Forest* he rejected the constructivist asceticism of his early productions. Canvas was used to cover the brick walls of the theater, and the stage was filled with furnishings and other stage properties. Something labeled "a bridge road" was hanging in the air and offered the actors a great range of possible uses. There was a dovecote with many living pigeons. Finally, street clothes were not used, but make-up was. Once again the stage used the variegated luxury of costumes and a variety of wigs and masks.

Meyerhold filled the presentation with acting virtuosity. He used real props and introduced "effects" everywhere, even in places where they contradicted the text and the sense of the action. A single phrase in Ostrovsky's text recalls that Neschastlivtsev had once performed some tricks, so a good number of them were shown on the stage. Aksiusha recalls, "Day and night, since I was six, I have helped my mother work," and so Meyerhold had her constantly working on the stage. When the merchant declares, "I shall give up everything," a flood of furs, shoes, and hats drops down on the stage from above.

Meyerhold loaded lyrical passages in the play with singing, dancing, and accordian music. And this helped to establish what was perhaps the most important aspect of the presentation—his assertion that his theater was, in terms of style, basically a theater of the mask. Every character was strictly bounded by a completely definite rhythm for his speech and motions; his gestures and pantomime were given a rhythm that was his alone. When he first appeared on the stage, he quickly acquainted the audience with his lietmotif, which remained standard in all situations.

The Forest began to crystallize the basic style of this most rebellious director. It clarified his pre-Revolutionary work and his innumerable excursions into the traditions of the *commedia dell'arte* in Italy, into the Spanish, Japanese, and Chinese theaters, and into the folk farce and Attic comedy. During all the years when he was becoming famous in arguments and for his agonizing experiments, he had been seeking a single path. He wanted to create a new theater of the mask. This new and absolute theater would be freed from the cheap literature and illusion that had been parasitic upon it. It would be organically hostile to the psychologizing theater that was true to life, and it would be cleansed of the age-old scum that was alien to it.

The human character was shown by means of the leitmotif and the scheme—the rest of the complex and variegated human heart was omitted. Meyerhold went through the years faithful to the idea of symbolism, to which he had been converted at the very start of his career. For him, the world remained an enormous puppet show in which Fate moved the marionettes according to whims of its own, and his theater always seemed to be a puppet show, with figures from a wax museum come to life in it. He did not need any actor with life and talent but only ideal marionettes who would be obedient. The chief feature of the actor under biomechanics was the precise fulfillment of the assignment given him by the director.

Meyerhold's work was frequently brilliant in terms of its directorial resourcefulness, and it proved capable of founding dozens of independent schools within the theater arts. Yet, the same idea goes right through it—there were no authentically living characters. There was rather the coolness of marionettes breathing from behind wonderful masks.

After *The Forest,* Meyerhold produced *The Give-Us-Europe Trust* and *Bubus the Teacher.*[16] These were not among the best presentations of the period, but they are worth examining because they constitute the intervening links in the evolution of Meyerhold and his theater.

In *The Give-Us-Europe Trust* Meyerhold tried to rework a typical Western "review" into political propaganda. Here, as in many of his other propagandistic presentations, he considered his theater a model workshop for developing new forms and devices for the entire Soviet theater, both professional and amateur.

The text of *The Give-Us-Europe Trust* was compiled by M. Podgayetsky from novels by Ehrenburg, Amp, Kellerman, and Sinclair. The play depicted the struggle of an American capitalistic trust with the radio trust of a Soviet republic. The American organization aimed at the complete "destruction" of Europe to eliminate a dangerous competitor. There were seventeen episodes, accompanied by political slogans. They satirized Poland, Germany, and France of the day, which were shown as disintegrating under pressure from "the trust for the destruction of

Europe." The production was of interest, but not for its coarse and deliberate propaganda depiction of the "disintegrating" bourgeoisie trembling epileptically from "fox trots." Nor did its interest come from the proletarians and other Soviet people who, in contrast, were healthy, and tanned by the sun that bathes Soviet stadiums. Its interest resulted from the new devices that Meyerhold introduced to the Soviet theater. He gave stage action a quality of almost motion-picturelike impetuosity by his rapid change of scenes, and he created tremendous and dynamic tension.

To attain this, Meyerhold and Ilya Shlepyanov—the set-designer—invented something that was as simple as it was effective. They used a system of wooden panels, which moved on rollers. These panels were heaped up in rapid combinations. They permitted the place of action to be shifted rapidly. A lecture hall was quickly transformed into a street with an endless fence. The street then became a chamber of a parliament. And this last was turned into a stadium within a few seconds. Meyerhold was allowed to enrich the theater with devices that were incredibly dynamic. One of the most wonderful scenes in *The Give-Us-Europe Trust* was a "chase," and during it the spotlights rushed about chaotically and suddenly all the panels began twirling around in different directions, creating an almost unbelievably dynamic picture.

Pantomime came to the fore in this production, even more than in Meyerhold's earlier efforts. There were a number of episodes that lasted altogether about ten or fifteen minutes and contained an insignificant amount of speech but much pantomime.

Bubus the Teacher provided Meyerhold with raw material for seeking a new form for a musical show. He was looking for a symphony of the theater, in which all the elements would be subordinated to rhythm and melody. Everything in the comedy—the motions and speeches of the actors, the props, the lighting, the sound effects, and the music—was a separate instrument in the scenic orchestra performing a synthetic symphony. First of all, the entire production took place to music. High above the decorative furnishings, one of the finest pianists in Moscow sat on a covered platform. During the three acts of the play, this frock-coated musician performed about forty-six pieces by Chopin and Liszt. All the motions of the actors were set against this musical background. At times, they were greatly prolonged, as if they were performing a tragic and solemn dance of the condemned. Meyerhold was aiming to show the doom of the capitalistic world in these careful and prolonged motions that faded into pauses as if the characters were listening to something going on inside them or outside of them.

Many of Meyerhold's earlier presentations had been done with the broadness of the market-place farce. In *Bubus the Teacher,* however, he created a refined production that was quite subtle. He turned aside from most of his ascetic and constructivist ideas and again used something resembling a pavilion on the stage. This was a semicircle of long, hanging, bamboo poles. The stage was decorated with a large basin and a flowing fountain. The floor was covered with a luxurious carpet. Furniture was brought in and a massive portal was erected at the entrance.

The presentation produced a strange and mysterious impression. There were agonizing leaps and fadings-out set to rhythm. The actors danced their long pantomime scenes slowly. With this production, Meyerhold put into practice his theory of "preacting." Preacting contained long pauses between the speeches. These breaks were filled with pantomime that strove to accomplish two things—to show the transition of the actor from one situation to another and to prepare the audience for a more correct and sharper perception of that which followed the preacting.

Preacting was based on a very important factor peculiar to the inner technique of acting—the laws of human conduct in life. In life a person prefixes his words with a short "overture" of gestures and pantomimes that transmit the sense of what he wants to say. The preacting in *Bubus the Teacher* was hypertrophied and deliberately prolix, as if Meyerhold were dealing with an exercise for actors rather than with a presentation. It was constructed on the same principle that he used for staging the dances in the play—not on a "legato" but rather on short rhythmic bits. After performing these bits, the dancers would pause motionlessly. The characters in the play would also freeze into the numbness of preacting before moving or uttering a word, as if they were trying first to listen for something before moving. The text merely furnished the sense of the pantomime to follow.

There was still another innovation, however, in this extremely subtle presentation. This was the virtuoso technique that Meyerhold used in conjunction with rhythm to reveal the social mask, the nature, and the psychology of his characters. A system of "rhythmic masks" was developed that belonged to Meyerhold's Theater alone. It revealed the essence of a character through the individual rhythms of his speech, motions, and gestures. Lunacharsky termed this feature "sociomechanics" in contrast to biomechanics.

Meyerhold staged Nikolai Erdman's *The Warrant* on April 20, 1925. This production revealed what was always one of Meyerhold's strong points—his flair for satire. In his production of *The Warrant* he reveled in his favorite theme—the animated exhibit, the enormous puppet show, the theater of "funny faces and grimaces," the theater of the grotesque. Here there was no boring and state-inspired bifurcation of the characters into "positive" and "negative" camps. Everyone was "negative." They were like wax figures from a chamber of horrors who had come to life under the spotlights of the theater.

Meyerhold gave each character a caricature as his leitmotif. Very frequently the characters betook themselves in their wax-museumlike poses from the blue haze of the stage to the rotating circle, or they froze with their eyes dully directed toward the audience. There were piles of furniture, trunks, coffers, and dresses that Meyerhold used to transmit the idea that the philistine world hoarded trifles and other items greedily.

Meyerhold found a new and somber kind of comedy in *The Warrant*. It was based on the incongruity between idol-like posing of the characters and their sudden transition from motionlessness to gesturing and loud talking. With the power and perception peculiar to him alone, he turned the ridicule of the early acts into a flagrantly grotesque "rebellion of the philistines." They sang the tsarist anthem and, in the catastrophic "Judgment Day" that transformed them into pitiful and unnecessary people, asked "So, how on earth are we going to live?"

Meyerhold used a revolving stage, a system of concentric circles that rotated in opposite directions to aid him in staging this animated exhibit. These circles "drove" persons and things from the rear of the stage to the foreground. Groups in frozen poses would use them to disappear in the fog. The circles often split groups of characters in two: some of them would remain downstage, while the others—no longer needed for the plot—would be carried off into the wings.

The Bolshevik critics considered that Meyerhold's treatment of *The Warrant* depicted the tragedy of "former people" unsparingly. These were individuals who had "slept through the Revolution" and "lost their last pitiful ideological baggage and their final illusions." The Bolsheviks felt that the play seemed to be limited only because it dwelt on the middle-class, dreaming of restoring the monarchy and living in the ready expectation that their lands and factories would be returned to them.

Meyerhold's theme in his production of *The Warrant* was, however, broader and more dangerous to the Soviet regime. He, like Vladimir Mayakovsky, felt that the idea behind the Communist Revolution was threatened most seriously from within by pettiness, philistinism, and bureaucracy. Both these great men foresaw that the Revolution would degenerate into a terrible bureaucratic state that threatened to stifle everything living. They foresaw the appearance of a new kind of philistine—the minor Communist functionaries and activists, the teamsters who would remain Stalin's faithful sycophants to their graves.

Guliachkin, with a Soviet "warrant" in his pocket, personified the petty and roguish philistine against whom Meyerhold was in revolt. The director's unsparing struggle through satire against this "Soviet trash" began with *The Warrant* and continued with Erdman's *The Suicide,* a play that the censors forbade.[17]

On December 9, 1926, Meyerhold offered Nikolai Gogol's *The Inspector-General* at the Vsevolod Meyerhold State Theater. This production was his "Song of Songs" as a director. If a description of this masterpiece alone is preserved of all his presentations, it would be quite enough to permit one to understand his creative personality. The production was the key to all the secrets of his work.

This production contained all the greatest features of Meyerhold as a director in classically polished form. Here the bold revision of the classics that accompanied his entire career was at its climax. He decided to reveal all of Gogol's writings in this *Inspector-General,* and so rearranged the scenes of the comedy and even incorporated a number of variants from Gogol's notebooks and some sections of Gogol's novel *Dead Souls* into *The Inspector-General.*[18]

In revising the play, Meyerhold worked on an enormous scale. He changed the locale from a remote town in serf-holding Russia to something that was almost St. Petersburg itself. Hence, all the classical characters in Gogol's comedy took on a new look. The local chief of police was changed from some minor official in the country to a young general who takes bribes on the scale of St. Petersburg or Moscow. His wife, Anna Andreyevna, was transformed from a silly, stupid and over-ripe lady of "provincial society" into a beautiful and experienced coquette, a hetaera of the St. Petersburg demimonde. Meyerhold introduced some civil-servants plus a number of officers, and the result was the brilliant and worldly society of the capital. Khlestakov was changed from a petty, procrastinating landowner's son given to stretching the truth into an unlovable adventurer whose rapacity did not stop at bribetaking, cheating, or flirting in a most underhanded manner. Meyerhold's goal was to show "everything bad in Russia" and to satirize the remote period of Nicholas I most harshly.

He made the presentation pompous throughout. The wood was varnished until it shone; the furniture was luxurious; the candelabra were gilded; the costumes were glittering and magnificent; the rooms and the partitions on the stage were enormous. He populated the comedy with a multitude of characters "introduced by the author of the presentation." They acted without speaking, but the pantomime of such characters as his captain—an officer in transit—were frequently as interesting or as important as that of Gogol's own characters.

Meyerhold gathered, not only all the work of Gogol and "everything bad in Russia" into one presentation, but also what was most important in his own work. *The Inspector-General* included the early Meyerhold of the period of "stylization" in the scene where Anna Andreyevna stood before the mirror in her silk dress. Her pose, her coloring, the lighting, and the furnishings transmitted the entire atmosphere of the early nineteenth century as presented in the genre paintings and realistic miniatures of Fedotov. Only Meyerhold could use iconography to such wonderful "effect" in stylization. Let us not forget either the brilliant "crowded setting" for the reading of Khlestakov's letter to Triapichkin. And here, too, we find Meyerhold's predilection for luxurious furniture, vessels, and costumes—which played roles all by themselves throughout the entire work.

For years Meyerhold had been searching for a rhythmical and musical principle to which all the acting could be subordinated, beginning with his work at the Marinsky Theater and continuing on through his work in *Bubus the Teacher.* His rhythmic principle acquired a symphonic polish in *The Inspector-General,* and he had reason to term this production "musical realism." All fifteen episodes of the play were parts of a suite on Gogolian themes. Language and gesture were subordinated to rhythm and a number of scenes were worked out on the lines of a chorus. Khlestakov or the chief of police would "sing" the verses, and

the mass of petty functionaries served as a chorus. Meyerhold added to
the length of the text by having the chorus repeat the remarks of
Khlestakov and of some of the others.[19]

Once again Meyerhold had boldly returned to mysticism in the cruel
world of Soviet materialism. This is what he had done in his first efforts
as a director. The entire production contained something invisible, fatal,
and "Hoffmannesque." The "officer in transit" whom Meyerhold had
introduced was very much like a devil controlling all the threads of
what was taking place.[20]

For staging the bribery episode, there were a number of doors which
formed a semicircle of redwood framing the proscenium. The ratlike
faces of the officials appeared from these doorways and gazed at the
drunken Khlestakov as he dozed in an armchair. The enactment of
terror and sycophancy, all the wonderfully effective folding doors, and
the planning of the approach and disappearance of the bribers constituted one of the greatest feats ever accomplished by a Soviet director.
Another such masterpiece was the "silent scene" at the end of the play.
This climaxed one of Meyerhold's main themes, the theme of "exhibits,"
of playing with masks and puppets. The thread of "figures from a wax
museum" also attained its most polished form in *The Inspector-General*,
and this idea was not disguised. Before the start of every episode the
characters froze in their poses as they came out to the proscenium on a
part of the revolving stage. They paused for a long time under the
spotlights and suddenly began to move and to speak. The actors seemed
like mechanical figures, while the motors of the revolving platforms
hummed. They thus showed themselves to the audience at the start of
every scene. In the concluding episode they froze in rigid, distorted
poses. The lights went out for a few seconds, and when they came on
again the audience saw not actors but mannequins in the same ridiculous
poses, mannequins whose costumes had been removed. With this closing
chord, Meyerhold for the first time revealed his secret to the audience.
For him, the world still possessed the young passions of symbolism.
Even in the "proletarian dictatorship" the world struck him as merely
an exhibit, a collection of benumbed puppets who were the playthings
and victims of Fate.

Perhaps no production of the Soviet theater called forth such a torrent
of polemics in the press as did Meyerhold's *The Inspector-General*. The

"cursing" critics won out. They accused this artist of "no longer hearing the music of revolution." They called the presentation mystical, reactionary, and symbolical. They said that he had shifted his center of gravity from satiric exposés to a "romantic, Gogolian-Hoffmannesque, and fantastic" treatment. The show was called "nonsocial," "asocial," and blatantly formalistic. The press printed irate protests by academicians and elderly dramatists who demanded that Soviet justice protect Gogol's rights as an author. The press had always howled at every new Meyerhold production, but after *The Inspector-General* its noise grew stronger and contained the same surplus of energy that Meyerhold himself had shown.

This was the reception given the greatest masterpiece in the entire history of Russian directing. And even today the Soviet theater press libels it by calling it "class-alien formalism." The Soviet critics have termed it a dark and shameful page in the history of the Soviet theater, claiming it was a reactionary phenomenon that "impeded the correct understanding of the classical heritage and the later development of a national and realistic scenic art." [21]

Meyerhold produced a second classic with the devices he had worked out for *The Inspector-General*—Alexander Griboyedov's *Gore ot uma* ("Woe from Wit"), which was presented on March 12, 1928. This is one of the greatest pre-Soviet plays, but Meyerhold revised its text with the same boundless boldness he had shown earlier. He began by changing the title from *Woe from Wit* to *Woe to Wit,* which is what the great dramatist had called his first draft. *Woe to Wit* was more dynamic and put greater emphasis on the struggle of an unrepentant society against the freethinking hero, Chatsky.

The play was Griboyedov's essay on the Moscow society of his day. Meyerhold made *Woe to Wit* into a malicious satire against the moldy and dignified Russia of the 1820s—inert, stupid, obese, and stifling everything that was new and freethinking. Just as he had done with *The Inspector-General,* Meyerhold changed the order of the scenes in Griboyedov's work. He included sketches and first drafts that the author had thrown out. He inserted verses by K. N. Ryleyev, the Decembrist, and by Pushkin. The director considered all this necessary to transform Chatsky into a freethinker of the Decembrist type. Meyerhold used still another method of "revising" the classics in this production, which even his defenders considered daring. He transferred the action to places that had nothing in common with the stage directions of the author.

Meyerhold was to deal the Communist functionaries a frontal blow with his productions of Vladimir Mayakovsky's two comedies *The Bug* and *The Bath*. These were done at a time when the Soviet theater had already started on the downgrade. They ought to be considered the final thunder-claps from the period of *Sturm und Drang,* and they climaxed the greatest thread in Meyerhold's career—the line of satire.

Meyerhold's satirical flair can be followed with perfect clarity as it matured during his career in the theater. His best work was with sarcasm, the grotesque, the acting of "funny faces and grimaces," the buffonade, the exhibit, and populating the stage with jeering phantoms. In these, he was peerless.

After the Revolution, the satiric aspect began to dominate his work. Except for *Les Aubes* by Verhaeren and *Komandarm 2* ("The Commander of the Second Army") by Ilya Selvinsky, all of Meyerhold's productions between 1920 and 1930 were satires.

Mayakovsky's *Mystery-Bouffe* and Crommelynck's *Le Cocu magnifique* were done in a style resembling the caricatures of posters. Meyerhold went on from these to two groups of satiric presentations. The first group consisted of merciless satires against the capitalistic West, such as *The Land Is on Edge, The Give-Us-Europe Trust, Bubus the Teacher,* and Faiko's *Lakes of Liul,* which was staged at the Theater of the Revolution. The second series of plays consisted of satires against tsarist Russia, such as *The Death of Tarelkin, The Forest, The Inspector-General,* and *Woe to Wit. The Warrant* stood alone as a kind of dangerous bridge—it satirized the "former people" and the real philistines of Russia. Thus Meyerhold had accumulated a number of satirical devices from material dealing with the past and the West. He then fired a double-barreled salvo at Soviet realities. *The Bug* and *The Bath* fell with great force upon the pettiness of Soviet existence and attacked the appalling and stupid Soviet dullards who were minor functionaries in the Party.

It was no accident that Meyerhold and Mayakovsky joined forces. They had both given their talents to Communism from the very first days of the Soviet regime. Soviet poetry has nothing more communistic than Mayakovsky's verses, and the Soviet theater has nothing more communistic than Meyerhold's productions. Both men were idealists who believed that the kingdom of Communist freedom was on the way. Until the day of his death, the poet remained outside the Party itself, but he gave his talent to the daily work of propaganda for building Communism. The director entered the Party, and had exposed and annihilated tsarist Russian and Western capitalism with the merciless antagonism of a Cheka member. But the two men shared their disillusionment with Bolshevism. They both foresaw that an All-Union Chain Gang was being constructed instead of a Commune of the Future. A "terrible, new, 'Arakcheyevlike' regime" was building a new dictatorship that would be obeyed by an army of millions of unthinking teamsters, petty officials with Party cards, and Soviet philistines. The two artists rebeled against Stalin's dictatorial distortion of Communism with *The Bug* and *The Bath*.

The Bug, a "fairy comedy," was first given on February 13, 1929, at the Vsevolod Meyerhold Theater. Its hero was Prisypkin, a member of the Communist Party, whom the Soviet censors insisted on restyling as "an ex-worker and ex-Party member."

This sluggish Party member decides that the time has come for him to "live in plenty." He marries a manicurist, the daughter of "petty-bourgeois barbers." His mother-in-law has no cause for regret because Prisypkin brings the household his "stainless proletarian origins" and his Party card (which the censorship changed into a trade-union card). He is "against the plebeian way of life—the canaries and the rest of it. . . . I am a man with important demands. . . . I am interested in a dresser with a mirror attached." His wedding to the daughter of a "petty tradesman" must be "ideologically useful" because it is the "marital union of a red toiler." There are "red groomsmen, a table laden with red ham, and bottles with red corks."

When this tasteless wedding feast of Comrade Prisypkin takes place, there is a fire and the entire gathering dies because so much vodka has been spilled and drunk. The firemen flood Prisypkin's body with water, and it freezes in the cellar. There it is found some fifty years later by those alive under Communism, and they decide by automatic vote to resurrect Prisypkin. He comes to life in the Federation of the distant future, but he makes a poor impression because of his Soviet jargon, his low tastes, and his ideas. A bug, which has frozen on Prisypkin, is brought back to life along with him. Both Prisypkin and the bug are considered by these new people to be frightful and extinct creatures.

Prisypkin's narrow-mindedness infects the people of the future with a passion for beer and vodka and for singing the most banal songs.

The bright people of the Federation must be saved from infection. Hence, it is decided to put both parasites—Prisypkin and the bug—into cages at the zoo that would be labeled "Bugus normalis" and "Philistinus vulgaris." Prisypkin's cage is surrounded with admonitory signs: "Careful—It Spits"; "Entry upon Advance Notice Only"; "Protect Your Ears—It Expresses Itself." Suddenly Prisypkin sees the audience and yells:

Citizens! Friends! My own folks! My very own folks! Where are you from? How many of you are there? When were all of you unfrozen? Why am I the only one in the cage? Take pity on me, friends and relatives! Why am I suffering? Citizens! . . .

This suggestion to pity all those in the Soviet audience who would be in the animal cage of future Communism ended the comedy.

The theme of *The Bug* was that the Revolution had grown narrow-minded, and the new Party functionaries had grown fat. Like Prisypkin, they could say:

What was I fighting for? I was fighting for a good life. Here it is, right at hand for me: a wife, a house, and real manners. I will always be ready to do my duty if it becomes necessary. Whoever has fought has the right to relax by a peaceful brook. Gosh! Maybe my planning will raise up my entire class. Gosh!

Meyerhold worked out two styles for the presentation. To depict the Soviet reality of what was then the present, he heaped piles of trifles on the stage. The narrow-minded people drowned in them, as they had in *The Warrant*. The masks were evil caricatures that seemed to have come from a nightmare. To depict the Federation of the future, he used metal and sparkling glass. The rooms were as white as the operating-rooms in a hospital. It was a sterilized future. The Soviet critics, considering the "sterilized future" to be almost a caricature of Communism, rebuked both Meyerhold and Mayakovsky because of it quite a few times. Mayakovsky even had to take an official oath that he had not been depicting socialist society.

The Bath had its première at Meyerhold's Theater on March 16, 1930. It was a strong satire that hit Stalin's Party bureaucracy directly. *The Bath,* in Mayakovsky's words, "washes—simply wipes out—the bureaucrats." Mayakovsky and Meyerhold used the stage to conduct their own private "purge" of Stalin's Party bureaucracy. As was true with *The Bug,* the purge occurred by transferring the action to the future, and for this occasion they used a "time machine."

The protagonist of this "drama with a circus and fireworks" is Comrade Pobedonosikov, the "Chief Agreement Administrator." He is a stupid, swaggering, inflated, petty tyrant—a civil-service grandee of Stalin's period. Mayakovsky uses him as a focal point for all the special features possessed by this appalling class of Soviet worthies. These traits include the most versatile timeserving, sycophancy, informing, cowardice, ignorance, petty spitefulness, and banality. Pobedonosikov is surrounded by bootlickers like his personal secretary Optimistenko and Isak Belvedonsky, an artist. (The name of Belvedonsky hints at that of Brodsky, a portrait-painter and Soviet laureate.)

The "Chief Agreement Administration" has as its purpose "the coordination and the preparation of questions for agreement"—itself a satire against the obtuse bureaucratic machinery of the Party and government. This was an establishment in which "the obeying of directives, the preparation of circulars, and the implementation of efficiency are executed by having papers lie around for years in a state of total chaos. For requests, complaints, and memoranda, there is a production line." This is the place in which the workers invent their "time machine," which is rejected because of "its failure to come within the scope of the plan for the next quarter." Besides, it is not "necessary to the broad masses of workers and peasants." Meanwhile, Pobedonosikov leads the life of a Communist grandee. He is surrounded by toadies and he buys antique furniture, although he knows nothing at all about it. (He even says: "Any Louis, only make it pretty old.") When all this is going on, Belvedonsky, the "artist-laureate," is "immortalizing" the Chief's features on canvas. The workers have by now invented the "time machine" by themselves. It is suggested that Pobedonosikov take his wife and his entire staff for a ride into the future. To this the Chief replies:

I am in favor of a time machine. All I have ever said was that in view of our limited budget there was no reason to race headlong into the past. Why burrow in our own dirt—in the dust of history, that is. But if it's a question of traveling to the future—to better positions and salaries—then let us make as many trips as we like.

Pobedonosikov demands that he and his wife be allowed to get on the time machine completely out of turn because they are "in charge." The apparatus, however, has a special feature: before it starts it throws back whoever does not come through the "purges" of Communism in the future. Thus, "time shakes off everyone who impedes progress toward Communism." Because of this, the entire pack of Party bureaucrats is rejected by the time machine. The play ends as Pobedonosikov irately attacks the author and the director: "Answer me. What did you want this to say? Why have you made such a fuss? . . . It's a propaganda skit, a poster! It's in-ar-tis-tic!"

When Meyerhold staged *The Bug* and *The Bath,* he did something else that was quite important. For the first time he rejected the risky experiments and the "leftist" innovations that had characterized his directing. He seemed to be afraid lest any innovations in form eclipse the irate satire. Instead of using stunning tricks, he merely concentrated everything that he had discovered earlier and had verified in the theater of satire. He refused to hire set designers and worked out primitive and symbolical stagings for himself. His directing centered on the character itself, and he caricatured the Bolshevik bureaucracy and the narrow-minded Soviet office workers as devastatingly as he could. In this regard *The Bug* and *The Bath* represent the zenith of Meyerhold's career as a satirist and are his most academic efforts as a director.

The Bolshevik critics reacted to these plays with fury. Stalin himself began to hate Meyerhold now that the director had satirized the dictator's bureaucracy, and the tragic end to Meyerhold's career became inevitable.

THE KAMERNY THEATER

Alexander Tairov's Kamerny Theater in Moscow was the second most important contributor to the heyday of the Soviet theater, and its influence on the stage of Western Europe even exceeded Meyerhold's. Like Meyerhold, Tairov had a program, which was indicated in his *Zapiski rezhissëra* ("Notes of a Director," 1921). Again like Meyerhold, Tairov rejected naturalism, perhaps even more intransigently than Meyerhold, who would occasionally introduce naturalism in his productions as a "visual attraction." Tairov wrote: "There are two truths: the truth of life and the truth of art." [22] He rejected the Moscow Art Theater, which he claimed, "tries to make both actor and playgoer forget the theater. It aspires to have them react as if the play being performed were just like real life." [23]

Tairov differed from Meyerhold in his attitude toward the place of literature in the theater. Meyerhold was faithful to the idea that "the new theater is growing out of literature," that "literature has always taken the initiative in quarrying dramatic forms," and that "literature creates the theater." Tairov, on the other hand, found literature pernicious. He considered that its maxims, its everyday quality, and its philosophizing withered and destroyed the art of acting. He felt that the theater must not be a faithful interpreter of a play but must rather create "its own, new work of art according to its own values." Tairov believed that the theater must use a dramatic work only as raw material. The genuine new theater "will, of course, create not literature but a new master-actor."

Meyerhold's biomechanics asserted that any person with normal reflexes could become an actor. On the other hand, Tairov's manifesto sharply and persistently struggled against non-professionals. He asserted that the actor must master his technique with the ardor of a musician. He considered the actor "chosen" and compounded, that is, equally perfect in juggling, pantomime, acrobatics, vocal technique, and inner technique.

Compared to the Kamerny Theater, Meyerhold's ensemble seemed on the surface to be a somewhat amateurish mixture of the "amateur" and professional theaters. Every one of his productions revealed a new étape in the development of all the theater arts.[24] His genius, however, did not produce "slick" and polished productions, especially during his stormiest period (right after the Revolution). He was born to tear up mountain ranges but not to polish stones. The pulverizing and finishing of Meyerhold's Cyclopean works were done by his disciples.

Both Stanislavsky and Tairov differed from Meyerhold in the skillful "analysis" of their productions, which showed great artistic taste and polish in every detail. During the Soviet period, Meyerhold's stage was always crudely assembled and gauchely adorned with the clumsy platforms and constructions of the carpenters. He would present diamonds in the rough: the lighting was primitive, the costumes were awkward, and all the stage-technicians were third-rate. Tairov's presentations, on the other hand, were always refined, well coordinated, brilliantly staged, masterfully costumed, and excellently furnished. To phrase it differently, Meyerhold "dressed" his productions like a tailor in a provincial town, while Tairov was like a master in the stylish ateliers of the capital. Despite his "sophistication," however, Tairov did not have a fraction of Meyerhold's theater ideas.

Like Meyerhold, Tairov opposed psychology. He ridiculed Stanislavsky's efforts to make the actors know life as it is lived and use it as a source for their work. He thought it unworthy of an artist "to walk about continually as if his heart and eyes were pocket cameras in order to transfer what he observes from life to the stage." [25]

The Stanislavsky System favored "effective memory," psychological analysis, and the search for genuine emotions and actions. Tairov found all this destructive of the actor's art. All Stanislavsky's naturalistic devices rob the actor of his creative quality, Tairov thought, and transform him from the sovereign of the stage to "a sweet and sensitive person who is not a bad psychologist but is certainly neurotic, [who] sincerely experiences his neighbor's woes and joys, but [who] creates nothing at all for the theater." [26] Language in the naturalistic theater is soiled with impurities copied from the drab speech of life, and gesture in such a theater is illustrative, everyday, and "tongue-tied." Truth to life triumphs in the naturalistic theater, but art is demolished. In general, Tairov felt that the naturalistic stage was a plague on the theater arts because it destroyed form:

There is no art at all—nor can there be any—without form. The naturalistic theater has suffered from the dysentery of formlessness. By concentrating on experience exclusively, by depriving the actor of the means to express himself, by subordinating his work to the truth of life with all its haphazardness, the naturalistic theater has annihilated the form of the stage. That form has its own laws, and they are not predicated upon life. Therefore, the naturalistic theater is essentially not a genuine theater and has never given finished works to the theater arts.[27]

Tairov, however, also rejected Meyerhold's Symbolical Theater. He felt that that theater had fled from its debasing captivity to "the truth of life" but had fallen captive to literature, painting, and the director's dictatorship. Meyerhold had transformed the actor into a puppet— a "colorful spot," a supplement to the excellent décor of the designers— and the "creative Ego" of the actor had been destroyed.

Tairov had rejected the thesis (the Naturalistic Theater) and the antithesis (the Symbolical Theater). He declared that he had found the synthesis. He first located his "scenic synthesis" in pantomime:

Pantomime is a concept of much scope, and of much spiritual nakedness. Words die away and are replaced by the birth of genuinely scenic action. Scenic action at first sight is a form that is filled with tense and creative emotion that flows into a suitable gesture completely.

Only the emotional gesture is strong enough to express the art of the genuine theater, the art of pantomime. It alone possesses the key to genuine form, form that is filled with creative feeling, emotional form.

The "emotional gesture," the "emotional form" is the scenic synthesis for which we have been groping in our work, and outside of which there is no exit to the contemporary theater, or even to the theater in general.[28]

Tairov's statement that the genuine theater was based on pantomime was not new. It repeated the chief point of Meyerhold's creative system. The new element was what Tairov understood by the word "emotion." His idea contradicted the "experience" and the "truth of feelings" found in the Moscow Art Theater.[29] It was also experience, but creative experience rather than the experience of life. As he explained: [Creative emotion takes] its juices not from real life (either the actor's or anyone else's), but from the life created for the stage character whom the actor summons forth from the magic land of fantasy to its creative existence." [30]

The sphere of the emotions is nobler than the "physiological experiences" that the Moscow Art Theater actors used to create a "physiological infection" within the playgoers. It lies in the "legendary realm of fantasy." The stage character is a synthesis of the emotions and the forms produced by the actor's creative fantasy.

Tairov never completely explained the mysterious word "emotion" or his idea of "stage character." He did not reveal what was most important in the scenic arts, and this is just what the Stanislavsky System had explained so thoroughly and so convincingly. Tairov never revealed how the creative process created the character on the stage but left the process enveloped in mystery: "The secret of how a stage character is engendered is as marvelous and as incomprehensible as the mystery of life and death. If the secret were successfully fathomed and analyzed, art would cease to exist." [31]

All this "sweet fog" tends to indicate that Tairov transferred the experiences of the actor to the stage only in terms of joy. Fantasy and personal inspiration were used to create the chimera of a stage character. The actor created from the purity of his own fantasy, and the resulting stage character is in no way connected with contemptible life. Like any actor of the "representational school," the Kamerny Theater performer divided himself into the "ego" and the "role." He allowed his "ego" to play the "passions" of the role, but for the "emotions" of a Herod, a Theseus, or a Romeo, he delved into his old trunk for the ancient stage stereotypes of all conceivable feelings. Only then did the process begin that was to give these stereotypes a new look. That process was Tairov's personal directing. He was essentially the sole creator and continuator of the Kamerny Theater style. He possessed great taste and a colorful esthetic sense, which he sometimes overdid. He used these to transform the usual costume-play acting stereotypes into something stylized, more elegant or more violent and spirited than the "representational stage" had seen before. Apart from Alice Koonen, a greatly gifted tragic actress, the entire cast of the Kamerny Theater was merely clay to be molded by the refined hands of Tairov.

The power of the theater trend and of the new school in the theater arts was not shown in its numerous followers who, cometlike, formed part of its tail. Its force was adjudged by whether it created a new group of actors and an original school. Stanislavsky alone succeeded in doing this. Neither Meyerhold nor Tairov left any real heirs, actors of his own school.

There is a better key to Tairov's creative method—music.[32] That word covers everything that distinguished the Kamerny from the other theaters. Music was its creative trunkline, and its most valuable contribution to the theater arts of the world. Tairov rearranged the theater arts on a musical basis. His theater—in theory—was like pure music in that it stood high above life and precluded any tie with naturalism. In his theater, the actors' speech and motions were basically melody and rhythm,[33] the colors, lighting, and sounds resembled the instruments that a composer uses to play the melodies and rhythms conceived in his own imagination. His devices were always cleansed of everything earthly, and they belonged to something outside of everyday existence.

The sound, Tairov told his actors, must go from *piano* to *forte,* from conversation to singing, from *stacatto* to *legato,* while harmonizing with their creative demands. He "orchestrated" the actors' voices in his productions. Thus, in his *Salome,* these were the "instruments": "double basses: soldiers; flute: the young Syrian; oboe: Salome; sounding brass: Iokanaan."

Motions and gestures were subordinated by the Kamerny Theater to the musical principle alone. The actor's body had to sing and resound "like a magic Stradivarius." [34] The actors sought the musical key "needed for the range" of every stage character. The décor, the lighting, and sound effects became musical elements organically connected with a symphonic composition of the theater.[35]

Finally, Tairov considered that the director should "sense the rhythmic beat of the play, locate its sound, its harmony, and then, as it were, orchestrate it." [36] It was no coincidence that several of the Kamerny Theater's productions even bore musical captions. *Princess Brambilla,* for instance, was termed "a *capriccio* by the Kamerny Theater."

The identification of the theater with music was both the strength and the weakness of this remarkable Theater. No other theater in the world made so many great contributions to rhythm in the theater or to constructing a synthetic presentation so organically subordinated to musical unity from start to finish. On the other hand, Tairov tore the actor away from everything human, lifelike, and psychological. Semantics and the sense of what was occurring were relegated to a minor position. Transferring the actor to a world of pure and abstract rhythms and melodies deprived him of the ability to influence the spirit and the psyche of the audiences. The playgoers considered the Kamerny Theater productions as something like the classical ballet.[37] The audiences found the productions very musical and quite pleasing to the eye and ear, but the presentations did not affect the heart. The spectacles were gay and astonishing, but they could not enrich the audience with experiences, or with new and profoundly disquieting thoughts.

Nevertheless, Tairov's persistent transformation of the theater into visible music was remarkable. He strove to return to the lost golden age of the ancient theater, which had developed from the dance and from music. He tried to restore the original theater, the dance set to music. He was bold enough to declare that not literature but music was the sister art of the theater.

Soviet Moscow at that time was a heaving sea of revolutionary hatred, hunger, poverty, and destruction. Tairov's Theater was a lone, variegated, and interesting islet lost in that sea. It was exotic; it never staged anything at all that resembled the gloomy realities of Soviet life. It was a greenhouse raising orchids in a city whose entire population was growing bloated from hunger and would avidly devour bad herring, rotten potatoes, and claylike bread. Tairov's Theater was completely isolated from Bolshevism. It was walled off from the unpleasantness of existence, reality, and politics, as if it contained the pure art of the theater within itself.

Tairov staged *Adrienne Lecouvreur* by Scribe and Legouvé in 1919, a year of famine, typhus, destruction, and civil war. In the Theater were sparkling satins, colorful silk dresses, lace, refined gestures, and a delicate melodious quality in the actors' voices. Tairov presented the wings of the Comédie Française, and the refined love tragedy of Adrienne Lecouvreur and Maurice, Duc de Saxe. The atmosphere was scented most subtly. What did this have in common with the many grim Red Army men or the hungry and sallow-faced civilians in the orchestra seats?

Tairov consciously chose this theme, with its forms and emotions, in the days of despair, famine, filth, and destruction. He wanted to contrast the presentation—which was refined, tender, lyrical, and colorful—with the coarse and gloomy environment. He wanted to elevate the hearts of the audience above the terror of reality and to a different world, which would be fine and pure. He contrasted satin, silk, and the most delicate lacework with the shabby clothes of the audience. There was an antithesis between the coarse gestures of the playgoers and the refined gestures of the actors, the gesticulations in the play having been worked out with a jewellike precision. The hoarse voices of the audience were quite unlike the minuetlike melodies of the actors. At the time when the Civil War brought bestial cruelty and death, the death of Adrienne Lecouvreur called forth a purifying smile of joy rather than tears.

Tairov used the presentation militantly to proclaim a theater that soared above the sinful earth and had nothing in common with life. His was a theater in which dreams materialized. It seemed to contain a cosmos within itself whose forms, motions, speech, and even its emotions were its own. Perhaps the complete break with the centripetal laws of real life contained all the greatness of Tairov's first reforms. The actor and the director were like divinities creating their own universe. This "theater world in itself" had two poles: tragedy and buffoonery. The theater was both a temple and a farce.

One of the Kamerny Theater's greatest contributions to the tragic genre was its production of Racine's *Phèdre* in 1921. Tairov's *Phèdre* scarcely resembled that of Racine, who had transferred his Hellenes to the Age of Louis XIV. Tairov restored *Phèdre* to the archaic period of the ancient Greeks, when the myth began.

A. Vesnin's maquette showed the dominance of inchoate forms during the ancient period. Angular steps, like bits of a seaside cliff, led down from two enormous columns. The entire acting platform, like the deck of a galley, sloped towards the auditorium. There were some elements— colored fragments of forms hanging in the air—that did not yet harmonize completely. Three brown warriors were as ponderous and as static as the columns against the limitless blue background. Thus Tairov succeeded in revealing the primordial atmosphere, along with the archaic and monumental quality of Greek mythology. Everything else on the stage was subordinated to it: the costumes, the poses, and the motions and gestures. Everything trifling and superficial was removed. Everything reminiscent of either existence or the shattered soul within contemporary man was taken away. These were severe statues in stone, animated only by niggardly motions and gestures that still were in the process of birth.

Tairov restored the same primordial laconicism to language and feeling on the stage. He changed the fumbling, fragmented, and complicated rhythm of contemporary speech into song, and he transformed the patches of old speech-forms into symbolical speech. All the psychological details and subtleties in the shadings and transitions had been removed from the emotions of the actors, and the passions shown were as unmixed as the multicolored fragments hanging above the stage.

Of course, not all the actors managed to accomplish the tremendous tasks that Tairov had set them to perfection. Nevertheless, this *Phèdre* was the one Soviet production—and perhaps the one European production—in which the director succeeded in transmitting both the great power of mythological tragedy and its archaic spirit.[38] On the maquette itself, the stairs resembled crags on a cliff, and the columns looked like the portal to a temple. The sloping stage floor seemed to raise the actors above the audience. The shining indigo background set off the characters and transformed them into statues. All this was in itself the discovery of a universal maquette for ancient tragedy.

Tairov created the theater of the "compound actor." These performers were able to play tragedy today, pantomime tomorrow, and a light operetta on the following day—and all with the same skill. Tairov enriched the theater arts with his innovations in buffoonery also. In his production of *Princess Brambilla,* which was based on E. T. A. Hoffmann's work, Tairov used the same actors who had done *Phèdre* and *Salome.* These performers demonstrated their virtuosity in acrobatics, juggling, and the techniques of buffoonery.

Princess Brambilla was a fantastic capriccio that made musical instruments from the elements of the theater. It was the first major "programmatic" presentation. Music completely dissolved the action on the stage. The presentation showed the victory of pure theater magic, which was sinister at times and burst out in harlequinades of unbridled joy on other occasions.

Charles Lecocq's *Giroflé-Girofla,* which had previously been almost unknown in Russia, was staged at the Kamerny Theater in 1922. The production of this operetta continued the innovations in buffoonery, and the result was a genuine masterpiece of the theater arts, the most ebullient buffonade that the Soviet theater has ever known. Theater was dissolved within music in the individual style of the Kamerny Theater, and Tairov's infinite imagination flavored the work. He filled the production with many theater jokes, bits of clowning, eccentricity, and acrobatics, and the presentation sparkled with gay colors and giddy choral dances.

Tairov managed to create a spectacle of light and continuous movements. The actors wore tights and sweaters and could be told apart only through the colors of their scarves. He thus outlined their bodies to use their entire range of expressive possibilities. He used all the lighting effects he could. During the scene in which Giroflé gets drunk, punch burned on the table. Both the characters and their surroundings were bathed in pink, violet, and sparkling gold. Everything was turned into a drunken cascade of light beams. This was the finest lighting achievement of the Soviet theater.

Tairov succeeded in creating a conglomerate spectacle in practice rather than merely in theory. The farce, the circus, the music-hall, the operetta, and the harlequinade were all blended into one, and the action raced forward in unrestrained happiness. He showed the glitter and the *joie de vivre* of the nonpsychological theater that used only the outer technique of the "representational theater" and was otherwise based on the pure "juggling" of comedians.

Giroflé-Girofla was powerful because it was organically connected with motion, dancing, singing, lighting, acrobatics, colored costumings, and all the other elements of the "representational theater" through rhythm. The entire symphonic buffonade was subordinated to the plan of the director. It was a triumph for dynamics within the theater.

In 1924 the Kamerny Theater set a precedent by experimenting with a drama that Tairov hated—*Storm,* by Alexander Ostrovsky. *Storm* was a true-to-life play that represented an artistic ideology diametrically opposed to Tairov's. The experiment calls to mind Meyerhold's attempt to do the same play back in 1915, which had also caused much commotion. Tairov's effort was most important in the development of the Soviet theater. He "cleansed" the play of material objects and other items that indicated the ordinary way of life. The stage contained a two-story construction which was quite ascetic. It resembled a wooden bridge, with ramps leading away from it. This was the basic décor for all the acts. The designers—the Stenberg brothers and Medunetsky—removed everything from the characters' costumes that might have suggested realism or the atmosphere of life. Only the basic plan for the costumes remained.[39] The acting was also cleansed of realism. Tairov's aim was to transfer some devices of the tragic theater, which he had discovered for *Phèdre,* to the Russian drama.

The purely Russian speech of Ostrovsky's characters was also purified of any normalistic traits, characteristics, or psychological motivations. The singing speech of the Kamerny Theater replaced the Russian of the old merchants.

Tairov did not completely succeed in breaking with the "land" and reality, or in transferring Katerina's entire tragedy to a nonrealistic and quasiabstract level. But his production of *Storm* did show the importance and the great esthetic value of staging classics with neither naturalism nor true-to-life trifles. It showed the possibility of changing a drama of milieu into a reverberating tragedy. And the production of *Storm* was a turning point for the Kamerny Theater. It marked the start of Tairov's "neorealism." This was the term for the original kind of "purism"— laconic, frugal, purged of everything petty in its style—that would later dominate Tairov's productions.

The next landmark on Tairov's creative path was his production, in 1924, of G. K. Chesterton's *The Man Who Was Thursday.* S. E. Krzhizhanovsky staged it. So far, Tairov's theater had played mainly pieces that were remote from reality. These dramas were used to assert the theater's superiority over life, to assert the timeless element, and a self-contained "skill for its own sake." The theater was militantly declared to be beyond the limits of life. With Chesterton's novella, however, something contemporary was undertaken, although the action did take place beyond the frontiers of Soviet Russia.

Chesterton's play is about a conspiracy of seven anarchists, each of whom is nicknamed for a day of the week. The group is planning to assassinate the King. All of them, except "Sunday," turn out to be Scotland Yard agents. The story tells how a single anarchist makes fools out of half a dozen detectives and compels them to chase each other while he prepares an act of terrorism and carries it out. Tairov used the story as raw material for a "symphony of the big city," with its fairyland of urbanism. He included the endless play of illuminated signs, sharply dynamic action, and racing elevators and escalators.

Tairov's work was based on the half-fantastic type of plot that is so typical of Chesterton, but it clearly shows that realism was influencing the Kamerny Theater. There were many characters in the presentation, but none of them was given the usual Kamerny Theater stylization so "unlike life." They were real inhabitants of a European capital, wearing the everyday clothes of ordinary people. All their accessories were also real. No doubt Tairov thought of this presentation when he took the Kamerny Theater on a tour of Europe in 1923. It must be considered a retreat from the Theater's policy. What inspired the presentation was reality itself, which Tairov had belligerently excluded from his theater for a number of years.

If it may be so expressed, *The Man Who Was Thursday* was part of the "urban infection" that was gripping many Soviet theaters at the time. Productions on Western European themes were created not so much to show the disintegration of the bourgeoisie as to show how infatuated the directors were with the cities of the West. There, tension was dynamic, mechanical techniques existed, and so did "American tempos." For most Soviet directors, the source for this romantic urbanism was not the realities of the West (which only Tairov had been lucky enough to feel and to observe), but literature and—even more—the motion pictures. This was where the noxious and dangerous—from the Bolshevik viewpoint—tendency to eccentricity, American qualities, machines, and the use of motion-picture devices came from.

With the staging of Chesterton's novella, Tairov began a series of productions based on Western European urbanism. This was no accident, and it was a change of the Kamerny Theater's principles. Tairov was turning to the works of dramatists from the West. From 1924 to 1928 he staged eight such contemporary plays.

Here we see one great service which he rendered the Russian theater and Russian audiences. The Soviet theater press does not mention it. From its very start and throughout the heyday of the Soviet theater, the Kamerny was always an outpost of European and other non-Soviet drama in Russia. Except, perhaps, for its years of agony, 90 percent of its repertory consisted of classical and contemporary plays by non-Russians.[40]

The Kamerny Theater was a point of contact between the West and the Russians living under the Soviet regime. It spoke with the voice of a world that an impassable abyss had separated from Soviet Russia. It played its Western European and American repertory on its three tours of the West (in 1923, 1925, and 1930) and thus accomplished a great cultural mission by using the arts as a means of friendly international contact. It enriched the theaters of the West through its discoveries of scenic form, and it enriched the theaters of the Soviet Union through its productions of new works from the West.

The Kamerny Theater staged Eugene O'Neill's *The Hairy Ape* in 1926. With this production, Tairov continued his "Western themes" and faced reality. This play, with O'Neill's inherent expressionistic power, showed two worlds in the America of those days. The first was the lower one, consisting of slaves to machines—the toiling stokers on a steamer. The other world was the higher one, the "topside world" of those who were fenced off from the proletariat by an insuperable wall. The absolute dichotomy between "black" and "white" was not very realistic, but it suited the Bolsheviks perfectly. It was no accident that Lunacharsky described *The Hairy Ape* favorably:

It is socially valuable. . . . It approaches the ideal of a genuine, finished, irreproachable social tragedy. The play tells us two things. First of all, it shows the colossal revolutionary potential of just this downtrodden proletariat, and secondly it shows how very solid are the walls of the American social cauldron.[41]

Tairov's greatest success in the presentation was with the mass scenes in the hold of the ship. The steam engines roared and thundered. Groups of stokers, their bodies half-naked and glossy with sweat, took turns feeding the fires. They were shown in varying perspectives and used striking motions to accompany their labors.[42]

In depicting the "bourgeoisie" Tairov maintained the canons that Meyerhold had worked out and that had become common for the entire Soviet theater of the period. The bourgeois characters were sharply caricatured and depicted as frightful dolls that danced the fox-trot incessantly.[43]

The Stenberg brothers were the designers for *The Hairy Ape*. Their work was done with the refined and elegant constructivism that was theirs alone. The basic construction represented a projecting cabin topside on the steamer. By opening the walls of the cabin and bringing in a small addition, it was transformed into the boiler room, the street, or the police station.

Tairov's production of O'Neill's *Desire under the Elms* in 1926 was much better artistically. For one thing, it was free of the propagandistic flights seen in *The Hairy Ape*. O'Neill transferred the story of Phaedra and Hippolytus to an American farm family, and the result contained no material for political propaganda. The production of *Desire under the Elms* continued and developed the devices used in *Storm*. It sought a tragic style to schematize reality, a "purism" in the theater, a drama purified from the dross and the trifles of existence, and a further assertion of neorealism.

In this production, Tairov again approached the terseness of tragedy. But this was a new step towards the real and the earth. The crowd scenes and the farmers' dances at the wedding were done with heavy "Flemish" pithiness. The Kamerny Theater, slowly but surely, was falling from the clouds and hovering above the land.

All God's Chillun Got Wings, a third play by O'Neill, was offered in 1929. Its external forms continued to strengthen "scenic purism," that is, sculptured brevity in the actor's motions and a background of the condensed and simplified décor. The combination of high screens, latticed shutters, angles, and staircases covered by a thin coating of rough stone hinted at a contemporary American city. But the urban décor was completely contradicted by the naturalistic costumes, the props borrowed from life, the street lamps, and so on.

The theme of American racial discrimination in the play suited the Bolsheviks. It jibed to a certain extent with the Communist propaganda slogans that stated that the white capitalists punished the Negroes.

Shaw's *St. Joan* was staged in 1924, and Walter Hasenclever's *Antigone* in 1927. The latter play was adapted by Sergei Gorodetsky, the poet. In these productions Tairov continued his most valuable reforms in seeking the forms of contemporary tragedy. He was, perhaps, the only Soviet director who persistently sought a way to the highest genre of the theater arts. In the process he maintained the earlier esthetic beliefs of the Kamerny Theater almost uncompromisingly.

Together with the Stenberg brothers—the designers for *St. Joan*—Tairov transformed the elements of Gothic architecture into a kind of primitive "Gothic constructivism." The costumes were like historical bits from the clothing worn during Joan of Arc's lifetime. The gestures of the characters were condensed, and only vital transitions were used. Alice Koonen played the title role with great skill and raised Shaw's play to the highest degree of the tragic. Tairov's entire production was directed at overcoming the realistic belittling of St. Joan's death found in Shaw. The presentation was extraordinarily static and ordinary, but it must not be simply rejected because it was a thing of beauty.

The production of *Antigone* raised the tragic genre to heights that the Soviet theater had never attained before. It turned out to be the last and crowning attempt of all the quests for the forms of classical tragedy. There was something prophetic in this 1927 production. Creon's palace rose in cubes above the abyss cut into the stage floor. It was like a "pillbox" from the cities or the "Atlantic Wall" of the Third Reich. The warriors were heavily armored from head to foot with iron mesh. The platform of the palace turned menacingly. The power of Creon's dictatorship annihilated everything, marking the peak of coercion and militarism. Such was the emotional theme of this uniquely powerful presentation, which showed the European reality of thirteen years later.

Tairov's particular skill at molding sculptured groups and crowd scenes was especially evident in *Antigone*. There were frightening interwoven lines of half-naked people in rags. At times they would come out of the numerous trapdoors and drag themselves up the walls and ladders of Creon's fortress. At other times they were thrown down and cowed by the firm step of the warriors. This was the one presentation of the Kamerny Theater in which the actors' voices, the noises, the whirlwinds of motion, the rumblings and the sounds of Creon's armored "robots" achieved superhuman power.

The productions that climaxed the Kamerny Theater's searchings within buffoonery were: V. Maas's *Kurikol* (1924); Charles Lecocq's *Le Jour et la nuit* (1926), and V. Zak's and Y. Dantsiger's *Sirocco* (1928). The tragic line of the Kamerny Theater rose steadily toward perfection, but the buffoonery line did not. None of the above-mentioned presentations could surpass *Giroflé-Girofla* in terms of acting or production.

There were two productions at the Kamerny Theater during this period that stand completely by themselves. Their distinction came, not from their formal novelty nor from the revelation of new horizons in the art of the theater, but from their civic qualities. These two plays—Mikhail Bulgakov's *Purple Island* (1928) and Mikhail Levidov's *Plot of the Equals* (1929)—concealed sharp attacks on the Soviet regime.

In *Purple Island* Bulgakov and the Kamerny Theater poked gay and satirical fun at propaganda potboilers and the cowardly Party members on the Main Repertorial Committee. But the Kamerny Theater also laughed at itself to some extent. Afraid of Bolshevism, it too had frequently staged propagandistic caricatures of old Russia and the world beyond the Soviet frontiers.

The press attacked this comedy, calling Bulgakov a counterrevolutionary, and soon forced the play off the boards. For a long time, however, the production was on the "list of offenses" committed by the Kamerny Theater, and it was recalled again when the Theater of Tairov was liquidated after the war.

It is almost impossible to find any reference to the *Plot of the Equals* in the Soviet press.[44] The production is not even mentioned in the publications of the Kamerny Theater itself. The play was forbidden by the Soviet censorship after its very first public performance.

Plot of the Equals dealt with the tragic death of "Caius Gracchus" Babeuf, the leader of the Babeuvists, which it treated with historical accuracy. It showed how the former revolutionaries degenerated under the Barras Directory after Thermidor. They became fat dictators who sentenced the last defenders of democracy and of the disinherited nation to the guillotine. The audience felt a chill run up its spine. They understood that the history of the Directory was really that of the present. *Plot of the Equals* was forbidden, and its author was branded a "Trotskyite."

THE MOSCOW ART THEATER

In 1919 the Moscow Art Theater suffered a catastrophe. A large part of the troupe had gone to southern Russia and was cut off from Moscow by the offensive of General Denikin's White Army. Many skilled members of the company remained with the White Army in retreat and finally left the country. In exile these people established the so-called "Prague Group of the Moscow Art Theater." Thus ended the wonderful ensemble with which Stanislavsky and Nemirovich-Danchenko had toiled for so many years. The Moscow group of "old-timers" suffered a great loss. It retained only Knipper, Lilina, Raevskaya, Korenëva, Kachalov, Moskvin, Gribunin, Luzhsky, Vishevsky, Podgorny, Burdzhalov, the two founders, and a group of studio trainees.

When the Theater requested permission to visit other countries, the Bolsheviks did not even detain this "fragment of Russian capitalism." Stanislavsky took the troupe for a tour of Europe and America, which began in September, 1922. Only Nemirovich-Danchenko and some apprenticed to the Theater's studios remained in Moscow. Stanislavsky and members of the Moscow Art Theater were free to join their colleagues of the Prague group. They could have preserved the entire former company, and the Moscow Art Theater would have been shielded from the coercion of art and artistic conscience that lay in store for them back in the Soviet Union. But Stanislavsky returned to Soviet Russia in August, 1924. Perhaps he felt that the Moscow Art Theater was a profoundly national Russian theater, which could exist and thrive only on Russian soil. Furthermore, he probably shared the belief held by most of the Russian theater experts at the time that the new regime was becoming humanized and that the NEP gave reason to hope for the "enlightenment" of the Bolsheviks. Whether Stanislavsky regretted his return during the last years of his life remains a secret. During those years the Bolshevik government seized control of his Theater.

On its tour abroad the Moscow Art Theater performed only Byron's *Cain* and Gogol's *The Inspector-General*. The première of *The Inspector-General* had taken place in Moscow on October 8, 1921, and it was the Moscow Art Theater's third production of the play, previous versions having been staged in 1908 and 1912. Meyerhold was not to produce it until years later.

The 1921 production contained many new elements. Unlike Meyerhold, Stanislavsky did not try to "revise" Gogol. There were no insertions from the author's notebooks and no change in the order of the scenes. The Theater was attracted by Gogol's satire, and the production shifted the center of gravity from local color and the truth of life to a forceful molding of the characters. The new version emphasized the truth of

Gogol's satire, not the truth of Gogol's own period. Stanislavsky freed the play from the fetters of its milieu. It now acquired a marvelous comic rhythm, new settings, colorful décor (by K. F. Yunin), and a bold, grotesque portrayal of Khlestakov by Mikhail Chekhov.

When Stanislavsky returned to the Soviet Union, he learned about the noisy activity of the Soviet theater reformers. His reaction was a mixture of sincere enthusiasm and paternal irony directed at children who were immeasurably mischievous and imaginative.[45] His keen eyes immediately noted whatever the innovators had contributed that was good.[46] He was pleased with the fervor and the boldness of all these experiments, but he well understood that most of them were superficial and external. They were not new devices for transmitting the life of the human spirit in artistic form.

His enthusiasm changed to apprehension at the idea that all these developments were becoming a goal in themselves and the spirit and the internal creative process of acting were being plundered.[47]

Perhaps no one could have reached a harsher conclusion about the entire noisy period than Stanislavsky did. He considered it a "tempest in a teapot." It was a revolution of the directors filled with victories by the directors, the designers, and the enlighteners. For Stanislavsky, the core of the theater arts had been and still was to use acting for revealing the internal world of the character. He viewed all the innovations as a flight from profundity to superficiality, which oppressed the creative spirit of acting.[48]

Stanislavsky felt that the absence of new plays was the tragedy that accompanied the scenic revolution:

Our collective work begins with the playwright; without him, the actors and directors have nothing to do. . . . Were a play to appear that brilliantly reflected the spirit of contemporary man and his life—regardless of whether its form were impressionistic, realistic, or Futuristic—all the actors, directors, and playgoers would jump upon it and would look for the best way to incarnate its internal and spiritual essence. The essence of human spiritual life nowadays is profoundly important. It has been created through suffering, struggle, exploits, and the most unprecedented and cruel catastrophes, including hunger and the revolutionary struggle.[49]

The lack of real talent among the contemporary dramatists has hurt the entire Soviet theater. It has caused all the desperate tricks in directing and the tailoring of the classics.[50] This was why they sought to make form alone contemporary and revolutionary. It was a series of hopeless experiments to change form into content.[51]

Stanislavsky sharply rejected replacing the absent poet with a propagandistic presentation created by the director, although this typified the period.[52] Everyone was intoxicated with the "external madness," and internal technique was considered reactionary, bourgeois, and "psychological."[53] The Moscow Art Theater was looking for other things. It wanted new means for bringing out the truth about human spiritual life through the classics, and it hunted most painstakingly for a new internal acting technique. It sought new technical and psychological means for the creative process known as the Stanislavsky System.

This is why the Moscow Art Theater exhibited no dazzling formal innovations. It did not glitter and did not strike the audiences or the critics with designers' coups, stunning lighting techniques and costumes, or alluring use of devices from motion pictures, the circus, or the music hall. All the innovations of Stanislavsky and Nemirovich-Danchenko took place in their search for new means to depict the actor's internal technique. There is no doubt that these covert innovations were much more important in the development of the theater arts than were the ear-splitting victories of the directors of the "Leftist Front" and of the "October in the Theater" movement.

This does not mean, however, that the Moscow Art Theater was astonishingly wise and successful or that its path was smooth. There were failures and frustrations that always resulted whenever the Theater abandoned Stanislavsky's ideas and suddenly decided to follow the style of the period or to try, as the poet Sergei Esenin expressed it, to "hitch up its pants and run after the Komsomol."

Stanislavsky's outstanding work during the period under discussion took place in 1926. He produced that year Alexander Ostrovsky's *Goriachee serdtse* ("Burning Heart"). This wonderful presentation has been inspiring the audiences at the Moscow Art Theater with fresh love and fresh joy for a quarter of a century. When it first came out, it was not only programmatic but even polemical. The Moscow Art Theater used *Burning Heart* to assert its own creative program. This responded to Lunacharsky's slogan "Back to Ostrovsky!" and observed the centennial of the great Russian dramatist's birth. It also answered Meyerhold's eccentric production of *The Forest*.[54]

It was programmatic because it really showed that Russian acting skill had been increased. This was at a time when technique was withering and dying throughout the Soviet theater under pressure from directors who sought spectacles and from the coercion of external forms. The Soviet critics had a standard accusation against the Moscow Art Theater—they accused it of wretched naturalism and "psychologizing." *Burning Heart* proclaimed the Theater's real personality, which was not a theater of naturalism or of truth-to-life but a theater of artistic truth. This theater created not only presentations that were psychologically realistic but presentations that imagination transformed into artistic and scenic fact.[55]

Burning Heart was polemical. It rebuked Meyerhold and threatened the "Meyerholdians." Stanislavsky brilliantly and convincingly showed how to give a new and contemporary interpretation of Ostrovsky without crudely and intolerably tailoring the text. The characters were not changed into Bolshevik propaganda posters. Nor were there any intrusions of futuristic devices into a dramatic text completely unsuited to them.[56]

Stanislavsky's major task was to find the satirical principle in Ostrovsky's work. This, however, had to be done without cutting up the comedy or mutilating it. Stanislavsky did not consider *Burning Heart* a "pretext for production," which was always the attitude of Meyerhold and Tairov. He sought to reveal in Ostrovsky's work the powerful source of the playwright's colorful and genuinely theatrical satire. The devices of the farce and of the folk comedy and all this pithy, inflated, and satirical comedy were profoundly justified and organized within Ostrovsky himself. This was satire staging facts—Stanislavsky transmuted the comic chimeras of the satire into reality, and he changed the ideal into the material. He showed "comedy from within," and the grotesque element came from the depths of the spirit. All this was the victory of the Moscow Art Theater and the Stanislavsky System over all the methods of the reformers, who always approached satire and fantasy from without, from the form, from movement, or from propagandistic notions.

Mikhail Bulgakov's *Days of the Turbins* was another revival that was presented by the Moscow Art Theater in 1926. The most important feature of this production was that it was done by the young people of the Theater. There were no performers in it who belonged to the old or even the middle generation. And everyone, including I. Sudakov, the director, had been trained by Stanislavsky and Nemirovich-Danchenko. These actors turned a "stage fact" into real life. They did not "punish" the characters—they "were" the characters. It was impressive because the Moscow Art Theater showed with unprecedented power the warmth, the sincerity, and the living breath of everything that was happening. This was a great triumph for the Theater in terms of its training of new actors—when most of the outstanding Soviet theaters could not create a new school of acting. With the production of *Days of the Turbins* the Moscow Art Theater presented the Soviet theater with new and expert actors completely trained by the Stanislavsky System.

This new production of *Days of the Turbins* marked another turning point in the history of the Soviet theater. Other theaters had approached the Civil War with propagandistic stereotypes. The Moscow Art Theater, however, now demonstrated that revolution and civil war could be staged with great brilliance, artistic power, and truth to life. This was the first presentation to give a contemporary Soviet theme with love, warmth, truth, and power in no way inferior to the same theater's presentations of the classics.

Recently, Soviet theater literature has tried to show that Stanislavsky, after all, tried to "correct" Bulgakov and make his play more "Soviet." [57] We are inclined to think that this is merely an easy falsification of the past because Stanislavsky has now been "canonized" by the Bolsheviks as a director. Even in *Days of the Turbins,* however, Stanislavsky and the Moscow Art Theater remained faithful to the principle that so sharply distinguished them from the bulk of Soviet theaters and theater experts. This principle consisted in not judging, not sentencing people or phenomena in life.

In 1927 another great event took place at the Moscow Art Theater —Stanislavsky's staging of *La Folle journée; ou, Le Mariage de Figaro* by Beaumarchais.[58] Stanislavsky considered the work a folk comedy, which had sounded revolutionary in the times of Beaumarchais.[59] He transferred the action from what was supposedly Spain to France on the eve of 1789, and he used every means he could to increase the role of the people. Every other production of *Le Mariage de Figaro* contained a faceless mob of opera-style supernumeraries, but Stanislavsky worked out an individualized character and profession for everyone in the crowd. All the external set-up—the furniture, the props, and the place of action—were carefully selected and checked against the flavor of the milieu. The director divided the five-act comedy into twelve scenes and used a revolving stage. The varied and ebullient life of the play was constantly connected with the liveliest of the live—Figaro. Stanislavsky preserved all the champagnelike froth and sparkle of the action as it developed spontaneously, and he retained its easy elegance.

His contribution to the play was not limited just to replacing the decrepit comic stereotypes with the warm blood of real life. Here for the first time he introduced new devices for the inner technique of acting and new laws for the "psychological technique of the actors." He demanded that each actor learn perfectly "the course of his day on the stage," the reasons for his every thought and action, an approach that concealed a most powerful method for advancing the inner technique of acting in a new direction and gave concrete clarity of purpose to every movement the actor made on the stage. Such self-examination absorbed the actor's whole being, and it demanded from him an unbroken chain of inner justification. All this made the stage action impress the audience as real. It was the source for something new and dynamic that would soon be incorporated into the Stanislavsky System—his method of physical actions.

Ordinary "physical actions" were studied on the stage. (They were really physical and psychological actions.) Every movement was examined, and the actor had to create the "given circumstances" and a number of hypotheses, using the idea "if this took place in my own, real life." Every elementary movement contained inner action and experience. The first étape of the Stanislavsky System had consisted of analysis. The new étape, on the other hand, began with the "method of physical actions" and was a synthesis. The System in the past had been strong in its profound treatment of the heart of a role, and this had frequently forced the body of the role into the background. The attainments of the first étape had been connected with the psyche, and their purpose was concrete action and motion. The new étape found a fusion of inner and outer action through physical action and movement.

Movement, clear in purpose and born of logic, became a "valve for the feelings," a "path to the life of the human spirit." "Physical action" made it possible to reach the hidden and complex heart of a character. His experiences could also be shown; movements produce both thoughts and experiences. The most difficult thing for an actor to do is to think the character's thoughts and to possess only the character's impulses to action. The "method of physical actions" made this possible. Concrete movements, concrete objectives on the part of the actor, tear him away from himself and bring him to a different reality. This is the reality of the character's spirit, along with his psychology. And it is not limited to psychology alone; the character of a person *is* his system of movements.

Although Stanislavsky had wanted to restore to *Le Mariage de Figaro* the revolutionary quality that Beaumarchais had given it, and although the result was a wonderful work which was filled with a noble and democratic spirit, nevertheless, the Bolshevik critics growled at it. They were not much interested in the fact that Stanislavsky had cleansed the comedy of stereotypes and falseness and returned it to the period of Beaumarchais. They wanted him to lie crudely by transforming Figaro into a confirmed Communist. Some Bolshevik reviewers were really ridiculous. They even denied seeing or sensing any *national* character in the presentation (which contradicted Stanislavsky).[60]

The première of Vsevolod Ivanov's *Armored Train 14–69* took place on November 8, 1927. It contained a number of "inner innovations" peculiar to the school of Stanislavsky. Stanislavsky decided that *Days of the Turbins* had not depicted "those who had really accomplished the Revolution and had borne on their shoulders all the weight of the struggle for the ideals of the Revolution." In Bulgakov's play, he continued, "The Russian people who carried out the Revolution and fought for it remain backstage and do not appear." [61] The Moscow Art Theater was now seeking to make up for its omission, and found a way to do so in Ivanov's play.

Stanislavsky's work on *Armored Train 14–69* was a major contribution to the Soviet theater. With this presentation, he greeted Bolshevism. He not only agreed to stage a "Party" presentation, but he showed the Soviet stage how the theater could ennoble the subject of revolution with profundity, sincerity, and humanity.[62] Vsevolod Ivanov himself pointed out what distinguished the Moscow Art Theater's treatment of Soviet plays from that of the other theaters when he wrote:

The more I scrutinized the Theater, the more it astonished me. Before it did my play, I thought that the most important thing in the theater was the ability to obtain something bulky, something—as it were—like a "city square," whether it was a medieval castle, an armored train, or simply an eight-story house. It turned out that these people considered something else important; they had an unusually serious attitude to a play, to the people acting in it, to the characters (whom they considered to be alive); they considered every phrase to be important, and they tried to understand it, to feel its full flavor, to give meaning to it the way a young lover gives meaning to his sweetheart's every word. Very frequently, I had people onstage by accident. . . . I found it most difficult to show a crowd on the stage—not only difficult but even impossible. . . . Then I saw that the actors wanted and were able to depict a crowd and in the process to examine every individual in it—and very frequently better than I could. The Moscow Art Theater conquered me.[63]

The most important "inner innovation" that the Moscow Art Theater brought to *Armored Train 14–69* was the many levels of action for its "positive" and "negative" characters. It showed the "revolutionary mass" as an assemblage of brilliant individuals. This in itself was a great revolution in the Soviet theater. Previously, there had been stereotypes. Communists had been "monolithic characters"; "Whites" had been beasts with shoulder straps; and the "mass" had been a "revolutionary proletariat" with but one character. It was a great innovation to show Peklevanov, a major Communist character in the play, as a nearsighted man with glasses. He was frail, an indoor man, sluggish, absent-minded, and at times a rather odd intellectual. It was an original revolt against the "hundred percent" Bolsheviks with their "leather jackets." The character of Vershinin, the muzhik leader of the partisans, also broke away from the packaged types with which Soviet actors had played revolutionary muzhiks. V. I. Kachalov played the role, and he condensed the wisdom, the complexity, and the spiritual beauty of the Russian peasant, giving in the process a fine psychological portrait rather than a cheap picture.

Stanislavsky and Simov—the designer—worked long and hard over every variant of the maquette and every detail of the staging. They attained extraordinary truthfulness and a most lifelike quality in the real details of the environment.

The production showed a new side to Stanislavsky's directing—the acceptance of Soviet ideas. It is difficult to say whether he was sincere or merely using the actor's technique of "getting used to a character." Stanislavsky's remarks at rehearsals did correspond to the realities, and —geniune or not—some of them are worth quoting. He told the "Whites" something that had nothing in common with his production of *Days of the Turbins* during the previous year:

You are not "crusaders," but traitors, betraying your country. As fine actors of our Theater depicting the belligerent remnants of the Russian bourgeoisie on the stage, you artists must make your hearts burn with indignation at them. For this, you must find a merciless and realistic attitude to your roles—especially if that work is to open the audiences' eyes to the ulcers of the past.[64]

These words sound like the speech of a theater director who was a Party member at a productional meeting. The "merciless attitude" to the characters portrayed by actors typified only the representational school. It completely contradicted the entire Stanislavsky System of the past. More important, it jarred completely against the System's later development and the Moscow Art Theater's later presentations. The Bolshevik attitude toward the White movement diametrically opposed *Days of the Turbins,* which the Moscow Art Theater was presenting at that very time. Let me repeat that this could be interpreted as Stanislavsky's "getting used" to his new role as a director of Soviet plays.

In finishing this survey of the outstanding productions at the Moscow Art Theater between 1921 and 1927, we ought to repeat that none of them used effective external devices. The performances were most important for the entire later development of the Soviet theater. Stanislavsky used them to erect, stone by stone, the greatest edifice of his entire life. This was the culmination of his system, a two-volume work entitled *An Actor Prepares.* Later, this study would become both the grammar and the syntax of acting throughout the Soviet theater.

STUDIOS OF THE MOSCOW ART THEATER

The First Studio of the Moscow Art Theater was established long before the Revolution. Stanislavsky despaired about ever using his System in the Moscow Art Theater itself because he was opposed by the outstanding actors and even by Nemirovich-Danchenko.[65] Stanislavsky decided, therefore, to create a new group composed of the young people in the Theater—the associates (extras) and trainees. They would be enthusiastic over his System and would accept it "literally and without checking." His partner in this enterprise was his friend and helper Leopold Antonovich Sulerzhitsky.

The First Studio was established in 1911. In addition to accepting and developing his System, the young offshoot of the Theater was given another task by Stanislavsky. They were to create an intimate theater, which would not be separated from the handful of playgoers by any footlights. "The young actor will not strain his voice, which is still weak," Stanislavsky wrote, "or his spirits, or his technique. Let the dimensions of the theater not force him to stretch and inflate his emotions. Let them not force him 'to tear a passion to tatters' for the sake of a large crowd." [66]

The nucleus of the new Studio on Tverskaya Street in Moscow comprised N. F. Kolin, G. M. Khmar, A. I. Chaban, V. V. Gotovstev, B. M. Sushkevich, S. V. Giatsintova, and S. G. Birman. They would later develop into most interesting and accomplished performers. The first brilliant adherent of the System in the new Studio was a young actor named Eugene V. Vakhtangov. He would later himself become a major innovator in the Soviet theater. The First Studio also began the development of a most remarkable contemporary Russian actor, Mikhail Alexandrovich Chekhov.

The First Studio of the Moscow Art Theater, with its tiny stage and auditorium, was the ancestor of a most fascinating movement during the Soviet period—the studio theaters. From 1918 to 1925 Moscow was filled with many studios, some of which were quite tiny and were hidden away in old buildings. In the evening, after a hard day's work at the factories and elsewhere, the young people would gather along with those who were not so young. They were all ardent and enthusiastic about the "new theater." They would rehearse from evening to late at night, and they searched for "new forms" with a fanatic passion. They sought the miracle of transmutation through the stage and of magic through the theater. Very frequently, after a rehearsal lasting until very late, they would remain to sleep in a group on the floor of the studio. They could then be up at daybreak to go to their factories and other places of employment. Hungry, ragged, greatly harried by office work and toil, they conquered their weak flesh through the great enthusiasm of their spirits. They searched for stage characters with spirit and absorption, grain by grain. They constructed the décor with their own hands, gluing the props together and sewing the costumes and curtains often until dawn.

The studios were almost like hermitages or monasteries, and the devotees who worked in them were a mendicant order of the militant faithful of the theaters. Frequently, all the reward they got for their enormous self-sacrifice and long, hard work was, one after the other, a "public preview," a "dress rehearsal," and a "première" of their presentation. A handful of close relatives and friends would comprise the audience, along with several people who themselves were enthusiasts from other chamber studios. These studios have for the most part disappeared by now, but they performed a great service in maintaining the burning flame of pure love for the pure art of the theater—especially among the young. The studios also retained much else that could not be found in the orthodox theaters.

In this atmosphere of obsession and self-sacrificing love for the theater the First, Second, Third (later called the Vakhtangov Theater), and Fourth Studios of the Moscow Art Theater came into being. They all came out of the studios set up within separate buildings in Moscow.

The earliest work of the First Studio of the Moscow Art Theater on Tverskaya Street was its production in 1911 of Herman Heijermans' play *The Good Hope,* performed in Russian under the title of *The Death of Hope.* This was supervised by Sulerzhitsky and directed by R. V. Boleslavsky and played by the young actors who had been raised on the Stanislavsky System. The production had sincerity, simplicity, and profundity in the acting and unprecedented warmth on the whole. The presentation scored a great hit with the Moscow public.

Anton Chekhov's *Sea Gull* had marked the birth of the original Moscow Art Theater's style. The adaptation of Charles Dickens's *The Cricket on the Hearth* did the same thing for the First Studio in 1912. Mildness, genuineness, and intimate humaneness such as the Russian theater had never seen before streamed forth from the stage to the small auditorium.[67] The heart and soul of the presentation was Sulerzhitsky. He blended the Tolstoyan idea with great love for life and the world. The devotion with which Sulerzhitsky preached the ideas of lofty dedication and service to art is not to be found in any of the other great personalities associated with the Russian theater. He brought to the theater the ecstatic spirituality with which he had once preached Leo Tolstoy's ideas to the Dukhobors in Canada. He alone, of course, was the spiritual leader of all the "theater hermitages," the little studios scattered through Moscow during those years.[68]

The Cricket on the Hearth showed the warmth, sincerity, and "pastel quality" in the style of the First Studio. It also revealed the group's faith in love, universal forgiveness, nonresistance to evil, and "peace on earth, good will to men." The Russian press and public were most enthusiastic over it and much was written on the subject. This victory of the Stanislavsky System produced a strong effect on the basic company of the Moscow Art Theater. It forced a review of their attitude to the "oddities" and "experiments" of Stanislavsky. The work of the First Studio won over all the former opposition to the "faith" of Stanislavsky.

After the Soviet upheaveal the First Studio played Ibsen's *Rosmersholm*. Vakhtangov staged the production in 1918, and the result was quite different from the pessimistic version of the play that the Moscow Art Theater had presented in 1907. In the earlier production death was the only way out for Rebecca from her struggle against the ghosts of Rosmersholm. Vakhtangov, however, stressed something else—Rosmer's and Rebecca's aspiration toward a new life. He wanted to show the spiritual death of the old world, and so he removed anything resembling life and replaced it with expressionism. He sought to use condensed devices for transmitting the spiritual moment of the drama, in which he saw "a step to the mystery [play]. This expressionism covers the acting, in which it attains abstractness in the psychological traits. It asserts the principle that actors create from themselves . . . through themselves, and by asserting themselves. This is how a character must be approached." [69] The staging of *Rosmersholm* was also subordinated to expressionism. It was done against a background of gloomy and severe cloths, with concentric rays of light that picked out the details of the furnishings and the figures of the performers.[70]

Strindberg's *Erik XIV* appeared in 1921 and marked the peak of the "Vakhtangov Period" at the First Studio. Vakhtangov tried to make the mystic Strindberg resound in a way that would be acceptable to the Bolsheviks. Vakhtangov's main theme was that a tragic death sentence had been pronounced against royal power. A "world of pale and bloodless courtiers" was surrounded with monumental abstractions.[71] The ordinary people were shown characteristically, "ethnographically," and with verisimilitude. The material world around them was also real. The characters in the "royal unit," however, were masked, "cubic," symbolic, and grotesquely tragic in their motions, make-up, costumes, and intonations. The entire production was worked out in two styles, which were mutually exclusive: "Cubism," with its symbolic quality, and realism.

Erik XIV was noteworthy for still another reason. Here, for the first time, the great talent of Mikhail Chekhov was presented in all its creative maturity. Chekhov played the title role—"a man born to be un-happy." For the first time, this actor showed the enormous range of his skills. In his intonations, in his outcry suddenly erupting from a whisper, in his hasty and impetuous motions, in his incredibly dynamic transition from shading to shading, he unveiled the character of a person torn apart by contradictions.

The Second Moscow Art Theater. When Vakhtangov died in 1922, Chekhov became the leader of the First Studio. In 1924, the First Studio was reconstituted as the Second Moscow Art Theater. Although Chekhov had been trained in Stanislavsky's theater, he gradually began to oppose the System. During the first years of the Soviet regime Chekhov began to develop his own theory and practice for the inner technique of acting. This was done within Chekhov's Studio in Moscow. Later on, he would set forth his ideas in *Put' aktëra* ("The Actor's Path"), and in *O tekhnike aktëra* ("On the Actor's Technique"). The latter study, his major work, appeared after he had gone abroad.

Chekhov began from the same "starting point" as did all the other Soviet theater reformers. He militantly rejected naturalism, "simplicity, such as exists in life," and "photographically precise transmission" on the stage.[72] He was a confirmed anthroposophist. Throughout his years on the stage, he remained faithful to Rudolf Steiner's idea of where work begins. Creativeness is awakened not by what *is,* but by what *can* be; not by reality, but by potentiality.

Chekhov tried to oppose the analytical Stanislavsky System and the creative method of the Moscow Art Theater (both of which he considered pernicious because they led to naturalism) with the synthetic principle. The actor's work must proceed not from the parts to the whole, but from the "preperception and perception of the whole." [73] This belief is behind the main difference between Mikhail Chekhov's method and everyone else's. Chekhov stressed the predominance of Fancy, Imagination, and Inspiration in acting.

Stanislavsky was a "monist," who blended the personal with the fictitious and the actor with the role in a single stage experience. Mikhail Chekhov, however, was a "dualist." He drew a sharp line between the actor and the emotions depicted. His actor depicts a character while standing aside and observing "it, its character, and its life." The actor can thus "approach the étape in which the artist purifies and ennobles his characters without bringing them any useless features from his own personal nature." [74] The actor must extinguish himself and let "inspiration act within him." [75]

At first glance, it would seem that Mikhail Chekhov had added nothing new with his "split consciousness." This was merely the ancient system of the "representational theater," deepened only by Steiner's philosophical terminology. Nor was Inspiration, to whose power the actor had to turn over his personality completely, anything new. It was a return to the old Russian school of acting, to the "internal school." Of course, Chekhov's value did not consist of his splicing the "internal" and "representational" schools together.

In the first stages of his research, this new item was revealed as quickly as possible in the power with which his students were submerged in a world of fantasy and inspiration. The activities in Chekhov's Studio had little in common with the "internal" school of lazy artisan actors but were activities in which the young actors used pure, Yoga-style concentration to seek renunciation of the environment, to liberate their "I" from its material casing, and completely to dissolve themselves within the creations of their own imagination. [76] Here too, however, Chekhov was unoriginal and only continued Stanislavsky's enthusiasm over Yoga (which was used in the System). The distinction between the two men was purely qualitative and involved the power and profundity with which Yoga was applied. The "ecstatic" quality was the new element in the internal technique of Chekhov's Studio. This was a complete manumission of fancy and inspiration, which transferred the actor's spirit into a world of different realities that had nothing in common with naturalism. The creative personality of the actor was liberated, the "Pythian quality" of his improvising was unleashed. There was a revolt against stereotypes and the limits of "common sense." [77] The resourcefulness of whoever creates characters on the stage was moved into the foreground. All this typified the first stage of the Mikhail Chekhov System. In contrast to Stanislavsky, Mikhail Chekhov proclaimed the *unreality* of stage experiences. [78]

One of the most interesting chapters in Mikhail Chekhov's works—for an actor or director—is the one dealing with the objective and subjective atmosphere as a significant factor in creating profoundly effective process in atmosphere—that is, the mood surrounding the actor on the stage as it surrounds a person in life. The atmosphere that an actor summons up from within on the stage is frequently in sharp contrast to the mood around him. Chekhov's atmosphere became important in realizing the tonality of the entire stage action and all the acting experiences.[79]

In the theaters of Meyerhold and Tairov, everyone and everything was eclipsed by the director. During the heyday of the Second Moscow Art Theater everything was subordinated to the great talent of Mikhail Chekhov as an actor. Beside his powerful portrayals of Erik XIV, Malvolio, Hamlet, Lear, and other roles, all the formal innovations of this Theater grow dim. What Chekhov showed in these phantasmagorical characters could not engender theater trends, schools of acting, or imitators. Everything was sealed within his own talent and creative personality.

His attitude toward the stage should clarify, however, the personality of this leading figure in the Second Moscow Art Theater. His artistic ideology completely contradicted the materialism of Bolshevism. The history of the struggle and death of the Theater is the history of a tragic conflict. The Theater tried to follow its own spiritual and ideological inclinations under a regime that was completely hostile to its philosophy and to Mikhail Chekhov himself. Neither the Tolstoyanism of Sulerzhitsky, the idealism and expressionism of Vakhtangov, nor the Steinerian attitude of Mikhail Chekhov could long survive under the belligerent materialism of the Bolshevik state.

From start to finish Chekhov found Bolshevism alien and frightening during his stay in the Soviet Union. He had no contact—nor could he have had any—with the world of militant materialists. His entire talent was turned to the spiritual, the ideal, the fantastic, and everything else that lay beyond existence. The dictatorship of the "baser I" was incompatible with the "loftier I" in the theater arts. More than any of the other actors at the time, Mikhail Chekhov saw the peril: "Danger threatened our art because of materialism. Accepted and carried out to the end, it was able to kill the living emotion of the actor, to lead him to re-evaluate the outer means of expression, and to cause him to lose the inner ones." [80]

All the tragic characters whom Chekhov played were filled with psychological expressionism. He seemed to lay bare the flowing blood, plus the living and palpitating human brain.[81] His comic roles were as ridiculous as they were frightening. It was always a grotesque kind of tragicomedy, slipping into phantasmagoria.

The most outstanding presentation of the Theater during the period under consideration was of William Shakespeare's *Hamlet*. For the first time the Russian theater treated the play with profound mysticism. During the rehearsals Chekhov discovered a new approach to the actor's handling of language. He trained actors to view the phonetics of a word as "motion transformed into sound." [82] After the production of *Hamlet* the First Studio was renamed the "Second Moscow Art Theater," and Mikhail Chekhov received the title of "Honored Artist of the R.S.F.S.R."

The Chekhov Period of the Second Moscow Art Theater lasted a short time. Mikhail Chekhov was hounded into exile. The agony of the Theater lasted for several years after his departure, and then the Soviet authorities ordered the Theater closed and finally liquidated it. We shall discuss in a later chapter the most significant productions given during the twilight years of the Second Moscow Art Theater.

The Vakhtangov Theater. Eugene Vakhtangov was one of the most important figures of the period. A few of his productions, a handful of his statements on the theater arts, and his lessons to his faithful students have proved enough to establish one of the most fascinating and whimsical Soviet theaters. His short life made the Soviet theater fruitful for years afterwards. While dying of cancer, he overcame frightful pain to give the theater Carlo Gozzi's *Turandot*. This was one of the gayest and sunniest productions in the Soviet theater.

Vakhtangov began as a fanatical adherent of the Stanislavsky System, and he developed according to this System even before the Revolution. Subsequently he was the only innovator who constantly retained the System's good qualities, even while sweeping away its weaker aspects. Unlike the others, Vakhtangov did not so much reject Stanislavsky's brilliant method as try to develop it further, to "revise it thoroughly" in his own fashion, and to base his own teachings upon it.

The weakest part of the work done by Meyerhold and Tairov was their sharp and intransigent rejection of Stanislavsky. They denied the great importance of the spiritual in the inner technique of acting. This is what led them to sterility, and why they failed to establish their own schools of acting. Vakhtangov was wise and sensitive enough to avoid their error. Both during and after his lifetime the actors associated with his Theater received their basic instruction through the Stanislavsky System.

Vakhtangov wished to accept all the good features of both Stanislavsky and Meyerhold:

[Stanislavsky] was carried away by genuine truth and brought naturalistic truth to the stage. He sought theatrical truth in the truth of life. Meyerhold went through the symbolical theater (which he is now rejecting) to the genuine theater. But Meyerhold was carried away by theatrical truth; he removed the truth of emotions. The truth, however, must exist both in Meyerhold's theater and in Stanislavsky's.[83]

Vakhtangov's work did synthesize the two and seemed to reconcile two mutually exclusive principles—Meyerhold's grotesquerie and Stanislavsky's truth-to-life. The synthesis produced an *irony* that belonged to Vakhtangov and his theater alone. Meyerhold's animated exhibit and merciless grotesquerie were lacking in this ironic theater, and so was the earthy realism of the Moscow Art Theater. Instead of using Meyerhold's suffocating masquerade or the Moscow Art Theater's ruthless psychological and realistic truth, Vakhtangov was theatrical. His comedies were permeated with warmth, genuine emotions, and the profound sincerity of the actors, as in his production of *The Cricket and the Hearth*.

Vakhtangov rejected the philistine art of everyday life, the "imitation of life," and the pettiness of realistic details. He did not, however, reject realism as a whole. He favored realism, but a realism that would "take from life not everything, but only what it needed for reproducing a given scene, that is, it would use only those items on the stage which play." [84] Vakhtangov proclaimed theatrical truth instead of truth-to-life. He opposed self-sufficient realism, but he favored a realism that would be subordinated to the unreal laws of the theater.

One of the strongest points in Vakhtangov's teaching was his belief in "theatrical realism." He felt that "the theater, like any other art, goes beyond the limits of ordinary reality." According to Zakhava, Vakhtangov had the following idea of "theatrical realism": "the tendency in the theater arts that aspired creatively to establish a special and theatrical life on the stage, a life that would strike the audience as a new reality. This theatrical life could be called *life* precisely because it would be presented with the *conviction* of real life." [85]

Vakhtangov strove to synthesize the romantic (or theatrical) with the realistic. This is shown in his teachings about the art of acting. He began by favoring the complete hegemony of the actor. Like Meyerhold and Tairov, he considered a play to be merely a "pretext" for the acting. The actor's highest task was to reveal "his own world of theatrical life on the stage through theatrical forms." [86] In Vakhtangov's Theater, as in those of Tairov and Meyerhold, the audience was not allowed to forget that it was in a theater. There was a difference, however. The actor in Vakhtangov's "theatrical theater" had to possess the "truth of scenic emotions" and an "inner justification" for his actions. This is why Vakhtangov accepted the bases which the Stanislavsky System used for working on a role, and made his actors learn them. [87]

If we may oversimplify, the synthesis of the real and the unreal subordinated the real elements to the unreal composition in the staging. In the technique of acting, it used all the complex psychological acting technique from the "theater of experience" to create characters of the "representational theater." Vakhtangov proclaimed an "attitude to what was being shown" which had to be attributed to the "representational theater." He declared that the actor and the director had the right to deform reality or history by showing their own attitude to it. Every artist had the unalienable right of showing his own thoughts and emotions about reality. Naturalists are not artists because they do not bring their individual attitudes to whatever they create. All the naturalists are alike, said Vakhtangov, the productions of one can be taken from the productions of any other.

Vakhtangov taught something that completely corresponds to the main point in the Kamerny Theater's program. He considered the theater to be a "gay festival of the arts" and emphasized the same militant theatricality that was inherent in Tairov. [88] Like Meyerhold, Vakhtangov believed that every idea and every play demanded its own special form of staging. [89]

This "permanent revolution" of forms was directed against the stereotyped traditions covering the theater. It strove to give the theater eternal youth and an inexhaustible wealth of newly created forms. Nothing could be more hostile to the later standardization of the Soviet theater and to its debasement by "socialist realism" than the eternal rebellion and curiosity of a Vakhtangov.

The productions done by the Third Studio of the Moscow Art Theater (later to be named for its director) sharply adhered to Vakhtangov's idea of seeking a new form for every play. All three of his efforts as a director (between 1920 and 1922) differed profoundly in their style.

He produced Anton Chekhov's *Svad'ba* ("Wedding") as a grotesque satire in 1920. Chekhov's characters appeared either as mechanized dolls or as Mardigras masks. Vakhtangov played havoc with Chekhov's skit, and turned it into a sharp satire against the world of the philistines.

Vakhtangov staged Maeterlinck's *Le Miracle de Saint Antoine* in 1921, which he turned into a satire on bourgeois society. Unlike *Wedding,* the Maeterlinck play was gloomy. Bigots, hypocrites, cynics, and stupid plunderers swarm around the deathbed of Aunt Hortense like vultures. They hope to be her heirs. Vakhtangov treated them like so many corpses, like so many cold and black puppets whose wooden hands and gestures were seen against the white background of the décor and the furniture.

St. Anthony wandered through the dead world of materialism in the rags of a stranger. He was alien and alone. Vakhtangov molded the crowd scenes, plus all the gestures and poses of the characters, with extraordinary laconicism. They had a sculptured quality, and showed the arid contrast between black and white. *Le Miracle de Saint Antoine* was gloomy and "Hoffmannesque."

Vakhtangov's next production, however, was the gayest presentation of the Soviet theater. The play was Carlo Gozzi's *Turandot,* produced in 1922—the director's last effort before his death. The work resounded with the joy of life. It contained the light, pure, and happy irony within Vakhtangov himself, which would later be the most charming feature of the theater bearing his name. He said:

In this presentation, the performers must not enact the tale of a cruel princess named Turandot; they must not bring the audience the content of the tale alone. Who cares whether Turandot loves Calaf or not? What is most important is one's contemporary attitude towards her, one's irony, and the smile provoked by the "tragic" contents of the tale.[90]

This gay and charming *Turandot* has been played over a thousand times. Even now, over thirty years later, it is in the repertory of the Vakhtangov Theater on the Arbat in Moscow. It is tremendously popular. Soviet audiences buy tickets for it a fifth and even a tenth time. *Turandot* stressed the joy of acting for acting's sake and lacked seriousness. It was not a presentation but a "day off" for the actors, who played theatrical pranks for their own pleasure and satisfaction. It was not a play, but rather light, elegant, prestidigitating—"play-acting."

Vakhtangov had his actors improvise merrily and spontaneously. The theme—haphazardly chosen—was the "tale for the theater" by Gozzi, that Venetian magician. In the first draft, Vakhtangov even wanted to scatter his performers—dressed in frock coats and evening gowns— throughout the auditorium, among their friends in the public. Suddenly, they would decide to go on the stage and would start playing "theater pranks."

In the final redaction, the actors were still clad in frock coats and evening dress (except for four traditional masks from the *commedia dell'arte:* Pantalone, Brighella, Truffaldino, and Tartaglia). All the performers came out on the stage to the sounds of the march and began "to get dressed" to the rhythms of the orchestra and chorus and in full view of the audience. Actually, all they did was to transform their clothes by adding items and materials that happened to be "at hand." Thus, instead of a luxurious turban, an actor wound an ordinary towel around his head, put on a pelerine, and became Prince Calaf. Another one tied a white scarf to his chin, and became King Timur. A bit of cloth and a letter-opener created Barach, the faithful servant. The one setting by I. Nivinsky was lightly fashioned in "Eastern" style.[91] In plain view of the public, make-up was applied by "proscenium attendants" clad in parti-colored silks.

There was a parade of the performers, who "ad-libbed" and cracked personal jokes at each other's expense. This quickly introduced the jesting nature of the impending improvisation. Some parti-colored silk remnants, a sign saying "Peking," and a round and yellow "sun" constituted the entire "localization" of the action. The acting itself showed a deliberate and derisive attitude towards the sense of the text. The performers did not act the text, but juggled words, melodies, and speech rhythms for their own satisfaction—or so it seemed.[92] The actors interrupted their "tragic soliloquies" with ad-libs and asides to the audience. They did not show their real emotions, but merely exhibited an easy and ironical ridicule in connection with those emotions.

All the primitive rearrangements of the "décor" were accomplished in plain view of the public. Even these, however, provided the actors with material for the happy rhythms of their motions. Rather than perform them seriously, they "played" at them. They jokingly changed the place of action so that the playgoers could see the joke that was taking place. At the start of the comedy, a scene is played almost to the end in "Peking." Suddenly, however, the actors catch sight of the audience, grasp their heads with exaggerated gestures, and sing out "Curtain!" in order to hide the "kitchen" of the theater from the public.

It was a charming mixture of elegant comedy and the naïve playing of children. The props and laughter had nothing to do with ancient China. The props included an accordion, a camera, a tennis-racket (instead of the emperor's sceptre), and so on. The music for the presentation was also quite ironic. The orchestra was made up of hair-combs in different sizes, which the Studio members would cover with cigarette paper and then "play."

Turandot was the one presentation of the Third Studio that removed all illusions of the theater, along with everything serious and absolute. Only the actors remained on the stage, and they played jokes on themselves and on each other. The spontaneity, the ethereal lightness of "playing theater jokes" for their own sake formed Vakhtangov's style of producing the comedy. It had a gay and charming flavor that the theater would later inherit from Vakhtangov in its productions of Lensky's *Lev Gurych Sinichkin* and Shakespeare's *Much Ado about Nothing*.

Turandot greatly resembled another presentation that opened the era of innovations within the Soviet theater—Meyerhold's treatment of *Le Cocu magnifique*. The premières of the two works took place only a few months apart. They both used the happy mischief-making of free comedians who seemed to have just awakened from a boring hibernation within the serious theater. They had been roused by the springtime atmosphere of freedom. There were only two distinctions between the productions, but both were important and favored Vakhtangov. Vakhtangov's childlike quality and warmth were alien to Meyerhold, who was not familiar with gentle irony, that is, irony without malice. Only Vakhtangov was able to use it.

During its first decade, the Soviet theater presented a dazzling surface picture. To those viewing it casually or from a distance, its brilliance and luster seemed unparalleled. Apparently those in power were exhibiting sublime intelligence in assimilating the best of the old theater and sponsoring its extension. The sheer physical development of the stage under

Soviet rule—the mushrooming of theaters in the cities, the same rapid expansion in the provinces, the countless amateur groups attached to farms or factories—all seemed proof that the Golden Age was at hand. Although even the most fanatical believers in this dream would admit that there was a dearth of contemporary playwrights, that the new plays were almost uniformly bad, and that it was necessary to fall back on a great number of classical plays or revivals to keep the theaters going, this was explained away by saying that it was easier for actors, producers, and technicians to "adjust" to the new way of thinking than it was for writers and like intellectuals, and that, with the passage of time, a new generation of writers would "grow up" with Soviet ideology, would find it a part of themselves, its themes closer to their hearts, would find their techniques more fluid and their characterizations more alive.

Certainly where vitality and variety of scenic design were concerned, the Soviet theater needed no defense. The electrifying experiments and astonishing presentations of Meyerhold, Tairov, and Vakhtangov seemed evidence that genius could and did flourish under the new dictatorship. But those who so lavishly praise Soviet theater policies conveniently forget two things: first, that all of these great artists had their roots and early growth in the pre-Revolutionary theater and that many of their so-called new experiments were merely continuations of experiments that had begun in the early twentieth century; and second, and more important, that Soviet leaders despised these innovators and their work because of its very originality and creativity, and that one by one, the experimental theaters—the great adornment of the Soviet theater—were closed by a relentless regime.

PART THREE

THE SECOND DECADE, 1927 TO 1937

CHAPTER VIII

THE FULL-SCALE ATTACK
ON THE THEATER

THE SECOND DECADE OF Soviet drama and the full-scale Bolshevik offensive against the theater began at the same time. The period of crusading directors was over, and the authors of "ideologically useful" plays came into power.

SOVIET CRITICISM OF THE CREATIVE THEATERS

We have examined but five important currents in the powerful flood that took place during the heyday of the theater. All five theaters were powerful reformers of the stage, and they had all mastered revolutionary forms. All their experiments and great achievements, all the titanic work done by the great talents of the Russian stage were, however, inevitably greeted with threats, maledictions, and persecutions by the Bolshevik dramatic critics and the Communist Party. The Party press never failed to brand their accomplishments as "art alien to the toilers," "reactionary," "typically bourgeois," "decadent," and harmful.

Meyerhold—the "leader of leaders" in the Soviet theater—has been the target for the wrath of Marxian dramatic critics over a number of years. It would be completely impossible to list the Bolsheviks' accusations against this brilliant revolutionary of the theater. In almost every Bolshevik review of his productions, we find their inevitable reproaches. He was accused of being linked to his own "dark past," to mystical and symbolical experiments, and to the theater of the "old regime." He was constantly rebuked for having dared to live and work before the bright and fine realm of Bolshevism existed, at a time when the "imperial stage" of "bloody Tsar Nicholas" did. Without Meyerhold's great work before the Revolution, the flourishing of the Soviet theater could never have taken place. Yet, this was termed Meyerhold's dark and pernicious past.

The Bolshevik dramatic critics' opinions of the Kamerny Theater and

Tairov were even harsher. This combination was termed even more alien to the Soviet state, and even more bourgeois and pernicious. According to the Soviet critics, neither Tairov nor his Theater had any connection with the toilers. The Kamerny worked for the remnants of esthetically recherché intellectuals, bourgeois gourmands, and the *nouveaux riches* who had just learned to say "pardon me" and not to blow their noses in their hands. Tairov's dilettantism was directed at a public which believed that Art with a capital "A"—was "sacred" and "eternal," but "had no content." [1] Its estheticism and especially its love for Western European and American drama gave the Bolsheviks a reason to consider this Theater as partisan to the "rotting bourgeoisie." And the Kamerny Theater was not helped by its numerous productions of militant satires on the Western bourgeoisie. The Bolsheviks had branded it a "bourgeois theater," and there was no room for such an institution under a proletarian dictatorship.

Although the Kamerny Theater had rendered a great service to the Soviet regime by raising the latter's prestige in the West during the Theater's triumphant world tour, the Bolsheviks considered that the tour was "to repair contacts" between the bourgeois Theater and its real masters, the world bourgeoisie. The organization was accused of serving "the different groups and strata of the European bourgeoisie, to which the Theater's earlier achievements were closer, of course, than they were to the dearest part of our own public—the proletarians." [2]

Tairov was a great expert, with lofty tastes and talents—a genuine revolutionary of the stage. The Bolshevik critics turn him into a "mere disciple," a "pitiful eclectic," a "complete dilettante" and a sterile "decadent."

In our own times, Bolshevism has put the Moscow Art Theater of Stanislavsky and Nemirovich-Danchenko on a pedestal as the classical theater for Soviet socialist realism. During the flourishing of the Soviet theater, however, this institution, too, was fired on from two sides. All the innovating directors scourged it indefatigably, and the Bolshevik dramatic critics also pounced upon it as a "remnant of Russian capitalism" and a "theater of the bourgeois public."

The critics defined the ideology of the Moscow Art Theater in various ways. First they would put one label on it and then another. They accused it of "petty-bourgeois liberalism," of "the merchants' ideology," [3] "the ideology held by the remnants of the Moscow middle class," and a "purely bourgeois ideology." They tried to invent some incredible stamp, such as the "naturalistic and impressionistic romanticism of the disillusioned, Russian, middle-class intellectuals."

The Bolsheviks' dislike for the Moscow Art Theater was not limited to the period of War Communism. It did not change either during or after the NEP years. The Soviet theater was at its zenith during the time of the official conference in 1927. Even then, there were voices saying "the Party has come into conflict with the Moscow Art Theater." Lebedev-Poliansky, a prominent Bolshevik, made a speech which called for pogrom against the Theater and all its studios. He stated:

If we examine the First and Second [Moscow] Art Theaters, we must resolutely declare that they are definitely conservative. They have undergone no change in the sense of approaching the Revolution. During the ten years of the Revolution, they have relinquished *Uncle Vanya*. . . . One must admit that they really gave it up under pressure from the theater censorship and would not have done so voluntarily. . . . If the Soviet regime had not used its Party members and censorship organs to interfere in the repertory of 1926 and 1927, the repertory of the Moscow Art Theater—and of other theaters—would have been overladen with Bulgakovism . . . and philistinism. . . . Their politics are very tricky because they are using it to form and to consolidate a new bourgeoisie.[4]

In other words, the Moscow Art Theater was a center for those enemies of the proletariat—the bourgeoisie—to consolidate themselves.

The great Stanislavsky System, which would later be canonized by the Bolsheviks, was also subjected to ruthless denouncing. The Marxist and quasi-Marxist critics found heaps of sins against the holy laws of "dialectical materialism," such as "unhistorical," "untemporal," "abstract," and "mechanical" approaches, "biologizing social phenomena," a full measure of "primitivism," "subjectivism in its creative work," and the replacement of "living dialectical analysis" with the actors' inner perceptions. The Theater was accused of "proclaiming the supremacy of the subconscious and the biological" while ignoring the "leading role of a conscious attitude toward life in the creative process." The Bolsheviks took the same absolutely hostile attitude towards Mikhail Chekhov, Vakhtangov, and all the other reformers in the Moscow Art Theater Studios. Lunacharsky—the "super-arbiter" of the Soviet theater —wrote that all the studios of the Moscow Art Theater "lack not only any kind of social or philosophical ideology, but even an ideology of the theater." [5] The First Studio was called a "mystical theater," a "sick theater," which was "alien and reactionary." All its productions were "discouraging, enfeebling, and corrupting." Mikhail Chekhov was a "sick actor" who spurted a mystical infection toward the entire Soviet theater. His best role—Hamlet—was a mystical nightmare alien to the materialistic cognition held by the toiling masses.

Eugene Vakhtangov's achievements were called "mystical," "decadent," "esthetic," "class-alien," "flight from revolutionary themes," and "bourgeois." Even his remarkable *Turandot* was not spared.

What were the motives behind the hostile attitude toward the creative theaters? First of all—and this is most important—Bolshevism did not need the theater as pure art. Art has lofty and universal aims and ideas. Bolshevism needed the theater as applied art, as a propaganda form for Party catch-phrases. Secondly, the creative freedom and artistic independence of most of the reformers were dangerous to Bolshevism. The "dictatorship of the proletariat" needs no great masters who have their own philosophies and their own ideologies in the arts. It needs directors and actors to carry out the political assignments that the Party dictates. It needs people who are not brilliant and whose outlooks on life do not differ. It needs petty functionaries whose theater work would be subordinated to the official precepts of the Bolshevik ideology. Any freedom of thought or of work must be branded immediately as "bourgeois" and "class-alien." There is no greater danger to the dictatorship of the Communist Party than the remnants of spiritual freedom. Thirdly, the theater policy of the Soviet regime and of the Soviet dramatic critics was indicated by the leaders of Bolshevism. These people were ruthless "orthodox," and intransigent in attaining their political aims. Most of them had no esthetic tastes whatsoever, nor did they have any conception of the specific features in art and creative work. It was a tyranny of tastelessness. This applied to all levels, from the District Committees up to Stalin himself. They were ignorant of art and oppressed their "subordinates"—those scribbling servants—and forced them to declare everything that showed the slightest taste or any good esthetics to be "alien," "hostile," and "bourgeois."

Under these conditions, a purely Bolshevik idea came into being that was frightful, genuinely reactionary, and killing. This was the notion that the masses understand and need a simplified and primitive form of art alone. Its form would be universally comprehensible, and it would be saturated "100 percent" with the orthodox catch-phrases of the Party.

The theater must not exceed the level of a grammar school. The need for a theater on a higher level was denied because "there is no need to spend the people's money on presentations for a handful of bourgeois intellectuals."

The twilight of the Russian theater arts began when the Communist Party started its ruthless offensive against the Soviet theater and against those remnants of freedom in work and thought that the outstanding theater figures still possessed.

"A CIVIL WAR IN THE THEATER"

The Communist Party stepped up its interference with the theater in 1927. The intensification of this meddling was not an isolated occurrence in the Soviet life of the period. The Fifteenth Congress of the Communist Party, held in that year, declared war on the peasantry. Collectivization began in earnest, and so did the liquidation of the NEP, private trading, churchgoing, independent publishing houses, other individualistic undertakings and enterprises, and the remaining leftist Socialist Revolutionaries and anarchists.

In that same year a conference on theater questions was held by the Department of Agitation and Propaganda attached to the Central Committee of the Communist Party. This meeting was most important for the later history of the Soviet theater. By this time speeches about a patient attitude toward "transitional ideological forms" had disappeared. The meeting was climaxed by resolutions that called for the Department of Agitation and Propaganda to make a militant attack on the final redoubts of free work and free opinions in the theater. The Communist Party based the need for attack on the statement that the NEP period had increased "the activity of anti-Soviet sectors of the intelligentsia, the petty bourgeoisie, and the remnants of the former bourgeoisie." [6]

In 1927 the Bolsheviks called for a ruthless civil war "to liquidate the class enemy in the countryside," and in the same year they shouted, "We will conduct a class war and—we shall not be frightened by the phrase—a civil war in the theater." [7] Between these two statements there was complete unity because the wish to transform every village into an official Soviet *kolkhoz* was directly related to the assertion that "we must try to make literally every theater our own and have it serve the proletarian revolution." [8]

The whole plan for the "civil war" in the theater was discussed at

length, and so were measures for completely suppressing all the freedoms of the theater. Targets were picked out to be fired at along the
entire front, and these included all plays that had been written under
the illusion that a "spiritual NEP" was in the offing. Bulgakov's *Days
of the Turbins* was one such play because it preached amnesty for those
who had fought in the White Army. Alexei Faiko's *Evgraf the Adventure-Seeker* was another because it timidly asked that dreamers and
romantics be allowed to exist in the Soviet Union even though they had
not yet managed to become 100 percent Bolsheviks. Bulgakov's *Zoika's
Apartment* was a third because it ridiculed the ghastliness of Soviet life.
They were all marked out for elimination and branded as "petty-
bourgeois," "bourgeois," and influenced by either the "urban Nepmen,"
or "the remnants of counterrevolutionary elements come to life." [9]

The chief sedition of the playhouses was their preference for the
classics and for nonpolitical plays. And the meeting of the Party members
on theater questions worked out tags and slogans for fighting the lack
of political orientation and for ruthlessly badgering whatever plays took
the audiences away from the swampy atmosphere of class-hatred and
lying policies. The time for pure art and for apolitical classics in the
theater was over.[10] The theaters belonged to the Soviet state and had to
obey their master's orders. The first instruction declared that the main
aim of the Soviet theater was "to re-educate the broad masses in the
spirit of Communism." It called for having the theaters propagandize
the slogans, ideas, and plans for "socialist construction" that Stalin—
the leader of the Communist Party—considered necessary. The basic
criterion of the theater's value would depend on the "political importance" of its work. Ideologically useful plays by Soviet dramatists
staged the current and repeated slogans of the Communist Party. These
had to constitute most of the repertory in all the theaters of the country.[11]

Hence, a number of resolutions adopted by the theater conference of
1927 discussed means for broadening the production of plays suitable
to the Department of Agitation and Propaganda. The method would be:
"to attract theaters to work with revolutionary playwrights [and] to
establish prizes and competitions for the best works in the drama that
respond to contemporary tasks." Of course, this meant the tasks set
by the Party.[12]

Censorship grew more important. "The organs for controlling the
repertory must in every way suppress the attempts to permeate the

theater with decadent and other antiproletarian trends." [13] The salutary protection that Lunacharsky and his influence had afforded the theater against the censors was now removed.[14] The foundation for the flourishing of the Soviet theater—the interpretation of plays on the stage—was retained by the censors. Hence, the Soviet government controlled form as well as content. The resolution stated: "Supervision by the organs of control must be broadened to include interpretation and staging of presentations, inasmuch as new and unacceptable features have been increased, emphasized, or introduced [through them]." [15]

The same theater session discussed numerous measures for a more direct control of the theaters. From then on, for example, all the theaters had to have confirmed Communists as their general managers. These people would help "to ease the theater onto revolutionary rails." "Artistic councils" within the theaters would indicate how to intensify Communist influence. Cells of the Party, the Komsomol, and trade unions would interfere at meetings to urge the "ideological reconstruction" of the theaters. The most important weapon against the independence of the theaters, however, would be dramatic criticism. The Party told the critics:

Promote those productions that reflect the characteristic features for the era of socialist construction through which we are living and that are permeated with the spirit of the proletarian class struggle. . . . Struggle against the intensified attempts by agents of the new bourgeoisie to win over the stage . . . to a repertory that is middle-class, salonish, boulevardish, and ideologically hostile. . . . Try to continue the ousting of the most harmful survivals from the art that originated in the feudal period of landed proprietors, and the period of bourgeois decadence.[16]

Party members should remember that

insufficient tact toward specialists and workers in these theaters can alienate them from the Soviet regime. The management and the critics of these theaters must nudge them adroitly and persistently to serve the tasks of the proletarian dictatorship and to win them away from the influences of social groups that are harmful to the proletariat and over to theater collectives that serve the proletariat [read: that serve the Party].[17]

The Bolsheviks were steadily aiming to use the theater for propaganda alone. This was and is the policy of the Soviet regime. The tactics used, however, changed from time to time, as do Bolshevik tactics in everything else. The theater was taken into custody, but the policemen who had to take it to jail were told by the Department of Agitation and Propaganda to do it subtly, like gentlemen. And there was a very important reason for the caution of the authorities. The Central Committee of the Party realized full well that the "old," "rightist," "academic," and "former bourgeois theaters" possessed *skill,* of which the Proletarian Culture Movement and the "proletarian theaters" did not have even a shadow. The Central Committee of the Party intended that Communist propaganda be carried out with convincing artistry. The Moscow Art Theater and other theaters possessed such artistry, but the miserable amateurs in the "proletarian theaters" did not,[18] and the Central Committee realized that the thoughts and feelings of the population were not to be influenced by incompetents.

The Bolsheviks well understood that they would make a major mistake were they to unleash an obvious "civil war" in the theater and to try seizing such "bourgeois specialists" as Stanislavsky, Nemirovich-Danchenko, Meyerhold, Tairov, and Yuzhin by the collar. These great artists and great individualists forced the Party to proceed gently and cautiously in its aim to have their artistic skill come under the control of the Soviet state. The Bosheviks' caution is called brilliant even today, but it was really a compulsory tactic, which the Party had to use in dealing with great talents of worldwide reputation. But the later history of the Soviet theater shows that the Party did not scruple at any means in attaining its ends. As a result, the Soviet theater, in terms of its arts, was destroyed. Let us examine the major weapons that the Communist Party used in the process.

THE METHODS AND RESULTS OF CENSORSHIP

From time to time, the works of some pre-Soviet Russian writer are republished in the Soviet Union. It has become standard practice to supply these works with an introductory article giving a Marxian analysis of the writer's work and invariably laying great stress on a description of the tsarist censorship. The pre-Revolutionary censors are said to have ruthlessly badgered the poor poets and prose writers of the Russian land. Authors were allegedly hounded and "driven to their graves." [19]

The complex Soviet censorship apparatus, however, will go down in history as unprecedented. It is called *Glavit* (The Central Administration of Literature and Publishing). Formally a part of the People's Commissariat of Enlightenment, it is really part of the organization that has frequently changed its name—Cheka, GPU, OGPU, NKVD, and MVD —but not its aims. The scale of *Glavit* is enormous, and in some years there were about 80,000 censors in it.[20] It is literally and absolutely true that not a *single word* can be printed, filmed, staged, or broadcast in the Soviet Union without the approval of the Bolshevik censorship. This applies to republications of works by Marx, Lenin, and Stalin, to every periodical, theater program, poster, official bookkeeping report, and blank notebook for Soviet schoolchildren. They all must bear the imprimatur of *Glavit*.[21]

Soviet censorship is not limited to the gigantic apparatus of *Glavit* alone. A second organ of political surveillance over Soviet publications is the Bureau of the Press attached to the Department of Agitation and Propaganda of the Central Committee of the Party. This organization appoints and is responsible for all the editors of publishing houses, periodicals, newspapers, and editorial boards. Only completely trustworthy Party members are named to such posts. The Bureau of the Press gives all the editors detailed instructions on everything permitted and forbidden and on the slightest change in Party tactics. A gigantic constellation of monitors reads everything turned out by every Soviet printing press, and it thus tightens the control over the editors and periodicals under the Bureau of the Press.

There is still more to Soviet censorship. The secret police has its own powerful Bureau for the Control of Literature known as *Litkontrol*. This organization keeps watch on the life, creative work, moods, friendships, and statements of all Soviet writers. Everyone has a "file" containing all the data received through spies and police informers. All works of a writer are attentively analyzed, all his dangerous thoughts noted, and all his heretical statements at discussions in public places and clubs are recorded. This material is "filed," and the man's "ideological portrait" is worked out most precisely. In this center of police surveillance the fate of all Soviet writers is decided, and from it instructions are issued to publishing houses and to Party secretaries of the Writers Union as to the measures to be taken in regard to anyone who does not want "to bring grist to the mill of Bolshevism." Must he be bribed with a glittering contract for publication, a generous advance, an "assignment," a prize won in competition, a luxurious apartment, or a flattering review—or must he be badgered by the press? One telephone call from this organ to the publishing houses soon shows a talented writer that he cannot get any of his new works published. The same *Litkontrol* draws up all plans for arresting writers and exiling them.

Such is the complex, frightening, and variegated machinery for reducing the Soviet press to a common denominator. Let us now show the complex control that the censorship exercises in practice. We shall make bold to illustrate it with a rather unusual situation. Let us imagine that William Shakespeare is living in the Soviet Union in the period under consideration. He has just written *Julius Caesar* and wants to place it in one of the Soviet theaters.

First, Shakespeare would like to mimeograph some copies of his manuscript to circulate among the theaters, and he immediately runs into a serious obstacle. He discovers that there is not even a single private or cooperative office in the country that does commercial mimeographing. Only government establishments possess mimeograph machines, and not a single mimeographing office in the state trusts will accept an order from Comrade Shakespeare. But he is in luck! There is an organization that has partial "jurisdiction" over Comrade Shakespeare inasmuch as he is a playwright, and that outfit has a mimeograph. It is the establishment that collects the royalties for Soviet playwrights from the theaters and motion-picture houses. At the time we are discussing it was called *Modpik* (the initals stand for the Moscow Society of Dramatists and Composers), but it is now called the Society for the Protection of Authors' Rights and is the sole central organization for mimeographing plays.

This is the starting point for getting *Julius Caesar* on the boards. But the Society for the Protection of Authors' Rights can accept and mimeograph only those manuscripts that bear the imprimatur of *Glavit*. Shakespeare has to put his manuscript back into his briefcase and start looking for *Glavit*. Once there, he hands in the manuscript of *Julius Caesar* at one of the narrow windows in this gloomy establishment. A month or two later he receives a summons to report to a room in *Glavit*. Since this censoring body is a branch of the secret police organization known as the State Security Administration, most of the censors are former investigators and operatives of the GPU. Their nerves have been completely shattered by their work, so they have been assigned to sedentary and more soothing tasks. They are exhausted and burned-out hangmen, masters of torture and "questioning under prejudice." Now, they are torturing and denouncing manuscripts instead of people, and they sniff out anti-Soviet subversion to be found between the lines and even letters themselves..

Shakespeare's very first meeting with the censor immediately shows him what freedom of speech is like within the Soviet Union. The censor uses precisely the same tone he had used in interrogating prisoners in the GPU, yelling coarsely and bitingly and trying to trip Shakespeare up, to catch him in some anti-Soviet intention. The censor demands that all the passages of *Julius Caesar* that are hazy and not explicit be spelled out to remove any possible loophole for other interpretations, and he requires that all the characters be shown with a more concrete "class orientation." Julius Caesar must be depicted as a fascist dictator from Roman times. Brutus must be turned into a spokesman for the oppressed Roman slaves and plebeians. Antony must be given the typical traits of a "compromiser." Only after Shakespeare has made all these changes and submits the revised manuscript for a new inspection can he count on an answer from *Glavit*.

After the revisions have been approved, all three copies of the manuscript are stitched with thread and the ends fastened together with the big wax seal of *Glavit*—lest Shakespeare insert some anti-Soviet page into the approved version. On the reverse side, under the wax seal, the number of pages authorized is written in by hand and it is stamped with this legend: *"Julius Caesar* by W. Shakespeare has been cleared for duplication in 300 copies by *Glavit* [the censor's number] on [month, day, year] in Moscow." *Julius Caesar* may now be mimeographed, but nothing else. It may not be produced yet because permission for staging must be granted by a different censorship organization, the *Glavrepertkom* (the Central Committee for Control over Repertory, or Central Repertorial Committee). So Shakespeare still faces several obstacles.

Shakespeare gives mimeographed copies of *Julius Caesar* to managers of literary sections of the Moscow theaters and distributes other copies to the provincial theaters. The managerial positions are usually filled by unsuccessful playwrights belonging to the Communist Party, and Shakespeare will not find it easy to pass inspection by jealous and untalented failures and captious followers of the Party line. He will be asked to make new revisions to "correct the ideology." For example, after Brutus' words, "As he [Caesar] was ambitious," Shakespeare will be asked to add, "and he oppressed the people and whipped the slaves."

But still Shakespeare is lucky. A non-Party "artistic director"—the chief director of the theater—has fallen in love with the tragedy. He helps Shakespeare to evade the new, stupid, and terrifying orders of the literary section manager of the theater. The playwright is now obliged to read the play to the Artistic Council of the Theater. The Council's "advice" is obligatory for all the theaters, and the body includes the "public representatives" who are for the most part orthodox Communists. Thus, there is another organ for surveillance over the repertory function of a theater, in addition to the "literary unit." The Council can remove some plays and can force others on the theater that will serve the Party line. In accordance with the Council's advice, Shakespeare mutilates his tragedy some more.

He has by now revised *Julius Caesar* so much that little of the original version remains. Finally, the Central Repertorial Committee grants permission for rehearsals. The theater spends much money on producing the historical play, and the time comes for the last ordeal with the censorship. This is the closed dress rehearsal for the members of the Central Repertorial Committee. The author, the director, the designer, and the Central Repertorial Committee are the only ones present in the auditorium. The chief of the Central Repertorial Committee himself finally arrives. He has not read Comrade Shakespeare's opus. And now the real tragedy takes place. *Julius Caesar* is forbidden and removed from the repertory of the theater. At a closed session of the Central Repertorial Committee the chief berates the censors who have "become a tool of anti-Soviet forces" by permitting the presentation of such a coarse and counterrevolutionary sortie. They have failed to see that Brutus' words and deeds furnish implicit propaganda for terroristic acts against the "leaders of our Party." They have failed to see that the entire story of "Caesar's will" is really, from start to finish, a Trotskyite trick, because the Trotskyites used "Lenin's will."

The censor guilty of the blunder is caught and quickly arrested, and the file on *Julius Caesar* is transferred to the other bureaus of the GPU. William Shakespeare is arrested and accused of being a Trotskyite and a counterrevolutionary and disappears forever in one of the camps in the far north.

Fear creates the incredible bureaucracy of this machine. Fear makes censors torment the author and his writings with endless revisions and corrections. They themselves are afraid of being "subversive," and so the play on a Soviet censor's table is a threat to his own personal welfare. If he permits it, he awaits its première and the reviews with a sense of dread. And woe betide him should the critics or—even worse—one of the "leaders" find it heretical. In such a case, the petty functionary inevitably is subjected to "administrative measures." He loses his job and is removed; sometimes he loses his Party membership as well. The cowards wish by all possible means to insure and reinsure themselves.

Most Soviet theater censors had no information whatsoever about the specific traits of the theater and plays. We shall not even mention taste. They placed any drama on a Procrustean bed of primitively "sociological" stereotypes. Everything that did not fit within the official formulas was lopped off ruthlessly. The stereotype was the same for all plays, themes, genres, and styles. The play must reveal the class struggle. The characters had to be spokesmen for the interests of their class and all were shown according to the stencils of the Department of Agitation and Propaganda.

The same "laws" of sociology gave the censors endless opportunities for ordering revisions. The "revelation of class interests" for all the characters could start a genuine *perpetuum mobile* of revisions. The censor's orders to change and revise plays were given without the slightest consideration for the idiosyncracies of the theater or the dramatist. Everything had to be written according to the stereotype of whatever "the broadest mass of the toilers" understands. Hence, the Soviet drama has developed a strange feature of its own over the years: You cannot tell one author's play from another's by the style. They are all cast in the same factory. The tens of thousands of censors and "Repertorial Committeemen" were the gravediggers of the Soviet theater and the Soviet drama.

The extent to which Soviet censors have hamstrung and perverted thousands of dramas can never be completely grasped. Hardly anyone can make a complete list of its victims—the forbidden plays that were burned by the NKVD or that rot away in its vaults.[22] *Glavit,* the Central Repertorial Committee, the Bureau of the Press attached to the Central Committee of the Party, and the Bureau for Control of Literature attached to the NKVD have created a "universal silence." The truth has disappeared completely from literature and the stage. All criticisms of the existing regime and the slightest mentions of its sins have been silenced. All the forms of art have been instilled with the servile flattery of slaves toward their masters.

MARXIAN THEORY AND THE CREATIVE PROCESS

Communism has produced no new, integral, or profound theory for the theater any more than it has for any of the other arts. Yet it has tried desperately to do so. The reason for its failure is simple. Dialectical materialism and historical materialism are incompatible with the creative process upon which any art is based.

The numerous militant efforts to standardize art deny the essence of the creative act. Art does not exist without spirituality. It is never isolated from the land, intuition, religious feelings, ethics, or idealism. The Bolsheviks, however, reduce all spiritual values to a reflection of the material processes that take place in the outer world, both physical and productional. Economics thus becomes a parody of an inexorable Fate that turns historic personalities into puppets. This denial of personality has nothing in common with art because art is based on the spiritual act of a creative personality.

Art does not exist without ethical and universal values, but the Marxian method tries to turn them all into something completely relative rather than eternal and immutable.[23] Marxists subordinate these values to the laws of development for the economic base and to the policy of the governing class. Good and Evil have lost their objective ethical value. Mercy and magnanimity to a fallen foe have become capital offenses.

Soviet art experts are all unfortunate in that neither Marx, Engels, nor Lenin had anything to say about Communist esthetics. There are a handful of lines dealing with what Marx and Engels happened to defend in literature and the arts. When compared to such a battleship of an idealistic theory of art as Hegel's *Vorlesungen über die Aesthetick,* the statements made by Marx and Engels look like driftwood on the surface of the ocean. Nor are there any solid and profound statements by the classical Marxist authors on the theater arts. Soviet Communist theater experts can only artificially transfer to the theater the laws that Marx propounded about economics and the class struggle.

Marxian study of art asserts that the theater, like any art, is merely an ideological superstructure erected on an economic base and directly dependent upon the latter. Like any other form of social consciousness, the theater reflects and expresses the ideology of some class, and this last determines the social relationships of production. The theater is not just a mirror of ideology for the class. It is also a weapon for the class struggle and aids the class to defend its own interests.[24]

Marx declared: "Philosophers only explained the world in different ways, but the important thing is to change it." Marxian theory of the theater has used this statement to forbid the Soviet theater from merely representing realities, as if it were a screen, but insists that the theater must dialectically reflect dialectical reality and actively change it: "The dialectical meaning of time is revolution, and therefore we must educate the people and teach them the best possible way to understand revolution. This is the aim for every theater presentation, both comedies and serious plays." [25]

The central problem of true theater arts is to create human character on the stage and in the drama. According to the Marxists, however, it is wrong to show the character's personal life—that is, "typical circumstances in the life of an individual personality, mainly in his private and individual interests." [26] Human psychology and a person's experiences must not be isolated from the class struggle, the socialist reconstruction of the world, and the "honor, bravery, and heroism of the working class." An individual's actions should reveal the changes of social relationships that arise from the actions and interrelationships between people.

Instead of creating its own Communist esthetic, Marxism has been limited to substituting dialectical categories (dealing with the development of society's economic base) for esthetic categories. It denies any forms, ideas, or spirituality in the arts that are independent of the "means of production." It denies that any ethical and spiritual phenomena are above the class struggle and are eternal for the human race. Thus Marxism negates art as a whole, for art is inconceivable without all these great values that the materialists despise.

Marxian terminology, then, became obligatory for articles on the theater arts, for speeches at panel discussions on the theater, and within the theater itself. All the actors and workers of the theater were made to study "diamat" (dialetical materialism) and "histmat" (historical materialism). Directors were ordered to "reconstruct" their work with the actors in accordance with this great method. Kirpotin stated: "In the field of art, distortions connected with the slogans of the dialetical materialist method have reached the point that actors, for example, have recommended the study of dialectical categories to replace the study of acting techniques." [27] Small wonder that Vsevolod Meyerhold testified:

It is now customary for some comrade to appear and say: "Take a look, he is not screwing that leg on the table dialectically," and some director, who has also read learned pamphlets, comes in, taps the actor on the shoulder, and says: "You are mechanical; you do not create characters dialectically at all." [28]

Soviet dramatic criticism aspires to retain the Marxian methodology of art. Only those works of art are considered full-blooded, generally useful, and artistic whose characters reveal the idea correctly. Only that man can be called an artist who thoroughly knows the objective truth of the idea that he tries to express in a series of images. All this might almost be acceptable and natural—but it implies an interesting corollary, which is that only the Party possesses the secret of objective truth. Only its loyal sons, the Bolshevik critics, possess the method of materialistic dialectics. The theaters, the directors, the playwrights, and the actors do not. After all, who are such people? The theaters and their cadres come from bourgeois and petty-bourgeois environments. They are apolitical and spoiled intellectuals who still have not mastered the world outlook of the proletariat. This arrogant contrast between the omniscient Communist Party and the ignorant artists of the theater has produced theater criticism peculiar to Bolshevism alone.

The main thing to be desired in the theater is not form but content, and so theater experts "must begin by defining the content—that is, by analyzing the play and revealing the ideas of whatever class has found expression in it." [29] Any attempt by a theater artist to turn off the bumpy road of politics, to go away from the terrible realities to a different and illusory world, to a world of dreams and fancy is immediately branded by Marxian critics as "rotten idealism," a "bourgeois outlook on life," and counterrevolution in art. The *index prohibitorum* includes: idealism, spirituality, contemplation, the unreal, illusion, phantasmagoria, refinement, subtlety, psychologizing, symbolism, impressionism, expressionism, primitivism, and exoticism. They are all different facets of the anti-Marxian heresy. A symbolic style is also taboo to the Marxists:

It was born of the mystical and idealistic bourgeois and petty-bourgeois intellectual outlook on life during the twilight period of capitalism. It aims to oppose the spirit to the body in order to make art express and propagandize the unreal most subtly. . . . It has made art a megaphone for reactionary ideas and for religion.[30]

The Marxian dramatic critics even attacked the theater of both pre-Revolutionary and Soviet times for being attracted to the comedies of Shakespeare, Molière, and Goldoni and for being interested in Hoffmann, the *commedia dell'arte,* and the buffonade. The theaters were accused of

striving, with the glitter of scenes, colors, costumes, and situations, to create a self-sufficient entertainment in the theater that was removed from life. They did not strive at all to reveal the class content included in the action of the play.

The great ideals that inspired the working class do not consist of the contemplation, oblivion, and penetration into the other world. They are a concrete and practical program for changing the world.[31]

The so-called Marxian theory of the theater was really only the theater theory of the Department of Agitation and Propaganda. Its purpose was to reduce the theater to a mere weapon for the use of the Communist Party. It was a weapon of literary terror used against those artists who did not belong to the Party. The ruthless persecution of the artists, the intimidations, and the accusations of counterrevolutionary ideology all had the same aim—to turn the free and non-Communist theater into a Party theater and to make it an appendage of the Department of Agitation and Propaganda.

RAPP AND TRAM

To some extent, RAPP (the Russian Association of Proletarian Writers) crowned the proletarian literature that had been started by the Proletarian Culture Movement and the *Kuznitsa* (Smithy), its union of poets and other writers. RAPP developed from the merging of the October Group of Communist writers with contributors to the magazine of criticism, *Na literaturnom postu* ("On Literary Guard Duty"), which for a time was favored by the Party. Its declarations were based on some logic. Soviet Russia, according to the statements by the Communist Party, was the land of the victorious proletariat. Therefore, it was natural that the leading literary role in the country should be played by Communist, proletarian writers. The Party proclaimed a "Leninist cultural revolution" whose program was to win all the most important positions in all fields of culture for the working class. It issued slogans about a "new proletarian intelligentsia," that had to replace the old intelligentsia (which consisted of bourgeois intellectuals who were "saboteurs" and "wreckers" hostile to the working class). It was there-

fore normal that a similar "seizure of the key positions" would sooner
or later be transferred to literature.

RAPP considered itself the vanguard of the working class, which had
to continue the offensive in those areas that had not yet been won—
literature and art. It was radical, militant, and maximalist to the same
degree that the Communist Party was. It was normal for the Party to
proclaim "the liquidation of the kulaks as a class" throughout the
country and the ruthless "collectivization" of the rural districts. This
being so, why should it be abnormal for RAPP to apply the same
methods to culture?

RAPP began by strengthening and consolidating a number of proletarian writers and appealing for "shock workers" in literature. All available means had to be used in the search for future proletarian Turgenievs,
Tolstoys, Gogols, and Pushkins among the factory workers and the rural
young people. These persons had to be taught and to be drawn into
literature to replace bourgeois writers.

RAPP later transferred the same methods to the Soviet theater also.
Its supporters waxed profoundly indignant over the fact that the Soviet
regime, through Lunacharsky, "nursed" and romped with the old bourgeois Russian theaters and its leading figures, who were "alien to the
working class." The old bourgeois experts should not be coddled or
patiently re-educated, they asserted. Their reactionary productions were
intolerable. The Soviet theater had to be won and subordinated to the
proletarian dictatorship with the same radical and ruthless methods with
which power had been seized in the country, the factories, the countryside, and all the institutions. Such was the "theater platform" of RAPP.[32]
What was needed to get rid of the bourgeois and the petty-bourgeois
tendencies in the Soviet theater once and for all and to transform it into
a purely proletarian theater? [33] Libedinsky wrote:

We need: (1) proletarian playwrights, who will write so that their plays
will organize the consciousness and emotion on the side of Communism;
(2) actors, who will perform those plays so that their content will not be
strange, and who will enrich the content of these plays with their own content; (3) directors, who will find the purpose of each complete presentation
and will build it in new and Communist fashion.

We must lift up the mass movement of the workers who are dramatists, the
mass movement of the actors and the worker-directors. We must also find
a new form for collective creative work and a new type of theater organization.[34]

RAPP's fatal error led to its downfall in 1932. It had a false proletarian-culture-style illusion that the country was really in the heyday of a proletarian dictatorship. What really existed was a dictatorship by Stalin's Party over the proletariat. There was also a most profound difference in principle between the Party and RAPP. The latter preached and practiced a program of seizing the theater "from below," through the power of the workers; it strove to replace the alien artists of the stage. The official policy of the Soviet state, however, was directed at seizing the theater "from above," through a "carrot and stick" policy; it was directed at "re-educating" the old theater experts and at making them obedient cadremen whose art and great technique were, in terms of influencing audiences, beyond the reach of the "shock workers." The official theater policy of the Soviet regime still in some measure retained Lenin's thesis about a cautious attitude toward the "cultural heritage." RAPP, however, was militantly and uncompromisingly opposed to the old theater.

According to RAPP, none of the former imperial theaters had any cultural value whatsoever—they had only been "subsidiary to the governmental apparatus of the state." At best, they had fulfilled only the needs of the "aristocratic and bureaucratic peaks." The Maly Theater in Moscow "was a tool of merchants and the aristocracy who were not in government service." The Moscow Art Theater was a "tool of the progressive bourgeoisie," and its method "stands on the level of bourgeois consciousness." [35] Stanislavsky was called "a naturalist, an empiricist, and—when all is said and done—an idealist of the worst sort." In his teachings, "we see no system at all." He did not know how "to understand the laws for the development of life, society, and human beings," and was not able "to proceed from his powerless art of 'vital truth' to a depiction of reality." The realism of the Moscow Art Theater "has always been encased in idealism and mysticism." [36] All the old Russian theaters, RAPP claimed, "distorted the correct conception of the relationship between form and content." They inflated "features of limited significance into absolutes," and they were infected by bourgeois idealism and formalism. Hence, the proletarian theater had to be protected from them.

Unlike its ancestor, the Proletarian Culture Movement, RAPP had a tempestuous and aggressive career in seizing all aspects of the theater arts for "narrow Party content." Because of this, it rendered a very important service to the Soviet regime's enslavement of the theater, despite the difference in opinion between the two groups on questions of theater policy.

RAPP spoke about the "leading role of the drama and the dramatist in the theater." This, of course, referred to the proletarian dramatist and was a powerful weapon for Bolshevizing the theater. The Communist Party retained this key to mastery over the theater after the routing of RAPP. Plays that were stanchly Bolshevik in spirit furnished the most effective weapon for rebuilding the Soviet theater along Communist lines. A compulsory assortment of Soviet plays was established. No theater maintained by the Soviet state could refuse to include such plays in its repertory. Communist criticism coarsely persecuted the apolitical plays in the repertory and praised the products of proletarian playwrights beyond all measure. These were the means used to achieve the ends.

The Marxian thesis that "content determines form" was added to the emphasis on new dramatists. This gave the critics occasion for attacking any "formalistic" treatment of plays that had been written by proletarian writers. Hence, directors could not flee doleful and official content for the free and happy creation of new forms. The leader of the Soviet theater was not the director, as was the case earlier, but rather the proletarian playwright. Any revolt against the dominance of the new "leader" was henceforth declared "a regurgitation of bourgeois decadence," "bourgeois formalism," "an idealistic break between form and content," "making form into a fetish," and so on. The ruthless war against the director conducted during the RAPP period aimed at suppressing innovations in the Soviet theater.

The group of leading dramatists associated with RAPP included Afinogenov, Kirshon, Nikolai Pogodin, Vishnevsky, and V. Bill-Belotserkovsky. They wrote articles on the theater as well as skillful plays and began to win the Soviet theater.

The second important act of RAPP was to consolidate Marxian dramatic critcism. It gathered the Bolshevik critics into a powerful fist and began to publish a periodical called *Sovetskii teatr* ("Soviet Theater"). Innumerable panel discussions were organized and so were many large "meetings on theater questions." Their tone was that used by the Department of Agitation and Propaganda. RAPP used its fist to start destroying all the remaining free-thinkers and all shadows of anti-Marxian heresy in the theater arts.

The outstanding directors and dramatists who were not Party members were summoned to the meetings and discussions of RAPP as if they were defendants before a tribunal of Bolshevik playwrights. Meyerhold and Tairov stood listening to accusations and demands before the lofty Areopagus containing "leaders of the Soviet theater." These two were supposed to confess their formalistic transgressions and to scourge themselves with self-criticism. RAPP's persecution of writers and poets was one reason for Vladimir Mayakovsky's suicide. Its members considered themselves members of a "Special Session of the Revolutionary Tribunal" that the Bolshevik regime had sent into art as a punitive expedition.

All the intolerance, ruthlessness, and fanaticism in the Marxian theory and criticism of the theater grew only because of RAPP's efforts. RAPP issued slogans declaring that Marxists had complete hegemony over theater criticism. It began to bait the theaters and directors and to campaign against non-Party dramatic critics and reviewers. These people, of course, were accused of possessing "features of bourgeois formalism, estheticism, and vulgar sociological oversimplification." These despicable non-Party people "preserved the fetish of taste and the guildlike limitations that typified the critics before the Revolution." [37] War was declared on the slightest traces of any nonpolitical or non-Party attitude in theater theory or criticism; war was declared on "all the class-hostile 'theories' that even now try to oppose the Marxist-Leninist theory of a cultural revolution." [38]

In creating the proletarian actors and directors that the Party needed to replace the "old bourgeois specialists," RAPP did not limit itself to catch-phrases and theories. The proletarian replacements in the theater arts had to come from the amateur theater. Every member of a local dramatic circle, every participant in a dramatic cell, had to feel that he was responsible for rebuilding the entire Soviet theater. RAPP considered the leading role in creating the Soviet theater to belong to the factory and rural-district amateurs. The amateurs had to raise the level of their acting to professional standards. RAPP helped in the birth of an organization that bridged a transitional state between amateur art and the professional theater. This was the so-called TRAM (the Theater of Working Young People). [39]

TRAM, a form of the "proletarian theater," was born in 1927 and became exceedingly widespread during the following four years.[40] The Komsomol was the active leader of the TRAM movement. TRAM issued an "appeal for shock workers in the theater" that seemed to resemble RAPP's earlier "appeal for shock workers in literature" but that was really quite different. The appeal for shock workers in literature was intended for selecting those young proletarians who were most talented and most inclined toward prose or poetry; these people would be given a broad "literary training" in literary circles and institutes created for the purpose. TRAM, however, even in its earliest days, continued the theories of the amateur theater that had been held by the "Leftist Front" during the first years of the Soviet regime. It was not a school for proletarian actors; it was rather a perfectly new form of the theater arts that belonged only to the proletarians. TRAM was the only way to dissolve professional art within amateur art inside socialist society.

TRAM made corrections in the theories about the amateur art of the past. It called for learning things from the professional theater, for blending with it and "dissolving it." Nevertheless, it retained the Proletarian Culture Movement's idea that a proletarian artist would be a "machine-tool worker" at the same time. Its circles thus had haughty pretensions to monopolizing the "authentic proletarian theater." This attitude later became the reef upon which the vessel that had been prepared in the shipyards of the Komsomol would founder.

The program and ideology of TRAM were almost completely acceptable to the Communist Party. From start to finish, it was a theater for the Department of Agitation and Propaganda:

The content of TRAM's work is determined by the tasks proposed by the Party and the Komsomol. . . . In this, TRAM does not so much depict or state the assignments and social changes given to it as it exerts an active influence after being summoned by the young working people to act; it pushes the young workers towards active revolutionary action.[41]

It was a propagandistic theater that staged current political problems and employed the fervor of Komsomol members in all the many theater devices that it used. It gave the "powder charge" to the working masses that the Communist Party needed.[42]

TRAM's methods met with no competition from any non-Party Soviet theater. Its work was strictly and orthodoxly based on dialectical materialism. It considered the theater a "method for reconstructing reality" according to the plans of socialism and stated that the "sole test for objective cognition of reality" was the "collective experience of the working class and the collective experience of the Communist Party (as expressed in the general line of the Party)." [43] The antagonisms between the individual experts and professions were to be replaced by a single "creative collective." TRAM revealed just the "artist" whom the Bolsheviks needed. He was no bourgeois creator, demanding something that smelled suspiciously of free work and free opinions. Such a person demanded his individual appraisal of reality and his subjective means of expression. The artist needed was the performer:

Therefore, the TRAM member is not subjective, is not individualized, and does not have any personal cognition of objective reality. The cognition of objective reality comes to him through the collective experience of the entire working class as made concrete by the general line of our Party.[44]

This ought to be considered the best formulation of what the Bolsheviks wanted to obtain from all artists in all the arts. We, they seemed to be saying, will give you, Comrade Artists, the ready-made ideology and appraisal of reality that has been manufactured by our wise Party. Your business does not concern philosophy but acting, sculpting, painting, or writing according to our recipes.

The experience of TRAM is most interesting for a historian of the Soviet theater. It attempted to create neither more nor less than a new "proletarian art of the theater" that could be firmly linked to the Party and the Komsomol and that would be based on the Marxian outlook. This would be a theater of party members. Its actors would be orthodox members of the Komsomol and its management and theoreticians would be Communists. Yet, despite the favorable confluence of "ideologically useful" circumstances, no new art was born. No new theater was created. No synthesis of the amateur and professional theaters was achieved. No new professional proletarian theater came into being. There was nothing but ordinary "amateurs" who tried to propagandize with a very amateurish duplication of the devices used by the old bourgeois theater.

ADMINISTRATIVE CONTROLS AND "PUBLIC PRESSURE"

In addition to the censorship, to Marxian theories and criticism, and to the offensive by RAPP and proletarian theater organizations, there was still another means for putting pressure on the theater. The administrations of all the theaters were centralized by a process that began after the theater conference of 1927.

Before that time, the administration of the theater network had been varied and decentralized, and theaters were run by the most different kinds of organizations: the Soviets of the Workers' and Peasants' Deputies, the provincial bureaus of national education, the local economic or trade-union organs, and so forth. The different bureaus of the People's Commissariat of Enlightenment dealt simultaneously with questions of theater policy. There were the administration for the academic theaters and the artistic bureaus of the main political enlightenment organization, the main science organization, and the Department of Agitation and Propaganda. The conference inaugurated a period in which a powerful Soviet bureaucratic machine was created to centralize and run the entire administration of the Soviet theaters.

The organization in question has changed its name several times. It has been called Main Art and the Committee for Art Affairs. It has grown into an enormous "main committee" that looms over the theaters and directs their ideological, artistic, economic, and administrative life.

The power of the general manager (*direktor*) in the theater has been expanded and intensified. He is almost without exception a Party member named by the "Cadre Bureau" attached to the Central Committee of the Party, in agreement with the organs for theater administration. The general manager represents the Party and the Soviet regime, and he controls all economic and administrative power. He is the first example of Party control within the theater, meddling with artistic and ideological questions. A process began that progressed rapidly. The outstanding artistic directors and other experts who were not members of the Party were to have their powers limited.

Before the change, if a Party member was named general manager of a theater, it was quite accidental. He had merely been "transferred" by the Cadre Bureau of the CPSU Central Committee. Sometimes the Party would send people from the economic or administrative branches of the Soviet apparatus and who had no understanding of the theater.[45] Before the change, such people did not dare to meddle in the artistic work of the theater and the directors. Their ignorance compelled them to yield to non-Party people. After the 1927 conference, however, the Party established courses and faculties for the general managers that were taught by the theater institutes. Party members were sent to be trained and equipped with a knowledge of the theater and the stage, and this made possible their future interference in the artistic work of the theaters.

The Party-member general-manager controlled the "seats" and the resources. Government subsidies were not the only hallmark of his power. As the political advisor of the theater, he could put pressure on the directors through the ruble, by forcing them not to exceed the estimate of expenditures for presenting a production in a new form. He was also the political monitor and thus carried out the tasks of the GPU. He kept watch against "subversive ideology" and "anti-Soviet tendencies," making sure that they did not take root among his subordinates lest he inform the proper authorities.

The Party-member general-manager sowed Party and Komsomol nuclei. He promoted members of the Party and Komsomol to responsible posts. He organized circles for studying Marxism. He instituted the system of wall newspapers that cluttered the walls with "self-criticism." He helped publicize every kind of "subversion" in the life and work of the theater and in the personal lives of the company. He established the "artistic councils" of the theater, the "activists' group," and the "sponsorship" by the theater of factories. He indefatigably saw to it that every actor and director had enough "social loads" of all kinds, including many kinds of bureaucratic and unnecessary duties. These people were thus robbed of the spare time they needed for their creative work and for learning their roles.

The "artistic councils" in the theaters formed one means of the many used in the struggle against the "No. 1 Enemy of the Theater"—the "artistic dictatorship" of the non-Party theater figures. Every theater set up a large-scale artistic council. The general manager and the secretary of the regional committee of the Party would compile lists. These would be introduced at the artistic councils by representatives of the Party, the Komsomol, professional organizations, the "activists' group" from the factories, the Red Army, and public organizations. The councils were termed organs of the "broad Soviet public." Nevertheless, most of them came from the omnipresent and omnipotent Communist Party. Under fire from this "public," the theater had to discuss its repertorial plan, the new plays that it intended to produce, the plans for the separate productions, and the resulting presentations.[46] The broad forum of the Party and workers criticized the plans and ideas of the theater and brought pressure to bear. Some additional Soviet plays had to be included in the repertory, and "formalist deviations," "estheticism," and everything else that the average semiliterate worker could not understand were criticized and "revised."

Sometimes, the artistic director of a theater would argue with the Repertorial committeeman and try not to agree. In such a case, "the voice of the Soviet public as a whole" precluded discussion since it was the "voice of the toiling masses." The artistic councils also had to defend the Soviet activists in the theater. They had to promote and consolidate the influence of those theater workers who backed the positions of the Party.[47]

Soviet activists' groups took shape within the theaters. The general manager and the Party nuclei selected for them Komsomol members, "public-spirited" technical personnel, actors inclined toward the opposition because of petty grudges, and supernumeraries who were "out-of-luck." The activists spoke at meetings, at the "artistic councils," and wrote for the wall newspapers. They criticized and unmasked bourgeois and anti-Soviet "deviations" within the theater. They branded the artistic directors and the production directors as "apolitical" and were frequently used to spy and inform upon them. These groups formed a fifth column to inflame the "class struggle" within the theater and to fight for a proletarian spirit and for a "genuinely Soviet atmosphere" within the theater.

The so-called productional meetings also helped the Party put steady pressure on the artistic guides and experts of the theaters. Sessions were regularly organized by local trade-union committees with the participation of the Party and Komsomol nuclei of the theater. All the technical and artistic staff members of the theater were present. The "activists" initiated the crudest kind of "self-criticism." They accused the artistic directors of mistakes and "exaggerations"; they accused the artistic directors of ignorance about running a theater, creating a repertory, staging a play, or economizing with the "people's money."

The Party-member general-manager also spoke at the production meetings. He threatened to burn out the remnants of bourgeois deviations with "red-hot irons." He demanded the introduction of "proletarian discipline." He required that the entire staff of the theater, "everyone included," study Marxism and Leninism. He called for the introduction and "activity" of all kinds of "circles," which ranged from rifle clubs and the Society for the Defense of the Soviet Union and for the Development of its Aviation and Chemical Industries to the International Aid Organization for Revolutionary Fighters. He stuffed the artists' heads with the same stereotypes that Communist bureaucrats used in their speeches. There was talk about the "need for mobilizing internal resources," "the correct placement of people," "streamlining the processes of production," and "the strict fulfillment of the industrial and financial plan." Party members put pressure on the directors "to get done with the lordly excesses taking place in items of expenditure for the production." They demanded "the expansion of shock work and competition," including the establishment of "brigades" that would "struggle for 100 percent fulfillment of the productional plan." And they made numerous other demands that slowly but surely changed the theater from a creative organization into a typical Soviet factory.

All these new measures forged a solid ring of steel around the theater, and its freedom was cut off. The Russian theaters were soiled with political intrigues, and they and their special creative personalities were herded into a single government stereotype.

Experimentation and the search for new forms were declared to be bourgeois distortions of content. The artistic incarnation of content was to be allowed only in the forms "that the masses could understand." Content, and Communist Party content alone, became the main thing for the theater. Finally, even the weakest attempts by artists to retain an iota of free choice in the forms used for their productions were branded as "a rebellion of petty-bourgeois groups in art using the name of the notorious 'freedom' of the artistic process and not wishing to work within the limits demanded by the proletariat." [48]

And this was the theater that had so recently given light to the entire world with its bold, great, stirring, and brilliant discoveries!

CHAPTER IX

PLAYS BASED ON PARTY SLOGANS

WHAT BOLSHEVISM WANTED WAS a theater that would merely illustrate the repeated slogans of the Communist Party on the stage. Productions of purely Soviet plays were becoming more frequent. In 1924 only 90 "Soviet" plays in all had been done in the Soviet theaters. In 1933 the number was 248. The Party, seeking plays responsive to its current political tasks, organized many contests with valuable prizes. Later it was to institute the Stalin Prizes. The Committee on Affairs of the Arts began to commission plays from outstanding writers. It gave them many substantial advances and sent them on different assignments for material at state expense. Earlier the Soviet theater press had concentrated on productions and directorial innovations, but it now focused on long and loud discussions of Soviet plays. The Party considered the play itself to be the most radical method for Sovietizing the theater, and it became most interested in the dramas, and the dramatist was placed in charge of the Soviet theater.[1] Nevertheless, the Party maintained a steady vigil to make sure that the new leader of the theater arts would strictly support its general line. The playwright had to pay for his power with his loyalty and obedience.

Soviet drama was exalted. In the future the process would lead to the proud and maniacal watchword: "The Soviet drama is the greatest and most human drama in the world." What were the special traits of that drama? V. Kirpotin wrote:

> Soviet drama differs from that of the pre-Revolutionary and the contemporary bourgeoisie in content. The pre-Revolutionary and contemporary bourgeois drama concentrate on the life of egoistic individuals. The self-infatuated savoring of narrowly individual experiences, the abnormally exaggerated individualistic principle . . . adultery, eroticism, and crime are most typical of the content of the bourgeois drama. The idea that private property and money are the highest blessings on earth . . . forms one of the basic themes of bourgeois drama. That is true both of its classics and of its period of decline.

> The ideas of Soviet drama are new. Its theme is collective toil and the collective struggle for socialism. . . . Soviet drama depicts man in a new way,

as a participant in the class collective, as a creator of new social forms, as the discoverer of new techniques that immeasurably expand his power over nature. . . . It concerns the class struggle of the working class against its exploiters, the civil war, socialist industrialization, the collectivization of agriculture, the role of the intellectuals in the revolution.[2]

The author of the above statement was one of the leading Party "critics," whose remarks were made at the First Congress of Soviet Writers. They clearly show that the main theme of the drama is "prescribed" for the authors from above. It is limited, for the most part, to current political tasks assigned by the Communist Party. It includes "the creation of new technique," "socialist industrialization," "the collectivization of agriculture," and "the role of the intellectuals."

That formula determined everything which has been and is now bruited about as "socialist realism." It was a realism that viewed the world according to the general line of the Party. A Soviet artist could take no other view. According to Lunacharsky, the Soviet "socialist realist" must be "convinced of mankind's Communist future and believe in the power of the proletariat, with its Party and its leaders." [3]

A great number of plays of the time concerned industrialization. They fit into one and the same pattern—there were politically "conscious" and "unconscious" builders. A "man on duty" and a concealed "wrecker" —a highly trained technician—were obligatory. The saboteur had to be contrasted with a Bolshevik "specialist." Of course, a member of the sage Communist Party was indispensable for steering the entire action toward a "happy ending." There was also a standard means for avoiding the routine boredom of propaganda. It consisted of an odd fellow "on duty." Generally, he was an old man or a comedian, who—despite his whimsicality—was an outstanding friend of the Bolsheviks.

One may change the names of such plays as *Temp* ("Tempo"), *Rel'sy gudiat* ("Rails Are Humming"), *Shakhtëry* ("Miners"), and *Piatyi gorizont* ("Fifth Horizon"). One may change the names of their authors—Nikolai Pogodin, Vladimir Kirshon, and Vladimir Bill-Belotserkovsky—yet their patterns are uniform, and their language contains the same Soviet jargon. The only "freedom" the playwrights have is in the background against which the hackneyed action takes place— the new construction may be a factory for locomotives (or for anything else) or a mine. But the important thing in drama is the treatment of the human conflicts, and that is stereotyped in these plays. All the plays were written according to formula. The rural group contains the same politically "conscious" and "unconscious" peasants. The "kulak" replaces the "wrecker," but the Party member remains the indispensable benefactor and savior of the countryside. Yuri Yuzovsky said: "The entire interest of a play is concentrated on unmasking the kulak [or the wrecker], in revealing him, catching him, punishing him, and executing him! As soon as that is done, the curtain falls and the play is over." [4]

Soviet drama is the only drama in the world that makes it almost ridiculous to study individual playwrights. They are not individual in style, language, or subject. Because of the standardization, there is no need to examine all of the two or three hundred Soviet plays written during the second decade of the Soviet theater. Their themes and styles are so uniform that it will be quite enough to study only the outstanding works connected with each group of Party slogans to obtain a comprehensive understanding of them all.

"THE LIQUIDATION OF THE KULAKS AS A CLASS"

Kirshon's *Khleb* ("Bread") is an outstanding play in the group dealing with the liquidation of the kulaks as a class. The idea behind the play is the application of the general Party line in the countryside. The background deals with the grain collections squeezed out of the rural districts, and the theme is the class struggle in the village and the Party's defeat of the peasants. The Soviet press published a good number of articles in praise of *Bread,* and it was declared almost the loftiest attainment of the entire proletarian drama. (Incidentally, that did not ease the author's later difficulties in the slightest—he was executed as an "enemy of the people.")

The protagonists of *Bread* are kulaks named Kvasov and Kotikhin. They are contrasted with two Party members, Rayevsky and Mikhailov. Party critics declared Kirshon's work to be the first play to show "kulaks" truly and powerfully.[5] The kulaks in it exert an enormous influence on the "middle peasants" and the "poor peasants."

Rayevsky is a Party member who is a "leftist exaggerator," a term applied to those who carried out Stalin's agricultural directives with utter ruthlessness. After Stalin's "brilliant" plan resulted in a complete fiasco, he blamed the "Rayevskys" for his own offenses. Mikhailov personified the Party line after Stalin's original plan had been corrected.[6]

Odinochestvo ("Solitude") by Nikolai Virta was a novel that was much discussed, and Stalin himself praised it. The author adapted it for the stage under the title of *Zemlia* ("Land") in 1937. The raw material for the work was Virta's recollections of his own childhood. His father had been a village priest who was shot by the Bolsheviks for participating in the great revolt of the Tambov province peasants in 1920. The rebellion was suppressed by Mikhail Tukhachevsky, later executed in the military plot of 1937. After Tukhachevsky was shot, Virta revised his novel and substituted Kotovsky for Tukhachevsky. They say that this was done on the advice of Stalin. Kotovsky, however, took no active part in the bloody expedition to Tambov province. This character in the play is of uncertain identity.

Solitude showed that the author sometimes tried to depict the rebelling peasants objectively. For this, the Party critics at first accused him of "apologizing for the kulaks." (Naturally, the accusations preceded the "very high" praise.) In the play, however, the entire situation was revised to become "ideologically useful." *Land* represents the debacle of the kulak revolt that Antonov and Storozhev led in the Tambov region. The emphasis was shifted from the lonely Russian peasants during the period when the countryside was enslaved to the "victorious union of workers and peasants" under the leadership of the Communist Party, which was leading the countryside to the world of the future. The minor and episodic figure of Grandpa Vasily in *Solitude* grows into Frol Bayev in *Land*. He personifies the "true line," according to which the peasants ought not to revolt against the workers, but must seek friendship with the proletariat. Frol Bayev is a "simple Russian peasant" who becomes entangled in the diabolical propaganda of the rebels and strays. But he is extremely fortunate in visiting a "human human"—Lenin. That opens Frol's eyes, and he understands that there is only one path for the muzhiks: with Lenin and against the kulaks. The scene in which old Frol Bayev perishes at Antonov's kulak headquarters was copied from Mikhail Glinka's treatment of Ivan Susanin's death in *A Life for the Tsar* (*Ivan Susanin*).

Storozhev, the instigator of the peasant rebellion, is pictured as a "hardened wolf" of a kulak. This spiritual leader of the peasants is filled with a black and unreasoning hatred. He dreams only of retaking the thousands of acres that the Soviet regime has expropriated from him. Virta changes Storozhev from a dedicated protector of the unhappy peasantry to a selfish and bestial landed proprietor. The play was devoted to the "destruction of his bestial proprietary philosophy." Antonov (the Cossack leader), Maria Kosova (the commander of a rebel regiment), Safirov (the chief of staff), and Ishin (a socialist revolutionary) are also repulsive. The shining hero of the work, of course, is Listrat Grigorevich—the commander of a partisan detachment.

"THE VALOR AND HONOR OF THE WORKING CLASS"

During the first Five-Year Plan industrialization was made "an affair concerning the valor and honor of the working class," and the drama was mobilized by the Party to show the mythological pathos of new constructions. N. Nikitin, whose *Liniia ognia* ("Line of Fire") came out in 1931, wrote about his play:

Two phalanxes of people are struggling in my play. One group is composed of the industrializers; the other, of people from the old capitalistic world. The second group is made up of people who bring the microbes of disbelief, sabotage, and demoralization to the constructions.[7]

Line of Fire shows the marvelous "reforging" of the politically unconscious seasonal workers into "conscious builders of socialism."

This same group of early plays on themes of industrial reconstruction includes Nikolai Pogodin's *Temp* ("Tempo") and Valentin Katayev's *Vremia vperëd!* ("Time, Forward!"). They both deal with "re-educating" the backward masses of seasonal and other workers, with the quickening of work tempos from Asiatic levels to "Bolshevik tempos," and with the change in the ignorant consciousness of backward people—a transformation engineered by the glorious members of the Party.

"BOLSHEVIKS MUST MASTER TECHNIQUE— TECHNIQUE DECIDES EVERYTHING"

Pogodin, one of the outstanding Soviet dramatists, wrote *Poema o topore* ("Poem about an Axe") in 1931. It illustrated the Party slogans that head this section of the chapter. Pogodin was a newspaperman turned playwright. During the first Five-Year Plan he made trips to new constructions for Party newspapers, and his early plays reveal journalistic qualities in their abundance of vital facts and keen observations in their depiction of reality.

Poem about an Axe deals with the struggle against technical backwardness. Technique was needed "to overtake and surpass the capitalistic countries," and it therefore had to be mastered.[8] The struggle was against "sleeping Asia" and the "Russian backwardness" of the workers and peasants. The people had to be awakened with Bolshevik ruthlessness and impelled to master technique. Without technique Bolshevism could not live. The play also shows the struggle waged by the Communists, the technicians, and the leading workers for reconstructing the factory. Of course "sabotaging specialists" put all kinds of obstacles in their way. Subsidiary themes are the struggles to involve women in production and to organize canteens at the factory.

"THE OLD INTELLIGENTSIA JOIN THE CAMP OF THE REVOLUTION"

There was a large group of plays devoted to the intellectuals during the second decade. The number itself bespeaks their importance to the Communist Party and the anxiety of the Bolsheviks about the intelligentsia. The "specialists" had to surrender. Formal conversion was not enough—they had to be enthusiastic about industrializing the country. Otherwise, the Five-Year Plans could not be fulfilled at all. The conversion of the intellectuals was one of the thorniest problems for Bolshevism and one of the commonest themes in Soviet drama.

L. Rakhmanov's *Besspokoinaia starost'* ("Unworried Old Age") was one of the most influential plays to deal with the conversion of a pre-Revolutionary intellectual to Bolshevism. Rakhmanov adapted the play from his scenario for *Deputat Baltiki* ("Baltic Deputy"), one of the best of early Soviet films.

Timiriazev, a member of the Academy, was the historical prototype upon whom the playwright based his old Professor Polezhayev, who is a Darwinist and an outstanding Russian scientist with a world-wide reputation. After several pre-Revolutionary scenes, in which the progressive Polezhayev's scientific efforts are frustrated by tsarist authorities, the Bolshevik Revolution of 1917 takes place. The October Revolution plunges old Polezhayev into a life of coldness, hunger, and searches by coarse Red Guardsmen. There are stories about mob rule and executions. The professor is appalled by the ignorance and vulgarity of the Red Guardsmen who have come to take away his "extra" because he is a bourgeois, and yet inwardly he sympathizes with them.

Professor Polezhayev hands the commissar who is directing the search of his house an article for the Bolshevik press. In the article the great scientist proclaims himself to be wholeheartedly behind the new regime.

Most of Polezhayev's colleagues decide to ostracize him. No one comes to his house on his birthday except for a faithful colleague Vorobëv (who is being shifted from one front to another) and a former student, Bocharov (who has become a Bolshevik). On the streets, the newsboys selling the non-Communist newspaper are shouting: "Former great scientist sells out to Bolsheviks!" The newspaper itself states: "It is with great sorrow that we announce the blinding of a famous scientist who, at the age of seventy plus, has gone over to the camp of the ravishers and enemies of culture." The students also are shocked by Polezhayev's decision, and they send a delegation to his home with an ultimatum. If he does not denounce his own article, they will boycott him at the university. The faithful Vorobëv has the only copy of Polezhayev's life work. Vorobëv threatens to send the manuscript abroad unless the professor denounces the Bolsheviks.

On Polezhayev's birthday Bocharov visits him. The old professor is weak and ill. He reads his lectures to sailors and Red Army men, however, and he exhorts the troops, who are bound for the front, to defend Petrograd from the Whites. The play ends with a telephone call. Lenin is on the line. He congratulates Polezhayev on his birthday and tells the scientist that, despite the war, Polezhayev's project for a botanical institute has been approved. Lenin also thanks the professor for the article supporting the Soviet regime.

The play was powerful, but the motion picture had been even better. Rakhmanov's picture of the odd, human, severe, and unbending professor and his moving and almost Chekhovian wife was warm and true. Polezhayev was such a fine and charming person that he moved even completely anti-Soviet people to tears. The play evoked a desire to emulate the scientist, to devote one's own life and fate to the simple and hearty workers.

Alexander Afinogenov's *Strakh* ("Fear") appeared in 1931 and is one of the best Soviet plays. Most Soviet dramatists are cowards in fulfilling the "social command" of the Party, and they are afraid of sinning against their customer's "general line." They are most interested in taking out insurance against future attacks by Marxian critics because they do not want to be accused of "deviations" or of lapses into heresy. Afinogenov, however, proposed and solved a problem. The old intelligentsia was divided into various strata, and its best members capitulated to the "conquering Galilean."

The hero of the play is old Professor Borodin, the director of a Soviet "Institute of Physiological Stimuli." His scientific experiments over the years in his "laboratory of social conduct" make him conclude that man's activity is determined by four stimuli: fear, love, hatred, and hunger. Scientific guidance of these "motivating forces" can change people and set their social activity on the right path. Borodin declares that, with the aid of his data, he is prepared to show that the "Soviet system of administration does not suit people at all" because it is founded on fear alone. The Soviet government must renounce its system of fear (or of blatant terrorism) and direct the masses through science. The protagonist of *Fear* revolted publicly against the class struggle that is the very basis of Bolshevism. One must give Afinogenov credit for great courage—but his courage ends with his mention of the problem.

Everything else in the play is profoundly Marxian. The author unmasks the feigned objectivity and non-Party principles of Borodin. Afinogenov set himself some dialectical tasks: "to remove 'the honesty' of the hero"; "to reveal his 'objectivity' as protective coloration that is harmful to the proletariat"; "to show that his 'pure science' has class motivations, is basically bourgeois, and inevitably serves the counter-revolution." [9]

The counterrevolutionary essence of Borodin comes to light through his "connections." He is isolated from the world and encased in his own office. The professor learns what is going on outside only from Vargasov, the secretary of the Institute. Vargasov is an ignorant and narrow-minded man whose contacts with foreign countries are suspicious. Later on, Vargasov draws up a protest for the "capitalistic press" against Soviet persecution of a scientist with a world-wide reputation. Professor Borodin's favorite pupil is Kastalsky, a sleek, "old-regime," career-minded graduate student and a bourgeois. Borodin dislikes the genuine proletarian change in science, as represented by a Kirghiz named Kimbayev. Borodin is too intolerant towards Tsekhovoi, a graduate student who passes himself off as a worker. When it comes out that Tsekhovoi is an admiral's son who has hidden his social origin, Borodin's antipathy turns into sympathy. The Professor stops shaking hands with his colleague Bobrov when he learns that the latter has decided to support the Bolsheviks. Borodin considers Bobrov's action a betrayal of the freedom to be nonpolitical in scientific research. Even Borodin's family contains a den of people who are "hostile to the proletariat." All these "connections" disclose the contradiction between the lofty, nonpolitical arguments in Professor Borodin's attitude toward science, and his purely "class practice," which is highly political. He reveals himself according to all the rules of dialectical materialism.

Hence, Afinogenov changed "fear" from a weapon of Borodin's against the Soviet regime to a weapon of the state's against its own enemies. All the characters of the play, it turns out, are divided by fear. Some fear for themselves, lest their shady pasts be disclosed. Others fear for their careers and positions. It is this fear held by the "class enemies" of the proletariat, which produces Borodin's counterrevolutionary theory of fear.

The struggle between Soviet and anti-Soviet forces is developing within the Institute itself. Despite this, Borodin is not afraid to read a paper at a scientific meeting that uncompromisingly sets forth his theory that the Soviet regime is based on fear alone. Fear is the sole stimulus for "socialist competition," "shock work," enthusiasm, and "Bolshevik tempos." The masses are constantly afraid of losing their jobs, their rations, their rights, and their freedom.[10]

Borodin is then overthrown. An old Bolshevik, Clara, mounts the rostrum. She shows the bankruptcy of Borodin's teachings as easily as if she were showing that two times two makes four. She concludes:

Yes, the working class knows what fear is . . . under capitalism and under imperialism. That fear has produced and is producing the fearlessness of the revolutionary struggle, the fearlessness of the struggle for a new, classless society, and the fearlessness of revolutionary victories!

The rhetorical downfall of Borodin means little to the author. He finishes the play by exposing the professor's actions. Borodin is arrested by the GPU. In the office of the secret-police examiner, Borodin learns that Kastalsky, his favorite pupil, has been caught at the frontier with the anti-Soviet "package" that Vargasov had handed him. Both the "counterrevolutionaries" ascribe their guilt to Professor Borodin. He is their leader and the reason why they became saboteurs. He is why they have become counterrevolutionaries and entered into communications with the "interventionists." "Him! Him! Him! . . . We were only a weapon in his hands, practicing what he preached."

Professor Borodin has never considered himself counterrevolutionary. He understands, however, that they are right—that he is "objectively guilty." When he is taken away from the office, he is destroyed morally and politically. The play ends with Borodin's renascence. Fabulously, he is liberated from the prisons of the GPU. He now starts a new life as a scientist "devoted to the Party and government." [11] Afinogenov fulfilled the "social command" of the Party.[12] The plot and the characterizations were skillfully done.

Boris Romashov's *Ognennyi most* ("Fiery Bridge") is also devoted to "rebuilding and re-educating the intellectuals." The heroine is a "petty-bourgeois" intellectual woman who accepts the Revolution romantically. When the NEP comes, she grows disillusioned, melancholy, and bored. The wise proletariat delivers her from the "blues" and despondency by showing her the new romanticism of Soviet daily life (which is frightful). It turns out that her doubts were not really so dangerous to Bolshevism. It is simply that her child had died, and she—being of a weak and "petty-bourgeois" nature—has become pessimistic and automatically transferred her attitude to the Soviet regime.

Yuri Olesha wrote *Zagovor chuvstv* ("Conspiracy of Feelings") in 1929 and *Spisok blagodeianii* ("List of Good Deeds") in 1931. These works also deal with "reconstructing the intelligentsia," but with a difference. They are works of art and were not written according to the standards set by the Department of Agitation and Propaganda. Olesha was one of the most talented and most original "fellow travelers" in Soviet literature.

Nothing more incompatible with the stereotypes of "socialist realism" can be found in Soviet literature than his works. He has since been silenced. Olesha was to literature what Vsevolod Meyerhold was to the theater. They were linked by a constant search for a way beyond the limits of existence. Olesha always aspired to break through to the world of the unreal, "to make the invisible country visible." For him, reality was only a "long shadow" from the other world.

The Communist critics did not spare paper or ink in discussing *Conspiracy of Feelings*. They discerned in it the inevitable death of petty reactionary passions, the "soot of dissatisfaction among kitchen philistines" who had to yield to such builders of socialism as Andrei Babichev, one of its characters. In fact, however, everything was somewhat deeper and more polemical.

Ivan Babichev, the hero in *Conspiracy of Feelings,* is "king of the vulgar." He rebels against his brother, Andrei. Basically, it is a rebellion against the doleful, official, and callous realm of materialism that the

Bolsheviks were building. Andrei Babichev is a fat and clumsy man, who sings in the bathroom every morning. He is healthy, optimistic, and narrow-minded. Andrei believes that all human happiness can be resolved by eating cheap sausages in a gigantic "public canteen" called "The Twenty-five Kopecks." He is shown as a genuinely and militantly vulgar conqueror. He builds a "socialism" in which the individual counts for nothing and the masses are only flocks of sheep herded into gigantic public canteens.

Olesha camouflages his own revolt against the stifling banality of materialism. Ivan Babichev—who is struggling against this materialism —is most unattractive. The leader of the *Conspiracy of Feelings* is masked as the "king of the vulgar." He is a flabby man in a derby and a greasy cutaway, who always appears with a pillow in his hands. Ivan wants to raise a final rebellion of the emotions that Bolshevik materialism is annihilating. They include "pity, pride, tenderness, and love— in short all the feelings that comprised the human spirit in the age that is past." He wants to direct them against the banal materialist whose narrow-mindedness is intolerable.

The materialist, on the other hand, dreams of creating a land on the earth whose people will have no dangerous emotions. It would be a sterilized, mechanical, utilitarian, and completely sober country where people would be happy—like the animals. They would enjoy gorging at the gigantic troughs provided by the state. Andrei has taken away Kavalerov (his brother's friend) and Valia. The Communist regards love as the "functioning of physiological demands."

On the rostrum at a meeting, Andrei Babichev promises to use "The Twenty-five Kopecks" to feed the Soviet masses. He talks about "unutilized potentialities," nutritiousness, and "profits from the communal canteen." His clumsy and ridiculous brother gets up, a pillow in his hands, and addresses the masses:

Comrades! They want to remove your main property—the domestic hearth. The horses of the Revolution are thundering up the dark staircases, oppressing your children and cats, smashing the stoves and bricks that you love, and breaking into your kitchens. Women, your pride and glory—the hearth—is threatened. . . . They mocked your pots and pans, your silence, and your right to suckle your own children. . . . They tear into your back streets; they slip along your shelves like rats. . . . Here is a pillow. I am the king of the pillows. Tell them each of us wants to sleep on his own pillow! Don't disturb our pillows! Our heads are not yet feathered or turning red with chicken down! They lay on these pillows! Our kisses fell upon them in nights of love. We died upon them and those whom we killed died upon them. Don't touch our pillows! . . . What can you offer us to replace our knowledge of love, hatred, hope, tears, pity, and forgiveness? . . . Here is a pillow —our coat of arms, our flag! Here is a pillow—bullets stick in a pillow. We shall stifle you with a pillow!

This speech by the "enraged philistine" is not silly, and it is far from being "narrow-minded." Between the make-up of the lines, concealed by the language of an Aesop, this is an accusation of the Soviet "devils" that is irate and truthful. But there is no rebellion of the "masses."

Ivan Babichev makes Kavalerov his weapon against the "sausage maker." Ivan, like Dostoevsky's Raskolnikov, craves to assert his own personality. Ivan Babichev perishes because his creator, Olesha, was compelled to compromise ideologically. Instead of slashing Andrei with the razor, Kavalerov kills Ivan. "I have killed my own past. . . . Give me the floor," he says in the curtain scene.

The Soviet critics, of course, did not fail to see the false denouement in *Conspiracy of Feelings*. They realized that Olesha's basic intention was not to solve the problem but to state it.[13]

List of Good Deeds opens right after a performance of *Hamlet* has supposedly been given in a Soviet theater. The main figure is a talented actress named Elena Goncharova. She has played the title role in *Hamlet* herself and joins the audience in a panel discussion. *List of Good Deeds* has an epigraph from *Hamlet*. In Olesha's play, the scene in which Hamlet asks Guildenstern to play the recorder is enacted twice—once upon the demand of the Soviet audience participating in the panel discussion, and again in Paris before Marjaret, the director of the music hall. Olesha paraphrases Hamlet's inner conflict (between duty plus reason and the heart plus emotion) in Soviet reality. For Elena Goncharova also, "the time is out of joint." The world is divided into two hostile camps. The actress says: "I am alone in the whole world, all alone! The struggle between the two worlds is all within me. And I am not arguing with you but with myself."

Goncharova's tragedy is that of the entire Russian intelligentsia. Their spirits, ideas, and emotions have blood links with the past that has been swept away. They have been forced to exist in the alien, Soviet world. Prudence, if not reason, demands their acceptance of it, but their hearts cannot comply.[14] Elena Goncharova's tragedy was that of Olesha himself or of any other talented "fellow traveler" in the arts. They are neither counterrevolutionaries nor anti-Soviet but are people "of the old world, who argue with themselves." They struggle with their consciences in an attempt to find a way to accept and justify the frightful Soviet realities into which fate had thrown them. They all, like Goncharova, made two lists: "a list of bad deeds" and a "list of good deeds" accomplished by the Soviet regime. Like Goncharova's, their "lists of bad deeds" did not include narrow-minded complaints about material shortages. They dealt with worse things—the crimes against the human personality that they considered to be the most frightening part of the regime.[15]

The prologue of the play shows us a panel discussion about *Hamlet* and the surroundings of Goncharova—or of any other "fellow traveler" in the arts—within the Soviet Union. The Party members are coarse and stupid. They hand Goncharova such a note as this:

The play which you have just shown us—*Hamlet*—was evidently written for intellectuals. An audience of workers does not understand it at all. It is foreign and deals with what happened long ago. Why is it presented?

Goncharova takes the floor, but she is closely watched by Orlovsky, the Communist chairman of the meeting. He clears his throat to "stop" her when she strays away from the "ideological line." Nevertheless, the actress does manage to mention important ideas that are relevant to the Soviet drama and may be taken as Olesha's own attitude:

Contemporary plays are false, schematic, and rectilinear. They contain no imagination. To play in them means to lose one's talent. . . . In an age of rapid tempos, an artist must think slowly.

Her final remark on the subject is her most important one. The "proletariat" and the Party coerce artists, but the latter can answer in Hamlet's words:

Why, look you now, how unworthy a thing you make of me! You would play upon me, you would seem to know my stops, you would pluck out the heart of my mystery, you would sound me from my lowest note to the top of my compass . . . though you can fret me, you cannot play upon me.

In her home, Goncharova is afflicted with all the stench and filth of Soviet life in a communal apartment. There are threats, insults, scandals, gossiping, and eavesdropping. She undertakes an assignment abroad and takes along her notebook containing the "list of bad deeds and good deeds" that is to become quite important in the play.

Starting with scene 3, Olesha's taste, boldness, and truthfulness desert him. As with *Conspiracy of Feelings*, he is content merely to state the question courageously. Later, the major artist "copies" capitalist Paris from the Communist propaganda posters. In Paris the actress feels how attracted she is to the "old stones of Europe." [16] She decides to remain and to become a "nonreturnee." This is where the second Olesha enters the scene—the one who works according to the prescriptions of the Department of Agitation and Propaganda and thus shows to what depths even such an artist as he can sink in the Soviet Union. He shows the entire bourgeois world of the West as vile, loathsome, and indecent.

When Goncharova has tasted "capitalism" and has been confused and compromised by the "White bandits," she "has her eyes opened," and the Soviet world strikes her as being a land of light and purity.[17] She returns to the "list of good deeds." Having lost her "Soviet home-land," she perishes in a skirmish between Parisian strikers and the police in using her body to shield a French Communist from the bullets of an undercover police agent. Thus, the Soviet actress fulfills her duty to the Revolution and dies in a pool of blood on the stones of old Europe. Olesha threw caution to the winds in capitulating to the Department of Agitation and Propaganda, but his "customers" were not satisfied. Meyerhold staged the play in 1931, and the Bolsheviks reacted crudely and harshly.

Faiko's play *Chelovek s portfelem* ("The Man with the Portfolio") came out in 1927 and dealt with the same theme. Its hero, Professor Androsov, is an honest specialist and a Soviet patriot. He is opposed by "a group of refined and contemplative intellectuals" who are "adjusting to socialist construction." Faiko's attitude to all the "people with port-folios"—intellectuals who serve Bolshevism in a formal and mechanical style without believing in it—is that of a prosecuting attorney. When the play was first presented by the Theater of the Revolution in Moscow, Faiko was accused of libeling the intelligentsia. A month later, however, the "miners' trial" broke, and the author was then praised for having foreseen the sabotage of the intellectuals.

"CADRES ARE EVERYTHING"

The so-called "cadre problem" was reflected in innumerable slogans. Among them were Stalin's phrase that "cadres are everything" and the various catch-phrases of the Party. The cadre problem has always been very important to the Bolsheviks. Right after their seizure of power the

Communists proclaimed: "The working class has acceded to power." But despite this and other fine slogans, the "ruling class" of the time had only brute strength. For any kind of production, and for any form of government, brains were needed. This meant specialists—such as doctors, teachers, and engineers. But the "brains" were hostile to Bolshevism.

The first weapon that the Bolsheviks used to break the resistance of the intellectuals and to force the "specialists" to surrender was terrorism. Terror led to the mass destruction of the intelligentsia. The intellectuals were the strongest and most valuable forces needed for construction, and so liquidating the intelligentsia as a class turned out to be more dangerous than destroying the peasantry. The best "fellow travelers" in all fields were terrorized into supporting the Soviet regime, but they did so with their lips, not with their hearts. Before entering any alliance wholeheartedly, they demanded something Bolshevism could not give them—the freedom of the individual.

From its very first days, therefore, the Communist regime tried to organize cadres of proletarian intellectuals. Here too, however, there were new obstacles. The new "specialists" could be created only with the aid of the old ones. In order to raise a proletarian intelligentsia big enough for such a huge country, the Communists needed an immeasurably stronger old intelligentsia than they possessed. The widespread executions of the early years now turned against the executioners themselves. Worst of all, the 100 percent proletarians—the proud fortress of the dictatorship—who studied at the various educational institutions soon became infected with a dangerous love for freedom and began to oppose the Soviet regime. This is borne out by the endless, large-scale repressions taken against Soviet students as a group. A horde of Red professors was needed to educate proletarian intellectuals who would remain loyal to the regime, but someone had to teach and develop the Red professors. It was a vicious circle. A generation of loyal and ideologically useful proletarian intellectuals could not be created by an intensive campaign whose tempo would resemble those of the "Five-Year Plans" because the process required decades. But that is why many Soviet plays deal—at least in part—with the headache of "new cadres" and the "re-educating of the old intelligentsia."

The Soviet critics always took a stern and nagging attitude toward the solutions of this problem presented on the stage. There could be no deviations or mistakes in producing plays based on such a theme.

Kirshon's *Konstantin Terekhin* was written in 1926 and showed the dangerous "demoralization" of a proletarian student. The Party dramatist "warned" against the danger of class degeneration in a proletarian who studies at an institute of higher education. This was the truth, the critics said, but Kirshon should have kept silent about it lest others follow such a bad example. The theater was supposed to depict ideal proletarian students for the young people in the audience to imitate. Hence, *Konstantin Terekhin* was not given a cordial reception:

> Where does the play show the genuine and positive type of proletarian student? Where is the type of student who matures in his work and study, who is concerned with real deeds and not merely with playing a guitar in the evening? The only student in the play who works and does not chatter is ideologically distant from the proletarian type. I declare that *Konstantin Terekhin* offers no positive type of proletarian student whose life harmonizes with the age in which socialism is being built.[18]

Many plays dealing with the new cadres were devoted to unmasking "class-hostile" elements that had wormed their way into Soviet universities and institutes. Bolshevism would not allow the sons and daughters of "former" people to receive any higher education. The endless "purges" of nonproletarian elements on the college level have been going on for years.

Mikitenko's *Light Up the Stars,* produced by the Second Moscow Art Theater in 1930, discussed the "proletarianization of higher education" and the need for "purging" the schools on the college level. It contains a scene in which the students debate the two viewpoints about new cadres at their meeting. One group maintains that any Soviet citizen should be admitted to college because the country needs millions of "specialists." The other viewpoint is the Party's. The Communists preached "selection," "purging," and "proletarianization" of higher education. They maintained that the "alien element" trained on the college level would replenish the cadres of the "wreckers" and thus bring about the destruction of the entire socialist system.

The outstanding work to discuss the new proletarian intelligentsia was Alexander Korneichuk's *Platon Krechet.* First produced in 1934, this work has since been acted on almost every Soviet stage, including even that of the Moscow Art Theater. Korneichuk is a Ukrainian Communist playwright, who since World War II has carved out a career for himself in the Soviet Foreign Ministry.

He too dealt with new cadres, this time in the field of medicine. He agreed completely with the changed tactics of the Communist Party on the question. Earlier, the problem had been solved by replacing the sabotaging, old intellectuals with a new and proletarian intelligentsia. *Platon Krechet,* however, discusses the struggle against bureaucrats who are backward specialists, directors, and Party members. Such people must be replaced by a new generation of bold reformers and Stakhanovites. The play corresponds to the altered policy of Stalin's dictatorship. In addition to purging bureaucrats from the Party, Stalin used shock workers and leaders to put pressure on Party members. He created a new class in the country—the "distinguished people" who were not Party members but had won medals as shock workers in all fields.

In *Platon Krechet,* the wise and alert Party of Stalin is represented by Berest, a member of the executive committee. Berest sees that Platon Krechet, a young surgeon who recently was a stoker on a steamer, is a Stakhanovite in medicine. Krechet is paving new ways for Soviet surgery. Berest takes Krechet under his wing and struggles ruthlessly against the backward Party members directing the local public-health service who want to drive Krechet out of surgery. They declare that his experiments have increased the number of unsuccessful operations. Through his characters, Korneichuk gives a rather truthful picture of what the Party members had done to the public-health service. All their "management" boils down to organizing the public in all kinds of "campaigns" to accomplish such harebrained schemes as turning the hospital into a "health factory."

The treatment of the old Russian medical personnel in the play is interesting. Both the district doctor—Bublik—and the old nurse are shown as warm people, and they have all the attributes of "positive characters." The work extoled Soviet medicine, but Korneichuk's predilections for "eloquence" gives the entire play a certain mawkish tone that is sometimes absurd.

"IN FAVOR OF A NEW AND SOCIALIST WAY OF LIFE"

A number of plays during the second decade discussed the "new way of life" and the uprooting of the petty-bourgeois way of life. One such work in 1933 was Shkvarkin's *Chuzhoi rebënok* ("Someone Else's Child," translated as *Father Unknown*). Shkvarkin proclaimed the new Soviet "freedom and equality of rights between the sexes" and the new attitude of parents toward each other and toward their children. The unmarried heroine, who is mistakenly suspected of being pregnant, emerges victorious over various manifestations of survivals from the "old way of life" with all its narrow-mindedness. Shkvarkin also wrote a play called *Vrednyi element* ("Harmful Element"), in which he contrasts bourgeois survivals and "Nepmen" with the new morality of a proletarian actor. Ilya Selvinsky, a poet, wrote a play called *Umka—Belyi medved'* ("Umka the White Bear," 1935), in which he seriously tried to justify the new Communist morality of a Party member named Kavaleridze. In order to accomplish the "class re-education" of a primitive chukchee from the polar regions, the Communist lets the other man sleep with Mrs. Kavaleridze. In other words, he puts the tasks of the Party above his own personal wishes. And in Afinogenov's *Chudak* ("Odd Fellow," 1929) the hero, Volgin, struggles alone against the "old world" and fights anti-Semitism, bureaucracy, and villainy in the style of a Don Quixote.

Valentin Katayev's play *Rastratchiki* ("Embezzlers"), produced in 1928, deals with a theme that is still vital today—embezzlement and peculation have plagued the country through the years. In his comedy Katayev utilized a theme that would be turned into a new form of terror several years later with the slogan "socialist property is sacred and inviolable," under which people would receive ten-year sentences for taking a handful of grain from a collective farm.

Leonid Leonov's *Untilovsk* also dates from 1928. The author was one of the most gifted "fellow travelers" in Soviet literature. His attempts to adapt himself to the Soviet system at first ran into severe criticism from Party members. His first novel on the subject, *The Badgers,* was made by him into a play. The critics accused Leonov of being "unable to depict the forces that made the Revolution. . . . Leonov shows the Revolution as something from without—a foreign body submerged in an alien milieu." [19]

In his later writings, however, Leonov revealed himself as a great and original artist with a fine style and a deep knowledge of Russian psychology. His devices are frequently reminiscent of Dostoevsky. He approached the Revolution in his own way rather than in the manner that the Party critics had urged upon him. For he considered the Revolution to be the development of something elemental within the depths of the Russian people rather than the planned accomplishment of the Communist program. Leonov's personal attitude, rather than the Party's attitude, shows up in all his plays. Unlike most Soviet playwrights, he does not write according to the recipes of the Department of Agitation and Propaganda. He raises problems and solves them in his own way.

In *Untilovsk,* Leonov rose against what he hated in the old way of life. But his discussion of the old included none of the general stereotypes found in Soviet drama. Somewhat in the manner of Saltykov-Shchedrin's *Gorod Glupov* ("Stupidville"), Leonov created a frightful town resembling a chamber of horrors. In it he gathered everything that he personally disliked, rather than what the Party disapproved. Leonov, through the characters, surveyed the "Russian abominations" —madness, lewdness, pettiness, garrulity, obscurantism, and narrow-mindedness. But he possessed enough taste not to insert any boring "positive characters" from the Party or the Komsomol into his half-fantastic and Dostoevskian work.[20] The new and Soviet element in the play is represented only by a chorus heard beyond the walls. It reminds us that a new way of life is coming to Untilovsk.

"STRENGTHEN THE DEFENSE OF THE U.S.S.R.!"

When Boris Romashev's *Boitsy* ("Fighters") appeared in 1934, it marked an outstanding event in Soviet drama because it was the first important play to deal with preparing the country for war by raising its defense potential. The new genre was called "defense drama" and was to have a great future in the U.S.S.R. With every passing year, the number of plays dealing with defense increased. The works called for military preparedness and vigilance.[21] During the war the Soviet theater gave all its energies to war dramas.

Romashev's play was first presented at the Maly Theater in Moscow. It called for reorganizing the Red Army. Lenchitsky (the chief of staff for a corps) and Gulin (the corps commander) personify the Soviet military leaders who are resting on their civil-war laurels. They are slow to learn about new advances in military technique, and their backwardness may aid the West in the coming war. (We know that this did happen in the wars against Finland and Hitler.) Berg, the young divisional commander, represents innovation in the Red Army. His victory over the out-dated heroes of the Civil War is the message of *Fighters.*

Nikolai Pogodin's defense and patriotic play *Piad' serebrianaia* ("Silvery Span," 1938) was based on some vital material of the time. There was a military clash with the Japanese on the Chinese-Far Eastern

44. Meyerhold used the devices and techniques of pantomime for Podgaetsky's *The Give-Us-Europe Trust*. A savage attack on Western capitalism, the play was based on novels by Ehrenburg, Kellerman, and Upton Sinclair.

45. Meyerhold's flair for satire found an excellent vehicle in Erdman's *The Warrant,* staged in 1925. A revolving stage and another new acting technique—"preacting"—were introduced.

46. In 1925 the Vakhtangov Theater presented *Virineya* by L. Seifulina. The theme was that the rural peasantry were Bolsheviks at heart even before the February Revolution. The play won personal approval from Stalin himself.

47. One of the most notable of all Soviet plays was Ivanov's *Armored Train 14-69,* produced by the Moscow Art Theater in 1927 in honor of the tenth anniversary of the Revolution. It has recently been revived in Moscow.

48. Ilya Selvinsky's drama-saga, *The Commander of the Second Army,* produced by Meyerhold in 1929, glorified the heroes of War Communism.

49. One of the heroes of *Armored Train 14-69* was Vershinin, the leader of the partisans, here played by V. I. Kachalov.

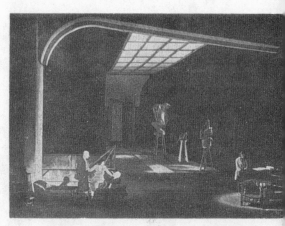

50. Alexei Popov's production of *My Friend,* by Nikolai Pogodin, at the Theater of the Revolution in Moscow in 1931, personified the Communist Party in the character of Gai, a Communist construction chief, whom the playwright made wise, benevolent, and endowed with all virtues.

51. Afinogenov's *Fear,* given at the Leningrad Academic Theater of Drama in 1931, pictured the intelligentsia of the old regime being gradually won over by the new.

52. Yuri Olesha's *List of Good Deeds* sympathetically portrayed the quandary of the intelligentsia, used to old ways, under the Soviet regime. All are converted at the play's end, the heroine finally giving her life for her new beliefs. A Meyerhold opus of 1931.

53. Trenëv's *Lyubov Yarovaya,* staged by Nemirovich-Danchenko for the Moscow Art Theater in 1936, extolled the virtues of a wife who turned her White Army soldier-husband over to Bolshevik executioners.

54. Vishnevsky's *Optimistic Tragedy,* produced by the Kamerny Theater in 1933, was a tragedy because every sailor in it was killed before the final curtain, optimistic because they were all happy to die for the New Russia.

55. Bulgakov's *Molière* was a disguised self-portrait attacking Soviet suppression of free speech and creative endeavor. P. V. Williams designed a gloomily symbolic décor for this Moscow Art Theater production of 1936.

56. Pogodin's *Man with a Gun* proved Stalin the true heir of Lenin. It was performed at the Vakhtangov Theater in 1937.

57. Nikolai Virta converted his novel *Solitude* into a drama called *Land* for the Moscow Art Theater in 1937. The novel had depicted peasants who resisted collectivization sympathetically, but in the play the peasants "learn" they should seek friendship with the proletariat.

58. Under Nemirovich-Danchenko's guidance, Tolstoy's wayward *Anna Karenina* became the symbol of "natural freedom" resisting the slavery imposed by a hypocritical society. Moscow Art Theater, 1937.

59. Stanislavsky's last work as a director was not a Soviet play but a famous classic, Molière's *Tartuffe*. The sketch for the décor is by P. V. Williams, Moscow Art Theater, 1938–39.

60. Another classic to gain "social significance" was Shakespeare's *Taming of the Shrew*, interpreted by Alexei Popov at the Central Theater of the Red Army, Moscow, in 1938. Katharine, it seems, was rebelling against her dull, stultifying, bourgeois environment.

61. The Moscow Art Theater's production of A. Kron's *Naval Officer* in 1945 was praised by Soviet critics for its utter realism.

62. The actor who played Lenin in Pogodin's *Kremlin Chimes* was nervous enough, but the actor who played Stalin with the real-life Stalin sitting in the audience was nervous almost to the point of speechlessness. Nemirovich-Danchenko produced it at the Moscow Art Theater in 1942.

63. Vishnevsky's *1919—The Unforgettable Year* was a cruder play on the theme of Lenin's friendship for and dependence on Stalin. Even the make-up was less subtle than that of the Moscow Art Theater presentation.

64. Chirskov's *Victors,* staged by the Moscow Art Theater in 1946, was one of a series of plays whose theme was that older worn-out generals should give way to the more up-to-date genius of younger ones.

65. Fadeyev's *Young Guard* was one of the best postwar plays dealing with the German occupation. The characters, patterned on real people, performed their deeds of heroism with almost incredible warmth and courage. Staged by Gl. Grakov, produced by Boris Zakhava at the Vakhtangov Theater in 1947.

Railroad. Mdivani's *Chest* ("Honor") propagandized for vigilance and preparedness on the part of the Soviet frontier guards. The play shows an ideal Georgian peasant who, despite ties of kinship, betrays a saboteur who has managed to cross the frontier, and the Bolsheviks capture the newcomer.

Vsevolod Vishnevsky's *Poslednii i reshitel'nyi* ("Final and Decisive") dates from 1931. The latter portion is connected with the defense motif. Vishnevsky had been a Communist sailor and was a specialist on the subject. These were the "pals" (*bratishki*) who had made the Revolution and fought in the Civil War on the side of the Bolsheviks, and Vishnevsky knew well the slang and customs of the coarse, pithy, and semianarchistic fleet "volunteers." He decided to make his play polemical. The first part attacks the "prettiness" and "opportunistic adaptability" of the theater, which had cheapened the Revolution and especially the Communist sailors. Vishnevsky's work was self-contradictory, illogical, and badly staged. Its episodes were crude, although the author pretended that they were a conscious departure from the stereotypes of the drama.

Vishnevsky recounts the story of two sailors "purged" from the Red Fleet because of their "immoral acts" with prostitutes in port, but his concluding scene is stylistically completely different from the others. In it, he shows the real heroism of the Red sailors who die while defending the frontier during the coming war against capitalism. For suddenly war breaks out against the Soviet Union. The frontier guards and sailors perish one at a time defending their posts. While the sailors are dying and bloody, the radio at the post blares forth fox trots and the songs of Maurice Chevalier, until one of the wounded men starts yelling: "Shut up, Europe!" He finished off the loudspeaker with a shot from his revolver. Bushuev, a fatally wounded sailor, is the last man left alive at the post. He crawls over to a wall, falling down and crawling once again as he stops up his wound with a bloody handkerchief. Feverishly, he takes some chalk and writes the number 162,000,000 on the wall. This was the population of the U.S.S.R. at the time. He substracts 27 from this number—27 people are killed at the post—and in his last spasm of life writes down the remainder to terrify the enemies of his country.

Both the title and the play itself caused great indignation among the Marxian critics. Vishnevsky had dared to take his title from the sacred

Russian words to the *Internationale*—the proletarian hymn. ("It is our final and decisive battle!") It would really be "final and decisive" if everyone were to die in it! [22] The heroics of the play should have matured from the "ordinary" and should not have been invented. And the ending should not have been so gloomy and ominous.

"UNDER THE WISE LEADERSHIP OF THE PARTY OF LENIN AND STALIN"

Pogodin's play *Moi drug* ("My Friend") came out in 1931. Its hero was a Communist construction chief named Gai, who personified the Communist Party. The dramatist fulfilled the worthy "social command" and showed the population that the Communist Party, as typified by Gai, contained concentrated wisdom, heroism, and humanity. Gai sees the "future in the present." He combines the romantic and poetic Communist of the future with the alert, ruthless, and thoughtful person whom the Party critics hailed enthusiastically. Gai is endowed with all the virtues, as befits an ordinary Bolshevik:

He is simple, sincere, and trusting with his comrades, and ironic with the foreign specialists. His irony clearly implies the value and superiority of Soviet people. He frequently breaks into the gay mischief of a healthy and strong person, and one constantly feels the intensity of his thinking, his concentration, and his profundity of emotion.[23]

The personification of the Communist Party is not limited to a complete set of human virtues. Gai assumes the functions of a divinity: he sees everything, knows everything, is able to do everything, and is sometimes even most gracious. He is full of pity for the weak, but he does not conceal his disapproval of offenders and squabblers. He has such a noble soul that he even nominates Monayenkov—who has just been conducting a campaign against Gai—to be his assistant. Gai builds socialism, keeps everyone warm, punishes the fools, liquidates the "human garbage," and feeds and clothes everyone. In short, Pogodin's supertask in the play was to say: Soviet people, the Party is most wise and virtuous! It is defending all of you and is taking you on a direct route to the paradise of socialist prosperity!

Alexander Bezymensky's play *Vystrel* ("The Shot") shows the Party in a somewhat different light. Meyerhold staged the piece by this Komsomol poet back in 1929. The protagonist—the "genius at getting along"—was named Prishletsov. He is a "theoretician of bureaucracy and political double-dealing." Bezymensky considered him the greatest threat to Bolshevik deeds. Prishletsov has his associates, such as Gladkikh (a Party pamphleteer and bureaucrat) and Bundia (a bootlicker). Bezymensky considered them to be the nucleus for Trotskyite and other anti-Bolshevik forces to group about. But the entire Soviet press, seeing it as a satire on bureaucrats in the Party, fell upon Bezymensky. He was accused of being "against the Party," "petty bourgeois," and a "masked Trotskyite." With all this persecution, the play could not long remain on the boards at Meyerhold's Theater. But there was one Party member in the country who decided to show the Communist critics once again that they were not the supreme judges of the arts. Stalin wrote a letter to Bezymensky to defend the playwright from persecution. It is dated March 19, 1930, and in it Stalin said:

I have read *Shot* and *Day of Our Life.* I have found nothing "petty-bourgeois" or "anti-Party" in these works. Both of them, especially *Shot,* can be considered models of revolutionary art for the present. . . . Their pathos consists in stressing the problems of the shortcomings in our apparatus and their deep belief in the possibility of correcting those shortcomings.[24]

Stalin prepared many "purges" for the Trotskyites and his other enemies in the Party to strengthen his own dictatorship. He wanted the Party to retain only loyal and flexible people; he would replenish its ranks with cadres of young people who were devoted to him. Bezymensky's *Shot* at the old Party bureaucracy was relevant to Stalin's objectives, so he complimented it.

Pogodin was the first playwright to discover a new theme for Soviet drama. He showed Lenin and Stalin together on the stage. Pogodin falsified the history of the Bolshevik revolution to the advantage of the dictator extant at the time. Long before the dramatist's *Chelovek s ruzh'ëm* ("Man with a Gun") appeared in 1937, "ideologically useful" Soviet paintings had dealt with the subject. A myth had been created that Stalin was Lenin's best and favorite pupil. There were many pictures painted in the oleographic manner of "socialist realism." They looked like enormous and ornate photographs. They invariably showed Stalin on Lenin's right at the Party Congresses, at the working out of brilliant plans, and even at the village of Gorky just before Lenin died there. All this is completely false. Stalin was never Lenin's "favorite pupil," and Lenin was not friendly toward him at all. Lenin's will is the best proof of our statement; on his deathbed Lenin warned the Party against the dangerous "master of sharp Caucasian dishes."

Pogodin's play, of course, was not written to show the fate of Ivan Shadrin (a "soldier from the front") as organically linking the 1917 victory of Bolshevism to the expectations of the entire Russian peasantry and working class. Nor was it written to show the frightful and miserable caricatures of Russian capitalists, generals, and Mensheviks condemned to death. The play magnifies and expands the role that Stalin played in the October Revolution. Such was the "social command." Small wonder that the critics considered the best scene in the play the one that shows Lenin working at night in his office. He telephones Stalin and tells him enthusiastically:

I have finished your draft of a declaration for the rights of peoples. I look at it like this: the declaration of the rights of peoples is the beginning of the end for racial and national inequality on the earth. It will be the basis for the future constitution of the Soviet state.

The plays of 1937 that sing of Lenin and Stalin include *Na beregu Nevy* ("On the Bank of the Neva") by Konstantin Trenëv, and *Pravda* ("Truth") by Korneichuk.

"THE HEROICS OF THE REVOLUTION AND THE CIVIL WAR"

The more the Revolution and the Civil War receded into the past, the more epic and monumental became the plays that treated these themes. Ordinary slaughter and despicable fratricide began to assume the qualities of sagas and myths. The Civil War had finished seven years before, and most of its participants were still alive and frequently went to the theater. On the stage, they were being transformed into legendary personalities and knights from Soviet folk-legends about the heroics of War Communism.

The first dramatist to use the saga technique was Ilya Selvinsky. His *The Commander of the Second Army* was staged in 1929 by Meyerhold. It was a tragedy about fighters who died in the Civil War, and its characters were sculptured images clad in Caucasian fur-caps and sheepskin coats. The strict and cumbersome verse of Selvinsky was like the epic song of a Scythian sentinel, and it gave the tragedy the flavor of "Red Nibelungs." The commanders and soldiers of the Red Army and the parade of the dead knights contrasted with the banality of contemporary Soviet existence. Whether the poet was conscious of it or not, his play implied that the romanticism and heroics of War Communism had yielded to an age of narrow-mindedness; the knights had been replaced by bureaucrats from the "regional committees," who carried portfolios tightly crammed with decrees and methods of procedure. The critics had reason to write as they did:

It is impossible to imagine any of them [the characters in the play] as studying at the Academy or commanding a regiment nowadays. These are people who disappeared on the battlefields in 1918 and 1919. They are just as legendary as the ancient Scythians. . . . In this case, the legend has taken shape shortly after the Revolution. While still warm and living in our memory and our life, they have been transformed under the present conditions of the class struggle into works of sculpture on the stage. The distinction from the rest of the past has been lost, and has petered out in our days.[25]

Vishnevsky's *Optimisticheskaia tragediia* ("An Optimistic Tragedy") also turned the Civil War into a saga. The Kamerny Theater presented that play in 1933. The tragedy showed a regiment of sailors, every man of whom was killed in action. The prologue stated that every one of them considered the regiment "to be a family. Each one had his woman. The women loved these people. . . . And each man vaguely sensed the imminent generation. . . . The fighters did not require you to become sad over their deaths." Hence, the tragedy was optimistic.

The play deals with the anarchistic and completely demoralized Baltic Fleet. The Party sends a woman to be its commissar. The sailors are insulted and infuriated at the fact that the Party has sent them a "dame." Someone simply decides to rape her. At the very first encounter, however, the commissar takes out her revolver and shoots the man. The woman brings to the Fleet the stern and ruthless discipline of the Communist Party, suppressing the anarchism that has become strong among the sailors. She then leads the former "Composite Anarchistic and Revolutionary Detachment" to the front and death.

The development of the "anarchistic rabble" and the modest woman into legendary figures constitutes the main theme of *An Optimistic Tragedy*. The characters could talk about themselves as simply as the ancient stele that said: "Wayfarer, if you go to Sparta, tell them that we lie here, as our nation commanded!"

The changing of the Civil War into an epic is stressed in other ways also. As he had done in his *Pervaia konnaia* ("First Cavalry Army"), Vishnevsky introduces a "Narrator" into his *Optimistic Tragedy*. The Narrator starts with the prologue and speaks in the name of the sailors who have fallen in battle. He talks about the future and comments on every scene. Sometimes he interrupts the actions with his ecstatic monologues. He introduces the element of saga. The Narrator binds the shallow episodes of the tragedy together. His remarks transfer the action from place to place. The symbolical and legendary quality in the play was, of course, accompanied by realism.

Vishnevsky's predecessor in treating Communist sailors on the stage was Boris Lavrenëv. For the tenth anniversary of the 1917 Revolution, Lavrenëv wrote *Razlom* ("Breach"). His theme was the rift in tsarist Russia that led to the Revolution. The breach took place among the naval officers. Either they could follow Captain Bersenev into the service of the Bolsheviks or they could be liquidated by the Bolshevik sailors led by Boatswain Godun.

Captain Bersenev's acceptance of Bolshevism is a complicated affair. Prompted by his feelings of honor as an officer, the old sea dog takes the blame for an offense committed by an officer of his crew on the cruiser *Dawn*. Godun protects Bersenev from the fury of the sailors. The Communist struggles for the soul of the Captain because the Red Fleet needs "specialists." The play is a stereotype from the group dealing with the "transition of the old intelligentsia to the camp of the Revolution." It gives a heroic version of the cruiser *Aurora* which, in real life, fired the first salvo against the Winter Palace in Petrograd during the October Revolution. The play ends when Godun ascends Captain Bersenev's bridge. The Communist gives the order to weigh anchor and join the fight for the October Revolution.

Another play in the impressive group dealing with Bolshevik sailors is Korneichuk's *Gibel' eskadry* ("Destruction of a Squadron," 1934), which shows the rebellion of sailors against their officers during the Civil War. A squadron is scuttled lest it fall to the Whites.

I. Prut's *Mstislav Udaloi* ("Mstislav the Bold"), presented in 1930, told about the heroism of an "ordinary son of the people." Suslov (a machine-gunner) and Lysenko (a commissar) inspire the crew of a beseiged armored train to resist the Whites heroically.

A civil-war play by Vsevolod Ivanov, however, was more important. This was his *Blokada* ("Blockade," 1929). As he had done with his

Armored Train 14–69, Ivanov wrote the play specifically for the Moscow Art Theater. *Blockade* dealt with suppressing the rebellion of the Baltic Fleet on Kronstadt in 1921. The sailors of the Baltic Fleet were the "pride and glory of the October Revolution," but they seized crucial forts and naval vessels in a revolt against the Soviet regime because the sailors "had finally realized what Bolshevism was." The Party sent the delegates of the Tenth Party Congress to suppress the revolt. Kronstadt was blockaded and the fight became unequal. The triumph was won by "courage, self-renunciation, devotion to the Revolution" and mainly by the genius of Stalin.

Ivanov crudely falsified the story of the rebellion. The rebels had to be shown most unfavorably, so Ivanov distorted the truth by stressing that, if you please, peace had just come to the country. Everyone was dreaming of peaceful construction and wanted a respite from the horrors of the Civil War. Along came the "Kronstadt gang," however, and brought the Civil War back again with all its chaos. Commissar Artem is the positive hero of the play; he is endowed with all the features of a legendary "iron Bolshevik" who fulfills the will of the "people." The chief negative character personifies the revolt—Rubtsov, a sailor of Kronstadt, who is shown to be an anarchist, a huckster, a coward, and a mercenary creature. The rebels are shown as self-seekers who dream only of establishing the "market place" and anarchy in the country. Ivanov did not hesitate to endow the Bolshevik executioners with cheap beauty and pathos, but for the conquered his palette contained only filth and soot.

"A SHADOW FALLS UPON EUROPE— THE SHADOW OF COMMUNISM"

A great number of "anticapitalistic" plays were written by Soviet playwrights, all of which repeat the identical Party theme in various ways. Any country in the West is shown with the same standardized "imperialists and capitalists." The weapon of these people is fascism, and their servants are the social democrats. The only bright force on the dark horizon of Europe consists of the members in the fraternal Communist parties. All the dark forces oppress the proletariat and drown it in blood. This leads the proletariat to open its eyes and go over to the Communist Party.

An analysis of one play from this group will adequately characterize this entire section of Soviet drama. We shall discuss Yuri German's *Vstuplenie* ("Introduction"), if only because it was produced by so great a master as Meyerhold. It was performed in 1932 and dealt with the "collapse of bourgeois culture."

Oskar Kelberg is a talented engineer and a specialist of major importance. The rotting capitalistic world compels him, however, to engage in completely degrading work—the manufacture of toilet paper. A worse fate falls to the lot of Nunbach, an unemployed engineer; he sells pornographic post cards near the walls of the enormous houses that he once built. The fear of unemployment hovers over the capitalistic world like a dark night.

The crisis and "twilight of the gods" in the West changes people's fate. Professor Kelberg flees from the "decline of Europe" to China, where he sees that Europeans are squeezing the last remaining strength out of the Chinese coolies. Kelberg realizes the European culture no longer exists, that capitalism is the same everywhere. The inhuman exploitation of man is concealed in the West but blatant in China. It is cosmopolitan, like capitalism itself. Professor Kelberg washes his hands of rotten capitalism and goes to the U.S.S.R.—the land of socialism and the real stronghold of humanism.

The author, the critics, and Meyerhold's Theater all considered the best scene to be the one in which Hugo Nunbach returns home after feverishly selling his post cards on the sidewalk. Nunbach stands alone before the spotlighted bust of Goethe. He turns its face toward him, kisses it, and says: "I forgot your face, Herr Goethe." The episode, one critic wrote,

reveals the real identity of present-day religion, morality, art, science, existence, society, and politics. In short, it shows the culture of those who consider themselves Goethe's heirs and thus closes the play with great power. Nunbach himself answers his own question: "Where is your culture?" [26]

Nunbach commits suicide. In the West are night and death. Light and life exist only in the Soviet Union. That is the meaning of German's *Introduction*.

"THE OLD LIFE IS DYING"

During all his years under the Soviet regime Maxim Gorky wrote only two plays: *Egor Bulichëv i dr.* ("Yegor Bulichev and Others," 1932) and *Dostigaev i dr.* ("Dostigayev and Others," 1933). Both of them deal with Russia on the eve of the Revolution. Gorky modestly called each of them "scenes," and they have no "intrigue" or brilliant plots. Nevertheless, they tower above the doleful valley of the entire Soviet drama, and they may certainly by called Soviet classics.

The power of Gorky's plays consists mainly in their language, in the great knowledge of life that he brought to the stage, and in his masterful creation of characters. He endowed the most minor persons in his plays with their own flavor and language. A few words brilliantly and precisely reveal the kernel of their natures. Gorky's characters are so pithy and interesting that he did not need any craftily woven intrigues or sensational twists and turns in developing his plots. He merely had to bring his characters together, and an interesting situation develops on the stage as his portrait gallery comes to life and starts moving.

Yegor Bulichev begins during World War I and ends with the Revolution of 1917. Bulichev is a merchant—a strong, original, and intelligent human being. He personifies the drama of those who have fallen "among strange people." Bulichev is dying of cancer. He is surrounded by the debris of a vain life, plunder, cheating, and rapacity in his own home. Just before his death, his house is invaded by everything bad and unclean in the Russian life of the time. Like Bulichev himself, the old life of Russia is incurably ill and is condemned to death.

Bulichev is a gifted man who is eager to live. He is a "builder of life" who hates the milieu to which he belongs. He despises the power of money, the existing regime, the rapacity, and the war. He is unable, however, to tear himself away from the milieu just as he is unable to stop the assault of death upon himself.

Bulichev has one weapon left—malicious mischief. He ridicules the devils around him. All his relatives are like vultures. They are anticipating his death and already are dividing his money. All the Zvontsovs and Dostigayevs are in a great hurry to get rich through the war and the national misery. Melaniya, the Mother Superior, is more concerned with investing the capital of the nunnery at a profit than she is with religion. They are quacks, bigots, charlatans, and chatterboxes. They form a parade of people who, just like the old order, are condemned to death—and the whole parade passes through the room of Yegor Bulichev.

The idea of the play was to show what the Revolution was going to smash. A story, intense action, and a keen-witted plot were not needed for Gorky's play. It was enough to give a death-bed vision of the living horsefaces who would soon turn into ghosts. "Look, the tsar is overthrown and the kingdom is perishing; sin, death, and stench hath come," says the "simpleton," and Yegor repeats these words as he dies.

Dostigayev is a continuation of *Yegor Bulichev*. It is more biased, more partial, and less skillful than the earlier play. *Dostigayev* reintroduces Zvontsov (Bulichev's son-in-law), Vasily Dostigayev (a merchant), and many other characters from the Bulichev milieu. The action takes place between July and October, 1917.

In the final scene of *Yegor Bulichev,* Dostigayev tells his wife: "Let's go home, Liza. Home! Bulichev is not well, not well at all. . . . And a demonstration is going on. . . . One must join it." Yegor Bulichev spent his life in "a strange land." Somewhere in the depths of his spirit, he has remained a peasant like his father, the raftsman. All Gorky's sympathies were with this talented and fiery Russian muzhik. Fate had not "decreed" that Bulichev could develop his talents in all their fullness. Gorky did not like Vasily Dostigayev, and he attacked the character from a democratic standpoint. Dostigayev is a higher and more predatory type of Russian capitalist. He is a merchant who has forgotten his roots in the peasantry. He is a European-style huckster, a calculating man who knows how to adjust himself to the political situation. Outwardly, he is fat and sleek. He seems to be good-hearted, but his jokes, his loquacity, and his facetious remarks mask a predatory individual whom Gorky considered a danger to the Revolution. Dostigayev hates the Revolution, but he wants to struggle to make it his "footboard." He worms his way into its midst and tries to play dirty tricks on it, to double-cross it from within.[27]

"Double dealing" and "adjusting" to the Revolution in order to throttle it from within form the main theme of *Dostigayev*. It is undoubtedly weaker than *Yegor Bulichev* and is more of a political pamphlet, a "chronicle of people," events, and groups with various social and political orientations on the eve of the October Revolution. *Yegor Bulichev* takes place within a single home. It centers around the mighty title figure. It was deeper, more psychological, and—most important—more sincere. *Dostigayev* bears the imprint of political partiality in its satiric depiction of the groups that were hostile to Bolshevism. Yet, Gorky's style, his "painting with words"—as he called it—remained as pithy and as powerful as it had been before.

"PRECURSORS OF STALIN IN HISTORY"

Alexei Nikolaevich Tolstoy's *Pëtr pervyi* ("Peter I") was an important event in Soviet drama. Tolstoy was a great stylist, and he used all his mastery in a brave attempt to consider the role of the individual in history. Earlier, Bolshevism had militantly maintained that the individual was only a minor weapon for the class and the masses, and it had denied any progressive significance whatever to the reforms of Peter the Great. The Bolsheviks had felt that he brought the land only ruin and had worsened the unbearable bondage of the peasantry. Bolshevik textbooks had shown Peter as a sick madcap. His conquest of the Baltic seacoast was regarded as a manifestation of the predatory aspirations held by the landed proprietors, serfholders, and trade capital. All this now changed. By some incomprehensible miracle, A. N. Tolstoy made the ruthless Russian emperor more "positive" than even the monarchists themselves had done. It was also a miracle that the play was not declared the work of a counterrevolutionary monarchist of aristocratic descent, or a thorough "distortion of the history of the class struggle in Russia." On the contrary, the critics hailed it as a masterpiece of Soviet drama.

This showed all the people of the Soviet Union that there had been a change in the Kremlin. There could be no doubt that Tolstoy's glorification of Peter's dictatorship had been approved by Stalin and his circle. The cult of Stalin as a personality was too widespread and sometimes reached a craze for cringing and bootlicking. Soviet people had to be shown that history has always had "progressive" state leaders very similar to Comrade Stalin. The brilliance of historical personalities had to be compared with Stalin's. Hence, a compromise could be reached with such drivel as the purely Marxian attitude to the role of the individual in history.

A. N. Tolstoy did not arrive at his Stalinlike conception of Peter the Great immediately. There are two other variants of his play that preceded the one "approved by the Party and the government." One of the first two variants almost corresponds to the old Marxian attitude.

In 1929 the play was still entitled *Na dybe* ("On the Rack"). That version showed the Age of Peter the Great as a thoroughly macabre period. Peter violated Russia. He suppressed everyone and everything as if he had been possessed by demons. He sowed fear, and put both his son and his entire country on the rack. He was left completely isolated from ignorant Russia's hatred of him. Everyone was his mortal foe, from the wild and enslaved muzhik to his own friends and family. Everyone betrayed him and deceived him, including his son Alexei, his wife (Ekaterina), and his best friend (Menshikov). It was a tragedy showing the isolation of a tyrant, and it depicted terror and solid barriers of resistance as the blood flowed on the executioner's block. It turned out that all the bloodshed was in vain; everything that Peter had constructed "on blood" was doomed to collapse when he died. His enemies were to gush forth like the waters of the Neva and sweep away the work of Peter's lifetime. The fleet symbolizing Peter's kingdom is destroyed. St. Petersburg, the city built on the blood and bones of hundreds of exhausted muzhiks, is flooded. The severed head of Mons is atop the only pole to stick out above the waves. "The water is rising. A terrible end!" This was the finish of the 1929 version.

Such a variant, of course, could only be viewed as using history to attack Stalin's dictatorship. It was an ominous warning that what Stalin had built on the blood of the peasants would also disappear. The GPU had spilled the blood of the martyrs in vain. Nothing is eternal, and there is the terrible question of "What is it for?" It was no accident that A. N. Tolstoy should have written such a play when Stalin was drowning Russia in the peasantry's blood with his "constant collectivization" and "constant industrialization."

The 1935 version, called *Peter I,* was almost completely different from *On the Rack.* Everything was transposed from a minor to a major key. First of all, Peter himself becomes the brilliant and indefatigable Hercules of the Russian nation. He is the builder-tsar, the carpenter-tsar, and the blacksmith-tsar. He rolls up his sleeves to build the Russian fleet, the cities, and the country. Tolstoy turns him into the prototype of a "Stakhanovite," and Peter becomes the "foundation-layer of Russia's military might." The construction of a ship becomes a symbol of the entire play. Pushkin had remarked that "Russia came into Europe like the launching of a ship—to the sound of the axe and the noise of the guns." The poet's observation became the motto of Tolstoy's play.

Peter I was filled with the fury and intoxication of toil. He is a "super-proletarian," masquerading as a Russian tsar. He wears the costumes and uses the material goods of the period when St. Petersburg was founded—but all by mistake. The tsar wears a leather apron to forge the anchor of a ship. He is unwilling to interrupt his work to hear reports. Everything grows and the rafters take shape high above the "tsar who is a worker." Tolstoy's Peter has a "toiler's psychology" and is democratic. Peter fears and respects the smith Zhemov. Sometimes the tsar learns from the smith; at other times Peter works as Zhemov's apprentice. The Russian emperor sometimes acts like a good member of the Communist Party. He gives rank to a proletarian Kalmyk. He has the lazy sons of the nobles hammer piles in the Wash at St. Petersburg. He follows the same procedure that the Bolsheviks used to chase "former people" and "dignitaries" into the "labor draft" during the first years of the Soviet regime. Peter hates war. He dreams of getting it over with in order to return to forging anchors, building vessels, and constructing docks—which he loves. Thus, Peter was "workerized" and "proletarianized" by A. N. Tolstoy. That was when they required "Stakhanovites," "rapid tempos in construction," and the fulfillment of the "Five-Year Plans."

Party policy changes, and so did A. N. Tolstoy's naughty game—not to say his mockery—with the history of Peter the Great. Tolstoy's third treatment of Peter came out in 1939, the year of the war with Finland. World War II was imminent, and the most important problem facing the Bolshevik state was defense. The patriotism of old Russia had to be instilled in the Soviet population. The obedient Tolstoy prepared a third version of his play, and this time he filled it with objects calling for patriotism and defense. His most important theme became the army.

Tolstoy tried to increase the importance of the masses and their patriotism. Mob scenes dominate the 1939 play and this is artificial. He brings in a muzhik named Vorobi, who is oppressed and exhausted by toil. Vorobi is a great hero protecting his homeland from its foreign enemies. After the battle of Poltava he tells Peter: "We did some work for you, tsar. . . . Don't you forget. . . . Take a drink for us."

Thus, one and the same play becomes a chameleon in the hands of the talented "Stalin laureate." Tolstoy reflected the tasks proposed by the Party's changing policy. He hastened to adjust himself to them. If the result of such loyal time-serving is bad for the history of Russia, then so much the worse for history. For the dramatist of Stalin's court, history was merely a stick to point in whatever direction the "master" desired.

MIKHAIL BULGAKOV'S *Molière*

Mikhail Bulgakov's *Molière* stands alone among the Soviet plays of the second decade. It was finished in 1931 and staged by Konstantin Stanislavsky at the Moscow Art Theater in 1936. It met an ordinary fate, and its production at the Moscow Art Theater brought consequences of its own.

At first glance, the talented Russian playwright merely seems to have wanted to be the first to show the personal life of the great French dramatist. One's first impression is that the love intrigue is the main theme of the plot. Molière's life was ruined by sinister and purely family circumstances. Bulgakov used the now-disproved story that without realizing it, Molière married his own daughter.

The prologue shows the wings during the première of a play in which Molière is participating at the court of Louis XIV. Molière tells his mistress, the actress Madeleine Bejart, that he is in love with her sister Armande and intends to marry the girl. Madeleine tells Lagrange, her lover's friend, that she has never told Molière that Armande is her daughter and not her sister.

The first scene shows us Molière at the peak of his glory as actor and director. His brilliant *Tartuffe* has already been played, and the clergy and the aristocracy are insulted and humiliated in the comedy, which is directed against them and the "cabal of hypocrites"—a secret society of reactionary feudal lords headed by the Archbishop of Paris.

Madeleine's secret gets out, and rumors begin to circulate that Molière has married his own daughter. Louis XIV withdraws his royal protection, and Molière is proclaimed something of an outlaw. He grows old and sick, and all kinds of blows rain down upon him. His wife leaves him, and his favorite pupil turns out to be an informer. The King subjects Molière to disgrace, and *Tartuffe* is forbidden. The persecuted playwright dies from a broken heart at a performance of *Le Malade imaginaire*. Such is the theme of Bulgakov's play.

Bulgakov was not writing, however, mainly about Molière's life. His principal theme was the "cabal of hypocrites"—a powerful party of people who imagined that they alone possessed the absolute truth, a party that did not stop at anything to silence the dangerous and freedom-loving playwright. Bulgakov's play was most powerful in dealing with the ruthless suppression of free speech and free creative endeavor. And so Bulgakov used non-Russian history as a weapon with which to strike at the "cabal of Marxian hypocrites."

Bulgakov was himself a victim of the Soviet cabal. Of his thirty-six plays, only five were permitted on the stage—and they for a short time only. The Soviet cabal understood the danger of *Molière,* and it was removed after a few performances.[27] Two years later the Russian dramatist who had cried out with the pain of Molière was dead.

CHAPTER X

LAST FLICKERS OF ORIGINALITY

DURING THE YEARS WHEN RAPP set the tone for the Soviet theater, the Party critics were incredibly "vigilant." Sometimes, plays written by Party members fell into the hands of non-Party directors who had originally been bourgeois or petty-bourgeois. Such people had to be watched lest they take it into their heads to mangle the "masterpieces" of proletarian drama. Sometimes, a play fell flat and the public stopped going to see it. In such a case, the Party critics invariably accused the theater and the director of being unable "to pull it up to the heights of the dramatist." The proletarian drama began to resemble the Party itself, which never makes mistakes or commits sins.

The unfortunate directors were persecuted for their inability to rescue the masterpieces of Communist drama despite all their efforts to do so. This theme runs like a red line through the hundreds of reviews written during the period. If the directors took strong measures to adorn the official boredom of Soviet plays with their own resourcefulness, they immediately came under the crossfire of other critics. The task of the second group was to wean the Soviet theater of dangerous esthetic deviations.

CREATIVE PRODUCTIONS OF PROLETARIAN PLAYS

An example of this was the Kamerny Theater's production of S. Semenov's *Natalia Tarpova* in 1929. The critics wrote that "Tairov gained a fall against the writer Semenov." Tairov had dared to profane a proletarian play with "bourgeois estheticism." He had tried to trim it prettily and to turn material from the socialist era into an "eternal, 'universal,' and personal problem."

Markish's *Piatyi gorizont* ("Fifth Horizon," 1932) was staged at the Vakhtangov Theater. The production was condemned as an "esthetic distortion of the stern realities connected with mining and miners." Perhaps half the Soviet plays staged at this Theater between 1927 and 1937 were declared "distortions of Soviet reality."

Vsevolod Ivanov's *Blockade* appeared at the Moscow Art Theater in 1929. The technique used to put it on was naturalism—which the Bolsheviks accepted. The sharp-eyed critics, however, noticed a spot of sedition. There was one dark scene in which the spotlight came to rest on a statue of Buddha. This was enough to accuse the theater of "dragging in contraband and class-alien philosophical generalizations."

Meyerhold was accused of estheticism because of a device he had used in staging Alexander Bezymensky's *Shot* in 1929:

The sparkling stream of paper very rapidly loses its significance as a satiric trait of bureaucracy, red tape, and paper sabotage, and it becomes purely esthetic. The paper that falls from above begins to act independently.[1]

With every new production Meyerhold seemed more "at a tangent" to the Bolsheviks. His struggle against naturalism was intransigent, and it now seemed aimed directly against "official realism." The packs of critics inquisitively rummaged in every new work of his in order to "nail down" the formalism. Their articles all grew more violent and emphasized more sharply that Meyerhold's work was full of distortions and perversions of "reality." In other words, they wanted to remove the nonrealism that Meyerhold had possessed all his life. They wished to "re-educate" him and "to reconstruct" him.

All the theaters had to stage the same Soviet plays in the spirit of "official realism," and so the Kamerny Theater, a showplace for theatricality and classical tragedy had to stage them also. In 1930 it was saddled with N. Nikitin's *Liniia ognia* ("Line of Fire"), a play about the reconstruction of politically unconscious seasonal workers employed at an electric power plant. The play was cold and false. The guilt for this, of course, was not attributed to the organs that made the Theater stage it but to the Theater itself. The colorful electric power project was illuminated with all the masterful lighting techniques of the Theater. But the politically unconscious characters were timid and impersonal and the conscious characters were energetic but also impersonal because even the Kamerny Theater could not breathe life into these ideologically useful schemes.

Tairov did not know any "new constructions" or "seasonal workers." He tried to chase them off the stage. He shaped skillful groupings from the heads and banners raised above the earth. He tried to conceal the wretchedness of the propaganda play and his own ignorance of "objective reality" with directorial techniques, brilliant lighting, and typical

Kamerny Theater devices. He, of course, received a "barrage" from the critics. They made the accusation that "esthetic and formalistic experimentation is present as an end in itself." [2] They said that the stage had too many "formalistic extras and esthetic affectations." The "seasonal workers" sometimes showed the characteristics of Harlequins. The lighting techniques had been used to make *Line of Fire* more beautiful and more spectacular, and they, too, were considered as most serious "deviations" by the theater.[3]

Any loophole that a Soviet director tried to use to animate the depressing boredom of the official plays was rudely attacked. One could no longer flee from "content" by means of lighting effects or directorial tricks. The Soviet director must not create—he must only fulfill his main work. He could merely try as best he could to make falsehood look like truth. That was all.

Tairov was also accused of estheticism in connection with his production of Kulish's *Sonata pathétique* in 1931. The décor for such a "theme from the Revolution" had not been based on naturalistic pavilions but rather on a "huge construction giving the cross-section of a many-storied house" quite symbolically. It would have been different if he had built a real house and taken off one of its walls. Tairov had committed an even worse offense—he had dared to combine the civil-war theme with "spectacular fantasy" and a "system of classic landscapes" that he had used in staging "bourgeois" plays. Tairov introduced some episodes of his own to show that "religion is the opium of the people." One critic wrote:

There was a silent procession of people carrying burning candles in the darkness as they walked through the city on Easter Night to the sound of the bell. . . . These people silently carry their flickering candles through terrible events. And the bell sounds in the dark night like the voice of a third power, a neutral voice of reconciliation and spiritual peace.[4]

This is what a Soviet director was preaching to his atheistic audiences!

The Kamerny Theater offered *Neizvestnye soldaty* ("Unknown Soldiers") in 1932. The play had been written by a Ukrainian named Leonid Pervomaysky. It was devoted to the workers' uprising in Odessa and the support given it by the French navy (André Marty) during the days of civil war and occupation. Tairov himself announced that he had consciously worked out the presentation in the style of a "naïve and concentrated poster." The critics denied him the right to any such experiment, however, and he was accused of "schematicism" and of making the settings commonplace. His introduction of novelty was "formalistic": he had, for example, used a motion-picture projector to show moving clouds on the horizon.

The artist's main offense, however, was that he had depicted the interventionist soldiers "from the viewpoint of their esthetic and biological relationship to France. France was shown as a land that was extraordinarily gay and giddy, whose people loved to sing and dance." This was almost anti-Soviet. It showed that there were nations on earth where people were happier than were the inhabitants of the Communist paradise.

The theater was also guilty of conducting "dynamic experiments": the platform containing the Red Army men moved; the clouds moved along the horizon. The sharp pikes of the interventionists, as they break into the city, were so effective that the audience applauded stormily. This permitted one to conclude that the playgoers were greeting the intervention. "The externally successful depiction of crowd scenes in no way identified the Theater with proletarian art," preached one Party critic.[5]

N. V. Petrov directed Alexander Afinogenov's *Fear* at the Leningrad Bolshoi Theater—the former Alexandrinsky Theater—in 1931. The designer was Nikolai Akimov. The two men considered the theme of the play to be of great importance, and so they decided to stage it on a large scale and to part with naturalistic details. The basis for the maquette was an enormous, sloping platform, rising in the depths of the stage and becoming lost in the darkness. A gigantic long table was placed upon it for the meeting scene at the institute. Behind it, there were a few seated characters. One of them was in the very back of the stage and seemed remote and lost in the wasteland of black space. The "roadway" was used to hold fanciful and expressionistic statues in the scene at the sculptress Valentina's workshop. It also served as a base for the corridors and gigantic libraries of the institute.[6]

Thus, a production whose central idea was that fear was the basic motivating power for Soviet people was given on a Cyclopean and "generalized" scale. The Party critics were greatly disturbed. Did they not want the director and designer to emphasize the "all-Soviet" significance of the dangerous theme? The critics' fear was implicit in their attacks on the "giantism" of Akimov's expressionistic manner. They demanded that the staging copy life—a requirement that typified the time. The designer had to limit himself to normal and lifelike scales, with less fantasy and hyperbole.[7]

Professor Borodin was played by Pevtsov, one of the leading actors in the Soviet Union. His work was quite remarkable. He played everything concerning the honesty and objectivity of Borodin and his chief belief— that fear was the plague of the Soviet Union—with stirring power and sincerity. On the other hand, he enacted the "renascence" of Professor Borodin unconvincingly and superficially. Perhaps this was conscious.[8]

The Moscow Art Theater did *Fear* later the same year. Its production had no trace of giantism or of expressionism, and the staging responded to all the conditions set by the Party line for "honest realism." This time, L. M. Leonidov played Professor Borodin. The Communist critics found that he too "amnestied" the scientist and justified Borodin morally. This was done by suborning the actor's own honesty and by treating Borodin like an intransigent man with an idea.[9]

Many productions between 1927 and 1937 showed a desire by the theaters to color the gray boredom of Soviet plays, even if the procedure had to be carried out surreptitiously. Almost every play had to be "rescued" by the director somehow. The audience had to be made interested in these works or else the theaters would be empty. Audiences were needed because the major part of the theater budgets come from the box-office and not from the state treasury.

The Vakhtangov Theater considered Soviet plays indigestible and of low quality. In many of its productions the Theater tried to season its fare with the sauces and garnishings of music and dancing. In 1936 Ruben Simonov staged Pletnëv's play *Shliapa* ("The Hat") at the Vakhtangov. (Pletnëv was a former chief of the Proletarian Culture Movement.) Its content was as colorless and orthodox as that of the other official Soviet plays. There is a "work stoppage" in the fulfillment of a "productional plan." The reason for the "work stoppage" was that shirkers, slackers, and vandals were "obstructing" the factory. Then, a new director comes who is loyal to the Party of Stalin, and the official miracle follows. The "harmful element" is arrested, and the factory "overfulfills" the plan. The director sought seasoning to make this gloomy sermon fit for the theater. He tried to bring in color by introducing a happy scene showing a drinking bout of the vandals and idlers. There were singing, dancing, and other features of "degeneracy." [10] The Committee on Affairs of the Arts and the Main Repertorial Committee, however, categorically removed all the directorial garnishings. The auditorium of the theater remained steadily and intolerably empty. This caused *The Hat* to be removed from the repertory very quickly.

The Kamerny Theater presented Venyamin Kaverin's *Ukroshchenie mistera Robinzona* ("The Taming of Mr. Robinson") in a "theatrical acting form." The critics did not like it at all. One Party member wrote: "The acting here is done by bottles, balls, turning tables, beds, shoes, dresses, couches, jackets, etc., etc. The theater is playing situations, but not attitudes or an idea." [11]

Tairov and his theater were accused of "Westernizing" the presentation. Thus, slowly but surely, a kind of state crime arose in the Soviet land:

The "Westernizing" is expressed in the search for new means of decorative expressiveness; it is also shown by regarding the actor as a simple element in the design of the production. The "Westernization" consists in a frantic savoring of devices for their own sake, for the priority of technique over meaning in a presentation. It is quite correct to state that in producing *The Taming of Mr. Robinson,* the theater thought more about such qualities of form as color and lighting than it did about people, who were the vehicles of ideas.[12]

In 1937 the Moscow Art Theater acquired a very rare honor. It was granted the "Order of Lenin." The award came for two productions that had been included in the repertory at the suggestion of Stalin himself. Gorky's *Vragi* ("Enemies") was staged in 1935, and Konstantin Trenëv's *Lyubov Yarovaya* was produced the following year. The decoration rewarded the Moscow Art Theater for its loyal and purely Communist interpretation of these presentations. It must not be forgotten that the Bolsheviks always knew how to combine the carrot with the whip in dealing with the theaters and their leading figures. Some theaters, directors, and actors always treated works and roles with the Party bias determined by the Department of Agitation and Propaganda. They were invariably encouraged with the titles of "People's Artist" and "Honored Artists" and "Art Figure," and with material indications of benevolence. This was so that others might learn!

Let us take a short look at the way in which the Moscow Art Theater won so rare and so honored an award and at its feats during those years. In 1932 the Moscow Art Theater took the title of the "Gorky Theater" and announced that from then on its work would be dominated by "Gorky's principle." In other words, it would start doing publicistic things with a Communist bias inasmuch as these exist throughout Gorky's work.

The theater had been nursed on the genius of Chekhov exclusively. It had even applied Chekhovian principles in staging plays by all other dramatists, including some by Gorky. It is very significant, therefore, that the theater_decided to consider itself not the "House of Chekhov" but the "House of Gorky." The decision was clearly a surrender to Bolshevism. In those years Gorky was the leader of Soviet literature, the "great artist of the proletariat," and the "proletarian writer of genius." The Theater then proceeded to stage a major cycle of his plays.[13]

Gorky's plays, of course, were important in filling the repertory of the Moscow Art Theater, which definitely abandoned its nonpolitical ways. It accepted Party partiality in depicting history and human beings on the stage. Now it could really accept Zhdanov's remarks on Soviet literature as its motto: "Our Soviet literature is not afraid to be accused of partiality. . . . In the age of the class struggle, there neither is nor can be a literature that is not class, not biased, or seemingly non-political." [14]

The new cycle of plays by Gorky at the Moscow Art Theater began with the adaptation of *Among People*.[15] Gorky's work clothed Party partiality and publicistics with a pungent and realistic language. All the characters are profoundly characterized. Pre-Revolutionary Russia, however, was depicted in biased and macabre shades, and the world of the *Lumpenproletariat* was idealized. But Gorky covered all this with his great mastery of language. He was really a model of what the Bolsheviks required because he made a propaganda play seem truthful by his pithy language, skillful craftsmanship, clarity, and strong traits.

Let us turn, however, from the suborned "talk" of Gorky's characters whose speech is full of provincialisms and direct our attention to the bias that filled the collection of Gorky's characters on the Moscow Art Theater's stage. The Party partiality in depicting the Russia of the past —which is so dear to Bolshevik hearts—becomes quite obvious. In *Among People,* the bestial baker of Kazan (Semenov) personifies the old Russia of private property and "masters." Semenov, who was played by M. M. Tarkhanov, was, according to a Marxist critic a "synthetic image of the predatory exploiter and the character of the 'master in general' that sprang up on a completely genuine soil." [16]

The "completely genuine soil" meant potent methods from the Moscow Art Theater's old arsenal of the "external truth-to-life." That is why the Soviet regime paid so much attention to this Theater, which it lured on with rewards and marks of respect. That is why the Soviet regime spoiled the Theater as doting parents do a child, and why Bolshevism has canonized the Stanislavsky System. The Communists were in urgent need of a great theater. The Moscow Art Theater possessed the best actors in the country, who knew how to influence the hearts of the Soviet audiences. The external naturalism of the Moscow Art Theater thus created a powerful illusion of verisimilitude for Communist lies. Party schemes in the theater seemed alive because the people seemed to have come directly from the street to play on the stage.

The Communist treatment of pre-Revolutionary Russia reached its limit in the Moscow Art Theater's production of Gorky's *Enemies*. The "trunkline" of the presentation was the "pathos of the class struggle and irreconcilability of the two camps—the masters and the workers, the reactionaries and the revolutionaries." Vladimir Nemirovich-Danchenko gave these instructions to M. N. Prudkin, who played the role of Mikhail Skrobotov: "[Enact the character] with a maximum of hatred toward the working class. He is a full-blooded and satiated capitalist who does not recognize any agreements. He craves only the harshest and most categorical of actions." [17] Sintsov, the old worker Levshin, and Nadia are the underground revolutionary characters in the play. They, of course, were surrounded with glowing halos. One could immediately guess that they were future loyal members of Stalin's Party. Such was the chief content of Stalin's "social command" to the Moscow Art Theater. How remote it seems from Stanislavsky's teaching that the divine principle, the good, ought to be sought even in a scoundrel!

The lie of bias burst upon the stage of the Moscow Art Theater. More diligence and more make-up were needed to clothe it in the "truth of life." As a result, the Theater now returned to the naturalistic forms that it had once condemned. For Gorky's plays, the Theater filled the stage with naturalistic trifles from life. With uneasy conscience it sought means to make the audience believe in the gloomy and unlifelike characters presented upon its stage. Minutiae and naturalistic junk were utilized as much as possible to make up for the lack of *inner* truth to life, which had been abandoned by the theater's acceptance of the Party bias. Stanislavsky had searched for something over the course of the years and finally found it. He discovered the truth of the spirit, the truth of inner character. The propagandistic plays which invaded the theater reduced it to naught. The decline of the Moscow Art Theater had begun.

Having lost the truth, the Theater rolled backwards into the vicious circle of its past—naturalism. The costumers, make-up men, and stage-hands were changed into skillful naturalists. They assiduously dressed up the falsehoods and publicistic vacuums of the Soviet drama in very truthful forms.

With its production of *Lyubov Yarovaya* in 1936, the Moscow Art Theater sang of the victorious Bolshevik Revolution. Lyubov Yarovaya does not lift a finger when the Bolsheviks drag her husband off to be executed even though under the "Whites" he had saved her from hanging several times. In this play the Theater saw "the triumph of Bolshevik ideas and Bolshevik morality," and so Nemirovich-Danchenko aimed high in presenting it. He wanted to interpret it as a "completely profound synthesis of political ideas depicted with splendid artistry." The result was an ordinary propaganda play. The splendid artistry of the depiction did not go beyond adorning the propaganda play with naturalism.

The great period of the Moscow Art Theater was over. It had once defended and justified people. It now sought "to reveal a keen, partial, and—one may say—a Party attitude to any character." [18] This was capitulation before the Bolshevik onslaught. The first "scapegoat" for the surrender was the Russia of the past. The theater had been perse-cuted by the Bolsheviks over the years as a "typical representative of the old Russian bourgeoisie." As if to answer these accusations, the Theater now wanted to "fence off" its own past. It wanted to separate itself from the Russia that had nourished it and raised it to the heights of the leading theater in the world. It wanted to serve the regime that had dug a grave for the theater.

Nemirovich-Danchenko was now a complete follower of the Party. Stanislavsky, however, still a power within the Theater, had always been quite sparing in his loyal enthusiasm for Stalin. When the Soviet theater was suffering disaster, Stanislavsky presented the theater arts with his two last and greatest works. They were Bulgakov's *Molière* (1936) and Molière's *Tartuffe*.

Nemirovich-Danchenko's productions at this time restored naturalism —so did the presentations of the other directors at the Theater. But not Stanislavsky's. All the props for *Molière* were gloomily symbolic. Theater costumes were hung on the racks, thrown across the railing, and piled on the floor in Molière's dressing room. They were like broken dolls, with the terrible grins of masks from the *commedia dell'arte*. Frightful and monstrous masks decorated the faces of the clowns painted on the portals. In the scene at the court of Louis XIV, monstrous and gilded caryatids replaced the clowns and dolls. In the scenes of the "Cabal of hypocrites," the colors, figures, and costumes were filled with a gloomy mystery. These scenes showed how tortures compelled the actors to betray Molière. The confession in the cathedral and the scene in the bedroom of the dying playwright were also gloomy. The entire stage was illuminated with strange patches of light from invisible and mysterious sources.

In working with the actors on *Molière,* Stanislavsky introduced valuable new methods for "rehearsal according to the scheme of the play." The skeleton was chosen that would support all the inner and outer action of the play. The actor, through his improvisational studies of the basis for the main "facts" and events, discovered the logic of the "trunkline" and his own attitude toward it. Aided by his work on the "skeleton of the play," the actors learned the "trunkline" profoundly well. The trunkline was the most important feature uniting the separate characters and "bits" into a single dramatic current. Stanislavsky kept expanding the use of his "methods of physical actions." The actors were no longer absorbed in delving within their own experiences but were entirely submerged in the concrete actions and deeds that flowed logically out of one another. He revealed a new method for working over the inner current of visions that accompany the actor's thoughts in playing a role.

These "internal innovations" completely disappeared when other directors staged Soviet plays at the Moscow Art Theater. Instead of looking for new paths, they only issued a complete parade of Party statements to the press. The pronouncements of Nemirovich-Danchenko and the others were not so devoted to questions of art as to stating the loyalty of the Theater to the Party and government. The directorial commentary to Nikolai Virta's *Land*, which was staged in 1937, is a case in point. Its style is indistinguishable from the homogenized Party newspapers in the Soviet Union:

The great union of the working class and the peasantry formed the basis for the new and happy life of our country. Only this union enabled the peasantry to learn in a practical way the greatness of those ideas in whose name the working class and its party summoned the peasantry to struggle against the oppressors. We have considered this idea of the union between the working class and the peasantry to be the basis of Nikolai Virta's play *Land*. All the positive characters of the play struggle to bring it about. Antonov, Storozhev, and all their adherents fight against it in every way. The chief line of the action consists in the fight for and against this "truth." [19]

Such a "trunkline" no longer had anything in common with the great truth for which Stanislavsky's theater had been fighting through the years. It was a pure lie, a deliberate falsification of reality on the stage. In the years of Antonov's revolt a decade earlier, there had been no talk about a "union" between the peasantry and the Communist Party. The bloody war of Bolshevism against the peasantry lasted for a decade. The production of *Land* contributed nothing new to the theater arts. It was a utilization of the old naturalism.

The many productions of 1937 that showed Stalin and Lenin did not contribute anything new to the art of the stage either. For the most part, they were gilded, patriotic, and toadyish pictures. There was cringing and there was the servile creation of a Stalin cult in the forms of art that was hardly distinguished from the mass production of lithographed portraits showing the "leader of the peoples," which were printed by the millions if not billions. One thing ought to be noted about this boot-licking genre. The actors who had to play Stalin on evenings when the living Stalin himself watched them from the government box experienced almost fabulous terror. We shall limit ourselves here to an incident from the memoirs of Yuri Elagin in which he describes an incident that took place during the staging of Pogodin's *Man with a Gun* at the Vakhtangov Theater:

The position of Shchukin was difficult; he had to play Lenin in Stalin's presence. The position of Ruben Simonov, however, was even more difficult; Simonov had to play Stalin in Stalin's presence! Where has there ever been anything like it in the history of the theater? . . . Simonov's nerves could not take it and they gave way. Some three days before the performance, he became unable to take food. His extraordinary nervousness did not permit him to swallow, and his stomach refused to work. His face became drawn, he grew thin, and his complexion turned sallow.

The worst moment came when Simonov, as Stalin, came onstage that fateful evening, looked at the government box directly before him, and caught sight of the real and living Stalin. Even Simonov's vocal cords stopped working. He was in so terrified a state that he had lost his voice. Simonov uttered his send-off speech to the Red Guardsmen who were going off to battle, in an inaudible whisper. He moved his lips ridiculously and gesticulated with his right hand like a broken toy.[20]

Nikolai Okhlopkov was a pupil of Meyerhold's who was in charge of the Realistic Theater in Moscow. Okhlopkov's productions were unusual and powerful during the period when the Soviet theater was being debased. His innovating ideas doubtlessly made a most interesting contribution to the development of the theater. His first idea, "activizing the audience," had been borrowed from Meyerhold, but Okhlopkov went further than Meyerhold had gone. Okhlopkov eliminated the stage entirely and re-equipped the theater so that the action took place in the midst of the audience, around it, and above it. The stage and the auditorium were blended together.

Okhlopkov's second idea was entirely his own. He now liquidated the traditional arrangement of scenes in a play with the same maximalism he had used in liquidating the picture-frame stage. The presentation consisted of a number of minor bits, scenes, dialogues, and both choral and instrumental selections, which were linked together more according to the rules of a novel rather than to those of the drama. The repertory of the Realistic Theater contained many adaptations of novels and tales. Among them were Vasili Stavsky's *Razbeg* ("The Start"), Alexander Serafimovich's *Zheleznyi potok* ("Iron Flood"), Maxim Gorky's *Mat'* ("Mother"), and Romain Rolland's *Colas Breugnon*. To defend these classics, and to make them absolutely and ideally "ideologically useful," Okhlopkov introduced some innovations that were quite risky for the times.

In *The Start,* Okhlopkov sat the audience in a semicircular hall, even utilizing the place where the stage had been. The members of the audience sat next to each other. An arched platform was constructed above the heads of the audience, and the action took place upon it. There were also platforms between the two groups of playgoers and behind them along the perimeter of the auditorium. The décor included genuine wooden gates, sunflowers, and fruit trees arranged throughout the premises. The audience seemed to be in the middle of a fruit orchard, or in the yard of a collective farm. The actors turned up anywhere, strolled among the audience, and played their scenes in its very midst. The playgoers frequently had to turn around in their seats to find where an actor's voice was coming from, or where a new episode of the action was starting.

Okhlopkov received a hostile reception:

The production was turned into a montage of visual attractions, a motley and noisy survey on the collective farm theme. The material was spectacularly illuminated, but this was done at the expense of a sharp debasement in the theme. The level of ideas was lowered, and there was an extreme simplification of those tasks that stand before the theater in its creative and ideational growth.[21]

But the keen eyes of the Party critics did not notice what was most important. The director had shown the theater new potentialities. A critical article on Serafimovich's *Iron Flood* at Okhlopkov's Theater shows the development of the director's two reforms:

The center of the presentation was not held by individuals but by a crowd, a raging and elemental people. When the theatergoer enters the hall, he is immediately submerged in the atmosphere of the action. He is greeted by the cracking of whips, the sound of singing, and the grinding of wheels. He has fallen upon a post of the Taman army, which is taking a break. After several short episodes played in different parts of the hall, the "iron flood" proceeds further, and the theatergoer feels drawn into it. He does not know where the flood is moving to or what motivates it. Phrases are audible about chasing the enemy, skirmishes, and assaults. . . . The people are horribly tired. Their sufferings are unbearable. Their wrath and despair are shown in laconic and fragmentary episodes. A child dies, and its mother throws herself on the ground, sobbing hysterically. A boy is killed, and he dies in the arms of the partisans, who are irate and grief-stricken. And then, the wild gaiety of the Taman group lets loose like a thunderstorm. This was a new element —unbridled, threatening, and furious.[22]

This quotation does not come from a laudatory review. The critic discovers quite a dangerous trait in all of Okhlopkov's work and reforms —anarchism. Everything in Okhlopkov was dissolved in spontaneity. The critic tried to show that abolishing the stage and activizing the audience were nothing but traits of Okhlopkov's anarchistic spirit.

Bolshevism no longer took into account the individual and stylistic traits of any theater. All the theaters were obliged to maintain the stereotypes of "official realism" that were produced by the forced homogenization of the theaters. This is especially noticeable in the fates of Tairov's and Meyerhold's theaters. Tairov's Theater slid into naturalism and Meyerhold's was pushed into it. Even the Moscow Art Theater surrendered. Capitulation, slowly but surely, gripped all the theaters.

Let us show the tragic struggle of individual theaters and their experts to maintain their rights in searching for forms and innovations. There was hidden resistance to the suffocation of free work and the sad necessity for staging propaganda plays. It took a form typical of the times—flight to the classics.

FLIGHT TO THE CLASSICS

The Bolsheviks never banished the classics outright from the Soviet theater. Percentagewise, however, they had to yield first place to the propaganda plays, and the Bolsheviks imposed a condition: the classical plays that the theaters planned to include in their repertories had to have "social value." There were, however, almost no classical plays that were "ideologically harmonious" with Bolshevism. The demand for socially valuable classics meant that the theaters had to "sociologize" them with pro-Communist interpretations. The revision of the classics in Marxian style was the tax the theaters and directors had to pay to the Soviet government for the right to relax with great plays. But the percentile relationship between the Party plays and the classics was frequently violated to the advantage of the latter, and the theaters often staged classical plays with more love and creative gusto than they used in putting on the compulsory assortment of propaganda plays.

The theater press was filled with statements between 1927 and 1937 accusing the theaters of "fleeing from reality" to the classics. When the Moscow Art Theater, for instance, staged Beaumarchais's *Mariage de Figaro* in 1928, the Theater was charged with not having found the "necessary social bite."

It is a comic satire that is keen, filled with the poison and emotionality of social passions. . . . The spectacle does not clearly sound the trumpet call of the coming revolution or the historical judgment and sentence. The imminent revolutionary thunderstorm is inaudible.[23]

The critic was, of course, discussing something that did not exist in the comedy of Beaumarchais but that was needed by the Bolsheviks. In general, however, because non-Soviet drama could appear on the Soviet stage only on condition that the life it showed was gloomier and more terrible than Soviet existence, the Soviet stage, under the social command of the Communist Party, mangled the classics in ways that were blasphemous, derisive, and sometimes even tragically absurd.

Meyerhold, for example, was accused of fleeing from reality to the classics and of using the absence of good Soviet plays as a pretext for doing so. In defending himself, he revealed the point of departure for Party falsifications of the drama:

In taking classical plays, I do so only to bring them closer to present-day audiences. I so arrange the characters in these plays that they become active in the class struggle. I define their destination in the structure of the presentation together with the class trend.[24]

During the years of the Bolshevik onslaught against the stage, the Moscow Art Theater staged a great number of classical plays, most of which were Russian. Between 1927 and 1939 it gave thirty-two premières, of which fifteen were classical plays. It offered an adaptation of Dostoevsky's *Diadiushkin son* ("Uncle's Dream") in 1929. The story deals with an evil dream in which Prince K. sees a row of philistines from the town of Mordasov. The theater changed it into a ruthless satire on tsarist Russia. The moribund prince, ravaged by softening of the brain, looked like a frightful and almost mechanical doll. The theater tried to use him to represent the physical and spiritual senility of the Russian aristocracy. The terrible monsters whom the Prince dreamed of, who surrounded him in the hope of tips, were vain, obnoxious, predatory, and insignificant—a satirical exhibit of tsarist Russia. What did such a presentation tell Soviet people? What, especially, did it tell the Soviet young people who had never seen the Russia of the past? That these dying aristocrats were once the flower and pride of the country. That these repulsive monsters had once been the masters of the country.

Nemirovich-Danchenko staged an adaptation of Leo Tolstoy's *Voskresen'e* ("Resurrection") in 1930, and in this production he turned away from everything that had once attracted the Moscow Art Theater to the great Russian writer's plays.[25] These ideas had once been part of the Theater's own ideology—it had been purely Tolstoyan to believe that every person bears a particle of godhead within him and must therefore be defended and justified.

The Moscow Art Theater's version of *Resurrection* was basically different from the novel. Gone were the religious themes, along with both the spiritual and the moral purification in whose name Tolstoy had written the novel. The viewpoint for adapting the novel was completely based on Lenin's words about the great writer:

Tolstoy lashed the ruling classes with enormous power and sincerity. With great clarity, he exposed the inner falseness of all the institutions which aided contemporary society to maintain itself: the church, the courts, militarism, "legal wedlock," and bourgeois science.[26]

Nemirovich-Danchenko changed Tolstoy from a philosopher to a vulgar sociologist. All the positive traits of Nekhliudov and all the inner reconciliation of Katiusha Maslova were removed, and replaced with the cynicism, banality, and ruthlessness of the tsarist courts. The jurymen were frightful satires. Nekhliudov "severely unmasks himself" and becomes a "negative character." Marietta, who suffers at the sight of the people's torments, is given humiliating traits. There was an incredible contrast between the courtroom, controlled by "transgressing tsarist justice," and the prison cells. The distinction was just as sharp between the poor and desolate Russian countryside and the European luxury of Countess Charskaya's aristocratic salon. There was also a great difference between the halts on the road to forced-labor and the manorial comfort of Nekhliudov's rooms. The Theater introduced a "Narrator," who was played by the great V. I. Kachalov. The Narrator linked the separate scenes and conducted the audience through a hell that had been designed by Lenin rather than by Tolstoy.

Resurrection was a profound tragedy of the human spirit, but it was turned into a propaganda play against tsarist justice and the "frightful mores" of pre-Revolutionary Russia. This was Leninist policy spilled over into Tolstoy's novel, making it a "revolutionary idea of *Resurrection*." It finished by having Katiusha Maslova become a revolutionary. One can completely agree with Nemirovich-Danchenko's statement:

I can state confidently that I would not have dared to put on such a presentation before the Revolution. And if I had dared . . . our entire intelligentsia would not have accepted it and would have hissed. I am not even going to talk about the high world of officialdom, which would have subjected the theater to heavy penalties.[27]

Nemirovich-Danchenko used the same Leninist technique on Tolstoy once again in the play adapted from *Anna Karenina,* which was produced in 1937. The director turned the work into a "social tragedy." Anna's *grande passion* was contrasted to the "pharisaical morality of society," and was treated as "natural freedom" resisting "triumphant slavery." The thirty-three scenes in the adaptation were so "dynamic" that they lost all of Tolstoy's profundity and leisureliness. They did away with his basic idea: "Vengeance is Mine; I will repay." The work was almost turned into a propaganda play directed against the repulsive high society of old Russia and the "evil machine," Karenin. Karenin personified the frightful bureaucracy of tsarist days, and Anna was idealized as a typical victim of the ruthless old regime. She incarnated "the sincerity and simplicity of an honest nature that has sensed the joy of pure truth and can no longer reconcile itself to the falsehood of Russian society." [28]

The Moscow Art Theater's version of *Anna Karenina* was performed at the 1937 International Exposition in Paris. Europeans were struck by the tasteless clumsiness of the staging. They disliked the absurd motion-picturelike rapidity with which the innumerable episodes were changed; such a technique had nothing in common with Tolstoy's work. They also observed the schematicism, the inner poverty, and the decline in the technique of acting. They could scarcely realize that the Russian performers belonged to the great theater that had once impressed the entire world with the profoundity and spirituality of its acting. The Russians were exceedingly shocked by their failure at Paris.

From the very first days of the Moscow Art Theater, there had been antagonism between Stanislavsky and Nemirovich-Danchenko. We need only recall the latter's stubborn resistance to all the former's innovations up to and including the Stanislavsky System. During the second decade after the Revolution, the antagonism grew. Nemirovich-Danchenko was capitulating to Bolshevism completely, and he became the chief Sovietizer of the Moscow Art Theater. He was the artistic guide for staging Soviet plays and, particularly, for staging Communist falsifications of the classics. In contrast, Stanislavsky's expressions of Soviet patriotism were exceedingly rare. Apart from *Armored Train 14–69,* Stanislavsky did not participate in directing a single propaganda play. He devoted most of his energies to teaching and occasionally to staging the classics. Some years before his death, he retired from the Theater completely. It continued in the hands of Nemirovich-Danchenko.

The Moscow Art Theater allowed falsehood, propaganda plays, and Party partiality to permeate its stage en masse. The decline of its skill became inevitable. The skill of the Theater troupe was based on a profound inner truth, and the assault of falsehood and bias began to force it out. It could no longer attain the heights that had been reached in *Inspector-General* and *Burning Heart*. (Let us not even mention the peerless perfection in its first stagings of Chekhov.) The skill of the actors had so declined that even as early as 1932, in his version of *Dead Souls*, all Stanislavsky's good intentions were reduced to naught.

Stanislavsky had made a bold and fine effort to reveal the satiric principle in Ostrovsky's *Burning Heart*. In contrast, his staging of *Dead Souls* was simple and very restrained. He stated:

Any directorial adornments for revealing the wonderful work by Gogol are unnecessary. The text must be so composed, and the actor must so perform it according to the sense of the action that he and he alone will reach the entire content of Gogol's text through his own art.[29]

This profound respect for the classic may have implied a protest against Nemirovich-Danchenko's bold revisions of Tolstoy.

For Stanislavsky, the production concentrated on establishing a portrait gallery for Gogol's types. The actors would reveal the complex natures of these immortal figures, and so the presentation would stress the actors rather than the director. Stanislavsky used Gogol's own words about how to perform *Inspector-General* as the key to staging *Dead Souls*. This was to find the chief and main concern of every character, upon which he spends his life. This method quite suited the actors' depiction of the types in *Dead Souls*.

Dead Souls was adapted by Mikhail Bulgakov. There had previously been many stage adaptations of Gogol's novel in Russia. But even when performed by leading actors, the adaptations were not very successful with the public. The stage showed Chichikov's visits to buy "dead souls" (serfs) and that finished it. Bulgakov was the first to succeed in getting a profoundly scenic culmination of the action. Chichikov plans to get rich from buying up and then selling the dead souls. His plans develop, mature, reach their peak, and then end in a complete fiasco. The setting that V. A. Simov designed for the production was also simple and restrained.

As might have been expected, the Bolshevik press disliked the presentation. In comparison with the Communist "sociologizing" of *Resurrection* and the ideologically useful productions of Soviet plays, the reserved and classical presentation of *Dead Souls* was a "step backwards." The Moscow Art Theater was accused of rejecting a "sharp portrayal of a

Russia that was terrible and frightful—politically, socially, and psychologically—a Russia that was asleep and awaiting the hour of its awakening." (Of course, the power that was to awaken and resurrect old Russia
was Bolshevism.) [30]

In 1933 Stanislavsky produced Goldoni's *La Locandiera*. This presentation was declared false because it did not let one sense the embittered
struggle of the Italian bourgeoisie in the eighteenth century against the
aristocracy, the degraded nobility, the privileges of class, and its moral
features.

In 1934 the Moscow Art Theater did an adaptation from Dickens entitled *The Pickwick Club*. Again the critics attacked the Theater. To
some extent, *The Pickwick Club* was a return to what the First Studio
of the Moscow Art Theater had done years before with *The Cricket on
the Hearth*. It revealed the warmth of human hearts and was therefore
attacked by the critics. The Theater was rebuked for having neglected
the "satiric and unmasking" aspect of Dickens who "lashed the mores
of his period."

The staging of *The Pickwick Club* was interesting. It was designed by
P. V. Williams, a very gifted artist, and it was quite different from the
three-dimensional realism that the Theater generally used in its décor.
It revived the painted flats that the Theater had used in its early years.
The scenes were built against a background of draperies, panels, and
frescoes that were supplemented by furniture and architectural details.
The beautiful panels at some times were soft and ironic, and at others
were grotesque and satirical. Essentially, they seemed to be enormous
illustrations to Dickens' novel, supplementing the stage action through
painting. Take the "maneuvers" episode, for example. There, the panel
depicted rows of marching toy-soldiers and a bold officer on horseback.
There were rows of tents on the horizon, and three military buglers set
in the clouds like angels. The foreground showed a group of people
watching the maneuvers. This was a continuation of the group of people
shown on the stage.

The revision of the classics has continued with energy throughout the
years of the Soviet regime. The production of Gogol's *Zhenit'ba* ("Marriage") at the Vakhtangov Theater was a bold example of revision,
which took place at the start of the period of debasement of the theater.
The Vakhtangov Theater played Gogol's comedy as a grotesque satire,
with a touch of mysticism. Gogol's characters received a sinister and

gloomy coating. Kochkarev was treated as a representative of the "infernal powers," and he was always accompanied by two "traveling companions"—his "doubles." Of course, such a revision of Gogol was condemned by the Communist press as "class-alien bourgeois mysticism."

The Maly Theater of Moscow was ultraconservative and known as the "House of Ostrovsky." But even it allowed a completely stupid "politicalization" of this great playwright to take place in 1935, when K. P. Khokhlov staged *Wolves and Sheep*.[31] The Bolsheviks needed antireligious propaganda, and so Murzavetskaya, the landed proprietress, was turned into "Mother Superior Meropya," the prioress of a convent. Pavlin, her overseer, became a nun, and the action took place within the walls of the convent!

There was also a production of Ostrovsky's *The Girl with No Dowry* in the city of Kalinin. The director dragged the Volga boatmen into the first act. One of them, oppressed by Russian capitalism, falls down on the stage. The merchant Vozzhevatov uses a stick to make the man go farther.

An effort was made to strengthen the antireligious principle in a production of Ostrovsky's *Storm* done at Gorky (formerly Nizhny-Novgorod) in 1935. A group of faithful pilgrims was shown whose purely clownish antics were to unmask the religious principle in Katherine, the heroine.

Soviet theaters and directors sought to enlarge the social scope of classical plays in fulfillment of the Bolshevik command "to unmask the ignorant Russia of the past." In their efforts to comply, Soviet theater people threw all caution to the winds. In Griboedov's *Woe from Wit,* for example, a chief of police was introduced in Act IV in order to arrest Chatsky as a "free thinker" and send him to jail. Thus, Chatsky was transformed into a "Decembrist," a revolutionary, and a Bolshevik prototype. The "degeneration" of the Russian bourgeoisie had to be shown. So, wild drinking sessions and bacchanales with gypsy songs were introduced in *Girl with No Dowry* and selections from other plays of his were arbitrarily introduced into this production. V. Toporkov, the gifted actor of the Moscow Art Theater, wrote:

The graceful and monumental works of our great classical playwrights have been shattered into fragmentary episodes. The tailored "works" made from them are like patchwork quilts. The director's caprice has distorted the characters so that they are no longer recognizable despite the common-sense traits that the author had given them. In one of Ostrovsky's plays, the "League of Nations" takes part for some reason; other characters perch on trapezes, climb ropes, and so on.[32]

During 1936 Alexei Popov staged Shakespeare's *Romeo and Juliet* at the Theater of the Revolution in Moscow. He made the feud between the Montagues and the Capulets the central theme of the presentation. The enmity had its "social roots" and "social contradictions." Of course, these eclipsed the more important theme of the love between Romeo and Juliet. For a Soviet director, it was more important to stay in the good graces of the Communist regime as a connoisseur of "social analysis" than to analyze Shakespeare with comparative humanity and literacy.

Three years later, D. Mansky did the same play at the Volkov Theater in Yaroslavl. Mansky decided to insert yet another Marxian correction into Shakespeare's tragedy. Shakespeare was politically "unconscious" and allowed himself to depict Friar Laurence—that grower of "opium for the people"—in a favorable light. Because of this, the toiling masses in the Soviet audiences might think that not all monks resemble the figures on the antireligious posters issued by the Department of Agitation and Propaganda. The "ideationally useful director" made Friar Laurence a "natural scientist of the Renaissance," a "thinker who is passionately interested in life."

Popov was making a habit out of the "ideological correction" of Shakespeare. In 1938 the director subjected *The Taming of the Shrew* to a sociological execution at the Theater of the Red Army in Moscow on the basis that Shakespeare had mistakenly set forth his plot in a gay comedy. Popov decided to correct the mistake, as well as to correct the purely bourgeois "light" approach that directors used in staging the play, in showing that the play is much more profound than Petruchio's clever and adroit taming of the shrewish and quarrelsome Katharine. The Communist director turned the gaily jesting comedy into a story of protest. Katharine revolts "against the despotic 'Domostroi' that dominates the household of old Baptista." She is a "head taller than the milieu around her," and she belongs to the future and is rebelling against the old world around her.[33]

The national record for revising Shakespeare was set by Akimov's production of *Hamlet* in 1936 at the Vakhtangov Theater. The talented designer also served as director and producer. Akimov's approach to

Hamlet was predicated on the assumption that Soviet audiences of the dynamic, Bolshevik age would find Hamlet's lengthy soliloquies difficult to understand and thoroughly boring. Akimov declared that the soliloquies "have no philosophical significance." After all, he asserted, the most vital and comprehensible part of Shakespeare's tragedy for present-day audiences is the adventurous struggle for the throne. There are duels, murders, intrigues, and the efficient Fortinbras, who conducts a war and wins victories for his country. "For Shakespeare and his character, the seizure of the throne is the vital thing." [34]

All of Hamlet's romanticism and poetic quality were removed. He was shown as a bald, stout, healthy, and plain-looking man. At times, he would sit in his study and apparently continue the scientific studies that he had begun back at the university in Wittenberg. At other times, he would drink like a playboy. Basically, however, he was a cold-blooded cynic struggling for the throne that Claudius had stolen from him. Akimov wrote: "A humanist of the late Renaissance could cold-bloodedly kill an uncle who stood between himself and the throne." The Ghost of Hamlet's father turns out to be a trick. It is instigated by the Prince in conjunction with his follower, Horatio. Their exact motive is to win the "wavering warriors" of Claudius over to their own side.

The tragedy was "cleansed" of any long passages that "hindered" the action. It became completely adventurous and dynamic. All the "philosophical ballast" of Hamlet's soliloquies was removed. The speeches left him were "made materialistic." Thus, the "to be or not to be" speech was heavily abridged, and Hamlet uttered it while holding a crown in his hands and examining it. What he meant was whether to be or not to be king.

Ophelia was shown as a "maiden" of seductive beauty. "After her father dies and her brother leaves, she is under no one's supervision . . . and leads a giddy life resulting in her drowning when she is drunk." [35] Indeed, the Ophelia of the presentation is a notorious courtesan of the palace who spends her time in orgies, and her "mad" speeches are merely the result of her dipsomania. [36]

All the monstrous profanations of Shakespeare which Akimov was committing as the director were generously decorated with stage effects and ornamental effects by Akimov the designer. A royal cavalcade moves across the stage on fine horses for a deer-hunt. Apparently the aim of the scene was to show what Hamlet was thinking of in the "mousetrap"

scene when he uses the image: "Why, let the strucken deer now weep, /
The hart ungalled play." [37]

Even Tairov was not immune to the poison of mocking the classics.
He created a strange presentation from bits of Shakespeare's *Antony
and Cleopatra,* Bernard Shaw's *Caesar and Cleopatra,* and Pushkin's
Evgipetskie nochi ("Egyptian Nights"). Tairov himself said that his
main idea was "the need to supplement and expand the content of
Shakespeare's *Antony and Cleopatra.*" [38] In other words, Tairov thought
that Shakespeare was not "full-blooded."

Nemirovich-Danchenko's fourth presentation of Griboyedov's *Woe
from Wit* took place in 1938 at the Moscow Art Theater. It was more
restrained but nevertheless was "sociological." He seemed to deny the
idea that many theaters had that Chatsky was a "prototype for the new
ideas of freedom." This attitude had led to performers of the role "trying to utter their speeches with the greatest power of social and political
indignation." Nemirovich-Danchenko wanted to present a Chatsky who
would "not only be the bearer of progressive ideas but first of all would
be a young man in love." [39]

Later, however, he defined the kernel of the play as the "clash between a person with a free outlook on life who clearly reflects the most
progressive ideas of his period and the conservatism in all the rest of
society." [40] He told the actors: "If I were playing Chatsky, I would play
him in such a manner that he would develop into a most potent political
figure." [41]

This version of *Woe from Wit* renounced the enormous dimensions
and the accumulation of naturalism and antiques on the stage that had
been used in its first productions. The rooms of the Famusov house
showed the snow of the Moscow streets through the windows. This and
the tile stoves created simple and warm surroundings for the characters.
It was a lifelike but, perhaps, a more "indoor" treatment of the comedy.

What the production accomplished in the way of "sociologizing" may
be judged from the following review by a Soviet theater "expert":

Woe from Wit has ceased to be a comedy of manners dealing with Moscow
society at a definite period. It has become a play that is moving because of
the firm faith of its protagonist (Chatsky) in the unconditional victory of
progressive ideas over any obscurantism. . . . The finale of the play convinced the audience that the best people of the past gave their powers to the
struggle against the negative aspects of life in their times. It suggested the

historical need for a new social structure to arise in which "there is a nook for insulted emotion." The play rang out afresh and was identified with the Soviet audience.[42]

There were productions between 1927 and 1937 that were not flavored with official Communist "sociology." Among them were some of the best work done by the Vakhtangov Theater, Meyerhold, and Stanislavsky.

There was one brilliant victory won by Akimov, the designer—rather than by the directors—at the Vakhtangov Theater. This was the 1931 version of Schiller's *Kabale und Liebe.* The presentation began by showing an old musician, Miller, who is directing an invisible orchestra. He is standing in the middle of a huge circle, which sparkles with silver and slopes sharply toward the footlight. The introduction is played to the tragedy about Miller's daughter, Louisa, and her lover, Ferdinand. The presentation ended with the bodies of Louisa and Ferdinand lying in the same glowing circle. Miller, the mad musician, is in a torn shirt and his gray hair is all disheveled. He is threatening some invisible individual in the sky as he directs the final chords of mournful music. The production gave other examples of Akimov's artistic resourcefulness, his good taste, and his expressionism.

The critics were not enthusiastic about the production of *Kabale und Liebe,* calling it dangerous "estheticism." Akimov himself described the expansion of the designer's work:

All too often, the idea of the designer lies at the basis of the presentation and thus turns the work of the director into a subordinate element of the presentation. The reasons for this are concealed in the fact that theater designers gradually proceed from work on settings to work on the presentation as a whole. The designer of a presentation not only shows the usual functions of an artist—the determination of form, color, scale, and illumination for the objects on the stage—but also the action and the actors connected with those objects.[43]

There was one shining example of joy and festivity. Sometimes, Soviet experts were able to do such works when, as it were, they could "take time off" from their official work in staging the compulsory assortment of Party plays and do a classic. We are referring now to I. M. Rappoport's production of Shakespeare's *Much Ado About Nothing* at the Vakhtangov Theater in 1936. For the audiences of the Vakhtangov Theater, *Much Ado About Nothing* is a favorite exceeded in popularity only by *Turandot.* Rappoport's work was a talented continuation of what

Eugene Vakhtangov had done with *Turandot*. It was a light, gay diversion for comedians who were "play-acting."

In this decade Meyerhold directed three classics, and it was quite indicative that he "sociologized" none of them. He staged Sukhovo-Kobylin's *Svad'ba Krechinskogo* ("Krechinsky's Wedding") in 1933. This was a mature and "classical" culmination for the devices that he discovered back in his St. Petersburg period. There, before the Revolution, he had staged the same dramatist's *Death of Tarelkin* in a grotesquely gloomy fashion. Krechinsky was enshrouded in something ominous and demonical, like a beast becoming tense before springing on its victim.

Chekhov's *33 obmoroka* ("Thirty-three Swoons") was produced in 1935 with the gaiety and malice of comic acting. It combined vaudeville and some of Chekhov's "jokes" in a "musical melodrama-bouffe."

One of Meyerhold's most outstanding works turned out to be his final one. This was his production of Dumas's *La Dame aux camélias* in 1934. The play was given with a Meyerholdian classicism, and there were no attempts to astound the public with directorial tricks. It was the swan song both for Meyerhold and for his wife (Zinaida Raikh, who played Marguerite Gautier). The Party critics were fierce and malicious in reviewing it, and a wave of persecutions engulfed the great master. It ended in the liquidation of his theater and in the subsequent death of both Meyerhold and his wife.

The most remarkable thing about the sea of indignation that surrounded Meyerhold's last production was that the staging was almost academic in character. One might have thought that it would be hailed enthusiastically. Meyerhold completely renounced the militant "formalism," which the Bolsheviks hated so. He almost returned to the Moscow Art Theater style that he had left in his youth. It was really a "return to Ithaca"—the Odyssey of the Russian theater.

Meyerhold had led the "October in the Theater" movement. He had been a rebel, a revolutionary, and a master of genuinely Bolshevik presentations. Then he returned to an easy, refined, and limpid impressionism. He had come back to the shimmering blue, pink, and lilac colors of Manet and Renoir. *La Dame aux camélias* was filled with leisureliness, moods, experience, the play of pauses, and half-tones. It displayed Meyerhold the painter for the last time. He transferred the entire atmosphere of French impressionism, with all its sensuality, to the stage.

The main stairway curved upwards. The white semicircle of the walls was almost transparent. The cream-colored curtains fell in folds on the ropes. These formed the background for Marguerite Gautier. The white and fresh expanse of the stage sparkled to the light of candles. It lent an especially strong touch to Marguerite as she floated about the stage. The Russian theater had never before seen such plenty or luxury. Meyerhold filled the stage with glowing crystal goblets of Venetian glass, which he spotlighted. There was also the warm gold of the glittering candelabra. The furniture of the period was beautiful and authentic. The dresses and other costumes were done with great taste and richness.

The first act finale was Meyerhold's masterpiece as a director. Marguerite, wearing a black dress, flailed about on the white marble staircase. The stage was half-dark, as the dying gold of the illuminated candelabra fell upon the white table that had been cleared, save for the heavy bowls of fruit.

In the finale Meyerhold renounced all stereotypes. He transferred Armand's last meeting with Marguerite behind the curtains. She runs to meet Armand like a white and limpid bird, like the angel of death. She raises her arms through the broad folds of her peignoir and stretches out her hands. Meyerhold had been using a naturalistic depiction of death in his revolutionary presentations. He had the death of Marguerite, however, take place in an armchair with its back to the audience. Only the gentle fall of a waxen hand betrays her end.

La Dame aux camélias was a final display of all Meyerhold's best accomplishments in his creative revolt. They turned up here in a purified, polished, and classical form. His final experiment was the first to omit any trace of experimentation; it was a finished work of art. The presentation implied an enormous protest against the wretched naturalistic debasement of the theater by the Bolsheviks. Meyerhold was protesting against the dismal truth of life in the staging of Soviet plays. His production was nonpolitical, refined, and impressionistic.

The Party critics howled at him. Their wails began the day after *La Dame aux camélias* had its première. Meyerhold had not shown the "social and tragic clash of the characters in its social content." Instead, the Bolshevik critics thought, he had dared to give the play a "lyrical treatment," with a "muted tone" for the "elegiac and esthetic drama of moods":

[The presentation] most typically indicated the condition of the so-called "directorial" and formalistic theater, and what this last has finally come to in our times. It cannot be characterized other than as a condition of barrenness and creative twilight in every sense.[44]

Other critics considered *La Dame aux camélias* a "capitulation to the naturalism of the Moscow Art Theater." The production lacked any trace of this. The level of the critics who wrote such things is shown clearly by their inability to distinguish impressionism from naturalism.

Meyerhold tried to defend his production of *La Dame aux camélias* by quoting from the memoirs of Liadov. It seemed that Lenin himself had wept when he saw Sarah Bernhardt play this "drama with no content" in Geneva. "Lenin sat in the back of the box and furtively wiped away a tear." Apparently the Communist leader was impressed by a play which dealt with the servile status of women under capitalism. But quoting Lenin did not help. Meyerhold was accused of apostasy, defeatism, unwillingness to participate in the construction of socialism, militant estheticism, un-Soviet beliefs, and formalism.

Stanislavsky's final work as a director was Molière's *Tartuffe,* which the Moscow Art Theater produced in 1938. This production also lacked any communist "sociologizing." Stanislavsky did not finish *Tartuffe,* but his students carried on after his death.

Stanislavsky viewed his work on Molière's comedy as exclusively pedagogic. It was directed at finding new ways for the internal technique of acting. He began work on it in the spring of 1938, some months before his death. He selected a small group of actors from the Theater and told them:

The art of the Art Theater is such that it demands constant renewal, and constant and steady work on oneself. It is built on the reproduction and transmission of living and organic life. It does not tolerate frozen forms and traditions, even if they be beautiful. It is living and, like everything else that exists, it is in constant development and motion. What was good yesterday is no longer fitting today. . . . Such an art demands a completely special technique. It is not the technique of studying particular devices of the theater. It is the technique of mastering the laws of creative human nature, of knowing how to influence that nature, of directing it, of knowing how to reveal one's own creative potentialities and intuition in every presentation. It is an artistic technique, or—as we call it—psychotechnique. . . . By moving away from life, I want to transmit all the bases of this technique to you.[45]

He made students again of even the major and most accomplished actors at the Moscow Art Theater. He proclaimed this method of returning experienced actors to their studies to be a sure way toward the eternal youth of acting techniques. A performer who followed this path would always advance and never become petrified in any of the numerous stereotypes or the stultifying traditions. The better the actor, the more steadily and modestly he had to return to the school bench every so often.[46]

The basic content to this new technique of acting is not to be found in writing or in theory but only in stage practice. It was the culmination of the Stanislavsky System. Stanislavsky's aim in *Tartuffe* was to give the actors the culmination of his life's work as their living heritage. He considered the key to his System to be the "method of physical actions." He told the actors:

Seek the truth of simple physical actions that are obvious to you. The truth of physical actions leads you to faith; everything goes further into the "I am." It flows into action and creative work. The method of physical actions enables an actor to acquire faith, to penetrate into the realm of authentic emotions and profound experiences. He creates a stage character in the shortest way possible.[47]

For Stanislavsky, "art begins when there is no role but when there is an 'I' in supposed circumstances." The loftiest quality of the scenic art is the actor's sincerity. To be sincere on the stage is scenic talent. Sincerity is the charm of a person, the charm of an actor, and is the uniquely potent means for influencing the audience. The way to sincerity is through the actor's faith in his actions. Conduct, action—even of the most elementary kind—form atoms of this sincerity. Belief in the inner justification of the slightest "physical actions" shows the way to sincerity and to "I am the role." It also indicates a lofty artistic process. Every "physical action" mobilizes the entire fantasy, psychology, and spirit of the actor.[48]

Stanislavsky wanted to help the actor's growth, the truth of his "physical actions," and the reality of his attitudes toward the other characters. He therefore transformed the rehearsal site at the theater to "Orgon's house":

The rehearsals did not take place in a separate room, or hall, or scenic platform, but used two artistically decorated floors backstage in the theater. It was to depict the two-story house of Orgon (a rich bourgeois), with its great number of rooms. The performers were supposed to become familiar with the location of the rooms in the house and to divide them among the members of the family. After some rehearsals, we dispersed to the various rooms, made ourselves comfortable, and began "to get used" to them. At the gong, everyone came down from his own room to the common dining room. Dorine served the diners, running up and down the staircase. Life was quiet and peaceful. This was before Tartuffe invaded the house.[49]

Later, Stanislavsky gave the actors "staying at Orgon's house" tasks that began to be more and more relevant to Molière's comedy. They had to play "Tartuffe's Appearance in Orgon's House"; "Orgon's Mother Leaves the House," and "Orgon Makes His Daughter Sign the Marriage Contract." Stanislavsky led the actors gradually from real and truthful "physical actions" with texts that they improvised to the text and situations of Molière. These last were in no way less truthful than the études in "getting used to Orgon's house."

The "method of physical actions" enabled Stanislavsky to make the conduct of the actors in the "supposed circumstances" sincere. He also led them away from the standardized acting of Molière's comedies. He said:

We must flee from what the theaters usually do and accept in performing Molière. . . . It is prejudicial to think that comedy must be played in that way. You must believe in the genuineness of whatever is transpiring on the stage and place yourself in the position of the characters acting in the play. Drama, comedy, and tragedy do not exist for the actor. There is an I, a person, in supposed circumstances.[50]

Let it be understood that the term "physical actions" was only conventional and temporary. They were really *psychological* actions. They were deliberately called by the more modest term in order to avoid all philosophizing and to make the term concrete and material. The accuracy, concreteness, and logic of the action were the score with which the actor had to become familiar. The creative process in the presentation could arise only on such a scoring. The way in which an actor acted according to this score, the way in which he painted the "physical action" depended on the audience, the inspiration, the uniqueness of every presentation, and the genuinely creative act.

Tartuffe had great significance in the development of the scenic art. It was Stanislavsky's first attempt to apply the entire complex of his System to the actor's work and included his new chapter on the "method of physical actions." It created the "scoring of the role" that enabled a noble creative act to take place on the stage.

PRODUCTIONS OF CONTEMPORARY WESTERN PLAYS

There was still another phenomenon typifying the gloomy second decade. Bolshevism began to resist with increasing intensity the staging of Western European plays on the Soviet stage. "Westernizing" was viewed as a noxious source for infecting Soviet directors and artists with "formalism." The Party critics gradually became more militant in their assertions that the themes of the West were alien and dangerous and that its forms were also alien.

A statement by Vsevolod Vishnevsky, the Communist playwright, created a furor among Party critics in 1933. Vishnevsky declared that Soviet dramatists and other authors must learn certain things from the West. He voiced this subversion in *Soviet Theater:*

In working, we cannot fail to look at the West. We cannot fail to observe that the West is changing under the influence of our Revolution. We cannot fail to see what is going on there. And we are obliged to study all the tendencies of Western art. Let us even take Joyce's *Ulysses.* We have to study the thing.[51]

Now Soviet directors could openly study things from the West and could stage Western plays in their theaters. Then Andrei Zhdanov—one of the most powerful figures in the Party and the government—spoke at the Congress of Soviet Writers. Zhdanov declared that bourgeois culture was completely rotten and characterized only by "a debauchery of mysticism, priestcraft, and a liking for pornography. The 'eminent people' of bourgeois literature . . . are now its thieves, detectives, prostitutes, and vandals, are they not?" [52]

In 1928 the Theater of the Revolution staged a German play, Toller's *Hoppla, wir leben.* Its tendency was "revolutionary" and pro-Communist. Yet, the critics attacked it as an effort to infect the healthy Soviet theater with the disintegration of sick German expressionism.

The Bolshoi Dramatic Theater in Leningrad offered Hasenclever's *Ein bessrer Herr.* Some of the critics thought that the production clearly showed "formalistic" tendencies. The theater, of course, had been infected by the Western playwright. It turned out that all this "formalism" merely boiled down to an attempt by the theater to depart from the truth of life and to subordinate the speeches and motions of the actor to music.

Some of Eugene O'Neill's plays were produced at the Kamerny Theater. These productions were proclaimed a flight by the "neobourgeois" theater from Soviet reality to drama in the "liberal bourgeois manner," with which it was esthetically infatuated. Tairov's production of Sophia Treadwell's *Machinal* in 1933 was also attacked for dragging in hypocritical bourgeois liberalism. It allegedly aimed at "eclipsing the genuine essence of capitalist society" for the Soviet playgoer.

Chicago, by Maurine Watkins, was given at the Moscow Art Theater in 1933 under the title of *Reklama* ("Publicity"). The critics' approach to it typified their approach to Western plays in general. First of all, the Moscow Art Theater was accused of putting on a play that did not "truthfully unmask the bestial nature of capitalism." The play they had chosen was declared to be a counterfeit and insignificant. It was bad enough that the Moscow Art Theater had chosen to do such a farce. It was even worse that the theater enacted it in a style similar to the one in which the play had been done upon the bourgeois stage. "Everything here is presented with a disarming, kind-hearted, thoughtless, and careless smile." [53] But it was strictly forbidden to show negative characters on the Soviet stage as being pleasant, human, and attractive. (And the entire bourgeois world is negative.) Were such portrayals allowed, Soviet people might think that there are some good people in the capitalistic world. The Soviet theater was obliged to be partial in its depiction of the capitalistic world—capitalistic countries had to be shown as they appear in the crude propaganda plays. One critic wrote: "The presentation in question was treated like a diverting comedy of manners and not like a social satire. Only a satiric comedy could show . . . what we need socially." [54] No merry comedy about bourgeois justice was needed. Instead, a malicious propaganda play on the subject was required. "Social perspective" was needed, along with a "critical surmounting of bourgeois culture." [55]

"Critical surmounting" of the West meant to falsify it according to the proper Communist slogans about the capitalistic world. It was the general line in the treatment of contemporary European plays and "Western themes" in Soviet drama during the second decade. The "anti-Western" movement began during those years. After World War II it was turned into a gigantic propaganda war against everything positive that could in any way be linked to the world beyond the boundaries of the Soviet state.

During its second decade the Soviet theater was slowly but surely engulfed by a primitive kind of realism that conquered even those leading theaters that had once had outstanding personalities of their own. Although experiment and innovation were not wiped out by the first decrees of the Party, and although directors who staged the official Soviet plays kept seeking any means at all to ornament the frightful and drab clichés with form and invention, the Party's policy of turning the theater into a machine for feeding its own propaganda to the populace rendered trailblazing, innovation, and experimentation fruitless and even dangerous. For Bolshevism, *what* the Soviet theater said was important. As for *how* a theater was to interpret a Communist subject, the Bolsheviks felt that the method must not eclipse their slogans and must be comprehensible to every Soviet citizen. These were the considerations that made any freedom of thought or philosophy on the part of the theater experts intolerable to the Bolsheviks.

PART FOUR

THE TRAGIC ENDING, 1937 TO 1952

CHAPTER XI

THE COMPLETE STANDARDIZATION
OF THE SOVIET THEATER

IN 1938 THE SOVIET THEATER was firmly and irrevocably enslaved to the Bolshevik state. Freedom of creative endeavor was shown only rarely and timidly. The enslavement of the theater was felt first of all in the complete standardization of the Soviet drama, which was now completely subordinated to a limited number of slogans that the Party had put forward. The central apparatus of "social command" had been adjusted so that the slightest shift in Party policy was instantly reflected in the great number of new plays. Standardized "official realism" made the stage interpretations of the most individual theaters indistinguishable from one another.

THE CAMPAIGN AGAINST FORMALISM

Freedom of creative endeavor itself was declared counterrevolutionary. Only class enemies could demand it in the Soviet land. One Party critic —I. Bachelis—wrote:

Incidentally, let us pause at the slogan, "freedom of creative endeavor." Is it not fitting to show that such a slogan could appear only among our class enemies—for the dictatorship of the proletariat limits only their "freedom of creative endeavor." [1]

Such counterrevolutionary freedom is inseparable from any artist's desire to interpret a drama in his own way, and no work of art is conceivable without it. But it was branded as "formalism," and with every passing year "formalists" became more synonymous with "anti-Soviet."

The reformers in the Soviet theater could not shield themselves from the "antiformalist" persecution even by pointing out something very interesting. In all the sciences, in all the technical fields, in production and economics, the Party was issuing heartrending appeals to everyone to experiment and seek new ways of doing things. All the workers of the entire country were encouraged to experiment and be inventive. Only

in art was innovation equated with an anti-Soviet sortie by class enemies
This is indicated by two clear quotations from the same source:

> Formalism is one of the most hostile and harmful manifestations of bour
> geois influence on our art. Its chief roots, of course, are broad, in bourgeoi
> culture, which is perishing and rotting alive. . . .
>
> It is also dangerous because it enables fascist agents, despicable Trotskyit
> degenerates, rightist renegades, and all the other enemies of the people sur
> reptitiously to drag in anti-Soviet and counterrevolutionary ideas under th
> protective cover of tricks, affectations and smug "esthetic values." [2]

What did the Bolsheviks want from Soviet theater people? The Com
munists wished the theater figures to become "materialistic artists." Yur
Libedinsky wrote: "From the viewpoint of subjective idealism, it is ;
very great constraint to follow the objective laws of reality, but from th
viewpoint of dialectical materialism, it is a very great liberty." [3] That i
what the Party members told the artists. It turns out that "objectiv
reality" is not given to theater people by life, but rather by the play of ,
Party dramatist: "The play, for example, is a phenomenon of objectiv
reality before the director sees it." [4]

Stalin himself thought up the ridiculous phrase "socialist realism."
The qualifying word "socialist" apparently implies that there is such
thing as "capitalist realism," or "monarchist realism," or "feudal rea
ism." What the phrase really meant could better be called "officia
realism." "Socialist realism"—an absurd term—became the fetish of th
Communist toadies, and all Soviet art was sacrificed before it. Bourgeoi
empiricists could be satisfied with objective truth and naked reality i
they liked, but "socialist realists" would evaluate reality from the view
point of the future Communist victory in the world.

The ruthless implanting of this "socialist realism" was invariabl
based on the idea that only such a form could be understood by th
masses. This shows how basely the Communist Party evaluated th
spiritual potentialities of the nation. Genuine realism can stir the hear
of peasants and members of the Academy to the same degree. Folklo
is many centuries old, but certainly it shows convincingly that th
"broad masses" love the imaginary and the unreal more than they d
the truth of realism.

REPRESSION, PERSECUTION, AND DEATH

The Central Committee of the All-Union Communist Party had adopte
a resolution on April 23, 1932, entitled "On the Reconstruction of Lite

ary and Artistic Organizations." Maxim Gorky had returned to the U.S.S.R. and had been placed in charge of all Soviet literature and other arts. It might appear that Gorky simply showed Stalin the absurd antagonism between the group of untalented "proletarian writers" who were Party members and the huge mass of talented writers who were not. It may have been suggested that a single union of Soviet writers should be established instead and that this union would succeed better in "recooking" all the literary men and preparing them for Bolshevism. At any rate, the decree proclaimed the need for establishing an organizing bureau for a union of Soviet writers.[5]

In 1936, at the threshold of war, Stalin set about completing the physical liquidation of all those who might potentially oppose his dictatorship. Art experts lost their positions, theaters were closed, and there was a terror of persecution and intimidation. All this merely continued the powerful waves of repression with which Stalin's dictatorship had attacked the theater. In that year *Pravda* published a series of articles, purportedly written by Stalin himself (certainly Stalin at least personally indicated what was to be said).[6] These articles included "Confusion instead of Music" on January 28, "Falseness in the Ballet" on February 6, and "On Slovenly Artists" on March 2. They began the "purge" of the formalists in Soviet art. The terror against experts in all the arts, including the theater, had begun in earnest. Soviet theater experts wrote about these articles:

They played a decisive role in unmasking the esthetic and decadent establishments in art. They helped the entire Soviet public distinctly to lay bare the formalistic tendencies and their orientation toward the different schools and subschools of the decadent art in the bourgeois West of Europe and America.[7]

The first victim of the campaign was the brilliant composer Dmitri Shostakovich. "Confusion instead of Music" accused him of formalism in his opera *Katerina Izmailova* (based on Nikolai Leskov's tale *Lady Makbet Mtsenskogo ùezda* ("Lady Macbeth of Mzensk"). The music, the article stated, "was built on the principle . . . according to which left-wing art in general denied simplicity, realism, comprehensibility, and the natural sound of language in art. . . . It is playing with nonsensical themes and can only end badly." As evidence of Shostakovich's subversion, the article mentioned that the opera had been successful among the bourgeois public abroad. Did not the bourgeois public praise the opera because it was confused and completely nonpolitical? Is not that the quality that tickles the perverted tastes of the bourgeois auditoriums with "twitching, flashy, and neurasthenic music?" "On Slovenly Artists" asserted: "Formalism takes a haughty and contemptible attitude to the real world. . . . The formalist takes a careless attitude to a large auditorium. He not only does not wish to be understood, but he regards comprehensibility as an insult to himself."

"Falseness in the Ballet" rose to the defense of reality on the collective farms, which had been blasphemously insulted by "futuristic tricks." Its conclusions were quite clear and were destined to be important in the complete devastations of the Soviet theater: "If they want to put a collective farm on the stage, they must study a collective farm, its people, and its way of life. If they decide to give a particular collective farm of the Kuban region, they should learn the characteristic traits of collective farms in the Kuban region." In other words, the moving finger unambiguously showed the Soviet theater that the only way permitted by the Party and the government was to copy reality.

During those years the vocabulary for baiting the art experts in the press began to resemble the jargon of Vishinsky in demanding punishment at the Moscow trials for the people he was prosecuting. Leading dramatists, theoreticians of the theater, critics, and members of literary bodies were proclaimed "double-dealers," "Trotskyites," and "agents of the class enemy." In addition to persecution by the press, the Party organized mock gatherings of theater people—sessions that resembled the compulsory self-flagellations and self-debasements that Party members had undergone before the tribunals in the "purges." The procedure was in accordance with the standards set in those terrible years. All the leading theater figures, one after the other, had to mount the rostrum, praise the wisdom of the Party's articles about formalism and double-dealing, slander Shostakovich, lash themselves for their own tricky formalism, and repent of their sins.

Nikolai Okhlopkov, the head of the Realistic Theater, "confessed": "Not having outgrown my petty-bourgeois ideology or my philistine ideology of the futuristic and sensationalistic artist, I was unable to bring the audience the real meaning of these presentations." [8] Tairov announced that his was a theater of the "petty-bourgeois intelligentsia." In the struggle against narrow-mindedness, he said:

I thought that the influence on the playgoer was exerted by the character acting on the stage. This conception was clearly idealistic. . . . I resolved the dynamics mechanically. Emotions and ideas were relegated to the back ground. Thus, idealistic conceptions gradually . . . led us to formalistic conceptions. . . . How did we reason? The Revolution destroyed the old forms of life. And we were destroying the old forms of art. Consequently, we were revolutionaries and could be in step with the Revolution. Of course, this was an illusion, but we sincerely believed that we were revolutionaries. Therefore, we continued our formalistic quests even after the Revolution. These quests were intended to destroy the old forms. . . . We, however, did not go on the high road of the Revolution, but along some idealistically reflected parallel road. . . . We understood reality statically [and we did not know] how to make corrections based on the great reality.[9]

Tairov had devised a theory which he called "structural realism" in the firm belief that it would meet the Marxism that was forcing its way into his theater. He wrote that having outgrown the formalistic attractions of his youth he was now striving for a "new and basic revision of the creative path and method of the Kamerny Theater as an artistic organism, and to base the development of this revision on an organic connection with the proletariat." Tairov, a great master of "art for art's sake," had been an esthetician and an apologist for art without politics. He now announced his unconditional surrender to Bolshevism. Basically, Tairov started his "structural realism" with an idea:

The dynamic process in which any character is revealed is not a mechanical cohesion of individual moments. It may, however, make partial use of cause and effect relationships. It is a complete structure and its completeness determines the separate elements going into it. . . . Our method for constructing a character in a presentation is based on the position that the whole—that is, the structure of the character—determines the parts and not the other way around.[10]

A dramatist writes a play because he has perceived the structure in the dynamic process of reality.[11] Form and content in art are resolved in the structure of a work of art. An artist receives the stimulus for his work from the "structure of authentic reality." The structure of his reaction to reality possesses a "formative power" that compels the artist to incarnate his invention in a character, in the "structure of the new creative reality."

Tairov was almost in complete agreement with the dialectical method. He asserted that the actor "corrects" the reality of a play according to his own ideas of "social reality." He continued:

The actor does not exist in isolation. He is revealed only in his mutual contacts with all the other characters. Hence, a specific trait of the actor's creative endeavor arises. It is determined by the creative process of the entire collective. The structure of the character whom the actor creates is legitimately determined by the structure of the presentation. We term the character who thus develops in the process of production a dynamic character.[12]

This was essentially Tairov's surrender. He was now seeking a new method that would be in accord with Bolshevism. He was trying to have his theater perform tasks for the Soviet regime. He wanted to transfer the devices that he had accumulated in the past into a "new quality, adequate to the new qualitative essence in the reconstruction period of our Revolution." [13]

Instead of praise, however, Tairov's surrender brought vitrolic accusations from the Bolsheviks. They declared that he was bringing in theories from structualistic psychology, which Marxism had condemned. His theater supposedly contained "a mixture of Mach's idealistic notions and electro-magnetic theory." Such ideas were a weapon of art experts in the rotten and bourgeois West. He was accused of preaching pure formalism rather than dialectics. It was said that he wanted to dissolve content in structure.[14] They declared that instead of "importing" any bourgeois *Gestalttheorie* from such damned capitalistic countries as Germany and America, Tairov ought to study the great, "tried and true" teachings of Marxism-Leninism. This too was absolutely typical of the Bolsheviks. Even those artists who surrendered and "repented" were humiliated in every way and received worse blows.

We have spent quite a little time on Tairov's "structural realism." It is the most serious and outstanding theory created by a person who was not a Party member in the history of the Soviet theater. Tairov was trying to meet Bolshevism halfway. He reached the apogee of his "self-criticism" by accusing his Kamerny Theater of a "naturalistic deviation," which it had never betrayed. He concluded with a panegyric to the fruitful interference of the Party: "To the degree that I have shaken off formalism, I feel stronger, gayer, freer, and happier." [15]

The Vakhtangov Theater also surrendered. Boris Zakhava, its general manager, announced that almost the entire repertory of his theater was pernicious, and conducted an experiment in "reforging" the teachings of Eugene Vakhtangov with dialectical materialism. And the best of the Russian theaters, the Moscow Art Theater, capitulated in practice if not in theory or through the press. Stanislavsky told the truth about this surrender only on the twentieth anniversary of the October upheaval:

From the very first days after the Great October Socialist Revolution on, the Party and the government have taken all worries about the Soviet theater upon themselves. This applies both to material cares and to ideas. It has stood guard for truth and national quality in art and has protected us from any false currents. After all, it was the Party and the government who raised their voices against formalism and in favor of genuine art. All this compels us to be authentic artists and to make sure that our art does not hide anything false or alien.

How comforting it is to work for one's nation and in close contact with it! This feeling is the result of the education that has been given to us by the Communist Party headed by our dear and beloved Joseph Stalin. He approaches all vital questions so simply and so sincerely, and he solves them so directly and so truly! Comrade Stalin is the genuine and solicitous friend of everything living and progressive; always foresees and anticipates everything. How much he had done for us actors! Thanks to him for all of it! (November 7, 1937).[16]

Nothing can be added to that! It does not ease the great sorrow of the Russian theater in the slightest. There is one final yet puzzling hope. The second part of this ode is stylistically similar to writing done by the secretary to the Theater's Party organization. Perhaps, therefore, it was not actually written by the great Stanislavsky.

Even Meyerhold was compelled to speak against himself. At the gathering of repentant theater figures in 1936 he said:

As soon as Comrade Stalin busied himself with the front of art, he immediately gave very valuable indications about what had to be done so that the artists might travel on the new path of socialist realism without trickery. The most important thing in art is simplicity. . . . Only a dialectical comprehension of reality can approach a genuine and creative revelation of that life that furnishes a means of nourishment for every authentic work of art.[17]

But Meyerhold was soon to redeem himself in the eyes of the creative, artistic world.

Bolshevism soon proceeded to the most obvious means of repression—closing the theaters. On February 28, 1936, the Council of the People's Commissars of the U.S.S.R. and the Central Committee of the Communist Party decided to close the Second Moscow Art Theater, whose leader, Mikhail Chekhov, had become a "nonreturnee." On December 17, 1937, *Pravda* published an article entitled "Alien Theater" in which Meyerhold's Theater was branded a "class-alien" theater, distinguished by a "systematic departure from Soviet reality, political distortion of that reality, and hostile slander against our life." Another article in *Teatr* declared: "In the ardor of his struggle against naturalism, he [Meyerhold] has shifted the front to fight realism. He turned formal innovation —one of his methods for struggling against naturalism—into an end in itself." [18] The Committee on Affairs of the Arts issued an order on January 3, 1938, closing the citadel of "October in the Theater." Thus ended Meyerhold's Theater, the most progressive and revolutionary theater in the land. The decree called it an "antinational theater alien to Soviet audiences and essentially hostile to them." Many of its productions had "distorted and slandered the representation of Soviet reality, and were filled with double-dealing, and even with open anti-Soviet malice." [19]

Every time a sentence was carried out against the victims after all the "trials," the Party immediately ordered all enterprises to hold meetings. Soviet people were forced to laud the deeds of the hangmen and to express their enthusiastic agreement with what had been done in the cells of the Cheka. In the same way, the secretaries of the Party cells ordered all the theaters of Moscow to "spring up spontaneously." A false rumor was started at these meetings. It claimed that all the theater people "entirely and completely" approved the decision of the Soviet government to liquidate Meyerhold's "hostile" theater.

There was only one great figure who called upon the disgraced genius, even though that figure had always personally found Meyerhold's work infinitely distasteful. The individual in question invited Meyerhold to work in his studios. His name was Konstantin Stanislavsky.

A year later, the last link of Meyerhold's fate was closed. The First All-Union Congress of directors was convoked in Moscow during June, 1939. The keynoter for the congress was the notorious Vishinsky—who had staged the bloody "trials" in Moscow. The appearance of the "superhangman" before the Soviet directors must have reminded them of what would happen to them should they dare to deviate from the "general line" in the theater. The sense of Vishinsky's report was that from then on the theater must unquestioningly subordinate itself to the tasks advanced by the Party and the government. Any deviation would be viewed as hostile and anti-Soviet. [20]

Meyerhold was also at the conference. His speech is still remembered. It led to his arrest and to his subsequent death. It is filled with the great courage that characterized the man. Russian theater figures keep it in their hearts as a memorial of the struggle that honest artists waged against Bolshevik coercion. It was Meyerhold's final speech to Soviet theater people. Courageously, he admitted a number of serious mistakes. He took the responsibility for the "Meyerholdism" with which a pack of giftless pupils and pseudopupils defamed the theater with banal and vandalic mockeries of the classics and with tricks for their own sake. He admitted that these distortions by his continuators had been caused by his own most questionable experiments with the classics. He said:

I have been cruelly reproached for distorting the classical heritage, for making impermissible experiments on the immortal works of Gogol, Griboyedov, and Ostrovsky. And there is some truth in the accusations. I really allowed myself too much experimentation in several productions that I did of classical plays. I gave too much leeway to my own fancy. At times, I forgot that the artistic value of the material with which I was dealing was always and in every case nobler than anything that I could add to it.[21]

Meyerhold thus admitted that the mistakes of which he had been accused were serious. He then proceeded to defend the artist's right to experiment and to maintain his own creative individuality. He accused Soviet practices of stifling the theater. The concluding part of his speech is so clear and stirring that I shall give it almost in its entirety:

I have been reproached as a formalist because I had forgotten about content in my creative work and in my hunt for a new and original form. In the search for means, I had forgotten the ends. It is a serious accusation. But I can agree with it only in part. In fact, through my creative biography, I have staged several presentations in which I felt like confirming several thoughts and ideas about theatrical form that I had recently discovered. They were experimental presentations. In fact, form was most important in them. But there were not many such presentations. They can be counted on the fingers of one hand.

But has a master—and I am still bold enough to consider myself as such—really no right to experiment? Has he really no moral right to check his creative ideas—even if they be mistaken—through experiments? And really, when all is said and done, has he no right to make mistakes? All mortals have the right to make mistakes, and I am just as mortal as everyone else.

I only rarely tolerated the confirmations and experiments that in fact deserve the adjective of formalistic. All my other creative work was not formalistic. On the contrary, all my efforts were directed at finding an organic form for the given content. Permit me to assert that I frequently did manage to find an organic form that corresponded to the content of the play completely. But it was my form—Meyerhold's form—and not Sidorov's form, or Petrov's or Ivanov's, or Stanislavsky's form, or Tairov's form. The form bore all the traits of my particular creative individuality. But is that really formalism? What do you think formalism is in general?

I would like to ask you the opposite questions also: what is antiformalism? What is socialist realism? Probably socialist realism itself is orthodox antiformalism. . . . What do you call what is going on in the Soviet theater?

At this point, I must talk bluntly: if what you have been doing with the Soviet theater recently is what you call antiformalism, if you consider what is now taking place on the stages of the best theaters in Moscow as an achievement of the Soviet theater, then I would prefer to be what you consider a "formalist." In my heart, I consider what is now taking place in our theaters frightful and pitiful. And I do not know what it is—antiformalism, realism, naturalism, or any other "ism." But I do know that it is untalented and bad. The pitiful and wretched thing that pretends to the title of the theater of socialist realism has nothing in common with art.

But the theater is art! And without art, there is no theater! Go visiting the theaters of Moscow. Look at their drab and boring presentations that resemble one another and are each worse than the others. It is now difficult to distinguish the creative style of the Maly Theater from that of the Vakhtangov, the Kamerny, or the Moscow Art Theater. Recently creative ideas poured from them. People in the arts searched, erred, and frequently stumbled and turned aside, but they really created—sometimes badly and sometimes splendidly. Where once there were the best theaters of the world, now—by your leave—everything is gloomily well-regulated, averagely arithmetical, stupifying, and murderous in its lack of talent. Is that your aim? If it is—oh!—you have done something monstrous! . . . In hunting formalism, you have eliminated art! [22]

The next day Meyerhold was arrested and disappeared inside the walls of the NKVD. After some time, his wife—Zinaida Raikh—was found dead in her apartment under mysterious and revolting circumstances. Her eyes had been gouged out and her body was covered with knife wounds. Her murder was attributed to robbers. Meyerhold did not die until after World War II. According to one story, he was tortured to death by the NKVD. According to another, he was set free after many years of imprisonment but, shattered and broken, he committed suicide. The theater of Russia and of the entire world lost perhaps the most brilliant innovator and director that ever existed.

The wave of terror that spread through the Soviet theater carried off many people. Those who were arrested and disappeared included dramatists, theoreticians, critics, and others. Among the dramatists were Nikolai Erdman, Isaak Babel, Sergei Budantsev, Artem Vselyi, Vladimir Kirshon, V. Maas, Ivan Mikitenko, Sergei Semenov, and Sergei Tretyakov. The persecuted Bulgakov died. The theoreticians and critics who disappeared included Piotrovsky, N. Chuzhak, K. Vronsky, Les Kurbas (the great innovator of the Ukrainian theater), Natalia Sats (the artistic guide of the Central Children's Theater in Moscow), and Amaglobeli (the general manager of the Maly Theater). Among the actresses were O. Shcherbinskaya, Z. Smirnova, and V. Vagrina. V. I. Meyer, the prominent actor at the Maly Theater, committed suicide. Yuri Olesha has long been silent as a dramatist. Which of the prisoners have been executed? Who have died in concentration camps? Who are still in those camps? In the Soviet Union, such questions are enshrouded in impenetrable fog.

The years, like a black plague, killed the last remnants of free thought in the Soviet theater. They drained its blood, crushed its innovators, and created a humble and submissive state bureaucracy. On the eve of World War II, the Soviet theater was firmly shackled to the government, an obedient weapon of the dictatorship.

CHAPTER XII

WARTIME PATRIOTISM AND
POSTWAR PROPAGANDA

IF YOU WERE to look at hundreds of photographs taken of stage productions in the Soviet theater from just before World War II to the present, your first impression would be that they are all shots of the same drab, wretched, and terribly Communistic play. They are done crudely in poor, provincial, and naturalistic pavilions. The trees have "real" flowers and foliage. There are the same slovenly costumes, shoes, and pants and the same false posing by the commanders, heroes, and shock workers. One is completely perplexed by the captions under this monotony when he observes that the titles and authors are quite different. It is even more terrible to realize that the photographs of the amateurishly arranged groups were also taken at different theaters—and not in the provinces either. They were taken at the same Moscow theaters whose experiments had once embellished the history of the theater.

Most productions of Soviet plays are very similar to paintings done by the Association for Artists of Revolutionary Russia (AKhRR). These portraits "reflect" marshals and bemedaled individuals, meetings of Party cells, shock workers in industry, and distinguished collective farmers at the early harvest. They are like bad photographs that have been so enlarged as to be measured in yards and that are then colored hastily by some painter-laureate. D. Brodsky, a great businessman, laid the foundations for such "art" in painting by putting his workshop on a factory footing. It was almost like a conveyor belt for transferring photographs to gigantic canvasses by the square foot. The industrial product was colored later. These cheap and mediocre oleographs were printed in official Party lithographs and became the only kind of painting in the Soviet Union. "Socialist realism" was inculcated "completely and entirely" not only in the theater, but in sculpture, the motion pictures, and literature as well.

Speeches, articles about "one's own creative work" by directors, dramatists, and actors have also been completely homogenized. During the heyday of the Soviet theater the statements of the outstanding figures to the press sparkled with individuality as they all talked about their philosophy of art in their own styles. The speeches of theater figures have now become as indistinguishable from one another as their productions, and their language cannot be distinguished from that of minor bureaucrats in the Party. Statements to the press by all the outstanding theater figures repeated the official "castings" that Stalin had made the theater "fertile," that the theater must be worthy of "Stalin's great era," and that the theater must "call for struggling on the side of Stalin's great ideals." [1]

All the theaters, playwrights, and directors were taken firmly in hand, and they were turned into divisions and obedient functionaries of the Soviet Ministry on Affairs of the Arts. To understand the Soviet theater from 1938 to 1952, it will suffice to examine some of the basic themes used in plays and productions. We shall also see how the final efforts of individual theaters to find loopholes in the wall separating them from real creative endeavor were frustrated.

RUSSIAN HISTORY AT THE SERVICE OF THE WAR

When the nation was being prepared for war, the Communist Party turned its entire Marxian historico-materialistic attitude toward the Russian past. Russian chauvinism and jingoism had been persecuted as evil facets of counterrevolution, but they were amnestied when the line changed. The Russian tsars, princes, and military leaders were freed from the detraction and damnation that Marxists had been heaping upon them for years. Earlier, a slip of the tongue—when an orator said the "Russian people" instead of the "Soviet people"—would be pounced upon as a chauvinistic sally.[2] Now there began to be all kinds of touching reminders about "Russian valor," "Russian soldiers," and "Russian people."

The shades of all the warriors and military commanders in the history of Russia were called to active service in the army of Bolshevism. Let us ennumerate only the outstanding works of the Soviet drama between 1939 and 1945 that aimed at stirring up patriotism through hailing Russian military leaders and tsars. It will then become clear how widespread the order of the Communist Party was. The list includes: *Suvorov the Commander* (1939) by I. Bekhterov and A. Razumovsky; *Field*

Marshal Kutuzov (1940) by Vladimir Soloviëv; *The Cruiser Ochakov* (1940) by N. Suptel and D. Ryndina; *Admiral Nakhimov* (1941) by I. Lukovsky; *Alexander Nevsky* (1942) by O. Litovsky and K. Osipov; *Dmitri of the Don* (1942) by S. Borodin; *Kuz'ma Minin* (1942) by V. Kostylëv and G. London; *General Brusilov* (1943) by I. Selvinsky; *Prince Vladimir* (1943) by O. Forsh and G. Boyadzhiev; *Russian General* (1943) by I. Bekhterov and A. Razumovsky; *The Battle at Gruenwald* (1944) by I. Lukovsky; *The Eagle and His Mate* (1944) by A. N. Tolstoy; *The Livonian War* (1944) by I. Selvinsky; *Nadezhda Durova* (1944) by K. Lipskerov and A. Kochetkov; *Peter Bagration* (1944) by G. Mdivani; *The Great Sovereign* (1945) by Vladimir Soloviëv; *The Sword of Gruenwald* (1945) by Apushkin; *Difficult Years* (1946) by A. N. Tolstoy.

And these are only the outstanding plays—the bad and mediocre ones are too numerous to be counted. It was a river that began to resemble a flood after the war with Hitler began. These plays sang of almost all the resolute Russian military commanders and the entire history of Russian arms. There is no need to analyze all these works because they are all constructed according to an identical scheme. They showed the infinite patriotism of Russians in the past as they defended their country. All the great military commanders and sovereigns seemed to be inseparable from the people, and they triumphed in the name of the nation for which the sacred soil was being defended. In all the plays historical truth was juggled and adjusted crudely to suit "the task of the current moment"—to defend the Soviet state that was reeling under the blows of the Germans.

The Bolshevik retouching of history in *Kuz'ma Minin* was especially crude and obvious. The Governor of Nizhegorod, who tries to bribe Minin, is depicted according to the propagandistic stereotypes for the old "White Guardsmen" and "diversionists sent by the imperialists." He promises the citizens of the city the blessings of foreign intervention. ("A foreign regime will make Russia a flourishing state; it will make us rich and enlightened.")

There was also a "foreign diversionist"—a woman—in *Alexander Nevsky*. Her aims, techniques, and nationality correspond precisely to the realities of 1942, when the play was written. Her name was Elsa, and she was "sent by the intelligence" of the German staff for the Livonian Knights.

Prince Vladimir was "modernized" in the same spirit. It turns out that in the ancient Russia of the Kiev period, there was a struggle raging against the aggression of "Aryans" and other dangerous aliens, foreigners, and traitors. The play showed the exploitation of the "workers" in old Russia by the "Varangians."

Contemporary Bolshevik policy really spilled over into history in a play dedicated to the events of 1410. This was Lukovsky's *Battle at Gruenwald*. Even Yuri Osnos, the Soviet theater expert, wrote:

The entire historical situation on the eve of the famous battle is fictitious; it is presented like the international situation at the start of the Second World War. The play contains a "fifth column"—in the spy Fabrias, who bounces around from capital to capital. It has a cowardly political figure named Jagiello, who seeks peace at any price and keeps repeating: "If only Krakow were not mine!" Wallenrod, the Grand Marshall of the Teutonic Order, is depicted as an ordinary Hitlerite bandit.[3]

All this shows that Soviet playwrights were interested in current politics rather than in history. They had to show examples for the Soviet people to imitate. In Soloviëv's *Field Marshal Kutuzov,* for example, the common people were shown to have saved Russia. Kutuzov himself was shown as an ideal son of his nation, a democrat, who had close and constant ties with the people. He never tires of thinking about the peasant partisans, and he gets rid of Barclay de Tolly, the Scot who served as field commander of the Russian army, "because the nation is against him.

Playwrights frequently transformed their "historical plays" into patriotic pictures under the caption "The thunder of victory reverberates!" Such a picture was Lukovsky's *Admiral Nakhimov,* which was staged at the Kamerny Theater. Nakhimov endlessly and needlessly strolls about under shellfire, and the sailors talk about the great admiral in golden tones: "When a shell flies, he only waves his hand at it, and it swerves around him."

M. Gus and Konstantin Fin wrote a play called *Kliuchi Berlina* ("The Keys to Berlin") that makes Frederick the Great a prototype of Hitler. Frederick wants to conquer Russia at a "cheap price," but it turns out that he is slightly mad. He gives the keys of Berlin to the Russians and wails hysterically: "Don't repeat my mistakes! Beware of the Russians." At the Theater of the Revolution Frederick was enacted by M. Shtraukh, who tried to stress the King's "hysterical aggressiveness" and to make him a duplicate of Hitler.

Against such a background, Ilya Selvinsky's *The Livonian War* stands out sharply. The play was a "philosophical poem" in which the author digresses partly in the direction of lyrical poetry. It presents the problem of Ivan the Terrible in a new light. The poet viewed Ivan's period as one of historical renascence, when the Russian people entered the world stage, and the idea of the unity of progressive mankind came into being. Ivan's struggle against the Livonian Knights was not merely a struggle for the outlet on the sea that sixteenth-century Russia needed so vitally. It was basically a struggle against the dark remnants of the Middle Ages waged by progress and humanism. Ivan is shown as inspired, ascetic, and unearthly—a man who was absorbed in his profound inner life. His emotions are highly developed, and he sees the exalted but remote destiny of mankind. "You are terrible, like God with the icons," he is told by Maria Staritskaya.

The Vakhtangov Theater staged *Velikii Gosudar'* ("The Great Sovereign") by Soloviëv in 1945. It was a second effort at extolling Ivan the Terrible. The play was completely contemporary politics thrust into the past.[4] The terrible tsar was shown as a great patriot who zealously defended his country. His terrorism was justified by profound historical necessity, and his aims were good for all of Russia. Historical necessity was even the protagonist of Soloviëv's play. In *The Great Sovereign* Ivan does not renounce any of his evil deeds. He is "unafraid of earthly judgment" and takes his sins on his own conscience. Let him be condemned as a tyrant. He will bear any sacrifice and shame through the ages, but he will not turn aside from a single murder or a single application of torture. Everything he has done was solely for the welfare of the country.

The third and most powerful "rehabilitation" of Ivan the Terrible's terror was done by Alexei N. Tolstoy. It consisted of two plays: *The Eagle and His Mate* (1944) and *Difficult Years* (1946).

The Eagle and His Mate begins when Tsar Ivan is gravely ill, and the boyars are neglecting him completely. When Ivan gets over his illness, he is ready to revolt against the boyars and the debased condition of Russia—parceled up within and despised by its foreign enemies. The boyars poison the "eagle's mate" Mariya Temriukovna, the Tsar's beloved wife. (This is just how the Trotskyites supposedly poisoned Alilueva, Stalin's beloved wife.) The finale of the first play shows the start of the ruthless war against the boyars and the campaign of the *oprichniki* against Moscow. Tolstoy thus transferred all the evil and nastiness of old Russia to the vile, greedy, and treacherous boyars. Ivan becomes a democratic and revolutionary tsar, struggling against reactionary butchers. He is opposed to the "obsolete class" that has kept Russia in poverty, given no rights to the people, and put the country in a degrading position in relation to the rest of Europe.

Difficult Years begins with a reception for foreign ambassadors. Russia has been raised up by Ivan. The dangerous Order of Livonian Knights has been thoroughly defeated in the West, and the country now possesses an outlet to the sea. But with every victory Ivan wins, new enemies rise up against Russia. The Crimean khan is marching on Moscow, and conspiracies and treason take shape and threaten to destroy the state. Ivan, like the official version of Stalin, is possessed by only one passion. He dreams of greatness for Russia, prosperity for its peoples, and peace with other nations. Like Stalin, Ivan lives modestly and works through the night on his plans for the welfare of Russia and for defending it against domestic and foreign enemies.

The Moscow Art Theater, in staging *Difficult Years,* was unable to correct the author's mistakes in writing (not to mention history). Ivan is a colossus, but the boyars are shown as weak dwarfs. It was no achievement to fight against such insignificant figures. The protagonist in the play, therefore, has no opponents with whom to come into dramatic conflict, and so the result was artificial and farfetched. The main theme—the struggle against the boyars—was suspended in the air.[5] The Moscow Art Theater tried somehow to cover up the falsifications with something true. It therefore made Ivan something of a religious fanatic—which is historically accurate. Ivan hysterically atones for his terrible sins through prayer. He is seized by terror at the thought of hell, which is waiting for him. The Theater's efforts were vigorously denounced by the critics:

It [the Moscow Art Theater] has simplified the historical process. It has presented Ivan IV as a strict and repentant monk, as if the great Russian military commander, diplomat, and unifier of the country, spent his time in atoning for his sins rather than in his great reforms.[6]

Truthful details were not allowed to destroy the completeness of the falsehood.

Despite all their deliberate falseness, these pseudohistorical plays were a mighty instrument for influencing the spirits of Soviet audiences. Most Soviet people had either been educated through textbooks that falsified Russian history, or they simply did not know any history. They considered what they saw on the stage to be true. The chief force that regenerated them at these presentations was not the truth of the past but the hope of the future. The Bolsheviks decided to sing numerous songs about the great national heroes of Russia, and they used for this purpose the Soviet stage, motion pictures, and literature. They utilized these forms to nurture an unshakable conviction that Stalin's dictatorship would turn around sharply, renounce persecution, resurrect religion, respect the past, and promise the abolition of serfdom after the war. This illusion produced the flaming patriotism of the Russians in their heroic and self-renouncing defense of their country against the German invasion. They were fighting for the freedom that the change of the Bolshevik course was promising them in the future, after they had defeated the enemy on the battlefield.

THE CALL TO DEFEND THE HOMELAND

The number of plays dealing with defense has grown throughout the period of the Bolshevik offensive against the theater. During the war this topic gave rise to plays dealing with the front, and the genre grew tremendously until it almost completely overshadowed the other themes in the repertory. (Historical plays about Russian military leaders were not eclipsed, of course, but then there was a close connection between the two genres.) And the "militarization" and "patriotization" of the Soviet theater became quite thorough. In one new production of Griboyedov's *Woe from Wit* the director turned Skalozub—a stupid and satirically conceived soldier—into a "positive hero who had participated in the battles of the Patriotic War during 1812." [7]

The best of the prewar defense plays was Leonid Leonov's *Polovchanskie sady* ("The Orchards of Polovchansk," 1939). Leonov took a Soviet state-orchard as his background, in which he showed Soviet patriots ready to defend their country. The main characters are Adrian Makkaveyev—the elderly director of the state orchard—and his sons. They are all devoted to the Soviet scheme of things. They smash such domestic enemies as the insects wrecking the fertile orchards, which are thus trying to corrode the Soviet regime from within. These people are also ready to meet any foreign enemies with fire and hatred. "Let them smash their heads on your breast." Such are the parting words of old Makkaveyev to his sons as they leave for the Red Army. Leonov immersed the entire patriotic Soviet theme in the sweet-scented world of horticulture, and he found something poetic in it all. A review of the Moscow Art Theater production should help us to ascertain the aims and meaning of the play:

The Orchards of Polovchansk breathes with the spirit of bright optimism growing from a deeply patriotic faith . . . in the victorious power of Soviet people. In this play, we meet representatives of the old way of life, and living corpses who try to hamper the construction of the new life. But they do not determine the atmosphere of the action. It concentrates on Soviet people who are honest and devoted to our country: the director of the Soviet state orchard—Adrian Makkaveyev—and his sons. . . . The play definitely rings with the conviction that Soviet people will resist the military threat with all the weapons in their power, with a fiery hatred of the enemy, and with a love for their socialist homeland.[8]

One of the first plays dealing with the war against Hitler was Alexander Afinogenov's Nakanune ("On the Eve"). The playwright himself was killed during a German air raid on Moscow in November, 1941. The action of On the Eve begins before the war. The entire play takes place at the country house of Timofei—an old smelter—and his family. All these people live an exceptionally happy life, as befits all citizens of the Soviet Union. They are happy because each of them is doing his favorite work. Then, war breaks out and everything changes. The peaceful country house becomes the scene of cruel battles. But the characters grit their teeth and survive various terrors and torments, quietly convinced of victory. They overcome all their difficulties and mature into victorious heroes.

Batal'on idët na Zapad ("The Battalion Is Going to the West") by G. Mdivani was staged at the Kamerny Theater in 1941. Mdivani took as his point of departure the happy prewar life of Soviet people—this time on a Georgian collective farm. War and mobilization come with the second movement just as in the play discussed above. The presentation showed the steadfast fearlessness of Soviet reconnaissance. The soldiers fight heroically to hold a bridge for the use of reinforcements bound for the front. Pravda wrote:

Hundreds of eyes in the auditorium were glued to the stage. Everyone became a participant in the action. Everyone saw his own home, his own hopes, his own good-byes, and his own military experience in his mind's eye. . . . The auditorium considered the presentation as a continuation of the military day. It breathed courage and conviction.[9]

Whatever the reasons, the reaction to the plays dealing with the front were truly tumultuous.

Krylatoe plemia ("The Tribe with Wings") by Arkady Perventsov offered no special dramatic skill. It describes the clash between an aircraft manufacturer and a test pilot. The latter demands certain changes in the design of a fighter plane before it is put into production. The chief distinction of this play is that it initiated quite an impressive number of cheap, Soviet, patriotic, print-style works. Inevitably, the "Stalin of the day" appears as the savior at the most confused and critical moment, like a *deus ex machina*. Often one merely hears Stalin's voice on the telephone.

Vladimir Soloviëv's *Front* ("The Front"), which came out in 1941 or 1942, was a typical stereotype of the front. The family of an old worker turns into a mighty assemblage of heroes defending the socialist homeland. One son falls in battle, while the other two—the tankman and the airman—perform miracles of bravery at the front. The old man and his daughter go off to the partisans, while the old mother remains with her baby son in the town occupied by the Germans. Everyone is heroic.[10]

Leonov's *Nashestvie* ("Invasion") was presented in 1942. This play, by a great master of language, was one of the outstanding dramas to deal with the German invasion. It may be the only one with any value as art. Gloomy, cruel, and malleable, it revealed the daily life at the start of the war and under the German occupation. Once again Leonov showed a certain similarity to Dostoevsky by intensifying the evil in the human heart to the limit. As he had always done, Leonov developed the theme in his own way rather than according to the clichés of the Party play. The work was most patriotic, and yet, the hero is a man most unsuited for heroism—Fëdor Talanov. Talanov is a Soviet citizen released from an NKVD concentration camp shortly before the Germans take the city in which he lives. This sullen and feverish person has a secret but ineradicable yearning to atone to the Soviet homeland for his guilt. Apparently, the fact that his life was crippled in the forced-labor camps is not enough. He offers to undertake dangerous underground work in the occupied town. However, Kolesnikov—the leader of the underground and the secretary of the Party Regional Committee— refuses the services of the "former political convict." Talanov then undertakes heroic and hazardous partisan activity, and he kills prominent Nazis. The Gestapo seizes him and becomes convinced that he is the legendary Communist named Kolesnikov. Talanov passes himself off as Kolesnikov and goes quietly to the gallows. He has atoned to the Soviet homeland for his guilt.

Leonov presents the enemies of the Soviet land with a cruel horror. Fayunin, a former merchant, is frightful and repulsive. Dressed in rags, he plays the fool and returns to his native town in the baggage of Hitler's soldiers. Slippery as a snake, he is protected by German bayonets and spreads his wings like a vampire. Kokoryshkin, who has sold out to the Germans, is also loathsome. The character of Mosalisky, a white emigré who has become a mercenary of Hitler's, is filled with a cold contempt. No one before or since *Invasion* has managed to draw a Gestapo official with the ruthless power shown by Leonov in creating his Spurre.

Leonov's positive characters are profoundly sincere. There are Aniska (who is tortured by the Gestapo), old Dr. Talanov, his daughter Olga, her husband Kolesnikov, the prisoners whom the Germans have condemned to death, old Statnov, and the boy Porfiry.

Leonov's *Invasion* was his greatest service to Bolshevism. He gave all his talent and imagination to the patriotic fury of this infinitely Communistic play. But the mastery of *Invasion* conceals a false character in Fëdor Talanov. The lie is almost blasphemous. Here is a Russian man who has been tortured by the NKVD. Yet, he becomes infinitely patriotic and sacrifices himself for the sake of his executioners.

Korneichuk's *The Front,* which came out in 1942, was greeted enthusiastically by the Soviet press. It was hailed as a masterpiece among masterpieces because it staged the slogans of Stalin's party exactly. The Party was using those slogans in a hasty effort to rebuild the Red Army. General Ivan Gorlov, the protagonist of *Front,* is the "scapegoat" for all of Stalin's mistakes. Gorlov personifies the "conservative" generation of Soviet military leaders, who had matured in the Civil War. Stubborn and limited, they did not want to learn anything or "to reorient themselves." "War is not an academy." "Soldiers don't write but fight." "Act without reflecting." Such were the aphorisms of this general, who feels that everything is decided by the personal heroism of the soldiers and their leaders.

General Ognëv, who has received his rank during the war, opposes Ivan Gorlov. Ognëv favors new methods of waging war. Miron Gorlov —General Gorlov's brother—visits the front and helps Ognëv's struggle. Miron Gorlov is in charge of an aircraft factory, and he ruthlessly destroys the military arts of his brother that are not leading to victory. It becomes clear that Miron is really only a messenger for the "Stalin of the day." En route to the front, Miron visits Stalin. This genius is also quite dissatisfied with Ivan Gorlov and is giving a new course in military strategy. As a result, the "conservative" Ivan Gorlov is removed. He is replaced by Ognëv, the young and forward-looking Soviet general. Ivan Gorlov represents "yesterday" and defeat. Ognëv represents "tomorrow" and Stalin's victories.

Konstantin Simonov's *Russkie liudi* ("Russian People") was given in 1943. The Soviet press considered *Russian People, Invasion,* and *Front* to be the three best plays about the war. *Russian People* was written when Bolshevik encouragement of Russian patriotism was at its height. Everyone and everything was shouting "Glory to Russian arms!" After the war, however, Stalin's clique found Russian patriotism superfluous. Then, Simonov was compeled to write some "self-criticism" for the press. He wrote that he "had not known how to raise himself above the idea of Russian patriotism in *Russian People* and had not shown what Soviet patriotism was." [11]

When the play was written and staged, all its characters were saturated with Russianism. The author considered the Russian people to have a profound feeling of its own value in regard to other nations in general and to the enemy in particular. Russians could "feel that they were not just the commander but the master of everything subordinated to them." [12]

A small detachment of Red Army men is surrounded by the Germans. They have no food or water. Under the circumstances, every man is valuable and the slightest carelessness would lead to the unit's destruction. The detachment, commanded by Captain Safonov, fights heroically. To a man, they are heroes who believe unshakably in victory and are ready to sacrifice everything in order to attain it. Captain Safonov loves Valia, but he sends her to the rear of the enemy—and to certain death —without batting an eyelash. The mother of Captain Safonov yells at the Germans before she dies: "Your mothers should be taken by the collar . . . and told: You see, you bitches, whom you have given birth to! . . . And if after that they won't curse their own sons, then I would kill them along with you, their sons." The wife of the traitor, Kharitonov, goes to her death wreaking vengeance for herself and for her son, and atoning for her husband's guilt. They all perish without surrendering, in obedience to the order: "Not a step back! Stand and die! Hold on and stay put! Take ten wounds, but stay put!"

Konstantin Paustovsky, a talented Soviet storyteller, wrote *Poka ne ostanovitsia serdtse* ("Until the Heart Stops"), which was staged at the Kamerny Theater in 1943. It deals with the sufferings of Soviet people under the German occupation and the liberating rebellion raised by some partisans. Tairov's propagandistic treatment of the Germans furnished the main interest of the production. The heroine is Anna Martynova, an actress, a role that Alice Koonen played. Her child is accidentally killed by a German soldier. The half-mad mother wanders about the occupied town with her dead child. Tairov intensified the dramatic effect with purely propagandistic devices. Harsh and bestial German soldiers in hobnailed boots surround the mother and her dead child. They laugh at her, sing obscene songs, and dance in a circle around her. Her attempts to break out of the ring and her delirium are in vain. The German officers hold a ball at a restaurant. Tairov treated this like a dance of ponderous machines. The officers danced like robots to the sounds of mechanical music. The finale of the play was just as posterish as the rest. The actress appeared on the empty stage of the theater in the occupied town, wearing a fluttering dress. With a red kerchief in her hands, she then called for a rebellion. The partisans tore through the theater building, their bayonets sparkling, and the furious figure of the actress appeared above them like a white angel of victory.

Tairov presented Vsevolod Vishnevsky's *U sten Leningrada* ("At the Walls of Leningrad") in 1944. The critics considered this play the weakest one to deal with the defense of that city. Plots and treason seemed to overshadow the heroic theme. Tairov resorted to the same "monumentally patriotic" style that was used by many other Soviet theaters at the time.

Y. Chepurin's *Stalingradtsy* ("People of Stalingrad") came out in 1944. It treated the daily life during the defense of the city. In genre, the play was a documentary report. The author had been a war correspondent with the Sixty-second Army. He said that most of the scenes in his play had been "painted directly from nature." He took down the speeches of his characters "word for word," like a reporter. "I wrote everything in the play from the words of the soldiers and officers." [13]

Despite all its naturalistic extremes, the documentary genre was popular with audiences. They considered such "documentations" to be living depictions of daily activity at the front—a counterfeit form of "television" from the battlefields. The enthusiasm of the critics over the documentary genre clearly shows that the descent to naturalism was continuing apace. This decline is peculiar to the contemporary Soviet theater.

Margarita Aliger wrote *Skazka o pravde* ("Tale about the Truth") in 1944. This was a naïve effort to turn a true story about a partisan girl from the woods near Moscow into something of heroic stature. The girl, Zoya Kosmodemianskaya, had been a member of the Komsomol whom the Germans hanged. In the play the heroine is tortured, but, on the eve of her execution, she sees a phantom of Stalin in her cell. It has come to inform her that the Red Army has launched a general offensive and that Moscow will not be surrendered. Zoya thanks Stalin for the information and tells him that now she is "afraid of nothing."

Mikhail Svetlov's *Brandenburgskie vorota* ("The Brandenburg Gate") was staged in 1945. It is not set in the past, but in the future of 1955. The play itself depicts events of 1944, however. In 1955 a Soviet state toy-store closes for a "memorial hour" rather than for a "dinner hour." The heroes assemble to recall their own great past. Svetlov needs to see the future in terms of the present in order to explain his intense infatuation with his characters. For him, they are poets rather than soldiers. Not only does the author adore his characters in a sentimental fashion, but they also adore one another. Inasmuch as everything is depicted quite lyrically, even the Soviet critics admitted that the plot could not be paraphrased. All this lyricism takes place against a background of war and victory. In the play "nothing is the way it is in life." The heroes praise themselves *a parte* with such remarks as: "We are the heroes of our time" and "We are fine people." The sniper sings songs instead of maintaining the deathlike silence prescribed in military regulations. "Without a song," he says, "the gunsight is inaccurate." Soviet soldiers who are fatally wounded and lying on the battlefield also sing, or as the author's stage direction has it: "The wounded lie motionless and begin singing." Dramatically, the play is quite weak, and the author's love for his characters knows no bounds, but despite all this the play is a spot of comfort against the drab boredom and naturalism in the plays of those years.

Ofitser flota ("Naval Officer") by A. Kron appeared in 1945 and showed the German blockade of Leningrad toward the end of 1941.

The blockade and the ice have marooned a Soviet submarine in the River Neva. Its commander, Gorbunov, the hero of the play, is determined to use all his and the crew's strength to free the submarine and bring it into action against the enemy. The action takes place against the harsh life of the blockaded and besieged city. Gorbunov's patriotic enthusiasm is contrasted with the official sangfroid of another commander who resists the process of freeing the submarine. There is a woman in the play, too, who loves the hero, who has no time for love. Rear Admiral Belobrov settles the conflict within the service in favor of Gorbunov, and the play finishes with the hero's triumph.[14]

The Moscow Art Theater staged B. Chirskov's *Pobediteli* ("Victors") in 1946. This play won a Stalin Prize. Its protagonist, General Muraviëv has the traits of a real Soviet military leader and is a man with an outstanding mind and great moral strength. He is contrasted to General Krivenko, a general with a good record who at the decisive moment shows himself to be "morally tired," nervous, and fussy. Krivenko is relieved of his command, "as a person who cannot master his tasks." Muraviëv, on the other hand, resembles Stalin in his military talents. Unlike the others, he feels that the victory over Germany was not won so much by the second front of the Allies as by the extent to which Red Army units succeeded in breaking into Europe and by the number of countries those units occupied.

Vladimir Soloviëv wrote his verse play *Doroga pobedy* ("The Road to Victory") in 1946. Its hero, an officer named Arseni, is verbose and expresses himself quite pompously. The Germans take him prisoner and promise him his life if he tells them all the military secrets. Arseni answers:

> Merely to live interests me not,
> When life is spent like an object. . . .
> And my life has remained
> Where women bestow smiles,
> Where people pay deserved honors
> Not to a person as a money-bags
> But to a person as he is.

The whole work is sustained in the same lofty tone. It shows the three stages of the war. The first stage—the endless withdrawals under German pressure—provoked dissatisfaction among the soldiers. The second stage was the organization of new units beyond the Urals in order to strike at Hitler's soldiers. The third stage was the collapse of the German hordes.

One of the main characters in *Road to Victory* is (again!) a general —Simbirtsev, whose wife Natalya, opens his eyes. General Simbirtsev was guilty of having fought with a personal heroism that was outdated and that miscarried. His wife understands his military backwardness, however, and aids him to become reoriented. He learns technique and finally takes the correct way to victory—Stalin's way.

Boris Lavrenëv's *Za tekh, kto v more* ("For Those Who Go to Sea") came out in 1947. Its hero, Lieutenant Commander Borovsky, is a "man with a kink." He dreams about personal glory and "drives himself boldly and persistently" in order to obtain it, saying, "Glory is capricious. . . . One must know how to seize it by its sparkling wings . . . and not to surrender it to anyone."

Borovsky has located a German submarine, but because of his "un-principled ambition," he does not summon a detachment of cutters. He does not want to share any glory. So he gives inaccurate coordinates to his "competitors" and goes to sink the enemy by using his own cutters exclusively. As a result, vice is punished. Fascist planes defeat him, but the submarine is sunk by the "real heroes." They are contrasted to him in the play. They preach: "Our business is not to chase after personal glory. This is not why the nation has raised us or what it has taught us. I do not need my own glory, but rather the glory of our cause."

The moral is this: "The successes of each individual are basically the successes of the collective which has nurtured him. The person who has torn himself away from the Soviet milieu, who gives himself over to individualistic moods, and who contrasts himself to the collective is con-demned to failure." [15]

Lavrenëv's play was given at the Maly Theater in Moscow. It was granted the highest awards and made the rounds of the Soviet stages. The actor playing Borovsky created a "psychological portrait of a person having a neurasthenic grimace, and who easily proceeds from exaltation to extreme depression." [16] The critics considered this a great achieve-ment.

Alexander Fadeyev's novel *Molodaia gvardiia* ("Young Guard") was adapted for the stage in 1947. Of all the postwar plays dealing with the German occupation, this was the one that provoked the greatest number of articles and discussions and the greatest amount of enthusiasm. The work played in almost all Soviet theaters, and afterwards, it was made into an outstanding Soviet film.

Fadeyev took his heroes from people who had really participated in the Komsomol underground organization at Krasnodon during the local German occupation, and his characters bear their real names. The group of stubborn Komsomol members received German permission to organize an amateur dramatic and musical circle to entertain German soldiers and officers. This masked their terroristic work of killing Hitler's men. An underground worker from the Party directed all the partisan activities of the young people. The "young guard" was discovered by the Gestapo, tortured, and executed.

Fadeyev endowed his young characters with incredible warmth and courage. The heroism with which they fought and went to their deaths was touching. Hence, the play was a success. Upon seeing either it or the motion picture, any spectator would completely forget that it dealt with Komsomol members and the results of underground Party work. The stage or screen showed how the occupation army killed wonderful Russian boys and girls. It was moving, provoked wrath, and produced pride in the glorious procession of Russian patriots.

The author made the facts romantic and heroic. The theater, however, did the reverse—which typified the Soviet postwar theater. It tried to return the romanticism to facts and naturalism. Boris Zakhava directed one of the best productions of the play at the Vakhtangov Theater in Moscow. He wrote that all the performers visited Krasnodon for a long period and studied for a long time at the places of the action. They also studied portraits, documents, and so forth. Zakhava wrote:

We tried for an extremely concrete depiction—concrete historically and geographically. The stage must show Krasnodon. Not Soviet young people in general, but those of Krasnodon. . . . All the actors who played young guardsmen had to learn the real biographies of their characters—the lives and specific traits of real people.[17]

THE CALL FOR SACRIFICE AND RECONSTRUCTION

Right after the war there appeared a number of plays based on the new slogans of the Party that called upon Soviet citizens for new sacrifices and new heroism in the war against destruction, ruins, and ashes. Nikolai Pogodin's *Sotvorenie mira* ("The Creation of the World"), which came out in 1946, is the only play of this group worth pausing over. It shows postwar Soviet people with their destroyed families and their cities wrecked by the Germans. A husband has been at the front —his wife, in the German rear. A lover learns that his girl has been in some kind of contact with the Germans, and he is troubled by jealousy and gloomy suspicions. People look for their wives, husbands, and mothers. The play shows primeval chaos in the ruins and in the lives of human beings.

Pogodin followed the patterns set by the Bureau of Agitation and Propaganda. He did his best to show that the war had not made Soviet people "worse," that they were the same devoted "non-Party Communists" that they had been before. But, in wholeheartedly accepting the official optimism, the author forgot to do any unmasking, the critics charged. He failed to show that those who had remained under the German occupation were scoundrels and "enemies of the people" if they had not joined the partisans. The playwright was guilty of "slurring over the baseness of others who had volunteered to serve the enemy and then hid their treason under the guise of devotion to the nation." [18]

Colonel Georgy Glagolin is the protagonist in *Creation of the World*. He is a disabled veteran, condemned to vegetate, who rebels, however, against the fate that kept him away from the battlefields. He craves exploits, and he soon performs them. The heroic conflict to restore his native town from the ashes is a battlefield on which this man shows his courage. As a new representative of the local Soviet, Glagolin begins to work in a cellar. Life bursts in on him in an endless stream. A line of people comes in, each one with his woes, misfortunes, complaints, requests for aid, and stories about his house and life that have been destroyed. These people live on the bare earth, on the burned-out wasteland left by Hitler's hordes. They have no dwellings, light, fuel, or anything else. But they do have Glagolin, who is a member of the Party. And, in the wasteland, Glagolin begins the "creation of the world." New houses and districts rise up on the map of the city like a phoenix from the ashes.

Incidentally, the vigilant Soviet critics found that the play listed dangerously—someone might suddenly think that the entire U.S.S.R. was in ruins. After the play was produced at the Maly Theater, a critic wrote:

The very theme of the "creation of the world" is a lightweight one because it turns out that the subject being dealt with is not liquidating the traces of fascist barbarism in the economy and in the consciousness of people, and not the restoration or the further construction of the state, but rather—to a large degree—building silos on a collective farm. Such is the scope of the emotions and pathos in the presentation.[19]

Stalin had something to say about the obstinate conservatives among executives and agricultural workers, and instantly a torrent of dramas—of a cast-iron mold—appeared to illustrate his words of genius. These works contained experimenters in industry and resolute discoverers of new methods in agriculture who were personal illustrations of the slogans concerning production advanced by the party. The series of plays about old-fashioned generals was thus succeeded by a mass of plays about old-fashioned factory supervisors and farm managers—the generals of production.

Of the plays dealing with this theme, the critics gave high praise to A. Surov's play *Daleko ot Stalingrada* ("Far from Stalingrad"), the background of which was a factory that produced aircraft engines during the war. There is a clash between the experimenters, represented by the Communist Orlov and the engineer Berezin, and the conservatives, among whom are Oseredko, the factory director, and the bureaucrat Krasavin. The author uses Krasavin to attack Soviet engineers who "are lacking in imagination" and do not admit the incredible potentialities of the Soviet people. This is done in the name of the Party because Oseredko, though a Party member, is a backward conservative who believes that "you don't propagandize technique." The Stalin Prize awarded the play suggests that the author had most diligently given "living pictures" and characters representing the slogans issued by the founder of those prizes.

Surov's *Rassvet nad Moskvoi* ("Dawn over Moscow"), which was produced in 1950 and which also won a Stalin Prize, concerns a woman—Kapotiliana Solntseva—who is directress of a textile factory and against whom the progressive workers and engineers struggle. Even though she is a Party member, the fight against her is led by a Party organizer. The progressives want the factory to turn out cloth to beautify the lives of the Soviet people, but the reactionary directress is not interested in beauty. She is only interested in more yardage because she wants to fulfill the production plans issued by the People's Commissariat of Garment Making. Kapotiliana Solntseva is also backward in her private life, and she refuses to understand her educated daughter's long-cherished ambition to become a Stakhanovite textile worker. This prize-winning play requires several acts for the progressives to re-educate the backward woman with their stern criticism.

Surov is a new star in the postwar Soviet drama, and the struggle against conservatives is his specialty as a dramatist. He has won several Stalin Prizes, and at first it is difficult to understand why. His plays suffer from unique drabness, conflicts that are boring clichés, stereotyped characters, and wretchedly official language, which is indistinguishable from the articles in *Pravda* and other official publications. His dialogue is schematic, and, instead of moving, the characters keep busy with depressing argumentation and, in fact, give reports. His diction is of the kind that is a coarsening and oversimplifying of the Russian language. Surov has won so many prizes, however, because he always deals with the most current and important tasks that the Party has assigned to production. His *Zelënaia ulitsa* ("Green Street"), which also won a Stalin Prize, deals with the merciless and labored offensive of the Party to increase the norms in production on the railroads.

Among other plays dealing with increasing industrial production were A. Safronov's *Moskovskii kharakter* ("Muscovite Character," 1949), Kron's *Kandidat Partii* ("Candidate for the Party," 1949), and O. Aleshin's *Director,* 1950. The best plays concerning agricultural production were *Osoboe mnenie* ("Opinion Reserved," 1949) by S. Klebanov and A. Mariamov, and *Khleb nash nasushchnyi* ("Our Daily Bread," 1950) by Nikolai Virta.

ANTI-WESTERN AND ANTI-AMERICAN THEMES

Soon after the war the Bolsheviks found out that their Allies did not intend to look the other way while Communism was engulfing one country after another in Europe. The Party then began a rabid propaganda campaign against the West and used every method to incite hatred. Day after day, the Bolsheviks hammered the idea into Soviet heads that the Western world was preparing for a war against them that would be more terrible than Hitler's, and an important part of this propaganda were the anti-Western and, especially, anti-American plays, which increased from year to year.[20] Englishmen and Americans became enemies in the Soviet plays—the enemies of all the nations in the entire world, not just of the Soviet people.

There was a whole ocean of plays unmasking "imperialistic schemes," "the instigation of war," and the "reactionary nature" of science and culture in the West and in America. There were irate exposés of "kow-towing" to the Western world and unmaskings of "cosmopolitanism."

Konstantin Simonov's *Alien Shadow* (1949) deals with a great discovery by a Soviet scientist, which is intended to liberate all mankind from a fatal disease. In the hands of American scientists, however, it is distorted into a weapon of extermination for the coming war.

The Maly Theater in Moscow staged in 1950 Boris Lavrenëv's *Voice of America,* another violently anti-American play. Its hero is Walter Kidd, a captain in the American army. During the war he became convinced that the Russian people were noble and self-sacrificing, and back home he falls victim to the Committee on Un-American Activities for his beliefs. A gallery of repulsive characters is contrasted to this "honest American intellectual who goes over to the camp of those who are actively struggling against the warmongers." There is Senator Wiler, an "American fascist," who appeals to the soldiers of Kidd's unit for a war against the Russians. There is a gangster named O'Leary who "lacks every human quality." Breasted is a policeman who is "ready to sell the law for a glass of whisky." Skundrell is an agent of the Committee on Un-American Activities who personifies the "fascist stratum" in the United States.

Through Skundrell, the Senate Committee presents Kidd with an ultimatum. If he does not broadcast that he is returning a Soviet medal awarded him during the war, and if he does not tell the American populace that the Russians want to seize America and annihilate the Americans, he will be treated like a Red. "You will die a slow death! From hunger and poverty! There will be no work for you in America."

Captain Kidd refuses to do what he is asked (of course). He threatens to unmask Senator Wiler in the press: "I will open American eyes," he says, "to his swindling with hard currency in the Occupied Zone, to his connections with German firms during the war, and to his rotten betrayal of American interests and the lives of American soldiers." In order to prevent this exposure, Senator Wiler hires a band of gangsters headed by O'Leary. They break into Kidd's apartment to kill him, but the Captain flees with a Communist and is thus saved from death.

That is the synopsis of the propaganda play. The Soviet critics declared unanimously that "it gives a truthful picture of contemporary America" and "mercilessly unmasks the encroachments of the American fascists."

The Maly Theater presentation of the play, like the dramatist, was completely responsive to the order that reality be falsified. The method of the Maly Theater was the old one of the propaganda poster: "The theater contrasts the human features of Kidd and his friends and the bestial appearance of powers-that-be. This is done truthfully; that is the way things are." [21] But in the staging of this anti-American play a subversive slip was made. Isaak Rabinovich, the designer, copied American illustrated magazines exactly in presenting the setting for the life of an average American. The critics found this disgraceful:

The luxurious halls and exotic views of the sea presented on the stage clearly do not correspond to the life of an honest toiler such as Walter Kidd and give a false and distorted presentation of life led by ordinary people in America.[22]

The Soviet theater since the war has become a brilliantly adjusted apparatus for carrying out the orders given by the Department of Agitation and Propaganda. Even the Stockholm Peace Appeal received an immediate and massive reflection in the drama. In 1951 a play by M. Volin and E. Shatrov—*Bitva za zhizn'* ("Fight for Life")—dealt with the French women who struggled to sign the Communist "peace" appeal. *Zvezda mira* ("Star of Peace") by Ts. Solodar and *Grazhdanin Frantsii* ("Citizen of France") by D. Khrabovitsky were staged in 1952. The latter deals with a French scientist (of the Joliot-Curie type) who struggles for the Stockholm appeal.

A number of plays were written to show the "bestiality" of the Americans in Korea. One of them is Mdivani's *People of Good Will,* and another is *Iuzhnee 38-oi paralleli* ("South of the Thirty-eighth Parallel") by Tkai Dian Chun. These plays used any lie, fairy tale, or propaganda-style terror. Their aim was to show:

The Americans, by their policy of colonial expansion, and their bloodthirsty subjugation of the aspirations of enslaved Korea toward freedom, are not securing a strong rear for themselves but are earning the fierce hatred of all honest people.[23]

A purge of the Western plays in the repertories of Soviet theaters began in 1946. Such plays as *The Circle* and *Penelope* by W. Somerset Maugham were declared dangerous bourgeois poison and were taken off the boards. The Kamerny Theater staged *An Inspector Calls* by J. B. Priestley in 1946, and it took every precaution not to fall under the cross-fire of the Communist critics. The Theater removed the mystic coating of Inspector Goole as a vague representative of some future

Judgment Day and turned him into a "public prosecutor," "a friend
of the people who have not yet acceded to power." In staging the work
the Theater resorted to the typical devices of antibourgeois propaganda
that had characterized its work. Even all this, however, did not save the
Kamerny Theater from the accusation that it had dragged a "typically
bourgeois detective" on the Soviet stage who typified the inner barrenness of the West.

GLORIFYING THE PARTY LEADERS

There was a constant increase in the slavish extolling of the Bolshevik
leaders in the drama during and after the war. The first place in these
ode-plays was held by Stalin. Soviet playwrights tried to transfer his
entire life to the stage, drama by drama. In 1951 *Iunost' vozhdia* ("Youth
of a Leader") by G. Nakhutsrishvili appeared and was followed by
Voskhodit solntse ("The Sun Is Rising")—the sun, of course, was
Stalin. A. Shtein's *Prologue* (1952) concerned young Stalin and his
great role in the Revolution of 1905. Two plays—*Kremlevskie kuranty*
("Kremlin Chimes") by Nikolai Pogodin and *Nezabyvaemyi 1919-yi*
("1919—The Unforgettable Year") by Vsevolod Vishnevsky—showed
Lenin with Stalin. Plays were also written about other Bolshevik heroes
such as Sverdlov, Volodarsky, Uritsky, Ordzhonikidze, Kirov, and
Frunze.

Let us examine two most valuable examples of this type of play.
Pogodin's *Kremlin Chimes* was written on the eve of the Soviet entry
into the war and followed his *Man with a Gun*. The Moscow Art Theater
production took place after the war had broken out. The plot deals with
the repair of the chimes on the Spasski Tower in the Kremlin, and, of
course, they play the "Internationale" at the end. The author wanted
this to symbolize Soviet Russian greatness arising from the ruins. In
fact, however, the story about the tower clock merely gives the playwright a pretext for extolling Stalin and Lenin on the Soviet stage once
more and in a slavish way. This time another Bolshevik "saint"—Felix
Dzherzhinsky (the first chief of the Cheka)—is added to the "iconostasis."
The plot also concerns an "old regime" engineer named Zabelin, who
refuses to acknowledge the Soviet regime and prefers selling matches on
the Moscow streets to serving the Communists. He is an erring and
"philistinized" man of some stature. Eventually he is placed on the path
to spiritual resurrection and becomes a participant in the great plan for

the "electrification" of Soviet Russia. This feat is accomplished by Stalin and Lenin, who are wise.

Vladimir Nemirovich-Danchenko carried out the most elaborate presentation of *Kremlin Chimes* at the Moscow Art Theater. As the director, he declared that he was seeking to combine "the most magnificent romanticism and the most simple form." Some of his statements should indicate what he considered as "romanticism":

I am eighty-two years old. I have seen very many people in my life. But I have never met such people as Comrades Stalin and Molotov. And what we see in the daily lives, in the lives and work of our leaders, with their mighty wills and powerful strength, gives us an example of the most magnificent romanticism in the most simple form.[24]

Apparently this "romantic" treatment applied in the director's suggestions to A. N. Gribov, who played Lenin:

I feel like having these bits in the Lenin line: "official lightnings" in his eyes and voice. . . . If one catches the lightnings throughout the role, they will show Lenin, the leader. And not as a goody-goody, sweet, or soft. . . . These are the lightning-quick and fiery ideas that show genius. When you grasp this lightninglike quality, I will say: this is a leader of genius, and not just a magnificent portrait. . . . No Lenin, no leader, can be shallow or a goody-goody. . . . Not a second of feebleness or friability; the most terrible thing would be Lenin and sentimentality.[25]

These words of Nemirovich-Danchenko's slightly raise the curtain on the "kitchen" in which the figures of Soviet leaders are baked for the stage. Everything living and ordinarily human has been annihilated. The buskins make them geniuses and demigods, and the entire role is covered with "flashing lightning."

The living and more-than-real Stalin was seated in the government box of the Moscow Art Theater. Before his eyes and the eyes of the others in the audience, the stage showed another Stalin, as immobile as a pagan god come down from the pedestal of a temple. Here is the prophetic finale in *Kremlin Chimes:* "Our country stands like an enormous rock in the ocean of bourgeois states. Wave after wave rolls up against it, threatening to engulf it and to erode it. And the rock stands firm. We will not yield, believe me, we will not yield." There was apparently only one thing needed to make the totalitarian dictatorship completely idiotic, and that was not lacking. After the presentation, the sovereign deigned to invite his incarnation on the stage to his box.

Stalin then gave the actor a few indications about how to transmit "Stalin" with even more genius.

Vishnevsky's *1919—the Unforgettable Year* was, of course, a more grandiose counterfeit of the "great friendship" between Lenin and Stalin. History was violated and Stalin was shown as Lenin's Siamese twin. They are inseparable. Lenin cannot think or breathe without Stalin. The prologue starts by showing the appearance of Stalin, whom the others have been awaiting a long time. Without him, Lenin cannot decide how to defend the republic. The country is in danger, and it can be saved only by Stalin. Lenin sends him to the front to suppress the rebellion at Kronstadt. And Stalin saves the republic. A telephone call from him about the ruthless suppression of the Kronstadt rebellion ends this false play.

POSTWAR COMEDIES

Satire and comedy in the Soviet Union have always been subjected to strict limitations. They have been permitted widely for defeating the class enemy abroad and for attacking the Russia of the past. There have been no classical comedies that failed to "sociologize," and there has been no contemporary satire directed at the ulcers of Soviet society. Socialist society has nothing to satirize!

The "Theater of Satire" lasted in Moscow for over twenty years. It was always an institution working under an alien name because real satire would attack the idiocies of Soviet life and the existing regime. Except for a poor staging of Saltykov-Shchedrin's *Stupidville,* everything which the Theater of Satire presented gently ridiculed the petty Soviet bureaucrats, the Nepmen, and the "base Soviet fools." It was all as toothless as the humor in the official magazine *Krokodil* because the censorship kept too sharp an eye on the Theater.

The lone comedy that can be considered a satire—and that with some difficulty—was Alexander Bezymensky's *Shot.* It was kept on the stage, although for only a short time, because the dictator himself defended it.

Even those comedies dealing with Soviet customs, which had been checked and approved in all the offices of the censorship, show a sharp decline. In 1930 the Theater of Satire could still find room for a rather malicious comedy about narrow-minded Soviet people—*Pervyi kandidat*

("First Candidate") by Alexander Zharov and M. Polikarpov. It showed the life enjoyed by the muddle-headed citizens in the town of Popliuisk. The main character was Morkovkin, the director of a printing-press and a candidate for membership in the Party. The critics even made some far-reaching generalizations about him:

Morkovkins get through all the cracks. They are careerists, cads, political double-dealers, maliciously narrow-minded, bureaucratic blockheads, and the triumphant philistine swine. Although Morkovkin is only a "first candidate," he delays the appearance of the Party newspaper in order hurriedly to print the appeal of churchmen in it. Although only in anticipation, he will "swear at" Karl Marx and adorn his holiday with "red caviar." But if you approve of Morkovkin, he will draw himself up to his full height.[26]

Alexei Diky directed *First Candidate* and E. Mandelberg was the designer. Back in 1930 hyperbole and the grotesque were still permissible. The scene showing the "decay" of the philistines was presented on an inclined floor, which depicted an enormous table that had been set. The tippling and falling characters swarmed over it like worms among the gigantic bottles and hors d'oeuvres. After the war, however, Soviet comedy was completely inoffensive, both in its dramatic material and in its interpretation on the stage.

Fakir na chas ("Fakir for an Hour") by V. Dykhnovnichny and M. Slobodsky typified this cachectic period. It was produced at the Theater of Satire in 1945. A famous Soviet writer arrives incognito in a little town. He passes himself off as a doctor and hypnotist. The various residents of the town come to his "reception." They take his advice and criticisms of their work. As they suggest, they are hypnotized by him. They try to correct the shortcomings in their work. The meaning of all this rubbish is that "people can be better if they themselves want to be."

Samolët opazdyvaet na sutki ("The Plane Is Twenty-four Hours Late," 1945) by N. Rybak and I. Savchenko was severely libeled by the theater press. The authors had dared to depict Pugovitsyn, a "supply-man," as buttering and flattering his chief. Pugovitsyn gets his boss something "illegally," and he does some pandering by "arranging" a liaison between his chief and an actress. He is not a completely negative character, and he tries to justify minor toadying in a country of great toadying.

N. Aduyev intended his *Bronzovyi biust* ("Bronze Bust," 1945) to be a light musical comedy. Like any other Soviet dramatist, however, he was not allowed to leave the "vital political problems of the day." The standard theme of 1945 was the war and the postwar reconstruction of the country. By using the "compulsory assortment" of "current problems" in a light musical comedy, Aduyev created something that was most stupid and most ridiculous. The heroine, Milochka Krotova, is a beautiful and sensitive girl who dreams of becoming a Soviet film star. The war, however, "reorients" her and she becomes a conscious worker —herding swine for a collective farm, where she is inspired to love her new "creative work."

As a rule, the new Soviet "comedy" always depicts some production seriously. It is also serious in the heroic and businesslike nature of its characters, its pathos, its enthusiasm, and the constructive activity of Party and Komsomol cells. The slightest comic lightness in developing the action or the dialogue brings an immediate attack from the critics: "The author smirks at what is most cherished." The "comic" element in such a play occurs only in the more verbose and lyrical love scenes, in the songs introduced, and in a few jokes.

CONVERTED INTELLECTUALS AND UNHAILED GENIUS

A number of plays since the war have served the decrees issued by the Central Committee of the Party dealing with literature, the struggle against the "formalists," and the "cosmopolitans." *Pamiatnye vstrechi* ("Memorable Meetings") by A. Utevsky, which came out in 1946, deals with the beneficial influence of the Party in reconstructing the intellectuals working in the arts. Its hero is a Soviet writer named Zavialov who has written a number of important works but has been silent for a while. He says: "To speak about our people at such a time in drab and dusty language—it would be better not to speak at all. . . . I try to write, but all I do is waste paper. It is a real shame." [27] Of course, the play does not reveal the real reason why many Soviet writers are "silent" —because they have been crushed by the press and censorship of the Party. As an orthodox Soviet patriot, Utevsky tried to show that Zavialov had "written himself out" because he had torn himself away from the Party and from Soviet reality.

A second play dedicated to the reorientation of the intellectuals working in the arts was Mikhalkov's *Ilia Golovin* (1948). Ilya Golovin is a major Soviet composer who is celebrating his birthday at his country place. He receives an unexpected present—a fresh edition of a Moscow paper in which his *Fourth Symphony* is denounced as "formalistic"— as happened in the actual case of Shostakovich. The composer falls into disgrace, grows quite sullen, and stops working. He is reformed by a Soviet general who has been billeted at the composer's country place during maneuvers. The general tells Golovin that the soldiers in his unit sang a song by him in all their battles, and when storming Berlin the soldiers sang it as they died. The general and an important Party member manage to return the stray sheep from "formalism" to folk songs and patriotic music.

Tret'ia molodost' ("Third Youth") by the Tur brothers was presented in 1952. The theater press wrote about it as follows:

The authors show the struggle of a major Soviet scientific figure, Professor Snezhinskaya, against the disciples of Virchow's reactionary theory that serves as a source for the views of Weissmann and Morgan. The play tells about the persistence of Soviet people who overcome difficulties in science through their mastery of the dialectical method of Marx and Lenin. They go forth boldly to seek new discoveries.[28]

There have been a number of postwar plays dealing with great Russian inventors, scientific figures, and people of cultural significance. They expanded the series of plays about scientists and continued the anti-Western propaganda of the Party. No doubt this series was ordered by the Bureau of Agitation and Propaganda. Soviet people had to be shown that Russia was always ahead of the West and that there was nothing to learn from the West. The West should learn from Russia because Russia has always outstripped it.

The entire series about great pre-Soviet Russians was constructed according to the same patterns. Old Russia did not recognize its geniuses. The greedy bourgeois of the West wanted to buy their inventions, but the patriotic inventors preferred to live in hunger without surrendering their brainchildren. They were preserving their inventions for the advent of Stalin's Russia.

One example of this mass-produced genre should suffice. Let us take Isidor Shtok's *Pobediteli nochi* ("Victors over the Night"), which was produced in 1950. The hero of the play was P. N. Yablochkov, a Russian scientist who perfected his own "electric light" between 1875 and 1879. The electric light is merely an excuse for an anti-Western propaganda play, which is shown by the fact that two of the main characters are William Gilard—"a representative of American capital"—and Deneyrouze, a French businessman and engineer, both of whom are completely repulsive and try to buy the unbribable Yablochkov. Incidentally, the play continued the very old type of propaganda play dealing with the terrors of life in ignorant, tsarist Russia. Yablochkov alone dreams about the advent of a bright paradise in the future, constructed according to the brilliant plans of Stalin. He exclaims: "Future generations will live well!"

AGAIN THE CLASSICS

Before the war the classical plays of the past were very important in Soviet theater repertories. In 1940 there were 24,240 presentations of the Russian classics alone, which played to more than ten million people. During the war the torrent of patriotic dramas all but drowned out the classics, but they were still given quite frequently. The coarse "sociologizing" of the old plays continued to grow stronger, however, and every passing year increased the naturalism of these presentations.

In 1940 the Moscow Art Theater staged a "revision" of Chekhov's *Tri sestry* ("Three Sisters"). The new edition was more "harmonious." It concentrated on the future socialism of Russia. The Prozorova sisters lost the elegiac and dreamy quality with which Chekhov had endowed them as the Theater made their "longing for a better life" into something active and courageous. They were convinced of the "bright future for those who work and cannot become reconciled to the monstrous banality of narrow-minded bourgeois existence." [29] Hence, the finale of the play was different:

The sisters take each other by the hand. Their faces are stern and solemn. They speak little about what is in their hearts. Their eyes talk. Their eyes sparkle, not with tears but with a stubborn belief in the future. And the three sisters here begin to show that they are great and strong. Their faces light up with a special glow, and we see that the modest Prozorova sisters are a magnificent type of Russian womanhood, with its suffering, self-renunciation, and moral strength.[30]

The Moscow Art Theater subjected Chekhov's *Uncle Vanya* to precisely the same sort of "revision" in 1946. M. N. Kedrov, the director, decided to "overcome" Chekhov's "stereotypes": In his work with the actors Kedrov tried to take them as far away as he could from experiences adorned with sorrow, martyrdom, and dreamy passiveness. In his interpretation, Chekhov's characters "tried for the life-asserting principle." They struggle against banality and for the "future liberation of their country's creative powers." The Bolshevik critics considered that the Theater managed to solve the main task connected with ideas. It protested "against the senselessness and gracelessness of life," and it wanted to create a "bright and courageous" spectacle about the struggle of these people for the bright socialist future of their country.

Soviet directors thus enriched the classics: "The productions of *Cyrano de Bergerac* at the Leningrad Komsomol Theater and at the Vakhtangov Theater, . . . the production of *Pygmalion* at the Maly Theater and *Twelfth Night* on the same stage ring loudly with the theme of Soviet humanism." [31]

During and after the war the Soviet theater finally transformed Alexander Ostrovsky, the great nineteenth-century comedy writer, into a "proletarian dramatist" and a Marxist. N. P. Khmelëv, for example, staged Ostrovsky's *Posledniaia zhertva* ("Last Victim") on the idea that the "social theme" of the presentation was the "theme of capital oppressing human life." He considered that in this play Ostrovsky

took and showed the seamy side of society everything that was hidden by the icon lamps and the ringing of the bells. Ostrovsky here reveals all the infinite insolence openly—this is where man is a wolf to man. There is a mad struggle between egoistic interests and passions. Everyone is for himself. Everyone wants to tear out a bigger piece.[32]

With this work, the Moscow Art Theater returned to its overscrupulous realism. The décor, as designed by Dmitriev, was in reddish brown. The merchant's living room was warm, with a tile stove and a table with a cloth on it. It was a quiet corner of the Zamoskvoreche district. One saw the reddening branches of the mountain ash and the gilded cupolas of the churches. The church bells were ringing, and there were warm patches of sunlight on the floor and furniture.

During the war Ostrovsky's patriotic chronicle *Kuz'ma Minin* made its first appearance on the Soviet stage. The theater used heroes from the national militia of 1612 as a means for instilling patriotism in the Soviet home guards. The latter were bound for the front without weapons, to become fodder for German cannon.

The "sociologizing" of Ostrovsky's plays took place in all the Soviet theaters of the time according to the same pattern. Characters who were "socially akin" were emphasized and magnified. They were advanced from secondary and even incidental characters to primary figures. There was a second device connected with this: all the "class-alien" figures were heavily satirized.

Leo Tolstoy's *Redemption* was interpreted in a new way by S. G. Birman at the Leninsk Komsomol Theater. The basic theme of the production was "Tolstoy's mighty protest against the mutilation of man by the monstrous laws of the capitalist world." Fedia Protasov is transformed into a struggler against capitalism, and he prefers death to compromising his moral principles.

The Kamerny Theater staged Maxim Gorky's *Starik* ("Old Man") in 1946. Most of the critics acknowledged that this production was a victory for the Theater, which had appeared on the "highway of realism." In other words, the Theater was completely renouncing its militant theatricality. The acting of P. P. Gaideburov in the title role was hailed by the theater press as one of the highest attainments of the Soviet theater. V. Ermilov, a critic, wrote:

P. Gaideburov creates a figure of broad and generalized significance, and the audience thinks about all the bearers of ignorance who hate mankind because of its aspirations toward good and happiness. Some of them cover themselves with their own papal "infallibility" and teach their flocks to accept humbly any suffering or torment inflicted on them by the executioners of mankind. They say that all people wallow in their sins and need to suffer. Others threaten entire nations with death because the nations do not want to endure torments and oppression. Such "old men" willingly appear as judges of humanity precisely because they refuse to condemn its enemies and exterminators.[33]

The Moscow Art Theater gave Oscar Wilde's *An Ideal Husband* in 1946. The Party critics, in connection with the new anti-Western political trend, considered it quite a positive phenomenon. Wilde's play was flavored with propagandistic tricks and turned out to be quite up-to-date and "anti-Western." The Bolshevik critics found but one fault in the production—the Theater had not reduced Wilde's work to a sharp political farce or a propagandistic caricature.

Somewhere in the vaults of the NKVD there are, perhaps, thirty-six of Mikhail Bulgakov's plays that were never produced. Or perhaps they were burned along with the archives of that department when Hitler was just outside Moscow. There is something profoundly moving and tragic in the fact that Bulgakov's last plays to be staged were *Molière* and *Poslednie dni Pushkina* ("Pushkin's Last Days"). One deals with the great French comedy writer, who was persecuted by the regime, the other with the genius of Russian poetry, who was also persecuted by the regime. The idea of the persecution and death of an author was a personal one for Bulgakov and his last one.

Pushkin's Last Days was produced at the Moscow Art Theater in 1943, five years after Bulgakov's death. The tragedy dealt with the death of Pushkin as a human being and as a victim of Nicholas I's regime and the impotence of the police state to kill Pushkin as a poet. Pushkin never appears on the stage, but instead we see his milieu and all his closest friends and worst enemies, including his wife and her lover D'Anthès. Bulgakov transmitted the isolation of Pushkin in the terrible emptiness around him with great power. The "world" was hostile to him. In the final scene, however, a crowd gathers at Pushkin's house, made up of poor, hungry, downtrodden, and anonymous people who know that the poet has been killed because he had fought for their freedom.

THE TRIUMPH OF "OFFICIAL REALISM"

The timid retreats from "official realism" that were undertaken by the Soviet theater during and after the war are like tiny oases in a tremendous desert. Only relatively speaking are they "innovations" because they paved the way for nothing new in the theater arts. Most of them were only quite modest repetitions of devices found in the pre-Revolutionary Russian theater and in the heyday of the Soviet theater.

Nikolai Okhlopkov and V. Ryndin, a designer, introduced a number of directorial tricks for their production of *Cyrano de Bergerac* at the Vakhtangov Theater, which provided a scandal for the orthodox Soviet press. In one scene a gigantic wooden figure of Roxane was erected on the stage, with a large-scale guitar in its hands. The real Roxane appears in its sounding board and is visible through the strings. She leans on the railing of the balcony and conducts a conversation with Cyrano. In this trick the director saw a "dream come true" and an expression of Cyrano's unsatisfied passion.

Vladimir Soloviëv's *Field Marshal Kutuzov* was also produced at the Vakhtangov Theater. At the climax of the play, Kutuzov has to decide whether to defend Moscow. Suddenly, the theater was filled with loud singing and instrumental music. An invisible and phantomlike choir— the "voice of the nation"—was advising Kutuzov through an oratorio.

Yuri Zavadsky staged M. Svetlov's *The Brandenburg Gate* at the Moscow Soviet Theater about 1946. It used "dynamic décor"—an old invention of Tairov's, which he had applied with his system of curtains in the production of *Salome*. This décor stresses the emotions of the action. The use of an old and alien device was viewed as a "revelation" against the drab, cheerless, and standard naturalism of the time.

Okhlopkov offered V. Gusev's "poem-play" *Synov'ia trëkh rek* ("Sons of Three Rivers"). The work dealt with the fate of three contemporaries —a Russian, a German, and a Frenchman—with posterish enthusiasm. Okhlopkov resorted to the old allegorical devices used in the "mass spectacles" of 1919 through 1921. He also used symbolism, which had been forgotten and condemned. He decided—neither more nor less— to present "man against a background of the universe." The background for the action was the sky. The stage represented part of the earth, which was sometimes changed into a hill pock-marked with shell-holes. The German "heaven" was low, oppressive, and a brownish-black. For the action in France, the sky became green and sparkling. For Soviet Russia, it was infinitely blue:

The stage [the land] moves, and the pictures of the three countries arise in turn. The music changes and the figures change. The drum beats as if you were hearing the mechanical movement of the German army; the footsteps of the German soldiers are heard and the figures of raging Germany take shape. There is a weeping German woman, who has just bade farewell to her husband who is out to conquer the world. And then the figures of France take shape—a young man who tries vainly to tear away from the grip of German soldiers. And then there is Russia. A Russian man looks forward, concentrating; his face is sad and stern, as if he is weighing his responsibility to the world. The orchestra plays a sweeping Russian melody. . . . The scenes again flow into one another. Somewhere in the distance, a Russian woman is waving a kerchief. A thin birch tree lies at her feet, cut down.[34]

The return to the cheap allegories of the "mass spectacles" sometimes became completely naïve and feebly "sensationalistic" in Okhlopkov's production. Transparent devices were used to show the "giants of Soviet industry" and both the Eiffel Tower and the Arch of Triumph in Paris. The skies were illuminated with the "rays" of a transparent sun. There were "heavenly bodies" moving along the backdrop. There were also other effects from the market-place farce and the ."panoramas." This cheapness and naïveté were praised by several critics as a "major and original work of the theater arts." The long quotation above describes the finale of the first act. A Soviet critic termed it a "major and powerful artistic form, perhaps the most powerful of all the presentations about the war." [35]

Perhaps the sole major innovating work was the last presentation at the Kamerny Theater. Tairov produced Chekhov's *Sea Gull* in 1946, and it showed Tairov's great courage as a creator. The play had been produced in the style of so great an organization as the Moscow Art Theater. Tairov used this play to affirm the style of his own Theater, which was directly opposed to naturalism and the "theater of moods."

The Kamerny Theater's posters for the première of its *Sea Gull* called it a "concert presentation." Tairov turned *Sea Gull* into a current discussion of naturalism and other trends in the theater and used Chekhov's play to present his esthetic credo. Tairov greatly abridged the play and removed everything from it that led to the "theater of experiences," the way of life, the "truth of life," and typicality. He laid bare the basic theme of the discussion—the struggle for new art forms. This was the discussion between Treplev as the representative of the new literature and Trigorin as the representative of realism. Treplev says: "You are rigid. You have taken first place in art and you consider only what you yourselves do to be legitimate and genuine. You chase away and stifle everything else."

Tairov doubtlessly used these words against all Soviet "socialist realism." Tairov used Treplev to assert to the Bolsheviks that the theater had a right to new forms, "and if there are none, then it would be better to have nothing." Treplev's sarcastic words were turned against drab Soviet naturalism: "The curtain goes up, and in the light of the evening, in a room with three walls, those great talents—the priests of hallowed art—depict how people eat, drink, make love, walk, and wear their jackets."

Tairov staged the *Sea Gull* as Treplev had dreamed of staging his own play—symbolically. The properties were reduced to a minimum. The indoor action took place against a background of black velvet drapes. All the performers were dressed in black, contemporary costumes. The scene in the garden near the lake was given quite symbolically. The spotlights picked out apparitions, vague silhouettes of birch trees, and woods seen through thin layers of muslin.

This was Tairov's final argument with Soviet naturalism. It was answered by Zavadsky, a bemedaled Party member, who produced the same play at the Moscow Soviet Theater. The answer was wretched, and it defended naturalism militantly. Suffice it to give a short quotation about Zavadsky's presentation in order to understand how old were the views which "medal-bearing" art maintained at the time:

Here are the park of the estate, the woods, the beautiful and "genuine" trees, the sunlight, the moon, and the lake. Everything is the way it is in life, in reality. Birds sing magnificently in different keys, like real birds of various kinds. They fill the entire presentation with their noise. It is hot at noon. . . . The people sit in comfortable armchairs. They have nothing to do, and they lazily toss their lines at one another, chatter, and fall asleep. . . . Outside the window, there is a genuine downpour. It beats on the glass and on the roofs. When the door to the veranda opens to admit a guest, the noise of the rain grows stronger. . . . The people draw out their words, they "eat" them, they swallow them, they minimize them, as in life. The director tears Chekhov's phrases—their music and their melody—to tatters. That is the way people talk in life.[36]

Let us return to the *Sea Gull* at the Kamerny Theater. It was a static "concert presentation." The actors stood in black, mournful costumes against black velvet backdrops. It was a quasi-mystical phenomenon about which the Soviet theater press did not carry a word. The production was a requiem for the Original Theater, a lugubrious concert of the hopeless struggle against naturalism on the stage.

The Moscow Art Theater had produced Konstantin Simonov's *Russian People* back in 1942. The designer (V. Dmitriev) and the directors (M. Knebel and V. Stanitsyn) trotted out the entire arsenal of naturalism. They showed the dark alleys of a squalid town occupied by the Germans, the wheezing and glowing lamps of the soldiers, the dark sky along which the spotlight glided, and an undecipherable jumble of Russian and German speech in the darkness. The finale began with the noise of an explosion. After this, the stage was filled with fragments, dust, and the ruins of a destroyed building.

The Leningrad Soviet Theater staged the same play. The designer was B. Volkov. In the prologue Volkov gave a three-dimensional landscape of a village as seen from the air. It was aglow with fire, and real puffs of black smoke drifted above it, now concealing and now revealing the village. The rooms were shown most naturalistically—with all their filth, rubbish, and neglect.

Chepurin's *People of Stalingrad* was given at the Central Theater of the Red Army. It was directed by Alexei Popov and designed by I. Shifrin. Every means was used to make the Volga countryside and the ruins of Stalingrad photographically exact approximations of lifelike reality. The rest of the directorial work in this presentation was subordinated to precisely the same naturalism. The stage groaned under a wealth of details and "sketches from life." The mass scenes were based on maximum typicality. The costume of every member in the crowd had an infinite number of naturalistic details.

The Pushkin Theater in Leningrad presented I. Shtok's *Victors over the Night* in 1950. The designer, N. Altman, who had once been a leftist artist, staged the presentation on a dolefully naturalistic level. Yablochkov's workshop was a half-dark, damp cellar with dirty and peeling walls. The French *pension* contained quite a number of reddish stage properties.

A. Kron's *Naval Officer* was produced at the Moscow Art Theater. With this presentation the Theater returned to naturalistic decorations "honestly" painted. The roofs were covered with snow from which "genuine" icicles hung down. The entire stage was filled with snow. Snow powdered the characters' overcoats.

After the war, the critics began complaining that the presentations were "drab and boring," that Soviet characters on the stage seemed "gray, boring, schematic, and monolinear." The critics did not, however, breathe a word to the effect that the Bureau of Agitation and Propaganda was responsible for it all. They tried to find a scapegoat outside the Party—the director. After all, the directors staged Soviet plays carelessly. They considered that the depiction of contemporaries did not require study or labor, and this led to a superficial depiction of contemporary themes and to anemic "transitional presentations."

It turned out that the guilt for the "pedestrian naturalism" and the frightful ennui of Soviet presentations did not fall upon the Soviet leaders who had demanded them. The guilty parties were the theater directors "sabotaging" the artistic front. The Central Committee of the Communist Party of the Soviet Union adopted a resolution on August 26, 1946, entitled "On the Repertory of the Dramatic Theaters and Measures for Improving It." The resolution declared that the productions of plays dealing with Soviet life had been deliberately consigned by the directors to second-rate directors who attracted to the presentations weak and inexperienced actors and who did not allot the necessary attention to the artistic staging of the productions in the theaters, as a result of which presentations on contemporary themes have been drab and of low artistic value.[37]

The designers worked coldly and listlessly, like petty functionaries, and the critics asserted that this was another important cause of the complete decline of the Soviet theater. "The actor must perform coldly on a stage where the décor" smacks of "drab and pedestrian naturalism." So wrote E. Kriger, a Bolshevik critic, about the production of Nikolai Pogodin's *Creation of the World* at the Maly Theater in Moscow. Such critics forgot that they themselves had clipped the artists' wings fully a decade earlier.

The betrayal of lofty artistic truth and the production of counterfeit Party-line plays inevitably caused the presentations to be phlegmatic and miserable. Vissarion Belinsky remarked over a century ago: "In art everything that is not true to reality is a lie and reveals not talent but mediocrity." All the demagogic appeals to theater experts to learn from real life were also false and counterfeit. All genuine artists have always drawn their material from life, and life has always enriched them. The Bolsheviks were not calling upon artists to follow life, but rather to follow the official Communist schemes: "Only that artist who looks at our Soviet nation and Soviet person from the viewpoint of Bolshevik Party spirit is able to show the Soviet person truthfully." [38] That is the key to the enigma of drabness. The artist must put Party spectacles between his eyes and life.

Later on, some of the critics even attacked the playwrights. They said that if you read the plays of some Soviet dramatists you will see that the playwright

knows life and the people in his play well, but they are covered with an impenetrable scab of dry and dead words. It is impossible to utter these words; they are official, ordinary, and featureless. . . . The dramatist turns the positive hero from a living person into an automaton who accurately tosses off boring quotations upon any stimulus and sometimes does not even need one. Such a "hero" cannot win the love of the audience, cannot inspire the audience with his own ideas, or convince it that his own ideas and actions are correct.[39]

The people who are called upon, according to the author's concept, to personify the features of the progressive person of our days, appear in these presentations as stilted schemes, abstractions, personifications of all the virtues, and as copybook maxims, but not as people who are real and living.[40]

The critics did not dare to say openly who was guilty of bringing the stage and the drama to such a miserable condition.

LATTER DAY REPRESSIONS AGAINST THE THEATER

Russians were heroic in defending their country against Hitler's hordes. Their courage came only partly from their patriotism and self-renunciation. It also came from their illusions and vain hopes. They believed that Bolshevism was beginning to change for the better. They thought that after the war the country would be given those freedoms that had been suppressed for over twenty years. Their profound faith in the arrival of freedom after the war had a number of causes. For one thing, the national heroes of Russian patriotism were honored once again. For another, the Comintern—the organ of "world revolution"—was liquidated. Again, there was a return to the former Russian military uniform and commissariats were restyled as ministries. There were widespread rumors to the effect that collective farm serfdom would be abolished. There was even supposed to be a project for organizing two new parties —for the workers and peasants. These hopes were encouraged by the fact that the Soviet Union was fighting side by side with the United States, Great Britain, and France. The country was very friendly with the peoples of the West, and the Soviet people believed that the "Great Wall" between the rest of the world and themselves was crumbling. They thought that the victory, won by Russian patriots, would cause the Bolshevik regime to renounce all its terror and intolerance.

The directors and heads of the Soviet theaters were short-sighted. Like all other Russians, they had not realized that "Russian patriotism" was only a temporary and tactical maneuver that Stalinism had used to avoid military destruction. Once victory had been won, the mask was removed and all the promises were broken. All the "freedoms" were suppressed and the Soviet population was shown that nothing had changed. The Bolshevik snake had only cast off its skin, but it could not and would not change its nature. This was the greatest deception ever practiced on the Russian masses.

A new offensive was launched against the "liberties" that had been allowed during the latter part of the war and during the first year afterwards. It heralded the return to prewar theater conditions. Once again, a wave of "purges" and "practical conclusions" swept through the Soviet theater. There were frightening decrees and theater closings. The Com-

munist Party was seeking to uproot the various "freedoms" in the theater. What were they? The Soviet theaters had believed that the war
would be followed by a period of peace with Europe and America. They
had, therefore, taken the liberty of increasing the percentage of Western
plays in their repertories by such dramatists as Pinero, Maugham,
Priestley, Kaufman, and Hart.

But there was to be no "friendship" with Europe and the "bourgeois
world." Did not any of the artistic leaders in the theaters really understand that "friendship" with the West was merely a tactical maneuver,
strictly limited in time? Plays by Western dramatists were acceptable
when the land was groaning under Hitler's attack—American soldiers,
tanks, ships, canned goods, and military equipment were all well and
good at that time, too. Now the comedy was finished, and the Allies
were seized by the collar:

Productions of plays by foreign and bourgeois authors have been, essentially,
a designation of the Soviet stage for propagandizing the reactionary bourgeois
ideology and morality. There has been an effort to poison the consciousness
of Soviet people with an outlook on life that is hostile to Soviet society and
to animate the survivals of capitalism in consciousness and existence.[41]

War and victory brought millions of Soviet soldiers their first direct
contact with the real people of the "bourgeois world." This was a greater
danger to the Communists than any defeat at the front because the cata-
racts were removed from millions of Soviet eyes. They saw the truth
about the West, and the falseness of Bolshevism's prolonged propaganda
against capitalism. The West was no hell, but compared to the West,
the Soviet Union was. The most powerful counterpropaganda had to be
carried on to counteract this new idea of Soviet people, and so once
again the West was declared a mortal enemy—murderous, aggressive,
and imperialistic. Its plays were poison. The anti-American and anti-
Western policy of the Communists began in 1946. The Soviet government hated its Allies who wanted to resist any further Soviet expansion
in Europe. Hence, the Bolshevik libels the very Allies to whom it is
partly indebted for its rescue from Hitler.

Several Soviet dramatists had become sick and tired of the official
boredom in the propaganda plays. They naïvely believed in the advent
of a "second NEP." These people had decided to write plays without
any excessive Communist content. The new wave of persecutions began
against them. They were attacked because they had allowed their plots

to center on love interest, theatricality, light comedy, and sentimentality. They were criticized because they had smiled and shown "erring" Soviet citizens and "Soviet fools."

Kazakov and Mariengof had written a comedy entitled *Zolotoi obruch* ("Golden Hoop"). They were berated because their heroine, who had won two gold medals, was sentimental. Once you get a medal, you must not have any emotions! Alexei Faiko had written *Captain Kostrov*. He had dared to show a Soviet officer who "throughout the play does not know what he wants and does not understand whom he loves." Faiko was also attacked because he had not "developed industrial motifs." Soviet man cannot be depicted unless his attitude to labor is stated.

Gladkov's *Novogodnaia noch* ("New Year's Night") was called a "trivial melodrama." Shkvarkin's *Prokliatoe kafe* ("Cursed Cafe") was a "trivial farce alien to the great theme" that an author must reflect. Nikolai Pogodin and the theater that had staged his *Lodochnitsa* ("The Boatwoman") were accused of having introduced a "ridiculous aquatic pantomime" in the hallowed theme of defending Stalingrad:

Some Soviet playwrights accepted the opinions of the businessmen in the theater about the wishes of the Soviet audience and were attracted toward diverting plays. . . . As a result of the complacency and the indifference of certain circles in the artistic public of our literature and art, there has been an infiltration of harmful "little theories" about nonpolitical qualities, the "right to err," and the right to "relax from the war." Individual workers in the arts have preached these views and considered themselves "independent" of politics. They have begun to create petty productions without any content of ideas.[42]

The final evidence of subversion was that the classics were overshadowing Soviet plays in general. As a result, official statistics reveal that native plays accounted for only 20 percent of the repertory.

As always, the new blow of the Party produced hastily organized meetings. Theater experts were compeled to show unbounded enthusiasm for the new repressions against them. The "coryphaei" of literature experienced their usual raptures. Alexander Fadeyev, for example, wrote:

When we have to discuss literature and art with foreign writers and talk about the decrees adopted by the Central Committee of the All-Union Communist Party, some of them say to us: "Tell us, please, does this not destroy freedom

of creative effort?" And we answer: "A free man tells the truth. And the
man who is least free is the one who is subject to the power of errors. We
possess the great truth of the world and therefore we are the freest artists in
the world. The resolution of the Central Committee not only does not con-
strain our freedom, but it even makes us freer.[43]

The Central Committee of the All-Soviet Communist Party adopted
another resolution on August 14, 1946. This one was called "On the
Magazines *Zvezda* and *Leningrad.*" It was followed by Zhdanov's
pogromlike report, which was published on September 30, 1946.

The resolution of the Central Committee and the speech by Zhdanov
called for persecuting "nonpolitical" figures and Westernizers. This
policy was instantly applied to all the arts. The Kamerny Theater fell
victim to the baiting of "cosmopolitans." Under the pressure of Bolshevism and "Zhdanovism," the Kamerny Theater almost completely renounced its earlier esthetic credo, and it adopted the standard Soviet
naturalism.

Tairov greeted "Zhdanovism" with a new loyalty oath to the Soviet
regime. He called on the theaters to

fight together against the vices that have been so precisely revealed in the
decisions taken by the Central Committee of the All-Union Communist Party
against banality, the lack of political content, and the lack of ideas on the
theatrical front.[44]

Tairov timidly tried to defend his theater's right to some realism
raised somewhat above life. He wrote:

Very frequently, we in the drama and the theater consider that we are showing an ordinary and average person on the stage. Unfortunately, this ordinary
and average person sometimes turns out to be neither ordinary nor average.
Sometimes he is not even human, but rather a scheme somewhat resembling
a person. He is a drab, flat, depersonalized scheme! [45]

Tairov enthusiastically quoted Stanislavsky's condemnation of naturalism and a statement by Gorky that said: "The narrow-minded person
is able to see and accept only the truth of facts. He does not understand
the truth of human aspirations to create facts." Gorky had been canonized, and Tairov hoped to quote him in order to win the right to genuine
realism from "official realism." Tairov observed that all the rest of Soviet
life called for inventions, quests, innovations, and a struggle against
stultifying routine. Why, then, should the Soviet theater not be allowed

to seek new forms, even if only modest ones? [46] Tairov ended his article
the way a sincere Soviet patriot should:

Our common task is to listen to the breathing of the people, to understand
what the people wants from us, to recognize afresh the enormous political role
of art in the present competition between our world and the capitalist world,
and to use all our powers and all our efforts so that the beacon of the new
communist society, created in our country by the Party of Lenin and Stalin,
illuminates the victory for the sake of which we are all living.[47]

This, however, was not enough to save the Kamerny Theater. It was
liquidated three years later, and Tairov himself was hounded and driven
to a premature death.

One of the strongest waves of repression hit the Soviet theater in
1950. The Party gave the signal, and all the newspapers and periodicals
began a frantic persecution and "unmasking" of "cosmopolitans without
kith or kin" and "people without family or tribe." Such persons were
declared to be "bourgeois agents." Cosmopolitanism was a weapon of
present-day "aggressive American imperialism." The "American monop-
olists" wanted to remove national identity and to deprive the people of
its patriotism. What was "cosmopolitanism" in art?

It is the desire to impede the progressive education of the people through
ideas, the desire to undermine national roots and national pride. Uprooted
people are easy to move from their places, and easy for imperialism to sell
into slavery.[48]

It was in this "anticosmopolitan" campaign that the Kamerny Theater
was termed a "manifestation of bourgeois estheticism and cosmopolitan
admiration for the bourgeois 'culture' of the West." It had been the last
representative of the great innovating period in the Soviet theater. The
Party declared publicly that "esthetic formalism serves only as a cloak
for antipatriotic activities." "Estheticism by its nature is against the
people . . . and antinational." [49] In other words, all estheticians were
"enemies of the people." The Soviet theater experts were not seeking
any pure paths to art—they merely wanted to stay alive.

Thus, the Communist Party had turned the free theater into an organ
whose chief purpose was to sing hymns to the Party and its members,
and the thirty-five year history of the Soviet theater was finished. Upon
reviewing that history we can credit it with one indubitable service. It
has made the theater accessible to the broad masses of all the nationali-
ties in Russia. But this accessibility—a purely formal one—is its entire

service. What it has given the broad masses under the guise of the theater belongs to Elena Goncharova's "list of bad deeds" committed by the regime.

In a few respects, Soviet Russia is ahead of many non-Communist countries. It has subsidized the theaters enormously, and state aid has insured the theaters' survival. Normally, this would seem to be a sign that the governmental structure is healthy. But, in addition to supporting the theater, the government has encroached upon freedom of creative endeavor. No other state has ever dared to do this. Bolshevism has changed the theater from an art to an official and bureaucratic establishment. The state machinery directs the creative aspects of the theater. The government has deprived theater experts of their power over the stage. Such artists had been people of great esthetic taste, and, for the most part, they either were not Party members or they stood above the Party. This is the condition of art in a healthy and normal state. Complete hegemony over the arts was given to Party members, however, and most Party members had absolutely no esthetic taste. They were soldiers, petty functionaries, or empty-headed "executives" and "organizers."

No one in the world today will deny that the lofty social ideas in art are above any lack of content. And history may, with some difficulty, justify the militant rejection of formalistic extremes. However, it will never justify the idea that "formalism" includes all quests for means of expression. Such quests form an integral part of any creative endeavor. Nor will history justify the merciless terror, purges, arrests, persecutions, starvings, and physical removal of artists whole sole offense was to have their own outlook on art.

Bolshevism has given the peoples a surrogate for the theater arts—the theater propaganda play. It has turned the stage into a weapon for Party falsehood toward tyrannical political ends—just like the entire Soviet press. The Bolsheviks have wailed for years about "national quality," "art for the masses," and "the theater of socialist society." This is all the crudest and falsest kind of demagogy. What Communism is creating now is not socialism but "Shigalevism." Dostoevsky foresaw this in his *The Possessed,* where Shigalev declares:

Every member of society keeps an eye on everyone else and is obliged to inform. Each one belongs to everyone, and everyone to each one. All are slaves and are equal in their slavery. In extreme cases there are slander and murder, but the main thing is equality.

The words of this great seer of the Russian land about Shigalevism can be applied to what the Bolsheviks have done to the theater:

The first thing is to lower the level of education, science, and talent. A high level of science and talent is accessible only to lofty capabilities; lofty capabilities are not needed. . . . Lofty capabilities . . . have always corrupted more than they have been of use. They are to be banished or punished. Cicero's tongue is to be cut out; Copernicus' eyes gouged out; Shakespeare will be stoned—that's Shigalevism! . . . We shall strangle the genius in his infancy. Everything to a common denominator—complete equality. . . .

NOTES

I. THEATER CONDITIONS IN THE NINETEENTH CENTURY

1. From the speech of A. A. Potekhin.
2. Iuzhin-Sumbatov, *Zapisi: Stat'i: Pis'ma*, p. 317.
3. *Ibid.*, p. 222.
4. Cited in Smirnova, *Vospominaniia*, pp. 78–79.
5. Stanislavskii, *Rabota aktëra nad soboi*, pp. 38–39.
6. *Zapiski aktëra Shchepkina*, p. 142.
7. *Ibid.*, p. 140.
8. Sergei Aksakov, *Raznye sochineniia* (Moscow, 1858), p. 358.
9. A. A. Stakhovich, *Klochki vospominanii* (Moscow, 1904), p. 57.
10. Stanislavskii, *Moia zhizn' v iskusstve*, p. 221.
11. *Ibid.*, pp. 200–201.
12. Vertinskii, *Artist*, No. 27 (1893), p. 46.
13. Iuzhin-Sumbatov, *Zapisi: Stat'i: Pis'ma*, p. 320.
14. A. N. Ostrovskii, "Dopolnitel'nye zapiski o teatral'noi shkole," *Polnoe sobranie sochinenii* (St. Petersburg, Prosveshchenie), IX, 709.
15. "In olden times, teaching was simple. . . . You want to go into the theater, to be an actor? Go to ballet school; an actor must first of all get straightened out. And people are needed there. If not to dance, then to march in processions and to act as page boys. If they make a dancer out of you—fine. But suppose your abilities do not lie in dancing but incline you to the opera or to the drama, let us turn to the training of a singer or actor. If it will not do, go back, play page boys, and then become a property man or a civil service employee." Stanislavskii, *Moia zhizn' v iskusstve*, p. 117.
16. L. Freidkina, "V. I. Nemirovich-Danchenko—teatral'nyi pedagog Filamonii," *Zapiski Gosudarstvennogo Instituta Iskusstva*, p. 101.
17. Stanislavskii, *Moia zhizn' v iskusstve*, pp. 125–27.
18. *Sovetskii teatr*, No. 11 (1936).
19. *Artist*, No. 7 (1890).
20. N. I. Tiraspol'skaia, *Iz proshlogo russkoi stseny*, p. 21.
21. Iuzhin-Sumbatov, *Zapisi: Stat'i: Pis'ma*, p. 228.
22. *Ibid.*, p. 229.
23. Stanislavskii, *Moia zhizn' v iskusstve*, p. 323.
24. *Ibid.*, p. 326.
25. V. A. Nelidov, *Teatral'naia Moskva*, pp. 101–2.
26. *Ibid.*, p. 106.
27. *Ibid.*, pp. 108–9.
28. A. Kugel, "Teatral'nye zametki," *Teatr i iskusstvo*, No. 1 (1900).
29. Stanislavskii, *Moia zhizn' v iskusstve*, pp. 335–36.

30. Nelidov, *Teatral'naia Moskva,* pp. 109–10.

31. *Ibid.,* p. 126.

32. Iuzhin-Sumbatov, *Zapisi: Stat'i: Pis'ma,* p. 29.

33. *Ibid.,* p. 224.

34. A. V. Lunacharskii, "Sotsializm i iskusstvo," *Teatr: Kniga o novom teatre,* p. 31.

II. THE MOSCOW ART THEATER FROM 1898 TO 1917

1. Stanislavskii, *Moia zhizn' v iskusstve,* p. 328.

2. *Ibid.,* p. 334.

3. *Ibid.,* p. 92.

4. *Ibid.,* p. 143.

5. *Ibid.,* pp. 142–43.

6. *Ibid.,* pp. 190–91.

7. *Ibid.,* p. 214.

8. *Ibid.,* p. 231.

9. *Ibid.,* p. 244.

10. Stanislavskii, *Rabota aktëra nad rol'iu.*

11. Stanislavskii, *Moia zhizn' v iskusstve,* p. 263.

12. *Ibid.,* p. 269.

13. *Ibid.,* pp. 281–82.

14. L. Freidkina, "V. I. Nemirovich-Danchenko—teatral'nyi pedagog Filarmonii," *Zapiski Gosudarstvennogo Instituta Teatral'nogo Iskusstva,* p. 96.

15. *Artist,* No. 12 (1891).

16. Freidkina, "V. I. Nemirovich-Danchenko—teatral'nyi pedagog Filarmonii," *Zapiski Gosudarstvennogo Instituta Teatral'nogo Iskusstva,* p. 100.

17. Vladimir Nemirovich-Danchenko, "Griadushchie sily," *Novosti dnia,* Nos. 2–4 (1891).

18. Nelidov, *Teatral'naia Moskva,* p. 298.

19. Stanislavskii, *Moia zhizn' v iskusstve,* pp. 375–76.

20. *Ibid.,* p. 522.

21. *Ibid.,* p. 524.

22. *Ibid.,* p. 523.

23. *Ibid.,* pp. 528–29.

24. *Ibid.,* p. 531. On the same page, Stanislavsky notes incidentally that the engrossment of the actor on the stage creates a more correct relationship between himself and the audience: "The more an actor wants to amuse the public," Stanislavsky writes, "the more the audience sits like a lord, leaning back and away from us, and waiting to be amused without even trying to participate in the action going on. But once the actor ceases to consider the crowd in the auditorium, it begins to reach out in his direction.".

25. *Ibid.,* pp. 536–37.

26. T. Ribo (Théodule Ribot), *Psikhologiia chuvstv* (St. Petersburg, F. Pavlenkov, 1898).

27. The first sketch of the System was a typescript of forty-six pages which Stanislavsky wrote between 1909 and 1912. It was not published, but Stanislavsky acquainted many of the actors at the Moscow Art Theater with his typescript. It has been preserved at the Museum of the Moscow Art Theater, where it bears the number VZh 19, No. 1972.

28. Letter from Stanislavsky to L. Gurevich, December 24, 1909. At the Bakhrushin Central Museum of the Theater, No. 73685/9331.

29. Letter from Stanislavsky to L. Gurevich, May 5, 1909. At the Bakhrushin Central Museum of the Theater, No. 73687/9329.

30. Stanislavskii, *Moia zhizn' v iskusstve*, p. 387.

31. *Ibid.*, p. 494.

32. *Ibid.*, p. 495.

33. *Ibid.*, p. 501.

34. *Ibid.*, p. 502.

35. *Ibid.*, p. 504.

36. *Ibid.*, p. 566.

37. *Ibid.*, pp. 567–68.

38. From a speech by Stanislavsky at a meeting of the Moscow Art Theater Studio personnel on Pozharskaya Street, Moscow, May 5, 1905.

39. Ibsen's plays included: *Hedda Gabler, An Enemy of the People, When We Dead Awaken, The Wild Duck, Pillar of Society, Ghosts, Brand, Rosmersholm,* and *Peer Gynt.* Hauptmann's dramas were: *Die versunkene Glocke, Führmann Henschel, Einsame Menschen,* and *Michael Kramer.*

40. Stanislavskii, *Moia zhizn' v iskusstve*, p. 442.

41. *Ibid.*, p. 444.

42. *Ibid.*, pp. 440–42.

43. *Ibid.*, p. 447.

44. *Ibid.*, p. 486.

45. Introductory speech by V. I. Nemirovich-Danchenko before the beginning of rehearsals for the 1940 production of the *Three Sisters.* (*Ezhegodnik MKhAT*, p. 151.)

46. In 1938, Nemirovich-Danchenko stated: "The art of Chekhov's dramatic works has become so enthroned among us that it would be difficult to name a single rehearsal of any play at all—not just contemporary or Russian classical plays, but even Shakespeare and Sophocles—in which we did not use the creative reserve which had been accumulated from our work with Chekhov." (Cited by N. Volkonskii, "Istoriia ne povtoriaetsia," *Teatral'nyi Al'manakh*, Book 6 [1947], p. 145.)

III. THE GREAT INNOVATORS OF THE PRE-REVOLUTIONARY THEATER

1. Stanislavskii, *Moia zhizn' v iskusstve*, p. 504.

2. *Ibid.*, p. 504.

3. E. Karpof, ed., *Sbornik pamiati V. F. Kommissarzhevskoi*, p. 93.

4. Cited by E. A. Znosko-Borovskii, *Russkii teatr nachala xx. veka*, p. 275.

5. Alexander Tairov, then a ~~young actor working with~~ Meyerhold at the Komisarzhevskaya Theater, wrote: "Meyerhold brought monographs on Botticelli and other artists to the very first rehearsals as, for example, of *Soeur Béatrice*. The pictures corresponded to various situations [in the play], and the performers borrowed their gestures and frequently whole groupings from this art, thus depicting not merely feelings, but even their external manifestation, i.e., the form itself." (Tairov, *Zapiski rezhissëra*, p. 27.)

6. Meyerhold, "Teatr (k istorii i tekhnike)," in *Teatr: Kniga o novom teatre*, p. 157.

7. Meyerhold, "Maks Reingardt" [presumably Max Reinhardt], *Vesy*, June, 1907.

8. Meyerhold, "Teatr (k istorii i tekhnike)," *Teatr: Kniga o novom teatre*, pp. 164–65.

9. *Ibid.*, p. 167.

10. "Motion is the most powerful means of expression in creating a theatrical presentation. The role of motion on the stage is more important than the role of the other elements in the theater. If it were deprived of words, acting attire, footlights, the coulisse, and the playhouse, and retained only the actor and his skillful movements, the theater would still be the theater. The audience learns the thoughts and motives of an actor through his movements, gestures, and grimaces." ("Klass V. E. Meierkhol'da: Tekhnika stsenicheskikh dvizhenii," *Liubov' k trëm apel'sinam*, No. 4/5 [1914], p. 94.)

11. Meyerhold, "Teatr [k istorii i tekhnike]", in *Teatr: Kniga o novom teatre*, p. 176.

12. In Meyerhold's removal of the coulisse, baring of the stage, and in the décor which flew upwards, it is not hard to spot the embryo of that complete baring of the stage to which he came in 1920, on the stage of the First Theater of the R.S.F.S.R. in Moscow. Transferral of the action to the proscenium, and the use of all kinds of devices for baring "the kitchen of the theater" began to be used in the Russian theater—after this production of *Farce*—by other directors as well as by Meyerhold.

13. Kugel, *Teatr i iskusstvo*, 1907.

14. *Ibid.*

15. Meyerhold asserted the three-dimensional quality of the stage for the first time in his "Teatr (k istorii i tekhnike)," *Teatr: Kniga o novom teatre*, p. 169.

16. Meyerhold took the word "grotesque" from painting and sculpture, in which the word denotes ornamental motifs which whimsically combine either natural or fantastic flora, fauna, and people, or portions thereof.

17. Meyerhold, "Balagan," *Liubov' k trëm apel'sinam*, No. 2 (1914), pp. 28–29.

18. *Ibid.*

19. From a chat with Meyerhold entitled "Novye puti" printed in the magazine *Rampa i zhizn'* in 1911. The same magazine published a letter from V. M. Bebutov (Meyerhold's future comrade and a Soviet director in his own

right) that declared: "The grotesque is not a style but an outlook on life in which caricature is evoked by the artist's solipsism and his alienation from the world." This is not a very faithful characterization of Meyerhold himself.

20. Meyerhold, Bebutov, and Aksenov, *Amplua aktëra*, p. 2.

21. A critic has observed, sarcastically: "The device of modernizing Ostrovskii almost beyond recognition was carried to such a degree of perfection, that Kabanova [the conservative and most Russian matriarch in the play] was, for example, quartered in some palazzo, *style moderne*. The action transpired somewhere between heaven and earth. There was not the slightest hint as to the period. The city street was borrowed from fairytales. Instead of costumes, the characters wore fantastic and colorful variations on Russian motifs." (Red'ko, *Teatr i evoliutsiia teatral'nykh form*, p. 71.)

22. "On the streets, the Revolution was already beginning; cries were heard; crowds with flags collected, and the streetcars were not running. It was deserted and frightening—and yet the theater was full." So writes Meyerhold about the première of *Masquerade* in the magazine *Teatr i iskusstvo*.

23. Znosko-Borovskii, *Russkii teatr nachala xx veka*, p. 310.

24. An example of this occurred when Meyerhold, in his quest for new forms, began not only with the poetry of the symbolists but also with the impressionism of the painting at the time. This is just how, in the Soviet theater, he would link his forms with the new literature, and the trends of the suprematists, futurists, cubists, and constructivists in painting.

25. The prospectus of the Old Theater was published in *Starye gody*, a magazine, during 1907. It declared: "The group of persons close to the art of the stage and its literature has set itself the task of presenting in chronological sequence, through a number of historical presentations, not only the history of dramatic literature but also the evolution of stage productions (in connection with the history of dancing and music in the theater), the recreating and incarnating of acting, costuming, and so on." The prospectus also states that the chief task of the Old Theater was purely one of restoration: "Archaeological and historical truth in the production and transmittal of the spirit and character of an age must, in the given case, be of decisive importance." Yet, the Old Theater departed from its "museumlike quality" in its initial phases. It had masters of modern painting stage the presentations.

26. Znosko-Borovskii, *Russkii teatr nachala xx veka*, p. 338.

27. Cited by Nikolai Evreinov, "Teatralizatsiia zhizni," *Teatr kak takovoi*, p. 27.

28. *Ibid.*, p. 98.

29. *Ibid.*, pp. 28–29.

30. *Ibid.*, p. 35.

31. Evreinov, *Teatr dlia sebia*, Preface.

32. Evreinov, "Teatralizatsiia zhizni," *Teatr kak takovoi*, p. 62.

33. *Ibid.*, p. 30.

34. *Ibid.*, p. 100.

35. Evreinov, *Zhizn' iskusstva*, December 24, 1920.

36. Cited in Kazanskii, *Metod teatra*, p. 78.

37. Suffice it to give an incomplete list of Evreinov's studies in order to understand the scope of his contribution to the knowledge of acting. These include: *O muzyke drevne-russkogo kozloglasovaniia* ("On the Music of Ancient Russian Goat-Calling"); *Proiskhozhdenie dramy: Pervobytnaia trage-diia i rol' kozla v istorii eë vozniknoveniia* ("The Origin of the Drama: The Primitive Tragedy and the Role of the Goat in the History of Its Beginnings"), Petrograd, Petropolis, 1921; *Pervobytnaia drama germantsev* ("The Primitive Drama of the Teutons") Petrograd, Poliarnaia Zvezda, 1922; "Teatral'noe masterstvo pravoslavnogo dukhovenstva" ("The Theatrical Mastery of the Orthodox Clergy"), in the book *Teatral'nye novatsii* ("Theatrical Innovations"), Petrograd, 1922; "Taina chërnoi maski" ("The Secret of the Black Mask"), in the anthology *Arena,* published by Vremia, 1923; *Azazel i Dionis* ("Azazel and Dionysos") [on the origin of the stage in connection with the beginnings of the drama among the Semites], Leningrad, Academia, 1924; *Teatr u zhivotnykh* ("The Theater among the Animals"), Leningrad, Kniga, 1924; *Krepostnye aktëry* ("Serf Actors"); *Proiskhozhdenie operetty* ("The Origin of the Operetta"); *Teatr i eshafot* ("The Theater and the Scaffold"); *Skandal, kak faktor razvitiia iskusstva* ("The Scandal as a Factor in the Development of Art"); *Imia bogu moemu—Teatrarkh* ("The Name of My God is Teatrarchus"), etc. He wrote most of these works before the Revolution and published them later.

38. Fëdor Kommissarzhevskii, "Pod filosofii," [introductory article] *Teatral'nye preliudii.*

39. From the review of the production in the magazine *Liubov' k trëm apel'sinam.*

40. "The principle of stripping the body helped us to arrange the costumes for *Sakuntala* with exceptional success. We made them so that they would neither interfere with nor distort the gestures of the actors but, on the contrary, they stressed and emphasized them. They constantly, both at rest and in motion, blended harmoniously with the bodies of the actors and set off the latter in ways suitable to the stage." (Tairov, *Zapiski rezhissëra,* p. 12.)

41. N. Krashenninikov, "Zametki pisatelia," *Rampa i zhizn',* No. 45 (1915).

42. *Rampa i zhizn',* No. 42 (1915).

43. *Ibid.*

44. "And just as the theater needs a poet as its creative assistant, so it needs a composer to make the self-sufficient part of the theater ring out in all the inexhaustible fullness of its many-faceted capabilities, to make the creative palette of the actor have new and stirring colors." (Tairov, *Zapiski rezhissëra,* p. 127.)

45. "A sound must go from *piano* to *forte,* from conversation to singing, from *staccato* to *legato* in accordance with your creative needs. And it need not disturb you that this is unnatural, if only it is justified by the scenic form. Such was the case in those stanzas of *Famira Kifared,* when the voice of

Famira sounded first in speech, then in some singing, and then again in speech." (*Ibid.*, p. 94.) "Every other construction of speech, both logical and psychological, must retire to the background behind the rhythmic structure." (*Ibid.*, p. 91.)

46. "The principle determining the structure of the stage platform is the principle of rhythm. . . . The construction of a maquette or, more exactly, the construction of its floor must be based on the rhythmic conception of any given production." (*Ibid.*, pp. 139, 142.)

47. Tugenkhold, *A. Ekster*, p. 20.

IV. FEBRUARY TO OCTOBER, 1917

1. Tairov, *Proklamatsii khudozhnika*, pp. 4–5.

2. Fëdor Kommissarzhevskii, *Teatr i iskusstvo*, No. 12 (1917).

3. Boris Glagolin, *Teatr i iskusstvo*, No. 28/29 (1917).

4. A. R. Kugel, *Teatr i iskusstvo*, No. 1 (1917).

5. I. Rabinovich, "Na rekakh Vavilonskikh," *Teatr i iskusstvo*, No. 1 (1917)

6. *Russkaia volia*, March 14, 1917.

7. V. Bezpalov, who was in charge of the former Imperial theaters after the February Revolution, has written in his reminiscences: "No one was concerned with questions of art; everyone was interested mainly in the way of life, or rather in its material aspects. Nothing new, responding to the revolution, was under way or even intended." (*Teatry v dni revoliutsii 1917*, p. 38.)

8. *Ibid.*, pp. 36–37.

9. *Ibid.*, p. 37.

10. "[This method] pulverized responsibility *ad infinitum*. . . . In essence, it abolished any responsibility. We have here all the sins of the old regime, painted over—as it were—in red. Here is the old bureaucratic evasion, the old system of "wrangling" which had been established in the days of Speranskii, as if that had to lead to the triumph of the truth. (*Teatr i iskusstvo*, No. 22 [1917].)

11. *Teatr i iskusstvo*, No. 20 (1917).

12. *Ibid.*

13. E. Stark, "Teatral'nyi bol'shevizm," *Obozrenie teatrov*, August 26, 1917.

14. *Teatr i iskusstvo*, No. 26 (1917).

15. *Teatr i iskusstvo*, No. 41 (1917).

16. *Obozrenie teatrov*, May 16, 1917.

17. *Teatr i iskusstvo*, No. 41 (1917).

18. Bolshevik headquarters were at the palace of Kshesinskaia, a ballerina.

19. V. Nabokov, "Revoliutsiia i kul'turnost'," *Rech*, March 15, 1917.

20. B. Nikonov, *Obozrenie teatrov*, July 7, 1917, and August 23, 1917.

21. A. R. Kugel, *Teatr i iskusstvo*, No. 24 (1917).

22. *Obozrenie teatrov*, August 23, 1917.

V. BOLSHEVISM ASSIGNS A ROLE TO THE THEATER

1. Karl Marx and Friedrich Engels, *Sochineniia*, XXV, 258–59.

2. Anatolii Lunacharskii, "Sotsializm i teatr," *Teatr* (*sbornik statei o novom teatre*), St. Petersburg, Shipovnik, 1908.

3. *Ibid.*

4. *Ibid.*

5. *Sbornik dekretov i postanovlenii po narodnomu obrazovaniiu*, Vol. 1 (1919), pp. 140–43.

6. *Ibid.*

7. It was published in *Izvestiia VTsIK*, September 9, 1919.

8. "All theater property (buildings, props), in view of its cultural value, is declared national property."

9. The Central Theater Committee was attached to the People's Commissariat of Enlightenment. It controlled all the theaters, including the state theater, the theaters of the military department, the cooperative theaters, and those belonging to the Soviet of Deputies. All theaters were divided into two categories. The first included theaters "whose cultural value is recognized by the Central Theater Committee and which are in the hands of steady and proven collectives." These theaters were given some autonomy, but the state retained for itself "the right to give the autonomous theaters certain indications of a repertorial nature in order to link them with the popular masses and their socialist ideal," i.e., the Bolsheviks retained ideological control. The other theaters "under the control of private managers or organizations that do not guarantee any elevated ideological level or, finally, of newly constituted troupes having no definite personality, used the national property placed at their disposal," but under brutal artistic and administrative state control. (*Vestnik teatra*, No. 33 [1919].)

10. *Ibid.*

11. Millin de Grandmaison, *La Liberté du théâtre*, Paris, 1794.

12. "We have no assistants. . . . Our intelligentsia, which has been much praised as being outside of the class structure [of society], has shown that its ideas were those of the exploiters. It values its privileges to culture no less than the landed proprietor values his lands." (*Griadushchee*, No. 1 [1919].)

13. History bears witness that this has dragged on over the decades. Because the resistance of an important part of the intelligentsia could not be overcome, many had to be liquidated in the torture chambers of the Cheka and the OGPU.

14. "Let us not deceive ourselves," wrote Lunacharsky in those years, "the nationalization of the theaters is certainly blocked because the state budget has new expenditures."

15. From Lunacharsky's speech, reprinted in *Puti razvitiia teatra*, p. 30.

16. "The attainments of the old culture must be preserved and made the property of all. So it is stated in our party program. Our party program has a shortcoming. Nothing is said therein about a new proletarian art. It talks only

about the need to preserve and disseminate the old art." (Lunacharskii, *Osnovy teatral'noi politiki sovetskoi vlasti*, p. 10.)

17. Lunacharskii, *Teatr i revoliutsiia*, p. 43.

18. *VKP (b) v rezoliutsiiakh i resheniiakh s'ezdov, konferentsii, i plenumov TsK*, Partizdat TsK VKP (b), 1936, part 1, p. 313.

19. V. I. Lenin, *Sochineniia*, XXIV, 409.

20. *VKP (b) v rezoliutsiiakh i resheniiakh*, part 1, p. 522.

21. "Classic artistic realism is the most suitable form for the new theater, but into this suitable form one must . . . pour new content." (Lunacharskii, "Kakoi teatr nam nuzhen?" *Komsomol'skaia pravda*, September 12, 1925.

22. A decree of the People's Commissariat of Enlightenment was published "about the establishment—for the accomplishment of cultural and educational tasks in the theater and in spectacles, of a union for general guidance and observation of the correct staging of all theater work on the territories of the R.S.F.S.R. of the Theater Section of the People's Commissariat of Enlightenment." (*Izvestiia VTsIK*, September 19, 1918.)

23. N. Zograf, *Vakhtangov*, pp. 64–65.

24. Circular of Peian, Nessidor 5, 1794.

25. "Proletarian culture must be a legitimate development of those stores of knowledge which mankind has worked out under the oppression of capitalistic society, landowners' society, and governmental functionaries' society." (Lenin, at the Third Congress of the Komsomol, in Lenin, *Sochineniia*, XXV, 387.)

"We are dealing with a *new* public. They have almost never seen the theater. They must see it and reorient its values. And among those values are the greatest things created by the intelligentsia at the time of its heyday." (Lunacharskii, "Kakoi teatr nam nuzhen?," *Komsomol'skaia pravda*, August 12, 1925.)

"The theaters are entrusted with producing only masterpieces from the culture of various periods and peoples that have preceded us. . . . If . . . the theaters fulfilled this role alone, they would be extremely valuable." (*Ibid.*)

26. Zograf, *Vakhtangov*, p. 65.

27. Five years later, the French surrealists were to preach: "We need revolution to overturn the realm of the bourgeoisie and the realm of reasonableness with it. Moscovites, bring on your innumerable detachments of Asiatics; crush European culture! Let us perish ourselves under the hoofs of the horses from the steppes, if only reason, the death-bearing principle of everything bourgeois, perish with us!" (Lunacharskii, "Predislovie," in Alexander Blok, *Sobranie sochinenii*, I, 45.)

28. "Scythianism was at the basis of the 'Vol'naia Filosofskaia Assotsiatsiia' " (Free Philosophical Association).

29. Belyi, Esenin, Kliuev, among others.

30. Sergei Radlov, the director, wanted to extol the "pedestrian, deserted, ancient cities, the shells of the houses taken apart at Pompeii, and the grass [growing] through the stones." (Sergei Radlov, *Stat'i o theatre*, p. 45.)

31. Lunacharskii, "Teatr budushchego," ~~Teatr: Kniga o novom teatre.~~

32. Shklovskii, *Khod konia*, pp. 23–25.

33. "The attraction of presentations can be compared to an epidemic of the Spanish Disease. It was that widespread. There were five hundred plays which toured the district without interruption." (*Vneshkol'noe obrazovanie*, No. 2/3 [1919], p. 170.)

"No one knows what to do with the dramatic circles. They propagate like Infusoria. Neither the fuel shortage, the food shortage, nor the Entente—nothing—could hold back their development." (Shklovskii, *Khod konia*, p. 59.)

34. Blok relates: "An illiterate peasant came to a private theater library where he had been sent to buy a play. He knew of but a single title: *Ne tak zhivi, kak khóchetsia* ("You Don't Live as You Feel Like Living")." (Blok, *Sobranie sochinenii*, XII, 128.)

35. Osnos, "U istokov sovetskogo teatra," in *Teatral'nyi al'manakh*, Moscow, Book 2 (1946), p. 42.

36. Shklovskii, *Khod konia*, p. 51.

37. "Pedagogy suggests new means of instruction, such as (for example) theatrifying it. The theater is accepted as a potent educational method essentially for the first time in Russia." (Blok, *Sobranie sochinenii*, XII, 170.)

38. Shklovskii, *Khod konia*, pp. 61–62.

39. From the notebooks of Eugene Vakhtangov for 1919.

40. Lunacharskii, *Stat'i o teatre i dramaturgii*, p. 123.

41. Later, the Hermitage Theater staged Schiller's *Kabale und Liebe*, Molière's *Tartuffe*, L. N. Tolstoi's *Pervyi vinokur* ("The First Distiller"), and V. R. Rappoport's *Tsarevna Vesniana* ("Princess Vesniana").

42. "This is how Annenkov felt about Tolstoy's text. He treated it like a scenario and developed it, inserting accordion-players, urban folk-rhymes (*chastushki*), an eccentric individual, acrobats, and so forth. The motivations for these insertions were as follows: the urban folk-rhymes were inserted as songs of the muzhiks, growing tipsy on the 'devil's swill.' The accordion players and the roundelay were also inserted in the drinking scene. The acrobats were presented as devils, i.e., the circus was brought into the play as a depiction of hell. And, finally, the eccentric individual, in a red wig and 'uniform' pants, was brought in without any motivation. He merely—this redhead—happened to be there, and he wandered about hell as if he were a café singer." (Shklovskii, *Khod konia*, pp. 125–27.)

43. "We glorify the Théâtre-Variétés because it reveals the laws governing life, the interweaving of the different rhythms, and the synthesis of speeds. . . . One must destroy any logic in the presentations and allow the unlikely and the ridiculous to prevail upon the stage." (From Marinetti's manifesto.)

44. The reworking of the classics may be justified in approximately these words (which Shklovsky used to review *The First Distiller*): "Of course the text of a work is not something inviolable, as was thought at the end of the nineteenth and at the start of the twentieth century. In any case, we have no right to say that freedom in treating someone else's text is a sign of 'poor

taste.' Why, Goethe reworked Shakespeare, and the Shakespearean text itself consists of layers of all kinds of reworkings, including, perhaps, some by actors." (Shklovskii, *Khod konia*, pp. 127–28.)

45. "The theater must be made mobile in all its elements, including light-weight scenery, and new devices for actors experienced in pantomime and in literary improvisation. These will restore the theater for which any [city] square was as suitable a place as a specially fashioned stage." (*Zhizn' i iskusstvo*, November 16, 1918.)

46. F. Stepun, "V poiskakh geroicheskogo teatra," *Literaturnyi sovremennik*, Munich, No. 1 (1951), p. 71.

47. *Ibid.*, p. 74.

48. *Ibid.*, p. 75.

49. "Downstage, he constructed an interesting combination of geometrically simplified staircases and platforms. He filled in the upstage area with a construction that rose steeply upwards and represented a cubified motif from the ancient theater." (*Ibid.*, p. 76.)

50. *Ibid.*, p. 76.

51. Thus, in Petrograd at the end of 1918, a certain Vadimov opened his "Teatr vechnykh problem" (Theater of Eternal Problems). He staged there, for the most part, plays on sexual topics which had previously been banned by the police. One of the was [Frank] Wedekind's *Frühlings Erwachen*. In 1920, the "Masterskaia revoliutsionnoi miniatury" (Workshop for Revolutionary Miniatures) or TAREM was set up. This wisely combined apotheoses and living pictures of "The Victory of the Commune" with little satires poking malicious fun at the contradictions of the "proletarian state." These theaters were closed by the People's Commissariat of Internal Affairs (the NKVD) as "theater dens for speculating bourgeois bagmen."

52. During the Civil War, Ivanov, a leading Russian symbolist, emigrated and became a Catholic. He had a brilliant career at the Holy See and eventually became a cardinal.

53. *Zhizn' iskusstva*, April 3, 1919.

54. Radlov wrote at the time: "In order to have national or folk comedy, it must be made dependent upon the national theater of past centuries. . . . We understand the charm of what was charming in the past. We are divining its lofty technique, which we wish to acquire afresh, sensing and hearing its living juices, which are ready to be infused into us and to burst through the dam of the deaf and blind nineteenth century." (*Zhizn' iskusstva*, November 12, 1920.)

55.
   "In Vienna, New York, and Rome,
      They esteem my full pocket.
   They esteem my loud name.
   I am the famous Morgan.
   Just now it's my time on the exchange.
      There is no time to waste.
   For precious stones
      I will exchange Negroes."

56. *Zhizn' iskusstva,* November 12, 1920.

57. "The aspiration that is ours alone, types remarkable for their grotesque exaggeration, eccentricity . . . all this must sparkle in twentieth-century folk comedy." (*Zhizn' iskusstva,* November 12, 1920.)

58. *Zhizn' iskusstva,* February 5–8, 1921.

59. *Zhizn' iskusstva,* September 20, 1921.

60. Vladimir Mayakovsky, a Futurist poet, had achieved a *succès de scandale* as early as 1913 with the staging of his tragedy, *Vladimir Maiakovskii.* The poet played himself. His "tragedy" suggested the isolation of the individual who is rebellious, anarchistic, egocentric, and who wishes to blow up the old society. He first went over to the Bolsheviks during the October Revolution, and during the years of War Communism, he was famous for his enormous labors, both as poet and as artist, in making propaganda posters for ROSTA (Russian Telegraph Agency).

61. A. Levinson, a critic, wrote: "The very claim of the Futurists to be the official art of the proletarian masses impresses me as being forced. They have to suit the new boss. That is why they are so crude and vehement." (*Zhizn' iskusstva,* November 21, 1918.)

62. He introduced a "Menshevik-conciliator," who constantly endured defeat in his attempts to make peace between the "clean" and the "unclean" characters.

63. B. Al'pers, *Teatr sotsial'noi maski,* pp. 22–24.

64. "Of the three groups which, according to the director's ideas, have to act in this diversion—the actors on the stage, the proletarian culture movement among the musicians, and the public in the orchestra seats—the public has stopped work. It is much more lively at any other meeting than it is at this one, in its costumes and 'contre-relief' cavalry trousers." (Shklovskii, *Khod konia,* p. 67.)

65. "Verhaeren has written a bad play. The revolutionary theater is being created in haste, and hence the play has been hastily accepted as revolutionary. The text has been changed. There is talk on the stage . . . about the regime of the Soviets. The action has been made contemporary, although I cannot say why the Imperialistic War takes place with spears and shields. In the middle of the second act, it seems, a messenger comes on and reads a dispatch about the losses of the Red Army at Perekop. . . . But because the action has been made contemporary, the dispatch is torn out of its context and the artistic effect which it was supposed to produce is not achieved." (*Ibid.,* p. 66.)

66. Natal'ia Krupskaia, "Postanovka 'Zor' Verkharna," *Pravda,* November 10, 1920.

67. "A theater is a theater, and neither a geographical atlas nor a motion picture. Its one place of action is the stage upon which the presentation is taking place." (Tairov, *Zapiski rezhissëra,* p. 154.)

68. *Ibid.,* p. 152.

69. In her paintings, Alexandra Ekster started from Cézanne and proceeded through cubism. But a thirst for synthesis distinguished her from the

analytic quality, the rejection of decorativeness and "applied use," and the assertion of painting for its own sake maintained by most cubists. All her efforts in painting sought to overcome the limitations of flatness, to enter the third dimension, to crave a comparison betwen painting and sculpture, and to open her paints to existence. Such was her motivation.

70. Mme Ekster not only covered the costumes with different paints, but in one and the same costume, she included materials of different weaves. In her search for rhythm, she created a costume from bits of silk, velvet, and linen, using their textures to create impressions of heaviness, lightness, glitter, or dullness.

71. Thus, for example, B. Al'pers—the Bolshevik dramatic critic and theater theoretician—writes (in his book *Teatr sotsial'noi maski*): "The Moscow Art Theater staged Byron's tragedy *Cain*, which it treated like a religious mystery. The presentation took place to the sounds of organ music, a church choir, and tones of penance. The theater deliberately used all this to stage and solve the problem of fratricide. . . . By pretending indifference to the Revolution, the theaters concealed their enmity towards it."

72. Stanislavskii, *Moia zhizn' v iskusstve*, pp. 676–77.

73. Alexander Blok wanted "to give a number of scenes from the general history of mankind using for this purpose all the means which science, art, and technique can offer today. The scenes ought to act upon the imagination and the will of the audience, to bring its ancestors closer, to show it that it is not alone in the world, that its life is accompanied by the same benedictions and damnations which have accompanied all of mankind. . . . Man must be shown in his entirety, not only with his upward flights, but also with his stumblings so that the picture of human life is given with [all] possible objectivity." (Blok, *Sobranie sochinenii*, XII, 170–71.)

74. As early as April 7, 1919, Lenin signed a resolution of the Defense Council to this effect: "All citizens of the R.S.F.S.R., without distinction as to sex or age, who are theater workers, are subject to registration so that they may be used in their professional capacities for service at the front and in the rear of the Red Army."

75. Osnos, "U istokov sovetskogo teatra," *Teatral'nyi al'manakh*, Book 2, (1946), p. 57.

76. Lunacharskii, "O narodnykh prazdnestvakh," in anthology *Stat'i o teatre i dramaturgii*, p. 166.

77. Examples of this are: *The Taking of the Azov Fortress by Peter the Great; The Glory of Russia;* and *The Taking of the Teok-Tepe Fortress—a Dramatic Presentation in Six Scenes, with Singing, Dancing, Battles, Living Pictures, and Apotheoses.* This last contained a living picture entitled, "Russia, Before Her Kneel the Peoples of Asia . . . [to] the Sound of Bells, Cries of 'Hurrah,' Artillery, Small-Arms Fire, and Music."

78. Examples of this are: *January 9, 1905; October; The Paris Commune; The Overthrow of the Autocracy;* and *Red Army Day.* There were also symbolic and allegorical motifs; such as *The Pantomime of the Great Revolution;*

The Mystery-Play of Liberated Toil; The Sword of Peace; In Favor of a World Commune; and *The Blockade of Russia.*

79. The left part of the oval was given over to a stage platform for the "reds"; the right, for the "whites." Both platforms were most complicated structures with steps, rostrums, and decorative backgrounds.

80. Nikolai Evreinov, "Vziatie Zimnego dvortsa," *Krasnyi militsioner,* 1920.

81. Shklovskii, *Khod konia,* p. 83.

82. *Ibid.,* p. 62.

83. The completely obvious truism that the Soviet amateur theaters were connected with the old dilettantes' theaters has been equated by Bolshevik critics with "counterrevolution" in the theater. When A. A. Gvozdev and A. I. Piotrovskii dared to assert, in their *Istoriia evropeiskogo teatra* ("History of the European Theater") that amateur art existed in the ancient world, under feudalism, and among the bourgeoisie, they were branded by "Marxist critics" as "agents of the class enemy." When Alexander Afinogenov, the playwright, spoke at the special meeting of RAPP in 1931, he explained Piotrovsky's subversion in this way: "The church mysteries are all described in suspicious detail, . . . [and so are] all the entrances and exits of the tsars. . . . When Piotrovsky talks about the circuses in Rome, he calls them colossal and enormous amateur festivals—'amateur' because no professional actors took part in them. This is how they hide the political sense of a 'theory' which castrates the real class content and idea of the phenomenon. According to this theory, a demonstration is nothing more than a theatrified play." This is "an attempt by militant [philosophical] idealism to take revenge while pretending to be discussing the ancient theater."

84. There were outstanding amateur theaters in very many plants and factories before the Revolution. Suffice it to mention such examples as the ones at the Bargunin Paper Factory, the Chekush Metal Works, and the Office for Preparing State Papers in St. Petersburg, the Rechkin Plant, the Thornton Textile Works, "Educational Institutions House," on the Obvodnyi Canal, etc.

85. "I have seen several places which acted plays that had been printed in 1885 as supplements to the magazine *Niva!* These supplements are still alive. Apparently they had been seized when the estates of the landed proprietors were destroyed. Also, several people turned up who had saved them and now gave them up willy-nilly." (*Puti razvitiia teatra,* p. 314.)

86. Lunacharskii, "O krest'ianskom teatre," cited in its revised form as printed in the anthology, *Stat'i o teatre i dramaturgii,* p. 160.

87. From Meshcheriakov's speech, in *Puti razvitiia teatra,* p. 311.

88. *Ibid.,* p. 314.

89. Speech of Krongauz, cited in *Puti razvitiia teatra.*

90. Lunacharskii, "O krest'ianskom teatre," *Stat'i o teatre.*

91. An example of this was the presentation of *Tsar Iudeiskii* ("King of the Jews"), a play by the Grand Duke Konstantin Konstantinovich. This was staged by the amateur theater at the Factory for Preparing State Signs in December of 1919.

92. V. I. Lenin, *Sochineniia,* XXIV, 276.

93. "The worker and the Communist find it easier to depict the workers' way of life than the way of life portrayed by any representative of the tsarist aristocracy or the bourgeoisie." (*Puti razvitiia teatra,* p. 289.)

94. From Edel'son's speech at the theater conference of 1927.

95. *Puti razvitiia teatra,* p. 297.

96. *Ibid.,* pp. 283–84.

97. *Proletarskaia kul'tura,* No. 3 (1918).

98. *Proletarskaia revoliutsiia,* No. 13/14 (1930).

99. From the speech of the worker-poet, Samobytnik-Mashirin, at the First All-Russian Conference of the Proletarian Culture Movement.

100. Pletnëv, "Na idealogicheskom fronte," *Pravda,* No. 2171 (1922).

101. *Gudki,* Moscow, No. 1 (1919).

102. *Gorn,* No. 1 (1919).

103. *Ibid.*

104. *Ibid.*

105. V. Kerzhentsev, *Tvorcheskii teatr,* Moscow, GIZ, 1923, p. 81.

106. The first "proletarian poets" were almost maniacally obsessed with capital letters. Apparently this was the only means which they possessed to give their verses significance. Ilia Sadofiev, for instance, wrote: "The solemn bells of the Socialist Revolution are ringing; a New World is arising; the Great Artist-Proletariat is creating a New Culture. . . . And soon we shall be on the Sunny Path of Proletarian Culture."

107. A. A. Mgebrov, *Zhizn' v teatre,* II, 324.

108. Kirillov wrote verses entitled "Zheleznyi Messiia" ("The Iron Messiah").

109. On August 31, 1918, *Zari griadushchego* ("Dawns of the Future"), a book of verses by Vladimir Kirillov, was staged.

110. Mgebrov himself tells how one aged proletarian woman understood the simple words "proletarians unite!" rather than any symbols: "She approached us . . . with her very pleasant old face beneath a white shawl. Her wrinkled face was as small as an apple. Her eyes were glittering, and she had a big smile. 'Ah,' she told us, 'how good it is, how darned well you sing. . . . And you make it come out well. . . . "Fly away and unite," [*Proletaite soediniactes*'] . . . fly away and unite. . . . It's impossible to say how good it is.'" (Mgebrov, *Zhizn' v teatre,* II, 399.) [The old woman has apparently confused the word *proletaite,* meaning "fly away," with the word *proletarii,* meaning "proletarians."—EHL.]

111. *Ibid.,* II, 430.

112. *Ibid.,* II, 488.

113. *Gorn,* No. 1 (1919).

114. Lunacharskii, "Teatr budushchego," in *Teatr: Kniga o novom teatre.*

115. Interview given by Leonid Andreev to the magazine *Rampa i zhizn'* in 1915.

116. Osip M. Brik, "Drenazh iskusstva," *Iskusstvo kommuny,* No. 1 (1918).

117. Brik, "Drenazh iskusstva," *Iskusstvo kommuny,* No. 1 (1918).

118. Brik wrote: "The proletariat, as a creative class, does not dare to sink into contemplation; it does not dare to give itself up to esthetic experiences [born of] contemplation in the old days."

119. In *Iskusstvo kommuny,* No. 7.

120. *LEF,* No. 1 (1923).

121. Lunacharskii, "Kakoi teatr nam nuzhen," *Komsomol'skaia pravda,* Dec. 8, 1925.

122. *LEF,* No. 1 (1923).

VI. ACCEPTABLE SUBJECTS FOR ACCEPTABLE PLAYS

1. "Finally, I would want us to say decisively that we demand Shakespeare, Goethe, Sophocles, and Molière, great tears and great laughter, and not in homeopathic doses but the real thing. . . . We must stand firmly for the classics; we must not yield our positions to the modernistic trends knocking at the gates." (Aleksandr Blok, "O repertuare kommunal'nykh i gosudarstvennykh teatrov," in anthology, *Repertuar,* Petrograd and Moscow, 1919.)

2. "The historical moment is genuinely exceptional, and art will be reviewed in the twenty-fifth century, but not by any of the Communist comrades." (Blok, "Doklad v kollegii otvetstvennykh rabotnikov teatral'nogo otdela," *Sobranie sochinenii,* XII, 129–30.)

3. "The stage of the contemporary theater needs a hero in the broad and true significance of the idea; it must show people the ideal essence. . . . Our times need a heroic theater, a theater whose goal would be to idealize the personality." (Maksim Gor'kii, "Trudnyi vopros," in anthology *Dela i dni Bolshogo dramaticheskogo teatra,* Petrograd, No. 1 [1919], p. 7.)

4. World history is shown in original Soviet dramas "as the legitimate movement by mankind towards the realm of freedom and justice to whose threshoid the peoples of the Soviet land have come as a result of the October Revolution. . . . The Soviet drama shows world history as the great pedigree of Soviet society." (Osnos, *Sovetskaia istoricheskaia dramaturgiia,* p. 19.)

5. Vasilii Kamenskii, *Sten'ka Razin,* a collective presentation in nine scenes. Published in 1919. Staged at the Theater of the Revolution in 1924.

6. Y. Iur'in, *Spoloshnyi zyk (Sten'ka Razin),* a folk tragedy, Petrograd and Moscow, Gosudarstvennoe izdatel'stvo, 1920.

7. V. Vol'kenshtein, *Spartak,* a tragedy, Gosudarstvennoe izdatel'stvo, 1921. Staged in 1923 at the Theater of the Revolution in Moscow.

8. "The performance was good but, alas, the task was unnecessary." (*Zrelishcha,* No. 54 [1923], p. 6.) "A noble, dry, and national spectacle . . . but it has no breath of revolution, no pathos of the struggle. It hits wide of the mark." (*Teatr i muzyka,* No. 32 [1923], p. 15.)

9. *Zagmuk* was staged at the Maly Theater in 1925.

10. *Puti razvitiia teatra,* pp. 148–49.

11. Osnos, *Sovetskaia istoricheskaia dramaturgiia,* p. 39.

12. Mstislavskii's *On Blood* was a hit at the Vakhtangov Theater in Moscow during 1927. The Soviet people began to feel a profound nostalgia for the Russia which had been destroyed and would never return. People began to understand that, instead of the realm of freedom, they had stumbled into a prison stronghold from which there was no hope of flight or liberation. This melancholy and greedy interest in their own "pre-prison" past, in the life of the country during its "freedom" was akin to the general craving of the masses for everything historical and foreign—everything which lay outside the terrible reality of Bolshevism and beyond the frontier posts of the Soviet Union.

13. Osnos, *Sovetskaia istoricheskaia dramaturgiia,* p. 84.

14. *Izvestiia TsIK,* January 15, 1926.

15. "The revolution as a historical action of the masses is, in general, weakly depicted and takes place for the most part offstage." (*Sovremennyi teatr,* No. 48 [1928], p. 77.)

16. Pugachëv was favored with the attention of Stalin himself, who said: "We Bolsheviks have always been interested in such historical personalities as Bolotnikov, Razin, Pugachëv, and so on. We see in the appearance of such persons a reflection of the spontaneous indignation on the part of the oppressed classes, a reflection of the spontaneous rebellion by the peasantry against feudal oppression." (Stalin, *Beseda s nemetskim pisatelem Emilem Liudvigom,* Moscow, 1933, p. 8.)

17. " 'To jump into Russia, to win it over to me completely, to set up new judges everywhere' (for, in his words, there was much injustice in the existing ones), 'and to ascend the throne of the Great Prince and Sovereign! I myself, he said, 'do not want to rule.' " (Aleksandr Pushkin, *Sochineniia,* Berlin, Petropolis, pp. 1230–31.)

18. I. B. Sobolev, "Pugachëvshchina," *Novyi zritel',* No. 39 (1925), p. 6.

19. Nemirovich-Danchenko, despite his defense of *Pugachëv's Rebellion,* later noticed its duality—its mixture of objectivity with bias—and said that, on the one hand, the play "frequently attains brilliant objectivity," while, on the other, it is saturated with a "revolutionary mood."

20. S. Durylin, "Khudozhestvennyi teatr v 1917–1945 godakh," *Teatral'nyi al'manakh,* Book 3 (1946), p. 83.

21. The Bolshevik critics noted a split within Trenëv: "On the one hand, he tried to dissolve the character of Pugachëv within the popular milieu surrounding him, while, on the other, he sensed the need to show him as a hero. The protagonist cracked from these unresolved contradictions, and the tragedy disintegrated into individual scenes." (*Izvestiia TsIK,* September 20, 1925.)

22. D. I. Pisarev, *Sochineniia,* F. Pavlenkov's edition (1894), IV, 523.

23. Pushkin, *Polnoe sobranie sochinenii,* Academia (1937), IX, 30.

24. One of the workers who attended the première wrote: "The actors on the stage, the storm on the stage, and I in the auditorium were blended into a single and indivisible whole. We were in with the play. There was no *Storm*

without me and no me without the *Storm.*" (*Zhizn' iskusstva,* No. 22 [1926].)

25. Konstantin Trenëv, *Liubov' Iarovaia,* album edition, p. 5.

26. Trenëv, "Moia rabota nad *Liubov'iu Iarovoi.*"

27. N. Abalkin, *Sistema Stanislavskogo i sovetskii teatr,* p. 205.

28. P. K——tsev, "Bronepoezd 14–69," *Pravda,* November 18, 1927.

29. The première of this play took place at the Moscow Art Theater on October 5, 1926.

30. *"The Days of the Turbins.* You know that this play has been condemned by the Marxist critics almost unanimously, but none of them has noticed one very special feature in it. . . . The play has an element in it which is not just musty but really putrid: it stinks of Russian chauvinism. . . . it contrasts the virtuous and honest Russian cadets with Petliura's bands." ("Sostoianie teatral'noi kritiki i eë zadach," in anthology *Puti razvitiia teatra,* p. 365.)

31. The Bolsheviks remarked maliciously that *The Days of the Turbins* "attracts the bourgeoisie, which goes to the Moscow Art Theater in order to lament Stanislavsky in a waistcoat and to mourn for itself." (From the speech by Mandel'shtam, the representative of the Department of Agitation and Propaganda of the CPSU, at the theater meeting in 1927, *Puti razvitiia teatra,* p. 77.)

32. Lunacharsky accused the Repertorial Committee at the 1927 meeting on theater questions called by the Central Committee of the CPSU. "He said: 'You allowed it. And when the theater had spent thousands on it and the actors had worked into their roles, you decided to take off the play which had gotten this far thanks to your . . . collusion!' What could we say? That our Repertorial Committee . . . allowed *The Days of the Turbins* up until the dress rehearsal and did not stop it before there had been enormous expenditures? The morale of the theater would have suffered a blow which would have had worldwide significance. Could we have said that, despite all this, we were forced to correct the error of the Repertorial Committee in regard to the state and the theater? . . . The People's Commissariat of Enlightenment had a discussion about it and decided that, these being the circumstances, *The Days of the Turbins* must be allowed. We decided to greet the play with certain criticisms." (*Puti razvitiia teatra,* p. 232.)

33. Cited from the reminiscences of L. M. Leonidov in *Sovetskoe iskusstvo,* December 21, 1939.

34. N. M. Gorchakov, *Rezhisserskie uroki K. S. Stanislavskogo,* p. 465.

35. *Ibid.,* p. 481.

36. N. Lebedev, *Shchukin—aktër kino,* Moscow, Goskinoizdat, 1944, p. 28.

37. B. Zakhava, "Vyvody iz opyta," in anthology *Rabota rezhissëra nad sovetskoi p'esoi,* p. 48.

38. Lenin wrote: "The peasant, as a toiler, inclines towards Bolshevism and prefers the dictatorship of the workers to the dictatorship of the bourgeoisie. The peasant, as a seller of grain, inclines towards the bourgeoisie

and towards free trade, i.e., back to the old, 'customary,' and 'primordial' capitalism." (Lenin, *Sochineniia,* XXIV, 314.)

39. *Puti razvitiia teatra,* pp. 35–36.

40. *Ibid.,* p. 151.

41. *Ibid.,* p. 72.

42. "One of these plays cost us twelve or thirteen thousand rubles. It was a hundred percent useful ideologically, but it was taken off at the end of· the year because only twenty or twenty-five people had come to see it." (*Puti razvitiia teatra,* pp. 89–90.)

43. "We are telling the theaters: 'Support our ideology,' and we not only fail to help them but even try to obtain some kind of income from them. But you know this is impossible; under these conditions, there is a great danger that the theaters will be [ideologically] useful—and shut down." (Lunacharskii, quoted in *Puti razvitiia teatra,* p. 234.)

44. According to official Soviet statistics, Soviet plays occupied only from fifteen to nineteen percent of the repertory during the years from 1924 to 1927.

VII. HEYDAY

1. Vsevolod Meyerhold's Theater was located on Sadovaya-Triumfalnaya Street in Moscow (the old Zon Operetta Building). Its name was changed five times in six years: It opened on October 7, 1920, as the First Theater of the R.S.F.S.R.; when it staged *Le Cocu magnifique* in 1922, it was called The Theater of the Actor—the Free Workshop of Vsevolod Meyerhold Attached to the State Supreme Theater Workshops; towards the autumn of 1922, the title became the Theater of the State Institute of the Theater Arts—Vsevolod Meyerhold's Workshop (the "Experimental and Heroic Theater" of Ferdinandov and Bebutov had autonomous status within this last mentioned "Workshop"); from 1923 through the winter of 1926, the Theater was called Vsevolod Meyerhold's Theater; the title was changed for the last time at the beginning of December, 1926 when it became the Vsevolod Meyerhold State Theater, which it remained until its liquidation by the Soviet government in 1937.

2. Reducing a passion to an absurdity typifies all Crommelynck's work. In *Tripes d'or,* for example, he has a miser eat his own gold so that it will not be stolen from him and will always remain at the bottom of his maw.

3. Boris Arbatov, a theoretician of "constructivism," characterized the origin of the movement in the depictive arts as follows: "The radical and leading part of the new intelligentsia, the so-called technical intelligentsia (to be precise), has been educated in the industrial centers of the present, and has been permeated with the positivism of the natural sciences, and has become 'Americanized'. . . . At the time when the former intelligentsia was soaring above the clouds in its 'pure ideology', the new and 'urbanized' intelligentsia was concentrating on the material world, the world of things. These

people wanted most to build and to construct. . . . The constructivists have declared that the basis and even the sole aim of art is the creative treatment . . . of materials. . . ." (B. Arbatov, "Iskusstvo i klassy," in a collection of his articles, *Sotsiologicheskaia poetika*, 1929, pp. 39–40.)

4. Chuzhak in *LEF*, No. 1 (1923), p. 30.

5. Meyerhold appends the following note to clarify the term "volitional": "The term 'feeling' is used in its technical and scientific sense, without any narrow-minded or sentimental connotations. The same is true of the term 'volitional.' This is done to separate the exposition from both acting of the 'internal' school (without systematic narcotics) and from the method of 'experience' (the hypnotic training of the imagination). The first of these methods coerces the will with an artificial incitement of feelings which have been enfeebled beforehand; the second coerces feeling through the hypnotic extraction of the will which has been enfeebled beforehand. Both of them must therefore be rejected as worthless and dangerous to healthy people subject to their influence. The term 'mimetic' indicates all the motions which arise on the periphery of the actor's body, as well as the motion of the actor himself within space."

6. Meyerhold, Bebutov, and Aksenov, *Amplua aktëra*, pp. 3–4.

7. Meyerhold, "Akter bubushchego," *Ermitazh*, No. 1 (1922), pp. 9–10.

8. In striving to show the "model human being of the new era" on the stage, Meyerhold wanted to expand "biomechanics." He wanted to proceed from the physical training of the actor to a new and purely Soviet conception of the beautiful.

9. "The bourgeois actor of the nineteenth century was basically a 'talking creature.' Meyerhold compared him to a phonograph which played different records every day. Today he uses a text by Pushkin; tomorrow, by Surguchev. In Meyerhold's words: 'With a change only in his wig and costume, an actor talks, talks, and only talks—now one text and now another.'" (Kryzhitskii, *Rezhissërskie portrety*, p. 32.)

10. Biological plasticity is a trait of every child and of every animal. There is but one difference: the child loses this natural and innate talent in the process of growing up, an adult becomes more and more stable with each passing year, while animals retain it even into old age.

11. "By the slogan 'Back to Ostrovsky,' I wanted to talk about the need for returning to the realistic theater which was socially psychological and . . . socially interesting. This was a suitable technique of expression." (A. V. Lunacharskii, *Stat'i o teatre i dramaturgii*, p. 125.)

12. The posters read: "Author of the presentation: Meyerhold."

13. A. A. Gvozdev, *Teatr imeni Meierkhol'da*, p. 27.

14. S. Mokul'skii, "Pereotsenka traditsii," in the anthology *Teatralnyi Oktiabr'*, pp. 21–22.

15. Gvozdev, *Teatr imeni Meierkhol'da*, p. 14.

16. The première of *The Give-Us-Europe Trust* took place on June 15, 1924; that of *Bubus the Teacher* on January 29, 1925.

17. Maxim Gorky wheedled permission out of Stalin to allow Erdman's *The Suicide* to be staged. The Theater had been working on the comedy for a year and a half when the permission was withdrawn at the insistence of L. M. Kaganovich. The play showed a Soviet philistine who has decided to close out his accounts with life. He assiduously spreads rumors to the effect that his suicide is inevitable. He engenders a whole movement among the "former people" burdened by Bolshevism. "Former people" make pilgrimages to see him and they implore him to use his suicide as an act against the Soviet regime. The main theme running through the work is that a Soviet individual can really feel free from the nightmare of Soviet realities only when he has chosen death. Shortly after *The Suicide* was forbidden, Erdman was arrested and disappeared into Soviet jails.

18. After the première, the Bolshevik critics wrote: "Meyerhold's dramatic concept of *The Inspector-General* is an interpretation not of Nikolai Gogol's five-act comedy as it was understood by the academic theater of the nineteenth century, but rather of Gogol's work in general. Gogol's 'truth and malice' is firmly preserved, but his wish 'to collect everything bad in Russia into one heap' was expanded very greatly and was revealed through the rich resources of contemporary directing." (R. Pel'she, in *Novyi zritel'*, December 21, 1926.)

19. "Thus, in the episode of the Procession, Khlestakov asks: 'What is the name of this fish?' The chorus of petty functionaries answers: 'Salt cod, sir.' This is repeated several times and is worked out by the chorus like a musical phrase. The voice of Zemlianika stands out from the chorus as he finishes the choral phrase with a flattering nasal sound to his 'Salt cod, sir.' And when the famous letter is read at the end of the play, the chorus of guests and petty functionaries grows nervous, making noise, laughs, gloats maliciously, exults, and cackles. Then, they grow quiet. The exertions—the noise, the outcries, and the laughter—start afresh. Such a use of the vocal retorts and gestures to build with can be compared only to the playing of various instruments in a large symphony orchestra." (Gvozdev, *Teatr imeni Meierkhol'da*, p. 53.)

20. Here Meyerhold was at last carrying out plans which he had thought of as early as 1908. He wanted "to introduce correctives in the treatment of the characters" according to "the original traits of the characters in *Inspector-General* as given by [Dmitri] Merezhkovskii in his penetrating article, 'Gogol' i chërt' ('Gogol and the Devil')." Meyerhold wanted to create a production of Gogol's comedy based on a realism "which does not flee life but overcomes it because it looks for only the symbol of the thing in its mystical essence." (Meyerhold, *O teatre*, pp. 98–99.)

21. Vl. Filippov, "Otechestvennaia klassika na russkoi stsene," *Teatral'nyi al'manakh*, Book 2 (1946), p. 141.

22. "Of course, they do have points of contact, but for the most part, the truth of life is false in art and, *vice versa,* the truth of art is false in life." (Tairov, *Zapiski rezhissëra*, p. 18.)

23. "Hence, it aspires to create scenic conditions to confirm this deceit;

hence, the odor of sour cabbage-soup and of a kitchen emanates from the depths of the stage on which a complete apartment has been erected." (*Ibid.*, p. 18.)

24. Vakhtangov wrote: "I am thinking about Meyerhold. . . . What a brilliant director—the greatest of any who have existed or exist [now]. Every production of his is a new theater. Every production of his could begin a new trend. . . . Meyerhold has given roots to the theaters of the future. . . . All the theaters of the very near future will be constructed and based on what Meyerhold has foreseen." (Evgenii Vakhtangov, *Dnevnik*, March 26, 1921.)

25. Tairov, *Zapiski rezhissëra*, p. 20.

26. *Ibid.*, pp. 20–21.

27. *Ibid.*, pp. 22–23.

28. *Ibid.*, p. 31.

29. Experience is based on the truth of life. In Tairov's words: "It leads the actor away from art and makes him a sick man, a neurotic, who delves into his own soul with the stubbornness of a maniac and performs home-grown psychological experiments on it." (*Ibid.*, p. 71.)

30. *Ibid.*, p. 75.

31. *Ibid.*, p. 76.

32. "Music! That was the thing, that was the magic whose rhythms enabled us to experience the sweet process of creating scenic synthesis, of perceiving in ourselves the first timid beatings of emotional form." (*Ibid.*, p. 31.)

33. "It has long since been time to stop looking at the literary material that the theater uses as if it were merely words to express this thought or that idea. . . . It is time, finally, to regard it the same way we do pantomime material: from the viewpoint of its rhythm, harmonies, and phonetic potentialities." (*Ibid.*, p. 125.)

34. "The body of the contemporary actor is no Stradivarius, but rather a three-stringed balalaika on which one can still play—although not without mistakes—'tipcat' or a 'lifelike motif' resembling it, but which turns out to be completely incapable of transmitting more complex harmonies." (Ibid., p. 85.)

35. It was no accident that Alexandra Ekster and Georgy Yakulov were the favorite artists of this Theater for a number of years. Ekster experimented greatly with "moving" colors and textures, while Yakulov used a furiously whirling "capriccio" of forms. They were both the most "musical" designers within the Soviet theater.

36. Tairov, *Zapiski rezhissëra*, p. 125.

37. Tairov considered it a compliment when a critic described Alice Koonen's debut at his theater with the phrase: "She danced through her role."

38. Lunacharsky always nursed an antipathy to the Kamerny Theater, but even he was conquered by this *Phèdre*. He wrote: "The presentation created an amazing impression of beauty. It is a monumental presentation; it is technically the first major step to an authentic monumental quality. Its vocal power, its clearness, the greatness of its gestures, and the brightness of its

colors should be viewed not in the darkish auditorium of the Kamerny Theater, but in a huge theater for three or four thousand people." (Lunacharskii, *Teatr i revoliutsiia*.)

39. This, of course, was nothing new in the Russian theater. Suffice it to recall Ibsen's *Hedda Gabler* at the Komisarzhevskaya Theater as produced by Meyerhold.

40. The Kamerny Theater existed for twenty years, but staged only one pre-Soviet Russian play (Ostrovsky's *Storm*). During this whole period, it produced only six plays on Soviet themes: *Bagrovyi ostrov* ("The Purple Island") by Mikhail Bulgakov in 1928; *Natalia Tarpova* by S. Semenov in 1929; *Liniia ognia* ("Line of Fire") by Nikolai Nikitin in 1930; *Pateticheskaia Sonata* ("Pathétique Sonata") by N. Kulish in 1931; *Neizvestnye soldaty* ("Unknown Soldiers") by Leonid Pervomaisky in 1932, and *Optimisticheskaia tragediia* ("An Optimistic Tragedy") by Vsevolod Vishnevsky in 1934.

41. Lunacharskii, *Iskusstvo trudiashchikhsia*, 1926.

42. Lunacharsky also wrote: "We in Russia have already seen many attempts to depict not only the dances of toil, but even those of the machine. However, no one else has succeeded in giving the sculptured and metallic rhythms of sound and motion so well as Tairov has in the first, the third, and the fourth scenes of the play. . . . [He shows] powerful bodies and exhausted bodies, the magnificent scope of collective work, the music of the machines, and all the conversations in which you constantly sense the collective more than the individual. These outbursts of gaiety, wrath, exhaustion, and joy in toil are all a purely proletarian reality, taken from the factory, from the chief determinant for proletarian existence." (*Ibid.*)

43. Let it be understood that this was organized by the Bolsheviks. Lunacharsky praised Tairov for the propagandistic caricatures: "No less interesting is Tairov's depiction of the bourgeoisie. . . . And, perhaps, the public, which was interested in this caricature of the ruling class, did not completely understand how accurate it was. . . . I personally returned from abroad only two or three days ago, and I was struck by the truthfulness and the profound realism of the depiction." (*Ibid.*)

44. *Plot of the Equals* was staged under the general artistic supervision of Tairov. The directors were N. Sokolovsky and M. Fedosimov. Ryndin designed the sets and Natalya Glan was the choreographer.

45. "As for the purely external technique of acting, I was genuinely struck by many major achievements. A new actor has indubitably appeared among us, although *actor* as yet retains its small initial letter. . . . He can sing a line or two from a song; he can recite verses, utter the text of a role, play a piano, a violin, or soccer, dance the fox trot, turn somersaults, stand or walk on his hands, and play tragedy and vaudeville. . . . Of course a clown's somersaults are better, and a *danseuse* from the *corps de ballet* dances better, and a pianist or a violinist in the orchestra plays better than the new actor can.

"Nevertheless, the variety of his behavior, the preparations of his body, his voice, and his entire depictive apparatus that are so essential to the theater, have recently achieved major results, just as the productions have." (Stanislavskii, *Moia zhizn' v iskusstve,* pp. 706–7.)

46. "The new art used the fine principles of sculpture, architecture, and constructivism on the stage. There is scarcely a theater which has not based itself upon them. The grotesque has been used to the utmost in the décor, the costumes, and the productions—and sometimes with great artistic talent. The bold sketches of make-up using gold and silver hair, Futuristic painting of the face, glued cut-outs, and the sculptured details are accepted with indifference and are repeated by almost all the theaters." (*Ibid.,* pp. 704–5.)

47. "Why, despite the success of the external quests and the success of the new theater, does it seem too old and worn out? Why is it so boring? Is it not because the contemporary new art is merely *stylish* rather than eternal? Or could it be that the external potentialities of production are extraordinarily limited and hence condemned to repetition which, of course, becomes a plague? . . . Is it not because the external, although its form is penetrating and beautiful, cannot come alive on the stage all by itself?" (*Ibid.,* pp. 707–8.)

48. The tasks that the new theater gives the actors are monstrous: In the first place, they must justify a form of production that is bold, and sharp to the point of artistic impudence. . . . Secondly, they must learn to revise the old dramatists in terms of new values, and free the theater completely from the poet and to replace his work not only externally but spiritually as well with the creations of the actors themselves. . . . Thirdly, they must tear the heart out of a work and . . . bring in bias or a utilitarian aim. . . . The creative feeling flees and is replaced by the coarsest, oldest, most naïve and forgotten stereotypes that the theater now passes off as its new declamation, plastic quality, and acting." (*Ibid.,* pp. 709–10.)

49. *Ibid.,* p. 695.

50. "Not having any new dramas, they have gone after the old classics. They talked about great people and great feelings, and began to tailor them according to a new measure. . . . The innovators have taken the new external form for a renewal of the internal substance." (*Ibid.,* p. 696.)

51. But what is most important—the life of the spirit—"will not be reached by . . . acrobatics, constructivism, blatant luxury, rich productions, painted posters, Futuristic boldness, simplicity (even to the complete removal of the scenery), false noses, circles painted on the faces, or by any of the other external devices and exaggerated effects . . . usually justified by the stylish word 'grotesque.' " (*Ibid.,* p. 695.)

52. "If the theater is able to fulfill utilitarian tasks as well as artistic ones, its usefulness increases and we can only rejoice at its variety. But it would be a mistake to confuse bias or generally useful knowledge—which people sometimes try to assert is the basis of the new theater—with its creative essence. This last comes from the spirit of a work of art. One must not take a mere spectacle, a sermon, or a piece of propaganda for genuine art." (*Ibid.,* p. 698.)

53. Stanislavsky remarked sarcastically that in those times: "Many people have decided that experience and psychology are typical attributes of bour-

geois art, and proletarian art must be based on the physical training of the actor alone." (*Ibid.*, p. 699.)

54. That Stanislavsky was using this production to dispute and to rebuke Meyerhold was shown by several of the stenographic reports containing his remarks at the rehearsals of *Burning Heart:*

"They say and write that acting skill is some kind of 'biomechanics.' Let us leave this assertion upon the conscience of whoever undertakes charlatanism in art. I have heard much about Meyerhold's *The Forest!* But what was it I heard? 'Ah, what gigantic steps he has in Act I!' 'Ah, he has them shooting at learned doves!' 'Ah, how wonderfully they play the waltz on the harmonica!' . . .

"This is disastrous for the work of the actors and the director. There is not a word about a person! There is not an exclamation about the sense, the idea of the play! . . .

"It is like a 'road of flowers' in the Chinese theater. . . . I must confess that I was astounded. Such a market-place farce in the middle of Moscow! Lentovsky in his time staged bold farces at the Hermitage. But Lentovsky could hardly allow himself to draw and quarter Ostrovsky, who is a Russian classic." (Cited from N. M. Gorchakov, *Rezhisserskie uroki Stanislavskogo,* pp. 308–9.)

55. "An authentic 'fact,' and genuine reality do not exist on the stage. Reality is not art. This last, by its very nature, needs artistic invention, which means first of all the work of an author. The actor's task and his creative technique consist in transforming the invented play into artistic and scenic fact!" (Stanislavskii, *Rabota aktëra nad soboi,* p. 113.)

56. For Stanislavsky no comic device was possible without major justification from within. "Ostrovsky's plot itself has many elements of folk presentations. . . . That is why I have used some risky settings for the first and second acts. But can we really draw back from the realism or the logic of events? Or from the idea of the play? In my opinion, we cannot. If our efforts to strengthen the expressiveness of certain scenes are not justified by the performances of the actors, I shall remove all our effective settings. . . . Our task is to struggle for realism. We must not give the 'stylish' critics the slightest reason to think that we have even the slightest sympathy for Meyerhold's tricks." (Cited from N. M. Gorchakov, *Rezhisserskie uroki Stanislavskogo,* p. 309.)

57. The following ought not to be taken literally, but it is worth mentioning: "Stanislavsky insisted on eliminating the 'nightmare' episode from the presentation. In this episode, a mystic figure sits for a quarter of an hour at the foot of Alexei Turbin's bed and conducts a reactionary conversation with the man about the fate of Russia. . . . Stanislavsky decided to stage the scene in the secondary school—the flight and destruction of the White Guards—as the central theme of the play. He demanded that Bulgakov have Col. Alexei Turbin strongly and directly assert, before his death, the uselessness and the senselessness of the White struggle against Bolshevism. Stanislav-

sky made the author rewrite the last scene, which was needed for drawing conclusions. He insisted that the scene show the genuine 'differentiation' of the Whites' ideas, so that Captain Myshlaevsky might be seen as a Russian officer who breaks with the Whites, acknowledges his mistakes, and is prepared to work honestly in the future for the good of his new, socialistic homeland." (*Ibid.*, pp. 317–18.)

58. The première of *La Folle journée; ou, Le Mariage de Figaro* by Beaumarchais took place on April 28, 1927. The designer was Golovin.

59. "Let us now look for its national and revolutionary element. Of course, we cannot point out any national uprising in the plot. There is, however, a nation that, a few years later, would arm itself with pikes, guns, or simply pitchforks and axes, and would take the Bastille and destroy the castles of the French feudal aristocrats. Beaumarchais has given the people a different weapon, but a very powerful one, in laughter. He is no longer afraid of those age-old enemies, the artistocrats. He laughs at them. He senses that feudal rights are dying out and changing into a hollow sound. And to get rid of them more quickly, he tries to discredit them in every way possible, to push them into a pond and into something 'which is a little deeper and a little filthier.' " (Gorchakov, *Rezhisserskie uroki Stanislavskogo*, p. 356.)

60. Kerzhentsev, a Communist who later became chief of the Committee on Theater Affairs, spoke on the subject at the theater conference called by the Central Committee of the CPSU in 1927. He attributed to *Le Mariage de Figaro* precisely what it did not have: "For the Tenth Anniversary [of the Bolshevik upheaval] *Le Mariage de Figaro* was staged. This is a social comedy about the eighteenth-century revolution that everyone has heard of. And what did the Moscow Art Theater do? It created friendly and peaceful relationships betwen the very pleasant aristocrats and the servants. . . . There was a total banishment of everything pointed which had been put in by Beaumarchais himself. . . . The aristocrats here were very sweet. Such pleasant lords, with pleasant servants! . . . an interpretation which contradicted what Beaumarchais had written in the eighteenth century." (*Puti razvitiia teatra*, pp. 96–97.)

61. Gorchakov, *Rezhisserskie uroki Stanislavskogo*, p. 460.

62. With *Armored Train 14–69* the Moscow Art Theater showed that it could dress a Soviet subject in the truth of life. And that marks the beginning of a most common dream among Soviet dramatists: to be accepted for production by the Moscow Art Theater and to have the assistance of that Theater in turning their own lies into the truth. Even Lunacharsky wrote about this: "That was the time when most of the dramatists who had been going along the path of revolution and really aspiring to create artistic dress for their ideas as soon as possible began to dream that Stanislavsky and his experts would select the theater clothes for this literary and artistic flesh." (Lunacharskii, *Sbornik statei o teatre i dramaturgii*, p. 88.)

63. Vsevolod Ivanov, "O 'Bronepoezde,' " *Teatr i dramaturgiia*, No. 3 (1924), p. 28.

64. Gorchakov, *Rezhisserskie uroki Stanislavskogo*, p. 485. An even stronger "politicalization" of the acting in the Moscow Art Theater can be found in the following statement, which apparently was made by Stanislavsky: "Today you and I have touched on an important problem, how the actor must create an artistic character that he considers socially and politically negative. Almost always, people who are hostile to progress have the negative characteristics of human individualism. . . . It is natural that an actor seems to love the positive characters, especially those who are his contemporaries. But this is only partially justified. . . . The contemporary artist must have extremely strong feelings of civic responsibility in his work and in his creative skill. He must kill the enemy of society, of the governmental structure, and of his country through art. This is as respectable as incarnating a positive hero of today with all one's strength. . . . To kill the enemy does not mean, in the language of the stage and of acting skill, to show one's own negative attitude as an actor toward that enemy. After all, none of the playgoers will ever think that you, a Soviet actor, are justifying this enemy of society, this negative character, in your heart.

"But to kill the enemy means to show the audience his entire inner nature . . . to show the audience all the viciousness of his psychology. This is an enormous and a respectable task for the artist of today." (*Ibid.*, pp. 487–88.)

65. Stanislavsky bitterly recalled his first attempts to introduce the System in the Moscow Art Theater: "For years on end, at all the rehearsals, in all the rooms, corridors, and lavatories, upon meeting people on the street, I preached my new [System], and I had no success at all. . . . They went away and whispered to each other: 'Why on earth has he begun to act worse? It was much better with no theory!' "

"A wall grew between the troupe and myself. I spent years on end with strained relations between the artists and myself. . . . I reproached them for their stagnation, their blind routine, their ingratitude, their faithlessness, their treason, and—with great bitterness—I continued my search." (Stanislavskii, *Moia zhizn' v iskusstve*, pp. 615–16.)

66. *Ibid.*, p. 623. This intimate theater studio was a prototype of the "chamber theaters" that have, in our days, sprung up over Europe (especially in Germany) and that are highly popular with audiences. These theaters have warmth, spontaneous contact between the actor and the audience, and sincerity. They have abandoned the intolerable shouting and racing about by the actors on the stage.

67. "I remember the feeling of unusually light gaiety, tender emotion, and gratitude which we all experienced when the curtains closed for the final time and we stood looking at each other. Many of us had tears in our eyes. . . . The performers had been first-class; they were permeated with the flavor of the story about the 'boiling teakettle.' Everything was unusual on the evening that *The Cricket on the Hearth* was first played. From the moment when we entered the small, cozy premises, sat down comfortably in our places, the lights went out in the hall, the teakettle began to whistle on the red coals

in the corner, and the voice of Sushkevich (the Reader) was heard, we entered a special world." (Smirnova, *Vospominaniia*, pp. 379–80.)

68. "On the Crimean coast of the Black Sea, a few miles from the city of Eupatoria, I bought part of a magnificently sandy beach and gave it over to the use of the Studio. Common buildings, a small inn, a stable, a barn, storehouses for the agricultural implements—along with the seeds, the produce, and the supplies—a cellar for keeping meat and milk were all built with the receipts of presentations in Eupatoria. Every member of the Studio had to use his own hands in building a house which he himself would have to live in during rainy weather.

"For two or three years, the Studio group would summer in Eupatoria. There, under the guidance of Sulerzhitsky, they would live a primitive life. . . . They themselves cut and carted the stones for building the public houses. . . . A tarpaulin served as a roof. Skins and textile curtains replaced the door and window frames. The floor was the sandy soil of the beach itself. Inside the house, the furnishings were comfortable—stone seats and couches covered over with pillows (as in medieval castles). There were textile panels along the wall, and Chinese lanterns illuminated the rooms in the evenings. The entire company of primitive people walked around half-naked, and soon were bronzed by the sun. . . . Each of the Studio members had his own duty. One was cook; another, coachman; a third, the domestic; a fourth, boatman, etc." (Stanislavskii, *Moia zhizn' v iskusstve*, pp. 630–31.)

69. Letter from Vakhtangov to A. I. Chaban, the actor, August 3, 1917.

70. "Fabrics, impregnated with the ages, fabrics having their own life and history. They possess silence and order, severity and stability, cruelty and inflexibility. Tapestries and portraits, faded and severe, gaze down from the walls. . . . The heavy divans, the tables, the massive armchairs, and the heirlooms all guard the silence. The only reason that they stand motionless instead of dying from shame because of the one degenerate in the Rosmer family is that they are wooden and cannot move." (Vakhtangov, in his notes "Chego mne khotelos' by dostignut' v *Rosmerskhol'me*," 1918.)

71. "The twisted columns of the palace, the spots of gold, the rust-spotted bronzes, gave an impression of Erik's decline and impending death. There were huge columns of straight lines, broken off here and there; these were fragments not of a palace, but of a prison—a prison for Erik. There was a labyrinth of passages, stairways, and small platforms that created a distinct deception in relation to perspectives." (P. Markov, "Sulerzhitskii—Vakhtangov—Chekhov," in anthology *Moskovskii Khudozhestvennyi Teatr—Vtoroi*, Moscow, 1925, p. 143.

72. "Naturalism is not art, for the artist can add nothing of his own to the naturalistic 'work of art' since his task is limited to knowing how to copy 'nature' more or less accurately." (Mikhail Chekhov, *Put' aktëra*, p. 55.)

73. "I never thought out the details and always was a mere observer of whatever emerged by itself from the perception of the whole. This future

whole engendered all the details and particles; it neither dried up nor vanished regardless of how long the revelation process took. . . .

"How much those actors suffer who underestimate this astonishing emotion, which is so needed in all aspects of their work. All the details and particles of the role are divided into thousands of bits and appear in chaotic disorder unless they are strengthened by the feeling of a single whole." (*Ibid.*, pp. 30–31.)

74. *Ibid.*, p. 148.

75. "The sincere creative state consists in the actor's experiencing inspiration. . . . His personality is handed over to inspiration, and he himself is infatuated with the results of its actions on his own personality. . . . It is often said that creative work must come from the depths of the artist's subconscious life, but this is possible only if the artist knows how to approach himself objectively without mingling his own coarse ideas and crude emotions with the work of his subconscious." (*Ibid.*, pp. 166–67.)

76. On the dichotomy in the actor between the "loftier I" and the "baser I," Chekhov wrote: "There is a constant struggle within a talented person between his loftier and his baser 'I.' Each of them seeks to dominate the other. In ordinary life, the victor is the baser, with all its ambition, passions, and egoistic agitation. But the other 'I' conquers (and must conquer) in the creative process. . . . A kind of dichotomy begins with the consciousness: the loftier becomes an inspirer, and the baser an agent and performer. It is interesting that the loftier one itself then also becomes an agent. . . . It observes from the side and directs the baser, guiding it and sympathizing with the imaginary passions and joys of the character. This is expressed by the fact that the actor suffers, weeps, rejoices, and laughs on the stage while personally he remains untouched by these emotions. Bad actors take pride in the fact that they sometimes succeed in 'experiencing' something on the stage to such an extent that they forget themselves! . . . And how tired they are after performing! Actors who play with a split consciousness and with 'sympathy' instead of with personal emotions do not tire. On the contrary, they experience a surge of new powers, which makes them healthy and stronger. These new forces flow out of the loftier 'I,' along with inspiration." (Chekhov, "Zhizn' i vstrechi," *Novyi zhurnal*, New York [1944], IX, 29–30.)

77. "Everything that you do on the stage is new and unexpected for you yourself because the loftier 'I' is improvising. . . . It appears in your acting only when your ordinary 'I' crosses the bounds of 'common sense' and tries to take an active part in the creative process." (Chekhov, *O tekhnike aktëra*, p. 166.)

78. "All the emotions, wishes, and experiences of your stage character, regardless of how strong they might be, are unrealistic. On the stage, regardless of how sincere and profound they might be, they will never become part of your daily spiritual life. . . . Actors' efforts to utilize personal emotions which they have not worked out completely but which 'are not yet forgotten' lead to sad results. The stage character becomes shallow and unesthetic. He

quickly uses stereotypes, and utilizes nothing new, original, or individual."
(*Ibid.,* pp. 160–61.)

79. "The actor who knows how to evaluate atmosphere seeks it in his daily life. Every landscape, every street, house, or room has its own special atmosphere for him. He goes differently into a library, a hospital, a cathedral, a noisy restaurant, a hotel, or a museum. . . . The same landscape 'sounds' differently to him in the quiet atmosphere of a spring morning, in a tempest, and in a thunderstorm. . . . Have you ever noticed that your motions, speech, posture, thoughts, emotions, and moods change involuntarily when you are gripped by a powerful atmosphere? And if you do not resist it, its influence over you grows. As in life, so on the stage. . . . In a materialistic and rationalistic era such as our own, people are ashamed of their emotions and are afraid to have them. They do not easily admit that atmosphere in an independently existing area of emotion. . . . A work of art must have a spirit, and that spirit is the atmosphere. The great mission of the actor is to save the spirit of the theater and thus to save the future theater from becoming mechanical." (*Ibid.,* pp. 34–35, 43.)

80. Chekhov, "Zhizn' i vstrechi," *Novyi zhurnal,* New York (1944), IX, 15.

81. B. Al'pers, a critic, wrote about Chekhov's portrayal of Erik XIV: "In this presentation on the boards of the Studio, which were not separated by anything from the auditorium, the racing about and shouting was not done by an actor in theater costume. The playing of Chekhov was not art in the ordinary sense. The palpitating human body, with its bared nerves and muscles, its open and pulsating heart, the thoughts running through the convolutions of its brain, beat convulsively before the astonished auditorium. . . . The next step must be to eliminate art, to remove the actor from the stage as a conscious creator and master, to change him into a maenad with a shattered conscience, and to draw the crowd into a circle of ecstasy." (Al'pers, *Teatr sotsial'noi maski,* pp. 20–21.)

82. "We are confused by the meaning, and the intellectual content of speech. We follow *what* a man tells us, and do not notice *how* his speech sounds. Having temporarily renounced the content of the words heard, we begin to grasp their sound and also the gesture which the sound implies. The artistry of speech is determined by sound and gesture and not by meaning. The sense of the words which the actor utters on the stage does not belong to him but to the author, and does not constitute the actor's service. But the way in which he pronounces these words, and how they sound from the stage—these comprise his service and determine his value as an artist. In working on *Hamlet,* we tried to experience the gestures of the words and their sounds, and for this we chose motions to suit the words and phrases. . . . A burning creative emotion and a volitional impulse flared up, and only after this did we utter the words and the phrases. Gestures passed over into words and sounded within them." (Chekhov, "Zhizn' i vstrechi," *Novyi zhurnal,* pp. 17–18.)

83. Vakhtangov, "Zapiski: Iz besedy s uchenikami," *Krasnaia nov,* Book 10 (1933), p. 218.

84. B. Zakhava, an actor and director at Vakhtangov's theater and a student of Vakhtangov's, points out the division between Vakhtangov's school and Stanislavsky's: "In the theater of psychological naturalism, emotion is frequently important all by itself, with no regard to its cause. It is an aim in itself. Here, with Vakhtangov, we have emotion because of the main content. They justify a character morally; we work out a character in relation to his social attitude. They blend completely with the character . . . we firmly guide the active part of the actor's personality . . . along with his entire life and conduct as the character. . . . Their main criterion of quality is a feeling of truth-to-life; ours is that the ideas and emotions of the artist reveal the social essence of the character. Their truth-to-life is in natural form; ours is in theatrical form. . . . The passive attitude of the natural and psychological theater to reality was changed by Vakhtangov to an active and creative attitude." (B. Zakhava, "Tvorcheskii metod teatra Vakhtangova," *Sovetskii teatr,* No. 129 [1931].)

Zakhava's statement clearly reveals the "sociologizing" and the terminology of dialectical materialism which he has used to tailor the teachings of Vakhtangov. These have nothing in common with the great mentor. The situation arose because Zakhava was defending the Vakhtangov Theater to the Bolsheviks after it have been accused of being (philosophically) "idealistic" and alienated from Soviet realities.

85. "Life on the stage acquires a convincing power equal to that of real life when all its elements are organically connected and form a single whole. . . . Theater life is something like a new reality brought about by the creative will of the given theater. . . . A special theater world takes shape that is different from the world of real life." (Zakhava, *Vakhtangov i ego studiia,* 1930, pp. 131–32.)

86. *Ibid.,* p. 132.

87. "K. S. Stanislavsky discovered a number of laws for the theater arts that are embedded in the biological nature of creative acting. We are correct in admitting that these lines are generally obligatory. . . ." Vakhtangov's theater considered the following laws from the Stanislavsky System as immutable: 1) To concentrate on the stage; 2) To disperse one's muscular energy along one's muscles in a suitable fashion; 3) To seek one's relationship to the milieu; 4) To move without worrying about emotions; 5) To motivate (scenically 'to justify') one's conduct on the stage; 6) To depend upon one's partner; 7) To reveal the inner meaning of the author's text (the 'subtext'); 8) To create a biography and the conditions of the character's life; 9) To act not for one's own sakè but for one's partner's; 10) To struggle against stereotypes." (Zakhava, "Tvorcheskii metod teatra Vakhtangova," *Sovetskii teatr,* No. 12 [1931].)

88. "Let the audience not forget for even a second that it is in a theater.

Let it constantly realize that the actor is an expert playing a role. Let the theater possess no 'mood' at all, for the theater must have joy alone. Participation in the gay festival of art and in the skill of the theater artists is the source of the audience's gaiety." (Zakhava, *Vakhtangov i ego studiia,* p. 119.)

89. "Vakhtangov taught that every idea demands its own form of expression and it developed that every play demanded its own form of theatrical staging, a form belonging to just that play. . . . Secondly, the form of the given presentation must satisfy contemporary needs. It must include a contemporary attitude on the part of the theater to the material that the author has given it. Thirdly, and finally, the form of every presentation must belong naturally, organically, and unalienably to the given theater. It must display the artistic personality of the theater collective and the degree of its development." (*Ibid.*)

90. *Ibid.,* pp. 140–41.

91. "We saw a constructivist platform which changed for every given situation in accordance with the locale. Little platforms were combined; so were curtains, and such gymnastic contrivances as rings, trapezes, and ladders. This gave every new scene a spatial effect. 'We must create a universal studio on the stage,' Vakhtangov demanded, 'in which any theatrical exercises which are easy and fitting would be used for enacting any play.'" (N. Zograf, *Vakhtangov,* p. 136.)

92. The apparently spontaneous and "haphazard" improvising attitude towards the text was really the result of long and precise work by Vakhtangov with the actors.

VIII. THE FULL-SCALE ATTACK ON THE THEATER

1. G. Kryzhitskii, *Rezhisserskie portrety,* p. 85.

2. Lunacharskii, *Stat'i o teatre i dramaturgii,* p. 53.

3. At the theater session which the Central Committee of the CPSU held in 1927, Lunacharsky had to defend even the Moscow Art Theater from the attacks of the Party members and to cry out: "It is not true that Stanislavsky is the ideologist of the merchantry because his father once made brocade!" (*Puti razvitiia teatra,* p. 231.)

4. *Ibid.,* pp. 213–14.

5. Lunacharskii, *Sbornik statei o teatre i dramaturgii,* p. 121.

6. "There was a time when the press repressed them more strongly and they went underground. They have now recovered, are organizing gradually, and are proceeding to struggle along our entire cultural front. The press, the schools, and literature are permeated with . . . definite anti-Soviet tendencies. . . . Is it really chance that a firmly united group of general managers and honored artists from the academic theaters turns up for a meeting of our theater workers at the People's Commissariat of Enlightenment, and that this solid wall has been advanced against the censorship at first, then against the Party's interference in theater work, and has gone so far as to

call for freedom of speech within the theater and for 'art for its own sake'? I consider that this is closely connected with all the groups that are observed among us in science, the schools, literature, and the theater. This is an offensive, the activity of anti-Soviet groups." (From the speech by Makarian, of the Department of Agitation and Propaganda, at the 1927 conference. Cited from *Puti razvitiia teatra*, pp. 164–65.)

7. From the speech by Pletnëv, *Ibid.*, p. 192.

8. From the speech by Leopol'd Averbakh, *Ibid.*, pp. 221–22.

9. "The complex process of developing a socialist economy and the relative growth of activity by the bourgeois groups in the country cannot fail to lead to efforts by these last to exercise their influence on ideology, particularly on the theater. That influence is here manifested either through a return to the decadent and socially unhealthy phenomena of the pre-Revolutionary theater, or through the birth of new phenomena that directly or indirectly reflect these opinions, which the proletariat finds alien and hostile." (From the Resolution adopted after Knorin's speech, *Ibid.*, p. 478.)

10. The classics could lead the Soviet theater "to surrender its positions under the pretext that the theater was self-sufficient, and under the pressure of elements alien to the proletariat." (*Ibid.*, p. 480.)

11. "The class war in the theater . . . is an important factor that must be considered in planning and accomplishing theater policy. Having intensified the struggle against all kinds of attempts to influence the theater in bourgeois and petty-bourgeois ways, the organs carrying out theater policy must, along with the critics, in every way possible further the growth, the consolidation, and the extension of theater enterprises that are directed at creating productions of art in response to the aims of the proletariat." (*Ibid.*, p. 478.)

12. *Ibid.*, p. 486.

13. *Ibid.*

14. "I have always indicated that 90 percent of the influence on the Main Repertorial Committee comes from the People's Commissariat of Enlightenment and—if you like—from the Commissar himself. The workers of the Main Repertorial Committee remember, and can perhaps present, a mass of notes by Comrade Lunacharsky in regard to the way various plays were staged. When a theater decides to stage some anti-Soviet play, and the Main Repertorial Committee forbids or excludes separate scenes, the theater appeals to the board of the People's Commissariat of Enlightenment for a review, and the play is permitted. We therefore consider that we must free ourselves from the self-sufficient influence of the People's Commissariat of Enlightenment or of the Commissar personally." (From the speech by Makarian, *Ibid.*, pp. 168–69.)

15. *Ibid.*, p. 487.

16. Resolutions of the conference about criticism, cited in *Ibid.*, pp. 503–4.

17. *Ibid.*

18. A certain Zorin represented the Department of Agitation and Propaganda. He openly told the meeting that it must be concerned mostly with

"a practical method for taking possession of the Moscow Art Theater . . . and its ideology, for penetrating the Moscow Art Theater, and for placing its experts at the service of the proletariat." (*Ibid.,* p. 217.)

19. Let us introduce here a description of the "terrors" perpetrated by the tsarist censorship, according to the Soviet editions of pre-Soviet authors: "The writer was forced to show his manuscripts to the censors lest even a single truthful word be printed against the regime of the time. . . . They literally stopped up the author's mouth. He spent all his great powers in the daily war with the censors, which went on from year to year, and he used all kinds of tricks to get by the obstacles that the censorship had placed in his way and to let his militant verses reach his readers. The censors hounded him to the very grave." (N. A. Nekrasov, *Stikhotvoreniia,* Moscow, 1936.)

Here is an account, however, of censorship in the age of Nicholas I. Faddei Bulgarin's *O tsenzure v Rossii* ("On Censorship in Russia") came out in 1826. In a note, he characterized the period in these words: "Considered as insulting the faith were: the Russian *heaven;* a *heavenly* look; an *angelic* smile; the *divine* Plato; for *God's* sake; by *God; God* gave him; he was *eternally* filled with the wish, and so on. . . . Any article containing the word government, minister, governor, or director was forbidden beforehand, regardless of its contents! But artificial periphrases could avoid the forbidden words and could frequently make the censors pass impermissible things. The censorship did not allow the public to learn about national happenings, parades, fireworks, outdoor parties, examinations in private or public institutions, or natural phenomena without approval. . . . Who would have thought that the Ministry of Internal Affairs would have to approve any mention of a drought, a hailstorm, or a hurricane? . . . In stories, one must not say the groom *kissed* his bride, but rather he looked at her; instead of he *loved* her, one must say he wanted to marry, and so on."

20. One can judge the number of censors from the workers' numbers that are used in issuing imprimaturs.

21. Eugene Bermont, a journalist, mentions the fact that *Glavit* had to approve initials to be engraved on a billfold beforehand. *Krokodil,* No. 14 (1939).

22. The Soviet censorship buried such outstanding works as Nikolai Erdman's *Suicide* and *Zasedanie o smekhe* ("Meeting about Laugher"), Mikhail Bulgakov's *Beg* ("The Race"), Valentine Katayev's *Univermag* ("The Department Store"), Alexander Korneichuk's *Bankir* ("The Banker"), S. E. Krzhizhanovsky's *Pisannaia torba* ("The New Toy"), and many others.

23. "For dialectical philosophy, nothing is permanent, unconditional, and sacred. On everything and in everything, it sees an inevitable decline, which nothing, except for the uninterrupted process of inception and elimination, can withstand." Friedrich Engels, *Sochineniia K. Marksa i F. Engel'sa,* p. 638.

24. "The theater, a synthetic art, is a form of consciousness, and unless you explain what kind and whose consciousness the theater expresses in the specific form of stage characters, you are bound to lapse into [philosoph-

ically] idealistic formalism." (S. Podol'skii, "Za leninskii etap teatrovedeniia," *Sovetskii teatr,* No. 4 [1932], p. 25.)

"At all times, art has been one of the social and ideological superstructures that plays an active role in the struggle of the classes. It is used by the governing classes to create a society in accord with their own interests. The classes opposed to the historical development of the ruling class also resort to it as a weapon of the class struggle." (Lunacharskii, "Sotsialisticheskii realizm," *Sovetskii teatr,* No. 2/3 [1933], p. 3.)

25. Lunacharskii, "Mysli o dialekticheskom materializme v oblasti teatra," *Sovetskii teatr,* No. 4 (1931), p. 4.

26. V. Kirpotin, "Problema obraza," in his anthology, *Proza, dramaturgiia, teatr,* p. 203.

27. *Ibid.,* p. 200.

28. Vsevolod Meyerhold, "Metod Meierkhol'da," *Sovetskii teatr,* No. 2/3 (1931), p. 14.

29. Podol'skii, "Za leninskii etap teatrovedeniia," *Sovetskii teatr,* No. 4 (1932), pp. 24–25.

30. Kirpotin, "Problemy formy v sovetskoi dramaturgii," *Proza, dramaturgiia, teatr,* p. 227.

31. *Ibid.,* p. 218.

32. "The working class is conducting a socialist offensive along the entire front. The socialist offensive in art is expressed through a mass movement directed at winning given sectors of art and at creating in those sectors military organizations of the working class. We, the members of *On Literary Guard,* have created such an organization in the RAPP, which is the support of the Party in literature." (Libedinskii, "Za platformu teatra RAPP," *Sovetskii teatr,* No. 2 [1932], p. 4.)

33. "Both in the practice and in the theory of the theater, we have no smaller bloom than the bourgeois, the petty-bourgeois, and the other phenomena that are hostile to the proletariat." (*Ibid.*)

34. *Ibid.,* p. 4.

35. "In striving for 'vital truth,' the [Moscow] Art Theater people have piled up a heap of observations. They have studied reality in good conscience as best they could, but because their consciousness was oppressed by trade fetishism, because they did not understand the dialectical development of the society which surrounded them, they elevated those observations to the level of esthetic canons." (*Ibid.,* p. 7.)

36. *Ibid.*

37. From the resolutions of the RAPP Secretariat on the theater in 1931.

38. Libedinskii, "Za platformu teatra RAPP," *Sovetskii teatr,* No. 2 (1932), p. 4.

39. Chicherov, the theoretician of TRAM, wrote: "TRAM stands at the junction of professional and amateur art. It experiences within itself the contradictory influence of both, and unites within itself, in the unity of contradictions, both amateur and professional art."

40. The TRAMs multiplied spontaneously for a few years. There were about ten professional TRAMs, thousands of "TRAM nuclei" and propaganda brigades in the factories.

41. From the Resolution of the First All Union TRAM Conference in 1929.

42. "A TRAM presentation is an original theater discussion of the problem posed. . . . The presentation is understood by TRAM to be a dialectical discourse by the TRAM collective based upon some particularly vital question. . . . A TRAM presentation ought to be understood as any actively propagandistic performance, whether it be an evening show before an organization, a mass outdoor party, a festival, etc." (From the Resolution of the First All Union TRAM Conference in 1929.)

43. Sokolovskii, "TRAM na perelome," *Klubnaia stsena,* No. 9 (1930), p. 17.

44. *Ibid.*

45. "We have not sent to our theaters the people who could carry out the political guidance of the Party in theater work or who could be the agents of our Party's influence. We are now sending them executives and administrators who do not know the theater. Such people discredit themselves and our Party." (From the speech by Obnorsky at the 1927 theater conference. Cited from *Puti razvitiia teatra,* p. 442.)

46. "What do I expect from the artistic councils, although they are advisory? They must air whatever is musty in the theater. The public will have its eyes there; the public will keep track of whether the work is going all right in terms of the plays chosen, whether good [that is, Party] plays are rejected, how all this is worked out by the directors, etc." (From the speech by Lunacharsky at the 1927 theater conference. Cited from *Ibid.,* p. 37.)

47. "The artistic councils of the theaters also have the task of establishing an atmosphere of public attention, guidance, and criticism around the theater without which the theater cannot be genuinely linked to the tasks of Soviet culture." (From the resolution of the theater conference in 1927, *Ibid.*)

48. *Na Literaturnom postu,* No. 16 (1929).

IX. PLAYS BASED ON PARTY SLOGANS

1. "The proletarian playwright is more or less mature and steadfast in relation to the petty-bourgeois playwright; he must stand up for his rights and take command." (Anatolii Lunacharskii, "Uzlovye momenty rekonstruktsii teatra," *Sovetskii teatr,* No. 2/3 [1931].)

2. V. Kirpotin "Uspekhi sovetskoi dramaturgii," *Teatr i dramaturgiia,* No. 8 (1934), p. 1.

3. Lunacharskii, "Sotsialisticheskii realizm," *Stat'i o teatre i dramaturgii,* p. 21.

4. From the speech by Iuzovsky, a critic at the congress of Soviet writers.

5. "There have been many kulaks on the various stages of our country, but

none of them has been satisfactory. Either they were schematic, posterish, and anecdotic, or they were frozen masks. Here we see a kulak in motion, struggle, and development. We see a kulak in the most primitive and elementary forms of the struggle. He intimidates Rayevsky; he flatters; he is shrewd; and he is deceptive. He is maturing into the final forms of the class struggle—revolt." (S. Podol'skii, "Proletarskaia p'esa," *Sovetskii teatr*, No. 4 [1931], p. 5.)

6. Kirshon wrote that, in *Bread*, he wanted to show the general problem and to contrast the "ideology of the proletariat (Mikhailov) with the ideology of the petty-bourgeoisie or, more exactly, of a petty-bourgeois intellectual (Rayevsky)."

7. *Sovetskoe iskusstvo*, No. 28 (1931).

8. "The enthusiam of the workers who have freed themselves from slavery through revolution, to rework the world in a new style clashes with the monumental sort of a figure who is unpolished and unarmed with knowledge." (A. Gurvich, "Poema o topore," *Sovetskii teatr*, No. 4 [1931], p. 26.)

9. I. Kruti, "Strakh," *Sovetskii teatr*, No. 7 (1931), p. 20.

10. "We have conducted objective research on several hundred individuals from different social strata. . . . The common stimulus in the conduct of 80 percent of the total is fear. . . . 80 percent of them live in constant fear of outcries and of becoming unable to support themselves. The milkmaid is afraid lest her cows be confiscated. The peasant fears forced collectivization. The Soviet worker fears the unending purges. The Party worker fears lest he be accused of deviating. The scientist is afraid lest he be accused of idealism. The technician is afraid lest he be accused of sabotage. We are living in an age of great fear. Fear compels the repudiation of mothers, the falsifying of social origins, and the wriggling into high positions. Yes, yes! . . . The danger of denunciation is not so terrible for a person in a high position. . . . Eliminate fear, and eliminate its causes, and you will see the great creative life that will flourish in the country. Permit me to stop here." So says Professor Borodin.

11. The curtain scene shows Borodin opening his Institute to Communists who have "won promotions in science." He tells them: "But now I am going to see those who are younger, who will authoritatively use the keys to all offices, and I shall give them all my own keys. . . . Say, you, new director, I am accepting your conditions!"

12. This "social command" stated: Show that the "struggle for collective forms of scientific endeavor becomes a form of the class struggle, because castes are a maneuver of the class enemy in his attempt to conceal his real intentions permanently from Soviet public opinion." (Kirpotin, *Proza, dramaturgiia, teatr*, p. 109.)

13. "The denouement of the play is Kavalerov's blow with the razor. Kavalerov kills Ivan Babichev and thus seems to resolve the conflict between the two Babichev brothers in favor of Andrei. But the denouement is false. . . . It is no culmination, and it does not solve the conflict within the play.

. . . Kavalerov could just as easily have killed Andrei Babichev, and then the conflict would have been decided in favor of Ivan Babichev." (Kirpotin, "Olesha dramaturg," *Proza, dramaturgiia, teatr,* p. 151.)

14. "The Revolution has deprived me of the past and has not shown me the future," says Goncharova. "I am thinking and only thinking. I wanted to obtain through thinking what I could not acquire through emotion. Human life is natural when thoughts and emotions harmonize. I have been deprived of that harmony and therefore my life in the new world is unnatural. . . . In my brain, I have come to believe that the triumph of the proletariat is natural and legitimate. But my emotions were against it. I was torn in half."

15. Goncharova remarks to her friend Semënova: "Do you think that these are selfish complaints about the lack of quality goods? . . . I am talking about the crimes against the personality. There are many things in the politics of our regime to which I cannot become reconciled. Do you think that I do not see or do not understand the good deeds of the Soviet regime? Now let us put the two halves together. That's my trouble, my dilemma. The two halves of the same conscience are so mixed up that they are driving me crazy. . . . We have people whose hearts contain only one list. If it is a list of crimes, if those people hate the Soviet regime, they are lucky. Some of them —the bold ones—rebel or flee abroad. . . . If a person has the other list— the good deeds—he becomes an enthusiastic builder of the new world. This is his country, his home. But I have both lists, and I cannot flee, lie, build, or revolt. I can only understand and be silent."

16. "I lived in a new world. Tears came to my eyes when I saw my shadow on the stones of the old. . . . I have accumulated the dust of the old world on the stones of Europe. They are ancient and powerful stones. The Romans built them. No one will move them."

17. "I remember . . . I remember. . . . I recalled everything. The gardens, the theaters, the art for the sake of the workers! I saw the glove in the hands of the shepherd. I saw the Red Army. . . . I saw knowledge in the eyes of the proletariat. I heard the slogan: 'Down with war!' I recalled everything."

18. *Puti razvitiia teatra,* pp. 204–5.

19. Kirpotin, "Romany Leonida Leonova," *Proza, dramaturgiia, teatr,* p. 30.

20. "Leonov has created in his play a complete series of useless, harmful, and superfluous people. But who needs the collection? Are these really people who determine life to any extent?" (*Pravda,* February 21, 1928.)

21. There is a clear indication of how plays on the defense theme grew between 1934 and 1938. The Union of Soviet Writers set up an autonomous section of "defense writers." This in turn was divided into subsections of defense writers called naval, air, and military.

22. "Bolshevism does not merely teach that one must die. Bolshevism teaches that one must conquer. . . . And if the play does not teach the need for victory, then what is left of Act IV except for an original kind of Remarque-

ism and anti-Bolshevism?" (L. Degtiarev, "Biurokraticheskaia otpiska," *Sovetskii teatr*, No. 4 [1931], p. 15.)

23. A. Karganov, "Put' sovetskogo khudozhnika," *Teatr*, No. 10 (1952), p. 99.

24. I. V. Stalin, *Sochineniia*, XII, 200–201.

25. Al'pers, *Teatr sotsial'noi maski*, p. 51.

26. A. Fevral'skii, "Dvadtsatyi spektakl' GOSTIM," *Sovetskii teatr*, No. 2/3 (1933), p. 23.

27. "After the statements of the central Party press and the Soviet public, Vladimir Nemirovich-Danchenko and Konstantin Stanislavsky withdrew *Molière* from the repertory of the theater. It was a presentation that did not respond to the tasks of truthfully showing the life and works of one of the outstanding classical playwrights on the stage." (N. M. Gorchakov, *Rezhisserskie uroki Stanislavskogo*, p. 386.)

X. LAST FLICKERS OF ORIGINALITY

1. Al'pers, *Teatr Sotsial'noi maski*, p. 59.

2. A. Gurvich, "Liniia ognia," *Sovetskii teatr*, No. 7 (1931), p. 18.

3. "The play of the lights in the presentation revealed an unconcealed, completely blatant, and cheap estheticism. How are we to understand the uninterrupted changing of the lights illuminating the sky in the background? How are we to understand night in the middle of the day, or the orange, indigo, lilac-colored, violet, and straw-colored sunsets and sunrises that are unnoticeably 'artistic' as they replace one another over several minutes?" (*Ibid.*, p. 19.)

4. *Sovetskii teatr*, No. 2 (1932).

5. *Sovetskii teatr*, No. 6 (1932), p. 15.

6. "The problem of the décor, which apparently gives the idea of a room, essentially enables the actor to talk on a theater platform of enormous dimensions rather than in a room itself." (From the pamphlet for the première of *Fear*.)

7. "Nikolai Akimov . . . made an enormous and sloping platform which turned people into pygmies and distracted the actors and the audience. The largeness of the sloping floor and the gigantic walls and doors drowned what was taking place on the stage. . . . Ordinary people wandered about in a lonely way among the lofty Pyramids." (I. Kruti, "Strakh," *Sovetskii teatr*, No. 7 [1931], p. 25.)

8. The party critics, of course, did not fail to notice this: "Pevtsov played Borodin. The actor created the 'absent-minded,' 'objective,' and 'honest' scientist with many details that had been skillfully worked out. But the character contained no inner struggle. The actor did not show his 'crevices' and therefore Borodin's 'conversion' was sudden and unjustified." (*Ibid.*)

9. "Leonidov showed us a scientist who was unwavering in his belief that his own ideas were correct. . . . The actor stressed this quality . . . with

exceptional expressiveness. The professor's attitude to everything going on around him was one of inner superiority. . . . The way in which Leonidov (as Borodin) gave his report at the Institute meeting was characteristic. The speech was clearly political, but he uttered . . . the conclusions to his observations in the calm and measured tones that he usually employed in his work as a lecturer." (B. Rostotskii, "Sovetskaia dramaturgiia na stsene Moskovskogo Khudozhestvennogo teatra," *Ezhegodnik MKhAT*, p. 134.)

10. "Simonov even introduced a special scene that was staged with major brilliance. The scene showed idlers, shirkers, and young vandals wearing the baptismal crosses of sailors and caps with shiny visors. Their muscular arms are tatooed, and they take some happy girls in white skirts and saucy berets by the arm. They sang songs of the Odessa underworld extraordinarily badly to the skillful accompaniment of a guitar. The entire picture had quite a good aim. It was supposed to show Soviet young people what laziness, drink, and neglect of socialist obligations could lead to." (Iurii Elagin, *Ukroshchenie iskusstv*, p. 130.)

11. *Teatr i dramaturgiia*, No. 2/3 (1933), p. 31.

12. *Ibid.*

13. It staged *V liudiakh* ("Among People") in 1933; *Yegor Bulichëv* in 1934; *Enemies* in 1935; and *Dostigayev* in 1938.

14. From Zhdanov's speech at the First All-Union Congress of Soviet Writers.

15. The adaptation of *Among People* also included bits from such of Gorky's stories as "Strasti-mordasti" ("Passionate Snouts"), "Khoziain" ("The Master"), and "Dvadtsat' shest' i odna" ("Twenty-Six Men and a Girl"). There were also some episodes from *Detstvo* ("Childhood"), and *Moi universitety* ("My Universities").

16. Sobolev, "M. M. Tarkhanov," in the anthology *Mastera MKhAT*, p. 306.

17. *Ezhegodnik MKhAT, 1947*, p. 248.

18. Rostotskii, "Sovetskaia dramaturgiia na stsene Moskovskogo Khudozhestvennogo teatra," *Ezhegodnik MKhAT, 1947*, p. 144.

19. N. M. Gorchakov, *Rezhisserskii kommentarii k knige Nikolaia Virty "Zemlia,"* p. 96.

20. Elagin, *Ukroshchenie iskusstv*, pp. 137–38.

21. Al'pers, "Razbeg," *Sovetskii teatr*, No. 5 (1932), p. 16.

22. A. Varshavskii, "Neverie v teatr," *Teatr*, No. 5 (1937), p. 112.

23. *Teatr i dramaturgiia*, No. 5 (1934), p. 49.

24. *Teatr i dramaturgiia*, No. 4 (1936), p. 208.

25. The Moscow Art Theater had produced Leo Tolstoy's *Fruits of Enlightenment, Redemption,* and *Power of Darkness.*

26. V. I. Lenin, "Tolstoi i proletarskaia bor'ba," *Sochineniia*, 4th edition, XXI, 323.

27. Vladimir Nemirovich-Danchenko, "Zerno spektaklia," *Ezhegodnik MKhAT, 1943*, p. 359.

28. Nemirovich-Danchenko wrote a letter to V. G. Sakhnovsky in which he discussed the idea of the play: "Anna is gripped by passion, but there are social and family chains. There is beauty—alive, natural, and in the grip of natural enthusiasm—and there is prettiness—artificial, invented, enslaving, and murdering. There is the truth which is alive and beautiful, and there is décor, which is impressive but dead. There is natural freedom and triumphant slavery." (*Ezhegodnik MKhAT, 1947,* p. 240.)

29. "K spektakliu: 'N. V. Gogol' *Mërtvye dushi,*'" Ocherk, V. G. Sakhnov-skogo, Moscow, Muzei MKhAT, 1937, p. 17.

30. "The blind alley that the Moscow Art Theater entered with its *Dead Souls* is a result of the effort to turn away from the major artistic achievements that the theater had accomplished with the very rich material of the Soviet drama . . . toward its own past and bourgeois realism. The results are here. We have a bad and naturalistic presentation." (Libedinskii, "Po osnovnym voprosam," *Sovetskii teatr,* No. 2/3 [1933], p. 11.)

31. Ten years earlier, the same Maly Theater was famous for another experiment in "rejuvenating" or "revising" Ostrovsky in "Party-style." N. O. Volkonsky, a director, decided to turn Ostrovsky's *Dokhodnoe mesto* ("A Lucrative Job") into an "unmasking of the social and political structure of tsarism." He transferred the action from the milieu of minor civil-servants to "high society." But Volkonsky did not dare to change the text, so there were a number of spots in the production that contradicted his objectives completely. In the unchanged finale, the "crowned" Vishnevsky was brought to justice for his crimes. This nullified all the "unmasking" of the tsarist regime and was almost considered counterrevolutionary.

32. V. Toporkov, *Stanislavskii na repetitsii,* p. 62.

33. In 1944 M. B. Korabel'nikov—director of the Dramatic Theater in the city of Gorky—decided to take another step toward "proletarianization." This time, Petruchio was the victim. Petruchio was given as an obvious democrat who showed up in rags at the wedding not out of mischief but rather out of "ideological conviction." He throws out the dress that the tailor has brought for Katharina, not to tame the shrew but to show her that poor clothes and a poor life—similar to Soviet poverty—are beautiful.

34. Gvozdev, *Nasha rabota nad klassikami,* p. 136.

35. *Ibid.,* p. 150.

36. V. O. Toporkov, an actor at the Moscow Art Theater, tells an interesting story about Stanislavsky's reaction to the rollicking *Hamlet* at the Vakhtangov Theater. "Stanislavsky then listened to the story about how Shakespeare's *Hamlet* was being produced. . . . [He] suddenly hung his head and, sighing deeply, said: 'Well, art has perished there.' . . . And then he set about working energetically. That day, he was particularly captious toward us. He made impossibly artistic demands and fell furiously upon the slightest blunder or manifestation of poor taste. At times he was cruel and unjust. We were being paid off for the outrage against Shakespeare's genius." (Toporkov, *Stanislavskii na repetitsii,* p. 98.)

37. Elagin, on p. 41 of his *Ukroshchenie iskusstv* ("Taming of the Arts") mentions that, after the première of this *Hamlet,* one of the magazines "printed a cartoon entitled 'A New Way for Obtaining Energy.' It showed the Vakhtangov Theater playing *Hamlet.* Next to the Theater was the grave of Shakespeare in cross-section. The great author was spinning in his grave from terror and indignation over the defilement of his work. Cables were attached to his body and led to a dynamo, which contributed the energy to illuminate the stage brilliantly."

38. *Teatr i dramaturgiia,* No. 4 (1936), p. 204.

39. *Ibid.*

40. *Ibid.,* p. 361.

41. *Ibid.,* p. 362.

42. V. Filippov, "Otechestvennaia klassika na russkoi stsene," *Teatral'nyi al'manakh,* Book 2 (1946), p. 163.

43. N. P. Akimov, "O tekhnike stseny," *Zhizn' iskusstva,* No. 27 (1929).

44. D. Tal'nikov, "Spetakl' *rasseiavshikhsia* mirazhei," *Teatr i dramaturgiia,* No. 4 (1935).

45. Toporkov, *Stanislavskii na repetitsii,* pp. 131–32.

46. "Remember," said Stanislavsky, "every major and exacting actor must start studying again after a certain period of time (four or five years). You know, one must exercise his voice (which takes time), and cleanse his creative essence of the dross sticking to it." (*Ibid.,* p. 132.)

47. *Ibid.,* p. 139.

48. Stanislavsky taught: "Emotions must not be recalled and fixed. One can only recall the line of physical actions. . . . In rehearsing the scene, begin from the simplest physical actions; make them extremely truthful; search for the truth in every trifle. You will then acquire faith in yourself and in your actions. . . . We know how to do the simplest physical actions, but these physical actions (depending on the supposed circumstances) go over into the psychophysical." (*Ibid.,* pp. 149–50.)

49. *Ibid.,* p. 143.

50. *Ibid.,* p. 171.

51. *Sovetskii teatr,* No. 2/3 (1933).

52. From Zhdanov's speech at the First All-Union Congress of Soviet Writers.

53. Del'ta, "Chuvstvo stilia," *Teatr i dramaturgiia,* No. 5 (1934), p. 47.

54. *Ibid.*

55. *Ibid.*

XI. THE COMPLETE STANDARDIZATION OF THE SOVIET THEATER

1. I. Bachelis, "Teatralnyi front," *Molodaia Gvardiia,* No. 21 (1929), p. 28.

2. Both quotations come from "Znamenatelnoe piatiletie," an editorial in *Teatr,* No. 1 (1937), p. 7.

3. Libedinskii, "Po osnovnym voprosam," *Sovetskii teatr,* No. 2/3 (1933), p. 17.

4. *Ibid.,* p. 12.

5. "To unite all writers supporting the platform of the Soviet regime and aspiring to participate in socialist construction into a single union of Soviet writers with a Communist faction in it. . . . To make analogous changes in the other arts. To have the Organizing Bureau work out practical measures for implementing this resolution." (*Pravda,* April 24, 1932.)

6. "The Party and Comrade Stalin personally guided art daily, directed the judgment of society against it, and, revealing its mistakes, indicated how to correct them. That was the case with *Katerina Ismailova.* . . . That was the case in the period of extensive discussions about *Warriors of Yore.*" (M. Levin, "O strastnosti i revoliutsii," *Teatral'nyi al'manakh* [1947], p. 55.)

7. B. I. Rostotskii, *K istorii bor'by za ideinost' i realizm sovetskogo teatra,* p. 64.

8. *Teatr i dramaturgiia,* No. 4 (1936), p. 196.

9. *Ibid.,* pp. 202–3.

10. Tairov, "Strukturnyi realizm—metod Kamernogo teatra," *Sovetskii teatr,* No. 2/3 (1931), p. 29–30.

11. Here Tairov launched a bold sortie against the respected Areopagus of Soviet dramatists listening to his report. He said: "There are, perhaps, some rare exceptions, but on the whole, all of the Soviet drama, despite its growth and quantitative success, does not structurally have an adequate structure of social reality in this reconstruction period." (*Ibid.,* p. 31.)

12. *Ibid.,* p. 31.

13. *Ibid.,* p. 34.

14. "If you attentively watch the artistic thought and trends in the West that are beginning to be shown in painting, sculpture, and architecture, you will see that a number of theoreticians there are operating according to this idea. Its formalistic meaning is completely real. It means obliterating the categories of content and form, and submerging them in the idea of structure." (Ermilov, *Sovetskii teatr,* No. 2/3 [1931], p. 34.)

15. *Teatr i dramaturgiia,* No. 4 (1936), p. 205.

16. Cited from *Teatr,* No. 10 (1952), pp. 25–26.

17. *Teatr i dramaturgiia,* No. 4 (1936), p. 196.

18. *Teatr,* No. 1 (1937), p. 28.

19. *Teatr,* No. 1 (1938), p. 5.

20. The speech of this new genius of directing was adorned by such stylistic gems as this: "Idealistic demands to shrink into oneself are alien to the Soviet drama and to the Soviet theater." (*Rezhissër v sovetskom teatre: Materialy Pervoi Vsesoiuznoi rezhisserskoi konferentsii,* Moscow and Leningrad, Iskusstvo, 1940, p. 20.)

21. Cited from Elagin, *Ukroshchenie iskusstv,* pp. 226–28.

22. *Ibid.*

XII. WARTIME PATRIOTISM AND POSTWAR PROPAGANDA

1. Aleksei Popov, the outstanding Soviet director, exclaimed with pathetic loyalty: "The content of the Soviet theater is to serve the great ideas of Lenin and Stalin." (*Rabota rezhissёra nad sovetskoi p'esoi,* p. 8.)

"The artists of our country cannot be mere observers. They must realize that they are communists and state workers," wrote a prominent theater expert. "It is correct to state that Bolshevism wants to turn all artists into 'Party workers.'" (P. Novitskii, "Obrazy Chekhova v ispolnenii N. P. Kheleva," *Ezhegodnik MKhAT,* II, 58.)

Belik, critic and Party member, thought up a brilliant interpretation of "Socialist realism"—"the Party's method for creative work in the arts."

2. "Ivan Alexandrovich Smorodin, the distinguished teacher from Bol'shaia Sosnova village in Sverdlovsk Province, has been working for forty-five years and has committed a serious offense. At a pre-election meeting, he concluded by saying: 'Long live the happy Russian people!' On the next day, I. A. Smorodin was dragged in to answer. . . . To cry 'Long live the Russian people!' is the most blatant and unbridled chauvinism. It is now clear to you, Citizen Smorodin, that you have committed a class-hostile sally. . . . Hastily, . . . they resolved that the old teacher . . . should be excluded from the number of sympathizers and that his immediate dismissal from his position should be discussed." (*Pravda,* January 19, 1938.)

3. Osnos, *Sovetskaia istoricheskaia dramaturgiia,* pp. 270–71.

4. Even the theater critics mentioned the "spilling" of politics into history. "The glorious present casts a bright light on the past of our Country. The greatness manifested by our country in the post-October years, and its invaluable services to mankind impel us freshly to enumerate and to interpret the pages of history. With a feeling of legitimate pride, let us pay its due to the centuries-old heroism of the Russian nation, and let us make a worthy evaluation of its sons.

"The historical role of Ivan the Terrible has been developed in a new light. He is presented to us as a highly talented statesman. He boldly entered the ruthless struggle against foreign and domestic enemies encroaching upon the power, unity, and welfare of Russia. The national tasks that he set the Russian state were enormous. The statesmanlike mind, the diplomatic art, the self-control, and the energy that were used to accomplish them were striking." (Vipper, "Novyi spektakl' ob Ivane Groznom," *Pravda,* November 21, 1945.)

5. The Soviet critics noticed this also. One of them wrote: "Alexei Tolstoy's mighty Ivan is contrasted to the weak boyars. . . . By lowering the characters of the boyars, he destroys the dramatic conflict and the chronicle-style feature which it communicates especially in Part II of *Difficult Years.* (Osnos, *Sovetskaia istoricheskaia dramaturgiia,* p. 237.)

6. M. Levin, "O strastnosti i ravnodushii," *Teatral'nyi al'manakh* (1947), p. 57.

7. D. Tal'nikov, "Problema rezhissury i russkaia klassika," *Teatral'nyi al'manakh* (1947), p. 184.

8. B. Rostotskii, "Sovetskaia dramaturgiia na stsene MKhAT," *Ezhegodnik MKhAT (1947)*, pp. 160–61.

9. *Pravda*, September 23, 1941.

10. One of the Soviet theater critics wrote: "However, it is vain to seek any simple, sincere, and human language in this play. Its characters lead an existence that is 'painted' according to pre-conceived rules. You do not believe in them regardless of their heroic exploits. Cheap theatricality and empty declamation have been raised above the strict and profound truth of human exploits." (I. Kruti,' "V gody otechestvennoi voiny," *Sovetskii teatr: k tritsadtiletiiu sovetskogo gosudarstva*, p. 213.

11. Konstantin Simonov, "Dramaturgiia, teatr i zhizn'," *Pravda*, November 22, 1946.

12. *Rabota rezhissëra nad sovetskoi p'esoi*, p. 130.

13. *Teatr*, No. 4 (1952), p. 97.

14. Belobrov was an ideal being. He was a "remarkable man who had passed through all the ranks of the navy. He had been an able-bodied seaman before the Revolution, and was now an admiral of the Soviet High Seas Fleet. The enormous experience of his life had made him very wise. He was a sensitive man who understood every movement of the human spirit from only half a word. He loved the navy and its people with a tender, paternal,. and solicitous love." (*Izvestiia*, May 19, 1945.)

15. Y. Lukin, "Za tekh, kto v more," *Pravda*, January 31, 1947.

16. M. Charnyi, "Spektakl' o chesti i slave," *Izvestiia*, February 1, 1947.

17. *Rabota rezhissëra nad sovetskoi p'esoi*, p. 70.

18. Levin, "O strastnosti i ravnodushii," *Teatral'nyi al'manakh*, p. 60.

19. *Ibid.*

20. The number of these plays is beyond calculation. Some of the outstanding dramas of this type which have appeared recently include: *Velikaia sila* ("Great Force") by Boris Romashev; *Zakon chesti* ("Law of Honor") by A. Shtein; *Dva lageria* ("Two Camps") by August Iakobson; *Russkii vopros* ("Russian Question") by Konstantin Simonov; *Tsvet kozhi* ("Color of Skin") by Bill-Belotserkovsky; *Mir* ("Peace") by Eugene Dolmatovsky; *Liudi dobroi voli* ("People of Good Will") by G. Mdivani; *Missuriiskii val's* ("Missouri Waltz") by Nikolai Pogodin; *Zemliak prezidenta* ("Man from the President's Home Region") by Anatoli Surov; *Chuzhaia ten'* ("Alien Shadow") by Konstantin Simonov; *Zagovor oэrechënnykh* ("Plot of the Condemned") by Nikolai Virta; *Ia khochu domoi* ("I Want To Go Home") by Sergei Mikhalkov; *Osobniak v pereulke* ("Lone House in the Alley") by the Tur brothers and L. Sheinin; *Mladshii partner* ("Junior Partner") by Arkady Perventsov, and *Golos Ameriki* ("Voice of America") by Boris Lavrenëv.

21. A. Anastas'ev, "V zashchitu demokratii," *Pravda*, May 16, 1950.·

22. *Ibid.*

23. I. Solov'ëv, "Na vakhte mira," *Teatr*, 1950, p. 55.

24. *Ezhegodnik MKhAT* (*1947*), p. 166.

25. *Ibid.*, p. 166.

26. *30 dnei*, No. 2 (1930), p. 94.

27. A. Koloskov, "Fal'shivaia komediia," *Pravda*, December 29, 1945.

28. *Teatr*, No. 2 (1952), p. 147.

29. *Ezhegodnik MKhAT* (*1947*), p. 244.

30. G. Boiadzhiev, *Teatral'nost i pravda*, pp. 33–34.

31. I. Kruti, "V gody Otechestvennoi voiny," in anthology *Sovetskii teatr k tridtsatiletiiu sovetskogo gosudarstva*, p. 239.

32. *Ezhegodnik MKhAT* (*1944*), p. 708.

33. V. Ermilov, "Novye gor'kovskie spektakli," *Izvestiia*, June 5, 1946.

34. Golovashenko, "Rezhissura spektaklei ob Otechestvennoi voine," *Teatral'nyi al'manakh*, Book 2 (1946), p. 219.

35. *Ibid.*

36. D. Tal'nikov, "Problema rezhissury i russkaia klassika," *Teatral'nyi al'manakh*, Book 6 (1947), p. 183.

37. E. Kriger, "Sotvorenie mira," *Izvestiia*, January 18, 1946.

38. Fadeev, "Obraz sovetskogo cheloveka," *Izvestiia*, June 28, 1947.

39. N. Bogoliubov, "Za tvorcheskoe sodruzhestvo," *Teatr*, No. 8 (1951), p. 49 .

40. "Itogi i uroki" (Moscow theaters in the 1950–1951 season), *Teatr*, No. 8 (1951), p. 56.

41. "O repertuare dramaturgicheskikh teatrov i merakh po ego uluchsheniiu," *Postanovlenie TsKVKP*, August 26, 1946.

42. Levin, "O strastnosti i ravnadushii," *Teatral'nyi al'manakh* (*1947*), pp. 56–57.

43. Fadeev, "Obraz sovetskogo cheloveka," *Izvestiia*, June 28, 1947.

44. Tairov, "Teatr i dramaturg," *Teatral'nyi al'manakh*, Book 6 (1947), p. 114.

45. *Ibid.*, p. 114.

46. "Our life and our statecraft have found a new form, which had not existed previously," wrote Tairov. "The Great October Socialist Revolution has produced a new type of state and a new state form—the Soviets. The socialist reconstruction of the countryside has found expression in a new form—collective agriculture, etc. Without a search for a new form, there will be no genuine and full-blooded method for expressing the new content of our life." (*Ibid.*, p. 121.)

47. *Ibid.*, p. 122.

48. Konstantin Simonov's speech, *Literaturnaia gazeta*, No. 17 (1949).

49. *Pravda*, February 3, 1950.

BIBLIOGRAPHY

Abalkin, N. Sistema Stanislavskogo i sovetskii teatr ("The Stanislavsky System and the Soviet Theater"). Moscow, Iskusstvo, 1950.

Al'pers, B. Teatr sotsial'noi maski ("The Theater of the Social Mask"). Moscow and Leningrad, OGIZ-GIKhL, 1931.

Belinskii, V. G. Polnoe sobranie sochinenii ("Complete Works"). S. A. Vengerov, editor. St. Petersburg, 1904.

Besedy K. S. Stanislavskogo ("Chats by Stanislavsky"). Moscow, Vserossiiskoe Teatral'noe Obshchestvo, 1947.

Beskin, E. Istoriia russkogo teatra ("History of the Russian Theater"). Moscow, 1928.

Bezpalov, V. F. Teatry v dni revoliutsii ("The Theaters in the Days of the Revolution"). Leningrad, Academia, 1927.

Birman, Serafim. Trud aktëra ("The Actor's Labor"), Moscow and Leningrad, Iskusstvo, 1939.

Blok, Alexander. Sobranie sochinenii. 14 vols. Moscow, Sovetskii pisatel, 1936.

Boiadzhiev, G. Teatral'nost' i pravda ("Theatricality and Truth"). Moscow and Leningrad, 1945.

Chekhov, M. A. O tekhnike aktëra ("On the Actor's Technique"). New York, 1946.

—— Put' aktëra ("The Actor's Path"). Moscow and Leningrad, Academia, 1929.

Chulkov, Georgii. Gody stranstvovaniia ("Years of Wandering"). Moscow, Federatsiia, 1930.

Elagin, Iurii. Ukroshchenie iskusstv ("The Taming of the Arts"). New York, Chekhov, 1952.

Evreinov, N. N. Teatr dlia sebia: Chast' tret'ia—prakticheskaia ("Theater for Its Own Sake: Part Three—Practical"). Petrograd, Butkovskaia, 1917.

—— Teatr kak takovoi ("The Theater as Such").

Ezhegodnik Moskovskogo Khudozhestvennogo Teatra (*Ezhegodnik MKhAT*) ("The Yearbook of the Moscow Art Theater"), 1944–1947.

Fevral'skii, A. Maiakovskii—dramaturg ("Maiakovskii as a Playwright"). Moscow, Iskusstvo, 1940.

Gorchakov, N. M. Rezhisserskie kommentary k knige Nikolaia Virty "Zemlia" ("A Director's Comments on Nicholas Virta's *Zemlia*"). Moscow and Leningrad, Iskusstvo, 1938.

Gorchakov, N. M. Rezhisserskie uroki K. S. Stanislavskogo ("The Directorial Lessons of K. S. Stanislavsky"). Moscow, Iskusstvo, 1951.

Gostinnitsa dlia puteshestvuiushchikh v prekrasnom ("An Inn for Travelers in the Beautiful"). Moscow, No. 1, 1922.

Griadushchee ("The Future"). Petrograd, Nos. 2, 3, 6, and 8, 1918.

Grinval'd, I. Tri veka moskovskoi stseny ("Three Centuries of the Moscow Stage"). Moscow, Moskovskii rabochii, 1949.

Gudki ("Whistles"). Moscow, Proletkult, No. 1, 1919.

Gurevich, Liubov'. Istoriia russkogo teatral'nogo byta ("A History of the Way of Life in the Russian Theater"). Moscow, Iskusstvo, 1939.

Gvozdev, A. A. Teatr imeni Vsevolod Meierkhol'da, 1920–1926 ("The Vsevolod Meyerhold Theater, 1920–1926"). Moscow and Leningrad, 1927.

Iskusstvo ("Art"). Book 2, 1925; Books 1 and 4, 1927; Books 3 and 4, 1928; Books 3, 4, 7, and 8, 1929.

Istoriia sovetskogo teatra: sbornik statei ("A History of the Soviet Theater: An Anthology"). S. S. Mokul'skii, editor. Leningrad, 1933.

Iuzhin-Sumbatov, A. I. Zapisi: Stat'i: Pis'ma ("Notes: Articles: Letters"). Moscow, Iskusstvo, 1951.

Ivanov-Razumnik, R. Pisatel'skie sud'by ("The Fortunes of Writers"). New York, The Literary Fund, 1951.

Kazanskii, V. Metod teatra ("The Method of a Theater").

Khudozhestvennaia zhizn' ("The Life of Art"). Nos. 1–15, 1919.

Kirpotin, V. Proza, dramaturgiia i teatr ("Prose, the Drama, and the Theater"). Moscow, Goslitizdat, 1935.

Kizevetter, A. A. Teatr ("The Theater"). Moscow, Zadruga, 1922.

Klubnaia stsena ("The Clubhouse Theater"). Nos. 1, 2, 4–6, 1927.

Kogan, P. S. V preddverii griadushchego teatra ("At the Threshold of the Future Theater"). Moscow, Pervina, 1921.

Kryzhitskii, G. Rezhisserskie portrety ("Portraits of Directors"). Moscow and Leningrad, Teakinopechat', 1928.

Kul'tura teatra ("Culture of the Theater"). Moscow, Nos. 6–8, 1921.

LEF. Moscow, No. 1, 1923.

Liubov' k trëm apel'sinam ("The Love for Three Oranges"), "Zhurnal doktora Dapertutto" ("Dr. Dapertutto's Magazine"). St. Petersburg, Nos. 1–3, 1914.

Lunacharskii, A. V. Osnovy teatral'noi politiki sovetskoi vlasti ("The Bases of Soviet Theater Policy"). Moscow, Goslitizdat, 1926.

—— Stat'i o teatre i dramaturgii ("Articles on the Theater and Drama"). Moscow, Iskusstvo, 1938.

—— Teatr: sbornik statei o novom teatre. St. Petersburg, Shipovnik, 1908.

Maiakovskii, V. V. Izbrannye sochineniia ("Selected Works"). Moscow, Goslitizdat, 1949.

Mastera MKhAT ("The Moscow Art Theater Experts"). Moscow and Leningrad, Iskusstvo, 1939.

Masterstvo aktëra ("The Expertness of the Actor"). Moscow, Goslitizdat, 1935.

Meierkhol'd, Vsevolod. O teatre ("On the Theater"). St. Petersburg, 1913.

—— "Teatr: k istorii i tekhnike," Teatr: Kniga o novom teatr. St. Petersburg, Shipovnik, 1908.

Meierkhol'd, Vsevolod, V. Bebutov, and Ivan Aksenov. Amplua Aktëra. Moscow, GVYTM, 1922.

Mgebrov, A. A. Zhizn' v teatre ("Life in the Theater"). 2 vols. Moscow and Leningrad, Academia, 1932.

Na literaturnom postu ("On Literary Guard Duty"). Moscow, No. 16, 1929.

Narodnoe prosveshchenie ("National Enlightenment"). Petrograd, Nos. 1–2, 1918.

Narodnye artisty SSSR ("People's Artists of the U.S.S.E."). Moscow and Leningrad, Iskusstvo, 1937.

Nelidov, V. A. Teatral'naia Moskva: sorok let moskovskikh teatrov ("Theatrical Moscow: Forty Years of the Moscow Theaters"). Berlin and Riga, 1931

Ofrosimov, Iu. Teatr ("The Theater"). Berlin, Volga, 1926.

Osnos, Iurii. Sovetskaia istoricheskaia dramaturgiia ("The Soviet Historical Drama"). Moscow, Sovetskii pisatel', 1947.

O teatre ("On the Theater"). Leningrad, 1927.

O teatre: Sbornik statei ("On the Theater: An Anthology"). S. S. Danilov and S. S. Mokul'skii, editors. Moscow and Leningrad, Iskusstvo, 1940.

P'esy ("Plays"). Moscow, Pravda, 1947.

Puti razvitiia teatra: Sbornik ("The Paths of Theater Development: An Anthology"). S. N. Krylov, editor. Moscow, Teakinopechat', 1927.

Rabochii i teatr ("The Worker and the Theater"). 1930–1932.

Rabota rezhissëra nad sovetskoi p'esoi: Sbornik statei ("The Director's Work on a Soviet Play: An Anthology"). Moscow and Leningrad, Iskusstvo, 1950.

Radlov, Sergei. Desiat' let v teatre ("Ten Years in the Theater"). Leningrad, Priboi, 1929.

Red'ko, A. E. Teatr i evoliutsiia teatral'nykh form ("The Theater and the Evolution of Theater Forms"). Leningrad, Sabashnikov, 1926.

Romashov, B. P'esy ("Plays"). Moscow, Sovetskii pisatel'.

Rostotskii, B. I. K istorii bor'by za ideinost' i realizm sovetskogo teatra ("Towards a History of the Struggle for Idea-Content and Realism in the Soviet Theater"). Moscow and Leningrad, Academia Nauk SSSR, 1950.

Sakhnovskii, V. Rezhissura i metodika ee prepodavaniia ("Directing and the Method of Teaching It"). Moscow and Leningrad, Iskusstvo, 1939.

Shapovalov, L. E. Tvorcheskii put' Malogo teatra ("The Creative Path of the Maly Theater"). Moscow, Pravda, 1949.

Shkhlovskii, Victor. Khod konia. Moscow and Berlin, Gelikon, 1923.

Smirnova, N. A. Vospominaniia ("Reminiscences"). Moscow, Vserossiiskoe Teatral'noe Obshchestvo, 1947.

Solov'ëv, V. P'esy ("Plays"). Moscow, Sovetskii pisatel, 1950.

Sovetskaia dramaturgiia: Sborniki ("The Soviet Drama: Anthologies"). 3 vols. Moscow and Leningrad, Iskusstvo, 1948.

Sovetskaia dramaturgiia, 1949 ("Soviet Drama, 1949"). Moscow, Iskusstvo, 1950.

Sovetskii teatr ("The Soviet Theater"). Nos. 2/3, 4, 7, 9, 1931; Nos. 1–12, 1932; No. 2/3, 1933; No. 11, 1946.

Sovetskii teatr i sovremennost': Sbornik materialov i statei ("The Soviet Theater and Today: An Anthology of Articles and Other Material"). Moscow, Vserossiiskoe Teatral'noe Obshchestvo, 1947.

Sovetskii teatr k tridstatiletiiu sovetskogo gosudarstva ("The Soviet Theater at the Thirtieth Anniversary of the Soviet State"). Moscow, Vserossiiskoe Teatral'noe Obshchestvo, 1947.

Stanislavskii, Konstantin. Etika ("Ethics"). Moscow, Muzei MKhAT, 1947.

—— Moia zhizn' v iskusstve ("My Life in Art"). Moscow, Academia, 1933.

—— Rabota aktëra nad soboi ("An Actor Prepares"). Moscow, Iskusstvo, 1951.

Stepun, F. Osnovnye problemy teatra ("Basic Problems of the Theater"). Berlin, Slovo, 1923.

Surov, A. P'esy ("Plays"). Moscow and Leningrad, Iskusstvo, 1949.

Tairov, Alexander. Proklamatsy khudozhnika. Moscow, 1917.

—— Zapiski rezhissëra ("Notes of a Director"). Moscow, Kamerny Theater, 1921.

Teatr. ("Theater"). Moscow, Nos. 1–9, 1937; 1939; 1945; 1950–1952.

Teatral'no-dekoratsionnoe iskusstvo v SSSR, 1917–1927 ("The Art of Designing Theater Sets in the U.S.S.R., 1917–1927"). Leningrad, 1927.

Teatral'noe obozrenie ("Theater Survey"). Moscow, Nos. 9–10, 1921.

Teatral'nyi al'manakh ("Theater Almanac"). Moscow, Nos. 1 (3), 2 (4), and 3 (5), 1946; No. 6, 1947; No. 7, 1948.

Teatr i dramaturgiia ("Theater and Dramaturgy"). Nos. 2–3, 1933; Nos. 4–12, 1934.

Teatr: Kniga o novom teatre ("The Theater: A Book about the New Theater"). St. Petersburg, Shipovnik, 1908.

Tiraspol'skaia, N. L. Iz proshlogo russkoi stseny ("From the Past of the Russian Stage"). Moscow, Vserossiiskoe Teatral'noe Obshchestvo, 1950.

Tolstoi, Aleksei. P'esy ("Plays"). Moscow and Leningrad, Iskusstvo, 1949.

Toporkov, V. Stanislavskii na repetitsii ("Stanislavsky at Rehearsals"). Moscow, Iskusstvo, 1950.

Tvorcheskiie besedy masterov teatra: S. G. Birman, S. V. Giatsintova ("Creative Chats of Theater Experts: S. G. Birman, S. V. Giatsintova"). Leningrad and Moscow, Vserossiiskoe Teatral'noe Obshchestvo, 1939.

Tvorchestvo ("Creative Work"). Moscow, No. 1, 1918.

Veresaev, V. Vospominaniia ("Reminiscences"). Moscow and Leningrad, OGIZ, Goslitizdat, 1946.

Vilenkin, V. I. I. M. Moskvin na stsene moskovskogo Khudozhestvennogo teatra ("Ivan Moskvin on the Stage of the Moscow Art Theater"). Muzei MKhAT, 1946.

Vishnevskii, Vsevolod. Izbrannoe ("Selected Works"). Moscow, Sovetskii pisatel', 1950.

Volkov, N. Meierkhol'd. 2 vols. Moscow and Leningrad, Academia, 1929.

Vsevolodskii (Gerngross), V. Istoriia russkogo teatra ("A History of the Russian Theater"). 2 vols. Leningrad and Moscow, Teakinopechat', 1929.

Zakhava, B. Vakhtangov i ego studiia. Moscow, 1930.

Zapiski aktëra Shchepkina ("Notes of Shchepkin, the Actor"). Moscow and Leningrad, Academia, 1933.

Zapiski Gosudarstvennogo Instituta Teatral'nogo Iskusstva imeni Lunacharskogo ("Proceedings of the Lunacharsky State Institute for the Theater Arts"). Moscow and Leningrad, Iskusstvo, 1940.

Znosko-Borovskii, Evgenii. Russki teatr nachala xx. veka ("The Russian Theater at the Beginning of the Twentieth Century"). Prague, Plamia, 1925.

Zograf, N. Vakhtangov. Moscow and Leningrad, Iskusstvo, 1939.

INDEX

About a Tub (Dabondance), 77
About the Cuckold's Hat (Dabondance), 77
Above the Land (Mayskaya), 169
Acting: nineteenth-century stereotypes in, 4-5; Stanislavsky on, 29, 222, 235-40, 346-49; Nemirovich-Danchenko on, 28-29; in works of fantasy, 42-43; Meyerhold on, 42-43, 54-59, 62-64, 70-71, 201-5, 210-11, 221-22, 428; Evreinov on, 79, 414; Komisarzhevsky on, 87; Tairov on, 88-89, 221, 222, 227-28, 359-60; Mikhail Chekhov on, 247-50, 436-38; Vakhtangov on, 252; *see also* Stanislavsky System
Actor of the Future, The (Meyerhold), 201
Actor Prepares, An (Stanislavsky), 24, 243
Actors: in nineteenth century, 3-13; effect of February Revolution on, 102-4, 118, 122-29; Communist attitude toward, 262, 276
Actor's Path, The (M. Chekhov), 247
Actor's Role, The (Meyerhold), 201
Admiral Nakhimov (Lukovsky), 368, 369
Adopted Child (Radlov), 131
Adrienne Lecouvreur (Scribe and Legouvé), 197, 226
Aduyev, N., 390-91
Afinogenov, Alexander, 278, 292-95, 323-24; quoted, 442
Akimov, Nikolai, 323, 340-41, 447; quoted, 341, 343
Aksenov, Ivan, 199
Aleshin, O., 384
Alexander I (Merezhkovsky), 169
Alexander Nevsky (Litovsky and Osipov), 368
Alexandrinsky Imperial Theater: in nineteenth century, 3, 11, 14-15, 17-18; apolitical character of, 47, 415; and Meyerhold, 64-65, 72-74, 205; after February Revolution, 97, 100-101; after October Revolution, 113; *see also* Leningrad Bolshoi Theater

Alexeyev's Circle, 21; *see also* Moscow Society for Art and Literature
Alien Shadow (Simonov), 385, 453
"Alien Theater," 361
Aliger, Margarita, 378
Alilueva (Mme Stalin), 370
All God's Chillun Got Wings (O'Neill), 232
Alpers, B., 132; quoted, 137, 421, 438
Altar of Freedom (Milyukova), 105, 169
Altman, N., 400
Amateur theaters, 151-57
Americans, depicted in Soviet plays, 184, 384-86
Among People (Gorky), 326-27, 448
Anarchists, 198
Anarchist Telegrapher, The, 105
Anathema (Andreyev), 100
Andreyev, Leonid, 43, 100; *Life of a Man,* 45-46, 62; quoted, 164
Andreyev, N. A., 141
Animated poster, 143
Anna Karenina (Tolstoy), 335-36
Annenkov, Yuri, 90, 125, 149, 418
Annexation and Contribution, 105
Antigone (Hasenclever), 232-33
Antony and Cleopatra (Shakespeare), 342
Apologia for Theatricality (Evreinov), 79
Apushkin, 368
Arbatov, Boris, quoted, 427-28
Armored Train 14-69 (Ivanov), 182-84, 241-42, 310-11, 336, 434
Artistic Council of the Theater, 270
Association for Artists of Revolutionary Russia, 366
At the Walls of Leningrad (Vishnevsky), 377
Aubes, Les (Verhaeren), 134-36, 216
Audience: in nineteenth century, 16-17, 48-49; Meyerhold's attitude toward, 58-59, 252; Evreinov's attitude toward, 79, 83-84; after October Revolution, 118, 122-24, 194-96; Vyacheslav Ivanov's theater of audience participation, 128; Tairov's atti-

468